FROMMER'S

DOLLARWISE GUIDE TO SWITZERLAND & LIECHTENSTEIN

by Darwin Porter

1984-85 Edition

Published by Frommer/Pasmantier Publishers
A Division of Simon & Schuster, Inc.
1230 Avenue of the Americas
New York, NY 10020

ISBN 0-671-49876-2

Manufactured in the United States of America

CONTENTS

MAPS

The author of this guide gratefully acknowledges the editorial contribution of Margaret Foresman of Key West, Florida.

For
Danforth Prince

INFLATION ALERT: We don't have to tell you that inflation has hit Switzerland as it has everywhere else. In researching this book I have made every effort to obtain up-to-the-minute prices, but even the most conscientious researcher cannot keep up with the current pace of inflation. As we go to press, I believe we have obtained the most reliable data possible. Nonetheless, in the lifetime of this edition—particularly its second year (1985)—the wise traveler will add 15% to 20% to the prices quoted throughout these pages.

A DISCLAIMER: Although every effort was made to ensure the accuracy of the prices and travel information appearing in this book, it should be kept in mind that prices do fluctuate in the course of time, and that information does change under the impact of the varied and volatile factors that affect the travel industry. Readers should also note that the establishments described under Readers' Selections or Suggestions have not in many cases been inspected by the author and that the opinions expressed there are those of the individual reader(s) only. They do not in any way represent the opinions of the publisher or author of this guide.

Introduction

DOLLARWISE GUIDE TO SWITZERLAND AND LIECHTENSTEIN

SWITZERLAND . . . the name conjures up a kaleidoscopic range of sensory perception—snowy Alps, happy yodelers, lakes whose quiet is broken only by the sound of chugging steamers, skiers schussing down mountains, watches and clocks, flavorful cheeses, the tinkle of cowbells in still mountain pastures, the scent and rustle of money on the way to numbered bank accounts. All these images and more are connected with the small but strong federal republic of Switzerland.

Neutral since the 19th century and thus avoiding becoming embroiled in the wars which have devastated its neighbors, Switzerland nevertheless has a fascinating history of external and internal conflicts since prehistoric tribesmen struggled to hold their tiny settlements along the great Rhône and Rhine Rivers and their many tributaries. The Swiss of today, at peace from the highest village in the Grisons to the biggest cities in the lowlands since the middle of the last century, are a happy, thriving, hospitable people.

In this introduction, I will give you a brief look at the country, with further exploration to follow. This may seem like a fat book to deal with a small country (15,830 densely populated square miles with nearly 6½ million inhabitants), but I've only skimmed the surface of establishments and attractions available. What I'm sharing with you are my favorites. Perhaps, using the book as your seed core, you'll find dozens more on your own.

Readers of this book will also be introduced to the tiny **Principality of Liechtenstein,** which nestles into a niche formed by the River Rhine on the west with Switzerland just across the water, Austria on the east, and Switzerland on the south. With a total area of 62 square miles and a population of 20,000 souls, Liechtenstein, like its western neighbor, is a neutral country. Also like Switzerland, it has lowlands and highlands, mountains and rich pastureland. Most of its people are descended from the early Allemani or Germanic tribes who settled there, but some are of Swiss immigrant stock. Switzerland is the representative of Liechtenstein in diplomatic affairs, and the close ties of the neighbor countries are reflected in many other areas.

The Principality of Liechtenstein will be discussed and its attractions described in the final chapter of this book.

THE COUNTRY: Switzerland occupies a position on the rooftop of the continent of Europe, with the drainage of its mammoth alpine glaciers becoming the source of such powerful rivers as the Rhine and the Rhône. The appellation "the crossroads of Europe" is fitting, as all rail lines, road passes, and tunnels through the mountains seem to lead to it. From the time the Romans crossed the Alps, going through Helvetia (the old name for part of today's Switzerland) on their way north, the major route connecting northern and southern Europe has been through Switzerland. The old roads and paths were just developed into modern highways and railroads.

The main European route for east-west travel also passes through Switzerland between Lake Constance and Geneva, and intercontinental airports connect the country with cities all over the world. London and Paris, for instance, are less than two hours away by air.

Today, motorists find an extensive network of good highways and superhighways, plus scenic mountain roads for the adventurous.

The tourist industry as we know it started in Switzerland, and the tradition of welcoming visitors is firmly entrenched in Swiss life. The first modern tourists, the British, began to come here "on holiday" in the 19th century, and other Europeans and some North Americans followed suit, so that soon the small federal state became known as "a nation of hotelkeepers," now hosting some 20 million visitors from abroad annually. Swiss catering, based on years of experience, has gained a worldwide reputation, and the entire country is known for its cleanliness and efficiency.

Switzerland has many great museums and a rich cultural life, but that's not why most people visit the country. They come mainly for the scenery, which is virtually unrivaled in the world, from alpine peaks to mountain lakes, from the palm trees of Ticino to the "Ice Palace" of Jungfrau.

With the rise of the dollar in recent years, Switzerland is not the lethally expensive country it was in the late 1970s. Restaurant and hotel prices have remained stabilized in the '80s. But it is never considered as a haven for the budget traveler. The Swiss rate of inflation has been modest when compared to many of the other countries of Europe, making it increasingly attractive to tourists who might in earlier years have made France or Germany their primary vacation goals.

Your reasons for coming here may be many, ranging from mountain climbing to opening a numbered bank account to learning to yodel, from skiing in winter to hiking through alpine meadows and along country roads. Although the country has four recognized national languages, many of its people, at least in the major tourist regions, speak English, so you'll find help in pursuing your goals.

THE BEST OF BOTH: I have set for myself the formidable task of seeking Switzerland and Liechtenstein at their finest, and condensing that between the covers of this book. The best towns, villages, cities, and sightseeing attractions are documented, as well as the best hotels, restaurants, bars, cafés, shops, and nightspots.

But the best need not be the most expensive. My ultimate aim—beyond that of familiarizing you with the offerings of Switzerland and Liechtenstein—is to stretch your dollar power . . . to reveal to you that you need not pay scalper's prices for charm, top-grade comfort, and gourmet-level food.

In this guide I'll devote a lot of attention to those old tourist meccas—Geneva, Zurich, St. Moritz, Zermatt—focusing on both their obvious and hidden treasures. But they are not the full "reason why" of this book. Important as they are, they simply do not reflect fully the widely diverse and complicated countryside of Switzerland. To discover that, you must venture deep into the "William Tell country" in the heart of Switzerland or perhaps to a chalet in the Engadine with its mountain-bordered valley and chain of lakes.

DOLLARWISE—WHAT IT MEANS: In brief, this is a guidebook giving specific details—including prices—about Swiss hotels, restaurants, bars, cafés, sightseeing attractions, nightlife, and tours. Establishments in many price ranges have been documented and described, although I am constantly searching for bargains. Along with the deluxe citadels, I am more interested in the family-run *gasthof*-type place where you can often bask in gemütlich warmth but at low prices.

In all cases, deluxe or budget, each establishment was measured by a strict yardstick of value. If they measured up, meaning if they were the best in their category, they were included.

Now more than ever one needs an accurate guidebook including tips for saving money. By careful planning and selecting from my listings, you'll find the true Swiss experience while remaining within a reasonable budget. This applies to independent travelers as well as those who visit Switzerland on a package tour. If you're one of the latter, and have already obtained your flight ticket and hotel, you'll still need a guide to direct you to restaurants, nightlife, and sightseeing attractions rarely covered on a package tour. If you're given a car, then you'll be in the market for suggestions of where to go in the country, once you leave either Zurich or Geneva, whichever is your "gateway" city.

SOME WORDS OF EXPLANATION: No restaurant, inn, hotel, nightclub, shop, or café paid to be mentioned in this book. What you read are entirely personal recommendations; in many cases the proprietors never knew their establishments were being visited or investigated for inclusion in a travel guide.

Unfortunately, although I have made every effort to be as accurate as possible, prices change, and they rarely go downward, at least in Switzerland. Always, when checking into a hotel, inquire about the rate and agree on it. That policy can save much embarrassment and disappointment when it comes time to settle the tab. If the prices quoted are not the same as those mentioned in this book, remember that my prices reflect those in effect at the time this edition was researched. As I said, prices change.

This guide is revised cover to cover every other year. But even in a book that appears with such frequency, it may happen that that cozy little wine tavern of a year ago has changed its stripes, blossoming out with cut-velvet walls, crystal chandeliers, and dining tabs that include the decorator's fee and the owner's villa at Davos. It may further develop that some of the people or settings I've described are no longer there or have changed.

THE ORGANIZATION OF THIS BOOK: Here's how the *Dollarwise Guide to Switzerland* sets forth its information:

Chapter I, directly ahead, deals with how to get to Switzerland, concentrating obviously on airplane transportation. That will be followed by a section on transportation within the country, including trains, car rentals, and lake steamers. Special bargain passes, such as the "Holiday Card," will be described.

Chapter II is a survey of Switzerland in general, its people, customs, four languages, and cuisine, plus a brief historical outline. Another section is devoted to sports, naturally focusing on winter skiing at alpine resorts, but there are also activities for the nonskier. Summer skiing (or glacier skiing) is described, along with such other sports possibilities as curling (rapidly gaining in popularity), ice skating, tennis, swimming, hang-gliding, horseback riding, golf, hiking, mountaineering, and cycling. The chapter concludes with the ABCs of Switzerland, all the details from electric current to legal holidays.

Chapter III introduces our "touchdown" city for Switzerland—Zurich, the gateway for the entire country. Accommodations here will range from two of the greatest hotels in the world to hillside-perching pensions run by kindly fraus that are both immaculate and charming. Zurich's most elegant restaurants are surveyed, followed by less expensive places, such as bierhalles and bargain-basement wine cellars. A discussion of Zurich transport is followed by practical ABC-type hints. A preview of shopping, including a walk along the Bahnhofstrasse, one of the world's great shopping streets, precedes an exploration of the city's cafés and nightspots. The chapter concludes with the most interesting excursions around Zurich, ranging from mountainside to lakeside.

Chapter IV takes us into the countryside of Switzerland, beginning in the northeast sector, which is the least known to North Americans. Our major stopover here is St. Gallen, from which it is easy to reach the attractions of Lake Constance. A trip through the Appenzell countryside, the heart of the cheese country, where ancient customs are still practiced, is included. Medieval Schaffhausen, built on terraces on the right bank of the Rhine, is explored, followed by an excursion to the Rheinfall (Rhine falls).

Chapter V visits the "second city" of Switzerland, prosperous Basle with its port, which is rich in sights (its art museum is ranked among the top ten in the world). It's also the center for exploring Switzerland's Rhineland. A full range of hotels and restaurants is previewed, including Drei Könige (Three Kings), the country's oldest hotel, founded in A.D. 1026. Following Basle, we'll go through the Jura mountains, a land of lakes, vineyards, and such charming old towns as Fribourg and Neuchâtel, once a haven for Dumas and Gide, among others. The cheese town of Gruyères gets the attention it deserves, for it's here that the Middle Ages live on. You'll get to see a model dairy where you can watch cheese being made, and, naturally, the restaurants will feature fondues and raclette.

Chapter VI highlights historic Berne, capital of the Confederation, a cosmopolitan city that still retains a medieval flavor. All of its major sights, including its famous bear pits, are surveyed, along with hotels that go from the historic and inexpensive Zum Goldenen Schlüssel in the heart of Old Town to the majestic deluxe Bellevue Palace. Since the cookery is exceptional, special attention is devoted to restaurants, followed by a range of cultural activities and nightlife. Shopping in nearly four miles of medieval arcades is included.

In this same chapter, we'll blaze a trail through the Bernese Oberland, one of the most popular tourist districts of Europe, with its glacier valleys, high alpine peaks, and lakes. Interlaken, the best known of the sports centers and health spas, will be our gateway city to this area. Methods of visiting Schilthorn at 9750 feet are described, as well as ways to get to Mürrenbach, Europe's highest waterfall. Interlaken can also be used as a center for exploring Jungfrau with its glacial slopes. Since the Bernese Oberland is one of the best equipped sports centers in the world, a full range of its winter activities is presented, including cable cars and ski lifts. All the major centers are spotlighted, especially Gstaad, at the point where five alpine valleys and part-time resident Elizabeth Taylor meet.

Chapter VII goes to the Valais, one of the great tourist attractions of the world, starting at Lake Geneva and following the river valley up into the mountains. Along the way, visitors pass the Rhine Glacier heading for Zermatt, the mecca of mountaineers (reached by cogwheel train) and the towering Matterhorn at a height of 14,780 feet. Another excursion can be taken to the Great St. Bernard Pass, with its famous monastery and kennels. We'll go through Sion, with its old ruins and vineyards. The trip ends at Brig, the start of Simplon, Europe's longest railway tunnel, the gateway to Italy. Its winter sports facilities are among the best equipped in the world, rivaling the Grisons and Bernese Oberland.

Chapter VIII, in the footsteps of Shelley and Byron, explores Lake Geneva (Lac Léman), in the southwest corner of Switzerland. Excursions by lake steamer, motorcoach, car, and train are detailed, plus a tour to the Mont Blanc tunnel. Lausanne, the cultural center of French-speaking Switzerland, is previewed, with its hotels that range from the Beau-Rivage (once a favorite of visiting royalty) to such inexpensive retreats as the family-run Beau Site. Entertainment, museums, shopping, and nightlife are all surveyed, plus excursions to such towns as Vevey, a small holiday resort known to Victor Hugo and Thackeray, and in later years to Charlie Chaplin. Montreux, once on the "Grand Tour" of Europe at the turn of the century, is the chief tourist center. Other descriptions will take in the vineyards of La Côte.

Chapter IX delivers us to Geneva, where a full range of accommodations is surveyed, beginning with the grand old Richemond, run by the great hotel family of Armleder, all the way down to that same family's little bargain oasis, the Grand-Pré. The food of Geneva is exceptional, and you'll discover where to find it, ranging from candlelit deluxe citadels with a view of the lake to inexpensive little bistros. The shopping section gives hints on what to buy (Geneva invented the wristwatch) and where to buy it, and the nightlife section previews the cafés, brasseries, and bars where the local people gather for apéritifs, followed by nightclubs, discos, opera, and movies. Following that, we'll explore the most immediate excursions possible on the doorstep of Geneva. The chapter concludes with a description of local transportation, along with practical ABC's of life in this French-speaking city.

Lucerne and Central Switzerland come up in Chapter X. A storybook Swiss city that is most favored by visiting Americans, Lucerne is also a center for winter and summer sports from such places as the deluxe citadel at Bürgenstock to such resorts as Engelberg, and to the mountain peaks at Rigi and Pilatus. Of course Lake Lucerne itself will be traversed on colorful little paddle-steamers. In Lucerne there is a full range of hotels, restaurants, museums, shopping, and entertainment possibilities. The ski resorts and facilities of central Switzerland conclude the chapter.

Chapter XI, the Grisons and the Engadine, covers the winter playground of the world. From historic Chur, excursions are possible to the legendary resorts of St. Moritz, Davos, Klosters, and Pontresina, and to the Swiss National Park. The Engadine is a valley bordered by mountains of the River Inn and its string of lakes, lying across the southern sector of the more frequented Grisons. A full survey of the Grisons, with its many hotels, restaurants, nightspots, and winter sports facilities, is included.

Chapter XII provides our final look at Switzerland, as we head south to Lugano, Locarno, and the Ticino. Lugano and Locarno share the lakes of Lugano and Maggiore with Italy and, as such, are among the most attractive sightseeing attractions in the country. Ascona is another one of its important tourist centers. The Ticino is the Italian-speaking section of Switzerland, and is completely different from the rest of the country. A full range of tourist facilities and sights is surveyed.

Chapter XIII journeys to the postage-stamp principality of Liechtenstein to visit the world's oldest living democracy. Methods of transportation are

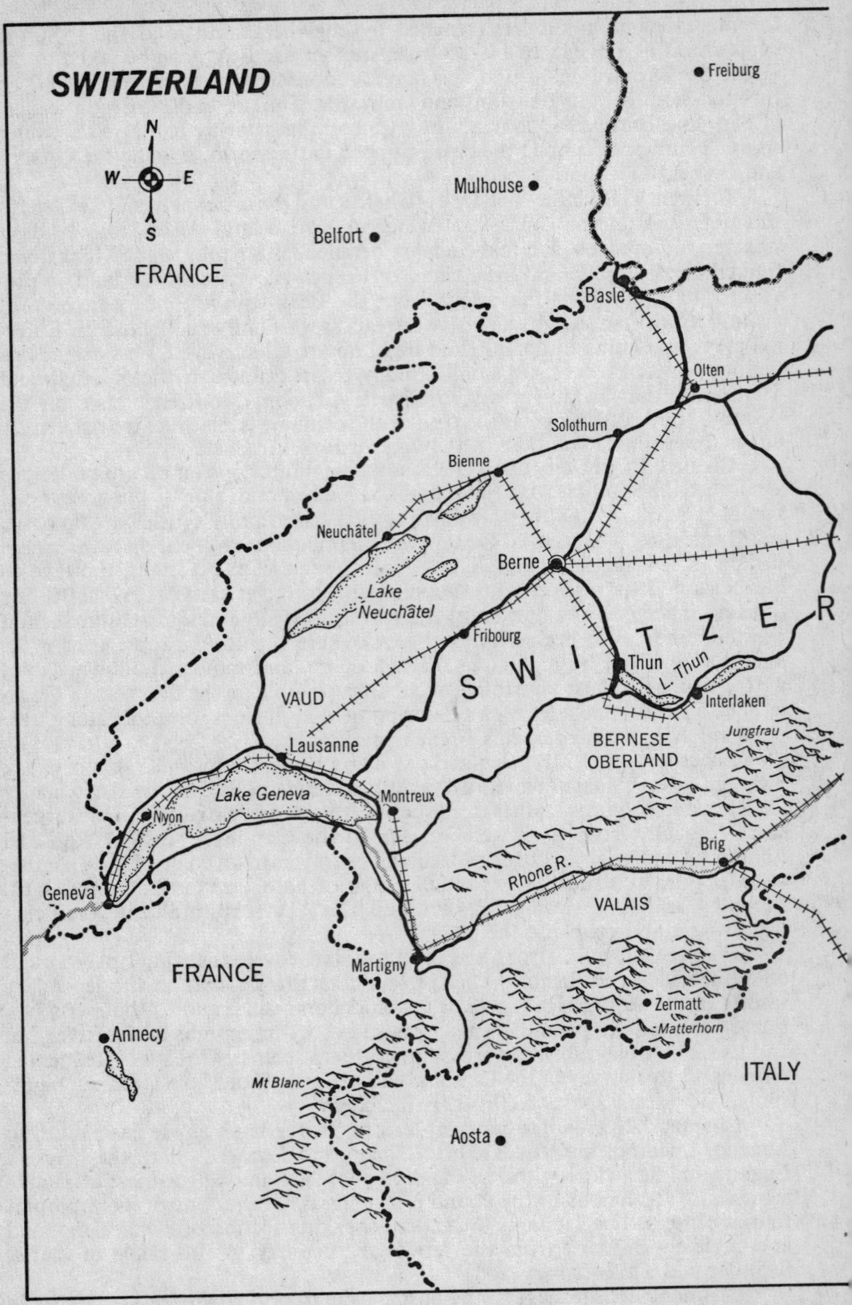
SWITZERLAND
N
W
E
S
Freiburg
Mulhouse
Belfort
FRANCE
Basle
Olten
Solothurn
Bienne
Neuchâtel
Berne
Lake Neuchâtel
Fribourg
S W I T Z E R
Thun
L. Thun
Interlaken
VAUD
Lausanne
BERNESE OBERLAND
Jungfrau
Lake Geneva
Montreux
Nyon
Brig
Rhone R.
Geneva
VALAIS
Martigny
FRANCE
Zermatt
Matterhorn
Annecy
ITALY
Mt Blanc
Aosta

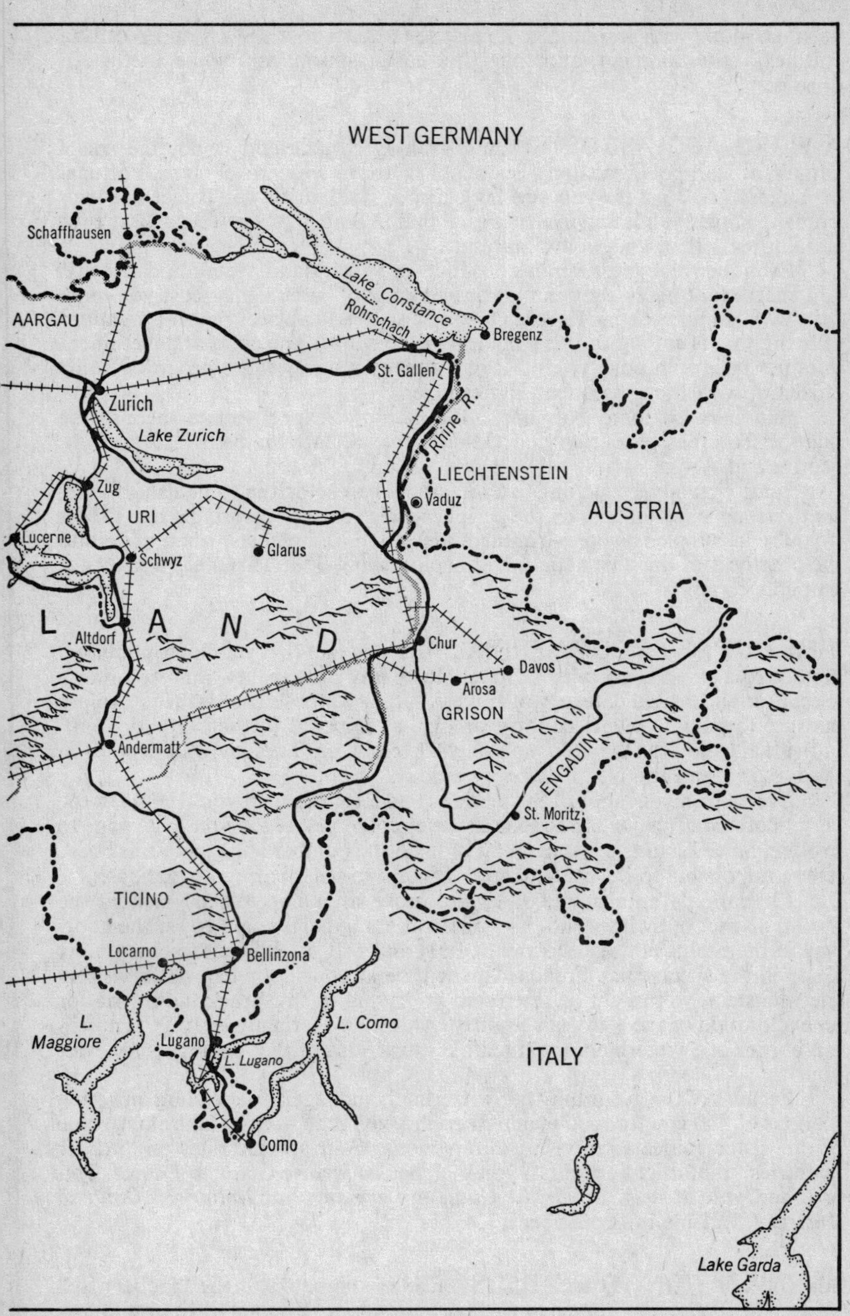
WEST GERMANY
Schaffhausen
Lake Constance
Rohrschach
Bregenz
AARGAU
St. Gallen
Zurich
Rhine R.
Lake Zurich
LIECHTENSTEIN
Zug
Vaduz
AUSTRIA
URI
Glarus
Lucerne
Schwyz
L
A
N
D
Altdorf
Chur
Davos
Arosa
GRISON
Andermatt
ENGADIN
St. Moritz
TICINO
Locarno
Bellinzona
L. Como
L.
Maggiore
Lugano
L. Lugano
ITALY
Como
Lake Garda

detailed, along with formalities, hotels, restaurants (both Swiss and Austrian cuisines), entertainment, shopping, museums, sports, and some useful addresses.

A WORD ABOUT COSTS: Quite frankly Switzerland is not the travel bargain of Europe. If economy is a major factor in your travel plans, Portugal or Yugoslavia, I assure you, are far cheaper. The tariffs you'll face are very similar to those you'll find in the United States. Sometimes you'll pay more for certain items than you would Stateside.

Even the three most famous products of Switzerland, watches, chocolate, and cheese (not necessarily in that order), might—just might—cost you more than they would back in Kansas. Of course staggering prices reflect a standard of living that is among the very highest in the world. The efficient government does not believe in poverty, and it offers many social welfare programs to its citizenry, with the subsequent higher taxes.

But there are many bargains, although don't expect to find them in the high-priced cities of Zurich and Geneva or especially in such resorts as St. Moritz and Arosa.

Since virtually everything in Switzerland can be driven to in a short time, try to stay at small villages on the periphery of celebrated resorts such as Davos if you're keeping costs bone-trimmed. Get up, have breakfast, then drive into the heartbeat of the chic action, and avoid paying 350F ($160.85) a night for a double room.

TIME OUT FOR A COMMERCIAL: The very fact that you have purchased a guide to a small country of Europe, plus a tiny principality, puts you into a special, sophisticated category of traveler—that is, those who want to explore and get to know a single country or two, as opposed to the "Grand Tour" individual who wants to do not only Belgium on Tuesday, but Rome on Wednesday, and the North Cape by Friday.

Even so, on your tour of Switzerland and Liechtenstein you'll come to the very doorstep of major attractions in other countries which you may want to explore. Since I had to set some limitation on the number of pages in this book, it was impossible to devote separate chapters to neighboring attractions.

I'll cite only an example or two to prove my point. When you visit the Ticino district of Switzerland, its Italian-speaking part, you'll be on the doorway of the beautiful Lake District of Italy and will surely want to cross it. At Geneva, the spectacular French Alps will be at your doorstep. After visiting Liechtenstein, you might be interested in driving to Innsbruck in Austria for an exploration of the Tyrolean country. And since Germany lies on the northern border of Switzerland, the manifold attractions of that country also await you.

Because of the geography of Switzerland, and, again, depending on which sections of that country you plan to travel in, you may want to take along some of our sister guides as traveling companions. Four specific ones on "border countries" that might appeal to you include: *Dollarwise Guide to France, Dollarwide Guide to Italy, Dollarwise Guide to Germany,* and *Dollarwise Guide to Austria* (available in September 1984).

AN INVITATION TO READERS: Like all the books in the "Dollarwise" series, the *Dollarwise Guide to Switzerland* hopes to maintain a continuing dialogue between its author and its readers. All of us share a common aim, I'm sure, and that is to travel as widely and as well as possible, at the lowest possible cost. In achieving that goal, your comments and suggestions can be of aid to other readers.

Therefore if you come across a particularly appealing hotel, restaurant, shop, or bargain, please don't keep it to yourself! It will be good for your soul if you share your gem with others.

Comments about existing listings are always helpful. The fact that a hotel or restaurant (or any other establishment) appears in this edition doesn't mean that it will necessarily appear in future editions if readers report that its service has slipped or that its prices have not only risen drastically but unfairly.

Even if you like a place, your comments are especially welcome, and have been known to brighten many a gray day.

Send your comments or finds—and, yes, those inevitable complaints that always arise—to Darwin Porter, c/o Frommer/Pasmantier Publishers, 1230 Avenue of the Americas, New York, NY 10020.

The $25-a-Day Travel Club—How to Save Money on All Your Travels

In this book we'll be looking at how to get your money's worth in Switzerland, but there is a "device" for saving money and determining value on *all* your trips. It's the popular, international $25-a-Day Travel Club, now in its 21st successful year of operation. The Club was formed at the urging of numerous readers of the $$$-a-Day and Dollarwise Guides, who felt that such an organization could provide continuing travel information and a sense of community to value-minded travelers in all parts of the world. And so it does!

In keeping with the budget concept, the annual membership fee is low and is immediately exceeded by the value of your benefits. Upon receipt of $14 (U.S. residents), or $16 U.S. by check drawn on a U.S. Bank or via international postal money order in U.S. funds (Canadian, Mexican and other foreign residents) in U.S. currency to cover one year's membership, we will send all new members, by return mail (book rate), the following items:

(1) The latest edition of *any two* of the following books (please designate in your letter which two you wish to receive):

Europe on $25 a Day
Australia on $25 a Day
England and Scotland on $25 a Day
Greece on $25 a Day
Hawaii on $35 a Day
Ireland on $25 a Day
Israel on $30 & $35 a Day
Mexico on $20 a Day
New York on $35 a Day
New Zealand on $20 & $25 a Day
Scandinavia on $25 a Day
South America on $25 a Day
Spain and Morocco (plus the Canary Is.) on $25 a Day
Washington, D.C. on $35 a Day

Dollarwise Guide to Canada
Dollarwise Guide to the Caribbean (including Bermuda and the Bahamas)
Dollarwise Guide to Egypt
Dollarwise Guide to England and Scotland

Dollarwise Guide to France
Dollarwise Guide to Germany
Dollarwise Guide to Italy
Dollarwise Guide to Portugal (plus Madeira and the Azores)
Dollarwise Guide to Switzerland
Dollarwise Guide to California and Las Vegas
Dollarwise Guide to Florida
Dollarwise Guide to New England
Dollarwise Guide to the Southeast and New Orleans
(Dollarwise Guides discuss accommodations and facilities in all price ranges, with emphasis on the medium-priced.)

How to Beat the High Cost of Travel
(This practical guide details how to save money on absolutely all travel items—accommodations, transportation, dining, sightseeing, shopping, taxes, and more. Includes special budget information for seniors, students, singles, and families.)

The New York Urban Athlete
(The ultimate guide to all the sports facilities in New York City for jocks and novices.)

Museums in New York
(A complete guide to all the museums, historic houses, gardens, zoos, and more in the five boroughs. Illustrated with over 200 photographs.)

The Fast 'n' Easy Phrase Book
(The four most useful languages—French, German, Spanish, and Italian—all in one convenient, easy-to-use phrase guide.)

Where to Stay USA
(By the Council on International Educational Exchange, this extraordinary guide is the first to list accommodations in all 50 states that cost anywhere from $3 to $25 per night.)

A Guide for the Disabled Traveler
(A guide to the best destinations for wheelchair travelers and other disabled vacationers in Europe, the United States, and Canada by an experienced wheelchair traveler. Includes detailed information about accommodations, restaurants, sights, transportation, and their accessibility.)

Marilyn Wood's Wonderful Weekends
(This very selective guide covers the best mini-vacation destinations within a 175-mile radius of New York City. It describes special country inns and other accommodations, restaurants, picnic spots, sights, and activities—all the information needed for a two- or three-day stay.)

(2) A one-year subscription to the quarterly eight-page tabloid newspaper—**The Wonderful World of Budget Travel**—which keeps you up to date on fast-breaking developments in low-cost travel in all parts of the world, bringing you the latest money-saving information—the kind of information you'd have to pay $25 a year to obtain elsewhere. This consumer-conscious publication also provides special services to readers: **The Traveler's Directory** (a list of

members all over the world who are willing to provide hospitality to other members as they pass through their home cities); **Share-a-Trip** (offers and requests from members for travel companions who can share costs and help avoid the burdensome single supplement); and **Readers Ask . . . Readers Reply** (travel questions from members to which other members reply with authentic firsthand information).

(3) A copy of **Arthur Frommer's Guide to New York,** a newly revised pocket-size guide to hotels, restaurants, nightspots, and sightseeing attractions in all price ranges throughout the New York area. (4) Your personal membership card which, once received, entitles you to purchase through the Club all Arthur Frommer publications, for a third to a half off their regular retail prices during the term of your membership.

So why not join this hardy band of international budgeteers and participate in its exchange of travel information and hospitality? Simply send your name and address, together with your annual membership fee of $14 (U.S. residents) or $16 U.S. (Canadian, Mexican, and other foreign residents), in U.S. currency to: $25-a-Day Travel Club, Inc., Frommer/Pasmantier Publishers, 1230 Avenue of the Americas, New York, NY 10020. And please remember to specify which *two* of the books in section (1) above you wish to receive in your initial package of members' benefits. Or, if you prefer, use the last page of this book, simply checking off the two books you select and enclosing $14 or $16 in U.S. currency.

Chapter I

GETTING TO AND AROUND SWITZERLAND

1. Plane Economics
2. Traveling Within Switzerland

IN THE GEOGRAPHICAL CENTER of Europe, Switzerland is a focal point for international air traffic which converges from almost every major city of the planet. The busy intercontinental airports of Zurich and Geneva can be reached in about eight jet hours from the East Coast of North America. Scheduled services to Switzerland are maintained by Pan Am and Swissair, with information on air fares available from both travel agents and the airlines themselves.

1. Plane Economics

Pan Am operates nonstop flights from New York's JFK airport to Zurich four times a week, on Tuesday, Wednesday, Friday, and Sunday at 7:15 p.m., arriving at 8:25 a.m. Zurich time. All flights are on a modern fleet of 747s, with excellent service, special meals, and advance seating assignments by telephone weeks in advance of your actual departure. Pan Am's newly inaugurated flights to Geneva began on December 15, 1983. They leave daily from New York at 6:45 p.m., making one brief stop in Paris before landing in the capital of French-speaking Switzerland.

Pan Am's price structure offers a wide choice of options for the budgets of most passengers. The following fares apply to passage to either Geneva or Zurich.

The **APEX midweek fare** is the most economical way to travel. Requiring a 21-day advance purchase, with an allowable stopover of from anywhere from seven days to three months, this ticket allows travel in both directions on Monday through Thursday only. Round-trip passage costs $548 in low season, $630 in shoulder season, and $730 in high season. A slightly more expensive **APEX weekend fare** also requires a 21-day advance purchase, with a minimum stay of 14 days and a maximum stay of three months. Travel is permitted on a Friday, Saturday, or Sunday in at least one direction, with travel in the other direction allowable on any day of the week a passenger prefers. Round-trip fares are $670 in low season, $700 in shoulder season, and $800 in high season. For the purposes of Pan Am's APEX tickets only, low season is from November 1 till December 14, and from December 25 till April 30. Shoulder season includes the entire month of May, and the period from September 15 till

October 31, and from December 15 to 24. High season is from June 1 till September 14.

Another form of ticket offered by Pan Am is the **excursion ticket,** which requires no advance purchase, and costs $901 round trip in low season, and $1135 in high season, with an allowable stay of from ten days to one year. A straightforward passage in **Cabin Class** requires no advance purchase, no minimum stay (you can deposit your funds into your favorite bank and return the same day, if you want), and a maximum stay of up to one year. This ticket costs $600 one way in low season, $730 in high season.

Pan Am's **Clipper Class** is the equivalent of what other airlines call business class, which might be considered a midway point between economy and first class. Seat width is only slightly less than in first class, with a definite increase in comfort over economy class. Passage on this frequently selected service costs $690 one way in low season, $835 in high season.

First-class passage represents an enormous fare increase, although your chair can practically be converted into a bed (they call it a "sleeperette") to help avoid the jet-lag hangover. One-way passage, which comes with a retinue of stewards and stewardesses who ply you with food and drink, costs $1514 in any season.

High and low seasons do not apply to first-class passage, but for every other type of passage *except APEX,* high and low seasons are as follows: For flights originating in the U.S., low season is from September 15 till April 30, while high season is from May 1 to September 14. For passengers originating in Switzerland, low season is from October 15 till May 31, while high season is from June 1 till October 14.

Passengers who are unable to take Pan Am to Switzerland can always fly Swissair, although Pan Am would probably be a better choice, especially since there is practically no fare difference between the two airlines. Swissair has a daily flight to Zurich from New York's JFK, and another daily flight from JFK to both Geneva and Zurich. Connections are easily made to Basle and Lugano with domestic flights within the country. In addition, Swissair operates a daily flight from Chicago via Boston nonstop to Zurich.

2. Traveling Within Switzerland

BY TRAIN: The comfort and cleanliness of Swiss trains, all of them electric, are widely known, and no less renowned are the numerous mountain railways which convey visitors to mountain resorts and summits, reaching the remote sections of the country with frequent, efficient service. Most trains carry two classes: first class for more comfortable travel and second class for economy. International through trains link many Swiss cities with other European centers. From your European gateway, many comfortable express trains carry you straight into the heart of Switzerland. Other intercity trains, those coming from Holland, Scandinavia, and Germany, require a change at Basle SBB station where a connection is usually offered on the same platform. Most intercity trains offer the fastest connections, and as trains leave the Basle station hourly, you don't have to wait there very long.

It is advisable to purchase transportation tickets for Europe before leaving home. This especially refers to made-to-order tickets issued for specific and complicated itineraries. Some advance notice is required for such tickets. All tickets are available from your travel agent or the Swiss National Tourist Office (SNTO) in New York, which acts as the official agency of the Swiss Federal

Railways. From other offices of the SNTO you can secure tickets as follows: Chicago—Swiss Holiday Card; San Francisco—Eurailpass, Eurail Youthpass, Swiss Holiday Card, Half-Fare Travel Card, and Senior Card; Toronto—Swiss Holiday Card, Half-Fare Card for 15 days and one month, Senior Half-Fare Travel Card, and one-month Junior Travel Card.

Addresses and phone numbers for these offices will be found under "Information" in "The ABC's of Switzerland," in Chapter II.

It is not possible to reserve seats on Swiss trains, except for groups of ten or more persons traveling together. Unlimited stopovers en route are permitted without formality.

Swiss Holiday Card

This is the most practical and convenient ticket for your Swiss trip. It entitles the holder to unlimited travel on the entire network of the Swiss Federal Railways, including most private and mountain railroads, on lake steamers, and on most postal motor coaches, linking Swiss cities and resorts. This pass also permits the holder to purchase in Switzerland an unlimited number of transportation tickets at a reduction of up to 50% for excursions to mountaintops. The Swiss Holiday Card is issued at half price to children over 6 years old and under 16.

With a Holiday Card, you don't need to plan in advance. Just get on a train, a boat, or a postal bus, show your card to the ticket collector, and enjoy your trip. You'll never have to wait long for your next travel link.

A first-class Holiday Card for four days costs $90; for eight days, $108; for 15 days, $137; and for one month, $190. A card for second-class travel is $61 for four days, $74 for eight days, $93 for 15 days, and $129 for one month.

Half-Fare Travel Card

The half-fare card is offered in three categories: **Elite, Senior,** and **Junior.** Each of the three cards entitles the holder to buy *in Switzerland* an unlimited number of full-fare transportation tickets, either round trip or one way, at half price on all regularly scheduled services by rail (including mountain railroads), postal motor coaches, and lake steamers. An Elite card costs $27 for 15 days, $34 for one month. Seniors pay $61 for a card valid for one year. The Junior Half-Fare Card is available to youths from 16 to 26 years of age and costs $17 for one month.

To purchase any of the three half-fare cards, you must provide a new passport photo and state the first day you wish the card to be valid.

Eurailpass

This ticket entitles bona fide residents of North America to unlimited first-class travel over the 100,000-mile national railroad networks of Western European countries, except Great Britain. It is also valid on some lake steamers and private railroads. For many years travelers to Europe have been taking advantage of the Eurailpass, one of the continent's great travel bargains. Passes may be purchased for as short a period as 15 days or as long as three months.

Here's how it works: The pass cannot be purchased in Europe. Vacationers planning a trip can secure the pass at $260 for 15 days, $330 for 21 days, $410 for one month, $560 for two months, or $680 for three months. Children under 4 years of age travel free if they don't occupy a seat (otherwise, they pay half fare). Children under 12 pay half fare. If you're under 26, you can obtain unlimited second-class travel, wherever Eurailpass is honored, on a **Eurail Youthpass,** which costs $290 for one month, $370 for two months.

The advantages are tempting. No tickets, no supplements—simply show the pass to the ticket collector, then settle back to enjoy the scenery. Seat reservations are required on some trains. Many of the trains have couchettes (sleeping cars) for which an additional fee is charged. Obviously, the two- or three-month traveler gets the greatest economic advantages; the Eurailpass is ideal for extensive trips.

Fifteen-day or one-month tourists have to estimate rail distance before determining if such a pass is to their benefit. To obtain full advantage of the ticket for 15 days or a month, you'd have to spend a great deal of time on the train.

Traval agents in all towns and railway agents in major cities such as New York, Montréal, Los Angeles, and Chicago sell the tickets. The Eurailpass is also available at the offices of CIT Travel Service, the Swiss National Railways, the German Federal Railroads, and the French National Railroads.

Glacier Express

Perhaps the most famous part of Switzerland's clean and efficient electrical railway system is the *Glacier Express,* connecting the highest peaks and glaciers of the eastern Alps around St. Moritz with those of the western Alps around Zermatt. This train has been running since 1928, crossing the Furka mountain, but because of the dangers from blizzards and avalanches, the mountain railroad bridges had to be removed in October and reinstalled in May, necessitating a long detour to Zurich in order to go from Zermatt to St. Moritz. Now, since the opening of the eight-mile-long Furka Tunnel in 1982, the *Glacier Express* runs one train each way between the two major resorts daily.

The 7½-hour, 150-mile trip between Zermatt and St. Moritz on the narrow-gauge railroad takes you through 91 viaducts and tunnels and over 291 bridges in comfortable coaches with restaurant cars. Seats are not reserved.

The *Glacier Express* leaves St. Moritz once daily at 8:55 a.m., arriving at Zermatt at 4:45 p.m. The train from Zermatt departs at 10:05 a.m., reaching St. Moritz at 5:52 p.m. From May 23 to September 25, a second train, which requires a change in Richenau, leaves each station daily.

A one-way first-class fare costs $72 per person and $48 in second class. With train connections to Geneva or Zurich, the fare is $147 in first class, $99 in second class.

For more information get in touch with the Swiss National Tourist Office at the addresses listed under "Information" in "The ABC's of Switzerland," Chapter 2.

BY BUS: The yellow alpine postal buses are popular and provide an unrivaled service over numerous and beautiful Swiss passes. Experienced drivers with special training operate these coaches, which have three independent brake systems. They go all around the country and will carry you from your railroad station to remote valleys and across the great alpine passes. A **Postal Coach Holiday Season Ticket,** available at offices of the Swiss Postal Passenger Service, provides half-fare travel for one month, including three days of free travel, on all scheduled Swiss postal bus lines. The price is 50F ($22.98) for adults, 25F ($11.49) for children 6 to 16 years old. **Postal Coach Weekly Passes,** for unlimited travel in the regions of Sion, Sierre, Upper Valais, Ilanz, Thusis,

Appenzell, Toggenburg, and the Principality of Liechtenstein, are available at the post offices of the regions in question. Hand baggage up to 110 pounds can be taken on a postal bus free.

The extremely dense network covered by the Swiss postal buses is useful for trips into the mountains and is a much safer and more comfortable way of seeing the Alps than trying to do your own driving in those regions.

BY BOAT: Passenger boats sail on all the major Swiss lakes and many of the country's rivers, ideal waterways for voyages to scenic spots, and most of the boats have excellent restaurants aboard. In summer more than 100 ships with accommodations for 60,000 passengers operate on many of the Swiss lakes and certain stretches of the Rhine and the Aare. Evening trips with music and dancing are popular. Pleasure boats and lake steamers are ideal means of transportation for the unhurried traveler. The old paddle-steamers on the lakes of Brienz, Geneva, Lucerne, and Zurich, all of which date from before World War I, are particularly attractive and provide a touch of unspoiled romanticism.

Your Holiday Card or Half-Fare Travel card entitles you to travel on lake steamers and on most postal motor coaches, as well as on trains.

The complete official **timetable** covering trains, buses, and lake steamers is available from the Swiss National Tourist Offices in New York and San Francisco at $6 per copy, or in Toronto for $8 Canadian. Addresses and phone numbers for the offices are listed under "Information" in "The ABCs of Switzerland," Chapter II.

BY CAR: Switzerland provides a dense network of well-constructed roads which are complemented by a system of superhighways to serve as quick connecting links between the big cities and the important border towns. Everywhere, at every turn of the road, the Swiss landscape has something new to offer. Travel is made easy by good signposts and clear road signs. Alpine passes are not difficult to cross, but drivers must remember to take reasonable care. Special rail facilities are provided for motorists wishing to transport their cars through the alpine tunnels of the Albula, Furka, Lötschberg, and Simplon. A timetable with rates is available from the Swiss National Tourist Offices. Apart from these facilities and the Great St. Bernard Tunnel, there are no road tolls in Switzerland.

If you are 18 years old, you can drive in Switzerland on your valid home driver's licence. However, car-rental companies set their own driving age, which is usually higher than 18.

You drive to the right in Switzerland, and with the exception of superhighways where the speed limit is 80 miles per hour, the national speed limit for passenger vehicles is 60 m.p.h. In built-up areas, such as cities, towns, and villages, the speed limit is usually 37 m.p.h., unless otherwise posted.

Headlights must be dimmed while driving through road tunnels. Passing on the right is strictly prohibited (even on superhighways), and seatbelts must be worn while driving. You cannot allow children under 12 to ride in the front seat. And *don't* take a chance and drive when you've been drinking.

The Swiss Automobile Clubs, **Automobil-Club der Schweiz,** 39 Wasserwerkgasse, 3000 Berne 13, and **Touring Club Suisse,** 9 rue Pierre-Fatio, 1211 Genève 3, and their branch offices will assist motorists at all times. If you have a breakdown, dial 140 for help. On mountain roads, emergency call boxes will allow you to call for help.

Car Rentals

The competition for the auto-rental business is tough throughout Europe, although many American companies cooperate with European affiliates to guarantee prompt delivery of cars upon your arrival in Switzerland. One of the best is **Budget Rent-a-Car,** which will reserve a wide range of autos for delivery at Basle, Bellinzona, Berne, and Chur. For pickup in Geneva, Lugano, and Zurich, you'll have a choice of getting your car either at the airport or downtown. The Budget Plan Europe is generally cheaper than a per-day rental offer by the same company. The only restrictions are that you need to reserve your car by calling Budget's toll-free number at least five days in advance and keep the car for five days or more.

Rates range from $169 per week and $24 for each additional day for a Fiat 127, going up to $380 a week and $54 for each additional day for an Opal Ascona with automatic transmission. Note that here, as in most car-rental companies, you pay dearly for a car with automatic transmission (the same Opal Ascona with a stick shift costs $280 a week and $40 for each additional day). For super-deluxe spenders, the day rate for a Mercedes 190 is $111 per day for seven days or more. All of the above rates include unlimited mileage. All you do is supply the gas.

Return to the original rental point is stated in the agreement, with the occasional exception of cars rented in Geneva or Zurich, which can sometimes be returned to Zurich and Geneva, respectively, and sometimes to Lugano. These rates change frequently, so be sure to learn the new prices before leaving home. The toll-free number in the U.S. is 800/527-0700. For most places in Canada, call 800/268-8900. In Alaska and Hawaii, call 800/527-0747.

Kemwell Car Rental is another company which, through a toll-free number, will reserve a car for you inexpensively upon your arrival in either Zurich or Geneva. Their Super Saver program offers a Fiat 127 or a Panda 45 with unlimited mileage for $139 a week. Their top-of-the-line automobile which falls into the Super Saver reduction is an Opal Ascona or a Ford Sierra, both manual shift, for $249 a week. You pay for the gas and an additional fee for full collision insurance upon your arrival in Switzerland.

To qualify for the Super Saver program you need to reserve and pay for your car 14 days in advance and return your vehicle to the original rental station. Kemwell is affiliated with rental companies in other cities throughout Switzerland other than Geneva or Zurich, but the Super Saver program doesn't apply there.

For information and reservations, contact the Kemwell Group, 106 Calvert St., Harrison, NY 10528. The nationwide toll-free number is 800/431-1362 (in New York State, dial 800/942-1932).

Chapter II

SETTLING INTO SWITZERLAND

1. The Swiss
2. Food and Drink
3. Sports, Winter and Summer
4. The ABC's of Switzerland

A PEACE-LOVING PEOPLE, the Swiss are friendly but reserved, much more so than Americans. For instance, they don't immediately call each other by their first names upon meeting. But I've found them outgoing and helpful to visitors, especially if you're struggling with a map. The Swiss love maps, and they understand those showing the dense network of well-constructed roads of their country.

For a motoring holiday in Switzerland, I suggest June as the ideal month, followed by either September or October, when the mountain passes are still open. In summer the country is often overrun with visitors. The Swiss are a law-abiding people, and they expect tourists to obey their laws, not the least of which involves drunk driving. For God's sake, don't drink and drive in Switzerland, not only because it's against the law but because you'll need to be not only sober but a skilled motorist to navigate some of those hairpin curves in the mountains.

The country may be peace-loving, having followed a course of neutrality during all wars since 1815, but it has compulsory military service. Its army, however, is devoted solely to the defense of the homeland. Unlike his counterpart in many countries, the Swiss soldier is ever ready. He keeps his military gear at home, including a gas mask, rifle, and plenty of ammunition, and attends obligatory shooting practice annually. In other words, he's ready to fight at any moment, as most Swiss feared would be the case in the dark days of World War II when the country was encircled by Axis powers. Many people believe that the Swiss "sat out the war." Actually, they helped hundreds of men of the Allied air forces find safety and eventual freedom. They also aided prisoners who escaped from the Nazis to find a haven behind Swiss lines.

However, their record in granting women's rights has not been the best. It wasn't until 1971 that Swiss women were granted the right to vote.

1. The Swiss

HISTORY: The history of Switzerland has not been all marked by happy yodeling and edelweiss, since such a strategically situated area was certainly an irresistible lure to empire builders since Roman times. The presence of mankind in the region of present-day civilization has been traced from the Ice Age through the Bronze Age and the Early Iron Age, with the first identifiable occupants being the Celts who entered the alpine regions from the west. The Helvetii, a Celtic tribe defeated by Julius Caesar when they tried to move into southern France in 58 B.C., gave their name to a portion of the country which was known as Helvetia to the Romans, who defeated the resident tribes of barbarians in 15 B.C. Peaceful colonization under Roman rule was ended about A.D. 455, when the history of the region began to be marked by frequent incursions of barbarians and later of Christian forces. Taken over by Charlemagne, the sector now known as Switzerland (then a hodgepodge of cantons with no centralized definition as a country) became a part of the Holy Roman Empire and through various land grabs and battles came eventually under Habsburg domination.

The Swiss may be peace-loving people now, but they have always jealously guarded what they considered theirs, and in 1291 an association of three small states (now cantons), the Perpetual Alliance, was formed and was the germ of the Swiss Confederation of today. In order to be rid of the greedy Habsburgs, the Confederation broke free of the Holy Roman Empire in 1439, but this did not bring freedom from attack by Austria, sometimes supported by France. It was as a result of a treaty with France during one of these allied attacks that Switzerland, now with a growing Confederation, began providing mercenary troops to a foreign power, a practice which at the beginning of the 16th century led to Swiss fighting Swiss. The agreement was ended in about 1515, and in 1516 the Confederates gave up their role as a belligerent force and declared their complete neutrality.

In 1814–1815 at the Congress of Vienna, with Switzerland consisting of 22 of its present 26 cantons (23, with three politically subdivided), the present-day national boundaries of the country were fixed and the perpetual neutrality of the country guaranteed. Free trade zones were set up on the borders of Geneva, and in 1848, by national referendum, a federal constitution was adopted, making Switzerland a federal state, which is today one of the safest and most peaceful countries in the world to visit.

This achievement and maintenance of peace and neutrality in time of wars involving even its closest neighbors has helped the country toward becoming one of the world's greatest tourist centers—small in area but with an extraordinary variety of natural beauty. Its tourists have ranged from Mark Twain to Queen Victoria.

LANGUAGES: The Swiss are vastly diverse as a people, comprising four separate linguistic and ethnic groups—German, Italian, French, and Romansh—with four different overlapping cultural influences. You can drive for less than an hour before a new language emerges. Most of the people of the country—some 70%—speak Swiss-German or Schwyzerdütsch. French is the second language at 20%, with about 9% speaking Italian (in the Ticino district). One percent speaks the esoteric language called Romansh, which contains a pre-Roman vocabulary of words and a substratum of Latin elements. It is believed to be the language of old Helvetia and is spoken mainly by people in the Grisons.

For some incredible reason Switzerland has formed a national identity despite this variation, and it is rare to find a Swiss who speaks only one of the four languages. In addition, many of the country's people speak English, so you might accurately say that Switzerland has five languages.

As well as the four national languages, each district, and in certain parts of the country even each village, has its own dialect. My visits there have begun to let me be able to distinguish (slightly) between the idiomatic vocabulary of a native of Berne, Basle, and other major cities, but I never expect to learn the patois of, say, the villagers in German-speaking Switzerland.

THE PEOPLE: The linguistic situation has brought about an abundance and variety of Swiss folklore, and since every Swiss belongs to a minority of some sort, I find that the people have an inherent tolerance toward different lifestyles, recognizing the right of each person to live as he or she chooses, if this choice is compatible with free will. The Swiss are opposed to any form of compulsion and subordination. They definitely do not like bureaucracy and autocracy.

Industry, crafts, and tourism contribute the major portion of the national income, giving employment to more than a million persons. Only about 7% of the Swiss are engaged in agriculture and forestry, and the country produces about half its food supply, its reputation as an agrarian state being gained through its dairy production, especially cheese. The engineering, chemical, and pharmaceutical industries, as well as makers of clocks and watches, spread Swiss products worldwide.

Three-quarters of the 6,365,960 people living in Switzerland reside in the central lowlands between the Alps and the Jura, more than two-fifths of them in cities and towns of more than 10,000 population, so that in this small country there are some 400 inhabitants per square mile.

RELIGION: As in other European countries, the Reformation, led in Switzerland by Ulrich Zwingli in 1519, brought about internal conflicts between Roman Catholic and Protestant cantons, spurred on by the arrival in 1536 of John Calvin, fleeing France. The spread of Calvinism led to the coining of the French term *Huguenot,* a corruption of the Swiss word *Eidgenosse* (Confederate). After Zwingli's defeat and death in a religious war in 1531, a peace treaty gave each territory the right to choose its own faith. Thus today, living peaceably together, 55% of the Swiss are Protestant, 43% Catholic, and 2% of other faiths.

GOVERNMENT: Swiss motor vehicles carry the international sign "CH," which stands for *Confoederatio Helvetica* and means Swiss Confederation. Depredations of various enemy forces led to a banding together of small Swiss states, now called cantons, some 700 years ago, a move which continued through the centuries as the people saw the value of being allied to defend themselves from attack by greedy outside powers. The present national boundaries were established in 1815.

The Federal Parliament of Switzerland consists of a National Council of 200 members, elected by the people, and the Council of States (cantons) in which each canton has two representatives, making 46 State Councilors in all. The two chambers constitute Switzerland's legislative authority. The executive body, the Federal Council, is made up of seven members who make decisions jointly, although each councilor is responsible for a different department. The presidency of the Federal Council changes annually and the *primus inter pares* ("first among equals") has the responsibility of acting as president of the Confederation. While not particularly flexible, this system of government does guarantee a measure of continuity and stability.

There are 3029 communes in Switzerland, each largely responsible for the independent administration of its public affairs, including the school system, taxation, road construction, water supply, and town planning, among other activities. The cantons were formed by communes joining together over the centuries for mutual advantages. Each canton and each of the three subdivisions has its own constitution, its own laws, and its own government. They have surrendered only certain aspects of their authority to the federal Parliament, such as foreign policy, national defense, and the general economic policy, including such matters as finance and civil and penal legislation.

All Swiss citizens, in general, are eligible to vote on federal matters at the age of 20. However, in the subdivided cantons of Appenzell and in a few small communes the vote is restricted to men, who vote only in cantonal and communal matters, not in the federal referendums or elections.

ART AND CULTURAL LIFE: The Public Art Collection in Basle, the Oskar Reinhart Foundation and Collection in Winterthur, and some private collections with limited public access are known throughout the world. The art museums of Zurich, Berne (including the Klee Foundation), and Geneva, as well as the Avegg Foundation in Berne (Riggisberg) and the Foundation Martin Bodmer (Geneva-Cologny), are also important. The Swiss National Museum in Zurich, the historical museums of Basle, Berne, and Geneva, and numerous local museums contain many valuable exhibits on history, archeology, and the history of art. There are museums of church treasures as well as ethnological displays at cities throughout the country, and an International Museum of Horology at La Chaux-de-Fonds.

Roman ruins are open to visitors at several sites, and churches vie with the thousands of ruined castles as tourist attractions. The architecture of cities and monasteries has been preserved, and examples of superb mastery of the building crafts of earlier days can be seen.

Every town of any size has a resident symphony orchestra and a municipal theater. The theater and concert season begins in September and continues until the end of May. In summer, music lovers from all over the world come to the many music festivals offered, as well as to film and folklore festivals. In some alpine valleys I've enjoyed joining the Swiss in old local costumes as they mark special holidays.

Switzerland's association with the cultural circles of its neighbors, Germany, France, and Italy, and the multilingual character of the country have been favorable to the development of Swiss culture.

2. Food and Drink

Switzerland's cuisine, like its languages, is varied, borrowing heavily from the kitchens of Germany, France, and Italy but with its own unique specialties that can only be called Swiss cookery. Overall, the cuisine is definitely international, but you'll want to try the repertoire of local foods.

CHEESE AND CHEESE DISHES: Cheesemaking is part of the Swiss heritage. Cattle breeding and dairy farming, concentrated in the alpine areas of the country, were pursuits of the inhabitants of the region some 2000 years ago, when the Romans ate *caseus Helveticus* (cheese from Helvetia, now called Switzerland). The St. Gotthard Pass was a well-known cattle route to the south as far back as the 13th century, and the Swiss have exported not only cheese but cattle and know-how to the world, and were important in the development of the dairy industry in the United States.

More than 100 different varieties of cheese are produced today in Switzerland, some of only local use. The cheeses are not mass produced but are made in hundreds of small, strictly controlled dairies, each under the direction of a master cheesemaker with a federal degree, to ensure that the product is made by strict manufacturing standards and properly cured to produce its own natural, protective rind.

The cheese with the holes, known as Switzerland Swiss or Emmentaler, has been widely copied, since nobody ever thought to protect the name for use only on cheeses produced in the Emme Valley until it was too late. Other cheeses of Switzerland, many of which have also had their names plagiarized for use by foreign cheesemakers, are Gruyère, Appenzeller, raclette, royalp, sap sago, and several mountain cheeses including sbrinz and spalen, which are probably most closely related to the *caseus Helveticus* of Roman times.

Cheese fondue is the national dish of Switzerland: cheese (Emmentaler and natural Gruyère used separately, together, or with special local cheeses) melted in white wine flavored with a soupçon of garlic and lemon juice. Seasonings used are traditionally freshly ground pepper, nutmeg, paprika, and Swiss kirsch. Guests surround a bubbling *caquelon* (an earthenware pipkin or small pot) and use long forks to dunk cubes of bread into the hot mixture, stirring them on the bottom of the pot. Other dunkables besides bread cubes are chunks of apples and pears, grapes, cocktail wieners, cubes of boiled ham, shrimp, pitted olives, and tiny boiled potatoes. These morsels are usually secured to the fork by spearing a bread cube after them.

Fondue tradition says that if a woman loses her bread cube in the pot, she owes the man on her right a kiss. If a man loses his morsel when dining in a restaurant, he has to buy the next round of drinks. If the feast is being enjoyed at home, a man owes his hostess a kiss if he loses his cube.

Raclette, another cheese specialty, is almost as famous as fondue. Popular for many centuries, its origin is lost in antiquity, but the word *raclette* comes from the French word *racler,* meaning "to scrape off." In Switzerland, raclette's home is the Valais, source of the Rhône River and one of the most picturesque of the Swiss cantons. Although originally raclette was used only for the dish made from the special mountain cheese of the Valais, today it not only describes the dish itself but also the cheese varieties suitable for melting at an open fire or in an oven. A piece of cheese (traditionally a half to a quarter of a wheel of raclette) is held in front of an open fire. As it starts to soften, it is scraped off onto your plate with a special knife. Diners do not wait until everyone is served, as the unique flavor of the cheese is more delicious when the cheese is hottest. Fresh, crusty homemade dark bread, potatoes boiled in their skins, pickled onions, cucumbers, or small corncobs are the classic accompaniments. You usually eat raclette with a fork, but if you need your knife, use it too.

Besides sampling the cheese fondue and raclette in Swiss restaurants (or homes, if you're lucky enough to get an invitation), you may want to discover favorite cheeses among the many more varieties.

OTHER FOOD SPECIALTIES: The most ubiquitous vegetable dish of the country is **röschti** or **rösti** (hash brown potatoes). I find this excellent when it's been popped into the oven coated with cheese, which melts and turns a golden brown. **Spaetzli** (Swiss dumplings) often appear on the menu.

Lake fish is a specialty in Switzerland, with ombre (a grayling) and ombre chevalier (char) heading the list, the latter being a tasty but expensive treat. From alpine lakes, among other varieties of fish you can enjoy trout or fried filets of tiny lake perch.

Country-cured **sausages** are another good food product in Switzerland, being offered for sale in many of the open markets you'll see as you travel around the country. The best known, air-dried beef, is called **bundnerfleisch,** a specialty in the Grisons. This meat isn't cured; it's dried in the clear, crisp, dry alpine air. Before modern refrigeration this was the Swiss way of preparing meat for winter consumption. Now bundnerfleisch is most often offered as an appetizer. My favorite place to order it is at one of those belvedere restaurants at the top of a chair lift on some alpine perch.

The **Bernerplatte** is the classic provincial dish of Berne. For gargantuan appetites, it's a version of the choucroûte garnie known to French citizens of Alsace. If you order this typical farmer's plate, you'll be confronted by a mammoth pile of sauerkraut or french beans, topped with pigs' feet, sausages, ham, bacon, pork chops—whatever.

In addition to cheese fondue, you may enjoy **fondue bourguignonne,** a dish that has become popular around the world. It consists of chunks of meat spitted on wooden sticks and broiled in oil or butter, seasoned as you choose. Also, many establishments offer **fondue Chinoise,** made with thin slices of beef and Oriental sauces. At the finish, you sip the broth in which the meat was cooked.

In Zurich and the northeast you'll get a German cuisine; in Geneva, French cookery; and in the Ticino, Italian foods, which always taste slightly different from what you're served south of the border. Typical Ticino specialties include **risotto** with mushrooms and a mixed grill known as **fritto misto. Polenta,** made with cornmeal, is popular as a side dish. The Ticino also has lake and river fish such as trout and pike. **Pizza** and **pasta** have spread to all provinces of Switzerland. If you're watching your centimes, either one is often the most economical dish on the menu.

Salads often combine both fresh lettuce and cooked vegetables such as beets. For a dining oddity, ask for a zwiebeln salat (cooked onion salad). In spring, the Swiss adore fresh asparagus. In fact, police have been forced to increase their night patrols in parts of the country to keep thieves out of the asparagus fields.

The glory of Swiss cuisine is its **pâtisseries,** little cakes and confections served all over the country in tearooms and cafés. The most common delicacy is gugelhopf, a big cake shaped like a bun which is traditionally filled with whipped cream.

WHERE TO FIND FOOD: Breakfast, usually included in the price of your hotel room, will probably be continental style and is often served as a buffet meal. You'll get rolls, butter, preserves, coffee or tea, and some fruit juices. If you order such extras as orange juice, bacon, ham, or eggs, you may be stuck with a stiff tab.

When in doubt about where to eat in Switzerland, try a railroad station buffet. They're generally excellent and medium in price. If you want a fast-food meal, head for an imbiss or snackbar, where the food is tasty, especially the open-face sandwiches. Prices are modest, as working people frequent these establishments.

HAVE A DRINK: Never order water, beer, or coffee with fondue. Your Swiss waiter will be horrified and will privately consider you a barbarian. White wine is the invariable choice of beverage with such a dish. If you don't like white wine, however, you might get by with substituting kirsch or tea.

There are almost no restrictions on the sale of alcohol in Switzerland, but prices of drinks such as bourbon, gin, and scotch are usually much higher than in the States, and bartenders are not noted for their generosity in pouring.

Swiss **wines** are superb, especially if you're in the region where the grapes are grown. Many I've tasted along, say, Lake Geneva are not even exported but are consumed entirely by the local populace. If possible, always try to ask for a local wine when ordering a meal. Unlike French wines, Swiss wines are best when "new." Wine in French-speaking Switzerland is as popular as beer to a Münchner. Instead of a martini before a meal, a Swiss business person is likely to order white wine as an apéritif. As you are unlikely to be familiar with the local Swiss wines of a particular canton, you should ask the headwaiter for advice. He'll usually be only too happy to recommend a good selection.

In this relatively small country, vineyards, stretching along the lakes, nestling in the hills, or tucked away on mountainsides, produce a variety of excellent wines. Most are white, but there are also good rosés and fragrant red wines. Most wines that are produced in sufficient quantity for export are from four wine-making areas: Valais (the valley of the Rhône), Lake Geneva, Ticino, and Seeland. However, more than 300 small wine-growing areas are spread over the rest of the country, especially where German dialects are spoken. You'll have to try these on their home ground, as quantities are so limited that the wines are easily consumed by the commune that produces them.

For information on where to look for wines, plus advice on taking some home with you, get in touch with the **Swiss Wine Growers Association,** P.O. Box 853, 1001 Lausanne, Switzerland, or in the U.S., from **Swissmart Inc.,** 444 Madison Ave, New York, NY 10022 (tel. 212/751-3768).

Swiss **beer** is an excellent brew, and is of course the preferred drink in the German-speaking part of the country. It varies in quality. If you want to face a mug of Hell, you'll be served a light beer. Dunkel is dark beer.

Swiss **liqueurs** are tasty and highly potent. The most popular are **kirsch,** the national hard drink of Switzerland (made of the juice of cherry pits), Marc, pflümli, and Williamine, my personal favorite, made of pears.

3. Sports, Winter and Summer

When you think of sports in Switzerland, it's a safe bet that the first thing that springs to mind is skiing, which is available in both winter and summer, although, of course, winter is the prime time. In fact in some resorts of the country winter is the "high season" and tariffs are higher than in summer, unlike most of the rest of Europe. However, Switzerland seems to have been designed with the sports person in mind. The country has everything from Swiss-style wrestling to "alpine baseball."

The abundance of magnificent mountain slopes guarantees every possible skiing thrill plus facilities for other snow- and ice-related sports. These include cross-country skiing, skating, ice hockey, curling, tobogganing, and ski-bobbing in winter.

SKIING: Ski schools, ski instructors, and the best ski equipment in the world are available all over, and Switzerland constantly improves on its skiing facilities. Nearly all resorts are blessed with ski-rental shops. *Warning:* Always carry plenty of suntan lotion, even in winter. I've seen inexperienced alpine visitors get badly sunburned because of the intense reflection of sunlight off the snow.

The best known areas for skiing are the Bernese Oberland, the Grisons, and the Valais, but there are many, many others. Skiing facilities will be previewed under these individual chapter headings. Skiing is big business in Switzerland—an estimated 40% of the tourist dollar is spent in pursuit of it. There are more than 1700 mountain railways and ski lifts to take you effortlessly to the starting point of downhill runs.

Summer skiing is most often called **glacier skiing.** This sport takes place on glaciers which still keep their snow even in the hottest months of July and August. Glacier skiing is best before lunchtime, especially in the early-morning hours. After that the snow might become a little mushy. The best glacier ski resorts are Zermatt, St. Moritz, Engelberg, Saas Fee, Gstaad, and Pontresina, although there are many more of course. Ski schools and ski lifts are open in summer.

Experienced skiers may wish to take a popular spring ski tour, the **Haute Route,** which crosses the French Alps into Switzerland via various routes, a week's tour which can usually be made from March to May. Led by a professional guide, skiers stop overnight and for noon rests at cabins maintained by the Swiss Alpine Club (see "Mountaineering," below, for more information on this club).

Cross-country skiing (called Langlaufing) is the fastest-growing sport in Europe. St. Moritz, Pontresina, and Montana are among the leaders in this field. A ski instructor told me that "it's hardly possible to break a bone" in this sport! You go at your own speed, and you never have to stay in your hotel if high slopes are closed when you ski cross-country. This sport allows many visitors who can't do downhill skiing to "be a part of things." There are no age limits and no charges for use of the cross-country trails, which are well marked.

From December 16 to March 31 you can get information on conditions in major ski areas in Switzerland before you leave home by calling the Swiss National Tourist Office snow report (tel. 212/757-6336), 24 hours a day.

For the Nonskier

Believe it or not, the so-called nonskier is now a major factor at all ski resorts. It's estimated that at such fashionable resorts as Gstaad, Pontresina, Arosa, and Davos, one out of two guests is a nonskier. That trend is growing rapidly too. If you don't ski, there are a host of other activities—not just après-ski. With sunbathing on mountain terraces, walks through forests, discos, sleigh rides, and sightseeing excursions, the nonskier manages to fill up his or her day.

CURLING AND SKATING: Curling is another "boom" sport in Switzerland. Professional skiers dismiss it as a "sport for the elderly," but this "ain't necessarily so." Curling requires team effort, is particularly popular at Davos, Villars, Gstaad, and Zermatt.

Ice skating is one of the leading winter sports of Switzerland, and nearly all major resorts have natural ice rinks. Also, there are dozens more artificial ones, of which Davos has the best.

GOLF: There are 30 golf courses in Switzerland at strategic spots throughout this small country, so you can almost always find one in easy reach. The altitude at which they lie ranges from 700 feet above sea level to the highest one at St. Moritz, 6100 feet up. You can enjoy your game at the same time as viewing beautiful scenery and breathing the bracing Swiss air. Visitors are welcome at local clubs, particularly on weekdays. Greens fees are from 15F ($6.89) to 38F ($17.46) per day, or you can get a weekly or monthly card for a reasonable fee. Golf clubs can be rented at the course's pro shop, and you can get instruction to improve your game if you wish. There are also many miniature golf courses to be found.

TENNIS: Tennis is popular, and there are many courts all over the country, both outdoor and indoor, including those at Saas-Fee and Flims. Most resorts have tennis courts, but if your hotel does not, you can probably use a local club for a nominal fee.

WATER SPORTS: You'll find opportunities for swimming at all altitudes in Switzerland, both at beaches along lakes and rivers and in pools. Most beaches are open from June to September or even longer in warmer regions, although if you grew up in Miami the water may be too cold for you in any season. Beaches are equipped for all manner of water sports. More and more of the big hotels provide indoor swimming pools, heated for use all year if you can't take the cold lakes. Sailing, waterskiing, windsurfing, and canoeing are all available.

HORSEBACK RIDING: St. Moritz and Arosa are both good centers for this recreational activity. Horse racing on the snow, in my opinion, is best left for connoisseurs. There are horses for rent at some 230 riding centers.

HANG-GLIDING: This dangerous and expensive sport is one of Switzerland's newest. The mountains and passes are subject to wind currents which may be exciting but are certainly scary, sometimes even for the most experienced gliders.

FISHING: The dedicated angler will find plenty of excitement in fishing some of Switzerland's abundance of rivers, lakes, and streams. Trout is found in most waters up to altitudes of over 6000 feet. Lake trout have been known to weigh in at 22 pounds. You need a license to fish, but municipal authorities can get you one easily. Regulations vary from place to place, so to be sure you're legal, inquire at a hotel or local tourist office.

CYCLING: Riding a bicycle is both a sport and an economical way of touring the country. You can rent one for a small fee at many railroad stations and turn it in at another station. A bicycle can be transported on a passenger train for a nominal fee. Rental rates for bicycles for both men and women are: with valid train ticket, up to 4 hours, 5F ($2.30); 4 to 12 hours, 7F ($3.22); 12 to 24 hours, 9F ($4.14); each additional day, 7F ($3.22). Without a train ticket, the prices are: up to 4 hours, 6F ($2.76); 4 to 12 hours, 9F ($4.14); 12 to 24 hours, 12F ($5.51); and each additional day, 9F ($4.14). Third-party insurance is included in the rental contract. You should reserve a bicycle at the station from which you plan to start a day or so ahead if possible.

The **Swiss Touring Club** maintains ten cycling centers throughout the country where you can rent bicycles and get brochures and maps of cycling circuits in the vicinity of the center. Rental is 8F ($3.68) for up to four hours or 12F ($5.51) for a whole day. The touring club directs you along routes where there isn't much motor traffic, taking you through villages and past castles and manor houses you might not otherwise discover. Even in remote areas you can usually find someone with good enough English to help you if you have a problem or if you're lost.

HIKING: With 30,000 miles of well-marked and well-maintained walking paths, Switzerland is ideal for hikers. The paths lead through alpine valleys, over lowlands, up hills to meadows, or into the heart of the Alps. Whether you choose a gentle walk or a rigorous trek to the high areas, you will see unspoiled beauty such as alpine meadows luxuriant with blooming wildflowers, which make your hike worthwhile. Many hotels offer walking or hiking excursions.

MOUNTAINEERING: Mountain-climbing schools where you can learn all about this exciting sport are found in Andermatt, Champéry, Crans, Davos, Les Diablerets, Fiesch, La Fouly, Glarus, Grindelwald, Kandersteg, Klosters, Meiringen, Pontresina, Riederalp, Saas-Fee, Saas-Grund, Schwende, Täsch, Zermatt, and Zinai, and guides are available at many other resorts. The peaks of the Swiss Alps offer challenges in both summer and winter.

Access to these peaks has been facilitated by the **Swiss Alpine Club,** which has built mountain huts at strategic spots throughout the country. Also, there are comfortable hotels and inns at favorable altitudes for alpine treks, many on high peaks and passes. The huts of the Swiss Alpine Club are modest, with bunkrooms sleeping 10 to 20, and are open to every alpinist. The average rate for a night's lodging (without food) is 22F ($10.11) for nonmembers of the club, 11F ($5.06) for members. The Swiss Alpine Club, founded in 1863, promotes mountaineering and ski tours in the high mountains and also organizes rescue service in the Swiss Alps. If you're interested in joining, write to the Swiss Alpine Club (SAC), Sektion Zermatt, Postfach 1, 3920 Zermatt, Switzerland.

4. The ABC's of Switzerland

Before you check into your hotel, you've got to reach it, and therefore, immediately upon your arrival in Switzerland, you'll need to know some "facts of life" to ease your adjustment into the country.

A number of situations, such as a medical emergency, might arise during your vacation, and there are various customs, such as tipping, you'll need to know about.

The concierge of your hotel, incidentally, is a usually reliable dispenser of information, offering advice about everything. If he or she fails you, the following summary of pertinent survival data may prove helpful.

Note: Much of this ABC-type data, such as how to get from the Zurich airport into town, will be listed under the individual cities.

BANKS: Banks are usually open Monday through Friday from 8:30 a.m. to 4:30 p.m.; closed Saturday, Sunday, and legal holidays. Foreign currency may be exchanged at larger railroad stations and airports until 10 p.m. daily.

BULLETIN: In a world of fast-changing developments, it's hard to keep abreast of late-breaking events that may affect your travel plans. For that reason, I recommend a new travel newsletter to readers who travel a lot and want "the latest word" on "what's happening" in Europe. *Travel Bulletin* is intended only for travel agents, but has also recently been made available to readers of the Dollarwise series. This way you'll learn the news the agents are getting at the same time they do. This four-page newsletter is mailed first class to its subscribers every month, and is augmented by a two-page supplement seasonally on some timely subject. It is completely independent of sponsors and advertisers, and seeks out bargains, particularly cut-rate air fares, as part of its "value for dollar" policy. You can subscribe by paying a yearly fee of $35 to Department SWI, *Travel Bulletin,* c/o Pinder Lane, 159 West 53rd St., New York, NY 10019.

BUSINESS HOURS (OFFICES): Most offices are open on weekdays from 8 a.m. to noon and from 2 to 6 p.m.; closed Saturday.

CIGARETTES: Most popular U.S. brands can be found. However, there are many British- and Swiss-made brands you may want to try, especially if you like a mild cigarette. Cigars and pipe tobacco are available almost everywhere as well.

CLIMATE: The temperature range is about the same as in the northern United States but without extremes of hot or cold. Summer temperatures seldom rise above 80 in the cities, and the humidity is low. Because of clear air and lack of wind in the high alpine regions, sunbathing is possible even in winter. In the southern part of Switzerland the temperature is mild year round, allowing subtropical vegetation to grow.

CURRENCY: The basic unit of Swiss currency is the **franc** (F) with banknotes issued for 10- to 1000-franc denominations, and coins being minted in 5-, 10-, 20-, and 50-centime values as well as for 1, 2, and 5 francs. One franc is worth 100 centimes. As a general guideline, the price conversions in this book have been computed at the rate of 2.1763 Swiss francs to $1 U.S. (1F equals $.4595). Bear in mind, however, that international exchange rates are far from stable, and this ratio might be hopelessly outdated by the time you arrive in Switzerland. As a guide only, I'll include the following equivalents at the exchange rate given above, which may be invalid at the time of your trip.

Francs	U.S.$	Francs	U.S.$
1	.46	100	45.95
2	.92	125	57.44
3	1.38	150	68.93
4	1.84	175	80.41
5	2.30	200	91.90
10	4.60	225	103.39
20	9.19	250	114.88
30	13.79	275	126.35
40	18.38	300	137.85
50	22.98	400	183.80
75	34.46	500	229.75

CUSTOMS: U.S. residents returning from abroad are allowed to bring back $400 in duty-free items for personal use only. To qualify, you must have been outside the U.S. at least 48 hours and not have claimed an exemption in the past 30 days. Articles valued in excess of $400 will be assessed at a flat duty rate of 10%. Antiques and original works of art produced 100 years prior to your date of reentry to the U.S. may be brought home duty free, but you must be able to prove their authenticity. Gifts for your personal use, but not for business purposes, may be included in the $400 exemption. Gifts sent home from abroad may be valued at $50. Liquor is limited to one 32-ounce bottle; tobacco, to 200 cigarettes and 100 cigars. Keep all your receipts for purchases made in Switzerland or elsewhere on your trip abroad as you may be asked for proof of the prices you paid.

ELECTRIC CURRENT: The current used in Switzerland is 220 volts, alternating current (AC), 50 cycles. Some international hotels are specially wired to allow North Americans to plug in their appliances, but you'll usually need a transformer for your electric razor, hairdryer, or soft-contact-lens sterilizer. Ask at the electrical department of a large hardware store for the size converter you'll need. You'll also need an adapter to channel the electricity from the Swiss system to the flat-pronged American system. Don't plug anything into the house current in Switzerland without being certain the systems are compatible.

GAMBLING: A number of Swiss towns and resorts have casinos which, while perhaps not enjoying the affluence of casinos in other countries because of certain restrictions, still offer a wide choice of entertainment, including folklore displays. Gambling in Switzerland is restricted to *boule* games, and the maximum bet that can be placed is 5F ($2.30). The minimum age for gambling in Switzerland is 20.

GASOLINE: The cost is about $2.25 per gallon, which, as I figure it, is about 4.2¢ per kilometer to drive around this mountainous land. Gas stations are usually open from 8 a.m. to 10 p.m. U.S. gasoline credit cards are generally not accepted.

HOTELS: The legend is that there's no such thing as a bad Swiss hotel. That's an old claim, and unfortunately it may not be as true as it once was. In most cases hotels in Switzerland are clean, comfortable, and efficiently run. On the deluxe level they are among the finest in the world (two in Zurich are, in fact, the very best in all of Europe). César Ritz, incidentally, who went on to other places, came from Switzerland, and indeed the country is known for its fine hotel schools. The hotel situation in general, however, isn't quite the same as it was in the good old days. Many Swiss citizens are lured to more attractive jobs (such as making Swiss watches) rather than scrubbing toilets. Foreign workers—many not as well trained as the Swiss—have been imported, and as a result many hotels report what is politely called "problems of staff." Even if standards aren't up to the legend, however, Swiss hotels are still among the finest in the world, taken as a whole. In one hostelry, when irate Yugoslav maids walked off the job, the manager rushed to scrub the bathtubs himself!

INFORMATION: Before you go, you can get the latest in tourist information from the **Swiss National Tourist Office,** 608 Fifth Ave., New York, NY 10020 (tel. 212/757-5944); 104 S. Michigan Ave., Chicago, IL 60603 (tel. 312/641-0050); 250 Stockton St., San Francisco, CA (tel. 415/362-2260); and in Canada, P.O. Box 215, Commerce Court Postal Station, Toronto, Ont. M5L 1E8 (tel. 416/868-0584).

LEGAL HOLIDAYS: In Switzerland, January 1 and 2 (New Year), Good Friday, Easter Monday, Ascension Day, Whit Monday, and December 25 and 26 for Christmas are celebrated as legal holidays.

PASSPORT AND VISA: Every traveler entering Switzerland must have a valid passport, although it is not necessary for North Americans to have a visa if they do not stay longer than three continuous months. For information on permanent residence in Switzerland, as well as on work permits, get in touch with the nearest Swiss Consulate.

PETS: Dogs and cats brought into Switzerland from abroad will require a veterinary certificate stating that the animal has been vaccinated against rabies not less than 30 days and not more than one year prior to entry into the country. This regulation also applies to dogs and cats returning after a temporary absence from Switzerland but is not applicable to animals transported through the country by rail or air traffic.

POST OFFICE: Post offices in large cities are open from 7:30 a.m. to noon and 1:45 to 6:30 p.m. on weekdays, from 7:30 to 11 a.m. on Saturday. If you have letters forwarded to a post office to be collected after you arrive, you'll need a passport for identification. The words "Poste Restante" must be clearly written on the envelope. Letters not collected within 30 days are returned to the sender. It costs 70 centimes to send a postcard to a foreign country from Switzerland by ordinary mail; 1F (46¢) for a postcard to the U.S. or Canada via airmail. Airmail letters up to 10 grams in weight to the U.S. and Canada cost 1.20F (55¢); 10 to 20 grams, 1.50F (69¢); and 20 to 50 grams, 2.70F ($1.24). Postcards and letters mailed to points within the country cost 40 centimes.

SHOPPING: Switzerland's superb products make it a shopper's paradise. English is spoken in most shops and department stores. Fine watches come in a wide variety and are likely to sell at about half the price you'd pay back home. Excellent buys are textiles, embroideries, fine handkerchiefs, wool sportswear, and linen. Those luscious Swiss chocolates are to be found in many sizes, shapes, and flavors. The craftsmanship for which the country has long been noted is to be found in precision instruments, drafting sets, multiblade pocketknives, typewriters, music boxes, woodcarvings, ceramics, and other handmade items. Antiques and art books, ski clothes and equipment, and shoes are just a few of the fine articles you can find in Switzerland.

SHOPPING HOURS: Shops are usually open weekdays from 8 a.m. to 12:15 p.m. and 1:30 to 6:30 p.m., from 1:30 to 4 p.m. on Saturday. In large cities most shops do not close during the lunch hour, although many do so on Monday morning.

SPAS: The spa treatment, a form of therapy many thousands of years old, is still in vogue despite the progress achieved in medical science. The natural curative springs of Switzerland are said not only to help restore the sick to health but also to ward off disease. Proponents of spa therapy point to the quiet and relaxation found in the health resorts as remedies for psychological stress and the pressures of everyday life.

Most resorts with the marked seal of approval by the Association of Swiss Health Spas and the Swiss Society of Balneology and Bioclimatology include a medical examination in their package plans for visitors, together with thermal baths and excursions.

There are 22 recognized spas in Switzerland, many of them open all year.

The following will provide you with information about spa vacations: Health and Fitness Vacations, 100 N. Biscayne Blvd., Miami, FL 33132 (tel. 305/379-8451); Health and Pleasure Tours, Inc., 165 West 46th St., New York, NY (tel. 212/586-1175); Odyssey Travel Ltd., 2050 Chestnut St., San Francisco, CA 94123 (tel. 415/567-9164); Ring International, P.O. Box 118, Novato, CA 94947 (tel. 415/892-3966); Selective Tours of Switzerland, 301 E. 48th St., New York, NY 10017 (tel. 212/758-4275 or toll free 800/223-6764); or Swissair, Tours Dept., 608 Fifth Ave., New York, NY 10020 (tel. 212/995-4400 or toll free 800/221-6644; in New York State, 800/522-9606).

TAXES AND SERVICE CHARGES: No taxes are added to purchases in Switzerland. Swiss merchants pay tax to the government, but the percentage is included in the price marked on any object. Likewise, service charges are included in restaurant bills. If a service charge is not indicated, ask the waiter or waitress. The only unclear area is in taxicabs. Signs will be posted in the cab, and usually the tip is included, but sometimes it isn't.

TELEPHONES: Always enter the phone booth with enough change since your call will be cut off once your Swiss francs run out. The telephone system is well organized, reaching everywhere in the country, and it's entirely automatic. Helpful numbers to know are: 111 for directory assistance; 120 for tourist information or in winter for snow reports; 140 for help on the road; 162 for weather forecasts; and 163 for up-to-the-minute information on road conditions. A call to the U.S. or Canada costs 5.40F ($2.48) per minute, or you can call your home collect. As in many European countries, it's considerably less expensive to make calls from a public phone booth, as substantial service charges are added for calls made at hotels.

TIME: Switzerland's clocks (and there sure are plenty of them) are always six hours ahead of Eastern Standard Time in the United States, only one hour ahead of Greenwich Mean Time.

TIPPING: The tip is automatically included on all hotel and restaurant bills. It's neither necessary nor expected for you to leave anything extra.

TOILETS: Most Swiss public rest rooms are clean and modernized. Except in this multilingual country, you'll have to know what you're looking for—be it WC, Toiletten, Toilettes, or Gabinetti. Women might be Damen or Frauen, Signore or Donne, Femmes or Dames, and men might be Herren or Männer, Signori or Uomini, Hommes or Messieurs. Most public rest rooms are at bus stations, railway termini, cable-car platforms, or wherever. There are never enough when you need one. You may have to rely on a café, as many Swiss do. Most of these public lavatories are free; if not, have a 20-centime (9¢) piece ready.

Chapter III

ZURICH

1. Accommodations
2. Where to Dine
3. What to See
4. Where to Shop
5. After Dark in Zurich
6. The ABC's of Zurich
7. Exploring the Environs

DEEP IN THE HEART of Helvetia, Zurich is the largest city in Switzerland. At an elevation of 1341 feet, it sprawls across 36 square miles, with a population of 380,000 Zurichers, a decline since its 1960 high.

At the foot of Lake Zurich in northern Switzerland, it is one of the most beautiful cities on the continent. Since it suffered no war damage, it still has very much a 19th-century appearance.

Called the city by the lake, Zurich lies on both banks of the Limmat River and its tributary, the Sihl. Quays line the riverbanks and the lake. In all it's like a capital "Y" formed by the corner of the lake and river. It lies between the wooded slopes of the Zürichberg and the Uetliberg.

The city is big enough to offer all the amenities a visitor would need, but it's also small enough to discover easily on your own.

Unlike French-speaking Geneva (which we'll visit later), Zurich is firmly German speaking (or rather, Zurichers speak "Schwyzerdütsch"). A *rue* becomes a *strasse* in Zurich.

Zurich is the capital of a canton of the same name, having joined the Swiss Confederation in 1351. However, contrary to what many visitors erroneously think, it is not the capital of Switzerland, or at least it hasn't been since 1848. That distinction belongs to Bern.

Surprisingly, Zurich is the leading tourist attraction of the country, and that's probably because it has the tiny nation's biggest airport. The city is also heavily industrialized, but it isn't the Manchester of Switzerland. The factories run on electricity, which keeps the skies over Zurich from being polluted. It earns a fifth of the national income.

That income is often stored in the banks of Zurich. The "gnomes" of Zurich, as they have been so unflatteringly referred to, is a reference to the city's bankers. The headquarters of five major Swiss banks alone lie on the Bahnhofstrasse (mountains of gold are literally buried in vaults underneath these banks). Zurich is a very wealthy city, and has been for centuries since it first prospered as a textile center.

But it's far from being a dreary city of commerce. Zurich was a great center of liberal thought, having attracted Lenin, Carl Jung, James Joyce, and Thomas Mann. The Dadaist school was founded here in 1916.

Yet when Zurich makes the headlines today, it's usually in reference to being a center of international finance. Today you see as many Japanese or Arabs as you do Americans. Its gold trading and stock exchange are part of the legend of the city, which has come a long way since it was a Roman settlement known as Turicum.

In the heart of Europe, Zurich doesn't enjoy Riviera-type summers. Often in July and August it's possible to swim in the lake (which is never warm enough for Miami-reared me). Many days are likely to be chilly and cloudy, obscuring the view of the Alps in the distance. Spring and fall can be quite nippy, but when a sunny, bright clear day dawns, Zurich is one of the most enjoyable cities of Europe. It gets cold here in the winter, but not as severe as it does farther north. The temperature rarely goes below zero at that time. The average temperature in January is 30°F, rising to an average of only 61°F in July. Climate, frankly, is not a major factor in determining a visit to Zurich since it's a livable metropolis all year round.

A former seat of the Reformation, Zurich is staunchly Protestant (some say Puritan). It's known for its hard-working people, who are good, honest, and industrious, and to many critics, too stiff and formal. But in spite of its press, it doesn't fold up at ten o'clock. Perhaps it would like to if it followed its own heart, but in the past two decades it has received far too many foreign visitors to go to bed so early. These visitors need entertainment, and being canny merchants, the Zurichers try to oblige.

I consider it one of the most rewarding sightseeing targets in the country (and a few pages from now we'll see why). In the meantime, we'll face the problem of finding an accommodation in Zurich. That can indeed be quite a problem.

1. Accommodations

Members of the international community of commerce, finance, and business often fill up the top hotels of Zurich, and in addition to that, the city is often the setting of conventions and fairs. I've had trouble finding an accommodation even in February. If possible, then, you should arrive with a reservation. And be prepared to pay handsomely for your stay in Zurich, although I'll survey an array of moderately priced lodgings for the economizer.

These warnings aside, know that Zurich is an ideal place to get acquainted with Swiss hospitality. You're faced with 120 hotels and some 11,000 beds. They range from the most deluxe and sumptuously furnished suites in Europe (rivaled only by a few deluxe hotels in Asia) to a lowly pension that isn't so lowly (likely to be perched on a hillside and run by a kindly frau who keeps everything immaculate).

It's hard to find a dirty hotel in Zurich. Some of the cheaper accommodations may be a little rawbone in decor, but, chances are, they'll be immaculately kept. You'll often end up in an *alkoholfrei* hotel, which means simply that they don't have a liquor license.

We'll start with a survey of the most expensive digs, then descend the price scale. In other words, if you want the best in the budget range, read from the bottom of the list.

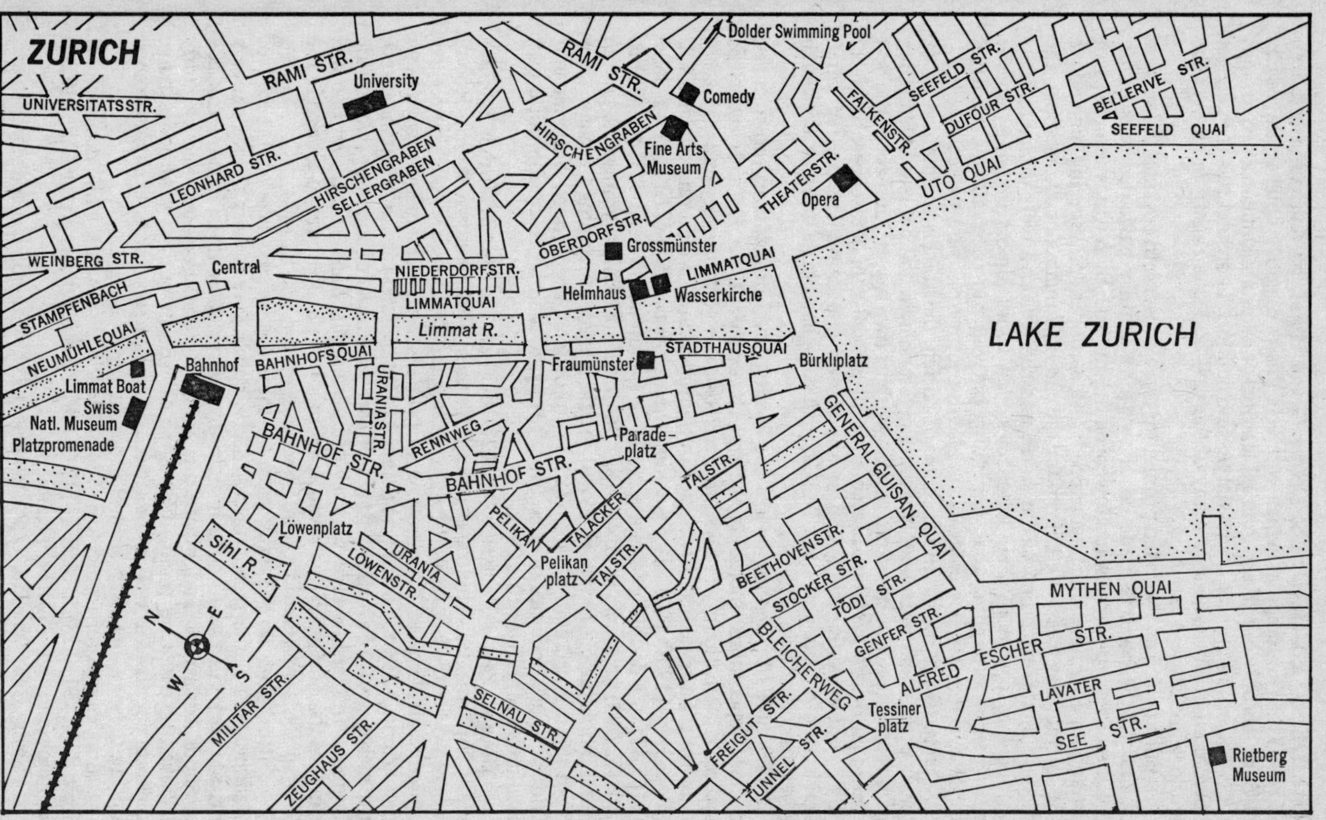
ZURICH
LAKE ZURICH
UNIVERSITATSSTR.
RAMI STR.
University
HIRSCHENGRABEN
SELLERGRABEN
LEONHARD STR.
WEINBERG STR.
STAMPFENBACH
NEUMUHLEQUAI
Central
NIEDERDORFSTR.
LIMMATQUAI
OBERDORFSTR.
Limmat R.
Comedy
Dolder Swimming Pool
Fine Arts Museum
Grossmünster
Wasserkirche
Helmhaus
Fraumünster
STADTHAUSQUAI
Bürkliplatz
THEATERSTR.
Opera
FALKENSTR.
SEEFELD STR.
DUFOUR STR.
UTO QUAI
BELLERIVE STR.
SEEFELD QUAI
GENERAL-GUISAN-QUAI
MYTHEN QUAI
Rietberg Museum
ESCHER STR.
LAVATER STR.
SEE STR.
ALFRED
Tessiner platz
GENFER STR.
TODI STR.
STOCKER STR.
BEETHOVENSTR.
BLEICHERWEG
TUNNEL STR.
FREIGUT STR.
TALSTR.
Parade-platz
BAHNHOF STR.
RENNWEG
TALACKER
Pelikan platz
PELIKAN
URANIA
URANIASTR.
LOWENSTR.
Löwenplatz
SELNAU STR.
ZEUGHAUS STR.
MILITAR STR.
Sihl R.
BAHNHOFSQUAI
Bahnhof
Limmat Boat
Swiss Natl. Museum
Platzpromenade
N
S
E
W

THE DELUXE CITADELS: Dolder Grand Hotel, 65 Kurhausstrasse (tel. 251-62-31). The funicular which connects this prestigious hotel to the center of Zurich is only one of the unusual features of an establishment noted around the world as the epitome of class, style, and comfort. I consider this the greatest hotel in all of Europe, as do many of the well-heeled clients from all over the world who frequent it.

Built on top of a wooded promontory in a conservative residential section of Zurich, the hotel is made up of two 19th-century balconied wings with half-timbered replicas of watchtowers on the far ends. Both wings seem to pivot around an enormous dungeon capped with a copper spire soaring high above the surrounding trees. Were it not for the carefully maintained flowerbeds, the modern annex extending off the back, and the conservatively dressed clients getting into or out of their limousines, you could almost imagine yourself gazing up at a building that, depending on your mood, is either a medieval fortress, a Renaissance château, or a 19th-century pleasure palace.

Only six minutes from the center of Zurich, the hotel is surrounded by six tennis courts, an immaculately maintained nine-hole golf course, a swimming pool that can only be described as vast (with its own waves), and about the best tended gardens to be found in a country full of well-kept landscapes. In winter you'll find a skating rink, and in any season you can enjoy the renovated ambience of the public rooms. The Gobelin salon has a huge tapestry in it worth several small fortunes.

Raoul T. de Gendre, one of the leading hotel directors in the business, oversees operations, including the superb restaurant, La Rotonde, which is staffed by a small army of Swiss technicians to serve your every culinary need. A continental breakfast is included in the room rates, which range from 140F ($64.33) to 190F ($87.31) in a single and from 230F ($105.69) to 360F ($165.42) in a double. Meals are available for anywhere from 42F ($19.30) to 50F ($22.98) for lunch, from 48F ($22.06) to 55F ($25.27) for dinner. A private hotel limousine charges 20F ($9.19) for six persons, including baggage, to or from the railroad station; 46F ($21.14) to or from the airport. The funicular and the sports facilities may be used free by guests on presentation of a pass available at the reception desk.

Baur au Lac, 1 Talstrasse (tel. 221-16-50), is the favorite Zurich hotel for many sophisticates, who travel miles for a meal at the renowned Grill Room, where no luxury is considered too extravagant. If, during lunch, you receive a phone call from say, Bahrain, someone will discreetly let you know where you can take it. A Zurich focal point since 1844, the hotel is cosmopolitan, grand, expensive, and a favorite with American stockbrokers soliciting worldwide business. In fact in a recent survey of international bankers Baur au Lac was rated as the number six or seven hotel in all of Europe, ranked alongside the Ritz in Paris and Claridge's in London.

Sitting like a good gray lady on the shore of the lake at the end of Bahnhofstrasse, the facade of this stone building rises four stories above a private park filled with modern sculpture and valuable trees. The interior is a spacious fantasy of Tudor paneling, massive stone fireplaces, and elegantly subdued colors. One room, offering stock market quotes from at least five different countries as well as the services of private secretaries, excludes women during the day, but they are welcomed in the evening.

Singles rent for from 140F ($64.33) to 200F ($91.90), while doubles cost from 240F ($110.28) to 320F ($147.04). Fixed-price meals go for 42F ($19.30) at lunch and 46F ($21.14) at dinner.

Savoy Baur en Ville, 12 Poststrasse (tel. 211-53-60), is a conservative and refined hotel conscious of its role as one of the premier hotels of Zurich, conspicuously located on the Paradeplatz and rising grandly six floors above the exclusive stores around. The Baur en Ville has always been a Zurich landmark, and after recent renovations it's better than ever. Owned by bankers, the hotel has rooms that are quietly dignified, decorated in a wide range of styles, from leather-upholstered modern to a subdued Louis XV. The public rooms are high ceilinged, decorated either in a somber forest green with lots of wood detailing or, in the case of the main salon, in a vivid scarlet with white and gilt rococo adornment.

All rooms are air-conditioned, although you'll be able to open the windows of those units with balconies if you want to catch a few minutes of sunbathing or choose to take breakfast on your terrace. Singles rent for from 130F ($59.74) to 170F ($78.12), while doubles cost 220F ($101.09) to 280F ($128.66), breakfast included.

You'll find that the sidewalk café is one of the most frequented daytime establishments of the city, while the Savoy Grill is a pleasant, top-notch restaurant.

Hotel Zurich, 42 Neumuhlequai (tel. 363-63-63), is my favorite among all the high-rise modern hostelries of Zurich. Rising high above the banks of the Limmat, a short pleasant walk across the river from the railroad station, the hotel looks from the outside like a tasteful black-and-white piece of concrete-and-steel modern architecture. The views from the top, by the way, are spectacular, showing to maximum advantage the spires and green parks of downtown Zurich.

The bedrooms are sunny, well decorated, and well appointed with all the modern conveniences you'd expect in a deluxe hotel, including attractive bathrooms, many dramatically tiled in black or midnight blue. When you tire of the view from your room, the public bars, salons, and restaurants cater to a sophisticated, well-to-do crowd from around the world. Singles here rent for from 130F ($59.74) to 170F ($78.12), while doubles cost 180F ($82.71) to 260F ($119.47). With 221 rooms to select from, you won't lack for choice accommodations. Breakfast and use of the futuristic swimming pool are included in the tariffs.

Hilton International, Zurich Airport (tel. 810-31-31), sprawling across several hundred yards of hillside near the Kloten Airport, has curving wings which look like an expanse of interconnected railroad cars joined at the center by the panoramic windows of the restaurant area and sun terrace.

The pleasantly decorated rooms are all air-conditioned, with TVs, minibars, phones, and radios, and have access to the swimming pool and the warmly furnished public rooms. Doubles with private bath rent for 158F ($72.60) per day, while singles cost 125F ($57.44). An extra bed can be set up in one of the hotel's double rooms at no extra charge. Breakfast is not included in the rates. This hotel, by the way, offers a three-kilometer outdoor exercise and jogging track, with 20 exercise or rest stations scattered along its length, plus an invigorating fitness program that many guests try at least once during a stay here. Live music is played in the bar, and service in the popular restaurant, Sutter's Grill, is meticulous.

Hotel International Zurich, Am Marktplatz (tel. 311-43-41). Everybody seems to take the tram, and this hotel is well served by four separate lines extending to all parts of the city. Owned by the Swissôtel chain, the International Zurich offers excellent service and a modern streamlined format to clients. The rooms are comfortably decorated in a style which the decorators probably thought would be as inoffensive as possible to as many people as possible, but everything is clean, efficient, and attractive. You'll find a swimming pool and sauna on the 32nd floor, and a panoramic bar, usually with a live orchestra, on the 31st. Elsewhere in the 700-bed complex are coffeeshops, snackbars, outlets of two Swiss banks, a news kiosk, and a small shop with everything you might have forgotten to bring with you.

Single rooms rent for anywhere from 120F ($55.14) to 140F ($64.33), while doubles cost 160F ($73.52) to 180F ($82.71), breakfast not included. The hotel is expensive for what a client gets for his or her money, and it tends to be largely commercial.

Atlantis Sheraton Hotel, 234 Döltschwieg (tel. 35-00-00), lies in a forested parkland at the foot of the Uetliberg. Bus service provided takes guests on frequent runs to the Hauptbahnhof, a 15-minute ride. With 320 beds, the hotel is part of a suburban office complex with enough amenities, including an Avis agency, to satisfy most of your needs. The lobby area is tastefully decorated in steel grays and reds, with a burnished metal chimney tube descending from the ceiling to funnel smoke from the open fireplace safely upward. The staff is discreet and efficient, and often includes local musicians who play Swiss band music.

The rooms are attractively decorated in shades of gray with wood detailing. Singles begin at 80F ($36.76), while the best double room in the hotel costs 220F ($101.09). Use of the pool is free for guests.

Hotel Eden au Lac, 45 Utoquai (tel. 47-94-04), is a grand hotel, with masses of ivy covering its ornate walls, turning in autumn to fiery orange and adding even more detail to the already ornamented facade. From certain vantage points you could almost imagine yourself sleeping in the Paris opera, because of the hotel's neoclassical columns, pediments, corner urns, and wrought-iron garlands of fruit and flowers. Everything is impeccably maintained to such a degree that many traditionalists return here season after season, insisting on the same rooms they've occupied for years. The walk from the hotel to downtown Zurich is like an old-fashioned promenade (be sure to allow plenty of time), winding along the borders of the lake among the hundreds of flowerbeds. You can bask in a little bit of nostalgia here, thanks to the efforts of the manager, R. A. Bärtschi, who was once described as the kind of administrator who has made Swiss hôteliers famous throughout the world. The hotel's French restaurant is one of the finest in Zurich (try their gourmet menu). The service is among the best I encountered in this city where the competition is keen for such a compliment.

Many bedrooms have a rose theme. Singles cost from 130F ($59.74) to 160F ($73.52) and doubles run 220F ($101.09) to 270F ($124.07), breakfast included. All rooms have baths or showers, air conditioning, radios, TVs, and private phones. The units in the rear are less expensive because they don't have a view of the lake. The hotel is owned by the Thurnheer family, which can boast generations of traditional Swiss hôteliers.

Hotel Europe, 4 Dufourstrasse (tel. 47-10-30). The telephone booth of this deluxe old-world hotel was fashioned from a 300-year-old sedan chair, and this is only one of the elegant details making this 65-bed facility near the lake popular with return travelers. Rising six stories above the first-floor awnings, the building is massively constructed of carved gray masonry, with wrought-iron balconies and gabled roofs. The interior is unpretentiously decorated with fine period furniture, tastefully patterned wall-to-wall carpeting, crystal chandeliers, and rococo mirrors. The suite next door to yours might be occupied by a visiting opera diva, because of the hotel's link with the Opera House next door. There is no room service, except for breakfast, and no restaurant on the premises. Whether you need it or not (and many visitors to Zurich do need it), you'll find a wall safe discreetly hidden behind a painting in your room for those gems you've been trying to smuggle out of hiding—or whatever.

Singles cost from 95F ($43.65) to 120F ($55.14), while doubles rent for 160F ($73.52) to 180F ($82.71), all rooms with modern baths and breakfast included. Ernest Schoch is the personable general manager and has been for 37 years, welcoming guests to the many conveniences of his hotel.

THE UPPER BRACKET: **Bellerive au Lac,** 47 Utoquai (tel. 251-70-10), is directed by the Simmen family who, with their many wildlife paintings, patterned carpeting, and rich Oriental rugs, show off their attractive building to its maximum advantage. This hotel stands next to the Hotel Eden au Lac and shares with it one of the best perches available on Lake Zurich. At your doorstep, you can join the Zurichers on their age-old promenade along the lake, and your proximity to the opera will make your stay all the more convenient.

The front rooms are obviously the more expensive ones, because of the view of the lake beyond the promenade's linden trees. All units have private bath, contain TV, radio, mini-bar, and telephone, and offer access to a first-class French restaurant on the premises and a comfortable bar for relaxing after a day downtown. Singles rent for 95F ($43.65) to 120F ($55.14), and doubles cost between 140F ($64.33) and 180F ($82.71). Breakfast is included in the rates.

Hotel St. Gotthard, 87 Bahnhofstrasse (tel. 211-55-00), is an older, more traditional hotel, long a favorite with the Swiss when they need to come into Zurich from their country homes. On one of the main shopping streets of the city, the St. Gotthard is only one block from the railroad station. The Hummer Bar specializes in lobster flown in from Canada and attracts a well-heeled clientele from all over the city. This and three other cosmopolitan restaurants—the Café Brasserie for snacks and pastries, the Steakhouse for the red meats you miss from back home, and La Bouillabaisse, a French restaurant known for seafood—make the St. Gotthard one of the premier rendezvous points on the Bahnhofstrasse.

Throughout all of the bedrooms there is a rather plush decor, although if you can get an accommodation on the upper floors it will be far superior. Singles cost from 105F ($48.24) to 190F ($87.31), while doubles rent for 190F ($87.31) to 230F ($105.69), breakfast included.

Hotel Im Park, 41 Kappelistrasse (tel. 210-65-65), is a real discovery lying outside the heart of the city in a residential district of fine homes and gardens. The building was probably at one time a private villa. Today a modern annex blends skillfully into the surrounding flower garden which adorns the 19th-century ocher mansion with masses of color in summer. Public rooms are high ceilinged, furnished with 19th-century antiques, and soothingly painted in clear, light colors.

Many of the modern units have balconies or open directly onto the garden. The establishment also has an attractive restaurant and serves a copious breakfast buffet that is included in the room price. Singles rent for 70F ($32.17) and 85F ($39.06); doubles go for 95F ($43.65) to 125F ($57.44). To get to the hotel, take the tram to the Billoweg stop.

Hotel Zum Storchen, Am Weinplatz (tel. 211-55-10). Important visitors to Zurich have been referred to this hotel by the city fathers since the 15th century. It sits on a bank of the Limmat looking across the river to the floodlit Rathaus and is undeniably romantic. My favorite part of this beflowered hotel is the café terrace cantilevered above the sidewalk on granite columns hundreds of years old. From the terrace you'll be able to see a sweeping panorama of old Zurich without ever having to leave your *kaffeeklatsch.* A large statue of an enraged stork decorates the facade of Zum Storchen, wrapping itself around a corner of the building and advertising the place to the river traffic passing below. The Rôtisserie restaurant inside offers first-class facilities, complete with river views and ornate stucco ceilings. In the cocktail bar, lots of pewter tankards, warm colors, and stained glass welcome you to converse with local entrepreneurs and bankers.

Singles rent for 120F ($55.14) to 135F ($62.03), while doubles cost from 180F ($82.71) to 230F ($105.69), breakfast included. Many in-the-know Swiss consider this place to be finer than any of the deluxe accommodations of Zurich. Since rooms are hard to get in summer, it's best to reserve ahead.

Hotel Schweizerhof, 7 Bahnhofplatz (tel. 211-86-40), is a gabled and turreted structure whose facade is covered with flags and ornate columns in high relief against the stonework. In one of the city's busiest areas, the Schweizerhof, through the tram system, is convenient to everything in town. The public rooms are pleasing and unpretentious, painted in clear colors with subdued furniture clustered into appealing conversational groupings. This is a grand old station hotel in the tradition so beloved at the turn of the century. People no longer arrive with trunks and maidservants as they used to (the doorman confided that some of today's guests bring a "change of underwear" and little else), but the Schweizerhof goes grandly on. Recent major renovations have been highly successful, keeping the hotel in step with the times.

The ideal rooms are the semicircular corner units which are understandably grabbed up first by clients familiar with the place. The 150 units cost from 110F ($101.00) to 170F ($78.12) for a single and from 220F ($101) to 270F ($124.07) for a double, each with breakfast, a modern bathroom, air conditioning, radio, TV, mini-bar, and direct-dial phone. A French restaurant and well-appointed bar area are to be found on the premises. Rainer Hüni, the front-office manager, proves helpful in answering any inquiries.

Hotel Simplon, 16 Schutzengasse (tel. 211-61-11), is opposite the Hotel St. Gotthard in a sought-after location, although a quick review of the prices will reveal that this is one of the special hotel bargains on this side of the river. The Simplon offers 120 beds priced at 64F ($29.41) to 90F ($41.36) in a single, from 104F ($47.79) to 150F ($68.93) in a double. Rooms are spacious, filled with modern furniture, with sunny views from most windows. The facade is one of those fine, incredibly solid pieces of masonry absolutely breathing reliability and punctuality as so many of the buildings in Zurich do. A disco, Birdwatchers, is a popular dancing spot for nightlife lovers (more on this under "After Dark in Zurich").

Hotel Plaza, 18 Goethestrasse (tel. 252-60-00), lies in a park in a tree-filled section of Zurich near the Opera House. The facade is nothing short of elegant, a two-tone gray-and-white building with neoclassical detailing above the windows and under the eaves. Goethestrasse, by the way, is one of the more interesting streets of Zurich, an occasional fountain splashing water near the green lawns where children play with the few older people who aren't wrapped up in their newspapers. The public rooms of this hotel are grandly decorated in a style that can best be called "manorial" (some of the pieces look vaguely Jacobean), with Oriental rugs, ornamented ceilings in geometric patterns, and heavy 19th-century furniture. The restaurant contains a steakhouse which looks like something you'd find in a wealthy part of Nevada, a rustically decorated bar area (the Horsestable), and an English-style pub called Piccadilly where you can eat indoors or out in an informal, colloquial setting.

You'll find that the rooms are very large, but not all of them have bathrooms, which gives you the chance to stay in a bathless single for a moderate 45F ($20.68) to 50F ($22.98), while singles with bath cost from 80F ($36.76) to 100F ($45.95). Bathless doubles go for 80F ($36.76) to 90F ($41.36), and from 110F ($50.55 to 170F ($78.12) in a double with bath, phone, mini-bar, and radio.

Hotel Zürcherhof, 21 Zahringerstrasse (tel. 47-10-40), across the river from the main railroad station, offers 50 beds in rooms with soundproof windows. Smack in the center of the old town, the five-story hotel sits on a corner one block from the famous Niederdorfstrasse, something akin to the Saint-Germain region of Paris. Painted in a vivid peach-russet color, it's one of the outstanding choices along this "street of hotels." Units inside are modern, efficient, and practically furnished with unfrilly, no-nonsense style. Singles rent for anywhere from 75F ($34.46) to 110F ($50.55); doubles cost 110F ($50.55) to 140F ($64.33). All rooms contain private baths and come with breakfast. Extra beds can be set up in any room for an additional 20F ($9.19). The attached restaurant, the Walliser Keller, serves culinary specialties from the Valais region in a rustically paneled cozy ambience of arched ceilings, sunny windows, and white napery.

Hotel Opera, 5 Dufourstrasse (tel. 251-90-90), offers 100 beds in a clean, well-maintained, and cozy atmosphere of Swiss efficiency. Next to the Opera House, the hotel has a large, attractive lobby area with an assortment of comfortable armchairs spread over a warmly patterned gold-and-red carpet. You should try for a room on the top floor here because they're the best, although the rooms on the lower floors are perfectly satisfactory too. Singles with modern bathrooms rent for 75F ($34.46) to 100F ($45.95), while doubles cost 106F ($48.71) to 150F ($68.93). Triples are available for anywhere from 126F ($57.80) to 170F ($78.12), and children's cribs can be set up for 15F ($6.89). The hotel maintains a bus departing for Kloten Airport every 1½ hours during the day.

Hotel Nova-Park, 420 Badenerstrasse (tel. 491-22-22). Sculpture and paintings adorn the rooms of this ultramodern hotel complex slightly removed from the center of town. You'll be connected to Zurich by a good network of bus and tram lines, and the availability of the sports and fitness facilities and the six restaurants might make the slight inconvenience worth it. The hotel offers 1000 beds in air-conditioned rooms with radios, TVs, mini-bars, and phones. The bedrooms, not large, are skillfully set up to create an impression of well-appointed luxury. They rent for 107F ($48.25) to 125F ($57.44) in a single, and 135F ($62.03) to 340F ($156.23) in a double. All rooms have audio-visual hookups where, through special arrangement with the hotel, more than 1000 movies can be transmitted into your room.

The effect of the decor of the public rooms, with spotlighting and boldly dramatic colors, is nothing short of a kaleidoscope. The Nova-Park is proud of its role as the first hotel possessing a comprehensive audio-visual installation in all of Europe, with in-house cable TV allowing more than 50 different programs to be transmitted simultaneously for viewing on 560 color TV sets or for projection onto a wide screen in the Nova Business center. A *Videothèque* lists a collection maintained by the hotel of some 1000 educational and entertainment films in German, English, French, Italian, Spanish, Japanese, and Arabic. Apartments are available here in a wide choice of sizes, for rent by the day or by the month.

Seiler Hotel Neues Schloss, 17 Stockerstrasse (tel. 201-65-50), lies conveniently near the Kongresshalle and the lake, convenient to trams lines 7, 8, 10, and 13 at *tramhalt* Stockerstrasse. From the outside the hotel is an unobtrusive modern gray building with balconies curving around its corners. The interior is comfortable, tastefully modern, and warmly decorated in autumnal colors with big sunny windows. The owners are Angela and Bernard Seiler, who also direct a small and intimate restaurant on the premises. You'll find lots of parks in your area, and views of the lake from vantage points. Singles rent for 105F ($48.25) to 120F ($55.14), and doubles cost 145F ($66.63) to 165F ($75.82), including breakfast.

Hotel Waldhaus, 20 Kurhausstrasse (tel. 251-93-60), is surrounded by verdant forests in the Dolder residential section of Zurich. A nine-hole golf course and 19 tennis courts, along with mini-golf and a swimming pool, make this a wonderful experience in country living. The hotel itself rises high above the surrounding trees, with balconies on every floor and red awnings protecting some from the sunlight. The spacious bedrooms are decorated in comfortably upholstered sofas and armchairs, with big windows to let in the forest light. Manager Hans Jorg Tobler rents singles with modern bathrooms, balconies, and views of the lake and the mountains for 110F ($50.55), with doubles (which actually comprise what is almost a two-room private apartment) going for from 200F ($91.90) to 220F ($101.09), with breakfast included. The rustic restaurant, by the way, has an interesting collection of 19th-century saws and woodworking tools hanging on the walls.

Hotel Ascot, 15 Lavaterstrasse (tel. 201-18-00), offers 60 air-conditioned and soundproof rooms near the lake, many of which contain expensive reproductions of elegantly upholstered Empire or Louis XV–style armchairs. Two restaurants on the premises include the intricately paneled Jockey Club and the Turf Bar, where a pianist accompanies the liquor and the appetizing light meals. Singles here rent for 98F ($45.03) to 130F ($59.74) while doubles cost 135F ($62.03) to 180F ($82.71), breakfast included. A sidewalk café covered with a striped awning is popular with locals in summertime.

Seehotel Meierhof, Horgen (tel. 725-29-61), a modern steel-and-concrete hotel, lies ten miles from the center of Zurich on the south shore of the lake. The management provides frequent speedboat trips from the hotel to the piers of Zurich, if you prefer to arrive by water. The restaurant offers a panoramic view of the lake, but the decor is angular, metallic, and somewhat stark in many of the public rooms. Guests have a covered swimming pool at their disposal, and several discos and shopping areas are nearby. Rooms inside tend to be small, and although a rail line separates the hotel from the lake, the units facing in that direction are still the more desirable ones. Singles rent for from 80F ($36.76) to 90F ($41.36); doubles cost 130F ($59.74) to 140F ($64.33). Accommodations contain private baths, phones, radios, TVs, and mini-bars, and include a generous breakfast in the price.

Hotel Airport, 30 Oberhauserstrasse, Zurich/Glattbrugg (tel. 810-44-44). If your schedule requires that you spend the night near Kloten Airport, this might be the ideal choice. Don't worry about being wakened in the night by the scream of jet engines. Zurich city ordinances prohibit airline departures or arrivals after 11 p.m. A hotel bus makes frequent trips to the airport (5 minutes away) and downtown Zurich (20 minutes away). A mural in the lobby shows a stylized map of the world in distressed metal relief, while the Japanese restaurant, Fujiya, offers artistically prepared food in an Eastern setting. If you've just returned from Tokyo and prefer Western food, the Town and Country Grill offers an intimate and warmly decorated European ambience which you can sample after leaving the marble-covered bar area.

Most people spend only one night here, but that needn't necessarily be your option. Singles rent for 100F ($45.95) and doubles cost 140F ($64.33), with an extra bed going for 30F ($13.79). A continental breakfast is included in the rates. Mr. Gehrig, the manager, verifies that all is running smoothly in his 50 rooms.

Hotel Glockenhof, 31 Sihlstrasse (tel. 211-56-60), is pleasant modern hotel halfway between the train station and the lake. A sunny courtyard contains a café-terrace with parasols, while the spacious lobby offers leather-upholstered chairs ideal for reading the local newspapers. Bedrooms are comfortable and invitingly decorated with dark carpeting and an occasional Oriental rug. They all contain full baths, mini-bars, and phones, with TV available upon request. The Glogge-Egge restaurant is warmly surrounded with wooden planks, hanging lights, and lots of brickwork. Singles rent for 86F ($39.52) to 96F ($44.11), and doubles cost between 118F ($54.22) and 144F ($66.17), with breakfast included.

Zurich Continental Hotel, 60 Stampfenbachstrasse (tel. 363-33-63), is a good example of the adaptibility of real estate to different uses. At one time this 250-bed hotel was an office building, but today its glass-and-steel facade shelters one of the most imaginative adaptations in Zurich. The lobby/reception area contains masses of comfortable armchairs upholstered in executive black, where guests sit in isolated groupings reading periodicals from around the world. The other public rooms contain some valuable antiques from the Valais. Bedrooms are sunny, carpeted in vivid natural colors, with modern tiled bathrooms. The hotel is only a stone's throw from the Hauptbahnhof, so the American Bar and the French restaurant are patronized by many of Zurich's business community who respond favorably to management's claim of being the city's "most cordial hotel."

Singles rent for 88F ($40.44) to 120F ($55.14), with doubles going for 144F ($66.17) to 197F ($90.52). A double can be rented to one person for 150F ($68.93), while an extra bed can be set up in any unit for an additional 20F ($9.19). Breakfast is not included in the price, but costs an additional 8F ($3.68).

Hotel Glarnishchhof, 30 Claridenstrasse (tel. 202-47-47), looks from the outside like one of those forbiddingly anonymous Swiss banks that seem to dot the street corners in downtown Zurich. The interior, however, is warmly paneled in light-colored woods, with patterned rugs and armchairs, well-maintained and in good condition, which were trendy and in vogue when they were installed in the early '60s. Each of the 70 rooms has its own bath and spacious, high-ceilinged dimensions. The establishment contains a grill room, a snack restaurant, and a bar. Since you're in the midst of the financial district here, you'll be close to everything in town. Single rooms rent for 110F ($50.55) to 120F ($55.14), while doubles cost 160F ($73.52) to 180F ($82.71), with breakfast included. Urs Mathys, the deferential manager, runs his hotel as part of the Best Western hotel chain.

THE MEDIUM BRACKET: **Hotel Kindli,** 1 Pfalzgasse (tel. 211-59-17). Dating from the 16th century, this hotel stands at the end of a steep little street in the old town, Rennweg. It mixes the antique with the contemporary in a blend that makes it one of my favorite little hotels in the city. Painted a pastel gray, the exterior shelters cozy and well-planned bedrooms furnished in an eclectic mix with, for example, polished provincial armoires next to black leatherette modern armchairs. The view from the windows reveals perspectives of the old town that can't be had from the street below. A favorite aspect of this place is the folkloric singing of Joe and Willi Schmid who, with their orchestra and an occasional international singing star, play to a full house practically every night of the week. (For more information, see the nightlife section.) The hotel charges from 90F ($41.36) to 105F ($48.25) in a single, from 105F ($48.25) to 160F ($73.52) in a double.

Hotel Ambassador, 6 Falkenstrasse (tel. 47-76-00). Staying here is about the most practical way to get a view of the lake but avoid paying the monstrous "lakeside view" prices so popular in Zurich hostelries. You'll be near the opera and the Bellevueplatz and within one block of the lake. The staff, directed ably by Mrs. M. Hoppeler and H. Raess, does everything it can to treat you "like royalty." All rooms are air-conditioned and soundproof, and contain baths, radios, mini-bars, and phones (TVs upon request). The Ambassador, frankly, is not as luxurious as its neighbor the Europe, just around the corner, but is nonetheless compared to it frequently.

The rooms tend to be irregularly shaped which lends character, and if you ever tire of the view from your window, you can descend to street level to sample the specialties of the popular sidewalk café below. Singles rent for 75F ($34.36) to 100F ($45.95), doubles cost from 106F ($48.71) to 150F ($68.93), and triples from 126F ($57.90) to 170F ($78.12). A crib can be set up in any room for an additional 15F ($6.89). Rates include breakfast.

Hotel Helm Haus, 20 Schiffländeplatz (corner of Limmatquai) (tel. 251-88-10), built in 1356, is a simple hotel rising six unadorned stories above the boat landing square, a block from the river. Shops fill the space on the ground floor, and in its category it's one of the best hotels in Zurich. The establishment, under the direction of A. Guler, is extremely well run and presents good value. Singles cost from 75F ($34.46) to 85F ($39.06), and doubles run from 92F ($42.27) to 126F ($57.90). All units have at least a toilet and shower, and many of them have bathtubs too. Since the hotel was renovated in 1976, many of the rooms contain mod/trendy/geometrically patterned curtains and space-age contoured chairs, and all are comfortable and impeccably clean. While there is no restaurant in the building, breakfast is included in the price of the room.

Hotel du Théâtre, 69 Seilergraben (tel. 252-60-62). The first thing you'll notice when approaching this modern hotel is the emphasis which management places on art. A life-size statue of a nude woman struggling to escape the captivity of the stone from which she's carved greets you near the entrance, while a dramatically colored abstract collage of intricately worked metal hangs over a 20-foot expanse of the facade. The rooms are comfortable and not without their own unusual prints and artwork. Even the lobby is a wonderfully original combination of mosaics, some of them on the walls and some dividing the floor space into abstract patterns of marble and river rocks. The hotel is attractively located near the central zone of the Zurich tram system, with direct lines to practically everything in town. Singles go for 54F ($24.81) to 74F ($34), while doubles cost from 100F ($45.95) to 112F ($51.46), breakfast included, all with private baths and soundproof windows.

Hotel Chesa Rustica, 70 Limmatquai (tel. 251-92-91), lies five minutes from the train station, about two blocks from the Rathaus. Some visitors have said that it's so cozy it could easily be an inn instead of a big-city hotel. The counter in the lobby is fashioned from an antique piece of Swiss cabinetry whose naïve designs reflect another era of craftsmanship. Throughout the hotel are placed items of genuine beauty, such as antique clocks and hanging cupboards containing hand-painted china. Rooms, comfortably furnished and spacious, cost from 85F ($39.06) to 105F ($48.25) in a single, from 135F ($62.03) to 155F ($71.22) in a double, breakfast included, with an extra bed going for 30F ($13.79). All units have baths, phones, private bars, radios, TVs, soundproof windows, and a rustic ambience that helps you to imagine yourself far away in the Alps.

Hotel Ermitage am See, Küsnacht-Zurich (tel. 910-52-22). Zurich is surrounded by several small suburbs, and Küsnacht is only seven minutes by car from the center of town. This hotel offers 50 beds in a lakeside ambience of panoramic windows, large trees, and all the character of a large country house. Many of the units open onto balconies which welcome in large doses of fresh air and sunshine, and all of them have bathrooms and modern conveniences. The public rooms are painted a clear white, and contain vivid blue carpeting and scattered Oriental rugs, fine furniture (I'm particularly fond of a ceiling-high pendulum clock in the lobby), and an airy, spacious feeling of well-being. A private lakefront beach and well-maintained grounds are for the use of guests, along with a warmly decorated bar area. The French restaurant offers candlelight dinners in an elegant setting every night. Single rooms cost 90F ($41.36), doubles rent from 120F ($55.14) to 160F ($73.52), and triples go from 150F ($68.93) to 190F ($87.31). Rooms facing the lake are of course more expensive.

Hotel Montana, 39 Konradstrasse (tel. 42-69-00), is three minutes north of the Hauptbahnhof in a six-story building with two bluish-white neon signs illuminating both the facade and the portico over the sidewalk. An underground garage is in the basement, to make arrival easy for motorists. The public rooms are streamlined and comfortable, thanks to the modern chairs of laminated wood with bright upholstery and the pin lights shining from the wooden ceilings. Bedrooms are impeccably clean and warmly appointed with brown and white monochromatic themes. The Beran family manages this attractive establishment, where singles cost 70F ($32.17) and doubles go for 95F ($43.65). All units have bathrooms and come with breakfast.

Hotel Buchzelg, 50 Bechzelstrasse (tel. 53-82-00), is a top-notch choice in its category, offering comfortable rooms, whose maintenance is supervised by the friendly English-speaking director, Irma Peters-Haas. The hotel stands in its own well-maintained grounds and contains 75 neat, attractive beds in well-kept rooms with radios, TVs, and private showers. However, for some, the toilet is in the hallway. Singles go for 52F ($23.89) to 64F ($29.41), and doubles cost from 76F ($34.92) to 88F ($40.44), with breakfast included. The lobby contains an elevator, a hairdressing salon, a restaurant, and a bar where service is generally excellent. From the central tram zone, take tram 3 or 8 to the Klusplatz, changing for a number 34 bus to the Witikon stop. This hotel lies a few minutes away on foot.

Hotel/Restaurant Berghalde, 341 Witikonerstrasse (tel. 53-24-50), is first and foremost a restaurant, although the Walter Hofmayer family maintains ten cozy rooms under the eaves of this comfortably proportioned quiet house. The restaurant is a favorite with the Swiss, so you won't be sorry if you stay in for dinner. Singles rent for 65F ($29.87), while doubles go for anywhere from 88F ($40.44) to 118F ($54.22), breakfast included. All rooms have showers or baths, but not all of them have toilets.

Hotel Royal, 6 Leonhardstrasse (tel. 47-67-10), is one of the most modern bed-and-breakfast hotels in downtown Zurich. Greeted at the front door by a rounded orange awning advertising the name of the hotel, you'll be served by a friendly and efficient staff who try to give personalized attention to the inhabitants of the hotel's 58 rooms. All rooms have modern bathrooms, phones, radios, and mini-bars, and there's an airport bus service and a round-the-clock Telex service for business clients. There's also an underground garage for easy parking. Singles here cost from 50F ($22.98) to 69F ($31.71), doubles go for 104F ($47.79), and triples, 129F ($59.28).

Spirgarten Hotel and Restaurant, Am Lindenplatz (tel. 62-24-00), offers clean and well-maintained rooms with the kind of oversize windows that are soundproof when closed and which pivot on a horizontal pin to let in lots of sunshine and fresh air. The hotel is set up to accommodate groups of people either for large conferences or small reunions, in a wide assortment of modern conference rooms serviced by an 800-space parking garage. Singles rent for 41F ($18.84) to 61F ($28.03), while doubles cost 92F ($42.27), and all units have baths, phones, and radios. If you choose this hotel, don't be surprised to see hordes of dark-suited businessmen in the lobby whenever you walk through it.

Hotel Seegarten, 14 Seegartenstrasse (tel. 252-37-37), lies just off the eastern shore of the lake in a pleasant residential section of Zurich built in the 19th century. The hotel is a renovated older building whose embellishments have unfortunately been replaced by a sheer facade of buff-colored stucco below the gabled mansard roof. A yellow awning identifies the restaurant section of the hotel, which serves well-prepared Italian food in a mellow atmosphere of brown and beige walls with wood trim and hanging brass lamps. Singles cost from 47F ($21.60) to 75F ($34.46); doubles go from 66F ($30.33) to 96F ($44.11). Each room is equipped with phone, radio, and in all but the cheapest units, private bath and toilet. Breakfast is included.

Hotel Franziskaner, 1 Stüssihofstatt (tel. 252-01-20). The symbol for this hotel is an illustration of a jovial, sympathetically venal monk who, by the looks of him, would certainly enjoy the good food and the comfortable lodgings of this old-fashioned hotel in the historic part of Zurich. The building is on a cobblestone square where a helmeted warrior stands above a Renaissance fountain. The interior is a classy combination of fine woodwork, warm colors, brass candelabra, and wrought iron, particularly in the detail-oriented French restaurant and bar. The bedrooms are clean and comfortable, and rent for anywhere from 85F ($29.09) to 110F ($50.55) in a single, for 110F ($50.55) to 145F ($66.63) in a double, with a breakfast buffet included. All units have private baths, and the relatively small size allows owners Christoph and Ruedi Suter to really take care of each guest's needs.

Hotel Olympia, 324 Badenerstrasse (tel. 491-77-66). The beige facade of this family-run hotel curves gracefully around a street corner in the northern part of Zurich. Easily accessible to the rest of the city (if you don't mind taking two or three tram lines), the hotel is comfortably furnished and decorated with wall-size murals of classical ruins. Astrid Hüsler, the genteel mistress, directs the bar area and the kitchen with first-class flair. Single rooms cost from 55F ($25.27) to 60F ($27.57), while doubles rent for anywhere from 60F ($27.57) to 90F ($41.36), which gives you a wide choice of plumbing options as well as a free breakfast.

Hotel Stoller, 357 Badenerstrasse (tel. 52-65-00), conveniently located next to several major tram lines, is an old-fashioned hotel offering 150 beds to travelers who are immediately placed at ease by the attractive staff, ably directed by W. Stoller. The salons are decorated in grained heavy furniture which seem to symbolize at a glance the esthetic tastes of the *haute bourgeoisie* 100 years ago. Some of the Oriental carpets are boldly patterned in muted colors, while the dining room is tastefully lit and decorated with wood paneling and forest-green walls. And if you're fond of color, wait till you see the bedrooms! Singles rent for 70F ($32.17) to 80F ($36.76), and doubles go for 135F ($62.03). Triples are available in limited numbers, for 135F ($62.03) to 150F ($68.93).

Hotel Rigihof, 101 Universitatstrasse (tel. 361-16-85), is on a busy street in the university section. It is modern, functional, and efficient, with an angular lobby area and a dining room crowned by an intricate geometrical ceiling. This is not the kind of hotel where the decorator went in for soft curves, but everything is clean, well run, and friendly. The outdoor terrace can be lovely on a hot day. Rooms are priced depending on whether they're on the street side or the "quiet side," and range between 68F ($31.25) and 85F ($39.06) for a single, from 88F ($40.44) to 110F ($50.55) in a double, with breakfast included, in rooms with private baths, radios, mini-bars, and phones. You'll even find an elevator and a hairdresser in the lobby.

Hotel Limmathaus, 118 Limmathaus (tel. 45-52-40), is easily reached by tram 13 or 4 to the Limmatplatz (it's only three stops, but it's really too long to do on foot when you first arrive exhausted in Zurich). The staff is friendly, and the rooms are modern and clean with a rather uninspired view from many of the windows. Single rooms cost 45F ($20.68), while doubles go from 65F ($29.87) to 100F ($45.95), depending on the plumbing. Triples cost from 90F ($41.36) to 120F ($55.14), and if you want it, a quad rents for 110F ($50.55). The hotel caters to lots of groups, so be prepared if all the guests on your hallway seem to know one another. Breakfast is included in the room price.

Hotel Florhof, 4 Florhofgasse (tel. 47-44-70), quickly gives a sense of being indeed a glamorous hotel. You'll arrive at a paved walkway leading to the double staircase of a large, patrician house which was formerly, I was told, a private residence. The blue of the facade is repeated in the blue and white Swiss tile oven which heats the dining room inside. Some of the bedrooms still have their high molded plaster ceilings, and all of them contain private baths. Singles cost between 85F ($39.06) and 95F ($43.65), while doubles range between 130F ($59.74) and 150F ($68.93), including breakfast.

Hotel Sternen, 335 Schaffhauserstrasse, Oerlikon (tel. 311-77-77), sits quietly in a Zurich suburb between the city center and the airport. Many of the tram lines pass through Oerlikon, so getting there is not a problem. The hotel, like many of the buildings around it, is constructed in a kind of internationally modern style, with an interesting facade broken into various planes of angles and colors. Rooms inside are predictably comfortable, while many of the public rooms are dramatically decorated in dark colors with lots of Oriental rugs. Singles go for anywhere from 45F ($20.68) to 62F ($28.49), doubles cost from 80F ($36.76) to 100F ($45.95), and triples go for 102F ($46.87) to 120F ($55.14), breakfast included. Not all units have private baths.

Hotel Trumpy, 9 Sihlquai (tel. 42-54-00). The octagonal spires of the National Museum rise only a block away from this grand old building near the railroad station. Its buff-colored facade usually flies a Swiss flag over its roofline, with an orange canopy sheltering the sidewalk café from the direct rays of the sun. The lobby has a large stone fountain spewing water from a human head in bas-relief against one wall, and there's a muted collection of Oriental rugs. Bedrooms are comfortably appointed, lushly carpeted, and sometimes come in a startlingly vivid choice of colors (I only saw the red one). All rooms have modern baths with accessories, TVs, soundproof windows, radios, and phones. The silvery blue-gray dining room serves good meals. Singles cost from 80F ($36.76) to 105F ($48.25), doubles range from 105F ($48.25) to 140F ($64.33), triples are priced from 138F ($63.41) to 160F ($73.52), and quads cost 150F ($68.93).

THE BUDGET CATEGORY: **Hotel Zelthof,** 18 Zeltweg (tel. 47-80-66). The Methodist Center of Zurich runs a clean, unpretentious, homey-type hotel near the Zurich art museum. They offer straightforward accommodations, in well-maintained, somewhat spartan rooms, none of which has a private bath. They don't accept credit cards, and there are no eating facilities other than for breakfast, which is included in the price of the room. Singles cost 48F ($22.06), while doubles rent for 70F ($32.17). Inhabitants tend to be friendly. Alcoholic beverages are not sold or consumed in the hotel.

Hotel Bristol, 34 Stampfenbachstrasse (tel. 47-07-00), for many years now has been one of the best known and most successful budget hotels of Zurich. It lies on a small hill near the main train station, in back of the major road to the airport, with a ramp at street level which leads you to the main entrance of the hotel. Bedrooms are well maintained, frequently renovated, and simply furnished, allow no alcoholic beverages, and provide no room service. The hotel has an elevator and a large TV room with a wide screen for the use of its guests in one of the public rooms. The Bristol offers 100 beds in singles that, breakfast included, cost from 40F ($18.38) to 60F ($27.57) and in doubles priced at 60F ($27.57) to 90F ($41.36). The range in prices is because not all rooms have private baths.

Hotel Leonhard, 136 Limmatquai (tel. 251-30-80), is in the old city, two minutes on foot from the main railroad station. The establishment is owned by the Leonhard family, who charge 90F ($41.36) a night, with breakfast included, in double rooms (there are no singles), all of which have twin beds and private baths. You'll see trees from your window.

Hotel Limmathof, 142 Limmatquai (tel. 47-42-20), is very often confused with another hotel, the Limmathaus. This one is on the active Centralplatz, the departure point for many of Zurich's tramlines just across the river from the railroad station. The hotel was formed by joining three town houses, each about 300 years old. Today this unpretentious establishment offers simply furnished tiny rooms with parquet floors and double-glazed windows. There are very few frills, but many budget-minded guests over the years have found the 55 rooms a good choice for the money. (Many visitors complain that the shower facilities are inadequate for the number of guests using them. Be forewarned that a "mechanical bandit" in each of the small tiled rooms requires a 1-franc piece before the water comes on. Woe to the hapless guest who finds the flow of water interrupted when he or she is in mid-shampoo. Bring more than one coin and be prepared for a hassle.) A rustic weinstube on the ground floor offers food and drink at reasonable prices. Singles without bath cost 40F ($18.38); doubles rent for 60F ($25.57) per day without bath and 75F ($34.46) with shower and toilet. Breakfast is included in the price.

Pension St. Josef, 64/68 Hirschengraben (tel. 251-27-57), is a Catholic hotel run by Sister Michelle, who welcomes visitors from around the world. Only six minutes on foot from the central station, the establishment is clean, strictly run, and represents good value for the money. The management may be a little straight-laced, but the price is right. Singles cost 35F ($16.08) to 40F ($18.38); doubles, 55F ($25.27) to 60F ($27.57); and triples, 66F ($30.33) to 75F ($34.46). Units are clean, comfortable, and safe, especially for women traveling alone.

Hotel Vorderer Sternen, Bellevueplatz (tel. 251-49-49), stands on the shore of the lake on the famous Bellevueplatz, which has excellent tram connections to every part of the city. The hotel looks like a small rectangular building with a gabled roof, the kind you'd find in dozens of typical Swiss towns, but in this case with the popular Boulevard Restaurant on the ground floor. Accommodations are very simple, but everything is carefully clean and scrubbed every day. None of the rooms has a private bath. Breakfast is included in the price set by Beatrix Behr, the English-speaking owner, of 45F ($20.68) in a single and 65F ($29.87) in a double.

Jolie Ville Motor Inn, 105 Zürichstrasse, Adliswil (tel. 710-85-85), was constructed in 1966 as part of the Mövenpick chain, in the suburb of Adliswil, south of Zurich on the southwest edge of the lake. You can get there by taking bus 87 or tram 7 from downtown Zurich, but many visitors tend to be motorists who don't want to negotiate city traffic. Most of the rooms are rustically paneled, and all of them are clean and comfortably furnished. From the outside the place looks like a low-lying modern building with fire-engine-red awnings. All rooms have twin beds that can be pushed together to form a double. For a single person staying in such a room, it costs from 68F ($31.25) to 78F

($35.84); for two persons, an additional 20F ($9.19). A rustically decorated restaurant (also managed by Mövenpick) lies in a half-timbered grange-like building 500 yards away.

Hotel Krone, 88 Limmatquai (tel. 251-42-22). The original building on this spot dates back to the beginning of the 17th century, although the hotel you'll see today has had many facelifts. You'll find yourself only 500 yards from the railroad station and a few steps from Bahnhofstrasse, and you'll have a view of the Limmat if your windows happen to face that way. The interior is freshly decorated in a series of pleasing beiges and creams, with warmly patterned Oriental rugs reflecting many of the sepia tones of the woodwork's detailing. The hotel offers only 25 rooms to 40 guests, priced at 43F ($19.76) in a single, from 73F ($33.54) to 85F ($39.06) in a double. Many of the plumbing accessories are on the second floor and scattered elsewhere throughout the building. Breakfast is included in the price.

Hotel Fischer, 520 Schaffhauserstrasse, Zurich-Seebach (tel. 301-27-55), is a rectangular modern building with a boxy facade broken by a double row of large glass windows. Awnings colored a vivid blue protect the terraced café from the direct sunlight and from a view of the nearby parking lot. On the ground floor you'll find a tearoom, and upstairs you'll see that most of the units are clean, sunny, and comfortable if somewhat bare. Singles cost 38F ($17.46), while doubles go for 78F ($35.84), all with bath and including breakfast.

Hotel Bahnpost, 6 Reitergasse (tel. 23-32-11), has the double benefit of being smack in the center of Zurich without being too noisy. With 44 beds, this place is among the best in its price range. Don't expect much in the way of a lobby or a lounge, but the rooms here are a good choice for people who like to spend most of their day out exploring, retiring to the hotel only for sleep—or whatever. Some of the rooms are covered with painted paneling, and all of them have hot and cold running water. Often, however, the bath is in the hallway. Singles cost 40F ($18.38) and doubles rent for 60F ($27.57), with breakfast included. An Italian restaurant on the premises, the Balestra, serves good meals.

Hotel Martahaus, 36 Zahringerstrasse (tel. 251-45-50). Because of its popularity with budget travelers, it's often very hard to get a room here during summer. The hotel offers 80 beds in rooms sleeping one, two, three, or six persons, none of which contains a private bathroom, although a sink is in each of the units. The establishment is ideally located, within walking distance of the main station. Rooms are not luxurious (the whole place has somewhat the aura of a youth hostel), but at these prices, who expects art? Singles go for 38F ($17.46), doubles for 55F ($25.27), and triples for 72F ($33.08). In the downstairs dormitories holding six bunk beds, each bed costs 20F ($9.19). Showers are on each floor, and breakfast is included in the price.

Hotel Rothaus, 17 Marktgasse (tel. 34-15-30), sits on a narrow street one block from the river in the old town. Its facade holds unpretentious rows of windows which allow lots of the outdoors into the rooms. Furnishings are an unusual blend of circa 1950 modern, with architectural details which are, in their own right, antiques (a tiled Swiss stove, for example, and a couple of armoires looking a lot like they'd be better off sitting in some church somewhere). The bar area is well-stocked with a long row of benches curving beside the countertop, and the dining room is pleasingly paneled in a somber kind of way. Not all the rooms have private baths and therefore the units range somewhat in price. Singles cost from 36F ($16.54) to 50F ($22.98), while doubles range between 65F ($29.87) and 85F ($39.06), with breakfast included. The hotel is in the Niederdorf section, convenient to Zurich's nightclubs, jazz houses, and a slew of budget restaurants. The accommodations are clean and basic, attracting a younger group of clients. The entrance is dreary, with a nightclub, the Red House, featuring erotic entertainment.

2. Where to Dine

More than 1200 restaurants, with a widely diversified cuisine ranging from Swiss to foreign, are at your culinary disposal in Zurich. Obviously I've had to do some powerful trimming to come up with my own preferred list, which, although modest in size, still covers a diverse gastronomic range that should also appeal to a wide range of purses.

As for Zuricher specialties, rösti (potatoes grated and fried) is one of my all-time favorite Swiss dishes. You might also try Züri-Gschnätzlets (shredded veal cooked with mushrooms in a cream sauce laced with white wine) and kutteln nach Zürcherart (tripe with mushrooms, white wine, and caraway seed). Another classic dish is leberspiesschen (liver cubes skewered with bacon and sage and served with potatoes and beans). Zouftschriibertopf is a potpourri of bacon, grilled meat, and mushrooms.

Among local wines, the white Riesling Sylvaner is outstanding (the vines were first cultivated along Lake Zurich). For his or her typical fish platter, a Zuricher often prefers a white räuschling. The light Clevner wines, always chilled, are made from blue Burgundy grapes growing around the lake too. Even in first-class restaurants you can order wine by the glass.

THE UPPER BRACKET: **Rebe,** 5 Schützengasse (tel. 221-10-65), is one of the most distinguished and fashionable restaurants of Zurich. Heinz R. Witschi, assisted by his wife Babette, is an outstanding chef (many food critics consider him *the* best in the city). The setting is sumptuously appointed, with lots of plants and paneled walls, creating a feeling of intimacy. The service on two floors is first class. Fish and shellfish are flown in by private plane, but Herr Witschi's establishment is not just a seafood restaurant, as he does meat dishes extremely well. However, you'll definitely think at first you're in a seafood restaurant when you see the live lobsters and oysters in Rebe's salt-water tank.

Nouvelle cuisine specialties include a salade de caille (quail) aux artichauts violets and a galantine de légumes (vegetables) au foie gras. And those are only to get you started on a meal where a certain dedication has gone into the preparation of each dish. Among Zurich's business community, patrons cite such selections as the pot-au-feu de la mer or the cassoulet of lobster cooked in Brouilly and served with black truffles. The Bresse pigeon in Médoc was my most recent rewarding choice, and my dinner companion selected an equally delectable platter of veal kidneys and sweetbreads. For dessert, a spectacular finish would be to order the soup of exotic fruit in Sauterne. A business lunch, consisting of three to five courses, costs from 35F ($16.08) to 48F ($22.06). Three special gourmet-caliber menus are offered—called "gastronomique," "patron," and "surprise" (this latter one consisting of ten courses!), at prices ranging from 85F ($39.06) to 135F ($62.03). Hours are daily except Sunday from noon to 2 p.m. and 6 to 10 p.m.

Agnès Amberg, 5 Hottingerstrasse (tel. 251-26-26), is one of the brightest luminaries of European gastronomy. The haute cuisine dispensed here is inspired by a woman author who has devoted most of her life to turning out epicurean delights and writing about them in her many books on cuisine. At her table in Zurich, you'll be served one of your most elegant and sumptuous repasts in Switzerland. The food is pleasing to both the palate and the eye.

A fine way to begin your meal is to order the fresh foie gras fashioned into a delectable terrine or a pâté of duckling. One of her salads, available seasonally, is made with sweetbreads. Or perhaps you might like to select her mussel soup with curry. Among the more recommendable main courses (if they're available on the night of your visit) are St. Pierre farci (stuffed John Dory) de poireaux (leeks) au beurre blanc (white butter), lobster in Sauterne, guinea fowl with honey, and sea bass in a saffron sauce. The restaurant is closed Sunday and Monday. Meals, depending on your selection, can range widely in price, but count on spending in the neighborhood of 55F ($25.27) to 80F ($36.76) for a meal. The wine selection, incidentally, is notable. If you can't arrive by Rolls-Royce, you can take the tram to Pfauen, anytime between 6:30 p.m. and midnight.

Chez Max, 53 Seestrasse (tel. 391-88-77), in the suburb of Zollikon. In an attractive house by the lake, about a 12-minute ride from Zurich, Max Kehl lures the world to his door. And with good reason. You don't come here by chance, and you definitely need a reservation. All the backdrop, including the decoration and the attention to china and table settings, has been planned by Herr Kehl himself. Gleaming copper blends with modern art. Regular customers, including the top business leaders of Zurich, treat themselves to some delicate and uncommon dishes. But Chez Max also knows the beauty and palate-pleasing allure of simplicity, particularly when the produce is very, very fresh, as his invariably is.

Two of his nouvelle cuisine concoctions—each one different, each one brilliant—included a puree of white eggplant and an equally memorable plate of truffles with Vacherin cheese. You might follow with crayfish in a cream and champagne sauce or filet goulasch with mustard or a pot-au-feu with duckling and vegetables. To finish, a soup of fresh fruits with sorbet is a celestial experience.

Chez Max is closed all day Sunday and for lunch on Monday, and it also shuts down in mid-July, reopening in August. Hours are noon to 2 p.m. and 6:30 to 11:30 p.m. Count on spending from 75F ($34.46) to 150F ($68.93). His wine selections, both Swiss and French, are among the best in Zurich.

Haus zum Rüden, 42 Limmatquai (tel. 47-95-90), is one of the historic Gothic guild houses of Zurich, dating from 1295. Renovated in 1936, the house was once frequented by lords and nobles, but today its Gothic room houses one of the best restaurants in the city, especially popular with foreign visitors, who ask for a table with a view of the Limmat. You'll enter under an arcade as you preview the posted menu on the sidewalk. You then climb an elegant stairwell. Medieval halberds decorate the walls, and other touches of decor include stag horns, polished balustrades, and Oriental rugs. The restaurant has a curved roof of elaborately crafted hardwood and exposed stone walls set in narrow strips between the huge, many-paned windows. The restaurant is spacious, yet somehow produces an intimate feeling of well-being.

The owner, Wilfried Keller, is respectful of the tradition of the house, but has hired a chef who keeps abreast of changing culinary taste. The house specializes in a cuisine du marché, which means "market-fresh cookery." Therefore, since all the foodstuff is likely to change by the time of your visit, I won't recommend any specialty. However, on my recent dinner visit with companions, several dishes were outstanding, including a salad of roebuck and sweetbreads, a soup of saffron-flavored mussels, snails in truffle sauce, a turbot soufflé with champagne, a ragoût of lobster with lime sauce, and lamb cooked with green peppercorns. Service is from noon to 1:30 p.m. and 6 to 10 p.m. A menu du jour ranges from 36F ($16.59) to 48F ($22.06), with à la carte dinners averaging from 50F ($22.98) to 80F ($36.76).

Jacky's Stopferstube, 45 Culmannstrasse (tel. 26-37-48), enjoys considerable renown, especially among the chic and fashionable. The owner, Jacky Schläpfer, a local celebrity, serves some of the best beef and veal steaks in town (priced according to weight). Many of the patrons order portions large enough to make a Texan envious. The veal cutlets, incidentally, are among the best I've ever sampled in Switzerland. You might also consider the veal shank, which is treated with consideration and delectably flavored. Daily specials are offered, and many of these meats are frequently braised. Assorted fresh mushrooms are presented, much to the delight of gourmet clients. The goose liver is superb, as is the fresh lobster salad. The wine list is most distinguished, with both Swiss and French vintages featured in a wide price range. Count on spending about 75F ($34.46) and up for dinner, and get there before 11:30 p.m. The restaurant is closed all day Sunday, serves lunch only on Monday, and shuts down from mid-July to mid-August.

Kronenhalle, 4 Rämistrasse (tel. 251-02-56), has for years been the major restaurant of Zurich, although in the past decade it has faced incredible competition. Still, Kronenhalle remains an enduring favorite, even if it has suffered an occasional bad review in recent years. Even if you don't like the food, you might want to dine here just to look at the modern art. On the walls hang original paintings by such artists as Chagall, Klee, Matisse, Miró, and Picasso from the Zumsteg family's own private collection.

Now into its second century as a restaurant, Kronenhalle consists of three separate dining rooms which have a lingering aura of the 19th century. Its bar is still a popular rendezvous point for local artists and an occasional visiting celebrity. The chefs specialize in Swiss and international dishes, including steak with mustard sauce, lamb in the Provençal style with green beans, and trout with herbs. For dessert, everybody in the know orders the chocolate mousse. Count on spending from 50F ($22.98) for a meal, and arrive before the last orders go in at 11:30 p.m.

Veltliner Keller, 8 Schlüsselgasse (tel. 221-32-28), in the old town of Zurich, has been a restaurant since 1551. Next to St. Peter's Church, it's expensive but worth every centime, and it literally reeks with atmosphere, a virtual museum of carved wood. The restaurant was once a wine cellar, and is paneled in a mountain pine called arve (grown only in Switzerland). The chef prepares many familiar Swiss specialties, including the classic chopped veal dish of Zurich, but he is also versatile, embracing many Italian dishes as well. The risotto comes with a mixed grill of sausage, liver, veal, kidney, and beef, and you might select crêpes made with cheese, meat, or spinach. Count on spending around 50F ($22.98) for a meal, served from 11:30 a.m. to 2 p.m. and 6:30 to 10 p.m. daily, except on Sunday and during vacation time for about three weeks in July. On Saturday the restaurant opens at 6 p.m.

Restaurant Piccoli (Accademia), 48 Rotwandstrasse (tel. 241-42-02), is one of the most elegant, most expensive, and finest Italian restaurants in Zurich. Service is skilled and efficient, and its many classic Italian dishes range from Venice to Naples. Chef's specialties include agnolotti alla piemontese and different types of spaghetti, as well as risotto with mushrooms. You might prefer the filetto alla napoletana among the meat courses, or veal liver alla veneziana. Furthermore, look for the daily specialties which in season are likely to include pheasant and partridge. The restaurant is closed on Saturday and Sunday until 6 p.m. and also takes a summer vacation in July. The average price for a very good lunch or dinner begins at 70F ($32.17) with wine included. Mr. Panardo-Piccoli runs an outstanding operation in every way, and always sees that only the finest meats and produce are used.

THE MIDDLE RANGE: Zumfthaus Zur Saffran, 54 Limmatquai (tel. 47-67-22). This building was constructed on the banks of the Limmat in 1740 as a headquarters for the spice merchants in apothecaries of Zurich. Renovated in 1971, it is one of the most interesting examples of updated 18th-century architecture in Zurich. You enter the front door from under an arcade, and follow the passageway past an abstract wall hanging to the elegantly curved stone stairs (the balustrades are shaped like urns). You enter one of those perfectly proportioned delights that millionaires have tried for centuries to recreate in their private homes. Opulent woodwork decorates the ceiling in voluptuous curves of natural wood, with a well-chosen blue-gray coloring the spaces in between. The far wall is pierced from floor to ceiling with glass overlooking the Limmat, with half columns with gilded capitals separating the many panes from one another. The tables and chairs are all of the most elegant sort, although you can sit in the attractively grouped series of Voltaire chairs for an apéritif before your meal if you choose.

A specialty of the house is zunfttopf served in old bronze pots with saffron rice; that is, filet mignon of beef with tomatoes and veal medallions with mushrooms. Or you might prefer sauteed minced veal with kidney in a mushroom cream sauce, served with rösti or minced calf liver with butter and fresh herbs. An eight-course dinner is offered for 38F ($17.46), and food is served from 11:45 a.m. to 2 p.m. and 6 to 10:30 p.m.

Fischstube Zürichhorn, 160 Bellerivestrasse (tel. 55-25-20), is ideal on a summer evening. A fish specialty restaurant, it is built on piles over the lake with al fresco dining in fair weather. The scenery is hard to beat, but the cuisine measures up admirably. Among the dishes I can recommend are the lake trout or turbot poached, the filet of Dover sole Champs-Élysées, perch filets with chopped almonds, the grilled lobster, or if you're a meat eater, the sirloin steak Café de Paris. À la carte prices begin at 40F ($18.38), and daily changing menus are featured from 19F ($8.73) to 24F ($11.03). The food and the service are top-notch.

Casino Zürich Horn, 170 Bellerivestrasse (tel. 55-20-20), has both an indoor restaurant and an outdoor dining terrace right on the lake. The place is large and popular, with excellently prepared food and courteous service. Of course, I prefer the outdoor dining spot in fair weather. From one of its tables you'll have a view of the night sightseeing boats with their strings of white lights. Count on spending from 40F ($18.38) and up for a meal here. Food is served from 11:30 a.m. to 2 p.m. and 6 to 10 p.m.

Oepfelchammer, 12 Rindermarkt (tel. 251-23-36), is for food, wine, and song, often to a guitar accompaniment. The house itself is from 1357, and over the years it's been frequented by students who have made it a virtual drinking fraternity. You raise your glass of wine in a toast at one of the carved wooden tables. The owner, Fred Tschanz, also has a winery, and naturally some of the bottles come from his vineyards. The place is smoke-stained and loaded with atmosphere—many famous professors and academicians have frequented the restaurant. The menu is in English, including such specialties as French onion soup, air-cured smoked beef, a pot of lentils with a choice of sausages, shredded calf liver in butter with rösti, and shredded veal Zuricher style. Desserts include a vodka sherbet and apple fritters with a hot vanilla sauce. Prices begin at 35F ($16.08), ranging upward. Remember to nail down a reservation before heading here. The restaurant is closed on Sunday, but open otherwise from 11 a.m. to midnight.

Restaurants Bahnhofbuffet Zürich, 15 Bahnhofplatz (tel. 211-15-10), owned by Martin Candrian, are nine railway station restaurants under one roof, lying at the end of your stroll down Bahnhofstrasse in the heart of Zurich. With so many restaurants and such different specialties and prices, this coterie of dining establishments caters to most tastes and pocketbooks. Its cuisine reaches its zenith at its prestigious French restaurant, au Premier, which has an elegant belle-époque atmosphere, with menus ranging in price from 22F ($10.11) to 55F ($25.27). A specialty is les médallions de filet de veau à la crème de Persil (medallion of veal in a parsley and cream sauce).

If you want something less elaborate, try traditional Swiss country cuisine at the wine restaurant, Trotte, in a rustic setting with prices starting at 7.50F ($3.45). Other restaurants include Da Capo (Italian specialties), Alfred Escher-stuve (try the grilled sole or salmon), Le Bistro de le Gare (entrecôte maître d'hôtel), the Cafeteria (roast veal sausage with french fries), the Brasserie (ten hash-brown potato dishes with garnishes ranging from cubes of vegetables to thinly sliced veal with mushrooms in a cream sauce) to the Winterthurer Stübli (sample pork Casimir in curry sauce) to the Chüechli-Wirtschaft (apple fritters with vanilla sauce). They're open seven days a week from 6 a.m. to 11:30 p.m. year round.

Hotel Florhof, 4 Florhofgasse (tel. 47-44-70), has a small, cozy, and elegant restaurant run by the Schilter family in an old patrician house renovated in 1973. The menu is limited, but carefully chosen. The soups are especially good, as are the appetizers, which might include risotto with mushrooms or air-dried prosciutto. Among the fish dishes, you can order filets of fera (a kind of trout) or shrimp Indian style with rice and curry. Among the special dishes of which the chef is rightly proud, try calf brains in butter or kidneys in mustard sauce. There is also a good selection of beef and veal dishes. Prices begin at 40F ($18.38) for a meal.

Restaurant Berghalde, 341 Witikonerstrasse (tel. 53-24-50), is a romantic garden restaurant in a cap-roofed villa in the quiet suburb of Witikon. The menu features specialties from the Black Forest, and with a fire blazing away in wintertime, it's easy to imagine yourself in a chilly woods somewhere in Germany. The restaurant has 27 kinds of meat dishes, including a fondue bourguignonne and fondue Chinoise, plus veal cooked in satisfying ways (try the veal filet of the chef with hollandaise sauce). There's plenty of parking around the house, and guests tend to find the place intimate and very comfortable, especially the Swiss themselves, who flock there, particularly on weekends. In summer there's a barbecued grill. Meals cost from 35F ($16.08). To reach the Berghalde, take tram 3 or 8. It's open from noon to midnight.

Conti, 1 Dufourstrasse (tel. 251-06-66), is the personal statement of Richard Rizzi, a well-known Swiss restaurateur. Next to the Opera House, it attracts devotees who often interrupt their dinner for a particular performance, returning for dessert and coffee. The carefully chosen menu is based on seasonal specialties such as venison. Food is served until 11:30 p.m. daily except on Sunday. Two persons can order Le Menu Gourmet "Saint-Pierre," at a cost of 74F ($34) each, which is a showcase treat where the chefs display their perfection and skills. This menu includes both meat and fish selections. Otherwise you can choose from the à la carte menu, selecting from such offerings as lobster, turbot, veal, and lamb. The perch is also outstanding. If you order à la carte, expect to spend from 35F ($16.08) to 60F ($27.57).

Le Dézaley, 7–9 Römergasse (tel. 251-61-29), is a landmark house which is practically a private club of French-speaking Zurichois. With a typical French-Swiss ambience, it lies in the center of town and has a long history, these two adjoining buildings dating from 1274. The city of Zurich acquired the house in 1916. Marianne and Pascal Ruhle, the managers, offer a carefully assembled repertoire of specialties from the Vaudoise region, including cheese fondue and fondue bourguignonne. A favorite of mine is a plate of sausages made with leeks, and the minced liver and kidney with rösti. Forty different wines from the canton of Vaud are offered. The menu is in English, and for dessert you can order a fruit cake which is based on the fresh fruit of the season. You'll most likely spend from 35F ($16.08), and you can do so from 9 a.m. to 2:30 p.m. and 5 p.m. to midnight daily except Sunday.

Ribó, 43 Luisenstrasse (tel. 44-48-64), is the best Spanish restaurant in Zurich, lying just off the Limmatplatz. It makes for marvelous change-of-pace dining, which is made even more inviting by the warm welcome accorded by the English-speaking host, Rodolfo Ribó, along with his wife Rosita. I suggest you begin your repast by ordering a glass of sherry such as Tío Pepe. You might then select the garlic soup or the Catalán salad with ham, eggs, sardines, olives, tuna, and asparagus tips. For a main course you might order the paella (made with chicken, mussels, squid, scampi, and shrimp), or a zarzuela (boiled seafood fisherman's style). The restaurant is fairly small, decorated in a regional tavern decor, and is known for its cozy atmosphere and well-prepared specialties. A menu costs from 18F ($8.27), but to order à la carte will average 45F ($20.68) or more. The restaurant is open daily except Sunday from 11:30 a.m. to 2:30 p.m. and 6 to 11 p.m. It closes annually from mid-August to mid-September.

Bodega Española, 15 Münstergasse (tel. 251-23-10), has been a well-known Spanish restaurant for some 20 years now. It's open throughout the year except Christmas from 10:30 a.m. to midnight daily. The ground-floor restaurant has what the owner aptly calls a "special bohemian ambience," where patrons order tapas (Spanish hors d'oeuvres) and drink the vino. The second-floor restaurant is more impressive, with original woodcarvings which must have been made more than 150 years ago. Both establishments, in fact, are in much the same style they were a century ago. A traditional Spanish cuisine is served here, including tortillas, calamares romana, and paella of the house with chicken and shrimp. Hot meals are served only from noon to 1:30 p.m. and 6 to 10 p.m. The price of a repast begins at 25F ($11.49), ranging upward, especially if you order the paella.

BUDGET DINING: **Bierhalle Kropf,** 16 In Gassen (tel. 221-18-05). The one thing you can say about "Die Kropf" (as it's affectionately called in Zurich) is that everyone in town eventually goes there, from the most conservative to the most liberal factions in the city. The food is generously served in an old-fashioned setting, and the waitresses are of the kind and motherly type. The overflow from the main dining room sometimes spills into the unpretentious entrance area, where some people specifically request to sit, and there's always a convivial hubbub. The decor is high-ceilinged and elaborate, with stag horns and painted hunting scenes. You'll see lots of well-polished paneling with late-19th-century embellishments, hanging chandeliers, and columns which could be made either of marble or of skillfully painted plaster. The restaurant is attractively located in a building with lots of stained glass in front, a few steps from the Paradeplatz.

In this venerated establishment—one of the oldest burger houses in Zurich—you face a choice of Swiss and Bavarian specialties, including chopped veal with rösti, stewed meats, pork shank, and pot-au-feu Zurich style, followed by palatschinken or apfelstrudel for dessert. Simple meals range in price from 13.50F ($6.20) to 18F ($8.27), but you could spend as much as 36F ($16.54) on the à la carte menu should you decide to go the whole hog.

Zeughauskeller, Am Paradeplatz (tel. 211-26-90). The proportions of this room, dating from 1487, are nothing short of vast, with a high ceiling covered with black and yellow rococo stencils between hewn timbers, all of it supported by massive round stone columns. The simple tables are made of wood, and even the chandeliers are crafted in massive wood with cast-iron chains, while the walls are decorated with medieval halberds and illustrations of Zurich noblemen of another era. The portions of typically Swiss dishes are more than generous, and are usually accompanied by steins of local beer. In fact many patrons come here just to drink.

In what was the former arsenal of Zurich, Kirt Andreae and Willy Hammer manage to keep 200 beer drinkers happy and well fed. It's estimated that the cooks make some 16 tons of potato salad a year. Many specialties of the Zurich kitchen are featured, including calf liver and bacon on a skewer. The kitchen also specializes in sausages of the various regions of Switzerland, including the original saucisson from Lake Geneva. Sausage is priced according to length. For 48F ($22.06), my party of four recently made a dinner out of one huge sausage. Set meals cost from 15F ($6.89) to 30F ($13.79). Daily specials are offered, and service is quick, efficient, and friendly. The beer hall serves weekdays from 11 a.m. to 10:45 p.m. and on Sunday from 11:30 a.m. to 10:30 p.m.

California, 125 Asylstrasse (tel. 53-56-80), has an unusual name for a restaurant in this city, but then, who wouldn't want to be in California during a cold Zurich winter? At least, that seems to be the mentality of the commercial and fashion photographers who come here with or without their models of that day for lunch. Super-hip, this is one of those low-key, high-tech establishments which could be in Milan, New York, or Los Angeles. Everyone seems to speak English. Three of the better known clients of this establishment are Zurich photographers Jürgen Tapprich, Gaston Vicky, and Eddie Kohli, although many other luminaries can also be seen from time to time. The food will certainly be familiar to you—hamburgers, cheesecake, corn on the cob, T-bone steak, and fresh mushroom salad. This is a fun address, with meals going for around 20F ($9.19) and up. It's open from 11:45 a.m. till 1:45 p.m. and 6 to 10:30 p.m. You can reach it by tram 3, 8, or 15, getting off at Hölderlinstrasse. No lunch is served on weekends, when the clientele, presumably, is in bed.

Hilti Vegi, 28 Sihlstrasse (tel. 221-38-71). The interior of this vegetarian restaurant is similar to Swiss establishments in that it's clean, orderly, appealing, and very neat. You can choose from two floors of dining areas here, the bottom one of which has a floor of roughly polished granite blocks set on end in semicircular patterns, a green and wood ceiling, and an elaborate array of vegetarian salads laid out American style on a stainless-steel rack. The entire room is filled with lime-green and red accents, which seem appropriate in the modern setting. Upstairs is sunnier than the downstairs, and it's decorated in maroon, with one wall completely covered with oversize windows.

Ever had a raclette vegi-burger? You can here, along with the very well-prepared and nutritious salads, good soups, and rich desserts. One of the least expensive items on the menu is spaghetti, which is served in five different ways. Many curry dishes are also featured. Set meals at lunch, served from 11 a.m. to 2:30 p.m., cost 12.50F ($5.74), and in the evening you can dine from 15F ($6.89) and up. The establishment became a restaurant in 1887, and in 1931 switched its menu to become strictly vegetarian. For your drink you'll have a selection of more than two dozen different blends of tea. Hours are from 11 a.m. to 8:45 p.m.

Raclette Stube, 16 Zähringerstrasse (tel. 251-41-30). It's hard to find good raclette in Zurich, and this is certainly one of the best places to try it for the first time. The restaurant is filled with simple tables and chairs in a format more modern than antique, on two levels of a white stucco room with an imposing

Louis XIII fireplace at the far end. A marvelously fashioned room divider of wrought iron adds visual interest, along with half paneling and lighting fixtures with pink lampshades. The establishment is well thought out and charming, and the service is sensitive and thoughtful.

Raclette, of course, is as traditional in Switzerland as fondue. It's made by holding a big piece of cheese in front of an open fire. When it starts to soften, scrapings are heaped lavishly on your plate and served with pickles, boiled potatoes, and pearl onions. The raclette costs 4.80F ($2.21) per portion, and you can keep ordering until you're full. I managed three. You can also order fondue bourguignonne, costing 47F ($21.60) for two, or a simple cheese fondue at 13.50F ($6.20). Tired of cheese? Order pork or veal sausages with rösti, from 8F ($3.68). Closed Wednesday.

Mère Catherine, Am Rüdenplatz (tel. 69-22-50). You'll have to negotiate some complicated back streets to reach this courtyard, which is anything but prominent on a city map, since it measures only about 35 feet on any side. In the daytime you'll find sunlight, ivy, and lots of quiet café tables, while at night a lot of attractive young people fill the bar area with quiet conversation, all of them casually dressed usually in leather or jeans. The bar area is marble topped with brass trim, filled with rock music and lots of Jean-Paul Belmondo look-alikes. Through a corridor to the back of the bar you'll see a high-ceilinged restaurant with stone floors, timbers, and a dimly lit ambience suitable for person-watching and drinking. A balcony area with a stenciled ceiling is connected to the ground floor by a gently rising staircase, and is usually filled shoulder to shoulder with young diners. The food, even the hand-scrawled menu, is bistro style. Salade paysanne is the most popular opener, and the chef also does good terrines. Specials change daily, but include such familiar fare as stuffed eggplant, fish soup, fried squid, and lamb cutlets in the Provençal style. Expect to spend from 25F ($11.49) for a meal.

Blockhus, 4 Schifflände (tel. 252-14-53), is a good typical old Swiss restaurant run by A. Baumann-Beck, who speaks English and gives guests a warm welcome. Cheese fondue, costing 13.50F ($6.20), is the specialty of the house, but other dishes are prepared equally well. These include beefsteak tartar and the ubiquitous minced veal with rösti, Zurich's most classic dish. The location is near Bellevueplatz. Lunch sees a choice of five menus priced from 8.80F ($4.05) to 17F ($7.81). The chef serves some costly items, but the majority of his meals are reasonable in price, the quality high. Hot meals are served from 11 a.m. to 11:30 p.m.

3. What to See

JUST WALKING AROUND: If you do nothing else in Zurich, walk along the world-famed **Bahnhofstrasse,** which has been called one of the most beautiful shopping streets on earth. Planted with linden trees, the street was built on the site of what used to be a "frogs' moat." The exclusive street is relatively free of traffic, except for trams, which Zurichers have labeled "holy cows."

Beginning at the Bahnhofplatz, the street extends for nearly 4000 feet until it reaches the lake. The drab **Bahnhofplatz,** the hub of Zurich's transportation network, is the railway station square. The Hauptbahnhof (the German word for central railway station) was built in 1871 on this square.

With your back to this railway terminus, you can head up Bahnhofstrasse, which is filled with shops selling luxury merchandise, such as Swiss watches, and banks, those "gnomeries" referred to earlier. You can select a favorite café and people-watch when you get tired of shopping. Incidentally, if you do shop, take along plenty of cash or else a gold-plated credit card. The merchandise is exquisite, but it's also some of the most expensive in the world.

At the end of the street you reach Bürkli-Platz, opening onto the shore of the lake. A pint-size Covent Garden–style vegetable and fruit market flourishes here, and in summer, on Tuesday and Friday morning, an active flea market.

To walk the **"Quays of Zurich"** is, in the view of many, an attraction rivaled in the city only by the Swiss National Museum. These promenades have been built along the Zurichsee (Lake Zurich) and the Limmat River. The most famous is Limmat Quai, in the virtual heart of Zurich, beginning at the Bahnhof Bridge and extending east to the Rathaus (town hall) and beyond. These quays for the most part have lovely gardens with beautiful trees such as the linden. The Swiss are known for their love of flowers, which is much in evidence as you join Zurichers in their promenade, especially invigorating when spring comes to the city. Uto Quai is the major lakeside promenade, running from Badeanstalt Uto Quai, a swimming pool, to Bellevue Square and Quai Brucke. (Incidentally, you can swim at this pool from 8 a.m. to 7 p.m. daily for 1.50F, or 69¢). The beautiful swans you see in the lake aren't just a scenic attraction. Zurichers have found that they're an efficient garbage disposal system, keeping the lake from being polluted as it laps up on their shores. If you stroll as far as Mythen Quai, you'll be following the lake along its western shore and out into the countryside where vistas open onto the Alps and, on the far horizon, the Oberland massifs.

Whenever I'm in Zurich, I always head for the **Old Quarter,** which is known for its romantic squares, narrow cobblestone streets, winding alleyways that aren't as sinister as they look, fountain-decorated corners, medieval houses, art galleries, boutiques, colorfully quaint restaurants, shops, a scattering of hotels (often budget), and antique stores. The old town lies on both sides of the Limmat River, and you might begin your exploration at the Münsterhof, or former swine market. Excavations have turned up houses here that date from the 1100s.

Once it was the tarrying place of Charlemagne, and to walk its old streets is to follow in the footsteps of everybody from Goethe to Lenin, from Einstein to Mozart, from James Joyce to Carl Jung.

Shaded by trees, the belvedere square of **Lindenhof** is one of the most scenic spots in Zurich, especially favored at twilight time by those who believe in "young love." It can be reached by climbing medieval alleyways from the Fraumünster. Once the site of a Celtic and Roman fort, Lindenhof is a good point to watch the crossing of the Limmat River. The lookout point is graced with a fountain of course. There's also a good view of the medieval Old Quarter, which rises in layers on the right bank. Many excellent restaurants are located in this vicinity.

Weinplatz is another landmark square you'll invariably reach in your exploration of Zurich. It lies right off the 1878 Rathausbrücke (town hall bridge) spanning the Limmat. Once this was the only river crossing in Zurich (not the present structure, however). The Weinplatz is named for its 1909 Weinbauer fountain depicting a "little ole Swiss wine-grower," basket of grapes in hand. Many visitors like to stop here to take a picture of the old burghers' houses with Flemish-style roofs on the opposite bank.

At this point you may want to cross the bridge for a visit to the **Rathaus,** the late Renaissance town hall of Zurich, erected in the closing years of the 17th century, and opening onto Limmatquai. Its rooms are darkly paneled, and it has those antique porcelain stoves so beloved in Switzerland and Austria. In a setting of rich sculptural adornment, cantonal councils still meet here. It's open Tuesday, Thursday, and Friday from 10 to 11:30 a.m. No admission is charged, but you should tip the guide who shows you around.

Directly south of Münsterbrücke is a Gothic church, rather austere, called the **Wesserkirche** or "water church." When it was built in 1479 it was surrounded by the river—hence its name. Here you'll see a statue of Zwingli, the famous Swiss reformer.

On the north side of the church is the **Helmhaus,** a 1794 building with a fountain hall, where the city shows changing art exhibitions. The address is 31 Limmatquai, and the gallery is on the second and third floors. It's open daily except Monday from 10 a.m. to 6 p.m. (also on Thursday evening from 8 to 10 p.m.).

Finally, I'd like to endorse a life-seeing program called **"Don't Miss the Swiss."** Sponsored by the Zurich Tourist Office, 15 Bahnhofplatz (tel. 211-40-00), it's a unique program that connects foreign visitors, such as Canadians and Americans, with personal contacts in Zurich. As much as possible, families of similar backgrounds and interests are matched (after all, you have to have something to talk about). After the red tape is out of the way, you're given an invitation to a Swiss home. I recently tested this program and was invited into the home of a Swiss writer and his family, his beautiful wife and two daughters. He was working on a biography of Carl Jung. An enjoyable evening was climaxed by coffee, Kirschwasser, and a dessert that one of the daughters had baked. He gave me some white chocolate to take back to my hotel. The next day, to reciprocate, I sent flowers. Obviously this is a noncommercial arrangement, and you should never go expecting a meal or an accommodation. Incidentally, you'll be matched with an English-speaking family. The tourist office will work out details, but give them a little time to set up your visit.

THE GREAT CHURCHES: The Romanesque and Gothic cathedral of Zurich, **Grossmünster,** was, according to legend, founded by Charlemagne whose horse bowed down on the spot marking the graves of three early Christian martyrs. Rising on a terrace above the Limmatquai, the cathedral has twin three-story towers, a city landmark. On the right bank of the Limmat, the present structure dates principally from 1090–1180 and from 1225 to the dawn of the 14th century.

The cathedral is dedicated to those Christian missionaries referred to, the patron saints of Zurich: Felix, Regula, and Exuperantius. Back in the third century they had a rough time converting the denizens of Turicum (the original name for Zurich) to Christianity. The governor of that day had them plunged into boiling oil and then made them drink molten lead, as legend would have it. The indefatigable trio refused to renounce their faith and were beheaded. Miraculously, they still had enough energy to pick up their heads and climb to the top of a hill (the present site of the cathedral) and dig their own graves in which to inter themselves. (The seal of Zurich honors these saints, depicting them carrying their heads under their arms.) The remains of the saints are said to rest in one of the chapels of the Münster.

The cathedral was once the parish church of Zwingli, one of the great leaders of the Reformation. He urged priests to take wives (he'd married one himself) and attacked the "worship of images" and the Roman doctrine of mass. Needless to say, he stirred up some Catholic ire. This led to his death at Kappel in a religious war in 1531. The public hangman quartered his body, and soldiers burnt the pieces with dung. That spot at Kappel is today marked with an inscription: "They may kill the body but not the soul." Almost to assert the truth of that, Zurich's Grossmünster, long stripped of the excessive ornamentation you find in the cathedrals of Italy, is austere looking, the way Zwingli would have wanted it.

However, if you visit the choir you'll come upon stained-glass windows Giacometti completed in 1933. In the crypt is the original (but weather-beaten) statue of a 15th-century figure of Charlemagne. A copy of that same statue crowns the south tower.

Visiting hours are from 9 a.m. to 4 p.m. weekdays only from April 1 until the end of September (until 5 p.m. on Saturday). For the remaining part of the year the cathedral is open daily from 10 a.m. to 4 p.m. If the weather's good, you'll be admitted to a tower from May 1 until the end of October for an impressive view, costing only 1F (46¢). If you want to know if the tower is open before heading there, phone 47-52-32.

Rising on the left bank, **Fraümunster,** with its slender blue spire, was founded as an abbey in 853, but dates mainly from the 13th and 14th centuries in its present reincarnation. The church overlooks the Münsterhof, the former pig market of Zurich. In the undercroft are the remains of the crypt of the old abbey church. The Emperor Ludwig (Louis the German) was the founder. He was the grandson of Charlemagne, and along with the Benedictines, he installed his daughter as abbess in 853. The chief attractions of Fraumünster are five stained-glass windows—each with its own color theme—by Marc Chagall dating from 1970. Obviously they are best seen in bright morning light. The Münster is also celebrated for its elaborate organ. The Gothic nave is from the 13th to the 15th centuries, and the basilica has three aisles. In the Romanesque and Gothic cloisters are 1920s paintings depicting old Zurich legends about the founding of the abbey. Visiting hours are weekdays from 9 a.m. to 6 p.m. May to September (on Sunday, from noon to 6 p.m.). For the remainder of the year, Fraumünster is open from 10 a.m. to 5 p.m. (closes at dusk or around 4 p.m. in winter).

After leaving the church, you might want to walk across **Münsterbrücke,** an 1838 bridge that leads to the already-previewed Grossmünster. On the bridge is a pre–World War II statue of Burgomaster Waldmann, who was beheaded in 1489. Under him, the city became a ruler of considerable lands.

The Münsterhof itself is one of the historic old squares of Zurich, well worth a visit. On the square stands the Zunfthaus zur Meisen, which we'll visit later. Buildings on the square are painted in pastels, lilacs and sky blues, with contrasting shutters. The rooftops for the most part are gabled and pointed, really Hansel-and-Gretel–type roofs that look as if a pencil sharpener has been at work on them.

On the left bank, **St. Peter's Church** (Peterskirche), from the 13th century, is the oldest in Zurich. The church is visited mainly by those wishing to view its mammoth timepiece, the largest clockface in Europe, measuring 28½ feet in diameter. The minute hands alone are four yards in length. The clock is gold faced, and is installed in the massive tower of the church. You'll easily spot the church rising to the south of the Lindenhof. Under the tower, its choir is in the late Romanesque style, but the three-aisle nave is baroque.

THE BEST OF THE MUSEUMS: If your time is limited, the three most outstanding museums of Zurich are the Swiss National Museum, the Fine Arts Museum, and the Rietberg Museum.

The **Landesmuseum** (Swiss National Museum) is an epic survey of the Swiss people, covering like a blanket their culture, art, and history. The saga of artifacts begins in dim unrecorded time and carries you up to the present day. The location, in a big, sprawling gray stone Victorian building, is in back of the Zurich Hauptbahnhof. It's like a storybook of all the cantons, and you turn it page by page as you go from gallery to gallery. You enter at 2 Museumstrasse, and you can do so admission free daily except Monday morning from 10 a.m. to 5 p.m. mid-June to mid-September. During the rest of the year it's open daily from 10 a.m. to noon and 2 to 5 p.m. except Monday morning. For information, call 221-10-10.

Religious art sounds a dominant theme, as represented by stained glass from the 1550s removed from Tänikon Convent. Some of the Carolingian art dates back to the ninth century. See especially the frescoes from the church of Müstair. Altarpieces—carved, painted, and gilded—bring back the glory of the Swiss medieval artisan. The prehistoric section is exceptional, dipping back to the fourth millennium. Switzerland as a Roman outpost is also revealed in exhibits.

Several rooms from Fraumünster Abbey are on view. The displays of utensils and furnishings of Swiss life over the centuries are staggering: medieval silverware, 14th-century drinking bowls, tiled 18th-century stoves, 17th-century china, Roman clothing, painted furniture, costumes, even dollhouses. Naturally, arms and armor revive Switzerland's military legacy, from 800 to 1800, although some weapons date from the late Iron Age.

In the basement are several workshops, showing the everyday life of 19th-century craftsmen such as the little old shoemaker. Naturally there's an exhibition tracing Swiss clockmaking from the 16th to the 18th centuries.

The **Zurich Kunsthaus** or fine arts museum is devoted to works mainly from the 19th and 20th centuries, although many of its paintings and sculpture dip back to antiquity. Dating back to Victorian times, the collection has grown and grown until it is today one of the most important in Europe.

The location is at 1 Heimplatz (tel. 251-67-65). Following its 1976 overhaul, the museum is now one of the most modern and sophisticated anywhere, both in its superb lighting and in its arrangement of art. Visiting hours are Tuesday to Friday from 10 a.m. to 9 p.m. and on weekends from 10 a.m. to 5 p.m. Monday hours are from 2 to 5 p.m. The regular admission is only 2F (92¢), rising to anywhere from 3F ($1.38) to 8F ($3.68) for special exhibitions, which are usually stunning and well worth the investment.

As you enter, note Rodin's *Gate of Hell.* Later on you can explore one of my favorite sections, the Giacometti wing, showing the artistic development of this amazing Swiss-born artist (1901–1966), whose works are characterized by surrealistically elongated forms and hallucinatory moods.

All the legendary names of modern art parade through the galleries: Picasso, Cézanne, Monet, Lipchitz, Marini, Mondrian, Bonnard, Braque, and Chagall (more than a dozen works). The gallery contains the largest collection of the works of the Norwegian-born artist Edvard Munch to be seen outside of Oslo. Old masters such as Rubens and Rembrandt are suitably honored, and one salon contains 17 Rouaults.

Among national artists, Ferdinand Hodler is an outstanding candidate, having "made waves" in the early 20th century. Pictures by Degas, Toulouse-Lautrec, and Utrillo are likely to brighten a gray day.

Rietberg Museum, 15 Gablerstrasse (tel. 202-45-28), is installed in the former Wesendonck Villa in the center of a garden, opening onto a view of Lake Zurich. The villa, enclosed by Rieter Park, is in the neoclassical style, having been modeled after Villa Albani in Rome. It was constructed in 1857 by a German industrialist, Otto Wesendonck, and in time it was visited by Richard Wagner who fell in love with the hostess, who inspired his *Tristan and Isolde.* The museum today, acquired by the city of Zurich in 1952, contains the collection of Baron von der Heydt, a vast assemblage of non-European art, one of the most stunning collections in Europe.

The collection is eclectic, roaming the South Sea islands, going to the Near East, dipping into mysterious Tibet, journeying by way of Africa and Java to pre-Columbian America. The Chinese and Japanese are represented, and of all the treasures, my favorite is the *Dancing Shiva,* a celebrated Indian carving. In addition to that, seek out the votive stelae of the Wei dynasty (dating from the archaic Buddhist period). Of course not all these treasures were collected by the baron; many have been donated by others, as the collection has grown considerably over the years.

Admission to the gallery is free. It's open Tuesday to Sunday from 10 a.m. to 5 p.m. (also Wednesday from 8 to 10 p.m.). The museum is reached after a 12-minute ride from the center of town (take tram 7).

Zunfthaus zur Meisen, opening onto the Münsterhof, across the bridge from the Wasserkirche, is one of the famous old guildhouses of the city. This one was owned by the wine merchants of Zurich, and it's a beautifully maintained structure with a wrought-iron gatehouse. The late baroque guildhouse dates from 1752, and has today been turned into a branch museum, an extension of the overstuffed Swiss National Museum. Along with some antiques, it's devoted mainly to Swiss 18th-century ceramics and the porcelain of Zurich. Frankly, the stuccoed rooms are so splendid that they compete with the exhibits. No admission is charged, and hours are daily, except holidays, from 10 a.m. to noon and 2 to 5 p.m. On Monday morning it's closed (as is almost everything else in Zurich), but it opens from 2 to 5 p.m.

SIGHTSEEING MISCELLANY: The **Zoological Garden,** 221 Zürichbergstrasse, is one of the best known in Europe, containing some 2400 animals belonging to some 350 species. It also has an aquarium and an open-air aviary. Hours in summer are from 8 a.m. to 6 p.m. and in winter from 8 a.m. to 5 p.m. You can visit the Africa house, the ape house, and the terrariums, along with the elephant house and the giant land turtle house. There are special enclosures for pandas, seals, otters, snow leopards, and tigers. Adults are charged 6F ($2.76) and 2.50F ($1.15) for children. The zoo lies in the eastern sector of the city, called Zürichberg, a wooded hill. From the Hauptbahnhof in Zurich, take tram 5 or 6.

Devotees of Thomas Mann, who won the Nobel Prize for literature in 1929, will be richly rewarded in Zurich. Mann, who opposed the Nazi regime and lived in the United States from 1938 to 1953, also lived in Zurich. The **Thomas Mann Archives of the Swiss Federal Institute of Technology,** 15 Schönberggasse, next to the university, contain manuscripts and mementos of the celebrated author of such works as *Death in Venice* and *The Magic Mountain.* Visiting hours are Wednesday to Saturday from 2 to 6 p.m.

If you're a true admirer, you might also want to journey to **Kilchberg,** four miles from Zurich, along the southwest shore of the lake. This town is more famously associated with the Swiss author Conrad Ferdinand Meyer, a 19th-century figure. However, Thomas Mann spent the last years of his life here, and was buried in south side of the small church in the village in 1955. His grave is marked, as is his wife's, who died in 1980.

The **Bührle Collection,** 172 Zollikerstrasse, is a jewel of a collection, an art aficionado's dream. However, it can only be visited on Tuesday and Friday from 2 to 5 p.m. The admission is 6.60F ($3.04) for adults and 2.75F ($1.27) for students. There is a limited but very special section devoted to medieval sculpture, but most visitors seem to be more interested in the French impressionists, including works by Monet, Degas, Renoir, and Manet. The collection also includes paintings by Rubens, Rembrandt, and Fragonard. The collection is private, but the owners have chosen to share it with the public.

4. Where to Shop

Zurich has been called a shopper's Valhalla, if that's not too pagan a term for such a Protestant city. Within the heart of Zurich is a square kilometer (or 25 acres) of shopping, including the exclusive stores along the **Bahnhofstrasse,** already previewed in the sightseeing section. Along this gold-plated street you can walk with oil-rich sheiks and their families in your search for furs, watches, jewelry, leather goods, silks, and embroidery. If your own oil well didn't come in, you can still shop for souvenirs.

Your shopping adventure might begin more modestly at the top of the street, the **Bahnhofplatz.** Underneath this vast transportation hub is a complex of shops known as **"Shopville."**

Grieder les Boutiques, 30 Bahnhofstrasse (tel. 211-33-60), is one of the chicest department stores in Switzerland, especially since its format includes both ready-to-wear and couture facilities of such designers as Ungaro, Scherrer, the House of Chanel, Ferré, and many others. The facility fills two floors of a stone building on Zurich's most fashionable commercial street, where the saleswomen tend to be bilingual, pretty, and formidably well dressed. The accessories are especially well selected, including a wide range of purses, scarves, and leather goods.

Heimatwerk, 2 Bahnhofstrasse (tel. 221-08-37). This is only one of a chain of similar stores throughout Zurich. Most of them have the same basic collection of, for example, hand-painted boxes in charmingly naïve patterns with or without music mechanisms, bookends, china, decorative stoneware plates, a wide range of textiles, and the obligatory cowbells in all sizes.

This particular store has a large selection of glass, embroidery, and woodcarvings, among other items. The items are wrapped in charming Swiss gift paper, and someone on the staff will label them for you. The English-speaking staff is particularly helpful in suggesting "little gifts."

Schuhhaus Bally Capitol, 66 Bahnhofstrasse (tel. 211-35-15), is the largest official outlet of this famous Swiss chain in the world, occupying a prominent place in a big-windowed store on this shopping artery. For lovers of Bally shoes, this is the place to buy them, although the merchandise, I've been told, is not necessarily cheaper than at other Bally outlets. You'll find the most complete line of Bally shoes here in the world, along with accessories and clothing (most, but not all, of which are made in Switzerland).

Jelmoli Department Store, 69 Bahnhofstrasse (tel. 221-21-42), is a Zurich institution, having everything a large department store should, from cookware to clothing. Founded 150 years ago by the Ticino-born entrepreneur Johann Peter Jelmoli, the store and the success of its many branches is a legend among the Zurich business community. Usually a huge portrait of the founder hangs above the main entrance.

Meister Silber, 28a Bahnhofstrasse (tel. 221-27-30). The location of this elite shop couldn't be more prestigious, directly on the Paradeplatz in the center of Zurich. It's the kind of shop where many people stop in to browse through the well-dusted showrooms, and where many of them return to buy that art object in silver or porcelain they never really needed but just had to have anyway. The prices are frighteningly high, although that doesn't seem to prevent the store from doing a brisk business anyway, particularly since they have one of the widest selections of flatware and gift items in the city. When I last visited, there was an exhibition of animalistic sculpture beautifully crafted from wrought silver and semiprecious crystals in stags, rams, deer, and fanciful and realistic birds, worth seeing as art objects alone. I was told there are revolving series of porcelain sculpture as well.

Beyer, 31 Bahnhofstrasse (tel. 221-10-80). If your heart is set on buying a timepiece in Zurich, try this well-established store midway between the train station and the lake. Besides carrying just about every famous brand of watch made in Switzerland, they also have a surprising museum in the basement, containing timepieces from as early as 1400 B.C. Exhibitions include all kinds of water clocks, sundials, and hour glasses. Another sure bet in Zurich would be:

Bucherer, 50 Bahnhofstrasse (tel. 211-26-35). A longtime name in the Swiss watch industry, this store carries an impressive collection of jewelry as well.

Sturzenegger, 48 Bahnhofstrasse (tel. 211-28-20), is a good place to buy the kinds of delicate hand-embroidered items which an age of polyester fabrics has conspired to make obsolete. A back room contains tall shelves of tablecloths, sheets, and napkins in all prices and sizes. Many of them are intricately patterned, while the room in front sells blouses, handkerchiefs, shawls, scarves, children's frocks, and embroidered curtains. The store is old-fashioned and wood-paneled, and much of the merchandise is partially concealed in drawers or high on shelves, so it's the kind of place where you'll need a salesperson, most of whom are friendly and professional.

Mädler, 26 Bahnhofstrasse (tel. 211-75-70), specializes in leather bags and suitcases at this most famous emporium of Swiss leather goods. You'll pass through the frosted glass doors leading to the Bahnhofstrasse and enter a modest-size showroom with a friendly battery of well-dressed women staffers. If you don't see what you like, be sure to take the elevator to the massively stocked second floor, where a medium-size leather bag will cost between 500F ($229.75) and 1500F ($689.25). Of course at that price it will be of the highest quality. Stephanie Mädler and her family have owned this shop (which has since become a famous chain) since 1951.

Musik Hug, 28 Limmatquai (tel. 47-16-00), is the kind of shop that musicians will love, particularly if they need sheet music for anything from flügelhorn concertos to yodeling duets. It might be the largest repository of alpine musical tradition anywhere, as well as a commercial music shop stocking woodwind recorders of all sizes and pitches (I saw one in the window at least four feet tall) along with flügelhorns and French horns. You'll find several other branches of this store around Zurich, although this one near the lake is the most interesting.

The **Travel Book Shop,** 11 Seilergraben (tel. 252-38-83), sells what could be called a very complete set of travel books, for anyone interested in going into great depth of research about an upcoming trip. Many of the books are in German, but some translations exist.

Buchhandlung Friedrich Daeniker, 11 In Gassen (tel. 211-27-04). If being in Zurich inspires you to reread excerpts from Carl Jung, this is the place to find them, along with the works of many other authors whose books have been translated into English. In addition to scholarly works, the friendly staff sells novels, periodicals, old-fashioned spellbinders, all of them in the Mother Tongue. It's between the Paradeplatz and the river, in an area where many of the shops are worth looking at.

The **Jade Dragon,** 20 Sihlstrasse (tel. 211-51-01), is on a well-traveled commercial street near the Bahnhofstrasse. This small storefront displays antique Chinese art which is exquisite. Some Mandarin probably paid a fortune for it, and so will you. You get valuable and unique objects along with friendly service.

Teuscher, 9 Storchengasse (tel. 211-51-53). If you have a sweet tooth and have ever noticed an epicurean chocolate shop in New York or Los Angeles selling the most divine chocolates in the world, then you'll be interested in seeing the original shop which began the empire years ago. It lies on a narrow cobblestone street in the old town of Zurich and is surprisingly small. You can tell you're in the area by the smell of chocolate truffles, which come in such flavors as champagne, orange, and cocoa. They sell for 5.20F ($2.40) per 100 grams. There's usually a seasonal theme in this store, where a decorator creates a fantasy.

Wuehre 9-Art Deco, 9 Wühre (tel. 221-18-70). If you're an art deco fan who has long ago explored most of the antique stores of America, this could be an insight into what was being made in the Teutonic countries in the '20s. It lies in a small shop on the quays of the Limmat, where you'll find other interesting stores nearby.

5. After Dark in Zurich

The city's nightlife is much more liberated than it was when I first checked it out as a college student. But, on the other hand, don't expect anything to rival Hamburg's Reeperbahn.

Since Zurich closes down fairly early, your nightlife might also begin early at one of the city's—

TEAROOMS, BARS, AND CAFÉS: **Confiserie Sprüngli,** Am Paradeplatz (tel. 211-07-95), founded in 1836, is the Zurich equivalent of the legendary Demel in Vienna. Many Zurichers remember episodes from their childhoods which took place at this quintessentially old-fashioned pastry shop on the Bahnhofstrasse. It's been said that listening to the chatter of the clients in the late afternoon is a good insight into the sociology of the city. It's open from Monday to Friday from 7 a.m. to 6:30 p.m. and on Saturday from 7:30 a.m. to 5:30 p.m. An area on the ground floor sells a staggering array of pastries (to go) and chocolates (the justly famed Lindt chocolates are about the best you'll ever devour). You can also order light meals here costing from 16.50F ($7.58), but most guests order tea from 2.10F (97¢). Desserts begin at 2.20F ($1.02).

If you like your tearooms more modern, try **Das Köstlichle Teehaus,** 7 Kuttelgasse (tel. 211-75-50). Even the matchbooks this teahouse distributes are tasteful and understated, as is the Japanese decor of the place. On a small street in the old town, it stands in an area filled with avant-garde boutiques and extravagantly dressed women. The shop is sensitively decorated with potted bamboos, live trees, and simple, well-constructed furniture in light woods and neutral colors. Established by the Weber family, the teahouse seems to have been warmly received by the chic community around it. All drinks are alcohol-free, although the choice of tea is very complete, a pot costing from 2.50F ($1.15). Simple menus range from 8.50F ($3.91) to 11.50F ($5.29). Hours are Monday to Friday from 6:30 a.m. to 9 p.m. (Thursday till 10 p.m.), and Saturday till 6 p.m.

Café Wühre, 11 Wühre (tel. 221-00-94), lies on the banks of the river on the Bahnhofstrasse side, with a view of much of the other side of Zurich which includes the double spires of the Grossmünster. It's in a neighborhood filled with unusual antique stores and super-trendy boutiques, with a clientele that's at the very least appreciative of the arts. The owner, Suzanne N'Gom-Cartier, is a statuesque brunette with a charming smile, who has decorated her sophisticated establishment with modern art. In summer, tables are set on the cobblestones facing a pedestrian walkway with no traffic. Coffee costs 2.20F ($1), with sandwiches priced from 3.70F ($1.70).

Café/Bar Odeon, 2 Limmatquai (tel. 251-47-60), is one of the most legendary turn-of-the-century bohemian landmarks of Zurich, and it might be fun to stop in for a coffee and check out the action, especially in the evening when it gets much singles action. Lenin discovered it in World War I and sat there late into the evening, uttering such pronouncements as "The neutrality of Switzerland is a bourgeois fraud and means submission to the imperialist war." The café is decorated in art nouveau, with an intimate format of banquettes and cubbyholes, plus a prominently curved bar and lots of tables on the sidewalk outside. It's open from 7 a.m. to 2 a.m. Monday to Saturday and from 11 a.m. to 2 a.m. on Sunday. Coffee costs from 1.50F (69¢), and you can also order light meals costing from 20F ($9.19).

Café Select, 16 Limmatquai (tel. 252-43-72), a gathering place of the so-called literati, is Zurich's closest rival to the Odeon. The restaurant has 350 seats on an outdoor terrace that is partially protected from noise and traffic because of its location in an open area surrounded by buildings. It's open daily from 7 a.m. to midnight. It doesn't serve alcohol, but offers other drinks such as coffee beginning at 2.10F (96¢). Café-style snacks and light meals cost from 8F ($3.69) to 14F ($6.43), with cakes and sandwiches averaging around 3F ($1.38).

Oliver Twist Pub (also Mr. Pickwick Pub), 6 Rindermarkt (tel. 252-47-10). The bartenders here speak with an Irish accent and are quick to give tips on life in Zurich. You can have intimate talks with your companion beneath portraits of QEII and the Duke of Edinburgh, which hang in regal detachment above the half-paneling on the velvet-flocked wall. In the back room, which is green, the dartboard is much in use with lots of visiting English or among the Anglophilic Swiss. Leather banquettes are usually occupied by sympathetic drinkers. An outer courtyard adds a charming Middle European touch, with marble pavement and a modern statue of a crouching laborer. Besides the friendly ambience, you'll find plenty of food and drink items. Daily specials, such as schnitzel, salad, and polenta, cost from 9F ($4.14). Sometimes for the same price you get spare ribs, and in season, "original curry." Two large beers cost 7.60F ($3.50).

James Joyce Pub, 8 Pelikanstrasse (tel. 221-18-28). Architectural purists might note that the interior of this pub would be more at home in Ireland than on the continent, and they'd be absolutely right. In the early 1970s the Union Bank of Switzerland acquired the interior decor of the bar area of an 18th-century hotel in Dublin (Jury's Bar) which was being demolished for urban renovation. Because the UBS wanted a suitable place near the Bahnhofstrasse to entertain business clients, they assembled the bar on a street near their main offices and named it after the quintessential Dubliner himself. Joyce, by the way, lived for a few years in Zurich and had described Jury's Bar (when it was still in Dublin) in passages of *Ulysses.* Today the banquettes are slightly more comfortable than they were before, and the entire establishment is impeccably clean, oiled, and polished with Swiss efficiency that even the Union Bank can be proud of. The blackboard menu contains daily specials (you can order complete meals here), and there's always a good assortment of soups, such as potato with shrimp, salads, cheese, and cold snacks. You can also order such pub specials as Irish stew and fish and chips, along with hamburgers and fried chicken legs. The menu is in English, and meals begin at 15F ($6.89), going up.

CULTURAL NOTES: Concerts, theater, opera, and ballet flourish in Zurich, reaching their peak of activity at the International Festival in June. The cultural tradition of Zurich is strong: it not only has 20 museums, of which we have visited only the most important, but nearly 100 galleries and some two dozen archives and galleries, including one devoted to Thomas Mann as I've outlined.

In June these cultural activities are spotlighted at the fine performances given at the Zurich **Opernhaus,** 10 Mühlebachstrasse (tel. 251-69-20). The opera is closed in July and August, and tickets (not very good ones) start at about 8F ($3.68).

Zurich has many well-respected theaters, but unless your German is proficient you won't understand the classic productions of *Hamlet* of Goethe's *Stella* presented at the **Schauspielhaus,** 3 Rämistrasse (tel. 251-11-11), where tickets range from about 12F ($5.51) to 40F ($18.38). The actors take a vacation from June until the beginning of September.

Big, splashy musicals such as *Hair* are often presented at the **Volkshaus,** on Stauffacherstrasse. For tickets and information, visit BiZZ on Werdmühleplatz (tel. 221-22-83).

For more experimental works—again, only if your German is proficient—catch a production at **Theater am Heckplatz,** Theaterkasse (tel. 252-32-34).

FOLKLORIC: **Baggli's Swiss Chalet,** 14–16 Marktgasse (tel. 252-59-40), is the kind of place where a Swiss business person might take one of his or her more informal clients for a "night on the town." The walls are rustically paneled, while the staff wears regional garb. When I last visited, the six-piece band did a convincing imitation of a '50s rock-and-roll piece to appreciative audiences. However, despite this heretical departure, on most nights you'll get the flag swingers, alphorn blowers, and yodelers. Flügelhorns and accordions weave intricate music through the timbered room. There's no cover charge, and a beer costs from 5.50F ($2.53) to 6.50F ($2.99). If you go earlier for dinner, it will cost about 50F ($22.98). Dance music is played after 10 p.m., although the restaurant and grill rooms open at 6 p.m.

Kindli Swiss Chalet, Rennweg/Pfalzgasse (tel. 211-41-82). Although yodeling is said to be the specialty of the bands that play here, their repertoires sometimes include everything from Dixieland jazz to Mozart, complete with flügelhorns and regional costumes. The owners, the Schmidt family, sometimes take to the platform to perform their own kind of alpine music. Dinner is served from 7:30 p.m., and the music begins at 8:30. An average meal usually costs 60F ($27.57) per person, although clients can visit just for drinks after 9:30 p.m., paying a cover charge of 8.80F ($4.05) plus 15F ($6.89) for the first alcoholic drink. The decor is pine paneled and rustic, with lots of timbers and hewn beams, while the food is gutburgerlich and alpine.

A much cheaper way to hear alpine music is to join the rowdy patrons at the **Bierhalle Wolf,** 132 Limmatquai (tel. 251-01-30). Folkloric music from an oompah band in regional garb greets you as you enter this large rectangular beer hall, decorated with triangular pendants from friendly nations hanging from the ceiling, plus flags from the different cantons. To the sound of a guitarist, trumpeter, accordionist, and tuba player, waitresses bring beer in tankards. You can go as early as 5 o'clock in the afternoon to hear the music. In between rounds the management shows slides on the wall of, say, happily laughing couples chugging beer in alpine meadows. The place is centrally located and one of the most gemütlich establishments in Zurich. Some of the beer halls in this section of Zurich can be dangerous, but the Wolf attracts a friendly, nonhostile crowd. Daily set menus are offered ranging from 7.80F ($3.59) to 10.80F ($4.97), with two large mugs of beer costing 7.80F ($3.59).

DISCO: **Birdwatcher's Club,** 16 Schützengasse (tel. 211-50-58), has been considered one of Zurich's smarter nightclubs since it was established about a decade ago. Its interior is filled with art nouveau murals, and there's a big bar area at the far end. You'll find plenty of dark velvet chairs for drinking. The cocktail hour between 5 and 8:30 p.m. attracts some of the most sophisticated 30-year-olds in Zurich, and after 9 p.m. weekdays there is disco dancing (on Saturday, this begins at 4 p.m. and on Sunday at 8 p.m.). The clientele is well dressed. Drink prices (no cover charge) begin at 9.50F ($4.37) for the disco. The place does a lively business.

La Ferme, 13 Stadthausquai (tel. 211-57-50). Besides being a restaurant, this is a popular dance hall and disco. On one of the quays on the Bahnhofstrasse side of the river, this lively establishment has a decor of rustic pine beams arranged to look like a barnyard fence. Paper leaves on the replicas of trees sprout from the middle of some of the wood tables. During the day this dark-hued place is a lunch restaurant and café, with sidewalk tables overlooking the Limmat and the Grossmünster across the river. At night, disco action takes place in front of a DJ's platform covered with rustic planks. On some nights you are likely to be titillated with "naughty" slides or even folkloric amusement. Top bands perform here in a high-spirited atmosphere. Dancing is from around 8:30 p.m. to 2 a.m. seven days a week, with a cover charge after 9 p.m. of 9F ($4.14), with beer costing from 6F ($2.76) a glass.

If you're a motorist, you may want to join a lot of attractive young Swiss and patronize the **Swing-Swing,** at the Holiday Inn in Regensdorf (tel. 840-25-20), a few kilometers from the heart of town. In this rustically decorated pub, Paul, the DJ, is proud of his tape collection. It's open daily from 8:30 p.m. to 1:30 a.m., except Sunday, charging from 8F ($3.68) for a drink with no cover.

Mascotte, 10 Theaterstrasse (tel. 252-44-81), has long been one of the leading discos in the city. It's known for its good bands and music. Open from 9 p.m. to 2 a.m., it charges entrance fees likely to range from 6F ($2.76) to 12F ($5.51). Drinks start at 10F ($4.60).

In the same price range is **Queen Anne Club,** 43 Dufourstrasse at Kreuzstrasse (tel. 251-94-22), one of the more luxurious and chicer discos of Zurich. It has disco dancing until 2 a.m.

JAZZ: **Casa Bar,** 30 Münstergasse (tel. 47-20-02), is the best place to go in Zurich to hear jazz, both English (90% of the performers come from Britain) and Dixieland. Some recent stars appearing here have included Bob Wallis and Jumbo Richford. Beer costs from 6.50F ($2.89) when the music is playing. The jazz is good, and people seem to have a good time.

COUNTRY WESTERN MUSIC: **d Börse z Züri,** 5 Bleicherweg (tel. 211-23-33). If you can picture Oklahoma with a Schweitzerdeutsch accent, you'll love it! It's a real cross-cultural example, with Confederate flags in profusion hanging from the heavy timbers of the trussed roof. The singers might yodel or switch to bluegrass. Beer costs 9F ($4.14) for a big stein. This entertainment emporium is in the midst of the financial district, with no fewer than six wining and dining establishments sheltered under one roof.

EROTICA: Red House, 17 Marktgasse (tel. 252-11-10), sponsors a little erotic theater with what the management claims are the "nicest girls in town." Inside, which resembles an old San Francisco bordello, show times are at 9 p.m. and again at 2 a.m. daily except Sunday. The entrance charge is 8.80F ($4.05). Drinks cost from 12F ($5.51).

Another "hot" spot is the **St. Pauli Bar,** 132 Langstrasse (tel. 241-98-19), which takes its name and its inspiration from the famed nighttime street of Hamburg. In fact I'm sure I've seen the same girls working both cities. If you like your girls nonstop *in natura,* you've arrived at the right doorstep. The patrons are very casually dressed, but not as casually dressed as the 20 or so disrobing girls who perform nightly. Curt, a well-known local DJ, is in charge of the music, and the place is known as "the working man's Broadway." It's open from 6 p.m. to midnight daily, including Sunday, and there's a cover charge of 13F ($5.97), including your first drink. On my most recent visit "Marlene" was the star, and patrons saw a lot of her!

6. The ABC's of Zurich

Before reading this, you may want to refer to the general ABC's of Switzerland in Chapter II, which may answer a question you have. However, in Zurich itself there are a number of local services, including transportation, that you'll need to know about to ease your adjustment into the largest city of Switzerland.

AIRPORT: Kloten Airport, the international airport of Zurich, is considered one of the ten most active in Europe—some 50 scheduled airlines use it (not to mention all the charter connections). It lies a long way from the center of Zurich, some seven miles in fact, and if you go by taxi you can count on paying a fare that may total $16 or more. A much cheaper way of going is by train, a feeder service operated by Swiss Federal Railways. For a fare of 3.60F ($1.66) you'll be delivered in less than ten minutes to the Zurich Hauptbahnhof, the main railway station. The train runs every 20 to 30 minutes, usually between the hours of 5:30 a.m. and 11 p.m. You can also go by bus (no. 68, Zurich Airport-Seebach), but this is more awkward, as you'll have to change to tram service (no. 14) for the center of town.

BANKS: In general, banks are open Monday to Friday from 8:15 a.m. to 4:30 p.m. (on Thursday, to 6 p.m.). Two well-known banks include the **Union Bank of Switzerland,** at ShopVille (tel. 234-11-11), and the **Swiss Bank Corporation** at 70 Bahnhofstrasse (tel. 211-31-71).

CAR RENTALS: All the major car-rental firms are represented at Kloten Airport. That includes **Avis** at 17 Gartenhofstrasse (tel. 242-20-40), and **Budget** at 9 Tödistrasse (tel. 201-26-70).

CHILDREN: Zurich takes good care of tots. For example, all the major department stores have babysitting services. You leave your child at a crêche, then proceed on your carefree way to shop. For information about this service, telephone 271-37-86. You might also want to check out the **Children Club,** which meets every Wednesday from 2 to 4:30 p.m. at the Hotel Nova Park, 420 Bedenerstrasse. For information about this activity, call 491-22-22. In the women's room at ShopVille, and at the Paradeplatz and Oerlikon railway stations you can change diapers free and you'll also find milk-warming facilities.

Restaurants, for the most part, are also aware of children's needs, providing special dishes for them or else half portions. Zurich has some 80 playground and recreation areas, suitable for children. The most central are **Lindenhof, Platzspitz,** and **Hohe Promenade.**

At the **Toy Museum,** 15 Fortunagasse, the collection accumulated by Franz Carl Weber can be seen. Many of these Swiss toys are centuries old. The exhibition is open Monday to Friday from 2 to 5 p.m.

If you're in Zurich in the off-season, there's a children's workshop at the **Kunsthaus** from October until June, every Wednesday from 2 to 4 p.m. It's suitable for children ages 6 to 12.

There are regularly changing programs for children at select theaters in Zurich. Ask at the tourist office or get a copy of *Zurich Weekly Official,* available at most newsstands.

CHURCHES: Zurich has a strong religious tradition, so there are some 100 churches and other places of worship in the city, including three synagogues. Of course they are far too numerous to document in this limited space. However, the times and addresses of various church services are given in a leaflet, *Zürcher Kirchen laden ein,* available at the tourist office.

CONSULATE: The **U.S. Consulate** is at 141 Zollikerstrasse (tel. 55-25-66). Go here if you lose your passport or have some other such emergency.

DRUGSTORE: An all-night chemist is the **Bellevue Apotheke,** 14 Theaterstrasse (tel. 252-44-11).

EMERGENCIES: In very urgent cases, call the police at 117.

HOSPITAL: There is an accident department at the **Cantonal University Hospital,** 8 Schmelzbergstrasse (tel. 255-11-11).

INFORMATION: The **Zurich Tourist Office** is at 15 Bahnhofplatz (tel. 211-40-00), the main railway station. From March to October it's open Monday to Friday from 8 a.m. to 10 p.m. and on weekends from 8 a.m. to 8:30 p.m. From November to February it's open Monday to Thursday from 8 a.m. to 8 p.m., on Friday to 10 p.m., and on weekends from 9 a.m. to 6 p.m. There's a branch office at the airport (tel. 814-05-65) which is open every day all year from 9 a.m. to 8 p.m.

LOST PROPERTY OFFICE: There is one at 10 Werdmühlestrasse (tel. 216-71-11), which is open Monday to Friday from 7:30 to 11:30 a.m. and 1:30 to 5:30 p.m.

MEDICAL AND DENTAL EMERGENCY SERVICE: For first aid, illness, and accident cases, phone 47-47-00 or the **City Ambulance Service** at 361-61-61.

MONEY EXCHANGE: Most banks and travel agencies will handle this for you. However, there's an exchange office at the Zurich Hauptbahnhof, the main railway station, open from 6:30 a.m. to 11:30 p.m., including Sunday.

PARKING: Before driving around Zurich, you should be armed with a street plan. Most such maps indicate multistory car parks within the city limits by a "P" sign for parking. The police of Zurich also publish a leaflet indicating all such parking garages.

PHONE AND TELEX: Your best bet is to go to the Zurich Hauptbahnhof, the main railway station, where a Telex and phone office are open from 7 a.m. to 10:30 p.m. Monday to Sunday.

POST OFFICE: The main post office in Zurich is the **Sihlpost,** 95–99 Kasernenstrasse (tel. 245-41-11), just across the Sihl River from Löwenstrasse, which has an emergency service window always open. Most post offices—listed under "Post" in the phone directory—are open during regular business hours from 7:30 a.m. to noon and 1:30 to 6:30 p.m. (however, they close at 11 a.m. on Saturday).

POSTAL CHARGES: Airmail overseas up to 10 grams costs 1.20F (56¢), up to 20 grams, 1.50F (69¢). It costs 1F (46¢) to send a regular postcard overseas.

PUBLIC TRANSPORT: The public transport system of Zurich is operated by VBZ Züri-Linie, which has a modern and extensive network. Trams and buses run daily between 5:30 a.m. and midnight every six minutes at rush hours. There is no subway or underground, but rather a network of streetcars and buses, which for the most part originate at the Zurich Hauptbahnhof, in the heart of the city, branching out to the suburbs.

Tickets are purchased on a self-service system from automatic vending machines which do not make change and are located at every stop. Tickets must be purchased before you get on a vehicle; and if you're caught without a valid ticket, you'll pay a fine of 20F ($9.19).

For a journey of up to five stops the fare is 80 centimes (37¢), and 1.20F (56¢) for anywhere from six stops to the edge of town. Best bet for visitors is to order a "one-day ticket," costing 3.50F ($1.61) and allowing you to travel on all buses and trams for 24 hours.

SHOPPING HOURS: Most shops in Zurich are open from 8 a.m. to 6:30 p.m. Monday to Friday and from 8 a.m. to 4 p.m. on Saturday. Some of the larger stores stay open until 9 p.m. on Thursday, and other shops are also closed on Monday morning.

SPORTS AND GAMES: The two golf courses nearest the heart of town are the **Golf and Country Club Zurich** at Zumikon (tel. 919-00-51), which has an 18-hole, par-72 course, and **Dolder Golfclub** (tel. 47-50-45), which has a 9-hole, par-60 course.

Zurich also has seven "Vita-Parcours" or keep-fit trails. The nearest woodland jogging route is on the Allmend Fluntern.

The closest ski region to Zurich is **Hoch-Ybrig,** which is about an hour's journey away from the Hauptbahnhof. Take the train to Einsiedeln, where a connection can be made by bus to Weglosen and the aerial cableway which will take you to Hoch-Ybrig, which has five ski lifts and two chair lifts.

You can go swimming in the lake of Zurich, which has an average summer temperature of 68°F. The finest beach here is the **Tiefenbrunnen,** which is enjoyed by topless bathers.

TAXIS: They are lethal in price, among the most expensive in Europe. Ride them only as a last resort. For a typical ride in the city, you'll spend around $8. The only good thing about that is that the service charge is included in the fare. Taxis can be phoned. **Taxi-Zentrale Zürich,** for example, can be called at 44-44-41.

TOURS: The easiest, quickest, and most convenient way to get acquainted with Zurich is to take a two-hour motorcoach tour with an English-speaking guide, costing 15F ($6.89). Departures are daily at 10 a.m. and 2 p.m. all year. From July 1 until the end of September there's also a noon departure, plus a 4 p.m. departure from May until the end of October. The tour takes in both the commercial and shopping center and the old town, and goes along the lake for a visit to see the Chagall windows at Fraumünster. It also stops at the Institute of Technology.

Another exciting tour is by both coach and aerial cableway, lasting 2½ hours and costing 17F ($7.81). This tour swings through the Reppischtal-Albispass-Adliswil recreational sector. The highlight is a ride on an aerial cableway, climbing to the **Felsenegg** at 2650 feet. From here, there's a panoramic view of the lake and the Alps beyond. The tour also takes in an animal farm and an indoor cactus garden. It leaves daily at 9:30 a.m. from May 1 until the end of October.

Tours leave from Postbrücke at the main station, and tickets can be purchased from the Zurich Tourist Office.

At some point in your stay you'll want to take a lake steamer for a tour of Lake Zurich. You can do this on your own if you wish, and a short trip costs 7.40F ($3.42); a round-trip ticket goes for 13F ($5.97). Walk to the end of Bahnhofstrasse and book your own ticket there at the pier. In peak season ferries depart about every 30 minutes.

A regular round-trip tour of the lake will cost 18.40F ($8.47) in second class, or 27.60F ($12.69) in first class.

You might also want to take a boat trip along the Limmat, looking close up at the historic buildings of Zurich. Departures are from the Landesmuseum at the Hauptbahnhof. After traversing the Limmat, the boat heads out into the lake for further views. In the far distance you'll see the snow-capped Alps. The boat lands at the Zürichhorn. Departures are every half hour in April and October daily from 1 to 6 p.m.; in May, June, and September, from 1 to 9 p.m., and in July and August, 10 a.m. to 9 p.m. The fare is only 5F ($2.30).

One of my favorite tours in Zurich is a stroll through the old town with a guide. The tour lasts 2½ hours, and the meeting point is at 9:30 a.m. and again at 3 p.m. in front of the tourist office at 15 Bahnhofplatz. The price is 9F ($4.14) for adults and 4.50F ($2.07) for children 6 to 12. Departures are June 1 through September 30 every Tuesday, Thursday, and Saturday.

7. Exploring the Environs

Zurich is encircled by some of the most interesting sightseeing areas in Switzerland. Many are close at hand. Out of a maze of possibilities I have picked a few of exceptional interest. When feasible, suggestions for food and lodging have been included as well. However, all of these attractions can be easily reached on a short day trip. A few interesting tours—all of which you can do on your own—make use of funiculars and trains.

The **Polybahn** funicular leaves every three minutes from Central, the square near the Main Station Bridge (Bahnhofbrücke) on the Limmatquai. The funicular, operating since 1889 and used daily by students attending the Federal Institute of Technology and the University of Zurich, takes you to the popular Poly terrace from which you can view the city and the Alps. Outdoor performances are held on the terrace, and it's a stopping place for official tours of the city. The Mensa restaurant of the technology institute and its coffeeshop are open to the public. The fare one way is .50F (23¢).

An interesting jaunt, summer or winter, takes you aboard the **Dolderbahn** for a short aerial cable ride to the Dolder Recreational Area, 1988 feet up above the city. Trains leave every ten minutes from Römerhofplatz, which you can reach by taking tram 3, 8, or 15. The recreational area has restaurants, nature trails, old rustic taverns, a path to the zoo, a miniature golf course, and from October to March, a huge ice-skating rink. Also in the area is a delightful place to swim, the Dolder Schwimmbad, which is carved into a hillside with a view over Zurich. To reach it, you have about a five-minute trek along a forest trail from the end of the cable-car line. Just follow the signs to Dolder Wellenbad. Even if you don't want to swim, the view makes this excursion worthwhile. Swimmers who wish to try the pool with its artificial waves will be admitted for a charge of 5F ($2.30). The Dolderbahn ride costs 1F (46¢). You buy your tickets from a machine.

If you're looking for rest and recreation close to Zurich, I recommend a trip on the **Forchbahn,** which leaves from the Stadelhofen station. The train takes you up to the city limits and out into the green country, where you find a strolling and rambling area with fine views and wooded paths leading down to the lake. There, if you wish, you can take a lake boat back to Zurich. Swiss woodlands, as decreed by law, are open to the public even if they are privately owned. Of course this means you should respect the rights of the individual property owners and not be a litterbug. Forchbahn trains run without conductors so you must buy your tickets from a machine at the stops. A round-trip ticket to Forch and back costs 5.60F ($2.57); to Esslingen, 8F ($3.68).

Another place you may wish to visit is the **Alpamare,** reached by Pfäffikon SZ on the lake of Zurich. Its attractions include a heated indoor swimming pool with artificial waves and a slide; an open-air thermal pool with underwater music, massage jets, and bubbling water "couches"; other outdoor thermal baths containing iodine and brine to relieve rheumatism; a well-equipped playground; free deck chairs; a snack restaurant; grills, saunas; and a large solarium. The Alpamare is open daily from 10 a.m. to 10 p.m., from 9 a.m. on Saturday, Sunday, and Monday. Admission for three hours for adults is 13F ($5.97), 14F ($6.43) on Saturday and Sunday. Children from 6 to 16 years of age pay 6.50F ($2.99) for three hours.

UETLIBERG: Southwest of Zurich, Uetliberg, the most northern peak in the Albis ridge, is one of the most popular excursions from the city. A mountain railway, called the Uetligbergbahn, travels from the Selnau station in Zurich to the site, a round-trip fare costing about 7.50F ($3.45). The station is on the

Sihl River, and the trip to a height of about 2800 feet should take about half an hour.

When the train lets you off, it's about a ten-minute hike up to the summit where there's a café and restaurant (many bring a picnic lunch with them). The tower is a climb of about 170 steps. From the lookout post, you can see as far away as the Black Forest on a clear day, as well as to the Bernese Alps and the Valais.

WINTERTHUR: An industrial town, only 25 minutes from Zurich, Winterthur is also a music and cultural center, with an art collection that makes it a worthy detour from Zurich. In the Töss Valley, Winterthur was once a Roman settlement and in time became the seat of the Counts of Kyburg. It later became one of the strongholds of the Habsburgs until falling to Zurich, to whom it was literally sold.

The ideal time to visit is on Tuesday or Friday when the narrow streets of the old town are busy with fruit, flower, and vegetable peddlers. Another exciting time to explore is on the last Saturday of every month when a flea market brings in people from the countryside who have merchandise to hawk.

The skyline of Winterthur is dominated by the twin towers of its parish church, the **Stadtkirche,** which was built from 1264 to 1515, although the towers date from a later period.

The **Oskar Reinhart Foundation,** 6 Stadthausstrasse, displays many of the pieces of art that this famous patron and collector assembled before his death in 1965. In his will, he gave his fabulous bequest to Switzerland, providing that they would let it remain in Winterthur, to which the government agreed. It is open from 10 a.m. to noon and 2 to 5 p.m. daily (except Monday morning), charging an admission of 3F ($1.38). The gallery is devoted mainly to works of Austrian, German, and Swiss artists, with a fine show provided by the so-called romantic painters, including Holder, Blechen, Friedrich, Kerstling, and Richter. The canvases by Holder, in particular, are plentiful. He died at the end of World War I. R. F. Wasmann has some outstanding drawings on display.

The other part of the collection is shown at **Am Römerholz,** 95 Haldenstrasse, which was the private home of Oskar Reinhart. The mansion, standing on its own grounds, is open daily except Monday (by now, you're learning that nearly everything in the area is closed on Monday). Hours are from 10 a.m. to 4 p.m., and the admission is 3F ($1.38). The collection of painting and related art here spans a period of 500 years, ranging from Cranach the Elder to Breughel. There are some fine drawings by Rembrandt and a painting from Toledo done by El Greco. Herr Reinhart was especially fond of French painters, and he collected quite a few, many of the biggest names such as Watteau, Fragonard, and Poussin. Daumier appears with some excellent drawings. A host of other more outstanding artists are also represented, with works by Delacroix, Manet, Cézanne, Van Gogh, and Corot, and dare I leave out Renoir? Some drawings from Picasso's "blue period," my favorite, are also shown. It's a worthy collection, and Winterthur is proud that the world now comes to its doorstep.

Herr Reinhart wasn't the only collector of art in the town. The **Kunstmuseum,** the fine arts museum of the city, also has an impressive collection as well. The location is in the Kunsthaus on Museumstrasse, north of the Stadthaus. The museum is a complex of galleries, ranging from numismatic to natural science. But the art and sculpture are the most important exhibitions, with a large collection of German and Swiss painters, ranging from Cranach the Elder to two dozen portraits by the Swiss artist, Anton Graff. Works by Swiss-born Giacometti are also shown, and the French artists are well represented, with such names as Bonnard, Van Gogh, and Vuillard. Some sculpture by Rodin is displayed, along with works by Marini and Maillol. Hours are daily except Monday morning from 10 a.m. to noon and 2 to 5 p.m.

If you can spare the time, I'd recommend a drive four miles from Winterthur to **Schloss Kyburg,** the biggest stronghold in eastern Switzerland left over from the Middle Ages. If you don't have a car, it can be reached on foot from the Kemptthal rail station, the Zurich-Winterthur line, or the Sennhof-Kyburg which is the Winterthur-Bauma railway line. This castle was the ancestral home of the previously mentioned Counts of Kyburg, who faded into history in 1264. It then became a stronghold of the Habsburgs, until it was ceded to Zurich in the 15th century. It's now a museum, displaying antiques and armor. There's a good view from the keep which is still standing, as is the residence hall of the knights. You can explore the parapet walk and visit a chapel as well. The admission is only 1.50F (69¢), and it's open March 1 until the end of October daily from 9 a.m. to noon and 1 to 5 p.m. It's closed on Monday. In winter it's open daily except Monday from 9 a.m. to noon and from 1 to 4 p.m.

The **Technorama Museum,** 1–3 Technoramastrasse (tel. 27-77-22), is roughly equivalent of an American museum of science and industry, with 6000 square meters of displays, many with tape-recorded explanations of what they are. These exhibits reveal current technological breakthroughs in metallurgy, electronics, physics, and building construction. Set into a natural green area, the museum offers pleasant walkways near its main building. A restaurant is on the premises.

Children ages 5 to 13 can be left in care of a supervised Mini-Technorama, with exhibits designed especially for them. By car, take autobahn N1 north of Zurich in the direction of St. Gallen, exiting at Ober-Winterthur. From there, go about 1.5 kilometers in the direction of Winterthur. By train, you can go from Zurich to Winterthur, from which you can take a double-decker bus from the station, which leaves a quarter to and a quarter past the hour (except at noon). Visiting hours are Tuesday, Thursday, Saturday, and Sunday from 10 a.m. till 5 p.m. On Friday, hours are 10 a.m. to 9 p.m. It's closed on Monday and holidays. The entrance fee is 7F ($3.20) for adults and 3F ($1.38) for children.

Food and Lodging

Garten-Hotel, 4 Stadthausstrasse (tel. 23-22-31), is the only hotel in Winterthur in the city park. You couldn't be more centrally located, and you have the advantage of being able to take many pleasant walks. The hotel, which is painted a well-maintained white, has up-to-date rooms with baths tiled in dramatic dark colors and big windows to let in the light. There's also an outdoor terrace for coffee and a well-known restaurant for intimate dining. All the comfortable rooms have private baths, renting for between 88F ($40.43) and 96F ($44.11) in a single and between 110F ($40.54) and 144F ($66.16) in a double, with breakfast included. An extra bed can be set up in any room for another 50F ($22.97).

Hotel/Restaurant Krone, 49 Marktgasse (tel. 23-25-21), can be identified by its elaborate gilt and wrought-iron bracket hanging over an embellished stone facade. The bracket is voluptuously curved, with a host of gilt ribbons and acanthus whorls, the hotel's trademark, an emperor's crown, hanging at its tip. The hotel is owned by the Schellenberg family and managed by the competent hotelier, Philipp Sigg. It offers doubles with bath between 85F ($39) and 90F ($41.35), singles with bath between 53F ($24.35) and 60F ($27.50). Bathless singles are a bargain at only 43F ($19.75), and a breakfast buffet is included in all prices. In the heart of the old town, the simple and comfortable rooms are far cheaper than the better known Garten Hotel, and consequently are heavily booked in advance. The restaurant, where my most recent meal cost 35F ($16.08), has polite service and several specialties, including the classic sliced veal dish in a cream sauce, Zuricher style, and a filet of beef in a peppercorn cream sauce. Try also the veal steak Ratzer.

Schloss Wülflinger, at Winterthur-Wülflingen (tel. 25-18-67), on the outskirts, is the best and most romantic place to dine. It was built in 1644 in a rustic stone, stucco, and slate style, and reeks with solidity and permanence. In summer, owner Walter Zimmerman and his family place garlands of greenery between the intricate shutters of the step-gabled house. Ivy grows over the door and café tables are set up in front. Aside from an extensive wine list, the restaurant offers a gastronomic menu costing from 52F ($23.89) per person, a good value since it consists of six courses. However, it's possible to order an à la carte dinner for around 35F ($16.08). Specialties include beef filet le Chef, medallions of beef in a tarragon cream sauce with gratin potatoes, or veal steak Ibn Saud, combining an excellent cut of veal with curry and fruit. Fish includes choices of trout, perch, and sole. A simpler menu is offered at lunch, slightly less elaborate, but with excellent meat dishes such as veal stuffed with country ham and a mousse of foie gras, served with tiny homemade noodles. You dine in an elegantly paneled ambience, where many of the rooms have their original ceramic stoves.

REGENSBERG: About ten miles northwest of Zurich, the village of Regensberg is a nugget from medieval days. It looks as if it has slumbered through the past centuries. Because of that, it's a national trust village of Switzerland, and nothing can be altered—not that anybody would want to anyway. It's best reached by car, about a 20-minute drive from Zurich, depending on traffic (take the road out of Zurich in the direction of Dielsdorf). If you don't have a car, you must go by postal bus from Dielsdorf, itself reached on the Zurich-Oberglatt-Niederweningen railway line. If you drive, you must park your car outside the town hall and walk into the walled town on its cobblestone streets.

Regensberg is a village of wine makers and vineyards, with some remarkably well-preserved half-timbered houses clustered around the main square, which is most colorful. The most famous of these old burghers' homes is the **Rote Rose house,** dating from 1540 and containing a museum of the painter Lotte Günthard.

The village church is from the early 16th century, but it was built on the site of a structure dating from the early 13th century.

Dominating the hamlet is a **castle** once owned by the Habsburgs. This was once the headquarters of the Barons of Regensberg, who dominated the town. The watchtower affords a view of the local vineyards and the Lägern hills. On a clear day you can see all the way to Zurich. The castle is from the 16th century, and today contains a children's home. You can climb the tower, the highest point in Regensberg, during most of the year. If it's closed, inquire at the castle.

The biggest half-timbered house in the village contains the **Restaurant Zur Krone,** Oberburgst (tel. 853-11-35), which serves both lunch and dinner, accompanied by wines from local vineyards. These wines are excellent, almost worth the pilgrimage from Zurich. You face a choice of dining rooms; my favorite is the Biedermeier salon, some of whose casement windows overlook the valley. But you don't come here for the view. The food is exceptional, with an emphasis on local and seasonal produce such as asparagus. It's also expensive, with a menu costing from 60F ($27.57).

The menu is in French, and the chef knows how to prepare all the classical French dishes, along with some innovative nouvelle cuisine touches. Try the country-style pâté, actually a terrine, followed by, say, veal kidneys or tournedos. The food and its preparation are excellent in every way, and the service is attentive and meticulous. Zur Krone is a surprising gourmet citadel for such a tiny hamlet. In summer you may want to enjoy the terrace. The restaurant is open from 11 a.m. to 11 p.m., although it doesn't serve hot food during all those hours. It's closed Sunday night and on Monday, and shuts down from December 20 to January 20.

RAPPERSWIL: A lake steamer from Zurich will take you to the "town of roses," Rapperswil, lying on the northern part of the lake, 19 miles away. If you're based in Zurich for just a short time and have no other chance to visit the rest of the country, then spend a day going to Rapperswil to see a typical Swiss town.

Many streets remain from the Middle Ages, and the town is dominated by a castle built about the year 1200 by the young Count of Rapperswil who had just returned from the First Crusade.

Rapperswil Castle is today the principal attraction of the town. Built on a rocky hill, it was an imposing medieval stronghold, with its towers, parapet walks, and inner ward. In 1869 it became a Polish National Museum, serving as a repository of national relics of that beleaguered country. One part is still devoted to Polish mementos, including those of Chopin. Other sections are devoted to relics left over from the "age of chivalry." It's open from 10 a.m. to noon and 2 to 5 p.m. in summer, charging an admission of 2F (92¢). In winter it's open only on Sunday and holidays.

On the north side of the hill is the **Hirschgarten** (or deer park) in the Linderhof. There's also a **Children's Zoo,** which is run by the Knie National Circus. The zoo is on the Strandweg, a road which runs along the lake, south of the railway station. Trained dolphins and other acts perform here.

On the Herrenberg, the **Heimat-museum** is a museum of local history, east of the parish church. It contains Roman artifacts and a collection of weaponry, along with paintings and antiques. It's open April to October daily except Friday from 2 to 5 p.m., charging an admission of 2F (92¢).

In the main square is the **Rathaus** (town hall), from 1471, with a richly embellished Gothic portal.

If you wish, you can go from Zurich to Rapperswil by lake steamer. A round-trip ticket costs 25F ($11.49).

Food and Lodging

If you're down just for the day, you may want to patronize the **Hotel Eden** (tel. 27-12-21), for either lunch or dinner. If so, you'll be following in the footsteps of many food connoisseurs from Zurich. The ample local vineyards produce a wine which, along with dozens of other vintages, is stocked in the cellars. The Ganahl family owns the six-story house and maintains it in a condition compatible with all the gourmet delicacies served inside. Specialties include fresh goose liver pâté, rack of lamb Eden, baby veal, lobster salad with artichoke hearts, and imaginatively prepared saltwater fish, along with an array of the freshest vegetables, always selected according to the season and market.

A plate of warm food is sometimes served for as little as 14.50F ($6.66), although many of the diners order fixed-price meals with anywhere from seven to ten courses, costing between 70F ($32.16) and 100F ($45.95). Desserts are consistently excellent. The Eden restaurant is closed Sunday night and all day Monday, but open otherwise from noon to 2:30 p.m. and for dinner after 5 p.m. It's in the old town.

Should you be fortunate enough to spend the night in Rapperswil, I have the following suggestions.

Hotel Speer (tel. 27-17-20) lies in a position to receive much of the resort traffic from Zurich. Its presence is announced by tastefully illuminated letters over the streetside terrace, which opens into a cozy modern bar with accents in green tile. The paneled dining area is attractively carpeted in green and red tartan. The 20 bedrooms at their best are furnished with elegantly upholstered rococo beds and Jacobean chairs, and in the less expensive ones, in attractive functional pieces. Singles with bath cost from 45F ($20.60) to 50F ($22.97), while singles without bath go for 34F ($15.62). Doubles with bath rent for between 90F ($41.35) and 120F ($55.14), and bathless chambers go for only 65F ($29.86), including breakfast.

Hotel Schwanen, 12 Seequai (tel. 27-77-77), is a beautifully ornate building with white walls and buff-colored shutters. The columns holding up the balconied portico have seen generations of vacationing Swiss pass between them, a function it continues to perform for the grandchildren of the original visitors. The interior has been tastefully modernized for a warm textured comfort. Kurt Zurflüh, your host, charges 120F ($55.14) in a well-furnished double room with bath, renting singles with bath for only 70F ($32.16).

Chapter IV

NORTHEASTERN SWITZERLAND

1. St. Gallen
2. Toggenburg
3. Walensee
4. Bad Ragaz
5. Appenzell
6. Braunwald
7. Schaffhausen and Rheinfall
8. Stein-am-Rhein
9. Lake Constance
10. Glarus

IF FIGURES MEAN ANYTHING, northeastern Switzerland is the most neglected part of the country from the standpoint of the North American tourist. What a shame! It's one of the most unspoiled regions of Switzerland, perhaps because of that oversight.

Old customs and traditions live on steadfastly here, as much of the green and rolling countryside is still deeply rooted in the past. The region is separated from southern Germany and Austria by the Rhine and Lake Constance. (The Principality of Liechtenstein is also part of the region, but because it's a separate country I've chosen to treat it individually in its own section—refer to Chapter XIII.)

In this part of Switzerland, you'll find the cantons of Appenzell, Glarus, St. Gallen, Schaffhausen, and Thurgau.

Many striking beauty spots abound, including St. Gallen Rhine Valley and the Rhine Falls near Neuhausen. St. Gallen is the cultural and economic center. There are many holiday resorts in the Toggenburg Valley, and some of the most splendid orchards in the country dot the shores of Lake Constance.

As for mountain peaks, the Säntis reaches a height of 8200 feet and Mt. Tödi in Glarus tops it at 11,880 feet.

If economy is a factor in your travel, then you should definitely consider exploring the region, as the prices for food and lodging in its old-world inns are among the lowest in the country.

1. St. Gallen

This is an ancient town, tracing its history back to when an Irish monk, Gallus, built himself a hermitage here in 612. In time a cloister grew from his "humble cell," and by the 13th century it was an important cultural outpost for the Western world. St. Gallen became a free imperial city in 1212, and in 1454 it joined the Swiss Confederation.

Today it's the capital of a canton that bears its name, lying 53 miles east of Zurich. St. Gallen is one of the primary sightseeing targets in northeastern Switzerland, mainly because of its old city, with its restored half-timbered houses with their characteristic turrets and oriels. Many lanes and alleys, left over from the Middle Ages (some closed to traffic) await the explorer. St. Gallen also makes a good center for exploring Lake Constance, the Säntis mountains, and the Appenzell countryside.

Pause in the **Klosterhof** (the abbey yard) to take in the splendor of the former Benedictine abbey. The present structures date mainly from the 17th and 18th centuries. Here are the major sights of the town, including the twin-towered Domkirche (the cathedral) and the world-famous Stiftsbibliothek or abbey library.

The **Domkirche** dates in its present form from 1756, and it grew up on the site of the more celebrated Gothic abbey from the 14th century. The interior is in the rich baroque style, reaching the zenith of its decorative beauty in its chancel.

From an inner courtyard you can enter the **Stiftsbibliothek.** This abbey library survived the secularization of the abbey itself, and it has a collection of some 100,000 volumes. Some of its manuscripts are from the 8th to the 12th centuries. It also displays some books printed in the 13th century. Several Renaissance manuscripts are stunningly illustrated. The library hall is a delight, built in a charming rococo style, with stucco art and ceiling paintings. The plan of St. Gallen abbey in 820 is exhibited under glass.

The library, charging 2F (92¢) for admission, may be visited from May to October daily except Sunday afternoon from 9 a.m. to noon and 2 to 5 p.m. (it opens at 10:30 a.m. on Sunday). In winter it's open daily except Sunday and Monday afternoon from 9 a.m. to noon and 2 to 4 p.m.

The **Industrie-und Gewerbemuseum** (museum of arts and trades), at 2 Vadianstrasse, might easily be overlooked were it not for the famous Iklè and Jacoby collection of needlework, considered the most complete collection in Europe. Its embroidery and lace, as well as tapestries, cover 500 years. Charging 3F ($1.38) for admission, it's open from 10 a.m. to noon and 2 to 5 p.m., except on weekends.

If you head south of St. Gallen for two miles you reach **Freudenberg,** at nearly 3000 feet. Once here, a panoramic view unfolds of the Säntis mountains, St. Gallen itself, and Lake Constance, which they call the "Bodensee" in this part of the country.

WHERE TO STAY: **Hotel Continental,** 95 Teufenerstrasse (tel. 27-88-11). Two minutes away from the train station by car, this hotel is warm and comfortable inside in spite of its bunker-like exterior. A garage is beneath the hotel, and many of the rooms have recessed balconies covered with awnings. Bedrooms are simply and sparsely furnished, and the beds are comfortable. All units contain phone, radio, color TV, mini-bar, and private bath. Doubles rent for 110F ($50.54), while singles cost 60F ($27.57), with breakfast included.

Hotel Sonne, 94 General Guisan Strasse (tel. 24-43-42), lies in a forested area on a hill above the city, where the principal advantages are peace and a lot of calm. The rooms are modern, clean, and functionally furnished, with a restaurant and a red plaid bar area where you'll probably meet some of the other guests. Singles rent for 43F ($19.75) without bath, going up to anywhere from 50F ($22.98) to 70F ($32.17) with bath. Bathless doubles are a good buy at 80F ($36.76), rising to 95F ($43.65) and 120F ($55.14) with bath, including breakfast.

Hecht Hotel, Marktplatz (tel. 22-65-02), rises like an elaborately decorated wedding cake in the middle of the old town. A flagpole pierces the roof of the facade's only tower. A Swiss flag proudly flies, matching the red-and-white banners fluttering from the top floor. The entire construction is painted white, shutters and all, and has been chosen as a prestigious gathering place for family celebrations in St. Gallen for years. All the bedrooms are clean and comfortable, and guests are usually tempted to have a drink under the vaulted ceiling of the Hechtbar before retiring for the night. Two restaurants inside, the Grill Room and the Stadt Restaurant, are both notable establishments in St. Gallen. The Studer family charges 48F ($22.05) in a bathless single and 78F ($35.84) in a single with bath. Bathless doubles cost 75F ($34.46), while doubles with bath range between 110F ($50.54) and 150F ($68.92), including breakfast. The rooms, by the way, tend to be rather large.

Hotel Dom, 22 Webergasse (tel. 23-20-44). The Els family directs this friendly hotel which is perfectly located near the cathedral of St. Gallen, as its name would suggest. All the rooms are simply but comfortably furnished, and the staff proves helpful and cooperative. Singles cost 46F ($21.13) without bath, rising to 62F ($28.48) with bath. Doubles without bath rent for 78F ($35.84), rising to anywhere from 102F ($46.86) to 106F ($48.70) with bath, including breakfast.

WHERE TO EAT: Schnäggehüsle, 31 Hagenbuchstrasse (tel. 25-65-25). Because of the intimate size of this unusual restaurant, it's best to phone ahead for a reservation. Even then, you're likely to find some of the best-heeled residents of St. Gallen climbing with you to the top of this hillock above the old town. The building which houses the restaurant is clean and attractively decorated, the perfect setting for a combination of a traditional and modern cuisine which has made this place so famous locally. Fixed-price menus run a wide range, between 37F ($17) and 126F ($57.98), the latter the gastronomic delight of the town. À la carte meals cost between 25F ($11.48) and 50F ($22.98), and might include such specialties as poached salmon in dill sauce, filet of sole in champagne sauce with crayfish sections, and an excellent cut of filet of beef with wild mushrooms sauce, plus a nouvelle cuisine creation: baby veal in raspberry vinegar sauce.

Schwartzer Bären, 151 Speicherstrasse (tel. 35-30-55), can be found after a ten-minute drive from the center of town, in a locale which is a wonderfully rustic blend of wrought iron, antiques, and textile wall hangings which look convincingly like something from Gobelins. The food items would tempt even the most traditional tastes, a conservative yet extremely well-prepared array of meats, fish, and vegetables which are always fresh. The filet of sole with capers and the cutlet of beef with homemade cabbage butter are particularly savory. The restaurant serves fixed-price meals from 29F ($13.32) to 70F ($32.16) and à la carte meals from 24F ($11.02) to 42F ($19.29). It's closed from the last week in July until mid-August.

2. Toggenburg

Once this part of Switzerland was independent, but it's now part of the cantonal district of St. Gallen. The valley of Toggenburg has some of the most varied scenery in eastern Switzerland. Lying south of Thurgau, it takes in the Upper Thur Valley and several little offshoot valleys, all rich in scenic attractions (but little else). The valley follows a curvy line between the Walensee and Mt. Säntis. A series of three resorts is spread out here, each one attracting a summer market, mainly German or the Swiss themselves, each of whom know of the charm of the place and the relatively low prices. The resorts are Alt St. Johann, Unterwasser, and Wildhaus.

WILDHAUS: This resort is built on a plateau over the Toggenburg. It was the birthplace of Zwingli, the great Swiss reformer. The modest cottage in which he was born in 1484 still lies in the hamlet of Lisighaus.

Wildhaus standing at a height of about 4000 feet, is both a summer and a winter resort. The gateway airport is usually Zurich. However, many motorists cross the Rhine from Vaduz, the capital of Liechtenstein, going through the town of Buchs. The scenery along the road from Buchs is magnificent, and in about 18 miles you reach Wildhaus. Zurich is some 40 miles away.

Wildhaus has an indoor swimming pool, a curling rink, an ice rink, and is a cross-country skiing center. It occupies a splendid setting on the south side of the Wildhauser Schafberg. A chair lift transports skiers to Gamplüt, at a height of about 4412 feet. Another chair lift goes to Oberdorf at 4165 feet, from which another lift goes to Gamsalp and from there to Gamserugg. Children are especially catered for at Wildhaus. You'll find a kindergarten, even a ski school for them.

The Resort Hotels

Hotel Acker (tel. 5-91-11) rises in two separate buildings, one older than the other, from the green meadows of the alpine foothills around it. The different sections are connected by a passageway containing an all-season swimming pool which, in winter, looks out through big windows onto the rolling hills in the distance. All of the bedrooms are modern, streamlined, and very comfortable, with competent management performed by Werner Beck. There are enough mountain trails in the vicinity to make anyone a sports enthusiast. Rates are slightly higher in the newer section, ranging from 90F ($41.35) to 175F ($80.41) in a double, depending on the exposure and the season, and from 75F ($34.46) to 120F ($55.14) in a single. In the chalet section doubles go for anywhere from 90F ($41.35) to 150F ($68.92), from 60F ($27.57) to 75F ($34.46) in a single, and all units contain private bath and breakfast. Half and full board are available for an additional 25F ($11.48) and 40F ($18.38) per person per day.

Hotel Hirschen (tel. 5-22-52). The rooms are unpretentiously furnished with comfortable pieces and there is rustic paneling on some of the walls. The setting is alpine, with good views in many directions. A sauna and a large swimming pool are also provided. The hotel is a small-scale resort, with such facilities as a hairdresser, a disco, a restaurant, and a snackbar. The Walt family offers double rooms with bath on the half-board plan for 75F ($34.46) per person, with full board costing an additional 10F ($4.60) per person daily. Singles with bath rent for 85F ($39.05) per person, with full board costing 95F ($43.65) daily.

Hotel Toggenburg (tel. 5-23-23). The designer of this hotel understood the technique of adding rustic touches to bring the outdoors inside. The bedrooms usually have areas covered with amber-tinted planks, often on the sloped ceilings under study areas or in the partially tiled baths. The big windows make the rooms bright and sunny, and the restaurant provides nourishing, well-prepared meals in a timbered room with a view over the countryside. Singles rent for between 50F ($22.98) and 60F ($27.57) in low season, always with bath, and for between 70F ($32.17) and 80F ($36.76) in high season. Doubles, also with private baths, rent for between 80F ($36.76) and 100F ($45.95) in low season, rising to between 120F ($55.14) and 150F ($68.92) in high season. These prices include half board. Peter Arn and his family are your congenial hosts.

UNTERWASSER: Two miles from Wildhaus, Unterwasser is another small resort in a tranquil setting, lying between the Mt. Säntis chain and the Churfirsten. Two streams merge here to create the Thur River. From Unterwasser you can take a mountain railway to Iltios at 4430 feet, which has a big restaurant with a sunning platform where skiers soak up alpine sun in winter. From Iltios, the cableway continues to Chäserugg at 7415 feet, from which there is a view over the Walensee to Flumserberg (see below). It offers suitable skiing for all grades.

Hotel Säntis (tel. 5-28-11) is recently constructed, very comfortable, and in the center of this fast-rising summer and winter playground. Deliberately designed for maximum balcony space, the hotel attracts many families who enjoy the sunny spacious rooms for their vacations, as well as local business people who use it for their conferences. Children receive special discount rates when they stay in a room with their parents. The rate structure is complicated, too much so to detail here, but prices are roughly from 80F ($36.76) to 95F ($43.65) in a single and from 65F ($29.86) to 75F ($34.46) per adult in a double, and from 60F ($27.57) to 70F ($32.17) per person in a triple, depending on the season. All units contain private baths, and breakfast is included in the price. Half board ranges in price from 10F ($4.60) to 15F ($6.89) per person.

3. Walensee

This nine-mile-long lake, one of the most beautiful in Switzerland, is nestled between the Glarus Alps and the Churfirsten, a relatively undiscovered area for Americans. Immortalized by Liszt, the lake is often glimpsed by tourists sailing from Zurich when they pass through the gap at Weesen-Sargans, heading for the Grisons, a much more popular destination. The lake is studded with some sleepy little resorts and in the mountains are some ski centers. My favorite follows:

FLUMSERBERG: This alpine district of grazing meadows and little mountain chalets is reached from Flums. Two small, winding roads lead up to it. It's both a winter and a summer resort, overlooking Lake Walensee. It offers good snow conditions throughout the winter, and in summer attracts mountain hikers. Ski courses are available. A vast network of marked hiking trails lead across wide alpine pastures, and the tiny resort also has an indoor swimming pool, tennis courts, cable cars, and, always, that view of Lake Walensee.

Flumserberg can be reached by way of the Zurich–Chur expressway or railway by using the cable car leaving from Unterterzen. It can also be reached by postal bus on a mountain road from Flums. The trip from Zurich is about an hour and a half.

The resort is connected with the fast-rising ski areas in the villages of Tannenheim at 4000 feet and Tannenbodenalp at 4595 feet.

The Resort Hotels

Hotel Gauenpark (tel. 3-31-31) is beautiful in any season, but is particularly dramatic in winter, when the snow on the alpine ridge behind the hotel makes the mountains look even closer. That's when the lights from the weatherproof windows of this place look especially inviting, and when you're likely to meet visitors from all over Europe. The interior makes use of every natural material it can, from the naturally finished vertical pine slats on the walls to the rough stone blocks of the floors in the snackbar. There's also lots of high-gloss wood in the intimately lit disco. Prices for bed and breakfast are on a per-person basis in a double room. From December to April you'll pay between 52F ($23.89) and 60F ($27.57), with a reduction ranging between 30% and 50% for children sharing a room with their parents. Between May and October guests pay between 44F ($20.22) and 50F ($22.98), with higher prices charged at Christmas, New Year's, and Easter. Singles are available for a 10F ($4.60) supplement. The cost for half board ranges between 60F ($27.57) and 76F ($34.92) per person, depending on the season.

Hotel Alpina (tel. 3-15-37) has exquisite views of the nearby alpine ridge from its many balconies, some of which are set at oblique angles to the main building for maximum advantage. The outside looks surprisingly urban for a village landscape (lots of contrete), but the interior is pierced with enough windows to allow views in many directions. The public rooms are warmly appointed with natural wood and well-chosen textiles. The Güller family are your hosts. On the half-board plan singles rent for between 52F ($23.89) and 68F ($31.25), while doubles range between 104F ($47.79) and 136F ($62.49), depending on the season. Full board is available for an additional 8F ($3.68), and is usually required of the guests who stay during the peak, peak season (December 1 till mid-January).

4. Bad Ragaz

This alpine Rhine Valley spa—one of the best known in Switzerland—has been famous for its mineral waters since the 11th century. Guests suffering from rheumatism and circulatory disorders are attracted to Bad Ragaz, but even if you're in perfect health you may want to make this a holiday center. The setting for the resort is a parklike landscape in the foothills of the Alps, and from a comfortable base here you can branch out on many a hiker's trail, especially through "the wild and romantic" Tamina Gorge.

The spa is well equipped with hotels, and chances are, your bedroom window will open onto a view of the rugged crests of the Falknis. The spa is also a departure point with cable cars and ski lifts to the Bad Ragaz–Pardiel–Pizol mountain railways, with connections to ski districts of the same name.

In summer you can enjoy the town's beautiful 18-hole golf course, along with tennis, riding, fishing, hiking (as mentioned), and mountain climbing, plus an open-air swimming pool. In winter, nature-lovers fill their days with ski runs, natural skating rinks, indoor tennis, riding, and footpaths, later soothed by a special concert. In other words, this is one resort that's in business!

The **Bad Ragaz Tourist Office** in town (tel. 9-10-61) will give you a map and outline excursions in the area, especially to spots such as Bad Pfäfers, with its public baths and buildings that date from the early 18th century.

The spa is mainly known for its two huge indoor swimming pools, where for an admission price of $2.25 you can swim in hot mineral waters, whether you have rheumatism or not. The springs from which the pools get their water were said to have been discovered by a knight in the Middle Ages. The 16th-century philosopher, Paracelsus, was once a "doctor in residence" at Bad Ragaz.

WHERE TO STAY: **Quellenhof** (tel. 9-01-11) is primarily sought out by persons suffering from rheumatic or circulatory disorders who come for the mineral water cures that are so famous throughout Switzerland. In its heyday the Quellenhof attracted the once-reigning king and queen of Hollywood, Mary Pickford and Douglas Fairbanks. Over the years much royalty has stayed here, including the crown prince of the Netherlands. Since the golden days many of the bedrooms have been modernized in a way that has little to do with the grand Europe of the 19th century (magenta carpets and upholstered barrel chairs in some of the bedrooms), although the service remains good and the gardens are beautiful. Rooms, whether single or double, rent for between 150F ($68.92) and 200F ($91.90), depending on the season and the type of accommodation. Full board costs an additional 20F ($9.19) per person.

Hof Ragaz (tel. 9-01-31) offers its own medical department with a host of physical therapy treatments. The location of the hotel is calm, beautiful, and scenic. The Hof Ragaz is actually part of a complex of therapy-related buildings, connected by covered passageways, including at least 34 separate hotel, cure, and sports facilities stretched over a landscaped garden. Rooms rent for between 55F ($25.27) and 90F ($41.36) per person without bath, and for between 90F and 120F ($55.14) per person with bath, including breakfast.

Hotel Cristal, 36 Bahnhofstrasse (tel. 9-28-77), is an imaginatively designed construction built of concrete with lots of glass and plants hanging from its prominent balconies and terraces. Easily reached from the train station, the hotel has well-appointed rooms, all with private bath, radio, phone, and refrigerator, plus a well-heated swimming pool open all day long. The hotel's restaurant, the Adler, is in a separate building just behind the hotel. Owned by the Reber family, the Cristal is open year round, charging from 63F ($28.94) to 68F ($32.25) in a single and from 55F ($25.28) to 60F ($27.57) in a double.

Gasthaus Zur Traube (tel. 9-14-60) is an appealingly proportioned building painted white with blue-gray shutters and a ruddy-colored hip roof that curves pleasantly at the corners. The inside is filled with artifacts that will make you feel comfortable, including an antique winepress in the lobby area that almost reaches the ceiling and lamps made from old carpenter's planes with frilly lampshades on top. A weinkeller in the basement has antique chains hanging as decorative objects over hewn pine beams, and the restaurant is popular, as is the sidewalk café, with local residents. Owned by the Good family, the hotel charges from 50F ($22.96) to 57F ($26.19) per person in single or double rooms with half board, and from 35F ($16.08) per person for bed and breakfast.

WHERE TO DINE: **Restaurant Paradies** (tel. 9-14-41) is one of those sympathetic restaurants where you'll want to return, especially if you love fresh- and saltwater fish cooked in a variety of original ways. The warm appetizers and meat dishes are also worthy of sampling. An attractive menu might include lobster and cognac soup, followed by a combination of trout with shrimp served with a white wine and tarragon sauce, topped by chocolate mousse for dessert. Prices are honest and fair, considering what you get. Fixed-price meals cost between 50F ($22.97) and 72F ($33.08), while à la carte dinners range anywhere from a low of 26F ($11.95) to an average of 50F ($22.98). The wine list is very complete here, although many guests order mineral water or beer.

Schlössli Büel (tel. 9-12-65) could serve as your destination if you need an excursion from Bad Ragaz. You'll drive between the rolling hills above the town before arriving at this spot which is woodsy enough to be idyllic, yet where the cuisine is good enough to be called intensely civilized. You could order a well-prepared plate of food if your appetite is small, although most diners prefer a complete meal, attractively priced at between 18F ($8.27) and 25.50F ($11.72), with à la carte meals costing roughly from 16F ($7.35) to 32F ($14.70). One of my favorite appetizers is melon with ham, which they do perfectly here, along with a very good veal pie and a series of vegetables fresh from the market. You might be interested in ordering the local wine (Büel), or any of the other vintages listed on the wine card.

5. Appenzell

Known for its baked goods and chocolates, Appenzell is one part of Switzerland where folk tradition lives on. Don't be surprised to encounter men with earrings but no shoes! Its folk costumes are distinctive, and I hope you'll get to see a woman in her ceremonial garb, wearing a coiffe with large tulle wings. The district has long been known for its Grandma Moses–type painters, and is also said to produce the best yodelers in the country.

As for the landscape, someone once compared the setting to a combination "of the rolling green hills of Vermont with a Yosemite-like limestone upthrust at its center." In the environs are several mirror lakes, and trusty cable cars haul visitors and locals alike over an otherwise inaccessible terrain. For centuries the district was relatively isolated from the rest of the world.

Set in the foothills of the Alpstein, the Appenzell district sweeps southward from Lake Constance. As you drive from hamlet to hamlet, you'll note artistically painted houses, inhabited by people who believe in keeping alive firmly rooted traditions.

The few Americans who visit the district reportedly are always in a rush, but perhaps you'll have time to stop over in the town of Appenzell itself. Try to visit the main street, the Hauptgasse. Here you can find shops selling the famous embroidery of the area (it's not cheap), but most women will want to make off with at least one souvenir of this exquisite craft.

The town has many traditional old painted houses which have been well preserved. At the square, the Landsgemeindeplatz, the men of the community, wearing swords, hold an annual meeting where you get to see democracy in action.

Appenzell is also a good base for excursions. From the town you can journey to **Ebenalp,** a distance of only four miles. Take the Weissbad–Wasserauen road until it ends. At the terminus, you can go by cable car, about an 11-minute ride to the summit at some 5400 feet. The cable car leaves about every 30 minutes in season, a round-trip fare costing 10F ($4.60).

The mountaintop promontory of Ebenalp, with its cliffs jutting out, affords a spectacular view of the Appenzell district with its contented cows. If you've wisely worn good, strong, and sturdy walking shoes, you can walk down to **Wildkirchli,** a chapel in a cave or grotto. It was once inhabited by hermits from the mid-17th to the mid-19th century. Around the turn of the century Paleolithic artifacts were discovered there, making it the oldest prehistoric settlement so far found in Switzerland.

If you're going to anchor in the district for two or three days, you may want to take more interesting excursions. The major attraction in the area is the climb up **Mt. Säntis,** the highest peak (8200 feet) in the Alpstein massif. It's the principal viewing platform for those wanting a panoramic sweep of eastern Switzerland. Spread before you will be the Grisons, the Bernese Alps, the Vorarlberg mountains, Lake Constance, even Lake Zurich. On the clearest of days you can see as far as Swabia in southern Germany. However, many readers are likely to be disappointed, as there are many hazy days, even in July, when the panoramic view is obscured.

To reach the cable car, drive first to Schwägalp, where the car will take you to the Säntis belvedere. The cable leaves about every hour year round, a round-trip fare costing 16F ($7.35).

FOOD AND LODGING IN APPENZELL: **Hotel Hecht** (tel. 87-10-26) is directed by the Knechtle family, who seem to know everyone in town and who keep their antiques, wood paneling, and the yellow-and-white facade of their cozy hotel in tip-top shape. Among the artifacts scattered throughout the wide hallways you'll see a spinning wheel, amusingly oversize cowbells serving as room dividers, and lots of chalet benches and chairs. The overall effect is gemütlich, and is enhanced by the good cuisine. A specialty is local freshwater fish, especially trout, served in the rustic dining room. Doubles without bath cost 35F ($16.08) per person, rising to 50F ($22.98) per person in a double with bath. Singles pay a 10F ($4.60) supplement. Full or half board is available for an additional 20F ($9.20) to 30F ($13.79) per person, respectively.

Romantik Hotel Säntis (tel. 87-26-44) has a facade which is stenciled and painted with dozens of symmetrical regional designs, and a series of small-paned windows that pierce the ruddy facade in long horizontal rows. In summer the Heeb family sets out a few café tables so guests can take in the alpine sunshine before retiring to the cozy bedrooms, many of which are filled with regional antiques. On the premises you'll find a snug dining room in the alpine style with a wood ceiling and colorful tablecloths. Bathless singles rent for between 35F ($16.08) and 45F ($20.68), while singles with bath cost between 45F ($20.68) and 64F ($29.41). Bathless doubles rent for between 65F ($29.86) and 75F ($34.46), while doubles with bath cost between 85F ($39.06) and 110F ($50.55). Half board costs an additional 20F ($9.19) more per person daily. The hotel stands on a small square in the heart of town, and the reception is friendly.

Restaurant Säntis (tel. 87-16-93) is on the first floor of the best known hotel in Appenzell, and sports a view over the elaborately detailed houses of the main square. The menu changes frequently, but usually has two or three specialties of the day, many of them regional, which are handwritten and inserted on a card into the regular menu. An appetizer might be a nourishing bouillon or a plate of alpine dried beef garnished with pickles and onions, followed by rack of lamb in Calvados sauce or roast filet of pork. You might also prefer the beef filet bourguignon or river trout with fennel. Even the noodles are homemade with eggs, carrots, and spinach, and beautifully served al dente as an accompaniment to some of the meat and fish dishes. The most popular dessert, according to the management, is melon sorbet or raspberry ice cream. Bottled wines are available, but the house wine, served in carafes, is also very good. Fixed-price meals are offered for between 23F ($10.57) and 50F ($22.98), while à la carte dinners begin at 24F ($11.03) and climb steeply from there. The chef, Joseph Heeb, is also the owner, and he has an annual closing from January 8 to February 8. Service is offered every day from 7 a.m. to midnight.

TROGEN: If you'd like to truly absorb the spirit of the Appenzell district, I suggest at least a night in Trogen, with its little historic hotel. The hamlet is the terminus of the St. Gallen–Speicher and Trogen tramway. The village has many frescoed 18th-century houses, and the people still cling to time-honored traditions.

Hotel Krone (tel. 94-13-04) lies about five minutes away from the railway station by foot, in an elaborately painted gem of a building, with five floors and a hexagonally capped tower, all of it covered with designs. Depending on your mood, you might call it trompe l'oeil, country baroque, or the product of a painter with a series of fanciful whims. In summer you'll see a few tables in front, which will give you a chance to sit down and observe the building more closely. The owner is responsible for the food coming from the kitchen, which is well spoken of in the region. The hotel charges 30F ($13.79) per person in a bathless single or double, and between 35F ($16.08) and 40F ($18.38) per person in a single or double with bath. Breakfast is included in these prices, although full and half board are available for an additional 15F ($6.89) or 27F ($12.41) per person daily.

6. Braunwald

For the relatively few Americans who venture into the canton of Glarus, Braunwald is a lovely little resort relatively undiscovered. It's rapidly developing, however, as a Swiss ski center. Mt. Tödi, at 11,900 feet, lies on its southern border.

The canton itself, south of St. Gallen, has several industrial towns, but is mainly characterized by mountain lakes, alpine meadows, and tiny hamlets, all set off against a backdrop of mountains lakes, with dunce-capped snow peaks.

Instead of anchoring into Glarus, the cantonal capital, an industrial town that will hold little interest for the tourist unless your relatives are from there, Braunwald is more appealing.

Go first to Linthal, which is enveloped by high mountains. There you can park your car in a garage and ascend in ten minutes on a mountain railway to Braunwald, the only traffic-free holiday resort in eastern Switzerland, which should make it attractive for parents with small children.

Braunwald is reached in about two hours from Zurich along the southern shores of Lake Zurich. The setting of the resort, which in winter attracts mainly beginner and intermediate skiers, is most attractive, especially its pine trees and, in summer, when the sycamores are at their peak.

The resort has a ski school. You and one other passenger can take a little two-seater gondola which rises over those pines and sycamores to Grotzenbühl at 5250 feet, which on my last visit was filled with British skiers. After some refreshment at the restaurant there, you can go on a chair lift to the ridge of Seblengrat at 5905 feet. It hooks up with the Bächital chair lift.

From another part of Braunwald you can take a chair lift north to Gumen at 6250 feet, which has a mountain chalet inn.

THE RESORT HOTELS: **Hotel Alpina** (tel. 84-32-84) offers, among other advantages, a spectacular view from a series of terraces of a range of mountains that look almost close enough to touch. The interior has been constructed with comfort and panoramic views in mind, so that some alpine features can be seen from practically anywhere inside. The hotel is owned by the Schweitzer family, who quote prices on a *per-person* basis. They usually prefer guests to stay at least three days. On the half-board plan in summer they charge from 49F ($22.52) to 53F ($24.35) in a bathless single and from 58F ($26.65) to 62F ($28.49) in a single with bath. Bathless doubles cost between 45F ($20.68) and 49F ($22.56) per person, while doubles with bath rent between 54F ($24.81) and 63F ($28.95) per person, depending on the size of the room and its exposure. In winter, still on the half-board plan, bathless singles range between a low of 58F ($26.65) and a high of 78F ($35.84), with doubles dipping to 55F ($25.27) per person and rising to 78F ($35.84) per person.

Hotel Bellevue (tel. 84-38-43) is a pastel yellow symmetrical hotel with black shutters and a glass-walled series of modern extensions which include a restaurant and a swimming pool. The hotel opens onto a view of the mountains, with large terraces covered with plants and café tables in summer. The bedrooms are comfortable with bright accents and big windows. The Bellevue offers a range of sports facilities and grants reductions for children who share their parents' room. Singles rent for between 45F ($20.68) and 80F ($36.76) without bath, and between 60F ($27.57) and 100F ($45.95) with bath, depending on the season. Doubles cost between 120F ($55.14) and 200F ($91.90) with bath, dropping to 85F ($39.05) to 130F ($59.73) without, depending on the season. Half board is included in the tariffs quoted.

Hotel Tödiblick (tel. 84-12-36) is built on a foundation of local stone sunk deep into the hillside. The masonary looks solid enough to allow you an untroubled sleep, and the views from the verandas are nothing short of spectacular. The Stuber family always keeps a Swiss flag flying, which is even more prominent in winter than in summer. The interior is a gemütlich collection of Oriental rugs, comfortable armchairs, and alpine knick-knacks, while the restaurant serves well-prepared meals in a panoramic setting. The bedrooms are usually wood paneled, and contain simple Nordic modern pieces. Bathless singles cost from 35F ($16.08), going up to 50F ($22.98) with bath. Doubles all have private bath, cost between 40F ($18.38) and 45F ($20.68) per person, with half board going for yet another 15F ($6.89) per person extra.

7. Schaffhausen and Rheinfall

An atmosphere from the Middle Ages still hangs over this old town constructed on terraces on the Rhine's right bank. The whole effect makes it one of the most charming little cities in the country. If that weren't reason enough to visit, it's also a center for visiting the Rhine Falls (Rheinfall), one of the most popular sights in this part of the country.

The city is modern and industrial, but it has integrated its industry into its physical setting in such a way that the ancient charm has still been preserved. The town has many romantic fountains and its brown-roofed houses are decorated with statues and paintings, and often contain oriel windows.

The capital of a Swiss canton of the same name, Schaffhausen lies about 31 "rail miles" to the west of Constance. Once an imperial free city, it was before that ruled by the Habsburgs. Many troops have marched through here, notably the Swedish and Bavarian armies. Today Schaffhausen is enclosed on three sides by Germany.

You can spend a morning touring the old town at your leisure. Crowning the town is the **Munot,** dating from 1564. Along the battlements, you'll have a good view of the old town. It's reached by stairs and a covered footbridge across the moat. This round fortress has a tower, platform, and parapet walks.

Built in 1564, it was the only fortress to be based on the ideas of Albrecht Dürer, which were published in a book in Nürnberg in 1527. It's open May to September from 8 a.m. to 8 p.m. and October to April from 9 a.m. to 5 p.m.

Back in the old town, visitors always like to photograph the frescoed **Haus zum Ritter** from 1485. Find your way to Vordergasse, which is the most charming street in the old town. The outstanding fountain is the Fronwagplatz, actually two fountains, both from the 1520s. The Rathaus (town hall) was built in 1632, but the crowning glory of Schaffhausen is All Saints' Church (or the **Münster** as the locals call it). Now Protestant, it was formerly a Benedictine monastery, consecrated in 1052. Its Romanesque architecture represents the sternest and plainest style. In a small courtyard nearby is the celebrated 15th-century bell that inspired Schiller's "Song of the Bell" and the opening of Longfellow's "Golden Legend."

The **Museum zu Allerheiligen** (All Saints' Museum), housed in a former abbey, today is one of the most important national museums in Switzerland. Its exhibitions range from prehistoric times to the present day. Look for the "Treasury" in the former abbots' salon. You'll see everything from the traditional regional garb of the province to old weaponry and period furnishings. It's open from 9 a.m. to noon and 1:30 to 5 p.m. April to October. Otherwise its hours are from 10 a.m. to noon and 1:30 to 4:30 p.m. It's closed on Monday.

Leaving the town, you can take the trail of beauty-lover John Ruskin to the **Rheinfall** (Rhine falls), the most celebrated waterfall in central Europe, certainly the most powerful, as 700 cubic meters of water per second rush over a width of 150 yards.

At this point the Rhine falls 70 feet, a sight that inspired Goethe to liken it to the "source of the ocean." The fall is most spectacular in the peak months of early summer when it's fed by mountain snows.

Most American visitors are based in Zurich when they decide to visit this fall. From the Hauptbahnhof in Zurich, they can travel by train to Neuhausen and the Rheinfall stop. The train reaches Neuhausen in less than an hour. From the train depot at Neuhausen you can walk to the waterfall in about 15 minutes. You can take a 5F ($2.30) boat trip to the rock in the center of the Rheinfall, a most dramatic experience.

Others prefer to view the falls from a belvedere provided for that purpose. On the left bank, this is best done at **Laufen Castle,** which has been converted into, naturally, a restaurant with a view of the falls. To stand on a belvedere, go inside the forecourt of the castle and down a staircase until you are on the same level as the falls (better carry a raincoat). Admission is only .50F (23¢).

You can also take a ferry across the river to the little **Wörth Castle,** which was a customs post at the falls, probably built in the 12th century. It too has been turned into a restaurant, and is open from the first of March until mid-November.

FOOD AND LODGING: **Hotel Park Villa,** 18 Parkstrasse (tel. 5-27-37), might be the closest thing you'll find to a cross between Balmoral Castle and a Teutonic fortress. The building is set among massive trees, many of them seemingly bigger than the hotel, on a green area close to the train station. The towers, steep roofs, and gables are covered with terracotta tiles, and the facade and the many chimneys are crafted of chiseled gray rocks, giving a pleasingly uneven texture to the surfaces. The interior is as elegantly graceful as the exterior is rough. You'll find crystal chandeliers, a bar area with wooden backdrops that are more like furniture than paneling, and a series of public rooms dotted with fresh flowers, comfortable chairs, and oil paintings. A few of the bedrooms are regally decorated with antiques, and for an unusual game of tennis, you'll find a well-maintained court only a few feet away from the brooding mass of the back side of the building. Frau Marga Müller is the owner, charging from 85F ($39.06) to 130F ($59.74) in a double with bath and from 55F ($25.27) to 65F ($29.87) in a single with bath. Bathless rooms rent for 48F ($22.06) in a single and from 65F ($29.87) to 75F ($34.46) in a double. A two-room apartment with bath suitable for three persons rents for 140F ($64.33).

Hotel Bellevue, Bahnhofstrasse at Neuhausen am Rheinfall (tel. 2-21-21), has the advantage of having a terrace where you can sip drinks and watch the waterfall without being drenched. There aren't a lot of other buildings blocking your view, so with the green countryside stretched out beyond the water, you can imagine yourself in an area more primitive than industrialized Europe. The interior of the hotel is unpretentiously modern, with large tile bathrooms and all the modern comforts. Singles rent for between 38F ($17.46) and 45F ($20.67) without bath, between 70F ($32.17) to 80F ($36.76) with bath. Doubles cost between 72F ($33.08) and 84F ($38.59) without bath, going up to 110F ($50.55) to 120F ($55.14) with bath. Breakfast is included, and the owner, Rudolf Nohava, does everything he can to make guests comfortable. The restaurant offers fixed-price meals from 14.50F ($6.66) which, with a view of the falls, might be a pleasant way to pass an early afternoon.

Restaurant Fischerzunft, 8 Rheinquai (tel. 5-32-81), was established in an unusually pretty town house at one of the best addresses in Schaffhausen, next to a riverside promenade that allows you to see the activity on this famous waterway. André Jäger is the well-known chef, and he's assisted by his charming wife in the dining room. As you'd expect from a riverside restaurant, the specialty of the house is fish cooked in many ways. Fish from the Rhine is often served in a pot-pourri and seasoned with fresh herbs. An exceptional dish is John Dory with coriander, and meat dishes include a well-prepared filet of roast lamb or pork. All portions are served on the family's beautifully painted personal china, and are usually followed by such desserts as raspberry soufflé with sorbet. The most expensive fixed-price meal is a gourmet regalia at 115F ($52.84), which changes monthly. Other fixed-price selections start at around 68F ($31.24), and à la carte meals run roughly between 30F ($13.78) and 68F ($31.25). The restaurant decor includes enough paneling and wood furniture to have kept a team of carpenters busy for months. It's closed every year between mid-January and mid-February.

Gerberstube, 8 Bachstrasse (tel. 5-21-55). In summertime this comfortably decorated Italian restaurant will greet you with cascades of flowers on its well-maintained facade, which should give a hint of the kind of pleasantly intimate ambience which has been established inside. Specialties include a tasty spinach ravioli, excellent cannelloni, along with virtually every kind of pasta imaginable, usually served with well-prepared meats such as saltimbocca. Another specialty is osso buco with risotto. Desserts include the classic favorite, a zabaglione laced with Marsala. À la carte meals cost between 36F ($16.52) and 42F ($19.30).

8. Stein-am-Rhein

Only 12 miles from Schaffhausen, on the right bank of the Rhine, Stein-am-Rhein is celebrated as one of the most authentic medieval towns of Switzerland and draws many visitors. It lies at the western edge of the Untersee, an arm of Lake Constance from which the Rhine leaves the lake.

Nearby was the first Roman bridge ever built over the Rhine. Records of the town go back to 1094.

Its principal sights are the **Rathausplatz** (the town hall square) and **Hauptstrasse** (the main street). Here the houses evoke that much-overused word "quaint," with their oriel windows, richly embellished frescoes, studded timberwork, and flower-bedecked fountains. They often have themes such as the house of the red ox or the white eagle. The townspeople love flowers so much that in summer the place virtually bursts into bloom.

The **Historische Sammlung** (historical museum) is in the Rathaus (town hall). It has the usual collection of a small Swiss town: weaponry, banners, and stained glass. Charging 1F (46¢), the museum is open from 10 to 11:30 a.m. and 2 to 5 p.m. weekdays. It's closed on weekends and holidays.

A Benedictine abbey was erected in the town at the beginning of the 11th century but was dissolved in 1524. Today it houses the **Klostermuseum St. Georgen** (St. George's abbey museum), which is devoted to local history and art. The rooms themselves are often more fascinating than the exhibits, with their rich ceilings and panelings and their 16th-century grisailles. The convent church of St. George, a 12th-century Romanesque basilica, has been renovated. It's now a Protestant parish church which can be visited.

If you're driving, perhaps you'd like to journey for two miles to visit **Hohenklingen Castle,** a medieval hilltop stronghold constructed in the mid-16th century. It's open from the first of March until mid-December daily except Monday. A tavern opened here in the 19th century, and at present a castle restaurant, popular with summer visitors, has been installed.

If you're stopping over, try the **Sonne,** 127 Rathausplatz (tel. 8-61-28), for food. It's one of the most famous establishments in this historic town, benefiting from its location on the well-preserved marketplace in the center. In the intimate dining room inside (it holds only eight tables), head chef and owner Philippe Combe practices a form of nouvelle cuisine which is likely to include fresh river crabs in a vinaigrette sauce, wild game in a Beaujolais sauce (served with wild mushrooms sauteed in butter), or roast hare with mustard sauce. Good wines complement a fine repast, all of it capped by a smooth dessert such as chocolate mousse. Fixed-price meals range from 68F ($31.25) to 100F ($45.95), while à la carte dinners cost from 38F ($17.46) to 65F ($29.87). Noontime meals are slightly less expensive, beginning at 30F ($13.79). The restaurant is closed Thursday and for the first two weeks of November and February.

READER'S HOTEL RECOMMENDATION: "The **Hotel Adler / Motel Roseburg** (tel. 8-68-58). We stayed at the motel, just across the river from the hotel, but within easy walking distance. Our room included the luxury of a well-stocked refrigerator. The food at the Adler is simply outstanding. The tab, including a liberal raiding of the fridge, was only 100F ($45.95)" (Thomas R. Emdy, Bloomington, Minn.).

9. Lake Constance

Even though three nations—Austria, Germany, and Switzerland—share the 162-mile shoreline of this large inland sea, the area around Lake Constance is united in a common cultural and historical heritage. The hillsides sloping down to the water's edge are covered with vineyards and orchards, and dotted with colorful hamlets and busy tourist centers. The mild climate and plentiful sunshine make Lake Constance a vacation spot for lovers of sun and sand, as well as for sightseers and spa-hoppers. A well-organized network of cruise ships and ferries links every major center around the lake.

Lake Constance is divided into three parts, although the name is frequently applied to the largest of these, the Bodensee. The western end of the Bodensee separates into two distinct branches, including the Überlingersee, a long fjord. On the other hand the Untersee is more irregular, jutting in and out of the marshlands and low-lying woodlands. It's connected to the larger lake by only a narrow channel of water—actually, the young Rhine, whose current flows right through the Bodensee. Tip: The blue felchen, a pike-like fish found only in Lake Constance, furnishes the district with a tasty and renowned specialty.

My favorite targets along the Swiss side of the lake are as follows:

ROMANSHORN: This town is one of the best centers on the Swiss side, and it's even convenient should you wish to explore the attractions on the German side. It has its own resort facilities, including a swimming pool, sailing school, waterskiing school, and tennis courts, but it's also a big excursion center.

A ferry runs all year from Romanshorn to Friedrichshafen, in Germany, with its castle which was a summer residence of the kings of Württemberg and its Zeppelin mementos. In summer, boat trips are organized to the island of Mainau, a German island, the former home of the Grand Duke of Baden, which lies about four miles north of Constance. Boats also visit Meersburg and Lindau.

Romanshorn has a beautiful park with stunning summer flora, plus a zoo. But mainly visitors come here because, as the largest port on Lake Constance, it's the base of the Swiss lake steamers.

Food and Lodging

Seehotel (tel. 63-42-94). The exterior of this family-run hotel is attractively paneled in rustically finished vertical wood slats which, because of the streamlined modern windows, give the hotel the appearance of an expensive private home in the Rockies. Well-maintained gardens surround the establishment, while the comfort of guests isn't forgotten in the cozy bar area and the well-appointed bedrooms. You'll also find an informal restaurant, an L-shaped pub, and a more formal restaurant called the Rôtisserie with wood accents and bright napery. The Oberlaender family, the owners, charge 32F ($14.70) in a bathless single, from 35F ($16.08) to 45F ($20.68) in a single with bath. Bathless doubles range between 55F ($25.27) and 60F ($27.57), while doubles with bath rent for between 70F ($32.16) and 90F ($41.36), depending on the season. Tariffs include breakfast.

Hotel Inseli (tel. 63-53-53). Anton Stäger is the friendly manager who, with his family, sees to the comfort of each of his guests at this dramatically modern hotel with red-trimmed extensions and big windows. Views from the comfortable rooms are out over an expanse of lawn, usually with a view of the lake. Many of the public rooms are appealingly decorated with wood, chrome, and metal accents, lots of plush carpeting, and the kind of informal ambience that lets you feel at home. Rooms in the old section of the hotel (which was an attractive but isolated house before the modern additions in 1977) are substantially cheaper than those in the newer part. In the older section, singles without bath cost 38F ($17.46); doubles go for 58F ($26.65) to 76F ($34.92) without bath, and from 67F ($30.79) to 88F ($40.44) with bath. In the new section all rooms have private bath, costing from 55F ($25.27) to 83F ($38.14) in a single and from 94F ($43.19) to 120F ($55.14) in a double. Half board is available for another 26F ($11.95) per person.

ARBON: One of the best spots on the lake is Arbon, from whose lakefront promenade you'll have a view over Constance, embracing the German shore opposite and taking in both the Swiss and Austrian Alps. Arbon is well equipped with many facilities, include a large boat harbor, swimming pools, a school for sailing and surfing. It's the starting point for many interesting excursions.

Arbon Castle was a medieval stronghold which has been turned into a local museum. Its keep is from the 13th century, and the residential wings date from the beginning of the 16th century. Arbon occupies the site of an ancient Celtic community. It was known to the Romans as Arbor Felix.

For food and lodging, your best bet is the **Hotel Metropole,** (tel. 46-35-35), a recently constructed hotel with prominent horizontal balconies and a series of sports facilities which include an outdoor swimming pool with grassy lawns around it, boating on the nearby lake, and a whirlpool and sauna much used by members of business conventions who occasionally meet here. The format is streamlined, modern, and efficient, the bedrooms decorated in vivid colors with their own loggias attached. The hotel is part of the Best Western chain, and is managed by an experienced hotelier, Charles Delway. Singles with bath cost between 60F ($27.57) and 85F ($39.06), while doubles without bath range between 88F ($40.45) and 100F ($45.95), rising to 94F ($43.19) and 136F ($62.50) with bath, depending on the season. Triples are also available, and half board is offered for 26F ($11.95) per person daily.

HORN: This ancient fishing village lies five minutes by car from Arbon. The hamlet belongs to the canton of Thurgau, and it's an idyllic little spot in which to base during your exploration of Lake Constance. The large port of Rorschach lies farther east.

For food and lodging, try **Hotel Bad Horn,** 36 Seestrasse (tel. 41-55-11), which stands in an idyllic position at the end of a small peninsula extending into the lake. The building is painted a vivid ochre, with big windows, a gabled tile roof, rooftop terraces, and an expanse of grassy lawn extending almost to the water. From the street side of the hotel you'll get an idea of how large it really is, because in addition to its 37 bedrooms the hotel offers conference rooms to the nearby community, two restaurants, and a bar, many of them decorated in saltily nautical themes. All units contain private baths, renting for between 39F ($17.92) and 58F ($26.65) in a single and between 34F ($15.64) and 53F ($24.35) per person in a double. Some especially luxurious doubles with two big beds cost between 60F ($27.57) and 85F ($39.06) per person daily, with breakfast included.

RORSCHACH: If you're planning to tour Lake Constance and visit the German side as well, Rorschach is a friendly harbor town on the Swiss side of the lake. The thousand-year-old port lies at the foot of the Rorschacher Berg at the most southerly part of the lake. If based here, you can virtually decide which country you want to visit on any given day, as the Principality of Liechtenstein, Germany, and Austria are at the doorstep.

Rorschach has had an illustrious past, as many of its buildings testify to this day. These include the Kornhaus, a granary built in 1746, the painted 18th-century houses along Hauptgasse with oriel windows, and the former Mariaberg cloister.

Of these, the Kornhaus is now the local museum, the **Heimatmuseum,** which has a collection of prehistoric artifacts as well as some examples of local weaving and embroidery. It's open from 9:30 to 11:30 a.m. and 2 to 5 p.m. (on Sunday, only from 10 a.m. to noon), charging an admission of 2F (92¢).

The town also has lakeside gardens, modern passenger ships which go for trips on the lake, an extensive promenade, plus facilities for sailing, rowing, swimming, fishing, and windsurfing.

For food and lodging, try the **Hotel Anker** (tel. 41-42-43). If you love boats, you'll love this hotel, especially since it sits across the street from a spot where many of the town's boats are anchored. Covered with flowers in summertime, the hotel is a substantial-looking building with a light-gray facade, a gabled red tile roof, and lots of balconies affording good views of the lake. The hotel is owned and managed by the Krähenbühl family, who oversee the staff in the hotel's restaurant, which turns out a long list of seafood specialties. Singles without bath cost between 40F ($18.35) and 45F ($20.67), going up to 45F ($20.67) and 60F ($27.57) with bath. Bathless doubles are tabbed at 60F ($27.57) and 70F ($32.17), climbing to 80F ($36.76) and 100F ($45.95) with bath. All these tariffs include breakfast.

HEIDEN: High above Lake Constance on a sunlit ridge in the canton of Appenzell, the little health resort of Heiden lies about four miles south of Rorschach. Virtually undiscovered by Americans, it's reached by cog railway in about 20 minutes. There's a 1960s monument to Henri Dunant, founder of the Red Cross, who lived here until his death in 1910, and gave the resort much publicity.

Even if you can't stay at one of Heiden's hotels (recommended below), you may want to take the cog railway just for the view of the valleys set against a mountain backdrop. You pass through an orchard setting, with an occasional castle in the background, and go across several viaducts to reach the little spa.

Once you're there, I have the following recommendations either for food or lodging.

Hotel Krone (tel. 91-11-27) is housed in an elegantly ornate building, painted almost exclusively white, with a red tile roof capped with ornate gables and a modified onion-shaped dome. The grounds around the hotel are well maintained with lots of flowers, and the public rooms have well-polished collections of delicate Victorian and Biedermeier chairs and beautifully aged cupboards and chests. The bedrooms have good views of the surrounding countryside, all the modern comforts, and enough personal touches to make you feel at home. Owned by the same family for the past 60 years (the Kühnes), the hotel charges between 68F ($31.25) and 90F ($41.35) for a double room with bath on the half-board plan for both occupants. Singles with bath rent for between 79F ($36.30) and 86F ($39.52), also on the half-board plan. A heated swimming pool is available to guests.

Hotel Linde (tel. 91-14-14) is housed in an attractive four-story building with gray trim, lots of shutters, and a sunny terrace extending out of sight off to the side of the house. A Swiss flag usually flies in front, hoisted every morning by the Ruppanner family, who charge full-board prices of between 74F ($34) and 78F ($35.84) per person in a double with bath, and 74F ($34) in a single with bath. For guests wishing to take only half board, a reduction of 10F ($4.60) is made. The comfortable bedrooms have phones and radios, while the meals in the dining room are carefully varied from day to day.

10. Glarus

In the foothills of the Vorder Glärnisch cliffs, Glarus lies to the south of the Walensee in a deep ravine, surrounded on three sides by mountains. The little town lies near a nature reserve and close to many of Switzerland's large winter sports resorts. It's also a center for excursions, including an eight-mile run to Lake Klöntal. An illuminated ski lift as well as a ski school, a skating rink, and a tobogganing run operate in winter.

The town has a historic hotel, the **Glarnerhof** (tel. 61-41-06), a recently renovated family-run establishment in a good location in a city park with a view of the mountains. The hotel looks like a generously proportioned private villa, with a red tile roof and three floors of buff-colored shutters. A jet of water spews foam into the air not far from the front door. The lobby of the hotel is filled with green and red draperies, a large Oriental rug, and a collection of invitingly upholstered Victorian armchairs. The renovated bedrooms are for the most part filled with nondescript modern, and are clean and comfortable, often with big windows. In a single or double, the rate is 46F ($21.13) per person with bath, 36F ($16.54) without. Breakfast is included in the rates. The Vogel family, the owners, enjoy welcoming visitors and are most hospitable.

Chapter V

BASLE AND THE JURAS

1. Basle
2. Targets in the Environs
3. Baden
4. Solothurn
5. Fribourg
6. Gruyères
7. Murten (Morat)
8. Neuchâtel
9. La Chaux-de-Fonds
10. Bienne (Biel)

NORTHWEST SWITZERLAND IS one of the most rewarding targets in the country. Your center is likely to be the old university and trading center of Basle (also spelled Basel) which straddles the Rhine, lying between Alsace in France and the Jura in Switzerland.

Most visitors from North America get to see only Basle, but if time is on your side you can motor into these hills, so rich in culture and tradition, weaving your way through valleys and zigzagging to the heights. You'll also be zigzagging between two cultures, and the names will often confuse you. If you ask a French person for directions, it's Morat (but Murten to a German).

Everybody has heard of Gruyères, known for its cheese, and many will want to visit it. But the old walled university town of Fribourg and historic Neuchâtel are just some of the other most rewarding targets. Numerous castles in the area recall the Middle Ages.

The Jura, a range of folded mountains between two great rivers, the Rhine and the Rhône, forms the frontier of Switzerland and France and extends from Geneva to Schaffhausen. Very different in height and character from the Alps, the Jura mountains do belong to the alpine system geologically, and the same forces which built up the Alps produced the folds and faults found in the Jura.

Few peaks in the Jura range exceed 5000 to 5500 feet, and the region is made up of lush pastures, pine forests, and deep valleys. Until the coming of rail- and vehicular roads, farmers of the Jura lived in relative isolation, and beef and dairy cattle raising, as then, are still a major economic resource.

Motorists or railroad passengers will find a trip through the region worthwhile for its panorama of scenic delight. The highways have great belvederes from which the Alps can be seen to the southeast, as well as broad views of the surrounding land.

The center of the Swiss watchmaking industry is here, with little pockets of industry located particularly in the part of the mountains to the south as you travel from Basle toward Geneva.

Thriving winter sports resorts can also be found throughout the mountains, although most of them draw a clientele from local rather than international sports people. Despite its beauty and its obvious attractions the Jura does not as yet have a heavy tourist industry, with travelers passing it by to frequent the more famous places.

A new canton of Jura was established in January 1979, becoming the 23rd member of the Confederation. A total of 82 communes make up the canton, with Delémont as its capital. This is a strongly Roman Catholic section of Switzerland, with nearly 88% of the population following that faith, and the language is mainly French, as is to be expected from its location along the French-Swiss border country.

A region of picturesque valleys, waterfalls, old-world villages and churches, lakes, rivers, and mountain crags make the Jura a part of Switzerland travelers should make a special effort to visit.

1. Basle

Basle (Basel in German), the second-largest city of Switzerland, stands on the Rhine at the point where the borders of France, Germany, and Switzerland meet. Grossbasel (or greater Basle) lies on the steep left bank and Kleinbasel (or lesser Basle) on the right bank. The old imperial city stood at Grossbasel on the left bank.

The city is linked by half a dozen bridges, plus three ferries which don't have motors but cross on power supplied by the current of the river. The first bridge (no longer standing) was erected in 1225. Called the Mittlere Brücke, it was for centuries the only one spanning the Rhine.

The town was a Roman fort in A.D. 374, and it was ruled by prince-bishops for some 1000 years. The Great Council met within the walls of Basle between 1431 and 1448, and a pope was crowned here. After it joined the Swiss Confederation in 1501 Basle became Protestant. At the advent of the Reformation in 1529 it became a haven and a refuge for victims of religious persecution. They flooded in here from Holland, Italy, and France, bringing renewed vitality to the city and laying the foundation for its great "golden age" in the 18th century.

Today Basle is an important banking and industrial city. It is said that half the millionaires of Switzerland live here. Its chemical and parmaceutical industry is one of the most important in the world. Basle is also the headquarters of the Bank for International Settlement (and these transactions often are phenomenal). The BIS tower for that bank stands near the railway station, and is irreverently nicknamed "the cotton reel" by the people of the town.

Basle is also one of the most important cultural centers of Switzerland. A city of humanism, it saw the rise of the printing machine and the book trade within its borders. It was in Basle that Erasmus published the first edition of the New Testament in the original Greek text in 1516.

To illustrate Basle's love of art, in 1967 its citizens voted by referendum to purchase two well-known works by Picasso: *L'Arlequin Assis* and *Les Deux Frères.* Picasso was so moved that he donated four other paintings to the town. Basle is wealthy in museums, containing a total of 27.

Basle has three railway stations—Swiss, French, and German—making it one of the largest railway junctions in Europe. It's also an international motor-

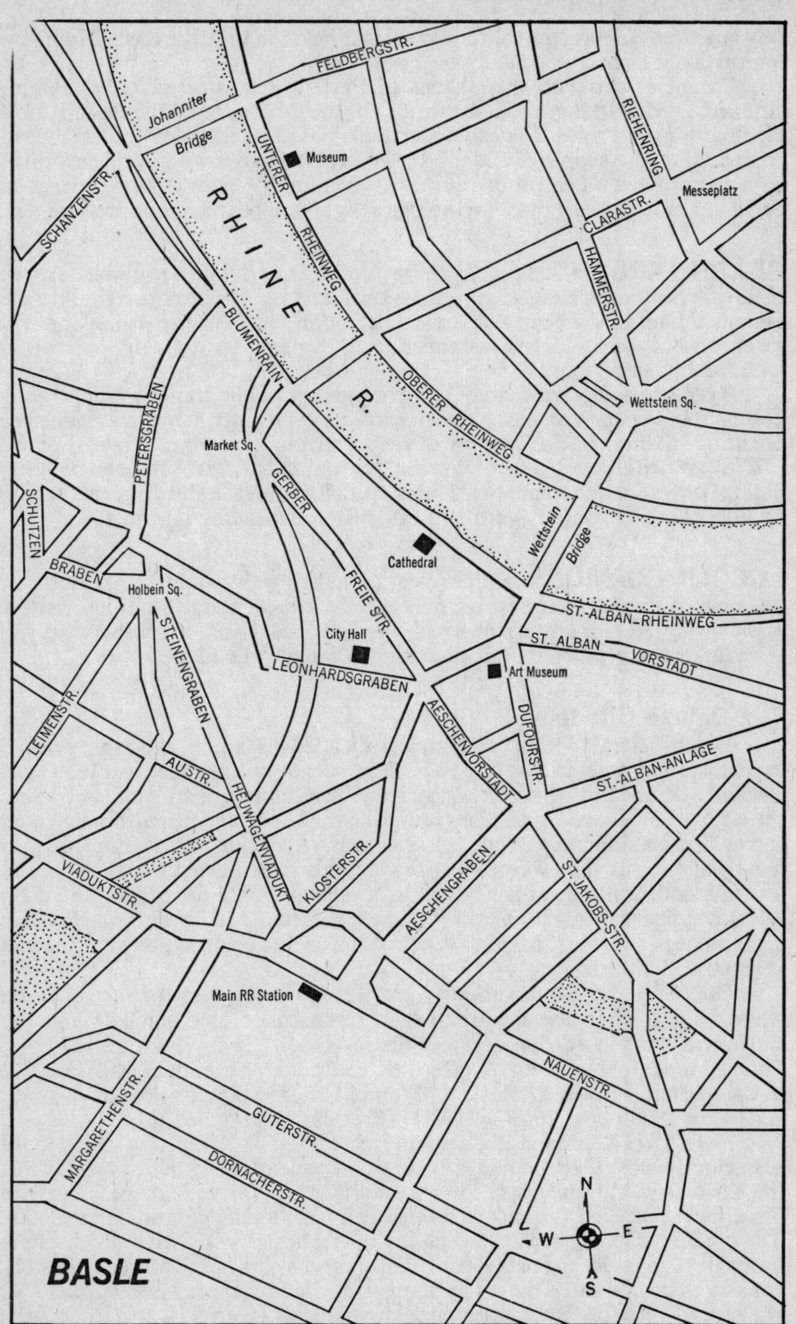
FELDBERGSTR.
Johanniter
Bridge
UNTERER
Museum
RIEHENRING
Messeplatz
CLARASTR.
SCHANZENSTR.
RHINE
RHEINWEG
HAMMERSTR.
BLUMENRAIN
R.
OBERER RHEINWEG
Wettstein Sq.
PETERSGRABEN
Market Sq.
GERBER
Cathedral
Wettstein
Bridge
SCHUTZEN
BRABEN
Holbein Sq.
FREIE STR.
ST.-ALBAN-RHEINWEG
STEINENGRABEN
City Hall
ST. ALBAN
VORSTADT
Art Museum
LEONHARDSGRABEN
LEIMENSTR.
AESCHENVORSTADT
DUFOURSTR.
ST.-ALBAN-ANLAGE
AUSTR.
HEUWAGENVIADUKT
KLOSTERSTR.
AESCHENGRABEN
VIADUKTSTR.
ST. JAKOBS-STR.
Main RR Station
NAUENSTR.
MARGARETHENSTR.
GUTERSTR.
DORNACHERSTR.
N
W
E
S
BASLE

way junction. Because the canton in which it lies is so tiny, the Basle-Mulhouse international airport is actually on French soil.

Except at carnival, the citizens of Basle are considered rather self-restrained, hard-working, and industrious, for the most part. Of the Baslers, Rolf Hochhuth once wrote: "English understatement looks like megalomania when compared to the people of Basle." However, Basle goes wild during its three days of carnival, when no one in town—seemingly—goes to bed. Festivities begin in January, when three mythological figures appear to chase away winter.

GETTING AROUND: Should you fly into Basle, arriving in Mulhouse across the Swiss frontier in France, you can take a bus from the airport right into the Hauptbahnhof in the center of Basle, costing 6F ($2.76) per person. You will rarely be hassled by Swiss Customs during this frontier crossing, unless you look mighty suspicious!

Basle has a good, relatively cheap system of public transportation, using both bus and tram. You purchase your tickets in advance at any station before boarding. Clear, concise maps will help you pinpoint your target. For 6F ($2.76) you can buy a ticket allowing you unlimited travel for one day and night. Otherwise, most inner-city fares cost .70F (32¢). Fares in general begin at .70F (32¢), ranging upward to 1.80F (83¢), depending on the zone.

ACCOMMODATIONS: Hotel reservations are tight, almost impossible, at the time of the Swiss Industries Fair which attracts about a million visitors every spring. Rooms are also impossible to find at carnival time. Otherwise, you shouldn't have a problem, but reservations are always advised.

The Deluxe Citadels

Hotel Euler, 14 Centralbahnplatz (tel. 23-45-00), is everything you'd expect a grand hotel in this city to be. The outside is a symmetrical rectangle, elegantly detailed in white with gray stone half-columns and window frames, set off by a blue awning on the ground floor. The chandeliered dining room serves first-class dinners, while a less expensive snackbar offers nourishing if less formal meals. The warm-hued bar is richly ornamented with leather and lots of wood, while a garden terrace is a relaxing place for coffee. The main salon is supported by red marble columns, the kind you have to touch to see if the stone is really just painted wood, with a ceiling painstakingly crafted into geometrical patterns.

The bedrooms are luxuriously paneled, some of them painted lilac on white, all of them impeccably up to Swiss standards of good hotelkeeping. The Euler was built in 1865 near the railroad station. Today it's directed by J. Pernet-Monkewitz who, for his 65 rooms, charges a maximum of 140F ($64.33) in a single and between 180F ($82.71) and 210F ($96.50) in a double. A junior suite here would cost 260F ($119.47). Breakfast is included in the price.

Hotel Drei Könige, 8 Blumenrain (tel. 25-52-52). A tapestry which looks suspiciously like a Gobelin hangs in the wood-paneled lobby of this hotel, while the bar area might quickly become a favorite place for your rendezvous with Swiss locals, paneled and accented the way it is with pin lights and brass detail. The hotel is officially recognized as the oldest hostelry in Switzerland, established in 1026 under the name Zur Blume ("at the sign of the flower"). History records that soon after the establishment of the inn, three kings (Conrad II, emperor of the Holy Roman Empire; his son, later Henry III; and Rudolf III, the last king of Burgundy) drew up a treaty which divided up western Switzerland and southern France. Since that time the political and literary figures who have signed the guest book (now a museum piece) include Voltaire, Napoleon, Princess (later queen) Victoria, Kaiser Wilhelm II, King Farouk (how did he get in with this crowd?), Don Juan, pretender to the throne of Spain, and scores of monarchs from dozens of European and Asiatic countries.

History aside, you'll find this an impeccably run and updated hotel. Some of the rooms have their original ornamentation on the ceilings and irreplaceable furniture, while others have been renovated with attractively modern decor. One of the salons has a surprisingly lifelike mural covering the entire expanse of one wall, interrupted only by the vertical expanse of cerulean-blue half-columns with gilded capitals that appear vaguely Corinthian. The hotel sits directly on the Rhine, at a point where it flows quickly past its stone banks, in a white, generously proportioned building with great dignity and what seem to have been several additions. A yellow-and-white canopy covers the river-front café (many of the barges you'll see will be carrying some kind of slag or gravel), which has dozens of miniature Swiss flags fluttering at its borders.

Guerin Janna, the director, charges from 130F ($59.74) to 160F ($73.52) in a single, from 180F ($82.71) to 280F ($128.66) in a double. All units have baths, air conditioning, radios, mini-bars, TVs, and phones. Breakfast is included in the tariffs, which fall into the lower range of the above-mentioned prices during off-season.

Hilton International, 31 Aeschengraben (tel. 22-66-22). Visitors are treated to typical Hilton style and service from the moment they disembark from their vehicles under the massive steel portico which, lit in a gridwork from underneath, extends unsupported from the glass-and-steel cube of the main building. Constructed in an elegantly streamlined format of matte black and glass, the Hilton offers 231 luxurious rooms and suites, each of them air-conditioned, with TV, phone, mini-bar, and refrigerator. Accommodations are comfortably furnished in shades of brown, beige, and wheat, many with interesting views of the city below. Singles rent for anywhere from $49 (U.S.) to $77, while doubles cost from $70 to $105.

The staff is multilingual and will direct you to the sauna, massage rooms, fitness club, and the popular swimming pool. The hotel is connected via an underground shopping arcade to the main railroad station, so you'll be within reach of everything. The Old City Bar, decorated with whorls of autumn colors, often has a pianist. You'll also find two restaurants and a Polynesian-style disco.

The Upper Bracket

Hotel International, 25 Steinentorstrasse (tel. 22-18-70), is a first-class hotel with 200 spotlessly clean rooms, all of which have been improved in the last several years. The well-trained management (which includes Mr. Gasteyger and Mr. Schuh) does everything it can to keep the hotel well groomed, which means replacing furniture when it becomes worn out and maintaining the many fitness facilities, such as the gym, sauna, and indoor swimming pool. All rooms are air-conditioned, many with a view, renting for 160F ($73.52) to 200F ($91.90) in a double, 110F ($50.55) to 150F ($68.93) in a single, breakfast included. You'll find an appealing rôtisserie on the premises. This and the timbered and rustically appointed dining room seem to be particularly popular with the Basle business community. A less expensive tavern on the premises is popular too, with a less formal crowd.

Hotel Europe, 43 Clarastrasse (tel. 26-80-80). Besides the obligatory Swiss flag, you'll find an enormous half-rounded purple-colored canopy sheltering this establishment's entrance from the busy sidewalk. A modern, informal hotel, owned by the ETAP chain, the Europe has a decorating scheme which borders on ideas that were trendy last year. The 175 rooms, fully air-conditioned, include baths tiled in dark colors, radios, and mini-bars, plus TVs upon request. Gathering places include the "oldtimer bar," a sidewalk café, and a restaurant, the Bajazzo, furnished with wooden banquettes and decorated with unusual murals which are brilliantly lit, while the rest of the room is left in semi-darkness. Accommodations, both in the main building and in the annex, are usually compact units of bed and bathroom, priced at 108F ($49.63) in a single and 166F ($76.30) in a double. An extra bed can be set up for an additional 30F ($13.79). A generous breakfast buffet is included in the price.

Hotel Alexander, 85 Riehenring (tel. 26-70-00). Aside from the hotel, which is directly across from the Swiss Trade Fair and the Basle Congress Center, you'll find a popular dancehall with live music and occasional disco. The appointments at the Alexander are modern, with a curved bar area and warm hospitable colors. A big-windowed restaurant with rustic half-timbering and a six-lane bowling alley complete the facilities. Singles rent for 70F ($32.17) to 100F ($45.95) while doubles range from 100F ($45.95) to 170F ($78.12), breakfast included. You'll be only ten minutes from the train station. Olivier Junod is the director.

Hotel Basel, corner of Spalenberg at Münzgasse (tel. 25-24-23), is ideally situated in a modern building which has been skillfully designed to blend tastefully with its surroundings, sitting in the old town on a street of buildings roughly the same height. Many of its 72 bedrooms have wood paneling on the walls, even on the sloping parts under the eaves of the gabled roof, and all of them are comfortably carpeted and decorated in clean, simple designs. The public rooms are high-ceilinged, with crystal chandeliers and, in one of the salons, a panoramic mural of some waterside agrarian theme. A café with bright parasols serves drinks and coffee in front of the hotel, while a rough-walled weinkeller and a brasserie offer light snacks or full meals.

O. Bäriswyl, the manager, directs the eating, lodging, and sports facilities with professional panache. He charges from 82F ($37.68) to 125F ($57.44) in a single, from 155F ($71.22) to 185F ($85.01) in a double. Prices are increased to the upper levels of the scale during trade fairs. An extra bed can be set up in a room for an additional 40F ($18.38).

Hotel Merian am Rhein, 2 Rheingasse at Greifengasse (tel. 25-94-66). The history of this establishment is intimately wrapped up in the history of Basle itself. The hotel is in a spot just off the quay where a bishop in the 13th century commissioned the construction of the only bridge across the Rhine, between Lake Constance and the sea. Today the Merian is a sympathetic hotel in the oldest part of the city, with atmosphere, charm, and updated conveniences such as comfortable beds. The more expensive double rooms (the ones with private baths) are on the Rhine side of this 60-room hotel. Singles without bath cost 85F ($39.06) to 95F ($43.65), while doubles with bath range from 115F ($52.84) to 155F ($71.22), breakfast included. A TV can be placed in your room upon request. The friendly manager, B. Skrobucha, does everything he can to make his guests comfortable.

Hotel Schaeizerhof, 1 Centralbahnplatz (tel. 22-28-23), has been in the same hotelkeeping family for the past three generations. Near the train station, not far from the old town, the hotel contains a bar, a restaurant, a pleasant sun terrace, and several conference rooms which are sometimes used for wedding receptions and business meetings. The building, across the street from a landscaped park with a fountain, rises six ornamented stories and has a few wrought-iron balconies and the obligatory Swiss flag flying on top. The salons are decorated with Oriental rugs and some 19th-century antiques, while the bedrooms are clean and pleasingly appointed in a simple modern format of understated good taste. The host Goetzinger family charges from 92F ($42.27) to 98F ($45.03) in a single and 155F ($71.22) in a double, all with bath or shower and breakfast.

The Medium Price Range

Hotel Bernina, 14 Margarethenstrasse (tel. 23-73-00), a modern hotel in downtown Basle next to the railroad station, is closer to the zoo than any other hostelry. All the modern rooms have baths and comfortable beds. Jo Scheurer, the director, is ably assisted by B. Braschler. They maintain the six-story facade in impeccable condition, frequently changing the collection of international flags hanging over the sidewalk in front. Singles with breakfast cost 80F ($36.76) per night; doubles go for 150F ($68.93).

Hotel Münchnerhof, 75 Riehenring (tel. 26-77-80), lies close to the Bahnhof in a brownish-ocher-colored building with white trim around the well-designed modern windows, some of which are arched over small balconies. The interior is attractively decorated in an unpretentious streamlined sort of way, keeping the ambience attractively traditional although everything looks recently updated. The owners are the Früh family, who also operate the two restaurants attached to the hotel, one with live music. Prices begin at 65F ($29.87) in a single, 100F ($45.95) in a double.

Hotel Flügelrad, 22 Kuchengasse (tel. 23-42-41), is the kind of family-run hotel that many tourists dream about, with flowers in the window-boxes, a Swiss flag flying over the narrow street in front, and four floors of immaculately maintained, cozy rooms. The public rooms, including the friendly restaurant decorated with pieces of painted furniture from the region, are attractively ornamented with full or half-paneling, colorful rugs or carpeting, and big sunny windows. The owners, the Wiemers-Schmid family, charge 45F ($20.68) in a bathless single, 65F ($29.87) in a single with bath, 80F ($36.76) in a double without private bath, and 100F ($45.95) in a double with shower and toilet. Breakfast is included in all the tariffs.

City Hotel, 12 Henric-Petri-Strasse (tel. 24-78-76), lies near St. Elisabeth's Church, not far from the railroad station. It's informal and modern, with lots of oversize windows looking either over the street or onto a tree-filled central garden. In summer a ring of flowers circles the hotel in a continuous planter approximately 12 feet above the ground. The lobby has a gray marble floor, a vividly patterned Oriental rug, and an attentively polite receptionist who does everything possible to make your stay pleasant. Bedrooms are up to date and well equipped, with two-toned white and natural-grain furniture and bathrooms. Singles cost 70F ($32.17) per day, while doubles rent for 120F ($55.14), breakfast included.

Hotel Jura, 11 Centralbahnplatz (tel. 23-18-00), is found near the train station in a building replete with so much modern art that you'll imagine yourself in a museum. The English-speaking Hess family directs this place, generously displaying the works by Léger and Matisse, which they own, plus the collection of Etruscan art maintained in the restaurant. This is indeed one of my favorite hotels in its category in Basle. Rooms are well maintained, tastefully appointed, and comfortable. Singles without bath cost from 45F ($20.68) to 55F ($25.27); with bath, 65F ($29.87) to 75F ($34.46). Doubles range from 80F ($36.76) to 90F ($41.36) without bath, from 100F ($45.95) to 140F ($64.33) with bath, breakfast included. If you plan to visit Basle during the autumn, be aware that hotel space is at a premium because of the many trade fairs. Reserve ahead.

Hotel Kraft am Rhein, 12 Rheingasse (tel. 26-88-77), is easily reached from the railroad station by taking tram 1 to the Rheingasse, where you'll be across the river from the old town's Rathaus and Münster, in a quiet ambience caused partly by the riverfront location. An attractive café/sun terrace gives you an opportunity to watch the summertime sunbathers on the stepped banks of the river, while the tastefully modern rooms (Oriental rugs and black-and-red plaid curtains) offer comfortable lodgings, often with a view. The public rooms are spacious, tasteful, and decorated with 19th-century antiques, oversize gilt mirrors, and Oriental rugs. The Waldmeyer-Schneiter family, the owners, spend much of their time maintaining the hotel, seeing to the needs of their guests and directing the service in the well-known attached restaurant, Zem Schnooggeloch. Rooms without bath rent for 34F ($15.62) to 48F ($22.06) in a single, for 58F ($26.65) to 90F ($41.36) in a double. Rooms with bath cost from 51F ($23.44) to 75F ($34.46) in a single, 82F ($37.68) to 125F ($57.44) in a double.

Hotel Drachen, 23 Aeschenvorstadt (tel. 23-90-90), is artfully maintained by Joe and Pia Dietlin, who offer pleasant rooms which are rather small but comfortably furnished. Many repeat visitors have come to know this well-established hotel. The 65 beds are in rooms with modern and spacious baths dramatically tiled in dark colors with checkerboard floors. All units also have radio, TV, and phone. Some apartments are offered to guests who plan to stay a long time. Two restaurants are connected to the hotel (see my dining recommendations). The hotel lies on a commercial street close to the Kunsthaus and the old city. Singles rent for between 42F ($19.30) and 80F ($36.76), while doubles range from 105F ($48.25) to 125F ($57.44), with a wide series of plumbing options and a free breakfast included.

Hotel Victoria, 3–4 Centralbahnplatz (tel. 22-55-66), across the street from the train station, is in a yellowish-buff-colored building with six floors of windows protected from the sun with red-and-white striped awnings. The hotel has its own parking lot, and the multilingual staff seems to know everything worth knowing about Basle. The windows of the 115 rooms are double-glazed to keep out the noise. Units are attractively furnished with low wooden beds, rattan-covered chrome and wooden chairs, radios, phones, mini-bars, and TV connections. Maintenance is generally on a high level. A bar area, attractively decorated in wood tones and latticed wooden ceilings, is patronized by the kinds of people you'd want to meet. The hotel contains two restaurants—a gaily painted, formal dining room with mirrors and excellent service, and a less formal Stanzlerstube, with a rustic wooden ceiling and hand-carved masks from the famous Basle "Fassnacht" festival.

The Gehring-Kleinert family manages this attractive hotel, where singles rent for anywhere from 60F ($27.57) to 90F ($41.36) and doubles go from 90F ($41.36) to 150F ($68.93). The less expensive units in both categories don't have private baths, but a breakfast buffet is included in either event.

Hotel Admiral, 5 Rosentalstrasse (tel. 26-77-77). If you're athletic, you'll be happy to discover the heated open-air swimming pool on the eighth floor of this commercial hotel, next door to the massive bulk of the Swiss Trade Fair. On clear days the view from here covers much of the surrounding area. The hotel itself is a balconied rectangle, and the roof section not covered by the pool is capped by a modified mansard roof of brown tiles. The 200 rooms are sunny and decorated in pleasing, coordinated colors, usually browns and soft oranges. You'll also find a bar, accented in key areas with black-and-white zebra stripes, and a pleasant restaurant. Single rooms cost from 40F ($18.38) to 70F ($32.17) (the lack of private bathrooms accounts for the low rate of the less expensive ones), while doubles range from 70F ($32.17) to 120F ($55.14), with breakfast. All units contain toilets, phones, radios, and TVs, and allow free access to the pool.

Hotel Spalenbrunnen, 2 Schützenmattstrasse (tel. 25-82-33), is an old-fashioned shuttered and gabled house sitting on a public square a few buildings from the green checkerboard roof of the Spalentor. The red stone fountain you'll see from many of the windows has the octagonal basin and the central statue on an ornate column you've seen often in Switzerland, but the setting is nevertheless charming and especially convenient, thanks to its location near a tram line. The house dates from the Middle Ages. Today the bedrooms are comfortably carpeted, with modern appointments, tiled baths, phones, TVs, radios, and mini-bars. The attached restaurant has lots of vaguely Spanish wrought-iron room dividers and pink napery, while a surprisingly intimate bar area looks like an up-to-date urban nightclub, with midnight-blue walls, pin spotlighting, and deep orange couches. Singles rent for 65F ($29.87) and doubles cost 120F ($55.14), breakfast included. Peter Allemann is the owner/manager.

Hotel Helvetia, 13 Küchengasse (tel. 23-06-88), is a recently renovated hotel on a small street one block west of the periphery of the public square facing the SBB train station. Its street-level entrance is almost entirely filled with a sympathetic restaurant in a Victorian theme of mirrors, blond paneling, maroon banquettes, and classical Roman busts in wall niches. This theme is repeated throughout the hotel, which charges 80F ($36.76) in a single and 120F ($55.14) in a double. All the fairly simple rooms have private baths plus all the modern comforts. The restaurant charges from 10.50F ($4.82) for a fixed-price meal, although no one will mind if you just stop in for a drink as it is one of the most attractive bars in Basle.

Economy Oases

Hotel Engelhof, 1 Stiftsgasse (tel. 25-22-44), looks back on an illustrious past as an upper-class residence dating from the 14th century. The facade breathes an aura of solid construction, with visible stone corner mullions, an entrance archway of carved stone which ushers guests into the cobblestone central courtyard, and an elegantly curved gabled roofline. Stiftsgasse is a small street about two blocks west of the curve in the Rhine. The comfortable rooms, which you can reach by elevator, are cozy, well decorated, and give a sense of well-being. Showers and toilets for some of the units are in the hallways, although some rooms have private facilities. Accommodations come with breakfast, which you'll take in the updated high-ceilinged dining room. Singles cost from 29F ($13.33) to 55F ($25.27), while doubles range from 60F ($27.57) to 86F ($39.52). There is no reception service after 1 a.m., although guests can let themselves in with their private keys.

Pension Steinenschanze, 69 Steinengraben (tel. 23-53-53), offers clean, safe, comfortable lodgings to "young maidens" under the age of 30, in a modern five-story building with lots of big windows, only ten minutes by foot away from the train station. Rooms are simply furnished, quiet, and sunny. The hotel sits on its own grounds, with a slightly overgrown garden behind the building. The director is Marcel Pierroz, who also offers tentative reservations to families, provided that they appear subdued and respectable. Singles rent for 40F ($18.38), while doubles go for 60F ($37.57) per day, which includes a continental breakfast.

Hotel St. Gotthard-Terminus, 13 Centralbahnstrasse (tel. 22-52-50), might be perfect for late-night arrivals in Basle. Opposite the train station, the hotel is identified by the five arched canopies in green fabric that stretch above the two doors and three picture windows on the facade of the building. Its two restaurants (one is less formal than the other) are open till midnight. One restaurant is in a warmly tinted brasserie style, while the main dining room has an elaborately patterned plaster ceiling suspended over turn-of-the-century bentwood chairs and lighting fixtures. The bedrooms might be considered slightly cramped, but you'll find them clean, comfortable, and safe. Many of the units have tiled baths, and those rooms which don't are, of course, cheaper. Singles rent for between 45F ($20.68) and 65F ($29.87), and doubles go for 75F ($34.46) and 95F ($43.65), breakfast included. The Geyer family owns this establishment and does everything possible, within reason, to help newcomers navigate Basle.

Hotel Bristol, 15 Centralbahnstrasse (tel. 22-38-22), facing the train station, rises like a baroque town house, with an embellished step pediment capping the facade's roofline, an ornately carved stone loggia between the windows of the third and fourth floors, and heavy stone detailing around the arches on the ground floor. The restaurant inside looks like a woodworker's dream because of its meticulously covered ceiling, walls, and floor, in polished paneling with dozens of architectural motifs worked into the designs. Not all the rooms upstairs have private baths, but singles rent for anywhere from 32F ($14.70) to 80F ($36.76), while doubles go for 55F ($34.46) and 105F ($48.25), breakfast included. You'll find the staff accommodating and helpful, and the units are a bit threadbare but clean.

Hotel Merkur, 7 Stänzlergasse (tel. 23-37-40), lies in a quiet part of town, an attraction for this hotel which is augmented by its discreet, unassuming management. Run by Frau R. Schneider, the hotel is housed in a five-story mustard-colored and brown building with pleasantly furnished, comfortable, and clean bedrooms. The Merkur is convenient to everything in town and should prove to be a solid and reliable choice, especially for women traveling alone. Singles with bath average 45F ($20.68); doubles, around 85F ($39.06).

Hotel Cavalier, 1 Reiterstrasse (tel. 39-22-62), is a small hotel (27 rooms) in a residential area west of the train station in a less congested part of town. The hotel sits at the end of a grassy plot of land, on a tree-lined street. It can be identified by its unpretentious white facade and its boxy, unadorned shape. All rooms have bath or shower, phone, and radio. A ground-floor restaurant is a little bare but serves satisfying meals to local residents. W. Gehrig, the owner/manager, charges 48F ($22.06) in a single, 82F ($37.68) in a double, breakfast included.

Park Hotel Bernerhof, 62 Elisabethenstrasse (tel. 23-09-55), is a park hotel in the sense that it lies across the street from the park which more glamorous hotels, such as the Hilton, also share. You'll be about a five-minute walk from the SBB train station here, as well as within walking distance of the old town and most of the art museums. The management usually consists of a colorful group of spry elderly women, who permit guests to park on a side street. The rooms are irregularly shaped, high-ceilinged, with weatherproof windows which, if you close them tight, keep out a lot of the noise. The furniture is interestingly old-fashioned. The major disadvantage is that the shower area for the bathless rooms is far away on the top floor under the eaves. In all, the price is right, and the location and cleanliness can make your stay pleasant. The hotel's 70 beds cost between 27F ($12.40) and 32F ($14.70) in a single, and between 50F ($22.96) and 65F ($29.87) in a double, all bathless.

Rooms with bath go for 55F ($25.27) in a single and 82F ($37.68) in a double. A simple restaurant is found downstairs.

WHERE TO DINE: Nearly 500 years ago Basle had an illustrious visitor, Aneas Silvio Piccolimini, who later became pope. About Baselers, he wrote: "Most of them are devotees of good living. They live at home in style and spend most of their time at the table." Not that much has changed today!

The Upper Bracket

Restaurant Bruderholz (Stucki), 42 Bruderholzallee (tel. 35 82 22). The gardens which surround the house serve as a backdrop for those diners who prefer to eat on the backyard terrace, but even the most elegant of gardens might not be the best format for the delicious cuisine cooked up by Hans and Susi Stucki in their gourmet restaurant a few kilometers outside of town. The house was a former private residence, which is today decorated with a gemütlich and patrician collection of antiques, oil paintings, and carefully crafted details which add considerably to the well-planned ambience. My favorite room is the salon vert, with its green napery, its Empire chairs, and the light-patterned Oriental rug whose colors are reflected in the cream-colored wooden walls, although there are two other well-appointed rooms at your disposal.

The restaurant enjoys renown all over Switzerland, and is considered the Basle citadel of haute cuisine, each dish prepared with artistry. Specialties are likely to include a filet of saltwater red mullet with coriander, a terrine of foie gras, a tomato stuffed with frog legs and served in a thyme cream sauce, or a lobster ragoût with truffles and baby leeks. The selle d'agneau (lamb) is cooked with a gratin of green beans, and the sweetbreads are masterful, as is the duckling with pesto and ratatouille. For dessert I'd suggest a compote of pears or a soufflé made with the fresh fruits of the season. Count on spending 100F ($45.95) for a gourmet repast here. It's open for lunch and dinner five days a week, from Tuesday through Saturday, except for the annual closing from mid-July until August 8.

Schloss Binningen, 5 Schlossgasse at Binningen (tel. 47-20-55), is the personal creation of Mario Hermann and his charming and chic Italian wife from Parma who have lavished attention upon the 16th-century château they acquired many years ago. The entrance hall is appropriately baronial, with a high ceiling and a carefully crafted loggia looking down onto the tile floor. The dining rooms are grand enough for a retinue of courtiers, packed with real antiques (the owner collects them), with an attractively understated service area of the most modern sort of stainless steel for efficient and excellent service. The grounds look almost like those of a private park, with a glass of wine, and from the terrace you could almost transport yourself back to another century.

Mr. Hermann's wine cellar is among the best in the region. There are at least 50 vintages not listed in the carte (the wine steward will make appropriate suggestions depending on what you order). The menu changes at least three times a year, so I hesitate to make specific suggestions. The fare, however, is likely to include such delectable dishes as a timbale de langoustines with caviar, a selle de chevreuil rôti (roebuck), a flan of salmon flavored with parmesan and served with an eggplant sauce, followed by a cold soufflé with kumquats, truly a celestial cuisine.

The menu gastronomique costs 85F ($39.06), and you can also order simpler meals or more elaborate à la carte suggestions. Usually the last orders go in at 9:45 p.m. On Sunday it serves lunch only, and on Monday only dinner.

Golden Gate, 42 Steinengraben (tel. 22-04-13), is a rendezvous for gastronomes in Basle. In summer you can dine in its attractive garden, retreating when the wind blows cold into its rustic interior, where you can order good-tasting and attractively served French specialties. It's open from 9 a.m. to midnight daily except Sunday. The interior, especially in winter, is very cozy, and the staff is most accommodating. Every Saturday evening there's a dinner dance. The Markus Hauenstein family, the owners, are proud of their many specialties, beginning with foie gras de Strasbourg, followed by those wide-flapped mushrooms in the Provençal style. It's on to escargots Bercy, coquilles St. Jacques, filet of beef with three types of mushrooms, scampi, sole meunière, veal kidney with mustard sauce, and entrecôte Strindberg. An excellent meal will cost from 60F ($27.57). There's a direct entrance from the second floor of the Steinenparking (elevator).

The Middle Bracket

Restaurant Schlusselzunft, 25 Freiestrasse (tel. 25-20-46). In summertime a café sits in front of this restaurant which lies in a street usually reserved for pedestrians. Clients enter an unpretentious street-level door and climb a flight of stairs, which is a woodworker's fantasy of massive balustrades of urn-shaped oak, before finding a high-ceilinged room with carved columns, simple tables, and lots of paneling, which during the daytime is flooded with light from the big windows. The building dates from 1486, and offers regional specialties, such as shredded veal and kidney in cream sauce, sirloin steak with pommes frites, and stuffed escalope of veal. Complete meals go for around 40SF ($18.38). The owner is Helmut Müller-Weber.

Restaurant Zum Goldenen Sternen, 70 St. Albanrheinweg (tel. 23-16-66), is the oldest pub in Switzerland, with a continuous history stretching back to 1421. You'll find it on the banks of the Rhine, in an unpretentious building which shares a common entrance with the apartment house next door. Wide planks are on the floor and wood beams and stenciled flowers cover some of the walls, while in some sections of the ceiling you'll notice lots of small panels with a star *(sternen)* carved into the center of each of them. Some Oriental rugs are scattered across the floor, the tables have blue tablecloths, and the front windows are covered with leaded strips of rounded glass. These details, plus the nonworking green tile ceramic stove against one wall, make up the decor of a historical locale that every Basler knows about.

The dishes are not outrageously complicated, but they're classic and good, with meals costing from 35F ($16.08). The appetizers are especially tempting, particularly the smoked eel and smoked trout. I've visited this establishment on several occasions over the years, and have also been fond of the terrine maison and the lobster soup. For the main course I'd recommend one of the following: carré d'agneau (lamb), filet of veal with citron, vol-au-vent, or Hungarian goulash with spätzli.

Pfauen, 13 St. Johanns-Vorstadt (tel. 25-32-67). This restaurant is known for its fish specialties, both freshwater and seafood. Of course you can also order traditional favorites such as rumpsteak, choice sirloin, and tournedos, each prepared only from U.S. beef. The restaurant has been honored with a local gastronomic award, the "Golden Fish Award." Set lunches range from 10F ($4.60) to 18F ($8.27), and at dinner you can order à la carte, spending from 13F ($5.97) to 35F ($16.08). The restaurant, run by Karl Ostertag, is open from 11 a.m. to 2:30 p.m. and 5 p.m. to midnight. It's closed Sunday evening and all day Monday. By the way, it's been under the ownership of the same family for the past three generations. The facade is similar to that of a narrow town house in a large city, with a view into the restaurant from the partially curtained windows on the ground floor. The interior is half-paneled and up-to-date, with immaculate white napery, simple chairs, and hanging lamps.

Restaurant Kunsthalle, 7 Steinenberg (tel. 23-42-33). This is one of my favorite restaurants in Basle. Located near the Kunsthalle's Tinguely Fountain, a huge rectangle of water set at ground level with amusing machines which electrically rotate to paddle, spray, agitate, or spit out water, presumably in mock battles with one another, the restaurant is exactly my fantasy of the kind of place where artists congregated in the early 20th century to talk about visual theories and politics.

You'll enter a beautifully paneled, vaulted room with huge murals filling the curved spaces with voluptuous nudes in a style like that of Rubens. A bar is at the far end, while a larger room to the right has higher ceilings and full-length windows with a view of the garden where tables have been set up as part of the outdoor café. Amusingly grotesque Fassnacht masks, complete with warts, leer at the diners above the stone arches, while prints and oversize oil paintings, presumably on loan from the nearby museum, decorate the walls.

It's possible to dine here for 15F ($6.89) to 30F ($13.79) and up, but many locals spend far more when they come for special celebration dinners. The Theaterteller plate is popular, consisting of Cordon Bleu maison, pommes frites, and a salad. Favorite dishes include the gazpacho, ravioli al pesto, and scampi with rice créole. Among the lavish chef's specialties are sweetbreads and scampi in champagne served with rice créole, lamb chops Beaucaire, and tournedos with small vegetables. A fine dessert is the sorbet vodka. Closed Sunday.

Café Spitz, 2 Rheingasse (tel. 25-94-66), is one of Basle's more prominent cafés, located near one end of a busy cross-river bridge (which has, by the way, a madonna's station midway across it). The building is designed to permit maximum views of the river traffic a few dozen feet away. The outside is elegantly airy, with big graceful windows, pleasing proportions, and a 19th-century construction of cream and light-mauve stonework in a style that is vaguely Moorish. The outdoor terrace is palatial, covered with many plants and flowers, with a green canopy over part of it. I always come here to sample one of the chef's six specialties of Basle, which range from salmon to beef goulash. For an appetizing beginning, try either the smoked river trout or the smoked morels. Among the fish dishes, the pike with tarragon sauce is generally excellent, as is the sliced veal Zurich style (prepared in a cream sauce). Count on spending around 50F ($22.98) for a big, filling meal here.

Restaurant Safran-Zunft, 11 Gerbergasse, (tel. 25-19-59). While admiring the medieval facade of this sprawling building, be careful not to step back into the narrow street—you might get run over by a tram. The entire structure is elegantly proportioned, with anywhere from four to five floors (depending on how you count the stairwells) of carved stone. On either side of the main entrance you'll see replicas of scholars or students crouched slightly above head level, while a fleur-de-lis graces the top of the archway. A wrought-iron sign hangs over the street with the logo of the restaurant, showing a gluttonous monk smelling the aroma from a goblet of wine. Inside, the restaurant is set up in a tavern style of red-checked tablecloths, paneling, simple chairs, and oversize Gothic windows with a stained-glass medallion set into the middle of each of them.

Most guests seem to visit this place to order the fondue Bacchus, done with veal with all the condiments, costing from 32F ($14.70) per person. The soups are usually good, most often clear broths such as oxtail with sherry. Irma and Jakob Stähli supervise a kitchen that turns out many other more elaborate specialty meals which might begin with such elegant appetizers as caviar or smoked salmon. You'll regularly find veal steak and chateaubriand on the menu. Meals cost from 40F ($18.38).

Hotel Drachen, 24 Aeschenvorstadt (tel. 23-90-90), serves some of the finest meals in the city. There's an expensive snackbar restaurant downstairs, with menus costing from 11.50F ($5.29), in a decor of stippled stucco and hanging lamps, (open 6 a.m. till 11 p.m. weekdays, from 11 a.m. till 9:30 p.m. on Sunday and from 7 a.m. till 11 p.m. on Saturday). Upstairs you can enjoy elegantly served and well-prepared food, with meals costing as much as 50F ($22.98) or more. Many French dishes appear on the menu which is international in scope. Favorite orders include filet goulash Stroganoff, selle d'agneau (lamb), ris de veau (sweetbreads) with morels, and veal piccata along with truite (trout) au bleu. The decor, by the way, is very appealing, with a personalized blend of modern tables and chairs in rigidly defined but pleasingly ordered rows. Serving accessories include lots of wheeled trays with cognacs and after-dinner drinks, plenty of warm colors, and a long wall of big windows with views onto the elegant buildings on the far side of the street.

Walliser Kanne, 50 Gerbergasse (tel. 25-70-17), attracts a local crowd rich in government and business leaders, soccer stars, and local show business types. The owner was a former resident of Zurich who moved to greener pastures in Basle, and today owns and directs this popular eatery where every dish is impeccably fresh and well prepared, and invariably seems to arrive with spätzle. It will cost from 12F ($5.51) to 17F ($7.81) for a fixed-price meal, and between 25F ($11.48) and 45F ($20.68) for an à la carte meal, which might begin with an hor d'oeuvres plate loaded with fresh salad, foie gras, shrimp, and a curry salad, followed by a three-meat main course (veal, beef, and pork covered with a savory sauce) accompanied by fresh vegetables and rice. Dessert could be a form of apple tarte with vanilla cream. Closed Sunday.

Escargot, Buffet de la Gare, (tel. 22-53-33). From the street the only thing you'll notice is a potted andromeda on the green terrazzo steps leading into the cellars of the SBB (where the trains to the rest of Switzerland leave). Don't be put off by the fact that this restaurant is in a train station. Inside it's warm and cozy, thanks to the hanging blue-and-white ceramic pots with ornate lids and handles which hang on heavy chains, illuminated from within. These, along with some discreetly placed spotlights, serve as lighting fixtures over the elegant bar area, whose walls are decorated with provincial illustrations of castles and trees, all very Swiss and very folkloric. The waitresses wear black vests and vertically striped skirts.

This is one of the best restaurants in Basle for la cuisine bourgeoise. A special part of the menu is devoted to French regional cookery, including tripes à la mode de Caen and other dishes. In honor of its namesake the kitchen prepares snails in three different ways. My favorite European vegetable, endive, is braised and served with butter here instead of just appearing in a salad. You'll find such French specialities as filet de sole bonne femme and coq au Morgon. In season you might order roebuck, and all year round unusual dishes appear, perhaps eggplant gratinée in the Egyptian style. I've always found the apfelstrudel the most reliable dessert. Expect to spend from 35F ($16.08) and up for a complete meal. Hours are from 11:15 a.m. to 2:30 p.m. and 6:15 to 11:45 p.m. daily except Sunday.

Restaurant Glogge, 3 Brunngasslein (tel. 23-32-75). A blue-and-white striped hanging awning, along with a recessed porch on the ground floor of this modern building, identifies the Glogge. When you enter you'll see a long narrow room with big windows looking into a sunny green garden area in the rear. In an ambience of heavy beams, red plaid tablecloths, and modern globe chandeliers, you find simple meals ranging in price from 8.50F ($3.91) to 12.50F ($5.74). However, should you partake of the à la carte menu, ordering some of the many top specialties, you're likely to spend from 50F ($22.98). For that you'll get several courses, including such main dishes as escalopes viennoises, grilled steak, sole meunière, and turbot with hollandaise, finishing with "omelette surprise" for dessert. The restaurant is popular for its district, and service is tactful.

Schlüsselzunft, 25 Freie Strasse (tel. 25-20-46). After a quick glance around the dining room you'll believe the claims that this is one of the oldest guildhouses in Basle, lying in the middle of the old town. Against one wall of the main room you'll see one of the most ornate ceramic tile stoves in Basle, embellished and painted over wide areas of its intricate surface. The wooden ceiling is supported by a centrally placed wooden beam, long ago worn smooth by the thousands of polishings it's received since it was first set in place. After you're seated, look for a special menu which lists seasonal specialties such as various types of fish or, in the autumn, venison. The menu has explanations in English. Strasbourg in Alsace moves a little closer to Basle when you order the foie gras, real goose liver, from that area. Soups include all the familiar ones, such as clear oxtail broth and lobster cream, but each one is well prepared. A fine selection of pasta is also featured, including cannelloni au gratin. The standard grills can always be ordered, but the chef has any number of other meat specialties including shredded calf kidney in a Madeira sauce. Specialties include veal curry, tenderloin steak with goose liver and morels, and shredded veal and kidney in a cream sauce with spätzli. If you're dining with a partner you can order two types of fondue, both chinoise and bourguignonne, or a double sirloin steak. Expect to spend from 35F ($16.08) for a complete meal.

Chez Donati, 48 St.-Johanns-Vorstadt (tel. 57-09-19), is a rendezvous point for Baslers, who come to savor the Italian specialties known throughout the region and who seek out the intimacy of the brasserie-style tables and chairs interspersed with statuary and elegant columns. The food here is among the best in the city. The chef's favorite specialties are homemade lasagne verdi and ravioli ricotta, followed by scaloppine in purgatorio and fegato (liver) alla veneziana. From October to December the chef is able to obtain white truffles which he uses with style and flourish. He also makes a spicy scampi maison. The price for an average meal ranges from 40F ($18.38) to 60F ($27.57), and hot meals are served from noon to 2 p.m. and 6 to 10 p.m. The restaurant is closed in July and every Monday.

The Budget Range

St. Alban Eck, 60 St. Albanvorstadt (tel. 22-03-20). Some of the original stonework can still be seen at the corner of this half-timbered house with the symmetrical glass windows. From the street you'll open a beautifully refinished oak door to reveal a small intimate restaurant with many graceful touches. The wooden tables with turned legs have without a doubt witnessed more than a few generations of Baslers sipping Warteck beer, the local brew of the region. The sign in front is in Victorian-style gilt lettering, and is set in a district with lots of architectural charm. This restaurant could be both a budget choice or an expensive place, depending on what you order. For example, if you go here for lunch you can select a soup and main course, beginning at only 10.50F ($4.83). However, should you elect to order from the à la carte speciality menu it takes no talent to spend from 50F ($22.98) and up. For that, you're likely to be tempted with such superb dishes as filet of perch with almonds, mignons de veau in Calvados, veal kidneys with morels, osso buco (the classic dish from Lombardy), or grilled sole with a remoulade sauce.

Da Roberto, 3 Kuchengasse (tel. 23-46-80), is housed in a series of rooms where you'll immediately feel at home, especially since you'll have a choice of three separate seating areas, all of which you might prefer to casually check out before finally selecting your favorite. Decor includes brown-and-white checked tablecloths, rustically paneled walls, and several kinds of hanging lamps shaped either like persimmons or like 1890s mid-Victorian fantasies. With their informality the casual staff will make you feel like one of Basle's younger crowd, particularly if you just prefer to sit at the mahogany bar with the comfortably padded suede chairs which, incidentally, give views of the entire warmly tinted establishment. The restaurant is only one block from the SBB train station, on a narrow side street with lots of activity.

At night much of young Basle often drops in here for the tasty pizzas, costing from 7.50F ($3.45) to 10F ($4.60). You can also order a daily special which is likely to range from gnocchi with gorgonzola at 10.50F ($4.83) all the way to filet of beef with fresh mushrooms and homemade fettuccine at 25F ($11.49). Naturally, soups, costing from 4F ($1.84) to 5.50F ($2.53), are a good buy, as are the spaghetti dishes, ranging from 6F ($2.76) to 11.50F ($5.29). Therefore, depending on what you order, you can dine here relatively inexpensively, enjoying the good food, lively atmosphere, and polite service. It's open Monday to Saturday from 11:30 a.m. to 2 p.m. and 5:30 p.m. to midnight (on Sunday from 11:30 a.m. to midnight).

Pagode, 32 Steinenvorstadt (tel. 23-80-77), as its name suggests, serves Chinese specialities, in this case from the Cantonese kitchen. It stands near the center of town, close to a major theater, cinemas, and the leading concert hall, so it might be ideal for an after-theater dinner. There's a wide selection of well-prepared dishes at moderate prices, a meal costing around 20F ($9.19) per person. The place always seems to be open, even on holidays (except Christmas). Waiters are polite and efficient. The same management also runs the slightly more expensive **Restaurant Hong Kong,** 91 Riehenring (tel. 26-88-14), near the Swiss Trade Fair and the Basle Congress Center. This is a very distinguished Chinese restaurant, offering both Cantonese and North China specialties, with meals averaging about 30F ($13.79) per person. It's closed on Monday and in the month of July.

Mövenpick, 30 Marktplatz (tel. 25-31-00). While many of the seats in this restaurant are out of sight of the buildings around the historic square where it's located, you'll still have enough of a choice usually to get a seat with a view. The room is an extended series of brick walls, rustic beams, dark paneling, and above the bar, an enormous inverted copper dish looking like a brewery kettle. The restaurant caters with efficient Swiss service to a middle-class crowd of locals. Chefs turn out the typical Mövenpick menu, which is international in scope, ranging from curry dishes from India to chili con carne from Texas to lasagne verdi from Italy. You can always get a rumpsteak or a mixed grill. Expect to spend from 14F ($6.43) to 21F ($9.65) for an average meal.

Pfeffermuehle, 4 Grunpfahlgasse (tel. 25-22-12). In an ambience of thick walls, massively beamed ceilings, antique pewter, and leaded windows, Nora Barabas and Jean-Carlo Erba have established an attractive luncheon and dinner restaurant with style and warmth. Even the menus are filled with amusing illustrations designed to make you smile. Hanging above the well-stocked bar are dozens of frequently burnished copper vessels, and behind the bar you're likely to see Jean-Carlo himself grilling meats over the enormous wood-burning fireplace of what looks like very old masonry. Everything is clean, imaginatively displayed, and friendly. It's open every day except Sunday and major holidays.

There's a wide à la carte menu, but if you're watching your francs, it's best to order from the daily menu, where set meals range in price from 9.50F ($4.37) to 17F ($7.81). Appetizers are intriguing, including air-dried beef from the Grisons, smoked trout or salmon, and snails. Fondues are also a specialty, and an unusual one is made with Calvados and green peppercorns. A couscous royal is prepared for two persons only, and there's also a selection of many classic Italian dishes, such as piccata milanese, and also French selections, including coq au vin or carré d'agneau (lamb) with gratin Dauphinois. Of course your tab will be far more if you order à la carte.

Restaurant Markthalle, 8 Viaduktstrasse (tel. 23-64-64), stands near the central railway station (SBB) in the heart of Basle in a long building whose facade curves around the bend in a busy city street, with four rows of massive windows edged in smooth-cut stone. The interior has decorative items like biorhythm and weight scales in the vestibule, followed by a series of rooms big enough to feed half of Basle. The first room is decorated in orange-and-white tablecloths, while another room has wood paneling and a square format. Clients who prefer to be more intimate can sit on a raised dais, semi-separated from the main room, but many prefer a table in the large main room near the heavily bordered windows. You can dine here very cheaply, paying only 15F ($6.89), or more expensively if you select from among the à la carte specialties. Watch for the daily specials, your best bet. In season the wild game dishes include, for example, peppersteak wild stag prepared hunter's style with homemade spätzli. The chef is equally adept at preparing both Swiss and French dishes. The filet de boeuf Markthalle is exceptional, and I like the filet tartar patron. You can also order a fondue bourguignonne.

Rialto, 45 Birsigstrasse (tel. 23-18-30). You can enter this restaurant from two levels, either from the bridge on the Viaduktstrasse, or from the Birsigstrasse three levels below. Strangely enough, the only way to get from one level to another is through the interior stairwell of the building itself, and no one will mind if you do just that. The exterior of the building was constructed in a style laughingly referred to as "Mussolini modern" in 1934. The freshly updated interior has modern parquet floors, and weathered timbers standing at random vertical heights as free-form room dividers.

A row of huge windows floods the entire length of the restaurant with light, and offers a view over a mass of treetops to the other edge of this small urban valley. An interesting feature inside is the large inverted copper dome hanging over the horseshoe-shaped bar. It has brass fittings all over it, any one of which would cost a small fortune today. The structure was probably used as a fermentation vat for a brewery before hanging above the bar. Open from 7 a.m. till midnight every day of the week, the restaurant serves filling meals, costing from 25F ($11.49), which are likely to include veal Cordon Bleu accompanied by spaghetti and a salad. You can also order more elaborate specialties, especially in the evening, for which you'll pay more. These are likely to be rumpsteak Madagaskar or entrecôte Café de Paris. The chef also does a fine scampi dish served Indian style, followed by his most classic Italian dessert, zabaglione. Service is competent and efficient.

Restaurant Elisbethenstübli, 34 Elisabethenstrasse (tel. 23-11-05). Rita and Ruedi Forster are the congenial owners who themselves prepare the well-seasoned budget-oriented fare served on the red-and-gray checkered tablecloths. The intimate lighting, beamed ceiling, and the green trim make the whole place cozy and effectively gemütlich. The restaurant is a decidedly local eatery, and if you have the good fortune to be there at closing, you'll see almost a cliché of one of the staff aggressively polishing every chair, table, and lighting fixture for the upcoming day's business. Meals from 19.50F ($8.95) include the range of standard Swiss dishes with such specialties as fondue at 11.50F ($5.28) per person.

Batterie, 18 Rappenbodenweg, in the suburb of Bottmingen (tel. 34-29-80), is good for another view of Basle, in an area where very few tourists ever venture. This eatery is similar to many other country restaurants in this part of Switzerland, although this one might be considered somewhat friendlier and more sympathetic than the norm. After driving down roads bordered with semi-rural houses and acres of crops, you'll see a sprawling country house with café tables in front and a graveled area for parking. The inside is filled with an unpretentious red-checkered decor where the windows are big, the bar is well stocked, and the service is friendly. This is a country eatery par excellence.

Many of the young people who patronize this out-of-the-way place come here at night to order pizzas, costing from 6.50F ($2.99) to 12F ($5.51), or the large number of various spaghetti plates, ranging from 6F ($2.76) to 9.50F ($4.37). However, you can order a complete Italian dinner for around 25F ($11.49) and up, enjoying such familiar dishes as Parma ham, stracciatella (the classic egg-drop soup of the Roman kitchen), piccata milanese, beefsteak pizzaiola, climaxed by a tasty zabaglione al Marsala.

WHAT TO SEE: The citizens of Basle have worked hard to preserve their old sector, which is one of the finest in Europe. Towering over this old town is the **Münster** (cathedral). This red Vosges sandstone building was consecrated as far back as 1019, but after an earthquake destroyed it in 1356, it was rebuilt along Romanesque and Gothic lines with a colorfully tiled roof in green and yellow. The cathedral (actually an abbey church since 1528) was founded by the Emperor Henry II.

The view of the cathedral from the right bank of the Rhine is renowned, as is the view from the Pfalz (palace), a 65-foot terrace in back of the building. From that terrace, you'll have a splendid view of the Rhine and can see into Germany's Black Forest.

The Münsterplatz, on which the cathedral sits, was built on the site of an old Roman fort. This 18th-century square is celebrated as being one of the most perfectly proportioned in Europe.

There's also an excellent view from the twin Gothic towers of the cathedral for those who pay the 1F (46¢) admission to go up. The facade of the cathedral is richly decorated, with figures depicting everybody from prophets to foolish virgins. Inside, the church has five aisles. One of its many treasures, seen at the end of the south aisle, is an 11th-century bas-relief. Its 1486 pulpit was carved from a single block of stone. There's a monumental slab on one of the pillars honoring Erasmus, who died in Basle in 1536. The church also contains the tomb of Anna von Hohenberg, wife of Rudolf of Habsburg.

The double cloister is entered on Rittergasse, and was erected in the 15th century on the foundations of the much earlier Romanesque structure.

Visiting hours are Easter to mid-October from 10 a.m. to 6 p.m. Monday to Friday; from 10 a.m. to noon and 2 to 6 p.m. on Saturday, and from 1 to 5 p.m. on Sunday. Otherwise, hours are from 10 a.m. to noon (not on Sunday) and 2 to 4 p.m.

Kunstmuseum (fine arts museum), 16 St. Alban Graben, contains one of the most remarkable collections of paintings in Europe, certainly the greatest in Switzerland. It has everybody from the old masters to 20th-century artists, and became a repository of many paintings labeled "decadent" by the government of Nazi Germany. Visiting hours are Tuesday to Sunday from 10 a.m. to 5 p.m. June to September, and from 10 a.m. to noon and 2 to 5 p.m. Tuesday to Sunday from October to May. Entrance is 3F ($1.38).

The gallery has an outstanding collection of the works of Holbein the Younger, who lived in Basle between 1515 and 1538, and came to the city when he was only 18 years old. For centuries the people of Basle have been able to view superb works of art by German and Swiss artists from the 15th and 16th centuries. Among these, Konrad Witz is a worthy candidate. But there is also a stunning collection of modern art, especially the impressionists. Picasso and Braque are followed by Chagall and Dali. Experimental works by contemporary artists are frequently changed.

Zoologischer Garten (zoological garden), adjoining the Hauptbahnhof, is known for its success in breeding in captivity wild animals on the endangered species list. It has some 2000 animals and 600 different species in a park right in the middle of the city. The zoo is one of the greatest in the world, enjoying wide acclaim. You can get *very* close to the animals. Trained elephants and sea lions perform tricks. The Vivarium is filled with everything from penguins to reptiles, and the monkey house has the an array of orangutans and gorillas. Visiting hours are from 8 a.m. to 6 p.m. (closes an hour earlier in winter). Admission is 7F ($3.22) for adults and 3F ($1.38) for children.

Spalentor (Spalen Gate) is one of the great monuments of Basle, dating from 1400 but much restored in the 19th century, and is considered one of the most beautiful in the country. It has two battlemented towers and is crowned with a pointed roof. The location is to the west of the university, marking the end of the medieval sector.

At some point in your sightseeing you'll want to take a ferry boat, the Münsterfähre, costing 6F ($2.76), to the right bank of the Rhina. Once you get off, you can stroll along the **Oberer Rheinweg,** a river esplanade filled with wood-frame houses pressed tightly against each other.

Historisches Museum (history museum), at Barfüsserplatz, is installed in a former 14th-century Franciscan church, containing many relics of medieval Basle among other exhibits. In this "church of the barefoot friars" on "barefoot square" are magnificent 15th-century tapestries and ecclesiastical art, including some removed from the cathedral. One of the best known sculptures is in the late Gothic style, depicting a *Babbling King.* Many treasures from the old Basle guildhouses rest here, as do upper-Rhenish Gothic sculptures. Its greatest exhibit is a reliquary bust of St. Ursula, in silver and gold, commissioned by the people of Basle to contain the saint's relics. The museum also displays mementos of Erasmus. It's open from 10 a.m. to noon and 2 to 5 p.m. daily except Monday. It charges 3F ($1.38) for admission, but is free on Wednesday afternoon, holidays, and weekends.

Haus zum Kirschgarten, 27 Elisabethenstrasse, is an 18th-century mansion turned into the "cherry orchard" museum, which may be visited from 10 a.m. to noon and 2 to 5 p.m., daily except Monday, for a 3F ($1.38) admission. It has an antique watch collection, plus some stunning porcelain, along with many old toys and period furnishings, including a kitchen. Look for the Aubusson tapestries.

The **Rathaus** (town hall), on Marktplatz, dominates the market square of Basle. It was built in the late Burgundian style in 1504, and is decorated with shields of the ancient city guildhouses. The sandstone building is adorned with frescoes, and has seen several later additions.

Mention should be made of the **University of Basle,** which lies on the south side of Petersplatz. Built during World War II, it was actually founded in 1460, making it one of the oldest citadels of learning in Switzerland. Its library, with one million volumes, has a rare collection of manuscripts, including works by Martin Luther, Erasmus, and the reformer Zwingli. The charter was signed by Pope Pius II, who participated in the Great Council which first met in Basle in 1431. The university has had some distinguished associates, including the cultural and art historian Jakob Burckhardt, the philosopher Friedrich Nietzsche, the physician Paracelsus, mathematicians Jakob and Johann Bernoulli, and, of course, Erasmus.

The **Jüdisches Museum,** (Jewish museum), 8 Kornhausgasse, contains an exhibition of valuable items connected with Jewish worship and religion. The museum has mementos of the first Zionist Congress, which was presided over by Theodor Herzl in Basle in 1897. It's open Monday and Wednesday from 3 to 5 p.m. and on Sunday from 10 a.m. to noon and 3 to 5 p.m.

Museum für Gegenwartskunst (museum for contemporary art), 2 St.-Alban-Tal, is the leading museum of Europe for modern art of the '60s, '70s, and '80s, including the works of such artists as Bruce Nauman, Richard Long, Jonathan Borofsky, Frank Stella, and Donald Judd. It's open Tuesday to Sunday from 10 a.m. to noon and 2 to 5 p.m. Entrance is 3F ($1.38).

North of the center, the **Port of Basle** is the terminus for navigation on the Rhine. The "Hafen," as it's called, is home to barge people from many European countries. From the silo terrace of the Swiss Navigation Company, reached by an elevator ride, there's a panoramic view of the Alsace plain, the Vosges, the Black Forest in Germany, and the Jura mountains. It's open daily from 10 a.m. to noon and 2 to 5 p.m. March to October, charging an admission of 2F (92¢). In winter the terrace is open only on weekends. The port, incidentally, opened in 1924, paving the way for Basle to become a great city of commerce.

A promontory called **Dreiländereck** (three countries' corner) juts out into the Rhine. If you walk around a pylon marking the spot, you can in just a few steps cross from Switzerland into Germany and then into France—and you don't need a passport!

TOURS: You can take sightseeing tours of Basle at 14F ($6.43) for adults, 7F ($3.22) for children. Departures are at 10 a.m. daily in front of the Hotel Victoria at the railroad station. Tickets can be purchased in advance at the hotel reception desk. The tour lasts 1¾ hours.

From the end of May until the beginning of October it's also possible to take a guided stroll through the old town. Tickets, purchased from the guide, cost 6F ($2.76) for adults and 3F ($1.38) for children. Tours are conducted on Sunday and Monday, departing at 3 p.m. in front of the cathedral.

As the gateway to Switzerland's Rhineland, Basle is a popular embarkation point for cruises on the river. The Rhine is navigable to Rheinfelden, and in summer **Basler Personenschiffahrts,** 55 Südquaistrasse (tel. 65-33-75), conducts cruises which cost 48F ($22.06) for adults and 32F ($14.70) for children.

WHERE TO SHOP: The fashionable shopping street of Basle is the **Freie Strasse,** leading to the market square and the town hall.

Bally Pflug, 38 Freie Strasse (tel. 25-18-98), sells shoes and leather goods from the most important shoe manufacturer in Switzerland. The Rohr family, the owners, make every effort to keep well stocked with the most recent models. Their elegant store has big display windows set into a five-story building which is whimsically decorated with three-fourths columns and carved bas-reliefs.

Kurz, 39 Freie Strasse (tel. 25-26-20), sells an impressive display of watches, jewelry, and mantelclocks.

Löw Boutique, 29 Freie Strasse (tel. 25-43-22), sells very fashionable clothes in an ambience that reeks of high quality. Garments, when I was last there, included suede skirts, hunter-style boots, and purses.

Ernest Beyeler Gallery, 9 Bäunleingasse (tel. 23-54-12). Collectors from all over the world frequent this internationally famous gallery, which sells a rotating series of painting and sculpture.

Galerie Pidoux, 24 Aeschenvorstadt (tel. 22-10-41), lies in a shopping arcade below the Hotel Drachen. Run by Herr Gass, the establishment sells 19th- and early 20th-century glass, as well as a host of knickknacks and art objects. Check out the collection of Gallé lamps and vases.

Davidoff, 4 Aeschenvorstadt, stocks a collection of an item which every pipesmoker knows about—briarwood and meerschaum pipes, along with cigarettes and cigars from around the world, including Havana.

City Apotheke, 4 Aeschenworstadt. Dr. Meier and his staff stock just about every medication made in health-conscious Switzerland and will give helpful advice about over-the-counter Swiss remedies for common aliments which might afflict you while traveling. The drugstore is open Monday to Friday from 7:30 a.m. to 6:30 p.m. and on Saturday from 8 a.m. to 5 p.m., and is centrally located to points of interest in the SBB train station and old town area. On weekends and at night, call the emergency number in Basle for medical, dental, and pharmacological emergencies: 22-22-18.

BASLE AFTER DARK: **Stadt-Casino,** Barfüssenplatz (tel. 22-23-23), offers musical acts in the Hans-Hüber Saal, which are frequently televised. Drinks cost from 15F ($6.89). It also has a disco inside, which you enter through the massive concrete entranceway of this 1930s-modern downtown building.

Café des Arts (Kunsthalle), 7 Steinenberg (tel. 23-42-33), lies near the famous Tingueley fountain in front of the Kunsthalle. This is one of the finest places in the city for drinks. In summer you might choose one of the café tables set up among ivy-covered trellises and modern and classical sculpture in the forecourt, although the green-painted walls with white detailing are also very appealing. The walls are full of risque art, such as nudes in many manifestations, including that of artfully blindfolded maidens holding lampshades above their heads. There's lot of attractively stylized buttock photography below ornate brass chandeliers. As in many places in Basle, you'll hear a lighthearted blend of American pop/rock music playing while you drink wine at 2.20F ($1.12) per glass and soups at 5.50F ($2.53) for a filling bowlful. Daily specials such as pot-au-feu are offered, also for 5.50F and up. The café is open seven days a week, from 11 a.m. to midnight Sunday to Thursday, to 1 a.m. on weekends.

Singerhaus, Am Marktplatz (tel. 25-64-66), advertises its striptease acts as "tasteful." You might see such aspiring disrobers as Gloria Garten or Zoe Zambei. All the action takes place every day (but Sunday) from 5 to 9 p.m., when a DJ plays disco. On Sunday afternoon, a live orchestra plays oldtime dance music from 4 to 7 p.m. Drinks begin at 15F ($6.89).

Hazyland, Heuwaage (tel. 23-99-82), is a rock-oriented nightclub attracting an electronic music–loving crowd generally under 30. A rotating group of live musicians from over much of the Teutonic world is engaged to play here. The club is open seven nights a week from 9 p.m. to 2 a.m. Drinks start at 10F ($4.60), and there's a restaurant inside.

Città 2000, 7 Ochsengasse (tel. 25-55-85). When I was last at this club the management had engaged a Mick Jagger look-alike to camp it up in the famous Rolling Stones style, complete with imitations of Jagger choreography. You might greet this with skepticism, yet many of the acts are enthusiastically cheered by the under-30 audiences. The disco draws a lively crowd every evening, opening at 8 p.m., with drinks beginning at 10F ($4.60).

Hotel Euler, 14 Centralbahnplatz (tel. 23-45-00). The elegantly appointed bar area is covered with crimson fabric, with tables that look like teak and containing little brass lamps. It's known internationally as a chic watering hole in Basle for many members of the world business community. The ceiling is one of those elaborately coffered numbers which any of us would like in our private homes. Even when it's crowded you'll rarely hear more than a polite murmur throughout its appealing square floor area. The chairs and banquettes are in dark leather. Drinks cost from 8F ($3.68).

Café Atlantis, 13 Klosterberg (tel. 23-34-00). Through the amber-tinted glass of the street level's panoramic windows you'll be able to judge if the ambience of this up-to-date hangout is for you. The cover charge varies according to the popularity of whatever musical act is appearing. When I was last there it was 5F ($2.30). The interior has beams, columns, and is open even for coffee in the morning. While you're there, be sure to walk up to the second floor for a view of the cathedral in an ambience of psychedelic mirrors, two bars, and a red-painted coffee room. It's open seven days a week from 8 a.m. on weekdays, from 10 a.m. on weekends. It closes at 1 a.m. on Friday, midnight on Saturday.

Old City Bar, Hilton Hotel, 31 Aeschengraben (tel. 22-66-22), is one of the most elegantly and consistently attractive places for a late-night drink or a before-dinner cocktail. The decor is plush, intimate, and low-key, with a pianist thumping out music which ranges from sophisticated sambas to understated show tunes. The location is one floor beneath the Hilton's main lobby, which you'll reach via a curved illuminated staircase. Drinks start at 3.80F ($1.75) to 5F ($2.30).

Bora-Bora Disco, Hilton Hotel, 31 Aeschengraben (tel. 22-66-22), is a relatively small room with a Polynesian theme, plus a DJ who plays everything from regional music to disco to Elvis Presley to an occasional piece by Mozart if he feels the audience would appreciate it. Lying two floors below the lobby of the Hilton, the club has a plush ambience. First drinks cost 15F ($6.89), and from 7.50F ($3.45) for each drink after that.

PRACTICAL FACTS: Basle Tourist Office, 2 Blumenrain (tel. 25-50-50), is open Monday to Friday from 8 a.m. to noon and 1:30 to 6 p.m., on Saturday from 8 a.m. to noon.

American Express, 48 Aeschenvorstadt (tel. 23-38-00), is closed Saturday afternoon and Sunday.

Laundromat, 79 Holeestrasse (tel. 39-27-22), is open weekdays from 9:30 a.m. to 6 p.m.

2. Targets in the Environs

Actually, everything in this chapter could be safely visited on a day trip while based in Basle. You're not only on the northeastern end of the Swiss Jura, but also in quick driving distance of Germany's Black Forest and the Vosges mountains of France. If you'd like to drive east, you can travel along Switzerland's Rhineland, heading in the direction of Lake Constance.

Instead of staying in Basle, you might want to locate at one of the smaller towns or villages nearby. I have a few suggestions, and they'll be followed by the major sightseeing targets of northwestern Switzerland such as Fribourg.

LANGENBRUCK: Lying about 19 miles from Basle, Langenbruck is a small holiday resort set in the midst of meadows and woods. The mountain ranges, which rise to 3610 feet, shelter it from the east and north winds. The village lies on top of the Upper Hauenstein Pass, a meeting point of several mountain valleys. The tourist office estimates that there are 125 miles of walks. With its ski lifts and ski jumping, it is also becoming a modest winter resort.

For food and lodging, the logical choice is the **Landgasthof Bären** (tel. 60-14-14), a comfortably proportioned, very old inn with a hipped tile roof, green-and-buff-colored shutters, and a faithful clientele. It was built in 1577 and reportedly sheltered Napoleon during one of his junkets in this part of Switzerland. Owned by the Grieder family since 1898, the hotel celebrates its status with a wrought-iron bracket holding an ornate depiction of a bear hanging over the pavement. The interior is predictably rustic, and includes a restaurant with three distinct rooms and a dancing bar. A bathless single rents for 28F ($12.86) a night, going up to 41F ($18.83) and 60F ($27.57) in a single with bath, depending on the size of the bed. A bathless double goes for 54F ($24.81), while a double with bath ranges between 76F ($34.93) and 92F ($42.27). Triples go from 92F also up to 110F ($50.54).

OLTEN: This important railway junction and industrial town lies on the banks of the Aare River at the foot of the Hauenstein. Because of its ideal location, the Swiss use it for many conventions and conferences. Frankly, for the tourist it merits only a passing stopover.

Take the covered wooden bridge (for pedestrians only) to the Altstadt or old town, which has many interesting and colorful old buildings.

The **Kunstmuseum** (fine arts) is open to the public from 10 a.m. to noon and 2 to 5 p.m. (closed on Monday and from mid-July to mid-August), charging an admission of 2F (92¢). It contains mostly 19th- and 20th-century paintings and sculpture. However, the work of the 19th-century artist Martin Disteli makes the museum notable. He was a famed artist, painter, and political caricaturist of his day.

Food and Lodging

Hotel Europe (tel. 22-33-55) welcomes visitors with a warm display of neon signs advertising the restaurant, pub, café, as well as the Tropicana dancing bar. The interior is tastefully appointed in floral prints, autumnal colors, and wicker furniture, with lots of big windows. Doubles with bath cost 105F ($48.25), while singles rent for 70F ($32.17), including breakfast. The hotel lies right in the geographical heart of town.

Hotel Schweizerhof (tel. 21-45-71) is housed on the banks of the Aare in a grand stone structure with a mansard roof, many gables, and a prominent illuminated sign set onto the roofline. The 42 bedrooms are updated and modern, with immaculate linens and plenty of space. Only two minutes by foot from the railway station, the hotel charges 45F ($20.68) for a single with bath, the cost jumping to 76F ($34.92) for a double with bath, including breakfast.

Zunfthaus zum Löwen, 6 Hauptstrasse (tel. 21-21-17), is Olten's most colorful restaurant, housed in the former meeting place of a medieval guild. Modernized with a panache that brings it very much into the 20th century, the establishment serves a nouvelle cuisine selection of such delicacies as terrine of crab, cabbage soup with rosemary and herbs from southern France, filet of sole, navarin of veal with crayfish (offered with a delectable spinach soufflé), and a pot-au-feu made with seafood and shellfish. The restaurant is in the very center of the old town. Fixed-price meals range from 22F ($10.10) to 87F ($39.98), the latter an epicurean delight, while à la carte choices range between 28F ($12.87) and 48F ($22.06). It's open daily from noon to 2:30 p.m. and about 6:30 to 10 p.m.

Restaurant Felsenburg, 157 Aaraustrasse (tel. 21-22-20), is decorated with lots of pieces of original art on its wood-paneled walls. Everything here is clean, efficient, and professional, so much so that many residents of Olten make this their preferred restaurant, especially for those who like elegant Italian food. Specialties include homemade pastas of all sorts, grilled meats, and an Italian delicacy known as cappelleti à la crème. You might also try escalope of veal with Marsala, risotto with parmesan, and as a main course, an entrecôte scheck. Fixed-price meals cost between a modest 11F ($5.05) and 17F ($7.81), with à la carte prices ranging from a low of 15F ($6.89) to a high that rarely goes beyond 45F ($20.67). The restaurant is closed Tuesday and for three weeks at some point every summer.

RHEINFELDEN: Called "Royal Rheinfelden," this is Switzerland's lowest altitude health spa. It faces the southern slopes of the Black Forest. Its salt springs, the Rheinfelden natural brine, are considered one of the major salt springs in Europe. Chances are, however, you won't be coming here to take "the cure," but to enjoy the Altstadt or old town, one of the most colorful in Europe. Old towers and ancient walls rise above the turbulent river, and at sunset, if caught in the right light, this is one of the most dramatic town views in Switzerland. The town has open-air swimming pools and much modern therapeutic equipment. Just outside the city are the famous breweries of Feldschlösschen and Cardinal.

Food and Lodging

Hotel Eden (tel. 87-54-06). From the front this family-run hotel looks like an old-fashioned resort. Partially hidden by towering trees and painted white, it's capped with a complicated red-tile roof. From the rear you'll quickly see that the Wiki family has imaginatively added a modern extension flanked by a landscaped swimming pool. This forms an attractive combination of old architecture, as exemplified by the high-ceilinged dining room with its vaulted arches, with new expanses of panoramic glass, as seen in the main lobby and reception area. On a per-person basis, rooms with full board cost from 75F ($34.46) to 90F ($41.35) without private bath, and from 98F ($45.03) to 145F ($66.63) with private bath. These rates apply in both single and double rooms. A reduction of 8F ($3.68) is made for clients who prefer only half board.

Hotel Schützen (tel. 87-50-04). Some of the rooms here are delightfully old-fashioned, decorated with parquet floors, high ceilings, and genuine antiques. You'll reach them via the gently sloping staircase, which is adorned with curlicues of wrought iron climbing up its balustrade. All of this is housed in an elegantly restrained gray building with white trim, red shutters, and a roofline that looks like something from Paris in the 19th century. The hotel can arrange an impressive collection of water and massage therapies, any of which will be explained by Mr. Stadelmann, the manager. Singles with private bath cost between 57F (26.19) and 67F ($30.79), dropping to 35F ($16.08) and 45F

($20.68) without. Bathless doubles range between 60F ($27.57) and 80F ($36.76), rising to 90F ($44.95) and 110F ($50.54) with private bath. Breakfast, which can be delivered to your room, is included. Full and half board are available for an additional 30F ($13.78) and 15F ($6.89) per person respectively.

Hotel Schwanen (tel. 87-53-44) is an elegantly constructed modern building, with maximum attention paid to the inclusion of large panoramic windows overlooking a flagstone terrace and manicured garden. The well-planned public room has a gemütlich feeling. The framework is of early 1970s construction, but many of the accessories, such as the chandeliers, are traditional. The combination of new and old is attractive. You'll find a swimming pool and a sauna to help you unwind before dinner in the comfortable restaurant. A full range of massage and mineral springs facilities is available, with special prices offered for stays of more than one week. However, for tourists in transit, singles cost from 76F ($34.92) without bath and from 94F ($43.19) to 104F ($47.78) with bath. Doubles rent for 72F ($33.08) per person without bath, from 90F ($41.36) to 102F ($46.87) per person with bath. All tariffs, both single and double, include full board.

Zum Goldenen Adler (tel. 87-53-32) stands in a prominent position in the center of the old town, housed a four-story country baroque building with three different colors on its elaborate facade and modified mansard roof. The interior is rustically gemütlich, complete with chalet chairs, a beamed ceiling, and a friendly reception from the formally correct owners, the Schärli family. None of their rooms contains a private bath, but shared facilities are easily accessible on every floor. Since there's no elevator, the cheapest units are on the top floor. With full board, rates range from 44F ($20.22) to 50F ($22.98) per person. If you want your room heated in winter, it costs an additional 2F (91¢).

ZURZACH: This popular spa, with three open-air swimming pools, grew up on the site of a Roman fort. Once it was a big river port with lots of Rhineland traffic. It lies across from Rheinheim, a German village reached by bridge. In fact, Zurzach is a good base for exploring many of Germany's Rhineland attractions, including the city of Koblenz. The town today contains many old burghers' houses and a church whose origins go back to the tenth century.

For food and lodging, my preferred choice is the **Hotel Zurzacherhof** (tel. 49-01-21). In summertime its bright awnings and concrete balconies can be seen from many yards away, although it can only be really appreciated from one of its panoramic terraces, sipping a drink and looking over the old town. The interior of the hotel is a mixture of contemporary with traditional, in a combination that many repeat visitors find winning. The most expensive rooms are decorated in a plush combination of padded French-style armchairs, ruffled vanity tables, and gold and scarlet brocades. The dining room has a beautifully grained wood-beamed ceiling and an intricately patterned Oriental rug set against the far wall. A fitness room, a sauna, and a covered swimming pool are on the premises. Each of the units has a private bath, costing from 65F ($29.87) to 77F ($35.38) in a single and from 59F ($27.11) to 69F ($31.70) in a double, depending on the season. All these prices are on a *per-person* basis, and include breakfast. Half board goes for an additional 21F ($9.64) per person daily.

The dining room, one of the best in town, specializes in such dishes as filet of sole, scampi, veal steak South Seas style, regional dishes, and a gratinée of seafood chef's style. For diners not staying at the hotel, reservations are suggested. Fixed-price meals cost between 24F ($11.03) and 48F ($22.06). The restaurant serves from 11:30 a.m. to 2 p.m. and 6:30 to 11 p.m.

3. Baden

The Romans, who called it Aquae Helvetiae, came here to bathe in its hot curative sulfur springs, hoping for relief from their rheumatism. By the close of the medieval period Baden's fame had grown until it had become one of the most important spas in the country, attracting the aristocrats of Zurich. Today it's known as the center of the Swiss electrical industry.

That doesn't mean to suggest that it's a dreary industrial town. Far from that, it's a tourist attraction even if you aren't interested in "taking the baths." The town is well endowed with hotels, tranquil parks, and a gambling casino adding a touch of class.

The first railway line in Switzerland started at this spa, and the old town where those passengers got off is still there. From the modern road bridge you'll have a good view of this medieval sector, with its colorful roofs split by dormers, and its narrow streets and squares. Later you can explore it, discovering many boutiques, shops, and art galleries.

The spa enjoys a panoramic site in the foothills of the Jura, built on both banks of the Limmat River (the same river we discovered in Zurich). Although included in this section on Basle for touring purposes, Baden is much closer to Zurich, which can be reached in less than half an hour.

The old covered wooden bridge across the Limmat has been preserved. If you walk across it, you'll end at the **Landvogteischloss,** or governor's mansion. The bailiffs lived here from 1415 to 1798, and the schloss has been turned into a historical museum which is open from 10 a.m. to noon and 2 to 5 p.m. except Monday and in February. It has displays of pottery from the area, antiques, armor, excavated coins, and folk clothing from the Canton of Aargau, in which Baden is situated.

You can also climb to the ruins of the **Castle of Stein,** a much-photographed site where a Swiss flag flies during the day. That wasn't always so: it was once a seat of the Habsburgs, and was attacked and destroyed more than once. The spa's skyline will unfold for you, characterized by the parish church, **Stadtkirche,** originally constructed from 1457, and by the **Tower of Baden,** a city landmark.

From Baden you can take at least two excursions, the first to visit **Habsburg Castle,** ancestral seat of the Counts of Habsburg. About ten miles from Baden, it lies near either Brugg or Bad Schinznach. Built on the summit of the Wülpelsberg, the castle today—or what remains—hardly suggests the power and sweep of a family that was to play such a central role in European affairs. There is a good view from the 11th-century keep, and a restaurant with a terrace has been installed. The place seems to be open all the time, at least from 9 a.m. to midnight any day except Tuesday in the off-season.

If you're motoring and it's a good day, you might also want to visit the old Cistercian **Abbey of Wettingen,** which has been turned into a school for teachers. It lies only two miles south of Baden. Founded in the 13th century, it receives visitors from 2 to 5 p.m., March to October, charging a 3F ($1.38) admission. The cloisters are Gothic, and the stained glass is from the 13th to the 17th centuries, some of the most remarkable I've ever viewed in Switzerland. The original abbey church was destroyed, but the present building, in the baroque style, contains some finely carved choir stalls that are exceptional in their artistry and detail.

THE SPA RESORTS: Hotel/Restaurant Du Park, 24 Römerstrasse (tel. 20-13-11), enjoys an attractive location between the city park and the thermal baths. It benefits from the most modern architectural principles and partially encloses a massive copper beech. The rooms are tasteful, filled with warm colors and lots of light. The bar, the informal bistro, the restaurant, and the grill room are engagingly decorated with a maximum usage of natural materials such as wood, stone, and unglazed tile. Archeologists will be interested in the statuette of Silenus, companion god of Bacchus, which was discovered by workmen during excavations for the hotel. The bronze depiction of the wizened deity is displayed along with other ancient objects and has become the logo of the hotel. Du Park is affiliated with the Best Western chain, charging from 75F ($34.46) to 95F ($43.65) in a single and from 88F ($40.44) to 145F ($66.63) in a double. All units contain private bath, radio, mini-bar, and phone, and tariffs include breakfast. Peter Walter, the manager, does much to make his guests content.

Hotel Linde, 22 Mellingerstrasse (tel. 22-53-85), rises in a multitiered collection of dramatic angles and jutting balconies. The street-level floor and the two floors above it house restaurants, summertime terraces, and attractively decorated public rooms (one of which is surprisingly rustic for such a skyscraper). The bedrooms are unpretentiously decorated in simple functional furniture and fiesta colors. The Wanner family are your hosts, charging between 67F ($30.78) and 72F (33.08) in a single with bath and between 100F ($45.95) and 120F ($55.14) in a double with bath, breakfast included. The same family, by the way, runs a popular cafeteria and a pastry shop and bakery on the ground floor as well.

Badhotel Limmathof (tel. 22-60-64). Sections of this hotel still retain their 19th-century opulence and have plenty of romantic touches, from the wrought-iron detailing on the riverside terrace to the tapestries, antique carpets, and settees of the public rooms. The building is a well-constructed remnant of another era, with a beautiful two-toned facade complete with corner mullions and restrained detailing around the windows. The hotel also has a swimming pool and a formidable array of massage and hydrotherapy programs, which complement the good cuisine and attentive service. Singles with private toilet and running water cost 60F ($27.57), rising to 75F ($34.46) with full bath. Doubles with running water and private toilet range between 110F ($50.54) and 120F ($55.14), peaking at 130F ($59.73) and 150F ($68.92) with full bath. Half board costs an additional 16F ($7.35) per person daily.

Hotel/Restaurant Kappelerhof, 142 Bruggerstrasse (tel. 22-38-34). Although the management claims that this hotel is now in its fourth generation of family ownership, you'd never realize it by looking at its facade. The structure is designed around two huge concrete cubes. One holds the ground-floor restaurant, whose wooden ceiling and patterned carpet represent the latest in angular architecture, while another holds the more starkly furnished bedrooms. The basement contains two automated bowling alleys. Each of the 30 units has its own shower, radio, and phone. Singles cost between 55F ($25.27) and 75F ($34.46), while doubles range between 85F ($39.06) and 110F ($50.55).

Bade-Hotel Bären (tel. 22-51-78) has been under the competent management of the Gugolz family since 1904, although a historian recently found a document mentioning an inn on this site in 1361. The elegantly neoclassical facade of the present hotel rises grandly above a well-maintained park dotted with sculpture. The overall effect is calm and serene, everything enhanced by the calm surveillance of the female demigods adorning one wing of the building. The spacious public rooms inside are filled with a mixture of modern pieces with groupings of late-19th-century antiques. The 80 bedrooms are priced with full board included. In either a single or double, bathless rooms cost between 59F ($27.11) and 69F ($31.70) per person, going up to 69F ($31.70) and 89F ($40.89) per person with partial bath, or 80F ($36.76) and 98F ($45.03) per person with full bath. Béatrice Wüscher is the director, and she's happy to explain the many mineral and massage treatments available at the hotel.

Verenahof Hotels (same telephone for all three—22-52-51) are actually a well-planned complex of three hotels, all of them connected by a covered passageway to a thermally heated swimming pool and a well-equipped medical therapy center. The entire complex is beautifully surrounded by landscaped gardens, verdant lawns, and sunny terraces, making a calm oasis for travelers. The hotels making up this group include the following.

Hotel Verenahof dominates the Kurplatz with its imposing facade of 19th-century gray carved stone. Its interior is filled with tall Doric columns, discreet geometrically patterned carpeting, well-crafted paneling, and elegant bedrooms with well-upholstered antiques and big sunny windows. Bedrooms, either single or double, with full board cost from 85F ($39.05) to 95F ($43.65) per person without private bath and from 105F ($48.24) to 125F ($57.44) per person with private bath.

Hotel Ochsen looks more like a homey country inn than the others in the group. It has a red tile sloped roof and flowers on the ledges of the second floor. The hotel lies on both sides of Badstrasse, with a covered passageway connecting the second floors of both sections. The bedrooms have been completely renovated. Including full board, *per-person* rates range from 75F ($34.46) to 95F ($43.65) in a single or double without private bath and from 105F ($48.25) to 125F ($57.43) with private bath.

Finally, the **Hotel Staadhof** is the most recently constructed of the three hotels, and definitely the most imaginatively designed. The exterior almost resembles a cascade of gray stalactites clustered into symmetrical rows with tall narrow windows piercing the facade in hundreds of places. The entire edifice is capped with garlands of hanging greenery which grows in pots on the upper terraces. The interior is spacious and attractively sophisticated, with good color choices and ample use of natural materials. The most expensive of the three hotels, it charges from 115F ($52.84) to 135F ($62.03) *per person* daily in a room with a partial bath (sink and toilet), in single or double occupancy with full board included. Rooms with full bath range between 135F ($62.03) and 230F ($105.69) per person daily, with the most expensive room being a particularly opulent suite. These latter rates also include full board.

A SIDE TRIP TO BRUGG: Six miles northwest of Baden, Brugg was founded by the Habsburgs in 1232. It lies near the point where three rivers converge, the Reuss, Aare, and the Limmat (the latter flowing through Zurich). It's a minor tourist center and also a headquarters of industry. But mainly it's known for its bridge, as its name would suggest. Near the bridge stands the Schwarzer Turm or "black tower," dating from the 11th century. At no. 39 on the main street is the house in which Heinrich Pestalozzi, the educator, died in 1827. A local museum, the Vindonissa, contains artifacts excavated from a Roman fort.

For food and lodging, the preferred choice is **Rotes Haus** (tel. 41-14-79). You'll be surprised to find that this hotel is painted an appealing shade of pastel pink instead of red, as implied by its name. The entire edifice is painstakingly trimmed with white shutters and detailing. The interior contains no less than ten different rooms for eating and drinking, all of them with different teutonically inspired names (some, however, are used exclusively for private gatherings). The rooms are uniformly decorated in an updated rustic ambience of bright colors and heavy beams. Doubles with private bath rent for 70F ($32.16), and singles, also with bath, going for 39F ($17.92), including breakfast.

4. Solothurn

The capital of a same-name Swiss canton, Solothurn at the foot of the Jura is ancient. On the banks of the Aar, it is, according to a 16th-century rhyme, "the oldest place in Celtis save Trier." Roman inscriptions calling it Salodurum have been found, as have the remains of a Roman castrum. In its long history it has been fortified many times—and with good reason.

THE SIGHTS: Like most Swiss towns of its vintage charm, it has an old town, lying on the left bank of the river and still partially enclosed by its 17th-century walls. Inside are numerous Renaissance and baroque buildings. The town enjoyed its greatest prestige when it was the residence of the French ambassadors to the Swiss Confederation from the 16th to the 18th centuries. Solothurn became part of the Confederation as early as 1481.

The old town is entered through the Biel Gate or the Basle Gate. The heart of the old sector is the Marktplatz, with a clock tower, a pulsating place with a wide variety of fruits and vegetables. The **Rathaus** (town hall) is from the 15th century, although its doorway is in the Renaissance style. The two most colorful streets I found were Hauptgasse and Schaalgasse, where you'll see many wrought-iron signs and brightly painted shutters.

The **Cathedral of St. Ursus,** in the grand baroque style, dates from the 18th century. It is said to have been erected on the spot where its namesake was martyred. The cathedral lies just inside the 16th-century Basle Gate and was constructed by builders from Ticino, hence its Italian appearance. Try to visit the gardens on the east side of the church. Since 1828 this has been the seat of the bishop of Basle.

Nearby, slightly to the northwest of the cathedral, stands the **Altes Zeughaus** (old arsenal), said to house the second-largest collection of weapons in Europe. The most fascinating exhibits are the medieval weaponry. Many military uniforms of the Swiss are also shown. Charging 2F (92¢) for admission, it's open from 10 a.m. to noon and 2 to 5 p.m. daily except Monday. It's also closed mornings in winter.

You should visit the **Kunstmuseum Solothurn** (or municipal museum), if for no other reason than to see the *Madonna of Solothurn* by Holbein the Younger, a notable painting. Also outstanding is a 15th-century painting on wood from the Rhenish school, the *Madonna with the Strawberries.* The museum is open from 10 a.m. to noon and 2 to 5 p.m. except Monday, charging 2F (92¢) for admission.

The **Jesuitenkirche** or Jesuits' church, on Hauptgasse between the cathedral and the marketplace, dates from 1680. It should be visited for a look at its three-bay nave which is richly frescoed.

The Solothurn tourist office, the **Verkehrsbüro,** 69 Hauptgasse (Kronenplatz) (tel. 22-19-14), will provide you with a map and pinpoint several interesting day excursions, such as a trip by boat on the Aare River to Biel, with a stopover at the Altreu, the first stork colony in Switzerland.

But if you've got two hours to spare, take the six-mile run to one of the major attractions of the country, the **Weissenstein.** The panoramic view of the Jura from here is about as impressive as you'll see anywhere. Getting there by car will be difficult, even dangerous, on narrow roads with hairpin curves, so it's best to take the chair lift from the Oberdorf station, which will deliver you to Kurhaus Weissenstein.

In fair weather the lift runs from 8 a.m. to noon and 1:30 to 6 p.m. (on Sunday, from 8 a.m. to 6 p.m.). In winter service is curtailed to 9 a.m. to noon and 1:30 to 5 p.m. (on Sunday, from 8 a.m. to 5 p.m.). The round-trip fare is about 9F ($4.14). On a clear day you can't see forever, but you can view Mont Blanc. You can also see Berne and Neuchâtel Lake, among other horizon-spanning geography.

FOOD AND LODGING: **Hotel Krone,** 64 Hauptgasse (tel. 22-44-12). Because of the links Solothurn has traditionally maintained with France, the gilt lettering on the pink facade of this hotel spells the name out in French (Hôtel de la Couronne). Don't be confused, because it would be unfortunate to miss this one as it's one of the oldest inns in Switzerland. Elegant touches throughout the hotel, both in furnishings and architectural detailing, make it extra special. Judging from the business in the restaurant, the grill room, and the bar, many local residents think so too. Each of the spacious bedrooms has its own private bath, and is decorated either in Louis XV or Biedermeier furniture. Standing in the sunlight from the oversize windows, it's easy to understand why Napoleon's wife, Josephine, chose to stay here for several days in 1811. Singles cost between 50F ($22.96) and 80F ($36.76). Doubles range between 100F ($45.95) and 140F ($64.33), and all rates include an abundant morning breakfast buffet. Each of the units has a phone, TV, radio, and mini-bar. Mr. and Mrs. Kung, your charming hosts, also supervise the high-quality cuisine in the kitchens. Specialties include veal steak royal, ris de veau (sweetbreads), and stuffed breast of chicken.

Hotel/Restaurant Roter Turm, 42 Hauptgasse (tel. 22-96-21). The medieval logo hanging from a wrought-iron bracket over the sidewalk is of a red enameled tower, and the illuminated sign below it spells out the name of the hotel in French. And so you'll be sure to find it, remember that it's next door to the gargoyled clock tower of St. Ursus's Cathedral. The Lorenz family has added a row of floor-to-ceiling glass panels in the restaurant in the rear of the building, and have retained a very competent kitchen staff to prepare the well-planned meals. The bedrooms are predictably modern, with very comfortable beds. Doubles with private bath cost 78F ($35.84), while singles with bath rent for 52F ($23.89), including breakfast.

Hotel Astoria, Wengistrasse (tel. 22-75-71), is conveniently located just outside the old town in a contemporary building near the Solothurn west train station and the main post office. The interior is graced with many large windows, particularly in the roof garden restaurant, where diners can view sections of the old town. The Farese family charges from 43F ($19.76) to 49F ($22.52) for a single and from 67F ($30.79) to 73F ($33.54) in a double, including breakfast.

Restaurant Misteli-Gasche, 14 Friedhofplatz (tel. 22-32-81). The culinary combination of chef Peter Misteli and his son is a difficult one to beat, especially when much of the region travels long distances to sample their appetizing blend of French food and local recipes. Specialties include a variety of fresh seafood, especially lobster and oysters, rack of lamb with rosemary and Provençal herbs, and medallions of veal steak Jacquaise. The gratinée dauphinoise is a recipe many of us would like to duplicate in our own kitchens, but father and son probably won't part with their secret. The restaurant is closed every week from Sunday evening until Tuesday at 9 a.m. and for three weeks sometime in midsummer. You'll find the place near the center of town, in a very comfortable cadre where you'll probably feel immediately at ease. Fixed-price meals range between 20F ($9.19) and 27F ($12.40), while à la carte dinners cost anywhere from 19F ($8.73) to 36F ($16.52).

Restaurant Tiger, 35 Stalden (tel. 22-24-12), is easy to find, as it lies in the center of town near the Friedhofplatz. The establishment is owned by Peter

Klaus, who prepares such specialties as fresh- and saltwater fish, veal steak with aromatic herbs, filet of pork Portuguese style, and calf liver with the preferred potato dish of Switzerland, rösti. You might try some of the Swiss cheese selections you've heard about, since the cheese platter here contains some local varieties never exported.

Fixed-price meals cost between 13F ($5.97) and 20F ($9.19), while à la carte meals range between 17F ($7.81) and 30F ($13.79). In summer you might prefer to dine on the terrace of this restaurant which is closed every Wednesday and for two weeks in February.

5. Fribourg

One of the great medieval towns of Switzerland, Fribourg, a stronghold of Catholicism in the country for centuries, is decidedly bilingual. Its German name is Freiburg. Places on the left bank of the Sarine River possess French names and those on the right bank go by German titles.

Fribourg has been called a "flower of the Gothic age," and as that appelation would suggest, there is much to see and explore here. Allow at least a day for it, and know then that you will have only skimmed the surface. Once a sovereign republic, Fribourg today has a population of some 40,000 people, including many university students. It has not only a Catholic University, but a famous boys' college, and many other educational establishments which enrich its cultural life.

It's easily reached by rail or road, and is served by the Federal Railways express trains, lying less than two hours from the international airports of Geneva, Basle, and Zurich. It's at the hub of a network of motorways, the position so strategic that it's been called a veritable crossroads of Europe.

In a setting between lakes and mountains, Fribourg was founded in 1157. In medieval days it became known throughout Europe for its dyers, weavers, and tanners. Once it was ruled by the House of Savoy, but in 1481 it became a member of the Swiss Confederation and is today the capital of a canton of the same name.

The oldest part of town, called "the Bourg," lies just above the Sarine riverbank and is flanked by the Auge and Neuveville sectors. These, along with the Planche sector on the right bank, form what is known as the Ville Basse.

THE SIGHTS: Other than the wide panoramic view of the site of Fribourg, its single major attraction is **St. Nicholas' Cathedral,** whose lofty Gothic belltower from the 15th century dominates the rooftops of the medieval quarter. The nave dates from the 13th and 14th centuries, although the choir was reconstructed in the 17th century. The choir stalls are exceptional, some carved as early as the 15th century, and the Chapel of the Holy Sepulchre, built in the 15th century, has some remarkable stained glass, an Entombment from 1433, and a celebrated organ. Much about this cathedral impresses me, but especially the tympanum of its major "porch," which is surmounted by a stunning rose window devoted to the Last Judgment.

After leaving the cathedral, you'll be in a particularly fascinating architectural zone of Fribourg, with many old patrician houses. Hopefully, you'll have time to walk and explore at your leisure, taking in the high-ranging rows of houses from the Gothic era, the small steep streets, and the squares adorned with fountains.

Whether it's called the Rathaus in German or the Hôtel de Ville in French, the **Town Hall** of Fribourg is a notable building from the 16th century, with an octagonal clock tower where mechanical figures strike the hours. Outside the Town Hall, the seat of the State Parliament of Fribourg, farmers' wives sell their produce fresh from the fields nearby. Many are in traditional garb, and market days are Wednesday and Saturday, which I find the most colorful time to visit the city.

The **Église des Cordeliers,** or Franciscan Church, is the second ecclesiastical building of note, lying north of the Place Nôtre-Dame with its 12th-century church, the oldest in the city. The choir at the Franciscan church is from the 13th century, the nave constructed in the 18th century. The church has an outstanding triptych, gilded and carved in wood, which dates from 1513, but its pièce de résistance is the splendid altarpiece rising over the main altar. This was the work of the "Masters of the Carnation," two artists who signed their works with a white and a red carnation in the 15th century. Before leaving the church, try to find the carved oak stalls from the late 13th century in the chancel.

The city also has an outstanding **Art and History Museum,** housed in an imposing Renaissance building, the Hôtel Ratzé. Here the epic sweep of Fribourg's history comes alive, especially in the sculpture and painting left over from the Middle Ages. The stained glass, some dating from the early 16th century, is exceptional, as are the antique French furniture and the Gobelins tapestries. The museum is open daily, July to September, from 10 a.m. to noon and 2 to 7 p.m. except on Monday. On Thursday night it stays open until 10 p.m. In other months it's open only on Tuesday, Wednesday, and Friday from 2 to 7 p.m., from 2 to 10 p.m. on Thursday, and from 10 a.m. to noon and 2 to 7 p.m. on weekends; again it's always closed on Monday. In the peak summer months admission is raised to 6F ($2.75), dropping to just 4F ($1.83) in winter.

If your schedule can possibly accommodate it, the ideal time of the year to visit Fribourg is for the international folkloric meeting, usually at the beginning of September or perhaps earlier. Yodeling, wrestling, and a game called hornussen dominate the festivities, and hotel bookings are difficult to get.

To reach the **upper town** of Fribourg, you can take a funicular, and at some point in your discovery you'll want to seek out the covered wooden bridge, the **Ponte de Berne,** constructed in 1580.

Fribourg is also the center for some important tours, although the Freiburger will tell you, "One has everything here, one doesn't have to go anywhere." Nevertheless, an 18-mile, hour-and-ten-minute ride will take you to **Schwarzee** or "the black lake," at about 3500 feet. This is both a summer and a winter resort (a very minor one), and is known for its beautiful mountain setting with wooded hills.

Another excursion will deliver you to **Hauterive Abbey,** some 4½ miles southwest of Fribourg. This was a Cistercian abbey built in a bend of the Sarine River. Its church, dating from the 12th century, has some beautiful stained glass from the 14th century and some elaborately carved stalls from the 15th century. Visits are possible Easter until mid-September from 8:30 to 10:15 a.m. and 2 to 5 p.m. on weekdays (on Sunday from 11 to 11:30 a.m. and 3:30 to 5 p.m. Otherwise, hours are from 10 a.m. to noon and 2:30 to 4:30 on weekdays (on Sunday from 11 to 11:30 a.m. and 2 to 4 p.m.).

Hopefully you'll get back in Fribourg by sunset and can cross the **Zähringen Bridge,** from which you can enjoy a great view of this famous old city which has loomed so large in Swiss history books.

The **Office du Tourisme** is at 30 Grand-Places (tel. 22-11-56).

WHERE TO STAY: **Hotel Alpha,** 13 rue du Simplon (tel. 22-72-72), lies only 300 yards from the train station (CFF), behind an ultramodern facade that could as easily be found in the U.S. as in historic Fribourg. All the windows are big enough to allow a maximum amount of light into the plushly padded bedrooms, where ample use seems to be made of brown velvets. In addition to the beamed dining facilities and the Safari bar and grill, the hotel has a group fitness program, coupled with massage, that seems to be a popular event in town. Each of the accommodations has its own private bath, costing 55F ($25.27) in a single, 90F ($41.35) in a double, and 135F ($62.03) in a triple, including breakfast. The color TV in the room usually receives ten channels from at least three countries, which should give you an interesting experience in cross-cultural viewing.

Eurotel, 15 Grand-Places (tel. 81-31-31). From the look of it this appears to be the tallest building in town, rising above its neighbors in a flourish of well-designed concrete and glass. You'll be just two minutes from the main station, and your room will likely be cheerfully decorated in shades of orange and umber, with lots of space and views over most of the city. Under the same roof you'll find a swimming pool, a bar, a nightclub for dancing, and several sun-drenched terraces with waiter service. Singles cost between 60F ($27.57) and 85F ($39.06), while doubles range between 95F ($43.65) and 125F ($57.43) All accommodations contain private baths. The brasserie-style restaurant serves American-style beef in a nautical setting. Fixed-price meals cost around 60F ($27.57), with à la carte dinners beginning at 42F ($19.30).

Hôtel de la Rose, Place Notre-Dame (tel. 22-46-07). The building dates from the 17th century, which becomes obvious as soon as you descend into the vaulted cellars where the Vielgrader family has installed a cheerfully decorated bar. The edifice sits on a centrally located square near the cathedral, which you'll be able to see in all its illuminated glory from the hotel's flagstone terrace. Many of the architectural touches are charming (I particularly like the warm elegance of the upstairs cocktail lounge). The bedrooms are freshly painted, usually in white, with occasional touches of vivid color. The 82 beds rent for between 55F ($25.27) and 70F ($32.16) in a single and between 95F ($43.65) and 110F ($50.54) in a double. All units contain private baths, and tariffs include breakfast. Half board is offered for an additional 20F ($9.19). A French restaurant and a happily cluttered pizzeria are also on the premises.

Hôtel Duc Bertold, 112 rue des Bouchers (tel. 23-47-33), is centrally located in the old town between the cathedral and the Zähringen Bridge. The roofline of this historic hotel is so unusual that you'd easily think it's made up of two different buildings joined together. Once you're inside, there's no inconsistency to the generally good service and the tasteful modern decor. In addition to two restaurants, you'll find a bar and disco called "Disco Duc." Bathless singles cost 39F ($17.92), going up to 54F ($24.81) and 77F ($35.38) with bath. Doubles, all of which contain baths, cost between 82F ($37.68) and 104F ($47.79), including breakfast.

WHERE TO DINE: **Le Vieux Chêne,** 17 route de Tavel (tel. 28-33-66). Some four years ago Roger Bertschy opened a restaurant in an aging villa with a view of Fribourg, and ever since, his reputation has spread throughout the region. He serves a local favorite, fondue, along with a variety of more original recipes which include a delectable lobster salad with fresh mushrooms and artichoke hearts, a gratinée of fresh fish and crustaceans, sole with morels, a seafood pot-au-feu, a gratinée of fresh mussels with green peppercorns and spinach, and a risotto textured with shellfish. Meat dishes include suckling veal with raspberry vinegar and two kinds of lamb in a tarragon sauce. The restaurant is closed on Monday and from mid-August to mid-September. It's a good idea to phone ahead for reservations. Fixed-price meals cost between 30F ($13.78) and 69F ($31.70), while an à la carte dinner would range from 28F ($12.87) to 57F ($26.19).

L'Aigle Noir, 58 rue des Alpes (tel. 22-49-77), tends to attract a wealthy and conservative crowd of seasoned diners who appreciate the early-18th-century ambience of the former aristocratic residence which houses it. The owners are a gifted and dynamic couple named Raemy, who have established a brasserie on the ground floor and a more formal restaurant on the same premises. The restaurant's specialties are a ragoût of fresh mushrooms in a gruyère cream sauce, veal steak with tarragon, wild trout with caviar, filet of veal with a sherry vinegar sauce, game cock sauteed with fresh mushrooms, and a rack of lamb cooked in wine. The fresh- and saltwater fish dishes are particularly good. Fixed-price meals cost between 34F ($15.62) and 73F ($33.54), while à la carte meals usually range between 52F ($23.89) and 62F ($28.49). The restaurant is closed on Tuesday and for most of January.

Restaurant Français Buffet de la Gare CFF (tel. 22-28-16). Don't be put off by the fact that this restaurant is in the train station—it's considered by local diners to be one of the best restaurants in the city. The Roger Morel family operate both a snackbar and a good brasserie, all within the same building. However, the Restaurant Français serves first-class meals. Madame Morel usually greets guests with something the French might call élan, sometimes suggesting one of the specialties. These might include poached chicken in cider, duck with honey, an "epicurean" pig's foot in puff pastry, frog legs provençale, and a local fish called sandre (pike-perch). Many of the dishes bow gracefully to nouvelle cuisine, including the cassoulet of sliced calf brain in raspberry vinegar. However, Chef Gaston Brasey designates Tuesday as a special day for gutburgerliche pot-au-feu and Wednesday for a local lipsmacker, calf head vinaigrette. Fixed-price meals usually run between 25F ($11.49) and 62F ($28.49), while à la carte dinners cost about the same.

6. Gruyères

This small town, which once belonged to the Counts of Gruyères, is known for its castle, its history, its houses from the Middle Ages, but mainly for its cheese. It is a highlight for any of you who are taking the "cheese route" through Switzerland. It's also a good base for exploring the district of Gruyère (the region is spelled without an "s," the town itself with an "s").

In the canton of Fribourg, the little town of Gruyères still seems to slumber somewhere back in the Middle Ages. Enclosed by ramparts from the 12th century, it is dominated by its castle where those counts held sway, mainly from the 12th to the 16th centuries.

Because the town would be overrun by vehicular traffic, cars are forbidden to enter between Easter and the first of November (and on Sunday all year round). You park your car outside the gates and walk into this formerly fortified town.

THE SIGHTS: The Renaissance houses along the main street are in excellent condition. However, some of their charm is obscured in summer by passengers from all the tour buses that descend on the area. If you're here when the tour buses aren't, you'll discover all on your own one of the most charming villages on the continent, lying on a rocky crag with a single main street that leads to the town fountain which is much photographed.

The crest of the former Counts of Gruyères bears a crane, and you'll see the symbol much used even today in Gruyères.

The traditional lunch in all the restaurants is raclette, which is prepared and served in Gruyères with a certain fanaticism. A machine is usually placed on your table and you melt and scrape the cheese at your own speed and your stomach's capacity. You can eat right down to the rind, which is crunchy (many Swiss gourmets consider this the best part of the raclette). If you're in Gruyères in the right season, you can finish with a large bowl of fresh raspberries in extremely thick cream.

At the entrance to the town, the Swiss Cheese Union operates a **Model Dairy** for demonstration purposes. Here you can see workers produce the famed Gruyère cheese, which is a more piquant version of the equally famous Emmenthaler. A cheese wheel weighs about 75 pounds. An audio-visual show reveals how the cheese is made. The dairy is open from 6 a.m. to 6 p.m., daily except Sunday, but it's best to go between 8 and 10 a.m. or 1:30 and 3 p.m. when the cheese is actually made. The dairy lies at the foot of a hill near the railway station.

Just as Switzerland is associated with cheese, it is also famous for its chocolates. At neighboring Broc, Peter-Cailler-Kohler founded his chocolate factory in 1898, and conducted tours are possible (but consult first with the tourist office about changing opening hours before heading there).

You can walk to the **Castle of Gruyères** on foot along cobblestones, along the way passing the former house of the famed court jester, Chalamala. Some parts of the castle, with its keep, bastion, chapel, and outer walls, date from the 13th century, but it's mainly from the 15th century. Today it's the property of the canton of Fribourg, and has been since 1938. However, when the Bovy family of Geneva acquired it in 1848, they were responsible for saving it from demolition and were also responsible for many of its present embellishments. Many famous artists, including Corot, have lived here. The château contains many rich objets d'art, the most outstanding of which are three mourning copes from the Order of the Golden Fleece, which were part of the bounty grabbed up in the Burgundian wars. The castle is open to the public from June until the first of October from 9 a.m. to 6 p.m. In winter it's open only from 9 a.m. to noon and 1:30 to 4:30 p.m., charging an admission of 3F ($1.38).

A popular excursion outside Gruyères is to **Moléson-Village,** at about 6565 feet, a four-mile journey, plus an additional half hour by cable car which swings up from the village from 8:30 a.m. to noon and 1:30 to 5:30 p.m. at a cost of 16F ($7.35) round trip (there's no service from November to mid-December). Once at the peak you can see from Titlis to Mont Blanc, and the whole Gruyère countryside unfolds before you. In winter the slopes become ski runs, as Moléson-Village is emerging as a fledgling ski resort.

You can not only visit Gruyères from Basle, but it also makes an easy day trip from Berne, about a 40-mile drive, going via Fribourg and Bulle.

FOOD AND LODGING: Hostellerie des Chevaliers (tel. 6-19-33) nestles in a hollow between two forested hills, with the snow-covered Alps as a backdrop. The well-maintained neatness of the white exterior is repeated throughout the public rooms, where every effort was made to decorate them imaginatively. White lattice covers the wall space of one of the sunny dining areas, repeating the verdant alpine theme with its many green accents. The bedrooms are well heated, with lots of wood paneling to contrast with the white plaster walls. The hotel and restaurant close every year from January 10 to February 10, and the restaurant also closes every Wednesday. The entire establishment is conscientiously directed by the attractive Bouchery-Rime family, who take an interest in the well-being of their guests. Each of the 34 rooms has its own bath, costing between 70F ($32.17) and 95F ($43.65) in a single and between 100F ($45.95) and 140F ($64.33) in a double, including breakfast. Half board is available upon request.

Hostellerie de St-Georges (tel. 6-22-46). Many repeat visitors to this peaceful hideaway claim it's one of the best hotels in the region. Centrally located, it offers 34 beds. Owner Héribert Miedler can give any extra time not devoted to his restaurant to the well-being of his overnight guests. Bathless singles cost between 30F ($13.78) and 45F ($20.68), going up to between 40F ($18.38) and 50F ($22.96) with bath. Doubles without bath range between 60F ($27.57) and 75F ($34.46), or 65F ($29.87) to 80F ($36.76) with bath. Half board is available for only another 8F ($3.68). Specialties in the restaurant include filet of beef served on a slate platter, breast of duckling with green peppercorns, local hens cooked with tarragon, pheasant suprême, duck liver with capers, and a quiche made with you know what kind of cheese. You might also prefer a platter of cured alpine meats, thinly sliced and served with pearl onions and pickles. Meals generally cost from 27F ($12.40) to 38F ($17.46). The restaurant is closed Wednesday evening all through the year and on Thursday in winter only. It also shuts down during most of January, and for all of February, and sometimes during much of March.

Hôtel de Ville (tel. 6-24-24) is housed in a historic building in the center of the old town. Owned and directed by Michel Murith, it offers comfortable, pleasantly furnished rooms for 40F ($18.38) in a single and from 75F ($34.46) in a double with bath. An attractive restaurant serves regional specialties such as ham and trout, the latter kept in an aquarium on the premises.

Hostellerie Le Castel (tel. 2-72-31). Making an excursion to this hotel high in an alpine meadow above the town gives a view of the Alps near Fribourg, the town of Gruyères, and the famous castles which surround it. Many of the guests prefer the terrace precisely because of that view, yet even indoors on a cold night the food is well worth the trip. Specialties include gratinée of asparagus, tender calf liver with onions, and plump Bresse hen. However, other goodies may be substituted for any of these dishes according to what head chef and owner Christian Roth found that day in the marketplace. Many guests prefer the fixed-price menus, costing from 43F ($19.76) all the way to a gastronomic banquet at 105F ($48.25). You'll usually find Madame Canisia Roth welcoming guests in the dining room and seeing that everything is running smoothly. A limited number of rooms is available to overnight guests. The restaurant lies a short distance from Gruyères in a suburb called Le Pâquier, and is closed every Tuesday.

In Crésuz

If Gruyères is overrun and you can't find a room (highly likely in summer), try the hamlet of Crésuz, 15 minutes away. It's reached from the station at Charmey. The living is easy, and the setting is idyllic in both summer and winter. It is convenient for exploring not only the chocolate factory at Broc, but both Gruyères and Bulle as well, along with other targets along Lac de la Gruyère.

For food and lodging, your best bet is **Le Vieux Chalet** (tel. 7-12-86). You'll cross a footbridge spanning a rocky stream a few feet from the front door of this alpine-style hotel which has much rustic charm. From the rear you'll notice that someone has added an annex in the same style as the original chalet, located just right for a panoramic view of the Alps. The restaurant inside has a ceiling supported by one particularly massive beam, and illuminated by the fire which often glows in the fieldstone fireplace. The bedrooms are comfortable and warm, costing 40F ($18.38) per person daily, including breakfast. You're only a few steps from the village church.

In Bulle

In the district of Gruyère, Bulle lies some 17 miles south of Fribourg, on the banks of the Trême River. It stands in the midst of what is called "green Gruyère." The bishops of Lausanne, who used to hold sway over the town, built a large castle here in the 13th century which is not open to the public.

However, in this market town you can visit the well-known **Gruérien Museum,** which is open to the public from 10 a.m. to noon and 2 to 5 p.m., except Sunday morning and Monday, charging an admission of 3.50F ($1.61). A regional author, Victor Tissot, established the museum which is devoted to antiques and regional wear from 18th-century Gruyère, along with some works by artists such as Corot, who visited it. Mainly it's a folkloric museum. You'll also see works by Courbet. An audio-visual presentation further helps you understand life in the district.

For accommodations, try either of the following:

The **Hôtel des Alpes** (tel. 2-92-92). This family-run hotel appears somewhat anonymous from the outside, yet opens into a more imaginative decor in its interior. It's decorated with appealing modern hanging lamps and comfortable banquettes and warm colors. The walls of the dining room have interesting art and an 11-foot flügelhorn. Bedrooms are carpeted and decorated in attractive shades of blue and green, with an occasional reproduction of a daringly contemporary abstract painting. Across from the train station, the location is most convenient. Doubles with private bath cost 85F ($39.06), while singles with bath go for 47F ($21.60), including breakfast.

Hôtel le Rallye, 8 route de Riaz (tel. 2-84-98), rises seven orange-and-white stories above a surprisingly small lot for such a tall building. The thoughtful management does everything it can to be helpful. Each of the comfortably furnished bedrooms has a private bath, costing 43F ($19.76) in a single and 80F ($36.76) in a double, including breakfast. Despite its relatively recent construction, the entire hotel was renovated in 1978.

7. Murten (Morat)

This small medieval town carries a double name because it's bilingual, the denizens speaking either French or German, and often both. In Switzerland it's called "the language demarcation line." Murten forms a gateway into French-speaking Switzerland, lying on the southern side of Murtensee (or Lac de Morat if you're more French inclined).

Of all the old towns in Switzerland I've sought out, I found this one most idyllic and beautifully preserved, many of its houses dating from the 15th to the 18th centuries. Not only that, but the town is surrounded by ramparts with a wall-walk. In the Middle Ages, these were defensive walls of course, but you can stroll along them today, taking in a view of the roofs of the Altstadt, with the castle, lake, and Juras as a backdrop.

Peter of Savoy, a duke, built the **castle** or schloss in the 13th century. It's bleak and foreboding, but impressive nevertheless, and from its inner courtyard (which you enter free) there's a vista of the lake and the Jura foothills.

The main street, **Hauptgasse,** is the major attraction of Murten, running through the center of the old quarter and taking you to the **Bernegate,** a baroque structure with one of the oldest clock towers in the country, dating from 1712.

Outside Murten on June 22, 1476, a fierce battle was fought between the Confederates and Charles the Bold of Burgundy.

The lake has a maximum depth of 150 feet, taking in an area of nearly ten square miles. Between May and September you can take lake trips on motor vessels and circular tours on the three lakes from Neuchâtel to Bienne to Murten, with trips through the canals in the Great Marshes.

FOOD AND LODGING: **Hotel Schiff Murten** (tel. 71-26-44). The location is pleasant, at the edge of the lake near the harbor. Well-maintained parks surround much of the hotel, leading right down to the water where you'll be tempted to stop for a drink at the lakeside café. The building is a complicated collection of 19th-century gables and porches, with a hipped roof, a few arched windows, and a modern extension containing some of the well-decorated public rooms. The bedrooms are fairly plush, with frequent use of nostalgically patterned wallpaper and attractively muted shades of such colors as cerulean blue, dusty rose, and sunflower. All the rooms contain private bath, costing between 48F ($22.05) and 78F ($35.84) in a single and between 88F ($40.43) and 146F ($67.09) in a double, including breakfast. Half board is another 30F ($13.78) per person. The hotel's restaurant is considered one of the best in town.

Hotel Krone (Hôtel de la Couronne) (tel. 71-52-52). From the terrace of this historic hotel you can see most of the lake, including the famous vineyards on the other side. The interior has been attractively modernized in keeping with the rustic informality of the public rooms. The bedrooms have been denuded of any historical feeling, nevertheless they are clean and comfortable. The hotel sits on a cobblestone street in the center of town, behind a gabled, red-shuttered facade with plenty of character. Bathless doubles cost 58F ($26.65), going up to 70F ($32.17) and 125F ($57.44) with full bath. Bathless singles go for 36F ($16.52), rising to anywhere from 47F ($21.60) to 57F ($26.19) with bath. The most expensive units, of course, face the lake. A restaurant on the premises specializes in local fish and grilled meats.

Hôtel de la Croix Blanche (Hotel Weisses Kreuz) (tel. 71-26-41), is a clean, attractive, family-run hotel with a sense of history in the way it maintains its ivy-covered facade with a heraldic shield over the door. A sun terrace extends off the back of the hotel, offering waiter service and good views of the lake. Bathless singles cost 35F ($16.08), going up to 50F ($22.98) to 60F ($27.57) with bath, depending on the view. Bathless doubles rent for 60F ($27.57), rising to 90F ($41.35) to 100F ($45.95) with bath, including breakfast.

Le Vieux Manoir au Lac, Murten-Meyriez (tel. 71-12-83), on the outskirts, is constructed of one of those elaborately Swiss conglomerations of stucco, weathered planking, slate, and fieldstone, with half-timbered gables, covered chimneys, and a gurgling hitching post with a fountain splashing into a basin. The scene is idyllic, and the service is impeccable in both the hotel and the restaurant. From the back the hotel presents another unusual collection of floor upon floor of weathered planking. Balconies and windows open onto the grassy banks of Lake Morat. A parasol-dotted sundeck allows guests the chance to relax in the summer sun, while the restaurant inside collects reservations for local wedding receptions and business conventions with gratifying regularity. The comfortable rooms rent for 75F ($34.46) to 85F ($39.06) in a single, and 120F ($55.14) to 180F ($82.71) in a double, including breakfast.

The restaurant attached to the establishment is excellent, with fish specialties printed on a separate menu. You'll appreciate the decor of the regional antiques while waiting for your meal. A fixed-price menu ranges from 40F ($18.38) to 90F ($41.35), or between 30F ($13.78) and 65F ($29.86) if you order à la carte. Reservations are suggested. The restaurant is closed during most of December and January.

8. Neuchâtel

One of the most charming and elegant towns of Switzerland, Neuchâtel was a haven for such notables as André Gide, Alexandre Dumas, and Mirabeau. It stands at the border of a lake of the same name—the largest lake entirely within Switzerland—and at the foot of the green slopes of Chaumont (3871 feet). The majority of its population are French speaking and Protestant. Once a Prussian principality, Neuchâtel became a member of the Swiss Confederation in 1815, and is today the capital of a Swiss canton of the same name. By the end of the 18th century watchmaking had earned Neuchâtel fame throughout Europe.

At the foot of the Jura, Neuchâtel enjoys an idyllic setting in the midst of vineyards. Many of its limestone houses have a distinctive yellow or ochre color, conjuring up for Dumas an image of the town as having been carved out of a "block of butter."

Neuchâtel is a seat of culture and learning (its citizens are said to speak the finest French in Switzerland), and you'll see many university students on the streets and in the cafés. Its university was founded in 1838.

The historic old sector is traffic free in the center. The French influence is very evident in architectural styles. Many houses in the old town date back to the 16th century, and some were built with defensive towers. The spirit of old Neuchâtel is best seen at the Maison des Halles, the market square where you may want to buy some well-known local cheese, de Jura, to eat later at a picnic around the lake.

THE SIGHTS: The medieval section is dominated by the **Château of Neuchâtel** and the **Collégiale** (university church), which along with the **Tour des Prisons** (prison tower) form an architectural complex of great interest. The castle has been much changed and altered over the years. The earliest part, the west wing, goes back to the 12th century, but most of the building is from the 15th to the 17th centuries. From the castle, a panoramic view of the old town unfolds.

The university church goes back to the 12th and 13th centuries, although parts of it, the west towers, are from the latter 19th century when the church underwent (some say suffered) a major overhaul. The church is characterized by glazed tiles in many hues. The highlight of the church is found in the Romanesque choir, a monument to the Counts of Neuchâtel, created in the 14th century. With more than a dozen painted effigies, this is considered the most spectacular Gothic memorial in the country. These counts—actually there are 15—strike austere and dignified poses.

The prison tower also offers a magnificent view as well, and is open from mid-April to mid-October from 8 a.m. to 8 p.m., while to visit the church and castle you have to apply to the concierge (you'll find him at the gate to the castle under an arch).

The **Griffin fountain** from 1664 lies nearby on the rue du Château. It's one of the most famous in the country, owing to the generosity of Henri II of

Orléans who in 1657 had it filled with 1300 gallons of red wine to honor his entrance into Neuchâtel.

The **Musée d'Art et d'Histoire** (museum of art and history), near the end of Quai Léopold-Robert, northeast of the harbor, is open from 10 a.m. to noon and 2 to 5 p.m. except on Monday, charging 3F ($1.38) for admission. The museum has an excellent collection of paintings, many by local artists (a few of dubious talent), who worked mainly from the late 19th and early 20th century. You can see works by Léopold Robert, for whom the quay was named. Many works are also displayed by artists painting in Neuchâtel today. But for the three-star attraction of the museum you have to go back to the 16th century for a painting on wood, called *The Coronation of the Madonna.* It has been attributed to one of the "Masters of the Carnation," who signed works with either a red or a white carnation. Neuchâtel's role as a watchmaking city is honored by the museum's clocks and watches. There is also a collection of automata (mechanical figures), of which a trio from the 18th century, the work of one Jaquet-Droz, shows great talent and imagination.

You spend a lot of time in Neuchâtel walking the **quays,** and well you should: there are three miles of them! The finest view of the Lake of Neuchâtel, with the Alps as a backdrop, is from Osterwald Quay.

The little city also has an exceptional **Museum of Ethnography,** which can be easily reached from the castle by heading up rue de l'Écluse. It's open from 10 a.m. to noon and 2 to 5 p.m. except on Monday, charging 3F ($1.38) admission. A sophisticated museum designer arranged the exhibits for easy viewing. You're taken on a journey from the mysterious kingdom of Bhutan at the top of the world, to Egypt at the time of the pharaohs. In the annex a mammoth fresco, *Conquest of Man,* is by the artist Hans Erni.

Near the Faubourg de l'Hôpital, in the patrician part of the city, a **Musée d'Archéologie** (museum of archeology) displays artifacts discovered at La Tène, a late Iron Age site excavated in 1858 at the northern end of the Lake of Neuchâtel (incidentally, this site, near St. Blaise, can be visited). The museum is open daily except Monday from 2 to 5 p.m.

Nearby you can stroll into the garden of the **Hôtel du Peyrou,** dating from 1764. This excellent patrician house was constructed for Du Peyrou, who was a friend of Rousseau and published some of his works. *The Bather,* a statue in the pool, is by Ramseyer.

For a final look at Neuchâtel, you can take a funicular (approached from the rue de l'Écluse, on the border of the medieval sector, heading up for the **Crêt du Plan**) to a height of 1962 feet. Before you will be a great view of the Lake of Neuchâtel and the distant Alps.

Sights in the Environs

If you base in Neuchâtel, you can explore many sights in the environs, especially along Lac de Nauchâtel, the lake which inspired Gide. If you drive northeast of town, you'll reach **La Coudre,** a distance of 2½ miles. From there you can take a funicular to the top of **Chaumont** at 3862 feet. The round-trip fare is 7F ($3.22) and the ride takes about 15 minutes. From the summit you'll have a view of Mont Blanc and the Bernese Alps.

Back in Neuchâtel, you can strike out to the west this time, going along the lake to discover a number of stopovers. You'll come to **Auvernier** after about three miles. It's a fishing village (the lake is filled with fish), but mainly it's known for its vineyards. You can make purchases from wine makers and consume your drink later at a picnic along the lake. The town is also noted for its beautiful Renaissance houses.

Leaving it, continue west to **Colombier,** a small village with a large castle, which produces an outstanding white wine. The late Gothic Castle of Colombier, from the 15th century, has two museums, and guided tours are conducted Monday to Friday from the first of March until the end of October from 2 to 3:30 p.m. for 2F (92¢). The castle was built on the ruins of a Roman fort, and Frederick the Great stayed there, as did Rousseau. One museum is devoted to military artifacts, another to paintings.

Boudry, very medieval looking, is our next stop. The Castle of Boudry, from the 16th century, has a museum of viticulture, which is open from 9 a.m. to noon and 2 to 6 p.m. (on Sunday, from 10 a.m. to noon and 2 to 5 p.m.). It's closed on Monday and in August. Boudry is known mainly, however, as the birthplace of Marat, the French revolutionist.

FOOD AND LODGING: Hotel Beaulac, Quai Léopold-Robert (tel. 25-88-22), is built almost on top of the lake at the junction of the Quai Léopold-Robert and the Quai du Port. The location is tranquil enough to allow guests an easy afternoon on the terrace below the five floors of the two-toned facade. The bedrooms are predictably modern, clean, and comfortable. The establishment contains no fewer than four restaurants, one of them specializing in fish (Le Colvert). All rooms have private bath. Singles cost between 70F ($32.17) and 95F ($43.65), while doubles range between 85F ($39.06) and 135F ($62.03), including breakfast.

Hotel/Restaurant City, Place A. M. Piaget (tel. 25-54-12), is decorated in a very untraditional style of contoured velvet chairs, often with chrome swivel bases. The bedroom furniture is Nordic modern. The place is clean, with an excellent location, and many of its bedrooms overlook the lake. The restaurant has inexpensive fixed-priced meals, especially at noon, and the bar is a place where you can easily forget about art history for a while. Doubles with bath cost 98F ($45.03), and singles, also with bath, go for 60F ($27.57). All units contain radio and TV, and rates include breakfast. There's also a Chinese restaurant on the premises.

Novotel Neuchâtel-Est, route de Berne (tel. 33-57-57), is in a very modern building in a tranquil setting only six minutes by car from the heart of Neuchâtel (get off at the Thielle exit on the Neuchâtel–Bienne autoroute). The hotel is built on a large scale in an aluminum, glass, and concrete format familiar to Americans. The entire structure angles itself around an outdoor swimming pool, and contains two restaurants and a bar. All accommodations have private baths, costing 66F ($30.32) in a single and 108F ($49.63) in a double.

Hôtel des Beaux-Art, 5–7 rue Pourtales (tel. 24-01-51), lies between the English Garden and the lake, in a blue-gray and white six-story building with lots of windows and two rows of recessed balconies. Inside you'll find a restaurant, a brasserie, and a sun terrace. The bedrooms are clean and sometimes painted or decorated in vivid colors. All the modern and comfortable accommodations contain private baths. Singles cost between 48F ($22.05) and 52F ($23.89), with doubles going for between 80F ($36.76) and 92F ($42.27).

Restaurant de la Grappe, 77 rue de la Dime, La Coudre–Neuchâtel (tel. 33-26-26), was built in 1607 as a companion house for a similar structure from 1577. A single example of a primitive form of flying buttress still juts into the street in front. From the rear of the sympathetic dining room you'll have a good view of the lake. Lino Marini, the owner, supervises and welcomes guests with great charm, while chef M. Pasetti prepares Italian specialties. These might include calf liver Venetian style with saffron risotto, carpaccio, veal and beef dishes, or a delicately seasoned seafood salad. The restaurant serves every day except Wednesday from 8 p.m. to midnight. It's usually closed for the last three weeks of July. À la carte meals cost from 19F ($8.73) to 27F ($12.40), while fixed-price dinners range between 23F ($10.56) and 46F ($21.13).

Restaurant au Vieux Vapeur ("Chez Mirano"), Port de Neuchâtel (tel. 24-34-00). Mirando Di Domenico has become somewhat of a minor celebrity in town, thanks to his restaurant. The delicacies prepared by his chef, C. Frôté, have made the place very popular. The location inside a retired lake cruiser offers a bar, nightclub, and disco in addition to a fine restaurant. Specialties include baby lamb with truffles, lake trout with smoked salmon in a red butter sauce, raw lake salmon marinated in a lemon sauce, and sweetbreads braised in champagne. The restaurant closes every Tuesday in winter and for all of January. Fixed-price meals cost between 32F ($14.70) and 37F ($17), with à la carte dinners ranging between 22F ($10.10) and 32F ($14.70). The top of the line is the fixed-price gourmet meal which usually goes for around 50F ($22.98).

Buffet de la Gare, Place de la Gare (tel. 25-48-53), is about the closest thing to a food factory there is in Neuchâtel. It has a standup eatery in the train station, a catering service, and a less expensive brasserie. At the top of the list, however, you'll find a high-quality restaurant with excellent service, a functionally elegant decor, and a chef, Lucien Gétaz, who takes his cookery seriously. Specialties include such rarified dishes as baby crayfish in saffron, quail mousse, trout garnished with smoked salmon and served with a horseradish mousse, filet of sole with three kinds of mushrooms, pike flan, fresh local fish, sea trout with grapefruit, and either filet of spring lamb or young hare with cabbage leaves. Fixed-price meals cost between 20F ($9.19) and 27F ($12.41), while à la carte dinners range between 21F ($9.64) and 48F ($22.06). The buffet is open every day of the week from 6 a.m. to midnight.

9. La Chaux-de-Fonds

The birthplace of Le Corbusier, La Chaux-de-Fonds is a clean industrial town, where streets cross each other at right angles, the result of planning when the town was rebuilt in the 19th century after it was destroyed by fire in 1794. A new residential sector has grown up on the western side of town, with high-rise apartment blocks

It isn't much of a tourist town, but because it's the capital of the Neuchâtel mountains, lying in a valley of the Jura, many visitors base here while exploring the encircling district. The location is about 1¼ hours from Bern, and just 15 minutes from the French border.

A center of Swiss watchmaking, it seems to employ everybody in town in the industry. The town has a **Musée International d'Horlogerie** (an international watch and clock museum), which is open from 10 a.m. to noon and 2 to 5 p.m. except Monday, charging an admission of 4F ($1.84). The location is at 29 rue des Musées. In this museum you'll see a cavalcade of timepieces dating back to the Egyptians. Some of the clocks, especially the enamel ones, are works of art. The museum also displays a collection of automata (mechanical figures).

Nearby stands the **Musé des Beaux-Art** (fine arts museum), which is open from 10 a.m. to noon and 2 to 5 p.m. except Monday. It has a good collection of the great romantic painter, Léopold Robert, who was born in the town in 1794. A Le Corbusier tapestry, entitled *The Music Players,* is also shown.

FOOD AND LODGING: **Hôtel Moreau,** 45 avenue Léopold Robert (tel. 23-22-22), curves around a corner of a busy street in a commercial section of the city. Neon signs identify the hotel at least twice, perhaps a welcome sight on a cold night in the Juras. The least expensive rooms contain a sink and a toilet, costing 35F ($16.08) in a single and 65F ($29.86) in a double. Accommodations with full private bath range between 45F ($20.67) and 90F ($41.35) in a single and from 100F ($45.95) to 160F ($73.52) in a double, including breakfast.

Le Provençal, Place de la Gare (tel. 22-22-03). If you yearn for seafood, this is the place in town to go. The imaginative preparations include recipes for just about everything with gills. Large aquariums assure a maximum freshness. Since the chef makes frequent trips to the local market, this makes for a very good cuisine. Try the crayfish flambeed with Calvados or the turbot braised in champagne. Lotte with basil or a sour version of John Dory might appeal to you, as surely the shellfish platter will. Madame A. Mathieu is responsible for the tone set by this well-run establishment. À la carte meals range between 28F ($12.86) and 52F ($23.89). The restaurant is closed Sunday and for all of July.

Club 44, 64 rue de la Serre (tel. 23-11-44). The ambience is sophisticated and low-key at this restaurant which looks like a private club. On the same premises is an art gallery which you might visit before your meal. Gérard Riske, the head chef, used to live in East Germany and later spent time with the famed Troisgros brothers in France. His specialties include crayfish in verbena with a champagne sabayon, a crayfish cassolette, and sweetbreads and duck liver in puff pastry. Set lunches cost from 15F ($6.89) to 28F ($12.87), with à la carte dinners going for anywhere from 30F ($13.79) to 65F ($29.87). The restaurant is open daily except Sunday from 11:30 a.m. to 2:30 p.m. and 6 p.m. to closing. It takes off during most of July and August.

10. Bienne (Biel)

This is one of the most bilingual cities of Switzerland. Citizens often address you in French, and before they've finished a thought they've switched to German. The street names are in both French and German. An industrial town, noted for its watchmaking, Biel lies at the northeastern end of Lake Biel, from which many excursions can be taken. It stands in the foothills of the Jura.

The town has grown rapidly in recent years, and is now said to contain 300 watchmaking workshops or factories, employing thousands of people. Omega was launched here in 1879.

THE SIGHTS: Ignoring the industrial suburbs, the sightseer will want to head directly for the Upper Town, especially the attractive old square, the landmark of Biel, which is known as **"The Ring."** The square is surrounded by step-gabled houses, the most outstanding of which is the **Zunfthaus der Waldleute,** a former guildhouse with its tower crowned by an onion-shaped dome. When the town was ruled by the Prince-Abbots of Basle, they seated themselves in a half-moon position, judging the guilty and freeing the innocent. In time the square became known as "The Ring." The Banneret fountain in the center is from 1546.

Nearby, the **Rathaus** (town hall) was built in 1530, but much restored. It is step-gabled, like many buildings in this part of town, and in front stands the Fountain of Justice from 1714.

Other than the arcades and Burgundian homes along the High Street, the single most important attraction of Biel is its **Schwab Museum,** open daily from 10 a.m. to noon and 2 to 5 p.m. except Monday.

is named for a colonel who pioneered excavations to discover Romansh Switzerland. On display are artifacts relating to the prehistoric period when the country was inhabited by lake-dwellers. The rooms also contain relics of the Gallo-Roman period as well, and some cases showing tools of the Iron Age.

Outside Bienne

If you want to follow in the footsteps of Goethe, who stayed at the former inn Zur Krone, and make Biel your base, you can take a number of interesting excursions. My favorite is to **St. Petersinsel** (St. Peter's Island) in Lake Biel, called Bielersee. You can reach it by boat from Biel, a round-trip fare costing 10F ($4.60). For details, inquire at the Biel tourist office, the **Verkehrsbüro,** Bahnhofplatz (tel. 22-75-75). The boat ride and exploration will eat up most of your day.

Jean-Jacques Rousseau in 1765 chose this island as a place of refuge, which he recalled in his *Confessions.* He lived at the 12th-century Cluniac priory, which when it was dissolved in 1530 was turned into an inn (see below).

You can take many pleasant strolls around the island, which is really a peninsula, as the water level of the lake has been lowered. The little island you'll see off the coast is Rabbit's Island, which might more accurately be called "Bird Island." Some deer roam through this natural sanctuary.

If you wish, you can also take a cruise around **Lake Biel,** which is of glacial origin. It's 7½ miles long, and was the site of many lake dwellings. The little villages, such as **La Neuveville,** which dot the lake are known for their wines and gastronomy. That village, rather grandly, is known as the "Montreux of the Jura." Its church is 1000 years old.

On the north side of the lake the villages of **Twann** and **Ligerz** can be visited. Twann has many venerated old vintner houses, and the upper part of the village touches the vineyards. The adjacent village, Ligerz, in a setting right in the midst of vineyards, has a church dating from 1482. It also has a Wine Museum, and from there you can take a funicular to Prêles for a magnificent view.

Armed with a good map, you can seek out **Aarberg,** another interesting town. It's positively medieval, with a fortress towering over the town and old bourgeois houses. Its wooden bridge is more than four centuries old.

FOOD AND LODGING: **Hôtel Elite,** 14 rue de la Gare (tel. 22-54-41), has an imposing ocher-colored facade that curves, art deco style, around a bend in the street. The rooms are modern and conservative, with attractively patterned wallpaper and comfortably overstuffed armchairs. The public rooms include a masculine bar area, a restaurant serving both Chinese and French food, and a plushly upholstered nightclub which usually has a live pianist. All accommodations have private bath, costing between 70F ($32.17) and 92F ($42.27) in a single and between 95F ($43.65) and 135F ($62.03) in a double. Half board costs another 25F ($11.49) per person daily. The restaurant serves one of the best tables in Biel, specializing in such delicacies as baby veal with crabmeat in puff pastry, goose with glazed onions, lobster terrine, and turbot with young vegetables. Fixed-price meals range between 43F ($19.75) and 49F ($22.52), with à la carte dinners costing from 30F ($13.79) to 58F ($26.65). Reservations are suggested.

Hotel Continental, 29 Aarbergstrasse (tel. 22-32-55), is a recently built hostelry with a balcony outside many of the contemporary bedrooms, plus a warm color choice in the lobby and bar area. The location is halfway between the city center and the lake. Rooms are soundproof, containing TV, radio, refrigerator, and private bath. Singles range between 75F ($34.46) and 80F ($36.76), with doubles costing around 120F ($55.14), breakfast included.

Au Provençale, 54 Bahnhofstrasse (tel. 23-24-11). The cuisine here, as the name suggests, is inspired by Provence, but dishes are given a modern nouvelle cuisine twist. In an ambience of rustic antiques and warm colors, chef Henri Scheibli concocts such specialties as filet of trout in a rosemary-flavored vinegar, turbot in lobster butter with spinach, and veal steak with home-grown cherries. Fixed-price meals cost between 26F ($11.95) and 80F ($36.76), while à la carte dinners range between 30F ($13.79) and 80F ($36.76).

Poissonnière (Buffet de la Gare), 4 Place de la Gare (tel. 22-33-11). On the top floor of this busy rail station you'll find an ambience far more elegant than you might have expected. As its name implies, the restaurant specializes in fish. Specialties include mussels, fried shellfish with tartar sauce, fried carp, and a beautifully prepared sole. Meat dishes run the usual gamut of lamb, beef, pork, and veal which, while not particularly exotic, are nonetheless well prepared and very tasty. À la carte meals range between 23F ($10.56) and 51F ($23.43).

Restaurant Bielstube, 10 Rosius (tel. 22-65-88), prepares honest and traditional cookery in an old city location convenient to almost everything. Directed by Peter Jutzeler and Madeleine Hofmann, the restaurant serves a rotating series of specialties which usually depend on whatever is freshest at the market that day. À la carte meals range from 11F ($5.05) to 37F ($17). The restaurant shuts down every Sunday and over the Christmas holidays.

Goya, 11 rue Hôpital (tel. 22-61-61), is the place to go for the best Spanish food in town. The aura is enhanced by several reproductions of the works of the 19th-century artist himself. The Spanish wine, coupled with the personality of the owner, Jorge Guanter, helps everyone have a good time. Specialties include two kinds of paella, both Catalán and marinara. Beef is also served in a pungent Spanish sauce. Fixed-price meals range between 10F ($4.60) and 14F ($6.43), while à la carte dinners cost from 17F ($7.81) all the way up to 43F ($19.76). The Goya doesn't paint on Sunday.

On the Island of St. Peter

Hotel St. Petersinsel, Bielersee (tel. 88-11-15). This island, mentioned under "sights" to Biel, is the place where Jean-Jacques Rousseau stayed for two months in 1765. Today the inn where he lived has been converted into a hotel which is open from March until November. The writer's former room is still more or less intact. Dozens of holiday-makers come here in summer to eat on the hotel's terrace, or under the huge arches of the rustic dining room. The Stauffer family rents rooms for 56F ($25.73) in a double with breakfast, or 86F ($39.52) for two on the half-board plan. The ambience is very calm and tranquil, and the place is best enjoyed with a friend.

Chapter VI

BERNE AND THE BERNESE OBERLAND

1. Berne
2. Lake Thun
3. Spiez
4. Interlaken
5. Mürren
6. Wengen
7. Grindelwald
8. Lake Brienz
9. Meiringen
10. Lenk/Adelboden
11. Gstaad
12. Kandersteg

THE BEST KNOWN holiday region of Switzerland, the Bernese Oberland is one of the great tourist attractions of the world, and one of the best equipped for winter sports.

The beauty of the area has long been extolled by writers, including Jean-Jacques Rousseau and Goethe. Interlaken—the best center for exploring the Bernese Oberland—became famous and fashionable in the 19th century.

Over the years the district has attracted such distinguished company as Madame de Staël, La Rouchefoucauld, and others. The English were not far behind. Byron visited in 1816, and he was followed by Ruskin, Shelley, and Thackeray. Longfellow and Mark Twain came from America.

This famed winter sports area is not only the center of Europe, but the heart of Switzerland. More than 150 installations transport skiers to all grades of well-prepared and maintained downhill runs. The Bernese Oberland sprawls between the Reuss River and Lake Geneva, the Rhône forming its southern border.

The canton of Berne, in which most of it falls, is the second largest in Switzerland, with some 100 square miles of glaciers. The River Aare forms the lakes of Thun and Brienz, two of the most rewarding sightseeing targets in summer. But the Oberland also takes in the Alps, culminating in the Jungfrau at 13,642 feet and the Finsteraarhorn at 14,022 feet.

The most acclaimed summer resort is Interlaken, but Meiringen and Thun also merit listing. Others, such as Gstaad, Grindelwald, Kandersteg, and Mürren, are both summer and winter playgrounds. The fame of Lenk and Adelboden dates from the early 19th century at the beginnings of modern tourism. The district also takes in the cheese-making land of Emmental (see a description in the environs of Berne).

The Bernese Oberland is ideal country for both the sports enthusiast and the nature lover. You can ski in the mountains or, in summer, sail, surf, and waterski on Lake Thun. Yodelers, alpine horn blowers, and folklore musicians keep alive ancient traditions. Mountain forests and alpine pastures invite the rambler, and trout fishing is possible in mountain streams after you've completed a climb over a glacier the previous day. You're likely to see the mountain chamoix, the ibex, or marmot, and certainly some alpine toadstools, crocuses, and rhododendrons.

Getting there is often half the fun, whether you arrive at your destination by steam railway, cog-wheel railway, aerial cableway, or a steamboat across Lake Brienz. Once you've arrived at your hotel, you can enjoy mountain cheese and the wine of Spiez.

A Regional Holiday Season Ticket for the Bernese Oberland is available at 92F ($42.27) for adults, 46F ($21.14) for children from 6 to 16 years old. The ticket is valid on nearly all railroads including mountain trains, cable cars, chair lifts, steamers on Lake Thun and Brienz, and most postal bus lines in the Bernese Oberland. There's also a 25% reduction on the Kleine Scheidegg–Eigergletscher–Jungfraujoch railway and the Mürren–Schilthorn aerial cable line, and bus to Grosse Scheidegg and Bussalp. The ticket, valid for 15 days, allows you to use it as a general season ticket for unlimited travel on five days of your choice and as a season ticket entitling you to any number of tickets at half fare.

You must book your Regional Holiday Season Ticket not less than one week before your arrival. Get in touch with your nearest Swiss tourist office for more information.

1. Berne

In the heart of Switzerland, Berne, the capital of the Confederation, is a city of diplomats and one of the loveliest of Europe. The city is ancient, built between the 12th and 18th centuries. It is, in fact, one of the great medieval cities still left in Europe that hasn't been destroyed, either torn down or bombed in wars.

In spite of the fact that it's host to many international organizations, and is a beehive of activity, it still has many touches of a big country town, as reflected by the bright splashes of red geraniums on the window sills of many of the houses.

Berne is a city of arcades, nearly four miles of them running along the streets of the old sector, and they're weatherproof and traffic free. Underneath these arcades are shop windows, everything from exclusive boutiques to department stores, from antique dealers to jewelers. It's a city of fountains and oriel windows, and its old sandstone steps have been trodden for centuries. The buildings, for the most part, are built of a yellowish green sandstone as well.

But don't get the idea that all of Berne is dripping in antiquity. Modern-day residents have discreetly imposed contemporary living over their centuries-old environment, showing a healthy respect for the past. Beginning with your arrival at the new Hauptbahnhof (railway station), you'll encounter "New Berne" right away. It has many modern houses, bridges, and streets.

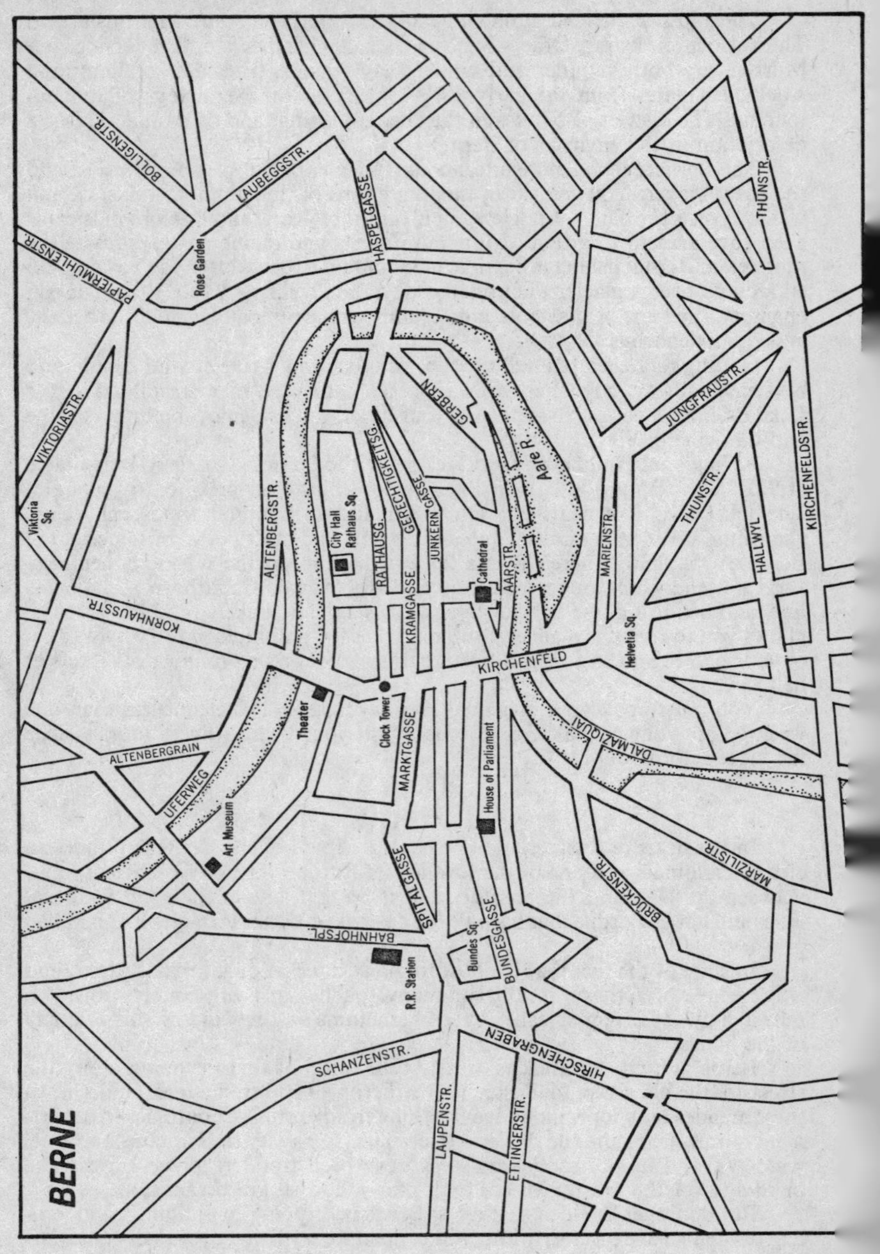
BERNE
BOLLIGENSTR.
LAUBEGGSTR.
HASPELGASSE
THUNSTR.
PAPIERMÜHLENSTR.
Rose Garden
VIKTORIASTR.
Viktoria Sq.
GERBERN
JUNGFRAUSTR.
Aare R.
GERECHTIGKEITSG.
ALTENBERGSTR.
City Hall Rathaus Sq.
RATHAUSG.
GASSE
JUNKERN
Cathedral
AARSTR.
MARIENSTR.
THUNSTR.
HALLWYL
KIRCHENFELDSTR.
KRAMGASSE
KORNHAUSSTR.
KIRCHENFELD
Helvetia Sq.
Theater
Clock Tower
MARKTGASSE
House of Parliament
DALMAZIQUAI
ALTENBERGRAIN
UFERWEG
Art Museum
SPITALGASSE
MARZILISTR.
BRÜCKENSTR.
BAHNHOFSPL.
R.R. Station
Bundes Sq.
BUNDESGASSE
HIRSCHENGRABEN
SCHANZENSTR.
LAUPENSTR.
ETTINGERSTR.

A university town, Berne is one of the centers of Swiss culture and education. Its research workers have been pioneers in many scientific fields. Among their achievements was a device used to measure solar winds on the moon. And breaking with centuries of tradition, the city often hires young policewomen to direct traffic.

Berne stands on a thumb of land, surrounded on three sides by the River Aare, to which it is linked symbolically as much as Paris is to its Seine. Many bridges, often sightseeing attractions in themselves, connect Berne to its newer sections.

Berne joined the Swiss Confederation in 1353, becoming the seat of the federal government in 1848, replacing Zurich. It is easily reached, either by motorway or rail. The city publishes a map that puts Berne at the virtual crossroads of Europe. You can also arrive at the international airports at Zurich or Geneva, both within easy commuting distance, or at Berne's own airport at Belpmoos.

Berne is also the center for many excursions, especially to the lakes and peaks of the Bernese Oberland (this vast playland is reached in only minutes from the capital).

On Tuesday and Saturday Berne holds its market days when the country people come to town, and either day would be ideal to visit to see the city in full bloom. But from the point of view of revelry, Berne is more fun on the fourth Monday of every November when it stages the centuries-old Zibelmärkt or onion market. At that time Bernese housewives stock up on onions for the winter, and it's also turned into a popular festival, as the city has one last big fling before the onset of winter.

ACCOMMODATIONS: The city tourist officials say their range of accommodations is vast—everything from a park bench to a Louis XV four-poster. As the federal capital, Berne is the center of many conventions and international meetings, and at times its hotels are fully booked. Try to arrive with a reservation.

The Deluxe Choices

Hotel Schweizerhof, 11 Schweizerhoflaube (tel. 22-45-01), is directed by the Gauer family (some people even call this the Gauer Hotel), whose personal antique collection is probably better than anything else a tourist might see in the way of decorative arts in Berne. Throughout the hotel, in all the public rooms and in many of the better suites, you'll see rich patinas on many pieces ranging from naïve provincial to ultra-formal drawing room articles of the 18th century. Other architectural details give tremendous visual pleasure to anyone interested in arts and crafts, from the wall-size tapestries to the crystal chandeliers to the glowing pastiche of styles in the warmly masculine bar area. Even some of the upper-floor hallways are laid out like a museum of the folk arts, with polychromed statues of saints hanging next to weathered wooden chests from the 17th century.

Because of its location in the heart of the Swiss capital, you'll find a lot of upper-crust diplomatic guests staying here. You're likely to meet them in one of the formal restaurants or in the 16th-century Simmentalerstube, whose walls, ceiling, and furnishings came almost intact from a much older building. The Schultheissenstube is my personal favorite, offering a rustic elegance and an attentive service which rates high even by competitive Swiss standards. Each of the bedrooms and suites is differently decorated, but almost all of them offer a lighthearted combination of comfortably upholstered chairs and sofas with a fairly good chest, desk, or table. Jaylin's nightclub provides live music and an elegant, intimate ambience for one of your nights out.

All bedrooms have modern baths and all the accessories. Singles rent for between 125F ($57.44) and 160F ($73.52), while doubles range between 185F ($85.01) to 250F ($114.88). Breakfast is included in the price, and an extra bed can be set up in any unit for an additional 30F ($13.79).

The **Bellevue Palace,** Kochergasse (tel. 22-45-81), is what would have been called, even when it was built in 1913, majestic. Next door to the Bundeshaus, the seat of the Swiss government, the hotel could easily be mistaken for part of the governmental complex, especially since, with its carved Corinthian columns, its ornate detailing, and its gray stone facade, it looks solid enough to support an Alp. Parts of the inside literally make the first-time visitor gasp—especially the stained-glass ceiling which arches over the wide expanse of one of the salons.

The hotel offers 53 single rooms at 125F ($57.44) to 160F ($73.52) and 88 double rooms at 185F ($85.01) to 250F ($114.88), all of them with bath and luxuriously appointed, each different from the other, each opulently proportioned with lots of space. The views to the southeast, weather permitting, are of the Jungfrau and her surrounding forests. The setting is undeniably old world, and the service is impeccable. You'll find a beautifully monochromatic dining room with high arched windows, a sun terrace with laughing couples and green-and-white parasols, and a bar.

The Upper Bracket

Hotel Metropole, 28 Zeughausgasse (tel. 22-50-21), is conveniently situated in the heart of Berne within the loop of the River Aare which contained the medieval city. The hotel offers a series of public rooms, cleverly decorated with such artifacts as an antique water mill hanging over the full expanse of a wall in the Old Mill Restaurant and old photographs of political leaders in the President Club (you'll have to ask the bartender to identify many of them). Bedrooms contain modern baths in such trendy colors as tangerine, and the rooms are carpeted and, except for their cramped size, very comfortable. Breakfast is included in the prices of 85F ($39.06) in a single and 114F ($52.38) in a double.

Hotel City, 7 Bubenbergplatz (tel. 22-53-77), sits behind its gray stone facade near the railroad station. The front is accented with colorful awnings above a bustling sidewalk café. You'll find an elevator in the lobby, and a Mövenpick restaurant with direct access to the hotel. Owned by the Mövenpick chain, the hotel is managed by Ada-Maria Allemann, who is assisted by Beatrice Kofer. They usually fill all six floors to capacity. The 47 rooms rent for 85F ($39.06) to 94F ($43.19) in a single, 115F ($52.84) to 124F ($56.98) in a double, with an extra bed costing an additional 25F ($11.49). Children under 16 share their parents' room free. Breakfast is included in the price. Each of the predictably modern units comes equipped with radio, color TV, phone, and mini-bar.

Hotel Ambassador, 97 Seftigenstrasse (tel. 45-41-11), rises nine stories into the Bernese sky, in a well-proportioned format of modern windows and streamlined decorations. You'll notice that it's the tallest building around, its neighbors being older houses with red-tile roofs. You'll be able to see the Bundeshaus (seat of government) from the windows of many of the rooms. You can savor the food in the French restaurant and the snackbar or enjoy drinks in the liquor bar. The sauna and fitness room are at your disposal, as well as the pool. Singles cost from 77F ($35.38) to 90F ($41.36), while doubles rent for 110F ($50.55) to 120F ($55.14), breakfast included. Accommodations include baths, toilets, phones, refrigerators, and TVs. The hotel is popular for its conference rooms as well as its guest rooms, so you'll be likely to see lots of gray flannel suits during your stay here. The efficient and personable manager at the reception desk is B. Tanner.

Hotel Alfa, 15 Laupenstrasse (tel. 25-38-66), is housed in a futuristic concrete-and-glass building just to the west of the train station. A restaurant occupies a big-windowed annex which is raised above the street level on stilts. A Swiss flag usually flies high above this establishment, which is owned and managed by the Fezzardi-Vaucher family. Bedrooms are attractively decorated in shades of wheat and soft orange, with modern baths and lots of light. Most of them contain a radio, TV connection, alarm clock, phone, and mini-bar. A parking lot and an elevator are on the premises. Singles rent for 85F ($39.06), doubles cost 115F ($52.84), and triples are 130F ($59.74), breakfast included.

Hotel Bern, 9 Zeughausgasse (tel. 21-10-21). If you like art deco, you'll love the facade of this inner-city hotel. The gray front is a massive testament to the art form that was so chic in the 1920s and so valued today. It consists of a massively arched roof with smaller arches and half-columns repeated throughout the rest of the construction. Several iconoclastic sculptures flank the entranceway which leads to the reception desk and a series of seven attractive rooms for dining and drinking, each of them different in character. The 100 well-furnished rooms, often attracting a diplomatic crowd, all have private bath, mini-bar, phone, radio, and TV connection, costing from 80F ($36.76) to 95F ($43.65) in a single and from 55F ($25.27) to 67F ($30.79) per person in a double, including breakfast.

The Middle Range

Hotel Silvahof, 97 Jubiläumsstrasse (tel. 43-15-31). Visitors must walk an invigorating distance or take a five-minute bus or car ride before reaching this beautifully appointed apartment hotel on the south side of Berne near the American Embassy. Most of the rooms have generously proportioned balconies, which for at least the first morning of your stay might tempt you not to leave your room. Accommodations always include a kitchenette, modern bathroom, and a refrigerator. They're usually decorated with attractive furniture which, while comfortable, leaves a lot of room for movement. The public salons are sometimes very striking. The Great Hall has a bar invitingly curved around one corner, a high beamed ceiling, long couches pulled into logical conversational groups, and a fireplace with a gilt-framed baroque mirror above it. Many guests choose to take morning coffee in the well-maintained garden.

The convivial manager is Ms. P. Vuyk, who charges from 85F ($39.06) to 95F ($43.65) in a single and from 110F ($50.55) to 130F ($59.74) in a double, breakfast included. Triples are available for 125F ($57.44) to 150F ($68.93). Special rates are offered for longer stays. If you're arriving by automobile, get off the autobahn at the Ostring exit.

Hotel Wachter, 44 Neuengasse (tel. 22-08-66), is another Berne hotel efficiently managed by the Mövenpick chain. The Wachter is fairly small, offering 44 rooms on four floors of a pleasant corner building near the railroad station. A sidewalk café occupies most of the pavement in front of the building, whose windows are protected in summer with awnings. Each of the modern rooms has a bath, radio, color TV, mini-bar, and special outlets for American electric razors. Single rooms begin at 74F ($34.00), while doubles (all of which have twin beds) cost 110F ($50.55). Breakfast is not included in the room price. B. Hunold is the manager.

Hotel Krebs, 8 Genferstrasse (tel. 22-49-42), lies close to the train station in a relatively nondescript building with a storefront sharing part of the hotel's ground floor. The management is informal and unpretentious, charging from 45F ($20.68) to 70F ($32.17) in a single, from 85F ($39.06) to 110F ($50.55) in a double. Breakfast is included in the price. Some of the rooms have private baths, while others require occupants to use the shower and toilet in the corridors. Accommodations are sunny, often partially paneled with vertical slats of light-grained wood, and decorated with attractive utilitarian furniture.

Hotel Continental, 27 Zeughausgasse (tel. 22-26-26). This charming hotel is close to the railroad station in front of a square with a fountain. The building has simple windows and flowerboxes that are filled with blossoms almost constantly throughout the summer. The public rooms are functional and unpretentious, while the bedrooms are clean, safe, and more spacious than you'd expect. A restaurant is attached to the hotel. Bedrooms rent for a wide range of prices, depending on the view and the plumbing. Singles cost from 40F ($18.38) to 70F ($32.17), and doubles range from 36F ($16.54) to 55F ($25.27) per person. Triples, when available, cost from 30F ($13.79) to 45F ($20.68) per person. Breakfast is included in all the prices.

Hotel Stadthof, 27 Speichergasse (tel. 22-77-27), was built in 1961 close to the railroad station. The bedrooms are clean and comfortably furnished with wooden furniture sometimes laminated with a white Formica-type cover, big sunny windows, and small armoires. All the rooms have private baths or showers and toilets, phones, and radios. The public rooms are traditional, with lots of exposed wood, many reproduction Windsor chairs, and in the dining room, a massive stone fireplace. One of the conference/banquet rooms is paneled with rich hardwoods and ornamented with stag horns. Singles rent for 68F ($31.25), while doubles cost between 92F ($42.27) 105F ($48.25), breakfast included. Half board is available for an additional 20F ($9.19) per person. E. Fasnacht, believe it or not, is the name of the owner.

Hotel Gurten Kulm, Wabern Berne (tel. 53-21-41). Visitors to this country hotel in a suburb of Berne will quickly respond to scenery which is nothing less than majestic. You'll have a superb view from many of the well-marked footpaths around the hotel which, although only 20 minutes away from Berne, still gives the impression of being very much in the Alps. You can arrive here from the center of town by tram and by funicular (which you might find to be a lot of fun all by itself, especially if you have children with you). Near the end of the line, you'll see the elaborately gabled roofline of this dignified old hostelry, with its green shutters, parasoled sundeck, and generous 19th-century proportions. The hillside seems to fall away in front, giving hotel guests the impression of being wonderfully isolated from the problems of the industrialized world back home.

Inside, you'll find everything that can be expected in a well-run establishment, including a good restaurant, a bar, and tastefully designed rooms with a wide option of plumbing choices priced between 48F ($22.06) and 94F ($43.19) in a single, from 39F ($17.92) to 84F ($38.60) per person in a double. Parents receive a reduction of 70% for children under 6 years old, 50% for children up to 12 years old, and 30% for adolescents up to 16 years old. If, by the way, your days in Switzerland don't allow enough time for a few hill-climbing expeditions, you'll find that the region around the Gurten Kulm has carefully marked trails for walks ranging from 20 to 50 minutes one way to several hamlets and hilltops nearby, which could be the basis for an invigorating morning's outing.

Hotel Bristol, 10 Schauplatzgasse (tel. 22-01-01), sits next to its sister hotel run by the same management, the Hotel Bären, where visitors are sometimes directed when the main hotel is full. Both establishments lie a few steps from the Swiss Parliament, close to the train station. The hotel facade is ornamented with oval medallions set between garlands of what look like laurel leaves carved into the stone between the flowered balconies. The cheaper rooms tend to be up under the eaves, with gabled windows looking out over the old city. Parts of the interior have been remodeled and replaced with a streamlined, conservative modern decor, but the bedrooms are tastefully appointed, carpeted, and have a variety of plumbing options.

Singles cost between 55F ($25.27) and 90F ($41.36), while doubles are priced at anywhere from 80F ($36.76) to 124F ($56.98), with a breakfast buffet included in the rate. All rooms, by the way, have recently been redecorated with new furniture, phones, radios, TVs, and mini-fridges. Peter Marbach, the owner, does everything he can to see that his staff is as helpful as possible.

Hotel Touring, 66 Zieglerstrasse (tel. 45-86-66), is a few minutes by foot from the train station, next to the Eigerplatz. Everything here is modern, in working order, and well maintained (and if something isn't operating, the assistant manager, S. Cordier, will see that it's quickly fixed). The bedrooms are clean, fairly spacious, and sunny. Many of the rooms have balconies and wood-paneled ceilings, and all of them have tiled baths, some of them impressively well-proportioned. The bedrooms were refurbished as recently as 1982. They all contain radios, phones, and, if you request it, TVs. The attached restaurant serves attractive meals at attractive prices. Singles rent for between 50F ($22.98) and 70F ($32.17), doubles from 40F ($18.38) to 55F ($25.27) per person, and triples between 40F ($18.38) and 43F ($19.76) per person, breakfast included. Parents receive reductions of 50% for children under 6 and 30% for children under 12, if they sleep in the same room as their parents.

Hotel Regina Arabelle, 6 Mittelstrasse (tel. 23-03-05), is a tranquil choice set pleasantly on its own grounds. The easy-going management tries to be helpful in every way, doing what it can to make guests feel at home. A grassy lawn with roses and a fountain lies just to the side of the backyard sun terrace, which might be an inviting place to write in your journal or to send letters home. Some of the bedrooms have Oriental rugs placed over the parquet floor and unusual photographic murals of the architectural designs on an elaborately ornamented Renaissance building. Breakfast is included in the price of between 50F ($22.98) and 72F ($33.08) in a single, 83F ($38.14) to 110F ($50.55) in a double. Triples cost from 115F ($52.84) to 126F ($57.90), while quads go for 137F ($62.95). For longer stays in Berne, the management offers apartments for two to four persons priced at between 132F ($60.65) and 185F ($85.01) per day.

Gasthof zum Löwen, 3 Enggisteinstrasse (tel. 83-23-03), in Worb, is the kind of romantic country inn that devotees of nostalgia seek out. Set in the residential suburg of Worb, which lies 15 to 20 minutes from the center of Berne, the hotel is easily reached by superhighway. The inn is an ivy-covered, hip-roofed, elegantly furnished establishment that is 600 years old. It's been in the same family for 11 generations. It's also bigger than it looks. You'll see mementos of a bygone era throughout the hotel, fine examples of hand craftsmanship, including the gently sloping stairway leading to the reception area from the lobby of the ground-floor restaurant. Antiques are scattered throughout.

The 14 rooms cost between 30F ($13.78) and 35F ($16.08) in a bathless single, going up to 60F ($27.57) in a single with bath. Bathless doubles rent for

60F ($27.57), rising to anywhere from 75F ($34.46) to 110F ($50.54) with bath, including a breakfast buffet served in a wood-paneled room.

The ambience of the restaurant is elegant and rustic, with a large bar filled with locals who drop in to drink. It's closed all day Wednesday and on Thursday until 4 p.m. Specialties include côte d'agneau forestière, piccata milanese, mignon de boeuf, entrecôte Café de Paris, and in season, wild game. Lunch is usually served from noon to 2 p.m. and dinner from 6:30 to 9:30 p.m. Fixed-price meals range between 20F ($9.19) and 47F ($21.60), with an à la carte dinner averaging from 22F ($10.11) to 44F ($20.22), and going up. The restaurant is closed from mid-July to mid-August.

Economy Choices

Hospiz Zur Heimat, 50 Gerechtigkeitsgasse (tel. 22-04-36), is, from the point of view of both charm and price, perhaps the outstanding economy choice in Berne. You couldn't possibly be more favorably situated than here, in the very heart of the old city, almost in the center of the peninsula on which Berne was originally built. The arches on the street level face a painted and gilded fountain whose waters splash into an octagonal basin below an ornate column holding a statue of a regal figure. The windows are big and, weather permitting, contain window boxes laden with heavy masses of flowers. The bedrooms are clean and well maintained, with headboards and simple functional furniture. A pleasant restaurant serves nourishing meals in a cozy ambience of wood paneling, hanging lamps, and a wall-size blowup of a Renaissance map of Berne. No alcohol is served in the restaurant.

Prices for rooms without private baths (although you'll find a sink with hot and cold running water in each of them) are 38F ($17.46) in a single, 62F ($28.49) in a double, 81F ($37.22) in a triple, and 108F ($49.63) in a quad. Prices with private bath are 52F ($23.89), 80F ($36.76), and 99F ($45.49) for a single, double, or triple, respectively. Breakfast is included. For easy access to the hotel from the train station, you can take trolleybus no. 12 for a ten-minute ride, getting off near the Rathaus and Münster.

Hotel zum Goldenen Adler, 7 Gerechtigkeitsgasse (tel. 22-17-25), lies a few buildings away from its neighbor, listed above, the Hospiz Zur Heimat, sharing the same fine site from which to tour the old city, especially since the Rathaus, the cathedral, and the Bearpit are all within a few blocks. The facade of this hotel, which is efficiently managed by the Peter Balz family, hints at its former glory as a private residence. The lobby contains an elevator leading to the redecorated rooms containing the hotel's 50 beds. The decor is a bit threadbare but clean, usually sunny and cozy. Children are especially welcome here. Rooms with private bath are priced at 60F ($27.57) in a single, 90F ($41.36) in a double, breakfast included.

Hotel Arca, 18 Gerechitgkeitsgasse (tel. 22-37-11), is on the same street as several of the other budget choices of downtown Berne. Managed by the Gasser-Schenker family, who renovated an older building in 1962, the establishment offers small, unpretentious lodgings in a breakfast-only format of clean rooms with baths, phones, and radios. A single rents for 65F ($29.87), while a double costs 90F ($41.36) for the night, including breakfast.

Hotel Goldener Schlüssel, 72 Rathausgasse (tel. 22-02-16), looks from the outside like a beautifully maintained patrician house with barn-red shutters, Swiss flags, and a wrought-iron oval sign containing the hotel's symbol, a golden key. A sidewalk café does a thriving business in summer, while the other popular restaurants seem to be busy all year. Bedrooms in this hotel are comfortably carpeted, often with one wall covered with mellow wooden planking. Elisbeth and Max Haller are the accommodating owners of this establishment, charging from 42F ($19.30) to 46F ($21.14) in a single, from 62F ($28.49) to 82F ($37.68) in a double, breakfast included. Within those price levels you'll find a plumbing option for your taste (and pocketbook).

WHERE TO DINE: The cuisine of Berne is international. The famous Swiss potato dish, rösti, is served everywhere, and there are dozens of specialty restaurants serving every dish from paella to porterhouse. Or best of all, you might head for one of the charming country inns on the outskirts.

The Leading Restaurants

Schultheissenstube, Hotel Schweitzerhof, 11 Schweizerhoflaube (tel. 22-45-01). A curved horseshoe bar occupies the center of this elegantly rustic second-floor restaurant, which some food critics hail as one of the 20 best in the country. Brown walls, polished paneling, and lots of elegant accessories contribute to the feeling of an elite sophistication. The menu was designed by the late Jean Cocteau. A menu gastronomique, which changes daily, costs 90F ($41.36) per person. In addition there's a daily carte of *les suggestions du chef,* which is likely to include a terrine of foie de canard (duckling) naturelle to lobster soup flavored with tarragon to a blanc de turbot bordelaise. The regular menu is also superb in every way, featuring among other dishes my favorite, sea bass with fennel, or perhaps mignonnettes of lamb flavored with basil and lamb.

Bellevue Grill, 3 Kochergasse (tel. 22-45-81), is considered one of the best parts of the famous Bellevue Palace Hotel. In summertime many patrons decide to eat on the elegant terrace high above the river, which many Swiss politicians consider the most beautiful garden terrace in Berne. A waiter will bring you a host of French dishes to your perch, all beautifully prepared and served on tables covered with flowers and immaculately pressed linens. You can arrive at the grill through the lobby of the hotel, or you might instead use the street-level entrance to the right of the hotel as you face its main portal. It's fashioned like a greenhouse, with lots of glass, maroon-colored steel, and a large piece of industrial sculpture with bears crawling all over it. Expect to spend from 50F ($22.98) and up for a meal composed of such classic dishes as caneton rôti with pearl onions, loup de mer (sea bass), and shellfish soup with cognac. Other typical dishes might include a mussel soup flavored with thyme, a terrine of roebuck, and sole in a saffron cream sauce. Service is from noon to 2:30 p.m. and 9 p.m. to midnight (on Saturday, from 7 p.m. to midnight). On the same premises is the **Stadt Restaurant zur Münz,** which is open from 8 a.m. to 11 p.m., serving simple meals from 14.50F ($6.66).

Restaurant Bärenstube, Hotel Bären, 4 Schauplatzgasse (tel. 22-33-67), near the Parliament House, is a favorite rendezvous for government ministers. The restaurant is in an attractively proportioned room with lots of paneling and some interesting frescoes of Bernese hunting scenes. You wouldn't expect the cuisine in such an ambience to be as light and up-to-date as it is, but chef Roland Burri nevertheless cooks many savory dishes with sophisticated touches. The cuisine créative, as it is called, features such dishes as rognons de veau (veal kidneys) in a cream sauce with tarragon, a salad made with mushrooms and foie gras, turbot flavored with fennel and Pernod, and a freshwater fish, fera, from the Vaudoise. You can order a light menu at 38F ($17.46), a menu gastronomique at 48F ($22.06), and a menu "surprise" at 85F ($39.06), or else order from the regular à la carte listings.

Café-Restaurant du Théâtre, 7 Theaterplatz (tel. 22-71-77), is housed in a grand baroque building near the famous clock tower in the old city. The high ceilings of its interior are partially covered with lighthearted murals of courtly scenes from the 18th century, as well as a discreet placement of a few hunting trophies. Ernesto Schlegel, the proprietor, serves such specialties as a tégamino of turbot with a mousseline of salmon, quenelles on a skewer with spinach, goose liver salad with sherry vinegar, salmon steak with baby leeks, and sweetbreads with shrimp. Open every day but Sunday evening and all day Monday, the restaurant charges from 25F ($11.49) to 36F ($16.54) for a four-course fixed-price meal, and around 82F ($37.68) for a seven-course gourmet repast. An à la carte meal averages between 28F ($12.87) and 68F ($31.24). The annual closing is from the last three weeks of July until early August. Reservations are suggested.

Restaurant Della Casa, 16 Schauplatzgasse (tel. 22-21-42). Entering from under an arcade, you'll go into a low-ceilinged paneled room painted a mellow off-white. The room is usually crowded with tables, chattering diners, and well-seasoned hausfraus serving large platters of food. Some of the platters are kept warm on top of a hotplate set on each table. An inner room containes daily newspapers on sticks, which are quietly perused by an older generation of politically conscious retired persons. It's an attractive place, perhaps the only one like it in Berne. The menu is continental, with an emphasis on Italian dishes such as bollito misto, a mixed potpourri of boiled meats. Two of my favorite dishes are the ravioli maison and the fried zucchini. You might also prefer the piccata maison or the risotto chipolata. The featured meat specialty is a filet mignon à la bordelaise with créole rice. Lunch is likely to cost from 11.50F ($5.29) to 14.50F ($6.66). In the evening, dinners range from 35F ($16.08) and up. Hours are from 11:30 a.m. to 2 p.m. and 6 to 9 p.m.

Restaurant Commerce, 74 Gerechtigkeitsgasse (tel. 22-11-61), is a small and sympathetic Spanish tavern where the waiters wear vests and seem to know many of the satisfied regular patrons. The decor is appropriately Iberian and the paella is very good. Scampi, prepared in several different ways, is the specialty. You might also want to sample their zarzuela, a Spanish-style bouillabaisse. Their chicken dishes are very well prepared, and you could settle happily for an entrecôte. Everything is backed up by good rice dishes and salads. À la carte meals cost between 34F ($15.62) and 47F ($21.60), on the average. The restaurant, which is closed in July, serves Tuesday through Saturday after 6 p.m.

Mistral, 42 Kramgasse (tel. 22-82-77), is named after the scorching winds that blow through Provence. A quick look at the menu will tell you that the food is indeed appropriate for the restaurant's name. The Provençal specialties include pesto soup, salade niçoise, frog legs, spaghetti al pesto, and an array of pizzas, beginning at 9F ($4.14). The savory tortellini dishes are always a favorite. If you order some of the à la carte specialties, expect to spend from 40F ($18.38) and up for a meal. The restaurant has a big sidewalk café separated from the light traffic of the old city street with a border of geraniums in summer. Hewn timbers stretch across the ceiling, while the stucco walls are covered with copper pans and pots and a few decorative animal skins.

Räblus, 3 Zeughausgasse (tel. 22-59-08), is the premier French restaurant of Berne, serving extravagant specialties to the occupants of ten tables set up inside. On the first floor of an inner-city building, near the famous old clock tower, the restaurant usually suggests that guests have an apéritif at the ground-floor bar, which the piano players make a popular rendezvous place. You climb upstairs for dinner. Specialties include a gratinée of seafood, mignons of veal with morels, tournedos Rossini, Indian chicken curry, Chinese fondue, and veal kidney flambé. The restaurant is open daily except Sunday till 1 a.m., but closes from July 20 to August 20. Fixed-price meals cost between 25F ($11.48) and 31F ($14.24), while à la carte dinners average between 26F ($11.94) and 56F ($25.73).

Ratskeller, 81 Gerechtigkeitsgasse (tel. 22-17-71), is an attractive combination of old masonry with a conservative modern update. Tables and chairs are made of patterned wood surrounded by lots of mirrors and an airy, well-lit ambience. Oldtime waitresses serve the savory food, directing guests to a basement keller if they choose. A special menu at night costs 42F ($19.30), while a carré d'agneau (lamb) à la diable goes for 30F ($13.78) for two persons. Other specialties include an omelette soufflée aux fruits at 9F ($4.14) for two persons. Main-course dishes are likely to feature veal kidneys Robert or côte de veau in butter. The restaurant is closed on Monday.

Budget to Moderate Dining

Churrasco, 60 Aarbergergasse (tel. 22-82-88). You'll imagine yourself in Argentina here, as many of the Bernese seem to when they come here for "something different." The decor is ranchero, with hanging lamps fashioned from pierced tin drums and cowhide covering the banquettes. Rustic pine branches (supposedly) support the ceiling, and at the far end of the room a chef dressed like an Argentinian cowboy grills deliciously flavored meat over a wood fire. Dishes include rumpsteak and entrecôte specialties (medium and "grande"), along with gazpacho, sangría, fried potatoes, and a special coffee. Meals begin at 30F ($13.78). The restaurant is open Sunday to Thursday from 11:30 a.m. to 11:30 p.m. (Friday and Saturday until midnight).

Restaurant Goldener Schlüssel, 72 Rathausgasse (tel. 22-02-16), sets its tables under the massive wood vaulting of its renovated dining room, although some of the tables sit under the stonework of an even older section. The restaurant, run by Elisbeth and Max Haller, is part of a budget-priced hotel previously recommended. Specialties here are inexpensively to moderately priced and are well prepared. Try the tête de veau (calf head) vinaigrette, if you have a taste for it (many diners don't), or more safely, the veal piccata with saffron rice or sweetbreads in puff pastry. Grilled beef dishes are very good also. Lunch begins at 16F ($7.35), while dinners cost from 25F ($11.49) and up.

Restaurant Harmonie, 3 Hotelgasse (tel. 22-38-40), lies at the corner of Münstergasse, a few blocks from the Houses of Parliament. This art nouveau charmer is directed with poise by Fritz and Marlise Gyger. It evokes Paris in the 1890s, with wooden paneling, skinny blue trim, and earth colors. The new generation has operated this gathering place since 1981 and have tried to maintain it in the style of their grandparents, who took it over in 1915. All kinds of people patronize the place, including, on one recent occasion, a diner who looked like a renegade impressionist painter. The establishment encourages an efficient service to its many tables, which are set far enough apart to give one a feeling of intimacy. There are two separate entrances, two separate rooms, and a few sidewalk tables protected by ivy-clad trellises. Evening meals begin at 25F ($11.49), and might include such good hearty food as tripe in tomato sauce with rösti, fresh homemade egg noodles bolognese, spinach ravioli, and a variety of omelets. Other dishes, which might also be served at noon, include rösti with ham and eggs, cheese fondue, potato soup, curried rice, and ratatouille. Lunches usually cost from 12.50F ($5.74). The restaurant is open from 8 a.m., serving warm food from 11:30 a.m. to 1:45 p.m. and the main dinner meals from 5:30 to 8:45 p.m., although some warm food is available until 11:30 p.m. Saturday hours are from 8 a.m. to 2 p.m.; closed Sunday.

Gfeller Rindlisbacher, 21 Bärenplatz (tel. 22-69-44), serves wholesome meals in several different ambiences to a loyal crowd of Bernese who pack into almost every seat, especially at lunchtime. The ground floor is divided into three seating areas, all of them with waitress service. You'll see a large chrome-and-steel staircase at one end, a partially latticed ceiling, and a symbolic representation of the buildings of Berne in wood cutouts. Upstairs you'll find a self-service cafeteria, American style, with panoramic windows opening onto the Bärenplatz. Lunches begin at 12F ($5.51). On the premises is a Swiss-style tearoom with a patisserie buffet with pastries costing from 2F (92¢). The sidewalk tables are crowded in summer, almost spilling over into the nearby flower market. The food comes in large, filling portions.

Restaurant Vegetaris, 15 Neuengasse (tel. 22-46-16). You'll need to walk up to the first floor of this building between the clock tower and the train station if you have a yen for vegetarian food. Once you get there, chances are you won't be disappointed. A salad buffet offers 24 different kinds of well-prepared and flavored salads, while waitress service can provide gratinée dishes from most vegetables grown in central Europe. You'll also find specialties made with soya and tofu, often with Swiss twist. Since it's open for breakfast every day except Sunday from 7:30 a.m., this might be your chance to order the yogurt, grain, and fruit mixture—so popular all over Switzerland—called birchermüesli. Meals begin at 12F ($5.51). Closing hours are 9 p.m., Monday to Friday, and 5 p.m. on Saturday.

Confiserie, 31 Marktgasse (tel. 22-35-56), is a café/bar/restaurant/tearoom which attracts mainly a female patronage. It's set under the busy arcades of the Marktgasse, and there's usually a flower vendor just outside the front door, along with other street merchants. The establishment extends a long way toward the orange-and-brown-colored rear of the restaurant. A bar with leatherette stools flanks the corridor-like section leading to the back, and some clients prefer to take their meals here. Set lunches are offered for 9.20F ($4.23), with a supplement of 2.80F ($1.28) should you prefer dessert. Breakfast is 4.20F ($1.92), and rich pastries begin at 1.60F (74¢). One aspect of the menu offers guests a green card where they check the kinds of salads they want assembled on a platter: a small one, with six different salads, goes for 6.50F ($2.99); a bigger one, with ten varieties, costs 8.80F ($4.04). The main eating hours are from 11 a.m. to 2 p.m. and 5 to 9 p.m.

WHAT TO SEE: **Marktgasse** is the principal artery of the old town, and it's lined with luxurious shops and boutiques. The number of florists reveals the Bernese love of flowers. In this traffic-free sector you can stroll at your leisure, shopping and admiring the 17th- and 18th-century houses. Hopefully, you will eventually find **Junkerngasse,** the most prestigious street in Berne, lined with patrician houses.

Marktgasse rolls on until it becomes **Kramgasse,** the first street to the right of the clock tower. It has many antique shops and art galleries. You'll also see many turrets and oriel windows, and you'll come upon the Zähringen fountain, showing a bear, the city's mascot, in armor.

The **Käfigturm** (prison tower) on Marktgasse in the 13th century marked the boundary line of Berne. Restored in the 18th century, it stands at the top of the Marktgasse.

To the east stands the **Zeitglocken** or clock tower, which was built in the 12th century and restored in the 16th century. Until 1250 it was the west gate of Berne. Four minutes before every hour, crowds gather for what has been called "the world's oldest and biggest horological puppet show." Mechanical bears (the little bear cubs are everybody's favorite), jesters, and emperors put on an animated show, and it's one of the longest running acts in show business, staged since 1530!

The **Cathedral of St. Vincent** (Münster), on Münsterplatz, was begun in 1421, although its tower wasn't completed until 1893. Its belfry, dominating Berne, is 300 feet high, and at the top a panoramic sweep of the Bernese Alps unfolds. A young woman, living in the tower, is the latest in a long line of attendants. You can climb a staircase, some 270 steps, to the platform tower from 10:30 a.m. to 4 p.m. for a 1.50F (69¢) admission. You'll also have a great vista over the old town and its bridges and a view of the Aare.

The Münster is one of the newer of the Gothic churches of Switzerland. Its most exceptional feature is the tympanum over the main portal, with more than 200 figures (I lost count!). Some of them are painted, and the vanquished ones in this Last Judgment setting are singled out for particularly harsh treatment. The mammoth stained-glass windows in the chancel were created in the 15th century. The choir stalls from 1523 brought the Renaissance to Berne, and in the Matter Chapel is a curious stained-glass window, the *Dance of Death,* constructed in the closing year of World War I but based on a much older design.

Once you leave the three-aisle, pillared basilica, you come upon the 1545 Moses Fountain on the Münsterplatz. The cathedral is open from 10 a.m. to noon 2 to 4 p.m., except on Sunday afternoon and Monday from November to Easter Sunday.

The **Rathaus** (town hall) on Rathausplatz is ancient, but still a center of political life. Erected in 1406, it was restored in its original style during World War II, when there wasn't much overhauling of old monuments going on elsewhere in Europe! It was built in the late Burgundy Gothic style, with a double staircase and a covered porch.

The **Kunstmuseum** (the city's are museum), 12 Hodlerstrasse (tel. 22-09-44), is the proud possessor of the world's biggest collection of the works of Paul Klee. A German painter, born in Switzerland in 1879, Klee had a style characterized by fantasy forms in line and light colors. He combined abstract elements with recognizable images. The museum has both Swiss and foreign works, placing its emphasis on the 19th and 20th centuries. However, some of its painting goes back to the 14th century. There is a collection of Italian "primitives," such as Fra Angelico's *Virgin and Child.* Swiss primitives include one from the Master of the Carnation (Paul Löwensprung, who died in 1499), who signed his work with either a red or while carnation.

The romantic painter, Holder, is represented by allegorical frescoes, depicting *Day* and, conversely, *Night.* Several impressionists are represented, including Monet, Manet, Sisley, and Cézanne, and you'll find such other artists represented as Delacroix and Bonnard. There are the inevitable scenes of Montmartre by Utrillo, and we move up to more contemporary times in the works of Picasso. Expressionist painters include Modigliani, Matisse, and Rouault, and cubist artists are properly exhibited, from Braque to Léger to Kandinsky. But, as mentioned, it is the works of Paul Klee that form the three-star attraction. There are at least 40 oils and 2000 drawings, gouaches, and watercolors. The museum, built in 1879, is open from 10 a.m. to noon and 2 to 5 p.m. except Monday, charging 3F ($1.38) for admission.

The **Bundeshaus** (federal palace) rises on the Bundplatz, containing two chambers of the Swiss Parliament. A flower market takes place in front on Tuesday and Saturday mornings. The dignified domed building was constructed in the Tuscan Renaissance style. The legislators of Parliament can look out upon the city beach, and when they saw the country's first topless bathers, a nationwide debate began. Guided tours are conducted through the building except when Parliament is in session. They depart every hour from 9 a.m. until noon and then at 2, 3, and 4 p.m. The building is closed on public holidays.

The famous **Bärengraben** (bear pits) is a deep, moonshaped den where the bears, those mascots of Berne, have been kept since 1480. Beloved by the Bernese, the bears are pampered and fed. Everybody seemingly drops by here, throwing these hungry beasts a carrot. The pits are reached by going across Nydegg Bridge, which has a great view of the city. It was built over a gorge of the river and its major stone-built arch has a span of 180 feet.

The bears have long been adopted as the heraldic symbol of Berne. Legend has it that when the Duke of Zähringen established the town in 1191, he sent his hunters out into the encircling woods which were full of wild game. The first animal slain would be honored by having the city named after it. A Bär or bear was the first animal killed, and since then the town was known as Bärn or Berne. Many scholars discount this legend, but it makes for a good story nonetheless.

Right below the bear pits, you can visit the stunningly beautiful **Rosengarten** (rose gardens). From these gardens you'll have a splendid vista onto the medieval sector and the river.

Try to fit in a visit to the **Schweizerisches Alpines Museum** (Swiss Alpine Museum), at 4 Helvetiaplatz (tel. 43-04-34), which is open Monday from 2 to 5 p.m., Tuesday to Saturday from 9 a.m. to noon and 2 to 5 p.m., and on Sunday from 10 a.m. to noon and 2 to 5 p.m., charging an admission of 1F (46¢). It depicts man's conquest of the Swiss Alps, and there's also a section devoted to architecture in the mountains, including mountain chalets. The traditional costumes of the population of the inhabitants of these lofty mountains are also exhibited. You'll see photographs and drawings of mountain flora and fauna, along with relief maps and panoramas, as well as mountaineering equipment and many life-saving devices.

In the same building is the Swiss postal museum, the **Schweizerisches PTT-Museum,** which is open from 9 a.m. to noon and from 2 to 5 p.m. (closed on Monday and opens an hour later on Sunday, at 10 a.m.). It depicts the development of the country's postal system, and also contains one of the largest stamp collections in the world.

The **Bernisches Historisches Museum** (Bernese historical museum), 5 Helvetiaplatz (tel. 43-18-11), is housed in a neo-Gothic structure, built in the style of a 16th-century schloss. It's open from 9 a.m. to noon and 2 to 5 p.m. (closed on Monday and opens an hour later on Sunday, at 10 a.m.). It has many tapestries and much splendid antique furniture, but is visited mainly by those desiring to see the loot captured from the Burgundians in 1476 at Grandson. These treasures are stunning, including standards and tapestries that once belonged to Charles the Bold. Admission is 3F ($1.38).

The **Naturhistorisches Museum** (natural history museum), 15 Bernastrasse, is one of the great museums of Berne, ofter overlooked, regrettably, by the most hurried visitor to the capital. You can view stuffed African beasts in a simulated natural habitat, along with everything from Arctic mammals to local fauna. There's an excellent exhibit of the endangered whale, although the reptile collection seems to hold the most fascination. The museum is open from 9 a.m. to noon and 2 to 5 p.m., except on Sunday when it opens at 10 a.m. It's free on Wednesday, Saturday, and Sunday afternoon; otherwise it charges a 2F (92¢) admission.

If you like your animals live, head for the **Dählhölzli Zoo** in the Tierpark, one of the most charming zoos in Europe (entrance on Jubiläumsstrasse). In this 32-acre park the Bernese have some 1000 animals to feed. Its Vivarium shelters hundreds of tropical birds, such as birds of paradise. The reptiles are always stunning, and the zoo has one of the biggest aquariums in Switzerland. It's open April to September from 8 a.m. to noon and 1:30 to 5:30 p.m., charging 3F ($1.38) for adults and 1.50F (69¢) for children.

In the immediate vicinity of Berne, you can visit one of the most spectacular attractions, **The Gurten,** a panoramic belvedere, a distance of only 1½ miles from the city. Depart Berne on the Monbijoustrasse, the road to Thun, heading for the suburb of Wabern. At Wabern, take a right (the road is marked) turn toward the funicular platform. In about ten minutes you'll arrive at the summit of The Gurten at 2815 feet. Service is about every 30 minutes, a round-trip ticket costing 6F ($2.76).

SOME SHOPPING NOTES: **Heimatwerk,** 61 Kramgasse (tel. 22-30-00), is a tourist store deluxe, selling souvenirs from the Bernese Oberland. Typical objects include pewter tankards, brass coffeepots, copper gelatin molds, and textiles of all kinds, as well as music boxes. Ceramic and wooden objects are to be found in the basement. If you're a dressmaker, be sure to look at the bolts of yard goods which are brightly patterned in regional design. The shop can be found under the arcades of a gray stone building on a historic street near the clock tower.

Altstadt Galerie, 7 Kramgasse (tel. 22-23-81), is an antique shop which was established six years ago by the attractive blonde owner, Suzanne Käppeli. The store is loaded with two floors of Swiss chests and tables, many of them made from pine and many originating in the Bernese Oberland. If you like antiques and aren't familiar with this type, come in and look. Prices are clearly marked, beginning at 500F ($229.75). Ms. Kappeli also features a changing exhibition of works by Swiss painters.

NIGHTLIFE: Most of the Bernese are good, hard-working people who have to get up early for work. That means they have an early "last drink" in one of the city's historic cellars, such as Kornhauskeller or the Klötzlikeller, then stroll home under the lamplights through the lanes and byways of the old town. However, for the more "rowdy" international crowd, there are several clubs offering dancing and entertainment, perhaps cabaret, which remain open until the wee hours.

If you speak German, you can see some very good theater in Berne. The leading theater is the **Stadtheater** (municipal theater) at 20 Kornhausplatz (tel. 22-07-77). Even if you don't speak German you might want to attend, as it has a program of operas and ballets where the artistic language is universal.

Ballet, cabaret, and many other types of performances are presented at the **Theater am Käfigturm,** 4 Spitalgasse (tel. 22-61-00). Contemporary plays in German are presented at the **Kleintheater,** 6 Kramgasse (tel. 22-42-42). *This Week in Berne,* distributed free by the tourist office, has a list of current cultural events.

The **Arcady Bar,** in the Hotel Schweitzerhof, 11 Schweizerhoflaube (tel. 22-45-01), might be the best place to begin your evening with an apéritif. You can also drop in later for an after-dinner nightcap. Here you're likely to see ambassadors drinking champagne and eating oysters. The decor is centered below an elliptical wood-covered ceiling, where butler's tables and Chinese lamps are accessories to the elegantly restrained decor. The clientele is chic and well dressed, so you should be too. Snacks are available, including omelets at

10F ($4.60) and an assiette grisonnaise at 17F ($7.81), the latter consisting of plates of air-dried meats from the Grisons.

Casino, 25 Herrengasse (tel. 22-20-27). Since the largest wager legally allowable in Switzerland is 5F ($2.30), many guests come to the casino for reasons other than gambling. Perhaps it will be to have an inexpensive meal in the Brasserie, in a choice of four little cozy rooms, decorated Bernese style. Both seasonal specialties and regional cookery are featured, at prices beginning at around 20F ($9.19). You also have a choice of draft beer and a fine selection of wines. A classic French cuisine is served in the Casino Restaurant, including such dishes as tournedos Rossini, filets de soles Marquery, a terrine of homemade goose liver, and many lobster dishes (the lobsters come from their own sea-water tank). At lunchtime the chefs prepare a daily three-course menu for 30F ($13.79), the à la carte dinner prices rising to 50F ($22.98) or more. In the new bar, you might ask the barmaid, "Maggie," to prepare your favorite drink, which she'll do until 2 a.m. You might also investigate the concert hall to see what musical acts are being performed on the night of your visit. On a weekend night the entire Casino is virtually an entertainment complex and a hub of Berne's nightlife.

Jaylin's Club, 11 Bahnhofplatz (tel. 22-45-01), is the most elegant club in town, sheltered in the prestigious Schweizerhof in a plush and glittering ambience where the clientele seems to come from many parts of Europe. Entrance is free to hotel guests, but others pay an entrance fee of 6F ($2.76). Musical acts are likely to include a host of American and English jazz groups. Live entertainment is supplemented by disco music with dancing. The club sponsors a Saturday apéritif concert from 4 to 7 p.m., which draws an active crowd, especially toward the end. Drinks cost from 15F ($6.89). Closed Sunday.

Kornhaus Keller, 18 Kornhausplatz (tel. 22-11-33), was once a grain warehouse but is today the best known after-dark establishment in Berne. It's in the old city in a stone building with elegantly symmetrical proportions and an arched arcade on the ground floor. It's a huge beer cellar, seating hundreds of diners in a getmütlich baronial kind of ambience. Musical acts perform here frequently. Often there is a Sunday brunch concert from 10 to 11:45 a.m., as well as a changing schedule of evening entertainment, including, on one recent occasion, the "Red Hot Peppers." Of course the repertoire always consists of alpine melodies produced by a brass band and accordions. This is Berne's answer to the Hofbrauhaus in Munich. Dinners cost about 22.50F ($10.34), or a simple meal, 8.50F ($3.91). A Berner plate of smoked meats and sauterkraut is the classic dish to order, going for 19F ($8.73).

Klötzlikeller, 62 Kerechtigkeitsgasse (tel. 22-74-56), is about the hardest place to find in the city of Berne—but well worth the search. It's in the cellar of one of the old town's historic buildings. Watch for the small sign on the street side of the sidewalk, pointing to an angled cellar door like the one leading to the backyard of a Victorian house. This is the oldest wine tavern in Berne, dating from 1635. Technically the site is owned by the city, which has leased it to the sophisticated and attractive Isabella Gschwind, who fulfills a long-established tradition—a long time ago the town fathers decreed that only a divorced woman with children should get the job. Most people come here to talk and drink, although simple meals are offered. The menu is limited, wisely so, and includes tasty sausages with rösti, excellent salads, and a large beer, which will cost from 16F ($7.35). However, it's most customary to visit to drink the wines, which you can do by the open glass if you prefer.

Charley's Beef and **Cadillac Disco,** 10 Laupenstrasse (tel. 25-34-34), are a few blocks west of the train station, in a corner building with big windows and an attractive and informal ambience. Charley's is known for the best steaks and grills in town, costing from 40F ($18.38) for a meal which might include onion soup, a sirloin, a good salad, and such side dishes as baked potato with chives and bacon. Many of the dessert specialties are flambé extravaganzas, made with bananas or peaches. The restaurant is open seven days a week from 5 p.m. (6 p.m. on Sunday), closing at 2 a.m. Sunday to Thursday and at 3 a.m. on Friday and Saturday. In the same building (downstairs) is the Cadillac Disco, which is an amusingly avant-garde and fun place to dance and drink, with libations beginning at 9F ($4.14).

Mocambo, 10 Genfergasse (tel. 22-50-41). The decor is in an Aztec theme in red with pre-Columbian bas-reliefs on the walls. The cabaret theme includes music, vaudeville, acrobatics, jugglers, can-can, and strip. A round dance floor lit from underneath accommodates disco dancing between shows. A "scotch bar" opens at 5 p.m., while the club itself is ready for business every night except Sunday from 9:30 p.m. Guests pay a cover charge of 8.50F ($3.91), plus from 14F ($6.43) for drinks.

Swiss Chalet Restaurant, 75 Rathausgasse (tel. 22-37-71), is the setting for a popular folkloric show, where yodelers call to one another and a brass band goes oom-pah-pah in a setting of brick walls, beamed ceilings, and red-checkered tablecloths. The walls are hung with oversize cow bells and alpine farm implements. The singers sit or stand on a recessed area which, during lunch, is concealed by a curtain. At night the place is brilliantly lit and a lot of fun. The music begins at 8:30 p.m. on a quiet note as patrons finish their dinner. From 9:30 to 10:30 there's a full-blown concert, with dancing after 10:30. (There's no music between January and March, although by the time of your visit there could be.) Dinner averages anywhere from 35F ($16.08) and up, but no one will mind if you drop in for just a beer, costing from 3.50F ($1.60). There's no cover charge. The establishment lies in the Hotel Glocke.

Chikito, 28 Neuengasse (tel. 22-26-80), is an all-around cabaret club featuring everything from strip to "Swiss rock." It opens at 8:30 p.m. and sometimes imposes a cover charge, depending on which live group might be appearing. You'll find a Frisco bar, with a rotating series of DJs playing. The audience is lively, and beer costs 14F ($6.43).

PRACTICAL FACTS: The **Berne Tourist Office** in the new Berne Hauptbahnhof (tel. 22-76-76) is open from 8 a.m. to 8:30 p.m. Monday to Saturday and from 10 a.m. to 8:30 p.m. on Sunday. If you need help finding a hotel room, they'll make reservations for you in a price range you select.

The **American Express** office, 37 Marktgasse (tel. 22-94-01), is open Monday to Friday from 8:30 a.m. to 12:30 p.m. and 1:30 to 5:30 p.m., on Saturday from 8:30 a.m. till noon; closed Sunday.

You'll find a **laundromat** at 50 Militärstrasse. It's open Monday to Friday from 8 a.m. to 6 p.m. and on Saturday from 7 a.m. to noon, charging about 9F ($4.14) per load. Take the streetcar to Breitenrainplatz.

If you need a **pharmacy,** try Central-Apotheke Volz and Co., 2 Zeitglockenlaube (tel. 22-10-94), which has served Berne's residents since 1900. Near the clock tower in the old city, it employs English-speaking staff members who are happy to suggest over-the-counter substitutes for American drugs which may not be obtainable in Europe. It's open Tuesday to Friday from 7:45 a.m. to 6:30 p.m., on Saturday to 4 p.m., and on Monday from 1:45 to 6:30 p.m.; closed Sunday.

The phone number for 24-hour **medical emergencies** in Berne is 22-92-11. This includes dental and pharmaceutical information. Pre-set schedules for doctors, dentists, and open pharmacies providing 24-hour service are changed weekly, so you must phone for the latest information.

You can check the children into **kindergarten** while you shop. The Ryfflihof department store, 53 Aarbergergasse (tel. 60-01-11), has facilities for looking after youngsters during store hours. The Loeb department store, 47-51 Spitalgasse (tel. 22-73-21), will accept responsibility for children, including serving them a meal, from 2 to 4 p.m. on Monday, 9 a.m. to 6 p.m. Tuesday to Friday, and 9 a.m. to 3:30 p.m. on Saturday. Maximum stay at the Loeb is two hours. The fee is 2F (92¢) per child. For **babysitting** services at other times, your hotel or the tourist office can probably accommodate you.

Of several **swimming pools,** I especially recommend **Ka-We-De,** a pool with artificial waves, 101 Jubiläumsstrasse (tel. 43-01-75), which is open from May till September. Hours in May and September are from 8 a.m. to 7 p.m. daily, to 6 p.m. on Sunday. In June, July, and August, hours are 8 a.m. to 8 p.m. daily, to 7 p.m. on Sunday. Admission is 1.60F (74¢). Another good choice is **Hallenbad** (indoor pool with Turkish bath and sauna), 14 Maulbeerstrasse (tel. 25-36-56). Hours vary daily. Admission is 3F ($1.38) to swim, with another 3F charged to use either the sauna or the Turkish bath.

GETTING AROUND IN BERNE: The **Public Transport System (SVB)** operates a self-service ticket-purchasing system on all routes. You must obtain your ticket at an automat (there's one at each stop on the bus and tram network) *before* you board the vehicle as there are no conductors or ticket dispensers aboard. If you're caught traveling without a ticket, it'll cost you 20F ($9.19) in addition to the fare for the ride. To save yourself time, trouble, and possibly money, you can purchase a one-day ticket for 4F ($1.84), which entitles you to unlimited travel on the 38-mile SVB network during any 24-hour period of your choice. Just get the ticket stamped at the automat before you begin your first trip. One-day tickets are available at ticket offices at 5 Bubenbergplatz (tel. 22-14-44) and in the underpass of the main railroad station (tel. 22-62-04), as well as at some other sales outlets in the city, including newsstands.

Taxis are found at the public cab ranks, or you can phone for one: Casinoplatz (tel. 22-05-40); railroad station (tel. 22-04-40); Kornhausplatz (tel. 22-29-29); Hirschengraber (tel. 22-40-22); or Waisenhausplatz (tel. 22-18-18).

For information as to timetables and tickets on the **Swiss Federal Railways,** phone 22-24-04 daily between 7:30 a.m. and 8:30 p.m.

SEEING BERNE: A **city sightseeing tour,** conducted daily except Sunday at 2 p.m. in April and at 10 a.m. and 2 p.m. from May 2 to October 21 (Saturday only from November 1 to December 31 at 2 p.m.), costs 14F ($6.43) and leaves from in front of the tourist office at the main railroad station. An English-speaking guide will escort you on the trip to the Rose Garden for a view over the old city, through the city's residential quarters, past museums, and down to the River Aare which flows below the Houses of Parliament. You'll see the late Gothic cathedral and have a stroll under the arcades to the clock tower. The tour takes you to the Bearpits where you can see Berne's heraldic animals, through the medieval streets of the city, and back to the railroad station. This half-day look at Berne is highly recommended.

A SIDE TRIP THROUGH EMMENTAL: The district of Emmental, in the canton of Berne, is famous for its cheese. Just ten miles or so from the capital, you'll be plunged into a pastoral world that is the home of the famous "hole-filled" Swiss cheese. Some of these wheels of cheese weigh 180 pounds. Set against a backdrop of snowy Alps, it's a world of verdant fields and plump Swiss cows. Some of the farms set on rolling hillsides have been in the same family for generations, each new brood also becoming farmers as were their forebears. Even the smallest hamlet has its little ole local cheesemaker.

Emmentaler (sometimes spelled Emmenthaler) is the most famous cheese of Switzerland, and is more commonly called "Swiss cheese."

Much of the architecture is similar: large Bernese farmhouse complexes, embracing both a main house, the bauernhaus, and an adjoining stöckli, where the grandparents retire when they get too old to run the farm and turn it over to their children. Government officials from Berne often take special guests outside the city for a country dinner in one of the local inns, usually named after a lion or a bear (the sympol of Berne), and which are known for their good, hearty food and abundant hospitality.

If you're planning to visit Lake Lucerne after Berne, you'll find that the quickest way is through the Emmental, and you'll have a sightseeing adventure along the way.

The gateway to the district is:

Burgdorf

Northeast of Berne, this small town is known for its castle of the Zähringen family, characterized by a trio of towers which have been turned into a historical museum of only passing interest. However, the view of the Bernese Alps is memorable. This large stronghold stands on an isolated crag, dating from the 12th century when it was founded by the Dukes of Zähringen, who turned it into one of the country's most formidable bastions of defense. It's open April 1 until the end of October from 2 to 6 p.m. and on Saturday from 9:30 to 11:30 a.m. (from 2 to 4 p.m. on Sunday). Admission is 2.50F ($1.15). Burgdorf also has a late Gothic church from the end of the 15th century, and many attractive and well-maintained guildhouses.

If you're in need of food and lodging, consider the following suggestion:

Hotel Touring Bernerhof, Am Bahnhofplatz (tel. 22-16-52), was constructed in 1954 in front of the train station, but is considerably quieter than you'd expect for such a location. The bedrooms have been renovated in a cozy style, sometimes with Oriental rugs, and always with comfortable beds. A staff of cooks prepare food for the brick-walled pizzeria, rustic restaurant, and steakhouse. The staff is usually very friendly. Each of the 34 rooms has its own bath, radio, phone, and TV hookup. Alice and Georges Portmann, the owner/managers, charge 48F ($22.06) in a single and between 85F ($39.06) and 95F ($43.65) in a double, including breakfast.

2. Lake Thun

Occupying an ancient terminal basin of a glacier, Lake Thun (Thunersee) was once connected to Lake Brienz (Brienzersee) until they were divided into two at Interlaken. Over the years the Lütschine River deposited so much debris at Interlaken that the one body of water eventually became two.

Beloved by Brahms, the lake—not as well known as some of its more famous counterparts in Switzerland—is a discovery to many North Americans. The Swiss are rightly proud of it, keeping it as a "secret address' for a lakeside holiday. It's about 13 miles long and two miles wide.

It has a mild climate, earning for it the title of the "Riviera of the Bernese Oberland." The lake is a playground for waterskiers, the yachting set, and windsurfers. It also has excellent swimming pools (both indoor and outdoor), as well as windsurfing schools. There's plenty of activity along its shores too, including golf, mountain railways, underground caves, tennis, and horseback riding.

Two major centers are Thun and Spiez (see below), although there are many other towns and villages off the beaten track that are worthy of your attention. Because of space limitations, I'll document only the more interesting ones.

THUN: At the gateway to the Bernese mountains, the little city of Thun began on an island at the point where the Aare River flows into Lake Thun. Lying 19 rail miles southeast of Berne, Thun is the capital of the Bernese Oberland. It long ago outgrew its island origins and overflowed onto both banks of the river.

The most interesting sector is on the Aare's right bank. The curiosity there is the busy main street of **Hauptgasse,** where flower-decorated walkways have been built across the arcaded shops below.

At the Rathausplatz, with its 17th-century town hall, you can take a covered staircase up to the formidable **Castle Kyburg.** Built by the Dukes of Zähringen at the close of the 12th century, it was later possessed by the Counts of Kyburg, and became in time the residence of the Bernese bailiffs. Today it's a historical museum, open from the first of June until the end of September from 9 a.m. to 6 p.m.; otherwise, April, May, and October, from 10 a.m. to 5 p.m., charging 2.50F ($1.15) for admission. Inside its massive residential tower is one of the largest baronial halls in Switzerland. Exhibits include tapestries, antiques, ceramics, armor, but mainly it's the view of the town and the river that will attract you.

If you'd like to take an excursion, head for **Schloss Schandau,** a 19th-century manor house on Thun Lake. Grandiose and baronial in style, it was built by a French architect in 1848. It's been called, if you can imagine such, "English Tudor Gothic" and "French Early Renaissance." On the ground floor is a restaurant, and on the second floor changing art exhibitions are shown. It's open in July and August daily from 10 a.m. to noon and 2 to 6 p.m. except Monday, charging an admission of 2.50F ($1.15). It can be reached on foot if you're athletic, as it lies only a mile south of Thun in the village of Scherzlingen.

Where to Stay

Hotel Beau Rivage, Aare Quai (tel. 22-22-36), rises from the shores of the lake with everything that a 19th-century resort hotel should have. Its heavily detailed facade is painted alpine white, with certain accents made of natural stone. The configurations of the red tile roof probably couldn't be duplicated today. Guests enjoy the sun terrace, the indoor swimming pool, and the antique-filled public rooms. A garage maintained by the hotel will park your car, although if you arrive by train you'll be only five minutes by foot from the station. The hotel usually closes between mid-October and the end of April. The bedrooms most often face south, with a view of lake and mountains. Bathless singles cost between 30F ($13.78) and 45F ($20.68), going up to anywhere from 44F ($20.21) to 70F ($32.16) with bath. Bathless doubles range between 55F ($25.27) and 78F ($35.84), rising to anywhere from 80F ($36.76) to 110F ($50.55), depending on the season. Breakfast is included.

Elite Hotel, 1 Bernstrasse (tel. 23-28-23), is a modern and comfortable hotel in the center of the city. It's soundproof and equipped with an attractive restaurant, a dimly lit bar, and a sun terrace with meal service. The bedrooms, for the most part, are flamboyantly decorated with vividly patterned geometric wallpaper. In the basement are some automated bowling alleys. The Riesen family, the English-speaking owners, do what they can to make guests feel at ease. All rooms contain private baths, costing between 52F ($23.89) and 58F ($26.65) in a single in low season, between 63F ($28.95) and 80F ($36.76) in high. Doubles go for 95F ($43.65) to 108F ($49.63) in low season and anywhere from 105F ($48.25) to 125F ($57.44) in high. Half board costs another 17F ($7.81). A good Chinese restaurant is also on the premises.

Schloss Hotel Freienhof, 3 Freienhofgasse (tel. 22-46-72), is quietly situated on the Aare close to the center of town. The hotel consists of an older four-story symmetrical core with a vibrantly modern addition extending to the side. There balconied rooms give views of the river on one side and a landscaped park on the other. The public rooms are richly but unpretentiously outfitted with natural grained woods and tastefully modern furniture. The comfortable accommodations all have private baths, costing between 43F ($19.75) and 49F ($22.51) in the off-season and from 60F ($27.57) in summer. These tariffs are on a *per-person* basis in a double room. For a single, a supplement of anywhere from 6F ($2.75) to 13F ($5.97) is charged. Half board goes for 20F ($9.19) per person.

Hotel Krone, Rathausplatz (tel. 22-82-82), is a historic building with a prominently turreted extension projecting into the front yard. Owned and operated by the Lamprian family, the hotel has well-decorated rooms, each with private bath, plus a swimming pool. Singles cost between 50F ($22.98) and 70F ($32.17), while doubles range between 90F ($41.36) and 140F ($64.33). The Krone is very popular and fills up early in peak season.

Hotel Bahnhof (Maulbeerbaum), 2A Frutigenstrasse (tel. 22-50-22), is conveniently located close to the train station in a white rectangular building with lots of windows, especially on the fifth and sixth floors. The comfortable rooms are somewhat on the small side, but are tasteful and pleasant. Singles cost between 45F ($20.67) and 55F ($25.27), while doubles range between 40F ($18.38) and 48F ($22.06) per person, depending on the season. All units contain private bath, and tariffs include breakfast. A restaurant with a bar and grill are on the first floor, along with a few sidewalk tables.

Where to Eat

Simmentalerhof, 59 Bälliz (tel. 22-22-03), is an intimately proportioned alpine-style restaurant, with regional mementos hanging from its rustic walls. Everything served is of the freshest available products, which combine into a gutbürgerlich cuisine very popular with local residents. The limited menu features shrimp bisque, sole "in the miller's style," chateaubriand, trout, perch, and cock with morels and noodles. Wines include a good selection of French products. The restaurant is closed on Sunday. Fixed-price meals cost between 15F ($6.89) and 43F ($19.76), while à la carte dinners average between 25F ($11.49) and 47F ($21.60).

Restaurant Turm, Schwäbisgasse (tel. 21-88-95), is a gutbürgerlich restaurant with a rich and well-varied salad buffet. A daily fixed-price meal at lunch costs 9F ($4.13), while dinner menus usually begin around 25F ($11.48). This is very much a shopper's restaurant, serving local residents in a chain outlet attached to one of the canton's grocery/delicatessens. It's open from 8:30 a.m.

to 11:30 p.m. every day except Sunday and Monday and for the last two weeks in July. Portions are generally well prepared and generous.

Casa Barba, Rathausplatz (tel. 22-22-27), is the most popular place in town for Spanish food, such as paella, rice with seafood, and Spanish-style filet of sole. The grilled meats are especially good, as are the Iberian wines. Juan and Mirianne Barba are the congenial hosts of this sympathetic spot, which is centrally located and open every day except Monday. À la carte meals cost between 17F ($7.81) and 29F ($13.33). A quiet terrace is available should you wish to dine outdoors.

BEATENBERG: A modest high-altitude health resort, Beatenberg lies about six miles from Interlaken, reached by climbing a steep, narrow road (or else you can take the funicular up from Beatenbucht). Beatenberg is the end of the line, as there is no through traffic. On the north side of Lake Thun, Beatenberg, at 4265 feet, lies on the southern slopes of the Niederhorn, which can be reached by chair lift, taking you to a height of 6400 feet.

The winter season, lasting from December to April, appeals to both beginning and experienced skiers. The chair lift to Neiderhorn and four ski tows take skiers to various runs. The Swiss Ski School also operates in the resort, and a cross-country and ski touring track is permanently marked. All access roads are open throughout the year. In the heart of the village is an ice rink for skating, hockey, and curling devotees. There's also a heated swimming pool.

Once at Beatenberg, you'll have splendid views of the highest peaks in the Jungfrau region, along with views of Lake Thun, Eiger, and Moench.

Beatenberg also enjoys a brilliant summer season from May to October, with alpine flowers and mild autumn-like days. The area has 20 miles of signposted paths.

Food and Lodging

Hotel Kurhaus Silberhorn (tel. 41-12-12) is sheltered inside a five-story clapboard building with lots of windows and four floors of covered loggias strewn with geraniums and begonias in summer. The sunny terrace is an inviting spot for coffee and snacks, especially since it allows for views of the Eiger, the Jungfrau, the Mönch, and Lake Thun. The inside is pleasantly furnished, in some places with cambriole-legged chairs and Oriental carpets. A heavily beamed bar and a glass-walled restaurant might be restful places for stopovers. The Jansen family charges from 46F ($21.13) to 60F ($27.57) in a bathless single and from 61F ($28.03) to 85F ($39.06) in a single with bath. For doubles, they charge from 92F ($42.27) to 120F ($55.14) without bath and from 122F ($56.06) to 150F ($68.93) with bath. These prices include half board, and full board is available for an additional 12F ($5.51) per person. Diet meals are offered. There's an elevator on the premises.

Hotel Favorita (tel. 41-12-04). The Gurtner family maintains a pastry shop, café, and tea and lunch room on the ground floor of this Victorian-style house with its wooden balconies and extended eaves. Many clients choose to sit on the masonry terrace in front. Whether it's for lunch or just a glass of mineral water, you're likely to get a tan from the sunny exposure. Several comfortable rooms are located on the upper floors. Bathless singles cost between 24F ($11.03) and 32F ($14.70), going up to 42F ($19.29) with bath. Bathless doubles range between 48F ($22.06) and 64F ($29.41), rising to 84F ($38.60) with bath.

MERLIGEN: The major reason for staying here is the elegant resort hotel described below. Tiny Merligen (not to be confused with Meiringen) lies on Lake Thun, about six miles from Interlaken, at an altitude of 1863 feet. This lakeside resort is perched at the gateway to the Justis Valley, enjoying a sheltered situation, and is the center of many summer sports.

Hotel Beatus (tel. 51-21-21). The best view of this hotel might be from a boat in the middle of Lake Thun. (The hotel will rent you one, along with equipment for most other water sports.) The architect of the establishment designed it in long horizontal lines which, when coupled with its yellow awnings, give a pleasantly restful impression of well-maintained calm. The interior includes a host of well-staffed public rooms, many of them with panoramic views of the lake. The spacious bedrooms usually offer balconies which you can enjoy at breakfast. There's also an indoor swimming pool, plus a sauna and whirlpool, as well as a dancing bar with a live pianist. Paul Joss is the capable manager. Each of the accommodations has its own private bath. Depending on the season, singles begin at 75F ($34.46) in winter, rising to a high of 145F ($66.63) in peak season. Doubles begin at 140F ($64.33) in low, soaring to anywhere from 200F ($91.90) to 260F ($119.47) in high season, including breakfast, plus another 40F ($18.38) per person should you want half board.

3. Spiez

SPIEZ: Dominated by its castle and vineyards, Spiez is an easily reached resort on the left bank or southern shore of the lake. Pleasantly situated at the foot of the Niesen, Spiez is mainly a summer resort, offering fishing, windsurfing tennis, horseback riding, open-air theater performances, folklore evenings, and many hiking paths. It also has a sailing school.

The **Castle of Spiez,** near the landing stage, has a museum today, open April to October daily from 9:30 a.m. to noon and 2 to 4 p.m. (closed on Monday morning). The museum charges 3F ($1.38) for admission. The best attraction of the castle, frankly, is its panoramic vista over the lake and the Niesen. Otherwise, it contains relics of its former owners, three well-known Bernese families—the Bubenbergs, the Strättligen, and the Erlachs.

The town also has an 11th-century Romanesque church with frescoes, known simply as **Alte Kirche** or old church.

The major attraction, however, lies outside the resort. Near the end of town, take a road leading to Simmental, heading via Mülenen for about five miles to the funicular station. There you can board the funicular, paying about 22F ($10.11) for a round-trip ticket which will take you to the **summit of the Niesen** at 7750 feet. Allow about two hours. Departures are fairly often between 8 a.m. and 5 p.m. from May until the end of October.

Food and Lodging

Strandhotel Belvedere (tel. 54-33-33). Only a large open meadow separates this elegant hotel from the lake. Since much of it is planted with flowers and old trees, it's a pleasure just walking around. The hotel has been added onto several times over the years, so that today it resembles a 19th-century gabled house with a panoramic series of public rooms extending toward the lake. All of this affords a visitor the use of several sunny terraces, as well as a collection of attractive furnishings and carpets. A modern and very comfortable annex is set nearby to accommodate overflow guests from the main building. Bathless doubles cost between 40F ($18.38) and 50F ($22.98) per person, while singles or doubles with bath range between 50F ($22.98) and 80F ($37.76) per person, depending on the season and exposure. Rooms in the annex rent for between 35F ($16.08) and 45F ($20.68) per person, with half board costing an additional 25F ($11.48) per person daily. On the premises you'll find a tennis court, plus facilities for waterskiing, windsurfing, and sailing, along with instructions. There's also a heated outdoor swimming pool.

Hotel Bahnhof Terminus (tel. 54-31-21) is a curious mixture of a steep-roofed 19th-century core with a steel-and-glass annex extending toward the lake off to the rear. The public rooms in the old section are cozy, while those in the modern part are streamlined, functional, and panoramic. The simply furnished bedrooms cost between 58F ($26.65) and 85F ($39.06) in a bathless double and between 30F ($13.78) and 44F ($20.21) in a bathless single. Rooms with bath range between 78F ($35.84) and 110F ($50.54) in a double, between 42F ($19.29) and 58F ($26.65) in a single. Half board is another 18F ($8.27) per person daily.

Hotel Bellevue, 36 Seestrasse (tel. 54-23-14), has a tall shape with unusual proportions—higher than it is wide, giving it an unmistakably Victorian aura. Its facade is accented with brown shutters and a few centrally placed wrought-iron balconies. It's been owned since 1944 by the Maurer family, who have redecorated the interior in an updated rusticity, including the obligatory heavy beamed ceilings. You're only five minutes on foot from the train station, yet the sunny terrace gives good views of the town with an almost unobstructed view of the lake beyond. Doubles with shower cost 42F ($19.30) per person or 32F ($14.70) per person without shower. Singles rent for 35F ($16.08) a day, and half board is available for an additional 12F ($5.51) per person.

OBERHOFEN: This town, on the eastern shore, is visited because it is dominated by the most romantic-looking castle on the lake. The **Castle of Oberhofen** dates back to the 12th century, and was once owned by one of the Habsburgs. In private hands since 1798, its last owner was an American attorney, William Maul Measey of Pennsylvania, who turned it over to the Oberhofen Castle Foundation in 1940. Over the past centuries, especially the 19th, the castle has been reconstructed in a rather self-conscious historical style. Its museum has a wide collection of furniture and artifacts, ranging from the Gothic to the baroque. It can be visited from mid-May to mid-October daily from 10 a.m. to noon and 2 to 5 p.m., charging 3F ($1.38) for admission. It closes on Monday morning.

FAULENSEE: This is a small sailing resort that lies immediately east of Spiez and is less likely to be overrun in summer. In fact, it can be reached on foot from Spiez along a marked pathway, taking about 30 minutes.

Hotel Sternen (tel. 54-13-06). Whoever designed this hotel did it with just the right number of humorous touches. Examples might include the pier light fashioned from a nautical anchor to designate where the boats should moor, or the discreetly robust mermaid painted onto the paneling in the dining room. I always like the photograph of the owner and head chef, Theo Müller, in full chef's regalia (including a stovepipe hat) windsurfing across the lake. The decor of the hotel is invitingly warm and the reception is friendly. The hotel offers a range of lake sports as well. Bathless singles cost between 30F ($13.78) and 40F ($18.38), going up to anywhere from 39F ($17.92) to 49F ($22.51) with bath. Bathless doubles rent for between 54F ($24.81) and 66F ($30.33), while doubles with bath increase to 96F ($44.11) to 111F ($51).

AESCHI: A fast-rising winter sports resort in the Bernese Oberland, Aeschi stands on a sunny terrace overlooking Lake Thun. It's easily within commuting distance of Spiez, and is reached by a good road or by the post bus from the rail station at Spiez, which is the end of the autobahn, about four miles from Aeschi. It's also a summer playground, with walks in many directions (some of these are conducted, allowing you to visit an alpine cheese dairy).

Swimming and other water sports are possible in the indoor swimming pool at Aeschi or at nearby Lake Thun. The resort is very unspoiled, and has two ski lifts and two training lifts, offering skiing for beginners and those more advanced on mechanically prepared runs. Tobogganing is also possible, and there's a ski school as well as bus service to nearby skiing grounds.

Hotel Restaurant Baumgarten (tel. 54-41-21). Usually the flag of the canton flies above the hotel, which is painted a pastel yellow with black shutters. The interior is outfitted with a few well-placed Oriental rugs, furniture selected in the '60s (but still comfortable and serviceable), and a heavily timbered bar area where you're likely to meet some of the locals. The owner-manager, Hansjürg Bürki, charges from 30F ($13.78) to 35F ($16.08) in a bathless single (but with a private toilet), that rate going up to between 38F ($17.46) and 47F ($21.59) in a single with bath. Doubles cost between 50F ($22.97) and 60F ($27.57) without bath, and between 70F ($32.16) and 90F ($41.35) with bath.

4. Interlaken

A holiday resort for some 300 years, Interlaken is the tourist capital of the Bernese Oberland, the point from which visitors take dozens of excursions, including to the frozen Jungfrau. Interlaken, the "town between the lakes" (Thun and Brienz), lies below the north side of Jungfrau. The excursion possibilities from Interlaken are numerous, as cableways and mountain rails bring most of the dazzling sights of the Bernese Oberland within fairly convenient reach.

For years Interlaken was known mainly as a summer resort, but in recent years it has gained considerable winter business as well

An Augustinian monastery was founded here in 1130 and lasted until it was closed by the Reformation (the ruins can still be seen in the grounds of the castle and the Protestant church). Tourism to the area could be said to have begun in 1690 when Margrave Frederic Albert of Brandenburg undertook a journey into the snowy alpine world of the mountains and glaciers of the Jungfrau massif. However, tourism really dawned at the beginning of the 19th century. The festivals of alpine shepherds drew many artists and writers to the area who did much to publicize the resort. Steamer service on the lakes and the railway brought a steady stream of visitors, which over the years has included royalty, along with such eminent names as Goethe, Mark Twain, and Mendelssohn.

The view of the Jungfrau from the Höhenpromenade in Interlaken is justly famed. The Höheweg goes between the west and east train stations of Interlaken. About 35 acres in the middle of town, once the property of the Augustinian monks, was acquired in the mid-19th century by the hotelkeepers of Interlaken who turned it into a parklike setting.

As you stroll along the promenade, you'll pass the Kursaal (casino), where everybody stops to gaze at the flower clock. The clip-clop of the fiacres add a nostalgic touch, as they were so beloved by the visiting Edwardians. The promenade is lined with hotels, cafés, and gardens.

At some point in your exploration you'll want to cross over the Aare River to Unterseen, built in 1280 by Berthold von Eschenbach and standing opposite Interlaken. There you can visit the parish church with its late Gothic tower dating from 1471. This is one of the most photographed sights in the Bernese Oberland. The Mönch appears on the left of the tower, the Jungfrau on the right.

Each summer, while seated in a covered grandstand, visitors are enthralled to watch the saga of William Tell, according to Friedrich Schiller, relating his version of the formation of the Swiss Confederation.

Interlaken is well equipped for tourists, with its indoor swimming pools, cafés with calorie-loaded pastries, and animal parks. As a throwback to Victoria's day, afternoon concerts are still presented.

In addition to mountain trekking, many local sports are available, including sailing, windsurfing, rowing, fishing, golf, tennis, even glider flying. You can also go on many lake steamers across Brienz and Thun.

WHERE TO STAY: Interlaken has a wide range of accommodations suitable to most tastes and pocketbooks. Some of the leading hostelries were around long *before* grandmother's day, but others are new and modern and have kept abreast of the times.

The Leading Hotels

Hotel Victoria-Jungfrau (tel. 21-21-71) has been considered for generations one of the most important hotels in Switzerland. Catering to a resort type of customer, it services the needs of Swiss and foreigners alike who come to Interlaken to rejuvenate themselves in the alpine sunshine. This is one of the *grande-dame* hotels of the region, designed around a central tower capped by a relatively simple curved roof below a slender needle-shaped spire. The rest of the facade extends with a kind of restrained dignity in a series of recessed planes to either side of the main tower. In summer, colorful awnings stretch above the balconied windows toward the rigid symmetry of the well-kept gardens.

Your eyes will not linger long in the immediate vicinity of the hotel, however, unless you should spot someone who particularly attracts your gaze. Everywhere around this hotel, as happens all over in Interlaken, your attention is drawn to the mountains around you, whose savagery seems to dwarf the cultivated plants near the hotel. A swimming pool is within view of the colonnade of one of the porches, while indoor-outdoor tennis courts support a sports facility which is simply magnificent.

The interior is gracefully high-ceilinged, with ornate plasterwork and lots of antiques from several different periods. The bar area has comfortable settees, lots of space, friendly service, and might afford a pleasant diversion.

Singles with full bath and all the accessories rent for between 97F ($44.57) and 165F ($75.82), while doubles cost from 160F ($73.52) to 270F ($124.07), including breakfast. When you grow tired of your room, you'll find enough wining, dining, and musical facilities here to keep anyone entertained for many, many days. On the premises are two elegant restaurants, three bars (some of which serve snacks), a cabaret-oriented nightclub (where some of the acts go beyond—far beyond—being mildly risqué), and a disco with live music. For further descriptions, see the "Nightlife" section.

Grand Hotel Beau-Rivage (tel. 22-46-21) presents the advantage to guests of being in the center of town and of supervising a varied program of health, diet, exercise, and skin-care regimes for clients who are interested. The hotel is built in a vaguely Italian Renaissance style, with a central tower capped by a triangular pediment below a modified mansard roof. The rest of the central tower has an ascending series of covered loggias, bedecked with flowers and ornamented with restrained carving. Two wings radiate to either side of the loggias, with wrought-iron balconies and gables rooflines. The ceiling of the reception area is covered with elaborate designs in the plaster and supported by four garlanded columns in the center of the room.

Despite the promise of old-fashioned decor hinted at by the facade, the bedrooms have for the most part been renovated in a conservatively traditional style, with mostly modern pieces used against the backdrop of prominently displayed curtains and forgettable furniture. Service is fairly good, however, and this is above all a sports-oriented, health-conscious hotel. Rates include access to the indoor pool and the fitness club.

M. Steffen, the manager, offers a wide choice of rooms, ranging from 47F ($21.60) to 124F ($56.98) per person in a double, from 52F ($23.89) to 103F ($47.33) in a single, breakfast included. High season is from July 11 till September 10, during which half board costs another 28F ($12.87) per person.

Bellevue-Garden Hotel (tel. 22-44-31) looks a lot like an updated version of a fortified castle with windows, shutters, and a glass-fronted restaurant. The hotel sits directly on the banks of the Aare River in a grass-covered setting with flowering trees, landscaped walkways, and roses. The garden style is definitely English, of great appeal to plant lovers.

The Fink family, the nature-conscious owners of this place, prefer not to do business every year between mid-October and the first week of April. The rest of the time they are gracious hosts to guests who fill the single rooms at 41F ($18.84) to 84F ($38.60) per night or doubles at 64F ($29.41) to 146F ($67.09). Public rooms are furnished with comfortable late-19th-century chairs and couches, creating a cozy, old-fashioned ambience where your great-grandmother would feel very much at home. On the shores of the river a rustic gazebo stands next to a wrought-iron fence.

Hotel Royal St. Georges (tel. 22-75-75) seems to be adorned over most of the outside and inside with a confectionery type of elaborate decoration that only the 19th century could have produced. The roofline is delightfully capped with dozens of small hand-turned spires placed above each of the gables on the red tile roof. The lower floors have so many balconies, loggias, and lengths of wrought iron that most Americans will marvel at the craftsmanship it took just to create the facade.

You won't be disappointed by the public rooms either. the architectural details have been pampered, painted, preserved, and protected in their original rococo splendor of French Second Empire and art nouveau. The ceiling of the main dining room has been painted in a discreetly colored mural of alpine skies whose clouds seem to flow over the molded borders of its frame. Some of the more expensive rooms have been restored to their original high-ceilinged condition, while others have been updated to a conservatively modern format of utilitarian furniture and panoramic windows. Public rooms include a bar area in a well-proportioned salon-type room, and two restaurants. Hermann Kurzen and his family are the proprietors here. They charge approximately 130F ($59.74) in a double and 80F ($36.76) in a single, all prices including breakfast.

Hotel Metropole (tel. 21-21-51) rises almost 2000 feet into the alpine air, high above practically everything else in Interlaken. It could as easily have been placed in the financial district of, for example, Seattle, as in the Alps, yet it's surprisingly pleasant here, particularly since the views from the panoramic bar/café are strikingly beautiful. Each of the 100 accommodations has its own color scheme (the turquoise rooms are turquoise from top to bottom, for example, although all-orange and all-sunflower rooms exist also). Hopefully, yours will have a concrete balcony with a southern exposure toward the Jungfrau. Units also have baths, radios, and phones.

Public rooms include the wood-paneled Raclette Tavern, an up-to-date informal snack restaurant, a black-and-white striped dancing bar, three liquor/apéritif coffee bars, an indoor swimming pool, a sauna, and lots of outdoor games. Le Charolais restaurant serves formal meals in an oversize rooms with bright tablecloths.

D. Campbell, the general manager, charges from 100F ($45.95) to 115F ($52.84) in a single, from 170F ($78.12) to 200F ($91.90) in a double, with breakfast included. The hotel closes in winter from November to April, although an annex, the Residence, stays open all year long, charging from 60F ($27.57) to 80F ($36.76) in a single, 100F ($45.95) to 140F ($64.33) in a double. Rates go up at Christmas, New Year's, and Easter. Half- and full-board plans are available for 28F ($12.87) and 42F ($19.30) additional per person. Children under 12 get a reduced rate in their parents' rooms. For an extra person in any unit, the hotel imposes an additional 35F ($16.08) fee.

Stella Hotel (tel. 22-88-71) From the balconies of this resort-type hotel you'll get a good view of the mountains in any season. The orange awnings are removed in winter, when the hotel's white concrete superstructure seems to blend in with the snowy field around it. Inside you'll find a tile swimming pool, protected by a roof but with a glass wall to the outside which can be opened or shut according to the weather. The lounge/bar area is rustically decorated with a planked ceiling, heavy timbers, and a piano, while the unpretentious restaurant serves nourishing meals. Werner and Christine Hofmann-Frei, the couple who direct this place, are themselves interested in winter sports. They'll prove helpful in every way, perhaps even accepting an offer to play Ping-Pong on the table set up outside on the grassy lawn in summer.

Single rooms rent for 55F ($25.27) to 92F ($42.27) while doubles range between 90F ($41.36) and 242F ($111.20), including breakfast. The wide range of prices stems from the management's policy to increase prices by about 25% in high season (summer and the Christmas and New Year's holidays), and to charge much less during any season for rooms facing north with an inferior view. Full- and half-board plans are available, as are apartments. Reductions are offered for children.

Hotel National (tel. 22-36-21) rises seven floors above its lawns, in a format of horizontal aqua and white stripes that would be at home on the grounds of a university in California. A bar inside is dramatically upholstered in black leatherette, with a curtained wall of curving picture windows below a timpered ceiling. The salon is filled with sets of smallish Victorian chairs and a "grandmother's parlor" kind of feeling. The Kübler-Bongard family owns this hotel, providing good service and charging from 50F ($22.98) to 70F ($32.17) in a single and from 50F ($22.98) to 80F ($36.76) in a double, breakfast included. Full- and half-board plans are available for an additional 35F ($16.08) and 20F ($9.19), respectively. Rates for children are reduced by anywhere from 30% to 50%.

Hotel Krebs (tel. 22-71-61), owned by a family with the same name, looks over the shopping district of Interlaken. Set into its own gardens in front of a sidewalk with a fairly active commerce, it is very much a downtown hotel, although the mansard roof and the green shutters could almost make you think it's a private home. The interior benefits from the carpenters who, years ago, built beautifully finished wooden ceilings and walls, along with a skillfully crafted wooden staircase leading to the upper floors. Bedrooms are pleasant, often with timbered ceilings and enough space to feel comfortable in. From the terrace there's a good view of the Jungfrau. Singles rent for between 75F ($34.46) and 90F ($41.36), while doubles from 120F ($55.14) to 150F ($68.93). A triple ranges from 150F ($68.93) to 180F ($82.71). Breakfast is included in all the tariffs. Half- and full-board plans are available.

The Middle Bracket

Hotel de la Paix, 24 Bernastrasse (tel. 22-70-44). You'll find this family-run hotel a pleasant surprise, especially since it's only a block away from the Bahnhof (Interlaken West). The roofline is fairly ornate, gabled and tiled like a legend from Grimms' fairy tales. The relaxed atmosphere is partly the result of the efforts of owners Gillian and Georges Etterli, who do everything they can to help the guests quickly adjust to the slow pace of Interlaken. An elevator will carry you to one of the 45 beds upstairs, which are found in rooms which have a wide range of plumbing. A double with shower costs 70F ($32.17), while a single rents for 32F ($14.70) without shower, 40F ($18.38) with. Breakfast is included.

Park-Hotel Mattenhof (tel. 21-61-21) is a large, old-fashioned hotel in a secluded spot at the edge of a forest. The management guarantees a quiet and calm sojourn to its many guests who marvel at the manicured lawns and panoramic views of the Alps. The outside looks like a private castle, because of its high pointed roof, its several towers, and many loggias and balconies. Attached to the hotel are a swimming pool, tennis courts, facilities for amusing children away from their parents, terraces, bars, and restaurants. Many of the salons are sunny and airy, warmly decorated in a way that makes you want to sit down and enjoy the ambience. The proprietors are Peter Bühler and his family, who charge from 55F ($25.27) to 65F ($29.87) in a single and from 62F ($28.49) to 86F ($39.52) per person in a double. The rooms facing north fall into the cheaper range of the prices. All tariffs include full board. A reduction of 9F ($4.14) per person is made for clients who request half board instead of full.

Hotel Weisses Kreuz, Höheweg (tel. 22-59-51), is in the center of Interlaken, under the direction of the Bieri family. The hotel is built inconspicuously on a street corner at the end of a row of buildings. The interior is pleasantly decorated with white walls and half-paneling, with a few Oriental rugs for extra color. Open all year, the hotel rents singles for between 38F ($17.46) and 72F ($33.08), and doubles go for 30F ($13.79) to 57F ($26.19) per person per day, depending on the season, breakfast included. Half- and full-board are available for an additional 18F ($8.27) and 28F ($12.87) per person. A baby's cot can be set up in any room for an extra 12F ($5.51).

Eurotel, 13 Regenparkstrasse (tel. 22-62-33), is part of the well-known European chain. Its Interlaken link can be found in the center of the resort and identified by its corner location and wide horizontal stripes of gray and white. Many of the rooms have private balconies, private baths, kitchenettes, radios, and phones. Some units have fewer accessories, and these, of course, cost less. The rooms are warmly decorated in, for example, soft browns, and there is enough space to feel comfortable in. On the premises you'll find a bar, a lounge, and a breakfast room. You'll never get the ambience of a privately run family hotel here, but the rooms are clean and efficient. They cost from 47F ($21.60) to 63F ($28.95) in a single, from 36F ($16.54) to 53F ($24.35) per person in a double. Breakfast is included in the prices.

Hotel Bernerhof (tel. 22-31-31) can be found close to the Interlaken West train station in the center of town. Open year round, the hotel presents an interesting angled facade to the street. Each room has its own recessed balcony separated from the bedroom inside by a wood and glass door which is angled sharply enough to create a triangular balcony floor space. The main salon is vividly decorated with scarlet wall-to-wall carpeting and modish purple chairs with delta-shaped supports. An open fireplace in the center sends smoke through a tubular chimney. The Hanspeter-Anderegg family are the owners. They charge from 45F ($20.68) to 63F ($28.95) per person in a double room, 61F ($28.03) to 82F ($37.68) in a single, breakfast included. Full and half board are available for 38F ($17.46) and 20F ($9.19), respectively.

Hotel Beau-Site, Seestrasse (tel. 22-81-81), can be found after a short walk from the Interlaken West train station. Surrounded by its own spacious gardens, dotted in summertime with parasol-shaded card tables and chaise lounges, the hotel proves to be a pleasant and relaxing oasis in the middle of town. The owners are the Ritter family, who charge from 33F ($15.16) to 63F ($28.95) per person in a double room with breakfast, with a small supplement added onto those prices for persons wishing to rent a double for use as a single. Full- and half-board plans are available for an additional 28F ($12.87) and 18F ($8.27) per person per day. The wide range of prices here is because of the variety of plumbing facilities within the hotel and the difference between high and low seasons.

Hotel Central Continental, 31 Bahnhofstrasse (tel. 22-86-26). From the main street you'll glimpse this grand dowager of a hotel across a rushing river. It was built during a period when every architect wanted to construct the ultimate in Victorian embellishment. Unfortunately, the interior isn't as whimsical as the outside. Renovations have simplified a lot of it, and of course the original furnishings are long gone. However, it remains a comfortable and cozy hotel. The owners created a Bounty Bar, a 19th-century mariner's fantasy of fishnets, buoys made into lamps, and whaling harpoons. It's a popular gathering spot where you can let your hair down. The 48 rooms all have private bath, costing from 45F ($20.68) to 75F ($34.46) in a single and from 40F ($18.38) to 70F ($32.16) per person in a double, depending on the season and the exposure of your accommodation.

The Budget Range

Gasthof Hirschen, Matten/Interlaken (tel. 22-15-45), is a congenial family-run inn slightly outside of town on the road to Grindelwald. The place looks like a rustic chalet, set directly on the road but with gardens behind. The inside offers 40 beds to guests, who frequently choose to dine in the paneled and timbered dining room or in the less formal bar area. The Sterchi-Barben family, the owners, charge 30F ($13.79) per person per night for a double room, 32F ($14.70) in a single. The establishment is closed every year from October 10 till December 1. Breakfast is included in the prices.

Swiss Inn, 23 General Guisan Strasse (tel. 22-36-26), is a very small inn, offering 25 beds to tourists for between 30F ($13.78) and 35F ($16.08) in a bathless single, and between 40F ($18.38) and 50F ($22.98) in a single with bath. Bathless doubles cost between 54F ($24.81) and 68F ($31.25), while doubles with bath range from 66F ($30.33) to 86F ($39.52), depending on the season and the length of stay. Prices include breakfast. Mrs. Vieny Müller-Lohner is the charming and attractive hostess, who does everything she can to make visitors feel at home. The hotel is a five-minute walk from the Interlaken West train station. The building, by the way, is Edwardian, with all the elaborate detailing and gables you'd expect. Jazz plays softly in the sympathetic breakfast room. Of particular interest is the second-floor sitting room, a small jewel of a room surrounded by red-and-blue stained-glass windows. All rooms are tastefully decorated, and very comfortable.

WHERE TO EAT: Most guests dine at their hotels, which partially explains why such a world-famed resort as Interlaken has so few very good independent restaurants. But there are some should you be staying in a hotel "garni" or else want a change of fare.

The best known spot is the **Schuh** (tel. 22-94-41), which has long been celebrated for its pastries. It's an attractive restaurant, confiserie, and tearoom in the center of town. It's housed in an alpine-style building with a thick roof extending in an arch over the fourth-floor windows like a woman's bonnet. In the rear is a sunny terrace with globe lights and a well-kept lawn. Inside is an extensive glass case loaded with tempting chocolates, as well as a large restaurant with oversize windows and a live pianist. The ambience is almost Viennese, with heavy silver on the well-set tables, as well as candles in antique brass holders and lights with pink silk lampshades. The establishment is owned by the Beuter-Kropf family, who charge from 14.80F ($6.80) and up for set meals, although you could spend as much as 50F ($22.98) ordering à la carte. Hot food is served from 11 a.m. to 2 p.m. and 5:30 p.m. until closing. The restaurant is near the Hotel Victoria.

Pizpaz, 1 Bahnhofstrasse (tel. 22-25-33), is a pizzeria in the center of town. Its many outdoor tables make it a busy, bustling place, serving primarily Italian specialties. Enrico Zanette, the owner, charges from 30F ($13.78) for an average meal which might include any of the standard Italian specialties such as calf liver in Marsala, osso buco, plus at least 20 different types of pizza. Gelato misto, a mixed selection of ice cream, is the most popular dessert. The establishment is very popular with families. It's closed Monday but open every other day from 10:30 a.m. to 1 a.m.

Restaurant Burestube and **Ryter-Bar,** 57 Höheweg (tel. 22-65-12), is a rustically friendly bierstube, with red accents and lots of polished wood. This place draws a wide range of clients, and everybody is very democratic, often sharing tables. The hubbub of conversation competes with the rock music. You might have a drink at the crowded bar where a gregarious bartender entertains a retinue of customers while keeping up a brisk service. You'll see wrought-iron cages for wine, lots of timbered beams, and an occasional painted alpine chest.

The kitchen prepares very good salads, a giant plate costing only 7.50F ($3.45). Children's plates are also offered, ranging in price from 6F ($2.76) to 7.50F ($3.45). You can choose your favorite meat (priced by the gram) at a buffet. Here you'll find the finest quality veal steak, tenderloin, sirloin, or pork cutlet. There are at least eight chef's specialties, including the Bernese plate with smoked pork products, sausage, sauerkraut, and boiled potatoes. Meals range from 25F ($11.49). The restaurant is closed on Monday.

NIGHTLIFE: **Congress Center** and **Casino** (tel. 22-17-12) stands in the heart of Interlaken (you can't miss it), and it's the closest establishment the resort has to a total entertainment center. Open every day but Sunday from May until September, it has different establishments under the same roof, which includes a dancing bar with cheerful live music and light disco. There's also a gaming room, plus a large concert hall. The concert hall maintains a regular schedule of musical acts from Switzerland and Germany, as well as other countries. Every Monday and Thursday night from June until August they host a Swiss folkloric concert with yodelers, brass instruments, and an occasional flügelhorn. These concerts are performed in September also, but only on Monday. From June until August the casino hosts daily (except Monday) concerts, either in the garden or in the casino bar. All of this is in addition to Le Petit Casino, a gaslit garden restaurant which draws its own crowd. Remember that the largest wager permitted in Switzerland is 5F ($2.29), so you can't lose much. The schedule for each of these events changes frequently, but your hotel will know and many kiosks in town post the casino's programs prominently.

Cabaret, am Höheweg, Hotel Victoria Jungfrau (tel. 22-12-38), features a host of "the famous cabaret strip girls," who wear elaborate costumes which include everything from leather with chains to gossamer butterfly wings. There's a different allure (practically) for everyone's fantasy, as well as magic acts, perhaps a local starlet in pink feathers, and lots of hoopla. There's no cover and drinks cost from 18F ($8.27).

Barbarella, am Höheweg, Hotel Victoria Jungfrau (tel. 22-12-38), is a popular disco, with kleig lights, a nightly live act with local and international bands, and lots of comfortable seating. There's no cover charge, and drinks cost from 9F ($4.13). It's open from 10 p.m. until 2 a.m. weekdays and Sunday, on Friday and Saturday until 3 a.m.

Paul's High Life (tel. 22-15-50), next to the Interlaken West train station, is the hottest disco in town. It draws a wide crowd of everybody from tourists to locals, and is open every day from 9 p.m. until 3 a.m. Hard liquor begins at 9F ($4.13) a drink, and beer costs from 6F ($2.75).

PRACTICAL FACTS: Take a **horse-drawn cab** *(fiacre)* for a round trip through Interlaken, Matten, and Unterseen, about a half-hour ride. The cost is 15F ($6.89) for one person, 18F ($8.27) for two, 20F ($9.19) for three, and 6F ($2.76) for each additional person. The cabs leave from the Westbahnhof in Interlaken.

Need a **babysitter?** The tourist office (tel. 22-21-21) will help you find one.

For the services of a **pharmacy,** I recommend Apotheke Seewer, 4 Höheweg (tel. 22-34-26).

If you need some exercise to rejuvenate yourself after a lot of sightseeing and fondue dipping, I suggest the following:

Swimming: There's a public indoor swimming pool (tel. 22-24-16) behind the casino, with a solarium and a fitness room. It's open Monday to Friday from 9 a.m. to 9:30 p.m., on Saturday and Sunday to 6 p.m. (closed on Monday from September 9 to April 30). Adults are charged 5.50F ($2.53), 4F ($1.84) with a visitor's card, 5F ($2.30) with a season ticket, and 3.50F ($1.61) with a season ticket and a visitor's card. Children under 6 are admitted free; from 6 to 16 they pay 3F ($1.38), 2.70F ($1.24) with a season ticket.

Golf: You can play at the Interlaken-Unterseen course for 35F ($16.08), 30F ($13.79) with a visitor's card. For more information, phone the clubhouse (tel. 22-60-22).

Tennis: Use of an outdoor court at the Höhematte will cost 15F ($6.89) per hour, 12F ($5.51) with a visitor's card. If you're alone and willing to take your chances on being matched up with another loner, it will cost you half the court fee. For reservations, phone 22-14-72 from 8 a.m. to noon and 2 to 5 p.m.

EXCURSIONS FROM INTERLAKEN: Swiss engineering genius reaches its apex in the Bernese Oberland, as the mountains are filled with cogwheel trains, mountain cables, chair lifts, and aerial cabins. A network of roads and mountain railways—many of which were once thought impossible to erect—serves the Jungfrau district.

Jungfraujoch

For many, the highlight of every Swiss tour is the trip to Jungfraujoch at 11,333 feet, the highest railway station in Europe for more than half a century. It's also one of the most expensive, costing adults 89F ($40.90) and children, 6 to 16, 44.50F ($20.43) for a round-trip ticket. Departures are usually at 8 a.m. (this could vary) from the east station in Interlaken, the return scheduled for about 4 p.m.

The excursion is comfortable and safe, and packed with adventure. You first take the Wengernalp railway (nicknamed WAB), a rack railway which opened in 1893. It takes you to Lauterbrunnen at 2612 feet. At Lauterbrunnen you change trains, heading for the Kleine Scheidegg station at 6762 feet. This is avalanche country, as a view unfolds of the Jungfrau (named for the white-clad Augustinian nuns of Interlaken), Mönch, and the Eiger Wall.

At Kleine Scheidegg you change to the highest situated rack railway in Europe, the Jungfraubahn. You have six miles to go, and four of those miles will be spent in a tunnel ambitiously carved into the mountain between 1896 and 1912 under the direction of Adolf Guyer-Zeller. You stop twice, for about five minutes each, at Eigerwand and Eismeer, where you can view the sea of ice from windows built into the rock. The Eigerwand is at 9400 feet and Eismeer is at 10,368 feet. After leaving the tunnel, you are likely to be blinded if you forgot to bring along a pair of sunglasses. Incidentally, the Eigernordwand (north wall) is so steep it's been called "notorious."

Once at the Jungfraujoch terminus you may feel a little giddy until you get used to the air. You can take a free elevator behind the post office to a corridor that will lead to the famed "Ice Palace." Here you'll be walking on what is called "eternal ice."

The Ice Palace (Eispalast) is a cavern hewn out of a glacier by a Swiss guide in 1934. These caverns were cut 65 feet below the surface of the glacier. Everything—walls, floors, whatever—has been made of ice, and in various niches you can see ice sculptures, including one of a vintage automobile.

There's much to do once you're here, as Jungfraujoch forms its own little eerie world.

Once you return to the station, you can take another corridor, called the Sphinx Tunnel, to yet another free elevator. This one takes you up 356 feet to an observation station called the Sphinx Terraces, overlooking the saddle between the Mönch and Jungfrau peaks. You can also take in the expanse of the Aletsch Glacier, at 14 miles the longest river of ice in Europe. The snow melts into Lake Geneva and is eventually carried to the Mediterranean, where it has become considerably warmer.

A scientific station here conducts astronomic and meteorological research, and has a research exhibition which explains weather conditions and offers a video presentation. There's also a cafeteria, naturally with a view.

As a further adventure, you can take a sleigh ride, pulled by stout huskies.

On your way back down, you return to Kleine Scheidegg station but can vary your route by going through Grindelwald (see the description coming up), from which you'll have panoramic views of the "north wall' which has claimed so many lives.

Hopefully, the weather and the visibility will be ideal. You should always ask at the tourist office in Interlaken before making the trip. Remember, once again, that your body metabolism will be affected, and you may find the slightest body movement tiring.

Back in Interlaken, you can strike out again on a much less ambitious excursion, this time to **Harder Kulm** at 4337 feet. This belvedere gives you not only a view of Interlaken and the Bernese Alps, but of both lakes, Thun and Brienz. A funicular will take you up to Harder Kulm, the trip taking about 15 minutes and costing 12F ($5.51) for a round-trip ticket. Departures are about every half hour, and service is from May to October. You can have drinks or a meal at the Hotel Restaurant Harder Kulm, with its observation terraces.

You can also take a funicular up to **Heimwehfluh,** at 2215 feet, where you'll be rewarded with views of both the lakes of Brienz and Thun. The funicular station is about a six-minute walk from the west rail station in Interlaken, at the southern end of Rugenparkstrasse. From the belvedere at the top you'll also have views of Jungfrau, Mönch, and Eiger, the classic trio. There's a lookout tower at the top along with a café and restaurant. The funicular ride takes about five minutes, costing 10F ($4.60) for a round-trip ticket. Departures are May until the middle of October from 9 a.m. to noon and 1:30 to 5 p.m.

Wilderswil

Lying less than two miles to the south of Interlaken, Wilderswil stands on a plain between the lakes of Brienz and Thun at the foot of the Jungfrau mountains. It is both a summer and a winter resort, and the starting point for many excursions. The resort has 16 different levels of accommodations, ranging from hotels to guest houses, but most visitors stay in Interlaken, visiting Wilderswil to take the excursion to **Schynige Platte.**

Ruskin came this way, finding that the view of the Jungfrau from here was one of the trio of great sights in all of Europe. You may want to do the same, taking the train from the Interlaken East station, arriving in Wilderswil in about six minutes, maybe a little more.

Here you can switch to a cogwheel train for the harrowingly steep, nearly hour-long descent to the Schynige Platte at 6454 feet. The rack railway, which opened in 1893, travels a distance of 4½ miles, with gradients up to 25%. More than a dozen trips a day leave in season from May to October, costing 25F ($11.49) for a round-trip ticket.

Once you arrive at Schynige Platte, you'll find an alpine garden, charging an admission of 2F (92¢), with some 500 species of flowers. At the belvedere, you'll have a splendid view of Eiger, Mönch, and Jungfrau. You can find food and drink at the Hotel Restaurant Schynige Platte.

If you'd care to stay in Wilderswil instead of Interlaken, I have the following recommendations:

Hotel Jungfrau (tel. 22-35-31). The best part of this hotel is its location, surrounded by trees and meadows with an alpine backdrop which inspires you to begin a sports regime. The hotel is a boxy modern interpretation of a mountain chalet, with lots of rustically wooden balconies over a cement superstructure. The interior is attractively decorated with heavy beams, lots of wrought-iron detailing, and a sympathetic bar area near the restaurant. Three minutes from the train station, it has nearby bus and train connections not only to Interlaken, but to Grindelwald, Mürren, or Wengen. The comfortable and well-furnished rooms cost from 35F ($16.08) to 47F ($21.60) in a bathless single and from 45F ($20.68) to 70F ($32.16) with bath. Bathless doubles range between 62F ($28.48) and 83F ($38.14). Doubles with bath include a wide range of accommodations, from a simple room to a penthouse or apartment, and these cost from 80F ($36.76) to 130F ($59.74). The price of any room goes up or down the above-mentioned scales according to the season. Half board is offered for 17F ($7.81).

Hotel Bären (tel. 22-35-21) is buff-colored with green shutters in an older building with light gingerbread under the eaves. The big-windowed dining room has wrought iron and wood antique-style hanging lamps, while another dining room has white walls and a sparse but formal atmosphere. The bedrooms are cozy and comfortable, costing between 38F ($17.46) and 50F ($22.97) per person without bath, going up to 40F ($18.38) and 65F ($29.87) per person with full bath.

5. Mürren

This village, one of the most stunningly situated in the Bernese Oberland, is cut off from traffic. If you're driving, you can go as far as Stechelberg, which lies at the terminus of the Lauterbrunnen Valley road. From there you must take a cable care to Mürren, costing 18F ($8.27) for a round-trip fare. The ride, which is part of the fun, takes about ten minutes, and departures are about every half hour.

Mürren occupies a sheltered and sunny balcony high above the Lauterbrunnen valley, and once there you'll breathe pure mountain air, as you take in a trio of wonders, the peaks of Jungfrau, Eiger, and Mönch.

It's an exciting excursion from Interlaken in summer and a major ski resort in winter. There are 50 kilometers of prepared runs, consisting of 16 downhills. The longest run measures 12 kilometers alone. For cross-country skiers there's a 12-kilometer track in the Lauterbrunnen Valley, ten rail minutes from Mürren.

At 5414 feet, Mürren is the highest permanently inhabited village in the Bernese Oberland. If you're not driving, you can reach Mürren in one hour by mountain railway from the east rail station in Interlaken going via Lauterbrunnen and Grütschalp, and in half an hour from Lauterbrunnen via Grütschalp. The Lauterbrunnen–Mürren railway opened in 1891 and is made up of two sections: the cableway from Lauterbrunnen to Grütschalp and the friction railway from Grütschalp to Mürren. The Mürren–Allmendhubel cableway, which opened in 1912, is a 15-minute walk from the Mürren mountain station of the Lauterbrunnen–Mürren railway. It arrives in four minutes at the belvedere of the Allmendhubel, providing views of the snow-capped peaks of the upper Lauterbrunnen valley and the massif of Eiger, Mönch, and Jungfrau.

The most popular excursion from Mürren is to the famous **Schilthorn,** which is reached after a 40-minute cable-car ride, a round-trip ticket costing about 60F ($27.57). In summer, departures are about every 30 minutes. The Schilthorn, also called "Piz Gloria," after the James Bond film *On Her Majesty's Secret Service,* is known for its 360° panoramic view, extending from the Jura to the Black Forest and taking in Mönch, Jungfrau, and Eiger.

Once at Schilthorn you can enjoy a meal in the restaurant Piz Gloria, a revolving restaurant which in less than an hour will give you a view of Mont Blanc, the Bernese Alps, and the heart of Switzerland. The Schilthorn summit is the start of the world's longest downhill ski race.

Long enjoyed by the British, Mürren itself was discovered by the Romantics some 150 years ago. It has been famous as a skiing center since 1910. In fact, downhill skiing was developed at the slalom invented here in the 1920s, and Mürren is the birthplace of modern alpine racing.

RESORT LIVING: **Hotel Eiger** (tel. 55-13-31) is housed in a comfortable adaptation of a chalet, with two large peak-roofed buildings joined together by a low-lying passageway. The views from many of the windows are spectacular, and the public rooms are warmly decorated. Facilities include a bar, an indoor heated swimming pool (with glass walls looking out onto the snow), a sauna, a fitness room, and a disco. The von Allmen family, along with the Stähli family, are your hosts. They have set three seasons: low, shoulder, and high. Singles begin at 60F ($27.57), peaking at 118F ($54.22). Doubles start at 100F ($45.95) going all the way to 195F ($89.60). Half board costs an additional 15F ($6.89). All units contain private baths.

Hotel Jungfrau and **Jungfrau Lodge** (tel. 55-28-24) consist of a 19th-century four-story building with stucco and brick walls, green-shuttered gables, and a small-scale peaked tower plus a comfortable annex constructed in 1965. Both buildings have an invitingly modern decor inside, with open fireplaces, conversational groupings of armchairs, and a shared wood-ceilinged dining room. The bedrooms in both buildings are sunny and appealing (those in the newer unit cost more). A terrace offers lunch outdoors even with masses of snow on the ground, and a bar serves après-ski drinks until late at night. The entrance to the hotels' sports center is included in the price, and there are facilities for swimming, squash, and ice skating. Prices, *per person,* for newer rooms in the lodge begin at 55F ($25.27) in low season, peaking at 95F ($43.65) in high. The per-person rate for bathless rooms in the older section starts at 35F ($16.08) in low, scaling the heights to 65F ($29.86) in high season. However, rooms with bath in the older section range from a low of 45F ($20.67) per person to a high of 80F ($36.76) in high. Half board is an additional 15F ($6.89) per person daily.

Hotel Mürren (tel. 55-24-24) is a cream-colored hotel with a black mansard roof and several sets of indented loggias with wrought-iron balconies. The interior is trendily modern, with comfortable and imaginatively designed furniture in the 46 bedrooms. Tennis courts are on the grounds, and from the hotel you can take an inviting set of mountain trails for winter cross-country skiing or summertime treks. There's also a bar and restaurant, along with "Dancing Inferno," an on-site disco. In summer, doubles, depending on the accommodation and exposure, range from 55F ($25.27) to 80F ($36.76) per person, including breakfast. Singles cost between 65F ($29.86) and 75F ($34.46). All units contain private baths. In winter, prices are quoted *per person* with half board. Doubles range between 80F ($36.76) and 143F ($65.70), per person, while singles cost from 93F ($42.73) to 135F ($62.03)

Hotel Blumental (tel. 55-18-26) is a gracefully decorated family-run hotel where the exterior is crafted of a masonry base and a weathered clapboard upper section. The interior has lots of timbers and various sections of exposed stonework that combine into a pleasant ambience. The wooden walls of the bedrooms contrast tastefully with the bedcovers. The von Allmen family, who have innkeeper relatives all over the region, are the owners. They have a wide scale of different prices, depending on the season. These range from a low of 42F ($19.29) in a single to a high of 90F ($41.36), with doubles beginning at 84F ($38.60) in low season, climbing to a high of 170F ($78.11). Half board costs another 15F ($6.89) per person daily. Each unit has its own private bath.

Hotel Edelweiss (tel. 3-43-12) is boxy and flat-roofed, with red shutters and several Swiss flags fluttering against the white balconies. The architecture may not be inspiring, but the view is. The sun terrace is built over an extremely steep dropoff. Except for Swiss engineering, there might not be a hotel here at all. When you're not overcoming your vertigo on the terrace, you can drink in a modern attractive bar or eat in an alpine-style dining room with pine boards on the ceiling. Mrs. Affentranger, who obviously isn't bothered by heights, is your hostess. Depending on the season, she charges a low of 32F ($14.70) in a single to a high of 40F ($18.38) to 65F ($29.86) in high season. Doubles in low season begin at 64F ($29.41) to 100F ($45.95), going up to 100F ($45.95) to 150F ($68.93) in high. Not all the rooms contain private baths, but breakfast is included in the tariffs. Half board is an extra 15F ($6.89) per person daily.

APRÈS SKI: This activity is very informal in Mürren, taking place for the most part in the hotels previously recommended. One of the most popular is the **Hotel Eiger,** which has a lively Tächi-Bar, attracting a young crowd, and a room for dancing. Sometimes a live band is brought in, and a rapidly burning fire makes for a cozy atmosphere as snow falls outside.

There's also nightly dancing at the Gruebi bar at the **Jungfrau Hotel.** At one end is a restaurant, and there's dancing at the other section, often to a small band.

An attractive young crowd of skiers patronize the Inferno Bar of the **Hotel Mürren** for disco dancing.

Finally, several mountain chalet restaurants have fondue and raclette parties at the height of the winter ski season.

6. Wengen

A resort village at the foot of that monstrous trio, Mönch, Jungfrau, and Eiger, Wengen lies on a sheltered sunny terrace high above the Lauterbrunnen valley, at about 4160 feet above sea level. One of the chicest and best equipped ski and mountain resorts in the Bernese Oberland, it has 30 hotels in all price categories as well as 500 apartments and chalets to rent.

The ski area around Wengen is highly developed, including Männlichen, Kleine Scheidegg, Lauberhorn, and Eigergletscher, with three mountain railways, one cable car, one gondola, five chair lifts, nine ski lifts, and three practice lifts. In the center of the village is a beginner's slope, along with a Swiss ski school. Other facilities and sports include an open-air and an artificial ice rink, a curling hall with two rinks, cross-country skiing (a 12-kilometer track at the bottom of the valley), sledging, an indoor swimming pool, glacier skiing, and a day nursery.

Drawn to its location not far from the Matterhorn, the English were the first to popularize the resort after World War I. Some parts of it still look like the farm community it was back in the 19th century; however, the main artery of town is filled with cafés, shops, and restaurants, most of which are geared to tourists.

No cars are allowed in Wengen, although there's a lot of activity from service vehicles and those electric carts that carry luggage from the train station to the hotels. If you're driving, you can go as far as Lauterbrunnen, where there's a large covered garage. From there, you board a cog railway for the 15-minute ride to Wengen, a second-class ticket costing only 3.60F ($1.66), a first-class seat going for 7.20F ($3.32).

Skiers in winter take the cableway to **Männlichen** at 7335 feet, which opens onto a panoramic vista of the treacherous Eiger. From here, there is no direct run back to Wengen; however, skiers can avail themselves of a seven-kilometer run to Grindelwald (see below).

Before heading to Wengen by rail, many visitors linger long enough in the Lauterbrunnen valley to take some excursions. One is to **Trümmelbach Falls,** plunging in five powerful cascades through a gorge. You can take an elevator (bring a raincoat) through the rock to a series of galleries. At the end of the line you come to the bottom of a wall into which the upper fall descends. These falls can be visited from the first of April until the end of October from 8 a.m. to 6 p.m. for an admission of 5F ($2.30). It takes about 45 minutes to reach them on foot.

You might also want to seek out the **Staubbach Waterfall.** An early visitor, Lord Byron, compared this fall to the "tail of the pale horse ridden by Death in the Apocalypse." Above Lauterbrunnen, these falls plunge nearly 1000 feet, a sheer drop.

FOOD AND LODGING: **Hotel Regina** (tel. 55-15-12) is the best hotel in Wengen, catering to an upper-crust, well-heeled crowd of increasingly youthful patrons. It might be called the dowager empress of all the hotels at the resort. It stands near the cog railway station in an embellished Victorian elephant of a building, with great amounts of charm and dozens of balconies facing the valley and the alpine sunshine. Jack Meyer, the owner, has been known to arrange unusual concerts for his guests. Once when I was there a group of high school students from Oklahoma was giving a summertime concert on the front lawn. The public rooms are elegantly furnished, with a baronial carved stone fireplace usually blazing in winter. There's also a disco with live bands and an attractive bar. Meals are varied and interesting, with frequent substitutions made from the fixed-price meals. This hotel, like all the others, is mobbed in winter, so make reservations during the season. There's a wide range of prices, beginning at 56F ($25.73) for a bathless single in low season to a high of 118F ($54.22) for a single with bath in high season. Likewise, bathless doubles begin at 112F ($51.46) in low season, going up to 182F ($83.63) in high season. However, you'll pay as much as 230F ($105.68) for a double with bath in high season. These prices include half board.

Sunstar Hotel (tel. 56-51-11). Margrit and Erich Leeman are the congenial hosts of this many-balconied hotel. Each of the wooden balustrades around the weatherproof windows has a medallion carved into an alpine design, which is repeated above the ceiling of one of the salons. This salon, by the way, is filled with expensive leather and metal chairs and rustic timbers outlined against the white stucco walls. An oval-shaped bar area is a relaxing place for a few drinks, while an indoor swimming pool with panoramic windows of the snow-covered mountains allows year-round swimming. The hotel has a sauna and a high-quality dining room, and its location in the center of Wengen makes it especially convenient. The well-furnished and comfortable rooms, all with private bath, cost between 85F ($39.05) and 145F ($66.63) in a single, and between 70F ($32.16) and 185F ($85) in a double. Summer accommodations fall at the cheaper end of the above-mentioned scale, although there's a wide variety of rooms. Prices quoted are all *per person* daily and include half board.

Hotel Bristol (tel. 55-15-51) is a well-constructed five-story building whose brown color contrasts attractively with the surrounding snows in winter. Only a five-minute walk from the station, it offers accommodations in either individual rooms or in one of several large apartments suitable for six persons or more. Norbert Plaschy, the manager, charges a wide variety of rates. In low season singles cost between 42F ($19.29) and 62F ($28.48), with doubles going for 84F ($38.60 to 122F ($56.06). However, in high season these same singles cost from 54F ($24.81) to 77F ($35.38), with doubles going for 108F ($49.62) to 154F ($70.76). Half board is included in these tariffs.

Hotel Eiger (tel. 55-11-31). The walls and ceilings of this attractive hotel are almost always covered with some kind of rustic timbers or planking, giving a warmly decorated gemütlich ambience. Some of the posters in the public rooms are of local ski champions soaring through the air as if they're about to land on a dining table. The overall impression of the place is one of well-padded comfort in an environment conducive to outdoor sports. The entire facility was constructed by the Karl Fuchs family in the center of town in 1981, and has already begun to attract a local clientele. The bedrooms are spacious and for the most part attractively decorated in beiges and browns. Singles cost between 61F ($28.03) and 85F ($39.05), while doubles range between 61F ($28.03) and 95F ($43.65) per person, depending on the season and the exposure of the room. All accommodations contain private bath and balcony, TV connection, and phone, and all tariffs include half board.

Hotel Alpenrose (tel. 55-32-16). Years ago a Scottish tourist named Margaret came to Wengen on a ski vacation where she met Paul von Allmen, owner of the Alpenrose. They fell in love, were married, and together established the current management of this well-situated hotel. The rooms usually have balconies with views over the Lauterbrunnen valley, lots of light, and pine paneling over part of their surfaces. A good percentage of the friendly staff comes from Scotland, which makes communication easy. The hotel is efficiently run, with cozy public rooms and a large formal dining area where, if you've been gathering wildflowers that day, you'll probably find them in a vase on your supper table. The hotel closes its doors every year during October and November. In ski season, however, it's mobbed with sports enthusiasts from all over Europe. The rustic lunchtime restaurant serves good fixed-price meals from 25F ($11.48) if you're visiting only for the day. International dishes from the evening menu are likely to include fondue bourguignonne, trout with almonds, terrine maison, and grilled steak. Room tariffs are carefully separated into high, middle, and low season in winter, and there's an even cheaper set of rates in summer. Singles without bath cost between 49F ($22.52) and 77F ($35.38), rising to between 61F ($28.02) and 73F ($33.54) with bath. Bathless doubles range from 47F ($21.60) to 88F ($40.43), going up to 58F ($26.65) to 98F ($45.03) with bath. All these prices are *per person* and per day, with half board included.

Hotel Silberhorn (tel. 55-22-41), aside from having one of the most popular discos in town on its ground floor, is a pleasant hotel with a hairdresser, a sports shop, and several boutiques. The interior is soundproofed from the disco below, and attractively outfitted with exposed stone walls, heavy timbering on many of its ceilings, and an airy dining room. The 60 well-furnished rooms have an almost unending series of floor arrangements, many with balconies and private baths. The complex is about a minute away from the rail station. The hotel will also rent apartments which are suitable to friendly groups or families. Singles in low season cost between 50F ($22.97) and 72F ($33.08), going up to 100F ($45.95) to 144F ($66.17) in a double. In high season singles range between 65F ($29.87) and 95F ($43.65), with doubles costing from 130F ($59.73) to 190F ($87.30). These prices include half board. The Beldi family are the proprietors.

Falken Hotel (tel. 55-14-31), near the rail station, is in a symmetrical gabled building painted cream and gray-green. It has its own garden and is close to many of the public sports facilities in town. The salons are comfortable and filled with attractive groupings of 19th-century chairs and couches. Low-season rates are between 50F ($22.97) and 72F ($33.08) in a single and from 100F ($45.95) to 144F ($66.16) in a double. High-season rates go up to 65F ($29.87) to 95F ($43.65) in a single and from 130F ($49.74) to 190F ($87.30) in a double. These prices include half board.

APRÈS SKI: Nightlife, such as it is, begins early here—at sunset. Everybody seemingly turns out to watch the sun set over Wengen. Regardless of where you've seen the sun set before, check out this one. It's spectacular.

Sometimes there's night skiing, torchlit of course, following a raclette party at the Wengenalp, an untamed perch at 6140 feet at the foot of the glacial slopes of the Jungfrau.

Most of the nighttime diversions take place in the hotels, although little discos come and go, some hardly lasting through a season.

Tea dances take place at the **Tiffany** in the Hotel Silberhorn complex. This is Wengen's leading disco. The DJ plays what's called "evergreen" or mountain music as well as the latest hits. The complex also houses one of the best bars in town, the **Hörnli-Bar.**

After that, the best place in town to dance and meet people is the **Carrousel** at the previously recommended Hotel Regina. It almost always has the best band in town.

KLEINE SCHEIDEGG: A skiing center in the Jungfrau region, Scheidegg lies close to Wengen. A mountain resort, popular in both summer and winter, it stands on a balcony connecting the Grindelwald valley with that of the just-recommended Lauterbrunnen. As mentioned, it's the starting point for the excursion to Jungfraujoch at 11,333 feet. The highest cogwheel railway in the world leaves from here, taking you to "the top of the world." If you board the train in Scheidegg at 8 a.m., you'll get a fare reduction of 25%. Many guests spend the night at one of the Scheidegg hotels to get an early start on this trip.

If you're coming from Interlaken, you'll face a difference in altitude of some 10,000 feet. There's a difference of only 4500 feet between Scheidegg and Jungfraujoch.

In winter there's skiing from door to door, with thousands of meters of downhill skiing. Snow is virtually certain from mid-November until well into May.

In summer, visitors can go hiking, climbing, and rambling. There are no motor cars. The Wengernalp and Jungfrau railways, the Wengen–Männlichen aerial cableway, and the Scheidegg–Lauberhorn chair lift make hiking routes accessible, and you see not only alpine flora, but most likely ibex, chamois, marmots, or eagles. From your hotel room here you can watch high-altitude ascents and climbing parties.

Food and Lodging

Scheidegg Hotels (tel. 55-12-12). Since Kleine Scheidegg is little more than a railroad terminus and a handful of Swiss-style buildings, these hotels stand out, lying at a very high altitude between the massive rocks and the surrounding alps. Skiers love to stay here because of the proximity to the surrounding slopes, but even in summer it's the ultimate in isolated comfort. There are plenty of well-marked paths with spectacular views. This is one of my favorite spots for hill-climbing in summer, especially since the paths are well maintained and follow the safest possible routes. Warning: There is little to do here after dark, so expect to retire early after a day of exercise in the alps. Of course, you can always stop in for a drink at the hotel bar where music is sometimes provided. The director, Heidi von Almen, will answer your questions and be helpful in many ways. Singles cost between 60F ($27.57) and 100F ($45.95) while doubles range between 130F ($59.73) and 190F ($87.30), depending on the plumbing, the accommodation, and the season. Half board is included in the price. The interior is beautifully decorated with Oriental rugs, comfortable leather chairs, and often blazing fireplaces.

7. Grindelwald

Set against a backdrop of the Wetterhorn and the towering north face of the Eiger, Grindelwald is both a winter and a summer resort. And is it ever touristy!

The altitude of the highest "skiable mountain" is 12,000 feet, a vertical drop of 5010 feet. There's a total of 22 lifts, gondolas, and mountain railroads. For "intermediate" training before making the long descent, Oberjoch at 8226 is a good point.

Grindelwald is often called the "glacier village." Unlike Wengen and Mürren, which we've already visited, it's the only resort in the Jungfrau region that can be reached in your automobile. Because of that accessibility, Grindelwald is often overrun with visitors, many of whom come just for the day, preferring to stay elsewhere. The streets can get very crowded.

It's also easy to visit Kleine Scheidegg from here, which is the departure point for the final ascent to the Jungfraujoch by train. From Grindelwald-Grund, where there's parking, you can also take Europe's longest gondola cableway to Männlichen. Along the way you'll have a panoramic view of all the peaks of the Jungfrau. The round-trip fare from Grindelwald-Grund to Männlichen is 30F ($13.79).

If you don't drive to Grindelwald, you can take a train from the east station in Interlaken, the Bernese Oberland Railway (BOB), which will take you there in 40 minutes. Grindelwald lies 14 miles from Interlaken.

DAYTIME ACTIVITIES: For a close look at a glacier ravine, you'll find a gallery at the base of the Lower Grindelwald glacier which takes you on a trip for more than half a mile past glacier mills, striation, and marble to the glacier tongue. The ravine gallery is easy to reach on foot or by car up to the entrance. Bus service is available, and there's a car park and restaurant.

A visit to the **Blue Ice Grotto** may give you an uneasy feeling, as it requires entrance into the Upper Grindelwald glacier which is currently experiencing a great deal of movement. However, I was assured that it's perfectly safe, and I found the grotto, which gives the visitor a direct encounter with the glacier world, to be worth the visit. The blue ice walls of the grotto, almost 100 feet deep, are unforgettable. The grotto is open from the middle of June till the middle of September.

Other glacier tours are offered, on which you will spend two days traveling from Jungfraujoch on the Aletsch glacier to Lake Marielen to Kuhboden (Valais), with an overnight lodging at the Konkordia cabin. These tours are made from July to the end of September.

An exhibition of Grindelwald history is found in the **Museum of Local Arts and Crafts,** where an alpine cheesery may be visited, as well as a retrospective of mountain climbing and winter sports. The museum is open from June until the middle of September.

The tourist office has two **guided tours** a week from the end of June to the middle of September, free for those who hold a visitor's card, except for the cost of transport. A gamekeeper shows you mountain flora and fauna and an alpine cheesery. For one of these tours, register at the tourist office (tel. 53-12-12).

For a further look at the local plant life, I suggest you take a journey along the Grütll forest path, called the **Burglauenen/Grindelwald Nature Trail.** More information on this pleasant and educational tour is available from a brochure you can purchase at the tourist office or at the Burglauenen train station for 2F (92¢).

For an active holiday to suit your taste and benefit your health, you may want to try **hiking** along the many diverse Grindelwald paths and mountain trails which are well marked and well maintained. From a simple walk on the valley floor to a challenging mountain trek along the north face of Mt. Eiger or to the Gleckstein cabin, you can take your choice. A map showing the Grindelwald region's paths and trails is available at the tourist office for 6F ($2.76).

If you're courageous and adventurous enough to be tempted by peaks 13,000 feet high or higher, or if you'd like to learn the proper way to climb rocks and ice, get in touch with the **Mountain Guide Office,** CH-3818 Grindelwald (tel. 036/53-20-21), or the **Mountain Climbing School,** CH-3818 Grindelwald (tel. 036/53-21-15).

Faulhorn, 8796 feet high, has a historic vantage point from which you can view a panorama of untouched alpine beauty. There's also a mountain hotel which has been here for more than 150 years. It can be reached only by going on foot from Bussalp (2¾ hours), from First (2½ hours), or from Schynige Platte (4 hours).

A 30-minute ride on Europe's longest chair lift, via Oberhaus, will take you to **First,** 7113 feet up. You can stop at Bort and Egg intermediate stations as you cross the lovely alpine meadows to the First mountain terminal and sun terrace. You'll have many hiking possibilities into either the neighboring Bussalp or Grosse Scheidegg areas, returning by bus. An hour's brisk hike will take you to idyllic Lake Bachalp. Besides the 2½-hour trek to Faulhorn, cited above, you can also make a trek by foot to the Schynige Platte in six hours. A round-trip chair-lift ride between Grindelwald and First costs 28F ($12.87).

Grosse Scheidegg, at 6434 feet, a pass between the Grindelwald and the Rosenlaui valleys, can be reached after a 40-minute bus ride. There you can take the alpine trail to First, and from First return to Grindelwald by chair lift. Also from here you can make a 2½-hour hike to Schwarzwaldup on a panoramic hiking trail, returning by bus to Grindelwald via Grosse Scheidegg. Cost of the Grindelwald–Grosse Scheidegg round trip is 18F ($8.27).

A short aerial cable-car ride will take you to **Pfingstegg,** at 4564 feet, from which point you can make memorable hikes to the Lower and Upper Grindelwald glaciers. A hike to Bäregg-Stieregg (one hour) is highly recommended as a one-day journey, as is the trek to Bänisegg (two hours). You'll get a view of the Eismeer and the Fiescherwand, both worth the hike. A popular half-day journey on foot is to Milchbach. In about an hour, you find yourself at the base of the Upper Grindelwald glacier, with the Blue Ice Grotto nearby. You don't have to hike all the way back, as a bus trip is available. The round-trip fare between Grindelwald and Pfinstegg is 9F ($4.14), 7F ($3.22) if you have a visitor's card of Grindelwald.

Want to learn how to skate from Swiss experts? **A Swisskate Skating School** for beginners and advanced skaters is run by Karl-Heinz Zitterbart-Seger. For information on times and tariffs, get in touch with the Sports Centre, CH-8318 Grindelwald (tel. 036/53-33-66).

Other sports opportunities are:

Tennis: Six sand courts are available through the tourist office at a rental of 12F ($5.51) per hour per court. The Regina, Spinne, and Sunstar Hotels all have courts, and you can play indoors on one of four hard courts in the Sports

Centre from the end of April until mid-June. Other indoor tennis facilities are available at Wilderswil and at Interlaken all year.

Swimming: A heated open-air swimming pool is open in Grindelwald from June to August. The Sports Centre has an indoor pool and sauna open daily.

Fishing: With a permit from the tourist office, you can try your angling skill in the Lütschine and the Bachalpsee.

Summer ice skating: The big ice hall at the Sports Centre is open from the end of June until the following Easter.

FOOD AND LODGING: **Grand Hotel Regina** (tel. 54-54-55) has an architectural format attractively balanced between the country-style rustic and urban modern slick. One of the salons is filled with Victorian chairs pulled up around bridge tables, with a pink metallic ceiling and various pieces of sculpture placed in wall niches. The bedrooms are comfortable, running the range from rustically masculine to a more subdued format of pink quilts and flowery wallpaper. The facade of the oldest part of the hotel is designed with an imposing set of turrets capped with red tile. A steel-and-glass low-lying extension houses the large swimming pool and sauna. Another outdoor pool is near the tennis courts. The hotel is open every year from December to October, offering 120 rooms and several deluxe suites in the chalet-style buildings next door. The art collection of hotel owner Alfred Krebs graces many of the walls with etchings, gouaches, and oil paintings. An in-house disco attracts live bands and groups of happy drinkers. Singles are rented with a 10F ($4.60) supplement over the prices quoted for a double room. Rates are *per person,* based on double occupancy with private bath. Accommodations range between 120F ($55.14) and 160F ($73.52), including breakfast and depending on the season. Half board is another 30F ($13.78) per person.

Parkhotel Schoenegg (tel. 53-18-53). One of my favorite building materials is hewn stone, and this comfortable hotel uses it in some of the public rooms in abundance, along with thick slabs of native wood, sometimes with letters carved into them. The exterior is grandly expansive, with several tiers of balconies with wooden dividers between the sections pertaining to each room. It was established by the Stettler family in 1890, and is still under their wing. Many of the local ski runs terminate at the hotel, while a ski lift to the ski school is close to the front door. In winter the hotel gives fondue parties for its guests in the basement bar area, the Gydis-Bar. A swimming pool, fitness room, and sauna are available. Singles range between 43F ($19.75) and 90F ($41.36), while doubles cost between 80F ($36.76) and 175F ($80.41), depending on the plumbing, exposure, and season. Half board is available for an additional 18F ($8.27) per person daily.

Hostellerie Eiger (tel. 53-21-21) appears as a multiseried collection of balconies, each of them on a different plane usually facing the alpine sunshine, in contrasting shades of while stucco and natural wood. The interior is attractive, unpretentious, and simple, with lots of warmly tinted wood, hanging lamps, and strong areas of light and cozy shadow. You'll find lots of places for intimate drinking and a quiet rendezvous. A disco bar often has live music or recently released songs and also "evergreen" (mountain) tunes. Sports facilities include a sauna and a whirlpool, along with two bars and two restaurants. Owned and operated by the Heller family, the establishment charges from 68F ($31.25) to 100F ($45.95) in a double and from 73F ($33.54) to 110F ($50.54) in a single, depending on the season, plumbing, and exposure. The above prices are on a *per-person* basis, with half board included. The hotel prefers guests to stay for a minimum of three nights.

Sunshine Hotel (tel. 54-54-17). Set at the base of the mountains, this very large hotel is an adaptation of a long rectangular solid, with the strong horizontal lines of its gray balconies contrasting vividly with the white surface of the concrete. The decor inside is ornamented with Oriental carpets and wood furniture, all of which give an invitingly warm reception to summer and winter visitors alike. The bar area is popular in the evening, while an indoor swimming pool offers the chance to complete the range of outdoor activities which are abundantly available outside the hotel. In summer, rooms with breakfast cost between 65F ($29.86) and 78F ($35.84) in a single and between 55F ($25.27) and 88F ($40.44) per person in a double. All units contain private baths. Half board is available for another 20F ($9.19) per person. In winter, rates range between 72F ($33.08) and 90F ($41.36) in a single and between 62F ($28.49) and 100F ($45.95) per person in a double, with half board going for another 25F ($11.48) per person daily.

Hotel Spinne (tel. 53-23-41) is the kind of establishment that places brass candlesticks and fresh flowers on the tables of its dining room. Rustic is the byword for the decor, taking in the comfortable bar area and the panel-covered sitting rooms with an exposed stone fireplace. The nightclub in the basement draws a younger crowd in the evening. The breakfast buffet is set out in generous quantities over a regional print tablecloth. The hotel is a five-story, flat-roofed constuction with black bands encircling it both horizontally and vertically. Rudolf Märkle, the owner, charges from 70F ($32.17) to 80F ($36.76) in a single and from 110F ($50.54) and 150F ($68.93) in a double, including breakfast. All units have private bath. A guest house, part of the complex, offers rental apartments by the day, ranging from 120F ($55.14) to 150F ($68.93) per day for triple occupancy.

Hotel Weisses Kreuz and Post (tel. 54-54-92) is appropriately named, because the entire establishment is painted white, with the exception of the black balcony rails and black shutters. A particularly high window on the top floor illuminates the indoor swimming pool. The ambience of a nearby terrace seems to encourage guests to strip to their bathing suits even while patches of snow are still on the ground. The exterior is a streamlined modern, and the cozy interior has been carefully crafted to imply a building of much greater age. A selection of well-chosen antiques dots the attractively rustic public rooms, where parquet floors and flowery carpeting highlight the tasteful conversational areas. The Challi-Bar is warmly decorated, alpine style, with wood, brick, and stone. Each of the big-windowed and comfortable bedrooms has its own bath. They cost between 85F ($39.05) and 105F ($48.24) in a single with half board and between 80F ($36.76) and 100F ($45.95) per person in a double, also with half board.

Hotel Belvedere (tel. 53-18-18) has extensive public rooms decorated with comfortable Windsor chairs and leather armchairs. Oriental rugs, and a sunny terrace high above the ground with views over the mountains. On the premises you'll find an indoor pool, a sauna, a children's playroom, and a padded bar. The well-furnished bedrooms are carpeted and usually have balconies with views. The flat-roofed structure is skillfully terraced on a steep hill, with masonry walls holding up the landfills around it. The Hauser family charges between 43F ($19.75) and 75F ($34.46) for a single and between 80F ($36.76) and 150F ($68.93) for a double in low season. In high season tariffs go up to between 55F ($25.27) and 90F ($41.35) in a single and between 100F ($45.95) and 180F ($82.71) in a double. Half board is another 20F ($9.20) per person extra.

Hotel Silberhorn (tel. 53-28-22) is a big-balconied hotel painted white with oversize windows, a large garden with tables and chairs, and comfortably carpeted rooms with simple furniture. The public rooms are decorated with large windows or lots of paneling (or both). The 50 bedrooms all have private bath, phone, radio, and balcony. There's a synagogue on the premises and a special celebration of Jewish holidays if requested. Singles, depending on the plumbing and season, range from 55F ($22.27) to 105F ($48.25). Doubles cost between 110F ($50.54) and 200F ($91.90). Half board is another 35F ($16.08) per person daily. A new wing, soon to be completed, will include a series of public rooms, a sauna, a fitness center, and a whirlpool. The Wagner family are your hosts.

Derby Hotel (tel. 54-54-61) is a very large adaptation of a mountain chalet. It has two distinct roof areas, both of them peaked at the same angles. Several floors of sliding glass doors give access to the irregularly shaped balconies attached to most of the comfortable bedrooms. The interior is filled with wood paneling and warm-tinted fabrics. All units have their own baths. The Bar Cava and the rustically furnished restaurant offer low-key meeting places. Doubles cost from 46F ($21.13) to 85F ($39.05) per person, depending on the season and the room. Singles range from 50F ($22.96) to 65F ($29.87). Half board goes for another 18F ($8.27) per person daily.

Hotel Alpina (tel. 53-33-33) is a chalet-style modern hotel with symmetrical rows of wood-railed balconies covered with flowers in summer. On a hill above the town, three minutes on foot from the train station, it offers streamlined bedrooms decorated with functional furniture and bright colors. A sun terrace and a curved bar area are attractive resting points after a day in the mountains. Views are good from the windows. Each accommodation has its own bath, costing between 45F ($20.68) and 65F ($29.86) per person in off-season, the price going up to 56F ($25.73) to 80F ($36.76) per person in high. Half board is another 20F ($9.19) per person daily.

Hotel Lauberhorn (tel. 53-10-82). From the outside it isn't much different from other chalet-style hotels in the region. Inside it's very well maintained. The location is somewhat more isolated than some of my other selections. The modern bedrooms are attractively decorated in shades of beige, while the public rooms are modern, somewhat sparse but comfortable. The Howald family, your hosts, efficiently direct the hotel and can advise (in English) their guests about local attractions. The *per-person* rates range from 34F ($15.62) to 46F ($21.13) in a double and between 34F ($15.62) and 49F ($22.52) in a single, including breakfast.

Hotel Hirschen (tel. 53-27-77) has an unusually handsome facade, detailed with an exposed stone foundation and lots of wrought iron. The shutters are of natural wood, as are the multitiered balconies. The dining room repeats the stone and wood theme of the outside, and the accommodations are clean, orderly, and attractive. The Bleuer-Peter family, the owners, charge between 32F ($14.70) and 46F ($21.14) per person in a bathless double, from 38F ($17.46) to 60F ($27.57) per person in a double with bath. Singles pay a supplement, and half board is provided for yet another 22F ($10.11) per person daily.

Sporthotel Jungfrau (tel. 53-13-41) is an attractive chalet-style hotel at the entrance to the village, three minutes from the train station. A large terrace offers a view of the Eiger, while the public rooms are beamed, carpeted, and very comfortable. A restaurant offers well-prepared meals in a setting of white linen and efficient service. The bedrooms are warm, usually paneled in blond, light-grained wood. Doubles cost between 35F ($16.08) and 40F ($18.38) per person without bath and between 45F ($20.67) and 55F ($25.27) with bath. Half board is another 18F ($8.27) per person daily.

Central Hotel Wolter (tel. 53-22-33) is a very pretty hotel in the middle of town with white walls, yellow balconies, red-and-white striped awnings, and lots of summer flowers. The bar inside is wood paneled—not too large, very cozy, perfect for a quiet conversation. The dining room and main salon are clean and outfitted with lots of wood. The bedrooms are simple, unpretentious, and clean. Peter Balmer, your host, charges between 43F ($19.76) and 75F ($34.46) in a single and between 76F ($34.92) and 135F ($62.03) in a double. Half board is another 18F ($8.27) per person daily.

APRÈS SKI: After dark, Grindelwald is one of the liveliest towns in the Bernese Oberland (but that's not saying a lot!). The most formal place (that is, people aren't likely to show up wearing jeans) is Le Ferme, the nightclub at the **Grand Hotel Regina.** There's dancing to a live band and often solo vocalists.

If you're looking for a good bar with a really cozy ambience when it's cold outside, try the friendly Scotch Bar of the **Hotel Spinne.** There's disco dancing in the hotel's nightclub.

Ski bunnies are also attracted to the Cava Bar of the already-recommended **Derby Hotel.**

The **Sunstar Hotel** is one of the most active spots after dark, drawing many clients from neighboring hotels. In addition to its bars, it has a nightclub for dancing, often to live music.

And let's not forget the brightly lit **Hotel Weisses Kreuz and Post,** with its Challi-Bar, which is done in a wonderfully rustic style. You can drink at candlelit tables and dance later if that's your pleasure.

There are also "get-together" parties once a week on the open-air ice rink.

8. Lake Brienz

Once this lake was connected to Lake Thun, but that was long ago. Now it's its own lake, measuring about nine miles long and from one to two miles wide. It's the smaller of the two blue Oberland lakes (Thun, which we've already visited, is larger). Around its shores are many holiday areas and resorts little visited by North Americans, who seem to popularize the more traditional sightseeing target, Lake Thun.

However, Lake Brienz has much charm, and there are many vacationers, especially Europeans, who prefer it. You might make your center in the town of Brienz or, and I prefer this, the little resort of Bönigen.

BRIENZ: On the upper end of the lake, the town of Brienz is the center for many an excursion. The town faces Giessbach Falls on the opposite side of the lake (you can hear the roar). Among the excursions, one of the most popular is to take a cogwheel railway for the climb to **Brienzer Rothorn,** where you'll be rewarded with a magnificent vista of the Bernese Alps and Lake Brienz itself. It takes about 1½ hours to reach at an elevation of some 7105 feet. Service is from the first of June until mid-October, and there are usually about nine trips a day, a round-trip ticket going for 35F ($16.08) per person. To visit **Giessbach Falls** from Brienz, go to the principal platform at the railway. The ticket there and back costs 8F ($3.68), and you should allow about two hours for the journey. Part will be by boat, the rest by funicular.

Brienz itself is famous for its Bernese Oberland woodcarvers, as you will quickly testify if you've been to a souvenir shop in Switzerland. It's also known for its violin makers (the school is open to the public).

Hotel Bären (tel. 51-24-12) lies in a square, flat-roofed balconied building on the shores of the lake. A garden and a terrace offer guests a quiet diversion. There's a swimming pool on the premises. Directed by the Berthod family, the hotel charges between 46F ($21.13) and 70F ($32.16) per person daily, including half board.

READERS' APARTMENT SELECTION: "I would like to bring to your attention a great place to stay in Switzerland for those who want a quiet place near excellent scenery and hiking. We chose Brienz, only 15 minutes by train from busy Interlaken, and found a building of several three-bedroom apartments operated by **Frau Robi Trauffer** (tel. 51-19-14). We shared one apartment with two others. A large bathroom and completely equipped kitchen are used by all three bedrooms. Frau Trauffer lives in a big new house next door, where she serves a large breakfast. She charges 44F ($20.22) per day for a double room. The building also boasts a swimming pool and sauna, use of which is included in the rates. The building is clean and new, and the kitchen allows you to prepare evening meals. The house is a pleasant 15-minute walk along the lakeshore from the train station, but Frau Trauffer will gladly pick you up and deliver you with your baggage. She will only reply to reservations requests accompanied by deposits. Note: By staying on the outskirts of Brienz, itself only a village, you avoid the traffic noise of the main road and the train which go through the hotel district in the narrow center of town between lake and mountain. We stayed eight days and wish it could have been longer" (Mr. and Mrs. A. Belmont, Minneapolis, Minn.).

The Most Popular Excursion

A visit to the **Swiss Open-Air Museum of Rural Dwellings and Lifestyle** at Ballenberg, near Brienz, in the Bernese Oberland is like a trip back into Switzerland's rural history. Visitors are afforded the opportunity to see typical buildings from farms and tiny settlements in groups surrounded by gardens and farm fields cultivated in the old ways peculiar to the area represented. Seven scenic areas are open to visitors taking the good roads found in the recreation area encompassing nearly 2000 acres, which includes a nature park and Lake Wyssen, between the villages of Hofstetten and Brienzwiler.

The museum was developed after realization that changes in the old ways of farm and village life and methods have imperiled historic buildings all over the country. Each of the scenic areas already open to the public, and others which are in preparation or projected, present a view of life in other eras. You can see how life was lived in eight different cantons at different periods in their history, with the mementos of other cantons and epochs to come. Mittelland units include Central, Bernese, Eastern and Western, allowing you to learn about rural trades, farm products, forest life, folk customs, and other phases of country life from the Jura to Zurich to Berne and elsewhere.

A round trip through the museum will take about three hours, and I recommend that you wear comfortable walking shoes to allow you to go through the houses and farm buildings, the gardens and artisans' quarters, with ease. The museum is open daily in April, May, and October from 9:30 a.m. to 5 p.m. and June through September from 9 a.m. to 5:30 p.m. Adults are charged 7F ($3.22) and children and students pay 3F ($1.38) for admission. On request, a guided tour can be arranged, but reservations are necessary. The price of such a tour is 3F ($1.38) per person, with a minimum charge of 45F ($20.68). Unless you join with other travelers you may have met at your hotel or wherever, you'll enjoy the tour just as much on your own, I've found.

Car parks will be found at the Hofstetten and Brienzwiler entrances. To come here by train, take the Interlaken–Meiringen–Lucerne line to the Brienz railroad station where you can make a bus connection to the museum, or to the Brienzwiler station from which a forest path will lead you to the museum route.

For information, get in touch with the Ballenberg Swiss Open-Air Museum Foundation, Direction CH-3855 Brienz, Bernese Oberland (tel. 036/51-14-42), or call the main ticket office (tel. 036/51-11-23).

BÖNIGEN: On the south shore of Lake Brienz, the lakeside resort of Bönigen has many old timbered houses, some of which go back to the 16th century. The location is only five minutes from Interlaken. Opening onto Lake Brienz, Bönigen is ideal for many walks, excursions, and trips by lake steamer. Go here for peace and tranquillity—and don't expect a lot of excitement.

Food and Lodging

Hotel Seiler au Lac (tel. 22-30-22) is a pleasant, 60-room hotel on the shores of the lake. Many of its accommodations have views over the water, and all units contain private baths. The public rooms have wide, open windows with lots of green plants in summer. The Zingg family, the owners, maintain the old-fashioned building with a tile roof in a good condition, and that fact is appreciated by the older clientele who seem to return here regularly. Singles cost between 78F ($35.84) and 95F ($43.65), with doubles renting for 130F ($59.74) to 180F ($82.71), all half-board tariffs. Rate differences depend on the season and exposure of the room.

Park Hotel (tel. 22-71-06) is a pleasant 19th-century building with a mansard roof, many individual balconies, and a desirable location beside the lake. Nearby facilities include a swing set and lawn toys for children and a series of flowered walkways for adults. Operated by the Looser family, the hotel charges half-board rates of between 43F ($19.76) and 53F ($24.35) in a bathless single, between 82F ($37.67) and 102F ($46.87) in a bathless double. Accommodations with bath cost between 106F ($48.70) and 120F ($55.14) in a double, and between 57F ($26.19) and 64F ($29.41) in a single with bath.

9. Meiringen

If you plan to center in the eastern part of the Bernese Oberland, which contains the upper reaches of the River Aare, an ideal center in the Haslital district is the old resort of Meiringen, which is famous throughout the world for the dessert concoction meringue. Essentially the district attracts mountaineers, rock climbers, and just plain ramblers.

Above Lake Brienz, Meiringen is the major town in the Haslital district, lying about eight miles from the town of Brienz which we have previously visited. The resort is centered among the Grimsel, Brunig, and Susten passes. Among its attractions are excursions to the Aare gorge, the Rosenlaui glacier, and the Reichenbach Falls, as well as a folklore museum, a crystal grotto, a water mill, and a glacier path. There are some 300 kilometers of marked paths for hiking and walks in unspoiled nature, and a large network of lifts to reach panoramic vantage points.

Everybody seemingly visits the parish church in the upper part of the village which dates from 1864, although there has been a church on this spot since the 11th century (the remains of a crypt from that era can still be seen).

If you're staying in the town, you can ask your hotel to prepare a meringue dessert for you. However, if you're passing through, you can buy one or two at one of the local bakeries, perhaps enjoying it at teatime. My favorite spots for both tea and dessert are either **Brunner** (tel. 71-14-23), which is closed on

Tuesday, or **Lüthl** (tel. 71-18-21), closed on Monday. In the warmer months you can enjoy light fare out in the gardens of both places.

So the story goes, the dessert was created when Napoleon visited the town and the local chef had a lot of leftover egg whites. In an inspiration, he created these puffy mounds and served them in a saucer brimming with sweet mountain cream, much to the dictator's delight. Most historians, however, dismiss this tale as apocryphal, although it has many supporters.

After you've found a room in Meiringen, you can strike out the next day on any number of interesting excursions. One is to the **Aare Gorge,** a wonder of nature. It's reached by road from Meiringen or from the Grimsel–Susten road by the so-called Kirchet. The gorge, charging an admission of 4F ($1.84), is open every day from 8 a.m. to 6 p.m. May to October. In July and August night visits are also possible, from 8 to 10 p.m. You'll enter a world of grotesque nooks and recesses, grottos, precipices, galleries, inlets, and arches—all fashioned by the waters of the Aare in the course of thousands of years. The 1500-yard-long and 650-foot-deep cleft carved in the Kirchet is a unique natural wonder of the Swiss Alps.

Another excursion, which fans of Sherlock Holmes will want to take, is to the **Reichenbachfall.** The watercourses of the Rosenlaui Valley meet in the Reichenbach Falls. The beauty and impressive nature of the falls have lured many visitors, beginning with the British in the 19th century. One visitor, Conan Doyle, was so impressed with the falls that he used it in *The Final Problem,* in which the villain, Dr. Moriarty, struggles with the detective to toss him in the falls. A Sherlock Holmes commemorative plaque can be seen today near the upper station of the funicular.

The funicular, incidentally, takes visitors to the starting point of walking tours through the **Rosenlaui Valley** to Grosse Scheidegg and Grindelwald (already visited by us). At the lower station is a large car park. To reach the falls, leave Meiringen on the road to Grimsel. Take a right turn (the road is marked) until you arrive at the car park. There you board the funicular, the ride taking about 11 minutes and costing 5F ($2.30) for a round-trip fare.

WHERE TO STAY AND EAT: **Hotel du Sauvage** (tel. 71-41-41). This is the kind of hotel that makes special efforts to make guests feel at home. Clients are usually greeted with a welcoming drink shortly after their arrival, just before being ushered into their high-ceilinged bedroom, which, although renovated, still has much of the 19th-century charm of its original building. The structure dates from 1880. The breakfast buffet is served in a big are nouveau–style dining room, while a French à la carte restaurant, La Meringue, serves well-prepared specialties. On the premises you'll find lots of pleasant outdoor walkways with enough café tables to ensure a relaxing afternoon in the sun. The service is likely to be very good, since the establishment serves as the staff-training grounds of the Swiss Hotel Association. The hotel has weekly specialty evenings, such as fondue or raclette parties, which are usually followed by dancing in the bar with live entertainment. Most of the accommodations have their own baths, except for a collection of bathless rooms with a simple but clean decor on the fourth floor. Singles range from 54F ($24.81) to 90F ($41.35), while doubles cost between 84F ($38.59) and 150F ($68.93). Half board is available for another 18F ($8.27) per person. The hotel's indoor swimming pool is 300 yards from the hotel, while tennis courts are out back. The owner/manager is J. Musfeld-Brugnoli.

Sporthotel Sherlock Holmes (tel. 71-42-42). A silhouette of the profile of the detective himself adorns the wall above one of the entrances. The hotel is buff colored, with balconies that look reddish by contrast. A white extension sticks toward the approach road. The restaurant and pizzeria has wicker and bentwood chairs, hanging lamps of green glass, and lots of windows opening toward the tree-dotted park. A swimming pool and sauna are on the premises, and there are lots of sun terraces. The bedrooms, comfortably furnished, are decorated with angular modern pieces. Rooms rent on a *per-person* basis, with half board, ranging from 68F ($31.25) to 81F ($37.22) in a double and between 79F ($36.30) and 96F ($44.11) in a single.

Hotel Tourist (tel. 71-10-44) is a small hotel with room for only 30 guests, which ensures a maximum amount of attention for each of them from the owners, the Wyss family. The building is a brown-and-white four-story structure with a gently sloping peaked roof and an extension on the back. The family is happy to serve food and drink to hotel guests and to passing motorists on the parasol-covered terrace in front. Otherwise, the hotel is attractively outfitted with large windows and rustic beams in the public rooms and simple, small-scale furniture in the bedrooms. Many of the clean and well-kept accommodations have their own bath. Rates range from 20F ($9.19) to 33F ($15.16) in a single and from 40F ($18.38) to 66F ($30.33) in a double. Half board is available for another 12F ($5.51) per person daily.

10. Lenk/Adelboden

Tucked snugly into the western sector of the Bernese Oberland, Lenk, linked with Adelboden, lies at the head of the picture-postcard Simmental, the grazing range of some of those famous Swiss cows. In the background is the snow-capped Wildstrubel, but the mountains around Lenk are less formidable. In the area are several mirror-like lakes and some stunning waterfalls. In all, it's an idyllic setting, with glaciers as a backdrop.

LENK: Since the 19th century it's been a popular health spa, owing to its pleasant situation, mild climate, and the strongest alpine sulfur springs in Europe. These springs have been known for centuries, and today attract a thriving health-spa clientele to the new center dating from 1977, standing in a large woodland park.

In summer Lenk attracts those interested in mountain climbing, hiking, playing tennis, or those "taking the cure." In winter it's a sports area, and its major ski centers are at Betelberg, Metsch, Bühlberg, and Hahnenmoos. For the cross-country skier there's a choice of circuits at 3600 and 6500 feet. For the less adventurous, there are 20 miles of well-tended walks.

Where to Stay

Hostellerie Kreuz (tel. 3-13-87) is a more than usually attractive modern chalet which was built in 1979. The swimming pool is covered with pine slats and brick facing, while the sunshine streaming into the dining room is mellowed by the surrounding areas of polished pine. The architect planned this hotel around a massive tree, which has walls built around much of it. The sun terraces allow guests a quiet moment to get a tan. The wood theme is repeated in many of the bedrooms, which are skillfully crafted with weatherproofed and sometimes custom-made windows. The sloping roofline requires that they sometimes be irregularly shaped. The hotel is ably directed by the Tritten family. The fixed-price meals are well prepared and most satisfactory, or else one can order à la carte. Half-board rates, depending on the season, exposure of the room, and plumbing, range between 62F ($28.49) and 101F ($46.40) in a single and between 57F ($26.19) and 94F ($43.19) per person in a double.

Parkhotel Bellevue (tel. 3-17-61) is a white rectangular building that looks somewhat like a Mediterranean villa when the snow doesn't cover the red tile roof. It's a family hotel, with a large outdoor swimming pool set into the grassy lawns behind the hotel, out of earshot of the comfortable bedrooms. Many of the accommodations have private loggias or balconies, which permit views of the surrounding rocky hills. The location somewhat outside the center of town is one which many clients find restful. The sitting rooms are done in blues and greens, a combination of reproduction 19th-century armchairs with more modern angular ones. The bar and one of the restaurants are outfitted with somewhat garish hot-pink and red textiles with textured chrome "disco panels" set against the walls. The main dining room is more conservatively furnished. The Nussbaum family, your hosts, charge between 60F ($27.57) and 80F ($36.76) per person with half board in rooms without private bath and between 80F ($36.76) and 115F ($52.84) per person with bath, also on the half-board plan. Rates vary according to the season and reductions are made to children sharing a room with their parents.

ADELBODEN: Adelboden, on the other hand, has a real alpine atmosphere with lots of charming farmhouses. In lies in the western part of the Engstligen valley, and is known for its scenery. It's both a summer resort and a winter ski center.

This town of about 3500 permanent inhabitants has at least 30 hotels and guest houses, plus some 1500 chalets and holiday apartments. Its major ski areas are those at Geils, Boden, Birg, and Tschentenegg.

Its mountain transportation includes the Engstligenalp aerial cableway (2162 yards), Schwandfeldspitz chair lift (2131 yards), the Hahnenmoos cabin cableway (2152 yards), and the Elsigenalp aerial cableway (1980 yards).

Near the center of the village is a children's playground.

Where to Stay

Nevada Palace (tel. 73-21-31) is a grand hotel with an imposing facade covered with strong horizontal lines of many tiers of balconies. The two lower floors are made of solid masonry with huge arched windows and a five-sided extension stretching toward the grassy lawns and the covered swimming pool. The interior has beautifully crafted sitting and dining rooms. From almost every point, including the heated waters of the pool, you'll see an alpine wilderness stretching for miles. There's a host of sports facilities, including tennis, and several restaurants and bars, one of which is the most popular nightlife spot in the region. The Oestrich family, the busy owners, charge from 65F ($29.87) to 150F ($68.92) per person in rooms with private bath on the half-board plan. Units without bath rent for between 55F ($25.27) and 85F ($39.05) per person daily, half board included. The rates reflect a wide price range between low and high season. Management requests that guests wear suitable attire (i.e., cocktail dresses for women in the evening), especially in high season.

Hotel Huldi and **Waldhaus** (tel. 73-15-31). My favorite part of this hotel is its terrace, whose chiseled flagstones look down on the large swimming pool and an alpine valley dotted with trees. The hotel itself, as its name implies, is divided into two chalet-style buildings, both with big windows, lots of balconies, and a secure niche dug into the side of the hill. The interior is cozily rustic as you'd expect, with masonry detailing, warm colors, and hewn beams and timbers. The restaurant prides itself on its cuisine, which sometimes arrives at the table carved in elaborate sculpture-like designs. The management recently added a sauna to the list of facilities available. Depending on the season and the plumbing, singles on half board range between 55F ($25.27) and 95F ($43.65) without bath and between 65F ($29.87) and 130F ($59.74) with bath. Doubles cost between 105F ($48.25) and 145F ($66.63) without bath and between 125F ($57.44) and 175F ($80.42) with bath, half board included.

Parkhotel Bellevue (tel. 73-16-21) is an attractively up-to-date establishment with many balconies, a flat roof, and several low-lying extensions spreading out from the main building. Painted a prominent white, which is even more striking against the green backdrop of the hill behind it, the hotel is intelligently landscaped into that hillside, with flagstone terraces, lots of flowers in summer, and even a small reflection pool. The decor is pleasingly understated, with the kind of bar area where you'll stop for a beverage even if you're not a drinker. There's also a warm-hued brick- and wood-walled restaurant. The Richard family, your hosts, charge from 68F ($31.24) to 123F ($56.52) in a single and from 68F ($31.24) to 113F ($51.92) per person in a double, all tariffs including half board. The difference in prices depends on the plumbing, season, and room exposure. The above-stated rates are for guests staying for seven days or more. Otherwise a supplement of 10F ($10.60) per person daily is added.

Hotel Kreuz (tel. 73-21-21) is a roadside chalet-style building, formidably well maintained, with café tables set onto a narrow embankment in summer. In the center of town, it's near all the sports facilities. The bedrooms are immaculately neat, with wood ceilings and big windows. A rustic restaurant, which is attractive albeit somewhat bare, serves meals to guests on the board plan, while an à la carte pizzeria prepares Italian specialties for the general public. All the single units are bathless, which isn't a problem as there's a shower on each floor. Some of the doubles are also bathless. These bathless accommodations cost from 42F ($19.30) to 55F ($25.27) per person, depending on the season, with half board included. Doubles with bath, balcony, and southern exposure range between 50F ($22.98) and 63F ($28.95) per person with half board. Guests have free access to the nearby swimming pool and ice-skating rink.

Après Ski

There are several small nightclubs and bars, and the place isn't as sleepy as it first appears to be. The most exciting nighttime diversion, however, is the Alte Taverne in the **Nevada Palace.** On a good night this place can pack in at least 300 customers. A half-dozen antique wooden homes were converted into a big barn-like room, with a gallery overlooking the dance floor.

The Pizzeria at the **Hotel Kreuz** also draws a lively après-ski crowd (the oven is exposed to the patrons, and some of the world's tallest peppermills await your request).

11. Gstaad

Against a backdrop of glaciers and mountain lakes, Gstaad is a haven of movie stars and the wealthy chic of the world, including Elizabeth Taylor. The Aga Khan shows up, and in days of yore Princess Grace paid an annual visit. The resort lies at a junction of a quartet of sleeping valleys—practically at the southern tip of the Bernese Oberland, almost in the Vaudois Alps.

With its chalet-style hotels it somehow retains an old-world atmosphere. Many of these chalets are privately owned, and some of the bistros and cafés in town (which are only open in peak season) operate like private clubs. If they know you, fine. If not, forget it.

Gstaad has many winding narrow streets and fashionable boutiques which open and close with frightening irregularity. The hamlet also has many detractors. Lured by extensive media coverage, many unsuspecting visitors have arrived, especially at the "wrong" time of the year, and found Gstaad a "bloody bore," to quote one irate British reader. "Unless you're a house guest of Roger Moore, or are staying in a suite at the Gstaad Palace, you'll miss out on what's going on."

That, perhaps, is an overstatement. Actually, life flourishes on many levels in Gstaad, and although the resort is expensive, there are many moderately priced hotels, taverns, and guest houses as well.

Gstaad is at 3445 feet, and the altitude of its highest skiable mountain is 6550 feet, with a vertical drop of 3555 feet. In all, it has access to 65 lifts, mountain railroads, and gondolas. East of the village is Eggli, a ski area reached by cable car. Wispellan-Sanetch is favored for afternoon skiing, with lots of runs down to the village. At the summit is the Glacier des Diablarets. Wassern-grat, reached from the south side of the resort, is another area favored for skiing. Even though Gstaad's own skiing is limited, it lies near half a dozen major ski resorts of Switzerland. Many prefer to stay in Gstaad, visiting the actual ski areas farther afield during the day.

A lot of this has to do with fashion. In chicdom, Gstaad is equaled in Switzerland in the winter only by St. Moritz, Arosa, and Davos. Certainly there is nothing to equal it for fashion in the Bernese Oberland.

August is a great month to show up, for that's the occasion of the Menuhin Festival, which draws an international music-loving crowd.

To reach Gstaad, many fly to Geneva (although others wing in to Zurich). Geneva, incidentally, is only a 2½-hour drive away.

The resort is rich in entertainment and sports facilities, including the world-class Swiss Open Tennis Tournament. In addition it offers a 200-mile network of hiking paths, cable cars (to altitudes of 5250, 6560, and 10,000 feet—the last offering skiing even in summer), 20 open-air and covered tennis courts, and both heated indoor and outdoor swimming pools.

ACCOMMODATIONS: Don't come here if economy is a major factor in your holiday. The prices, as you'll soon see, are lethal, especially in high season. When business is slow, many (or most) of the hostelries shut down.

Gstaad Palace (tel. 8-31-31). There's an anecdote in the region that says that the finest hairdressers in the Bernese Oberland are to be found here. The reason for this is that the staff is by now accustomed to the world's most demanding clients. This is the jet-set hideaway par excellence, where the crowned heads of the world, both real and celluloid, come to romp and play. The clientele is frighteningly chic, both because the hotel demands it and because socialites from around the world virtually plan their winters around a stay here. Clients not wearing black tie are requested to dine in the less formal of the two dining halls, the Sans Cravate. The hotel commands a prominent position above Gstaad, with a view over the mountains and a series of facilities for the amusement of its guests. The massage facilities alone are supposed to be simply heavenly.

The palace is the social center for high society in the Bernese Oberland. Many residents of the private chalets nearby come here to meet their friends.

You're likely to see Elizabeth Taylor parading through the lobby, perhaps Roger Moore. The hotel is owned by Herr Scherz who, along with members of his family, reign as the most polished hoteliers and hosts in the region. Half-board is included in the predictably high rates which the hotel seems to have no trouble collecting. Naturally, each of the rooms has a luxurious private bath and is beautifully furnished. Singles cost from 165F ($75.81) to 380F ($174.61), while doubles range from 295F ($135.55) to 720F ($330.84), depending on the room and the season.

Grand Hotel Alpina (tel. 4-57-25) sits in an isolated position on a pine-covered hill slightly above Gstaad. The hotel is a half-timbered building with a well-maintained tile roof which curves slightly at the outer ends of its many gables and ridges. A square-based turret caps the entire structure with a happily Victorian symbol of another era. The interior has been renovated into a vividly modern style, with patterned carpeting and deep armchairs. Very little of the original embellishments remain inside, but the place is still warm, inviting, and restful. The Burri family are your hosts, charging from 90F ($41.36) to 145F ($66.63) per person with half board in accommodations with private bath. Over the Christmas holidays the per-person half-board rates zoom up to between 170F ($78.12) and 190F ($87.30).

Steigenberger Hotel Gstaad-Saanen (tel. 8-33-88) is one of my favorite hotels in the region. Its imaginative architect spared no expense in creating what looks like a cluster of modernized chalet-like structures, with a series of peaked roofs, all sloping at the same angles. The effect is attractively balanced, and a view of the inside reveals a careful craftsmanship and sense of design. Many of the ceilings are crafted of polished pine, with judicious placement of a series of stone fireplaces that crackle with heat in winter. The bedrooms and restaurants are attractively organized, while a high-ceilinged room with a swimming pool completes an impressive list of sports facilities. The kitchens prepare both hearty regional dishes and nouvelle cuisine specialties served in charmingly rustic dining rooms. The 156 rooms of this showcase palace rent for between 100F ($45.95) and 210F ($96.50) in a single and between 175F ($80.41) and 390F ($179.20) in a double, with half board included. Each of the accommodations has its own private bath. The hotel, like everything else in Saanen, is two kilometers from Gstaad.

Bellevue Gstaad Grand Hotel (tel. 4-32-64) is an elegantly gabled white building set in a flowered garden. The shutters are light green, and in summer the management sets orange awnings above the sunny windows. Five minutes from the village center and a five-minute drive to the cable cars, the hotel has comfortably furnished rooms with private bath and balconies with southern exposure. Ulf Höfle is the general manager here. Accommodations, either single or double, cost between 90F ($41.35) and 135F ($62.03) per person, with half board (which is required of guests over the Christmas holidays).

Hotel Cabana (tel. 4-48-55). By the looks of the dramatically modern facade of this place, which nonetheless retains a chalet ambience about it, you'll guess that something unusual might wait for you inside. And what that is is a series of rooms with unusually massive polished beams supporting the ceiling, a very complete exercise room, and an imaginative selection of textiles which include boldly patterned pieces from underdeveloped countries. The indoor swimming pool has lounge chairs and coffee tables placed around it, Caribbean style, while the heated outdoor swimming pool welcomes swimmers with clouds of steam, even during snow storms. This hotel is part of a Swiss chain, so although you might miss the sense of being part of a family-run establishment, you make up for it in the quality of the accommodations. Each of the very comfortable bedrooms has a private bath. Singles rent for between 95F

($43.65) and 195F ($89.60), while doubles cost between 155F ($71.22) and 335F ($153.93), including half board.

Parkhotel Reuteler (tel. 8-33-77) is one of those Victorian-style fantasy buildings, with lots of gently curved gables, magenta awnings, and big sunny public rooms looking over a very extensive park. The decor of the establishment is one of traditional folk art. Much of the furniture is carved and painted with regional floral designs, and some of the wall surfaces follow the same strategy. The comfortable bedrooms are usually somewhat more modern than the public rooms, but comfortable in every way. Rooms with private bath cost between 95F ($43.65) and 180F ($82.71) per person per day, while those with bath rent for between 80F ($36.76) and 120F ($55.14), including half board. The price of any unit, of course, will vary according to the season. A covered garage is on the premises.

Hotel Olden (tel. 4-34 44) is one of the most charming hotels in Gstaad, its facade painted over with regional floral designs, pithy pieces of folk wisdom, and the date of construction (1899). The interior has all the dozens of architectural delights you'd expect in a building like this, ranging from the embellishments carved or painted into the stone lintels around many of the doors to the elegant woodworking over the ceilings and walls. A summer terrace in front serves drinks and a menu of the day for 25F ($11.48). Should you choose to eat indoors you'll have a choice of four different areas, one of them with dancing (see my nightlife recommendations). Each of them is popular for hotel guests and independent eaters alike. La Cave is closed in summer. You might try tagliatelle maison, blue trout, pâté of wild hare, roebuck (in season), lobster bisque, steak tartar, or, especially good on a cold day, three types of fondue which usually cost from 60F ($27.57) for two persons.

Hotel Hornberg, Saanenmöser (tel. 4-44-40), is a very pleasant family-style chalet hotel about six miles outside Gstaad. In three separate buildings, all set very close together, the hotel is outfitted in a well-maintained format which is half rustic, half modern. The dining room has one wall of hewn native stone and a wooden ceiling, with white napery covering the sunlit tables. Outdoor and indoor pools on the premises offer a chance to use up the excess energy you didn't already burn off on your winter or summer sports regimes. Children are welcomed here as well. Peter and Elizabeth Siebenthal, the attractive owners, have set up a children's playroom. Fireplaces take off much of the winter chill. The meal plan here is called the "brunch-pension" arrangement, because the breakfast served is actually a very ample meal offered buffet style every day from 8 to 11 a.m. It's so generous that many clients prefer to skip lunch altogether and wait for the traditional meal in the evening. Bathless rooms range from 55F ($25.27) to 90F ($41.36) per person daily, while accommodations with bath cost between 75F ($34.46) and 145F ($66.62).

Hotel Arc-en-Ciel (tel. 4-29-33) is an attractively decorated alpine-style chalet ten minutes from the center of Gstaad, which many lovers of calm will appreciate in peak season. The bedrooms are tasteful, combining lots of horizontal wood planking with white plaster walls for a cozy, well-lit ambience of great comfort. All accommodations have private baths. Singles range between 50F ($22.98) and 155F ($52.84), depending on the season, and doubles cost between 85F ($39.05) and 205F ($94.19) per day, depending on the season. Half board is offered for an additional 25F ($11.48) per person daily. You'll also find a pizzeria on the premises.

Posthotel Rössli (tel. 4-34-12) is rustically authentic according to the Bernese Oberland style, but it's also well heated and furnished with modern conveniences. Huge acres of the interior are covered with paneling, including the bedrooms which are cozy behind the weatherproof windows. The establishment lies in the center of the village, in a chalet-style building with green shutters and a flag of the Bernese canton flying over the front door. The restaurant and bierstube inside welcome almost as many local residents as they do international guests. Singles rent for between 35F ($16.08) and 55F ($25.27) without bath, and between 43F ($19.75) and 83F ($38.14) with bath. Doubles without bath cost between 67F ($30.78) and 115F ($52.84), going up to 83F ($38.13) and 143F ($65.70) with bath. Half board is another 20F ($9.19) per person daily. Ruedi Widmer and his family, your hosts, also maintain the restaurant, where fixed-price meals cost between 20F ($9.19) and 31F ($14.24), while à la carte begins at 25F ($11.49).

Hotel Alphorn (tel. 4-45-45) was opened in 1970 at the base of the Wispile cable car. The chalet-style establishment is owned by Erwin Mösching, who earlier in his life served as the director of international hotels in Stockholm and Hamburg. The intimate hotel offers 21 cozy rooms to guests who pay between 35F ($16.08) and 70F ($32.16) in a single and between 75F ($34.46) and 165F ($75.81) for a double, including breakfast. Half board is offered for another 22F ($10.11) per person daily. The hotel has an indoor pool, plus a ski shop. Specialties of the restaurant include trout and cheese dishes as well as a "dish of the house" made with fresh mushrooms.

Hotel National Rialto (tel. 4-34-74). Like many hotels in Gstaad, this one was designed with as much wood as possible, covering the walls and ceilings. The hotel offers a series of pleasant public rooms, outfitted with comfortable sofas in autumnal colors. Adjoining the hotel is a pleasant tearoom with a sunny terrace warmed on cold days with infrared heating. A landscaped park area stretches out behind the building, which sits prominently on the main street of the village. The Burri family, the owners, charge rates with half board included: between 55F ($25.27) and 72F ($33.08) in a single and between 110F ($50.54) and 190F ($87.31) in a double, depending on the plumbing, season, and type of accommodation.

Hotel Christiana (tel. 4-51-21) is beautifully outfitted inside with a satisfying combination of white walls and glowing paneling, Oriental rugs, and tasteful furniture. The bedrooms are comfortable, but some of the suites are spectacular, especially one with white carpets and white upholstery. This is one of the smaller hotels of Gstaad, which presumably means the service will be more individualized. From the outside the establishment looks like a chalet, with particularly elaborate gingerbread under the eaves. Singles rent for between 40F ($18.38) and 120F ($55.14), while doubles cost between 80F ($36.76) and 220F ($101.09), depending on the plumbing, the exposure of the room, and the season. Half board is offered for an additional 28F ($12.87). In summer guests have free entrance to the heated swimming pool near the Palace Hotel.

Sporthotel Victoria (tel. 4-14-31) is the personal statement of the Oehrli family, who prove to be congenial hosts. Their pleasant five-story hotel is in the center of town, two minutes from the train station. The accommodations are tastefully furnished with simple furniture, some of it alpine, and the bedrooms usually have lots of paneling and every comfort. A musical group sometimes performs in the rustic restaurant and dancing bar. Singles cost between 55F ($25.27) and 95F ($43.65), while doubles range between 110F ($50.54) and 189F ($86.84), including half board. An à la carte pizzeria is also on the premises.

Hotel Bernerhof (tel. 8-33-66). The first detail you notice from the outside is the uninterrupted lengths of wood balconies stretching across the facade of the hotel. These and the many additional touches make a stay here very pleasant, especially with the restaurant (see "Where to Eat"). Your host is

Leonz Blunschi, who charges between 52F ($23.89) and 93F ($42.73) per person in a double room or a three-person suite, depending on the season and the accommodation. All units contain balcony and private bath. Singles rent for between 58F ($26.65) and 99F ($45.49). Half board is available for another 21F ($9.65) per person daily.

Hotel Alpenrose (tel. 73-11-61) is decorated throughout in clean, fresh shades of primary colors, in a simple, attractive, and up-to-date decor which includes amusingly grotesque Fassnacht masks fastened to the dining room walls. The establishment is a combination of an oldtime alpine chalet with a strikingly modern series of extensions which contain big-windowed rooms with expansive balconies. The view covers many of the chalets of Gstaad, with the valley below changing colors in every season. The Aellig family, your hosts, charge half-board rates ranging from 45F ($20.67) to 69F ($31.70) in summer and from 50F ($22.98) to 73F ($33.54) in winter.

WHERE TO EAT: Most guests take either half or full board at their hotel, which is often required in the very peak seasons. There are few independent eateries in Gstaad that are noteworthy, perhaps owing to that very reason. Some exceptions follow.

Hostellerie Alpenrose, in Schönried (tel. 4-12-38), is one of the most attractive alpine chalets in the area, lying seven kilometers from Gstaad. Everything about this restaurant and hotel is costly, from the regional artifacts hanging from the polished wooden walls to the ingredients going into the imaginative cuisine. The establishment is owned and operated by Monique von Siebenthal, who offers delicacies so good that Prince Rainier and his family seek it out whenever they sojourn in the region. The food items and decor harmonize beautifully, always accented by the antiques and a blazing fireplace.

You might be intrigued by the blinis in sour cream and caviar, or a salad of suckling veal in burgundy vinegar and walnut oil, or veal marinated in olive oil with onions and green peppercorns. There are also many excellent saltwater specialties, and everything is prepared in the lightest possible way, deeply influenced by the tenets of nouvelle cuisine.

The expensive meals are considered by the elite of Gstaad to be worth the price. Fixed-price meals range from 70F ($32.16) to 125F ($57.43), while à la carte dinners cost between 41F ($18.83) and 68F ($31.25). The restaurant is closed Monday and from mid-April to mid-June and from November 1 until mid-December. In winter dinners begin late around here, around 10 p.m. Reservations are absolutely essential at this much-sought-after establishment.

For anyone who wishes to combine a culinary experience with a quiet weekend away from the wintertime bustle of Gstaad, the hostellerie maintains five unpretentious rooms, which are well heated, cozy, and decorated for the most part with Provençal artifacts. Singles cost 50F ($22.98), with doubles renting for 85F ($39.06).

Restaurant Bernerhof, in the Hotel Bernerhof (tel. 8-33-66), is a pleasant tavern-style restaurant serving many Italian specialties, such as risotto with "fruits of the sea," excellent soups, sometimes with mussels and scampi, veal liver Venetian style, and some very good pork dishes. Meals cost from 25F ($11.49). On the premises is the popular Stöckli-Bar.

Chez Esther, Hauptstrasse (tel. 4-11-28). The doors between the rooms of this informal restaurant are on Star-Trek electronic slides, for maximum retention of heat in winter. When you enter, be sure to walk into the cozy inner room whose windows face a terrace. Larger than the outer section, its walls are covered with paneling. Chairs pulled up to the tables are nostalgically alpine. Billy Matti, the director, tries to greet customers as they come in the door.

Well-prepared meals begin at 25F ($11.49), and include meats grilled over the open fire, riz Cazimir, cannelloni at forno, assiette valaisanne (air-dried meats), hamburgers, and scampi curry. The establishment is next to a public garden. Sometimes busloads of tourists descend on the place (hopefully not at the time of your visit).

APRÉS SKI: Gstaad has the most fashionable après-ski scene in the Bernese Oberland. Many nightclubs, especially discos, come and go, but the Café Olden at the **Hotel Olden** is the most popular place in town (even guests from the Gstaad Palace go here for a lark). Open only in winter, La Cave has a rôtisserie where you can dine and dance by the fireplace. It's rustic in style. The Olden Bar on the ground floor is also popular, drawing an international clientele.

The **Gstaad Palace** has an outstanding nightclub, the Green Go, with an excellent band and modern decor. Many guests show up in black tie, others preferring to be very casually dressed.

A very attractive young crowd goes dancing at the **Hostellerie Chesery** (tel. 4-24-51), a chalet-like hotel with a good restaurant and a disco.

My favorite spot, about two miles outside Gstaad, is the **Restaurant Chlösterli,** run by Herr Müllener (tel. 5-10-45). This is an alpine-style inn, dating from the 1600s, which can hold hundreds of people (and often does on a winter's night). Sometimes a live band is brought in; otherwise you get disco. You can go here to dine or drink.

And surely you'll discover some newly opened bars and discos on your own. Some may last only six weeks, but during their heyday they can be quite fun.

12. Kandersteg

Between Grindelwald and Gstaad, Kandersteg is at a southerly point in the Bernese Oberland. It's a tranquil and lovely mountain village—spread over four kilometers so nothing is crowded—and characterized by its rust- and orange-colored rooftops and its green, green Swiss meadows where wildflowers bloom in spring. It's framed by mountain passes in almost every direction. From the village, about six alpine huts are not-so-easily reached.

Since 1977 Kandersteg has been free of car traffic (a bypass starts at the outskirts to the village). The resort, which is active in both summer and winter, lies at the northern terminus of the Lötschberg Tunnel which stretches for nine miles, making it the third longest in the Alps. Ever since the beginning of World War I it has linked Berne with the Rhône Valley. Cars can be transported on the railway going through the tunnel.

Once, however, Kandersteg was known all over Switzerland for another reason dealing with transportation. It was a stage on the road to the Gemmi Pass, which long ago linked the Valais with the Bernese Oberland.

The village still has many old farmer's homes and a tiny church from the 16th century. It seems proud of its traditions.

In summer, horses can be rented at the local riding school, and the environs of Kandersteg are riddled with an extensive network of level footpaths and strategically located benches. These paths are also open in the winter.

As for skiing in winter, top-speed skiers avoid the place, but it attracts both beginners and cross-country devotees. Facilities include an open-air ice rink and an indoor artificial ice rink. For the downhill skier, there are a cable car, two chair lifts, and four ski tows. Kandersteg is also the site of the National Nordic Ski Center, with its ski-jumping station. In winter it has a floodlit cross-country track of about 2½ kilometers which is open in the evening.

At the foot of the Blümlisalp chain (12,000 feet), Kandersteg is served by the Berne–Lötschberg–Simplon railway. Perhaps it no longer attracts the celebrities it used to (Gstaad has taken over that position), but it's very popular nevertheless.

The **Oeschinensee** (or Lake Oeschinen) towers high above Kandersteg, and experts call this the most beautiful lake in the Alps. It's surrounded by snow-covered peaks, dropping 6000 feet to the rim of the lake. This, of course, is the most popular excursion from Kandersteg. You can walk to it from the Victoria Hotel or take a chair lift, costing 5F ($2.30), to the Oeschinen station and walk down from that point. The lake, at the foot of the Blümlisalp, has extremely clear water.

Another popular excursion is to **Klus,** a journey of some two miles (park your vehicle at the cable station's lower platform at Stock). You climb the rest of the way on foot, going through a tunnel over this untamed gorge, filled with the rushing falls of the Kander River. The wildly flowing Kander creates a romantic setting. However, you must watch your step, as the path gets very slippery in places, the spray coating the stones and pebbles.

FOOD AND LODGING: Royal Hotel Bellevue (tel. 75-12-12) is graced with a free-form swimming pool in the back garden, where anyone who looks up from his or her lawn chair can see a magnificent mountain vista in all directions. The hotel is a four-story brown-and-white streamlined structure, with a chalet-style roof and big windows. A quick look at the interior will reveal that it's one of the finest hotels in the region. The interior is elegant, with flagstone floors covered with dozens of Oriental rugs, Louis XIII armchairs, rococo lighting fixtures, and a reception desk tastefully fashioned from blond woods and tufted beige velvet. A handful of interesting-looking fireplaces crackle during most of the winter, with carved Louis XV armchairs covered with gray brocades clustered into conversational groups around them. Other rooms include barrel chairs in supple leather in an ambience of live piano music and mellow antiques.

The Rôtisserie is undeniably glamorous, with French armchairs pulled around crystal chandeliers, paneling, and handcrafted tapestries. The Grill-Stubli is a gemütlich lunchtime restaurant. Guests are requested to wear dinner jackets and formal or semiformal dresses for dinner. On the premises are an indoor and outdoor swimming pool, a sauna, a riding stable with a host of well-seasoned horses (bring riding clothes, including boots, if you have them), and a well-maintained tennis court. On the lake, 20 minutes away, the hotel owns a ten-meter yacht suitable for six passengers and a motorboat for water-skiing. In a nearby park, the hotel owns three separate chalets, each with apartment facilities and suites.

In brief, this is one of the most elegant hotels in region. Rooms range from 90F ($41.36) to 190F ($87.31) per person daily with half board included. This includes a variety of accommodations during a full range of seasons. The hotel, a member of Relais et Châteaux, has been owned by the Rikki family for three generations.

Hotel Victoria Ritter (tel. 75-14-44) is an elegantly Victorian-style hotel with lots of chimneys, gables, and dormers, plus a modern extension in front containing an indoor swimming pool. Tennis courts are on the premises. The mountains loom up virtually in the hotel's backyard, so you certainly won't be without scenery here. The gemütlich and comfortable restaurant is in a chalet-style building a few steps from the hotel, which serves very good food in a rustic series of paneled rooms. Half board ranges from 70F ($32.17) to 90F ($41.36) per person in a double room, with singles paying a supplement of 5F ($2.30) daily. If you like to fish, the hotel offers free trout fishing in a nearby, well-stocked private stream.

Hotel Schweizerhof (tel. 75-12-41) is an imposing five-story building with red shutters, a covered arcade stretching across the facade of the fourth floor, and a cupola above the front porch—everything set against a jagged backdrop of the rugged Alps. The interior is furnished with a mixture of ornate antiques (one of the settees could be in a museum) and conservatively traditional furniture. The rooms are clean, well heated, and comfortable. The *per-person* rate for bed and breakfast ranges between 40F ($18.38) and 50F ($22.96).

Hotel Alpenblick (tel. 75-11-29). Verena and Heinz Ogi-Müller are the congenial hosts of this very small hotel with 25 well-maintained beds. In the center of town, five minutes from the train station, the hotel is attractively balconied in a rustic chalet style. Someone will pick you and your bags up at the train station if you call ahead. The renovated rooms rent for 25F ($11.48) to 34F ($15.62) per person, either single or double occupancy, these tariffs including breakfast. The hotel is closed in October and during the last two weeks of March.

Hotel Alfa-Soleil (tel. 75-12-58) is one of the best dining choices when you want to break the monotony of your regular hotel fare. It is ably directed by the Seiler-Schwitter family, who serve pizzas, grilled meats, and a tempting variety of gourmet specialties which include homemade lasagne, tortellini, ravioli, and blue lake trout, as well as chateaubriand with béarnaise sauce and such classic dishes as turbot, fresh seafood salad (with wild marjoram), and chicken livers flavored with sage. Other dishes include a range of flambé delicacies, including calf liver, tournedos, and marinated plums with ice cream. Meals begin at 30F ($13.79), going up.

APRÈS SKI: Your best bet is the disco "High Moon," at the **Hotel Alfa-Soleil.** Many of the other hotels, such as the **Adler** and **Victoria,** also have lively bars.

Chapter VII

THE VALAIS

1. Leysin
2. Champéry
3. Martigny
4. Verbier
5. Great St. Bernard Pass
6. Sion
7. Crans-Montana
8. Leukerbad
9. Grimentz
10. Zermatt and the Matterhorn
11. Saas-Fee and Grächen
12. Brig and the Simplon Pass
13. The Grimsel Pass

THE MATTERHORN . . . the Great St. Bernard Pass . . . Zermatt . . . all of these legendary names in tourism are part of the canton of Valais, called by Goethe "that wondrous beautiful valley." Its name, derived from the one given to it by the Romans about 2000 years ago, described what the region was: the valley of the upper Rhône, a great river that springs from a huge glacier near the Furka Pass and flows westward and northward to Lake Geneva and beyond, into France, and then southward to empty into the Mediterranean. The Latin name for that upper Rhône Valley was Vallis Poenina, and the Germans still call it Wallis.

The boundaries of the Valais are obviously the result of its topographical features. Carved out through the millennia by the Rhône, the river valley was the natural recipient of the waters from many tributaries making their way from the lofty glacial Alps surrounding it. More than 50 major mountain peaks tower around the Valais, with the Matterhorn (14,701 feet) as the reigning queen. The most considerable stretch of glaciers in Switzerland is here, as well as some five square miles of lakes. The Dufourspitze summit of Monte Rosa (15,200 feet) is the loftiest point, but the Dom (14,942) is the tallest mountain lying completely within the canton.

The Rhône corridor, protected from storms by the mountains, with lots of sunshine and a stable climate, was a choice place of habitation from prehistoric times, many tribes having happened onto it during migrations when they found their way through alpine passes. It has for centuries been a major route over the Alps. The Great St. Bernard and Simplon Passes saw the passage of

Celts before the Christian era, and it was held by the Gauls for some 500 years. Some historians say that Hannibal's elephants came this way long before Napoleon made the Simplon passable for his huge cannons. Pilgrim and merchant, beggar and emperor—all have traveled the alpine passes of the Valais. Today wide highways, many with tunnels going through the most forbidding mountains, provide motorists with the shortest route to and from Italy by way of the valley of the Rhône, many still going over the Great St. Bernard Pass (8094 feet) and the Simplon Pass (6591 feet).

Two languages are spoken in the Valais, with the two-thirds of the population living in the west—Lake Geneva to Sierre—speaking French and those on eastward to the Simplon Pass speaking a German dialect. Many of the inhabitants, however, speak both tongues fluently, as well as some English.

The vineyards of the Valais are second only to those of the Vaud, and the fruity bouquet and delicate flavor of the upper Rhône Valley wines are known to all connoisseurs. The canton is rich in *mazots* or *raccards,* small barns standing on piles and used for the storage of grain, as dairy farming is carried on here. The favorite cheeses for raclette, the Swiss dish described in Chapter II under "Food and Drink," is made of rich, unskimmed milk from the Bagnes Valley, near the Great St. Bernard Pass.

Perhaps they're inspired by the majesty of the Matterhorn and the magnificence of the landscape, but for whatever reason, the Valais people are strong adherents of the Roman Catholic faith, as indicated by their many churches with lofty spires, their abbeys, and their monasteries.

With a climate which has been likened to that of Spain and Provence, the Valais attracts skiers and followers of other winter sports. Zermatt and its neighbors are known for having good snow conditions even when other parts of Switzerland do not. The increasing popularity of this canton in both summer and winter has brought an increase in accommodations ranging from resort facilities to modest pensions. Tourism forms a major part of the Valais economy, and almost every tributary glen and alpine meadow seemingly has a hotel or at least a small inn. But I've observed that, through careful and realistic planning, the region has managed to keep its countryside intact, by and large. Many little valleys with their Rhône tributaries are tranquil havens even today, the silence broken only by the tinkle of cowbells from mountain pastures, the buzz of bees suckling alpine flowers, and the song of birds. The sounds of passing human beings are muted by the surrounding mountains.

Visitors can select from a wide variety of rooms and prices. You may find that you're well pleased with a wood-paneled room in a private home, which may cost as little as 22F ($10.11) to 25F ($11.49). Or you may choose to splurge, paying 200F ($91.90) in a superior resort hotel.

Swissair flies daily from New York to Geneva, and from there you can go by car or train to towns in the Valais. The second-class rail fare one way between Geneva and Brig, for example, is about 36F ($16.54). On the good Swiss Federal Railways, second class is my preferred way to travel. It's so comfortable and clean that first class seems to me to be an unnecessary extravagance.

Now, if you're ready for a journey through this "wondrous valley," we'll begin our trek from Lake Geneva, which is the major tourist routing.

1. Leysin

Our first stopover will be at Leysin, which is reached by turning left at Aigle, after you've left Lake Geneva, and journeying up into the mountains for about ten miles. It's also possible to reach it by taking a cogwheel railway from Aigle.

A year-round resort, Leysin overlooks a vast alpine panorama, with 180 kilometers of marked paths for walks. Views extend from the Bernese Alps to Mont Blanc.

At some 4760 feet, the resort is about the fifth-biggest winter sports playground in Switzerland. It has two centers, each on different levels. There's also a snow nursery for children.

FOOD AND LODGING: **Hotel Central-Residence** (tel. 34-12-11) contributes a bit of ultramodern styling to the alpine panorama around it. The six-story flat-roofed building has two floors of vividly upholstered public rooms capped with four levels of comfortably low-key bedrooms, all of which contain kitchenettes and southern balconies. The downstairs bar and sitting rooms alternate surfaces of distressed concrete with light-grained wood for a cheerful ambience that is improved with fires blazing in the round fireplace, the smoke from which is funneled through a metallic chimney in the middle of the room. Sports facilities include a covered swimming pool and outdoor tennis courts, as well as sauna and massage facilities. You'll find dancing in the Casanova Club, the most popular après-ski spot. Each of the accommodations has a private bath. They cost between 71F ($32.62) and 140F ($64.33) in a single and between 110F ($50.54) and 195F ($89.60) in a double, including breakfast. Half board is available for another 18F ($8.27).

Hotel Le Relais (tel. 34-24-21), in the center of the village, is an attractively boxy building with different series of wood-grained panels offset against irregular lines of the modern windows. Inside, a comfortable snackbar and restaurant looks vaguely English, with its half-timbering and Windsor chairs, while a more formal dining room is done in shades of dusty rose and scarlet. The decor of the bedrooms is comfortable and unpretentious. Open all year, the hotel has 100 beds and charges between 65F ($29.87) and 115F ($52.84) for a single and between 95F ($43.65) and 165F ($75.82) in a double, including breakfast. Half board is offered for an additional 20F ($9.19). Upon your arrival the management will present you with a booklet which allows free entrance to some of the village's sports facilities.

Hotel Mont-Riant (tel. 34-12-35) is a very pleasant 36-bed hotel made even more so by the concerned ministrations of the Ryhen family. Their hostelry is six minutes from the railway station in a quiet part of what residents call "the upper part of town." This affords views as far away as the Rhône Valley. The hotel is close to the chair lift of Solacyre. Guests receive passes for free entrance to a covered skating rink and a nearby indoor swimming pool. Many of the accommodations facing south have private balconies. Singles range from 30F ($13.78) to 60F ($27.57), while doubles cost anywhere between 50F ($22.98) and 107F ($49.17), with half board available for another 17F ($7.81) per person.

Hotel Restaurant Les Orchidées (tel. 34-14-21) is a small white-painted hotel landscaped into the hill on which it was placed. Many of its bedrooms face an alpine vista across a private balcony. The public rooms are very clean and trimmed in wood. The Haupt-Glinickes, the multilingual proprietors, prepare attractive meals and offer free mini-golf, use of a swimming pool, and ice skating to their guests. Singles range from 30F ($13.78) to 64F ($29.40), while doubles cost between 55F ($25.27) and 105F ($48.25), with half board going for an additional 15F ($6.89).

Hotel Universitaire (tel. 34-11-91) is owned by a reputable chain of hotels, with branches in six other Swiss resorts. This one is a large rectangle of a building with shutters and a big-windowed extension stretching off toward the panoramic vista. Most of the units are bathless doubles, although one of these can be converted into a single for an additional charge of 8F ($3.67). Good shower facilities exist on each floor. You're only a few minutes' walk from the train station. The management is sports-oriented and friendly. *Per-person* rates in a double range between 48F ($22.05) and 68F ($31.24), with half board available for another 9F ($4.14) per day.

2. Champéry

Near the French border, about a 1½-hour drive from Geneva, Champéry lies in the center of the so-called Portes du Soleil, a complex of 13 French and Swiss ski resorts, including the famed Avoriaz on the French side. In fact Champery is linked to Avoriaz by a lift system.

Champéry stands at the beginning of the Illiez Valley (the Val d'Illiez), at an altitude of 3450 feet. It's overshadowed by the Dents du Midi range. You find yourself in a setting of forests and impressive peaks.

The resort enjoys international acclaim, yet it's very small, and all the local inhabitants know each other. It's very much a family-type place, and there are ski classes for children as well as adults.

You can go by cable car to Planachaux, another kilometer higher up. A round-trip ticket costs 10F ($4.60). From there you can climb to the Cross at 6440 feet for a splendid view of the Alps. This is a very popular ski area, where there are several lifts opening onto some magnificent runs.

FOOD AND LODGING: **Hotel Beau Séjour** (tel. 79-17-01) is a beautifully rustic chalet with lots of handcrafted detailing. It's adjacent to the Planachaux cableway terminus and is very popular, especially in wintertime with skiers. Owned and managed by the Avanthey family, the hotel offers different levels of accommodation, some contemporary, some oldtimey in style. Even if you're not staying here you may want to patronize its Vieux Chalet for fondue and raclette. In season a musical group often provides entertainment, and it's one of the liveliest stops on the après-ski circuit. All units contain bath, costing between 50F ($22.97) and 70F ($32.16) in a single and between 83F ($38.14) and 120F ($55.14) in a double. Half board is offered for another 19F ($8.73) per person.

Pension de la Gare (tel. 79-13-29) is another establishment owned by Gerald Avanthey and family. Set in an alpine-style house with masonry detailing and a half-timbered upper floor, the establishment offers bed and breakfast in bathless rooms for between 26F ($11.94) and 30F ($13.79) per person daily, with half board in the sympathetic restaurant costing an additional 13F ($5.97) per person daily.

Pension Rose des Alpes (tel. 79-12-18) is a very attractive double chalet. One section is newer than the other, but crafted nonetheless in the traditional style. The interior has all the wood detailing and alpine furniture you've come to expect, along with a modern lounge with leatherette chairs. Managed and owned by the Delalay family, the hotel charges between 30F ($13.78) and 48F ($22.06) in a single and between 48F ($22.06) and 80F ($36.76) in a double, with breakfast included. None of the rooms contains a private toilet, but there are two bathrooms on each floor. Showers or running water are offered in each unit, however. Half board is available for another 14F ($6.43) per person.

APRÈS SKI: If popularity contests were held, **Le Levant** (tel. 79-12-72), would get the nod as one of the liveliest places to go after you've finished your day on the ski runs. The villagers themselves patronize the establishment, as well, for it is known for its raclette. You'll see a sign posted, "*Ici Raclette.*" The cost is about 18F ($8.27) for a meal here. The patron of this Valais tavern is Bernard Biolaz, who cuts wheels of cheese as large as pumpkins. In this room, decorated with wainscotting, you can also drink Fendant, the white wine famous throughout the Valais. In fact it's most preferred with raclette (never order beer!).

Among hotels, the most action is at the Beau Séjour.

MORGINS: There has been a collection of chalet-style farms on the steep hillsides of this region since time immemorial. However, a more formal classification of the village as an alpine station occurred in 1820, when the region became better known. Since then a steadily increasing flow of tourism has contributed to the prosperity of this place. Today the village is dotted with intricately crafted chalets and a few buildings of more modern design, all of which make Morgins both a summer mountain resort and a winter ski center. In winter, residents have the extraordinary choice of more than 150 ski lifts in the entire area. The motto of the town is "unbordered skiing" (that is, without frontiers), since you can ski to France without a passport.

Nightlife is not Las Vegas in dimension, but there are several bars, restaurants, and discos.

If you want to base here, try the following:

Hostellerie Bellevue (tel. 77-27-71) is a pleasingly proportioned chalet with balconies covering the front and back. It contains 160 beds in comfortably carpeted and upholstered rooms, each of which has its own bath and balcony, with a view of the green hills around the hotel. On the premises you'll find a disco/nightclub, a pool, a sauna, five different eateries, and a piano bar. There's also a kindergarten for childcare. All this is in addition to the electronically up-to-date conference rooms. The *per-person* rate for doubles ranges between 55F ($25.27) and 88F ($40.44), with an additional 10F ($4.60) for single occupancy. Half board is another 20F ($9.19).

3. Martigny

Everybody has marched through here, including Roman legions and, much later, the armies of Napoleon heading across the Great St. Bernard Pass. In time it attracted such personalities as Goethe, Byron, and Rousseau. The Gallo-Roman settlement was called Octodurus.

In the Rhône Valley, the town lies in a setting of vineyards, orchards, and forests, with mountain ranges in the background. It's completely different from the towns in the north of Switzerland, taking on a more southern aura, as reflected by its Place Centrale, with its café terraces shaded by large plane trees.

For centuries Martigny has been an international road junction. Dominating the town is the 13th-century castle—now in ruins—of La Bâtiaz, which was the property of the powerful bishops of Sion. The tower, most visible today, was restored at the end of the 19th century. As a memory of its Roman occupation, a amphitheater lies to the southeast of the town.

Chances are you'll be just like most motorists and pass through Martigny for the day. However, it merits a stopover, if only to see a number of sights in the general vicinity.

These include excursions to the **Trient Gorges,** which are open from May 1 until the end of September from 8 a.m. to 6 p.m., charging an admission of 4F ($1.84). You can drive your car to Vernayaz where there's a car park. At this site you can see where the Trient pours into the Rhône Valley. Also in the vicinity is the **Pissevache waterfall,** which plunges earthward from a large rock near Vernayaz. This waterfall gave Goethe much pleasure, as he later recorded, although we are told by guides that it was much more powerful in the author's day.

FOOD AND LODGING: As an alternative to staying in Martigny, you might want to consider one of the little satellite resorts in its environs which immediately follow.

Hotel du Rhône, 11 avenue Grand St. Bernard (tel. 2-17-17), is a modern white-faced building that looks very much like an urban hotel. It has big windows, plus one section with covered loggias outside each of the bedrooms. The ground floors are covered with curtained glass, which reveal comfortable public rooms filled with '60s-style furniture. The sunny bedrooms are carpeted, sometimes in an attractive forest green, with clean sheets and soundproof windows. This hotel accommodates 100 visitors in rooms, all with bath, priced between 48F ($22.06) and 68F ($31.25) in a single and between 85F ($39.05) and 125F ($57.43) in a double. The hotel is affiliated with Best Western.

Hotel de la Poste, 8 rue de la Poste (tel. 2-14-44), does everything it can to maintain the service of the 19th century in a modern format of a rectangular concrete building with big windows and a flat roof. The bedrooms are tastefully filled with striped bedcovers, an occasional Oriental rug, and modest furniture. The restaurant is a popular local eatery which serves food brasserie style in a format of red leatherette chairs and white napery. Marcel Claivaz and his family charge between 42F ($12.29) and 58F ($26.65) in a single and between 70F ($32.17) and 98F ($45.03) in a double. Half board is offered for another 16F ($7.35) per person daily.

Restaurant du Léman, 19 avenue du Léman (tel. 2-30-75), is owned and operated by a man with a lot of relatives in the district, Michel Claivaz. Near the exit to Martigny from the autoroute, the restaurant specializes in seafood, serving whatever looked freshest in the market that day, along with regional specialties familiar in the Alps. International dishes include beef with chanterelles, rack of lamb provençal, and rognons de veau (veal kidneys) if you have a taste for them. In summer you might prefer to eat on the garden terrace. The restaurant is closed on Sunday and Monday and for two weeks in both June and October. Hours are from 7 a.m. to 11 p.m. Fixed-price meals range from 15F ($6.89) to 50F ($22.98), with an à la carte dinner costing about the same.

CHAMPEX: This tiny resort, reached by taking a road south from Martigny, is popular in both summer and winter. It lies in the Mont Blanc massif, and opens onto what is called the most beautiful alpine lake in the Valais, Lake Champex.

The setting is in a mountain valley at a height of 4800 feet, about 30 kilometers from Martigny (head in the direction of the St. Bernard road tunnel).

Summer sports include riding, hiking, and fishing, certainly walking. Boat trips are possible on the lake, although motor boats are forbidden. Windsurfing is popular, and you can also hire pedal boats, or swim in the resort's heated swimming pool, later visiting an alpine botanical garden. One of the most thrilling adventures here is to go for a walk up to the glaciers.

In winter Champex naturally attracts skiers. There is rarely any waiting for the resort's two chair lifts or its ski lift.

Hotel Alpes et Lac (tel. 4-11-51). Guests are welcomed to this attractive place with a drink and the offer of assistance by the congenial owners, Karl and Bernadette Zimmerman. The majority of clients might prefer to stay on the graveled sun terrace below the blue-shuttered and gabled facade of this lovely spot, although more active ones will find lots to do. Dress is informal: ties are required only on New Year's Eve. Each of the elegant bedrooms was refurnished in 1980. The hotel provides many services and amenities beyond the call of duty, including dinners and parties where guests can meet each other. The public rooms are tasteful, furnished sometimes with Victorian antiques or tastefully updated setees and chairs. In summertime you'll enjoy the many well-marked paths around the hotel. Rates are 55F ($25.27) to 98F ($45.03) per person, based on double occupancy, with half board included. The tariffs depend on the season, plumbing, and exposure. Singles are available for supplements ranging from 4F ($1.84) to 10F ($4.60).

LES MARÉCTTES: One mile southwest of Salvan, you reach the mini-resort of Les Marécottes, which draws both a summer and a winter crowd. Known mostly to Europeans, it's a little undiscovered nugget of the Valais. At 3600 feet, it has both a natural swimming pool and a zoo of alpine animals. A chair lift takes you up to Creusaz at 5840 feet. When you reach Les Marécottes, you will have come to the end of the road, but a railway will take you to the famous ski resort of Chamonix in France.

Hotel Joliment (tel. 6-14-70) is a centrally located composite of an old-fashioned balconied hotel with plenty of charm. A nearby flat-roofed annex is built with a connecting passage. The roof of the annex is set with pink tiles and serves as a sundeck. The establishment is only a few steps from the village church, yet you'll still feel you're in the countryside because of the sloping garden leading off toward a view of the mountains. Many of the accommodations have balconies, and even the new annex is comfortably outfitted with rustic beams and pleasing colors. A tearoom and dancing bar under the same management lies 50 yards away. Singles rent for between 23F ($10.56) and 45F ($20.67), while doubles cost between 35F ($16.08) and 73F ($33.54) per person daily. Half board is offered for an additional 13F ($5.97) per person daily. The Délez family are your hosts.

4. Verbier

Within easy reach of Martigny, Verbier at 4920 feet has a charming chalet atmosphere and offers a large variety of pistes with ski lifts everywhere. It's the start of the Haute Route Verbier-Saas Fee. It stands on a sunny plateau looking south with views of Mont Blanc.

In the heart of the southermost Alps of Switzerland, Verbier is ruled by skiing: there are 80 mechanical lifts in four valleys, plus 300 kilometers of tracks, plus many other winter sports such as skating and curling.

Les Ruinettes/Attelas has a large choice of places to ski. Mont Gelé at about 10,000 feet is one of the most challenging and best known runs. Many skiers debate seriously before taking the plunge. The sunny bowl of Lac des Vaux has some gentle slopes for beginners.

The gondola to Tortin opens up one of the most difficult runs in Europe, the glacier skiing below Mount Fort. Savoleyres offers good skiing over the ridge of La Tzoumaz, facing north. It's my serious recommendation that this resort is for dedicated skiers. Nonskiers may find happier oases elsewhere.

In summer you can hike through alpine reserves, encountering everything from a farmer to an ibex to a mountain goat.

FOOD AND LODGING: **Hotel Rhodania** (tel. 7-01-21) is an unusually designed chalet in the middle of the village. It's made with a varied combination of wood and stucco, with an updated system of buttressing the overhanging eaves. The nightlife facilities are among the most popular (and sometimes the most raucous) in town, but you'd never know it from inside your soundproof bedroom. The interior is very comfortable, outfitted with wood trim, exposed masonry, and lots of comfortable velvet-colored chairs. Half board in the pleasant red-carpeted dining room is included in the following prices: from 110F ($50.55) to 140F ($64.33) in a single and from 175F ($80.41) to 235F ($107.98) in a double. All accommodations contain private bath. The hotel is affiliated with the Best Western chain.

Hotel Farinet (tel. 7-66-26) is a traditionally designed alpine chalet with touches of the American west. This is especially evident in the grill room, decorated Rocky Mountain style with wagon wheels and large slogans for rib-eye steak. The rest of the establishment is cozily outfitted with comfortable chairs, wall-to-wall carpeting, and stone detailing. In summertime dozens of rose-colored parasols cluster like pink clouds on the sun terrace and balconies. Singles range from 56F ($25.73) to 118F ($54.22), while doubles cost between 100F ($45.95) and 205F ($94.20), which includes half board. The prices, of course, vary with the season.

Hotel Grand Combin (tel. 7-55-15) is the kind of chalet where huge icicles suspend themselves from the eaves in the early spring when the snows are best for skiing. Although you'll probably have your own private balcony, you'll still end up on the sun terrace for snacks and drinks, especially since many of the guests choose to eat breakfast there in virtually any season. The interior is warmly decorated in the kinds of colors and chairs that look restful after a hard day of skiing. Bedrooms are romantically papered in flowered patterns, set off by scalloped bedcovers. Edouard Bessard and his family sometimes organize nature walks with informed explanation of the flora and fauna, and plan raclette excursions for the introduction of guests to one another. With half board included, singles rent for between 51F ($23.43) and 110F ($50.55), while doubles cost between 120F ($55.14) and 210F ($96.50), depending on the season and the plumbing. Full board is available for an additional 15F ($6.89) per person daily.

Hôtel Le Mazot (tel. 7-68-12) is an apartment hotel decorated with style and lots of exposed paneling. From the front it looks like two very similar alpine structures connected at the base with a reception area. This permits a maximum of balcony space for the simply furnished bedrooms. These usually have a large bed and a minimum of comfortably spartan furniture which, thanks to the warmth of the paneling and the autumnal colors, contribute to a comfortable room. The hotel is designed for young-hearted people who appreciate athletics. Singles rent for between 63F ($28.94) and 98F ($45.03), while doubles cost from 115F ($52.84) to 195F ($89.60), with half board included. Each of the accommodations has a private bath. Serge Tacchini is the owner.

Hotel Catogne (tel. 7-51-05). The upper half looks like a chalet; the lower half is masonry and stucco, with big windows and a modern extension containing the restaurant. The inside is as rustically paneled as you'd expect, with orange tablecloths near the well-stocked bar. Jean-Marc Corthay, the owner, charges from 48F ($22.05) to 68F ($31.24) in a single and from 85F ($39.05) to 138F ($63.41) in a double, depending on the season, with half board included.

Rosalp, route de la Tintaz (tel. 7-63-23). Some habitués of this resort hotel say that the cooking produced by head chef Roland Pierroz is nothing short of brilliant, and the cuisine is often judged the best in the Valais. A virtual mob descends on this establishment every night in high season. He prepares regional specialties for those who order them, but his light nouvelle cuisine is what is really the occasion. Seasonally adjusted specialties include oysters with caviar in puff pastry, turbot with crab, chicken with chervil, a host of game dishes, and imaginative renderings of lobster and salmon. Cheese platters and desserts are well assorted. The wine list concentrates on very good vintages from the Valais. Fixed-price meals range from 70F ($32.16) to 115F ($52.84), with à la carte meals costing from 95F ($43.65) to 130F ($59.73). The restaurant lies about 200 yards from the center of town and it's imperative to reserve a table. The restaurant is closed from May till June and from mid-October until the last week in November. In the off-season it's closed all day on Wednesday and on Thursday until 5 p.m.

APRÈS SKI: Before you order dinner (likely fondue), drop in for a drink at an attractive bar, **Nelson's Pub,** appropriately masculine in leather and mahogany. You'll mingle with many fellow skiers to discuss your run for the next day.

Later you'll adjourn to the **Pizzeria** for a beer and pizza. It draws an animated young crowd. Pizza and pasta are also served at **Le Bivouac,** downstairs.

On the disco circuit, the most popular place in town is the **Farm Club,** attached to the Hotel Rhodania, previously recommended. Before getting caught up in madness, you might also want to order a meal in its excellent restaurant, **Le Refuge.**

5. Great St. Bernard Pass

The St. Bernards are beloved in Switzerland, even though they aren't as in demand as they once were. Today motorists in general take the four-mile-long Great St. Bernard Tunnel between Italy's Aosta Valley and the Valais, instead of the road over the Great St. Bernard Pass. Alas, the dogs no longer carry brandy in their casks. But they're still bred by monks at the Great St. Bernard Hospice. If you wish to visit the hospice, you should make inquiries prior to your arrival: **Hospice du Grand-St. Bernard,** Le Grand-St-Bernard 1931 Bourg-St-Pierre (tel. 020/4-92-36).

This famed hospice was established in the mid-11th century to aid stranded travelers trying to make it across the pass. At the hospice you can visit the dogs in their kennels. Allow about an hour's drive from Martigny. You can also visit a small museum illustrating the history of the pass.

Many visitors in summer make the pilgrimage over this pass, following in the footsteps of Napoleon in 1800 when his army used it to cross into Italy. The road over the pass is usually open from mid-June (perhaps a little later) until October.

If you wish to stop over here, perhaps for nostalgic reasons, you can find a good accommodation in—

BOURG-ST-PIERRE: **Auberge de Vieux-Moulin** (tel. 4-91-69) is a very small, 30-bed roadside inn which was recently built by blasting away part of a rocky hillside beside the highway. Its bedrooms are clean, streamlined, and comfortable, usually with a private bath. A pleasant restaurant with big windows and wood paneling is on the premises, with a gas station and a currency-exchange office on the same grounds. This inn lies in a hamlet which you might not even notice if you blink, so you might consider this as a practical way station en route to somewhere else. Singles range from 22F ($10.11) to 38F ($17.46), while doubles cost between 34F ($15.62) and 65F ($29.87). Half board is offered for an additional 13F ($5.97).

6. Sion

The capital of the Valais, Sion is known for its glorious springs and falls (summer is considered divine all over Switzerland). Easily reached from either France or Italy, Sion dates from Roman times. Most of its population speaks French. The silhouettes of the castles of Valère and Tourbillon dominate this small capital.

THE SIGHTS: Crowning the north hillock is the **Castle of Tourbillon,** perched on a steep rock above the town. It's the ruin of a medieval stronghold built at the end of the 13th century by a bishop wanting to defend Sion against the House of Savoy. It was mainly destroyed by a fire in 1788 and has never been rebuilt, although you'll see the remains of a keep, watchtower, and chapel, among other sights. It makes an ideal place to go for a stroll. At a height of 2149 feet, there's a view of the Rhône Valley.

On the other hill, the **Château de Valère** at 2038 feet is more interesting, because this fortified church is in much better shape. In Roman times it was believed to have been a citadel. The church in its present structure is mainly from the 12th and 13th centuries. You must make a steep climb up to the church and museum (you can park down below). A three-aisle basilica, the church contains some splendid stalls from the 17th century, and what has been called "the oldest playable organ in the world," dating from the 14th century.

Standing beside the church is the **Musée de Valère,** with such Roman antiquities as a three-horned bronze bull and its medieval sculpture. It's open in summer daily from 8 a.m. to noon and 1:30 to 7 p.m. (it's floodlit at night), and in winter daily from 9 a.m. to noon and 1:30 to 5 p.m., charging an admission of 2.50F ($1.15). It's always closed on Monday.

After you've made this exhausting climb, you can descend to the town to check it out. The **Hôtel de Ville** (town hall) has beautiful doors and columns from the 17th century. On the main street of Sion, the rue du Grand-Pont, it has an astronomical clock you may want to photograph. The Roman stones on the ground floor date from A.D. 377, and are reputedly the earliest known evidence of the spread of Christianity in the country.

Northeast of the Hôtel de Ville is the **Cathédrale de Notre-Dame-du-Glarier,** reconstructed by 15th-century builders, although the Romanesque belfry remains, dating from the 11th and 13th centuries. Inside, look for the triptych in gilded wood, called *The Tree of Jesse.*

The **Supersaxo House** dates from 1505 and is sumptuously impressive. Built by a provincial governor of the same name, it stands at 7 rue de Conthey and is open to the public from 8 a.m. to noon and 2 to 6 p.m. except on Sunday and holidays. The house is richly decorated, including one room with a decorated rose ceiling that's stunning.

The **Majorie Museum** is also open to the public from 10 a.m. to noon and 2 to 6 p.m., daily except Monday, charging an admission of 2.50F ($1.15). It closes at 5 p.m. in winter. Once a residence of the "Major," an episcopal authority, it today houses a fine arts museum. To reach it, head up the rue des Châteaux in the direction of the hilltop castles (the museum will be on your left). Special attention is devoted to a Valais-born artist, Raphy Dallèves, who died in 1940.

Sion can also become an important excursion center for you, as you explore such places as Crans-Montana, covered separately in this guide, and Zermatt, which is a drive of only 1½ hours. The Office du Tourisme, 6 rue de Lausanne (tel. 22-28-98), in Sion will assist you in planning day trips.

WHERE TO STAY: Rising like a cement cube in the middle of town, **Hôtel de la Gare,** Place de la Gare (tel. 23-28-21), looks very much like a product of late-20th-century architecture. Each of the bedrooms is comfortably furnished with uncarved wood-grained furniture, big windows, and views over the city and the Alps. The building is air-conditioned, soundproof, and has two elevators, two restaurants, and underground parking. All units contain private baths. Singles cost from 45F ($20.67) to 60F ($27.57), while doubles range between 82F ($37.67) and 103F ($47.33). Half board in the comfortable restaurant costs an additional 20F ($9.19).

Hôtel Touring, 6 avenue de la Gare (tel. 23-15-51), one of the commercial streets of Sion, alternates horizontal bands of concrete with weatherproof windows in its facade. The interior is attractively and functionally furnished with understated chairs and tables. A comfortable restaurant serves well-prepared meals on white napery. Each of the rooms has its own bath. Singles rent for between 45F ($20.67) and 67F ($30.78), while doubles cost from 89F ($40.90) to 111F ($51), including breakfast. Half board is offered for another 20F ($9.19) per person.

WHERE TO DINE: **Enclos de Valère,** rue des Châteaux (tel. 23-32-30). You can just barely drive a car up the steep cobblestones leading to this restaurant, but if another vehicle happens to be coming down the hill, you might be in for trouble. Your destination is the small and intimate restaurant not far from the château. It's surrounded by a flowering garden, where many guests choose to sit in summertime to taste the creations of Gerald Henrion, who was strongly influenced by the famed Paul Bocuse of France. Specialties vary according to the season, but are likely to include gigot of lamb with Provençal herbs such as thyme flowers, a filet of beef with green peppercorns, a medallion of sea bass, and lobster ragoût with baby vegetables. Try also the three-fish terrine, containing essence of fresh crab. Roast goose is often served with fresh nectarines. The restaurant is open from 6:30 p.m. to midnight, closed on Monday except in summer, and reservations are strongly advised. A grand menu is offered at 68F ($31.25) with six courses. However, sometimes fixed-price meals begin at around 55F ($25.27). À la carte meals most often range from 52F ($23.89) to 72F ($33.08).

Caves de Tous-Vents, 22 rue des Châteaux (tel. 22-46-84), stands right next to Enclos de Valère in a pink stucco building with a cellar that dates from the 13th century. It serves specialties of the Valais region at moderate tariffs. These include raclette, fondue, air-dried alpine meats, gigot of lamb with Provençal herbs, and especially grilled meats. Count on spending from 35F ($16.08) and up. Desserts might include a tart made with the fresh fruits of the season or a chocolate mousse. Regis Favre is the owner, and he closes every Monday for a much-needed rest.

Chez Tchetchett (les Mayennets), 36 avenue de Tourbillon (tel. 22-18-98), is a sympathetic restaurant decorated with wood panels about two minutes from the train station. Michel Follonier created this relatively inexpensive eatery which for some 20 years has been known to everyone in town. Fish is one of his specialties, including young turbot with vegetables and fresh salmon with grapefruit. He also does an excellent sole in tarragon butter and, in season, mussels marinara. Some dishes are Italian inspired, including the lasagne and the triples milanese. Try, if available, the fresh frog legs. His major offering is a bouillabaisse prepared only for two persons. Fixed-price meals begin at 18F ($8.27), while à la carte dinners range from 20F ($9.19) to 45F ($20.67). The restaurant, which has sidewalk tables, is open from 7 a.m. to midnight every night but Sunday. It's closed for about a month in summer.

Restaurant Au Vieux Valais, 3 rue St-Théodule (tel. 22-16-74), is a rustic place, with pine chalet tables, carved wood paneling, and waitresses in regional dress. The walls are dotted with antique cowbells, old pewter, and a child's sled from the 19th century. You'll find this place on a narrow passageway in a cobbled street near the cathedral. Georges Lupet, the owner, stays open every day except Sunday from 9 a.m. to midnight, serving set meals starting from 13.50F ($6.20). These might begin with a tasty assiette valaisanne, a plate of air-dried alpine meat, and proceed to duck à l'orange. You can also order exceptionally good á la carte dishes, including various fondues (bourguignonne, chinoise, and tomato). Try also the terrine made with meats and green peppercorns or the rack of deviled lamb. The filet perch meunière is also excellent. On the à la carte, you can easily spend from 35F ($16.08) and up per person.

HAUTE-NENDAZ: Above Sion, facing the Bernese Alps, Haute-Nendaz at 4116 feet is steadily gaining in popularity. And when (or if) you get bored there, you can always go on to Super-Nendaz, a new tourist center at 5525 feet. Haute-Nendaz is both a winter and a summer resort. In fair weather, skiing is still possible, along with tennis, swimming, running, walking, and angling. But Haute-Nendaz's reputation is primarily as a ski resort.

It's rapidly emerging as a competitor to Verbier. There are more than 200 kilometers of walks taking you along bisses (irrigation channels), which are sometimes several miles long, and leading you to the edge of glaciers. Among other excursions, you can take a cableway to Tracouet, at 7220 feet, for skiing.

Food and Lodging

Hôtel Mont Calme (tel. 88-22-40) is a modern adaptation of a chalet, with a sunny restaurant, grill room, pizzeria, and disco bar. The hotel really is calm, as its name suggests, even though the tongue-in-cheek logo is an illustration of a small child raucously raising hell for everyone to hear. Véronique and Jeannot Fournier have filled their establishment with many attractive details, and they do everything they can to be helpful. Most of the comfortable bedrooms are fairly large and have enough wood paneling to make you feel at home in the country. Singles rent for between 48F ($22.06) and 62F ($28.49), while doubles cost between 85F ($39.06) and 111F ($51), with breakfast included. Half board is offered for another 19F ($8.73) per person.

Hôtel Sourire (tel. 88-26-16) was built in 1970 in the center of the village by the Schiess-Glassey family, who prove to be generous and responsible hosts. The public rooms have well-polished wooden ceilings and comfortable modern furniture, while the bedrooms contain private baths and a good view as far as the Rhône Valley. Singles range from 37F ($17) to 55F ($25.27), while doubles go from 68F ($31.25) to 93F ($42.74), including breakfast. Half board is available for an additional 17F ($7.81) per person daily.

ANZÈRE: Overlooking the valley of the Rhône, Anzère gets quite a bit of sunshine. The views from this pint-size resort are spectacular, opening onto the Alpes Vaudoises all the way to Mont Blanc. It draws visitors in both summer and winter. Summer activities include numerous walks in the forest, swimming in alpine pools, tennis, and fishing in the cold waters.

Lying to the north of Sion, Anzère is just beginning to emerge as a ski resort. It seems to have a bright future. The center has been carefully conceived, with the modern tourist in mind.

The resort lies at 4920 feet. A cableway will take you to the Pas de Maimbré at 7752 feet, where there's not only a panoramic vista, but ski runs as well.

In Anzère, traffic is forbidden in the main square.

Food and Lodging

Residence et Hôtel Grand-Roc (tel. 38-35-35) has beautiful views from the balconies of its well-furnished rooms, as well as a well-designed series of inviting public rooms. The bar area is my favorite, and the flagstone-covered tavern is attractive also. The Eliane Moos family help guests in any way they can. They've set up a three-kilometer fitness course in the nearby woods which, if you're not out promenading through the hills, might make a healthy diversion. Singles cost between 42F ($19.30) and 63F ($28.95), while doubles rent for between 73F ($33.54) and 124F ($56.98), with half board offered for another 17F ($7.81) per person daily.

Restaurant Les Premiers Pas, Place du Village (tel. 38-29-20), is on the central square of town, in a gemütlich restaurant open every day of the week in high season from 9 a.m. to midnight. In low season the place closes on Monday and also shuts down from the first of November until mid-December. Specialties are the best raclette in town, tournedos on a slate with morels, cheese fondue, and different items which are either flambeed or grilled over an open fire, as well as regional dishes. A noontime menu offers fixed-price meals beginning at 12F ($5.51), while evening dinners cost from 42F ($19.30).

EVOLÈNE: From Sion, another road heads south through the beautiful Val d'Hérens, a historic district, leading to Evolène at 4525 feet. The village contains dark-brown larch-wood-fronted houses which, in summer, blossom with brightly colored flowers in the windowsills. Women still wear their national costume at work (and not just on holidays or to awe the tourists).

As you drive through the valley you'll see a crown of mountain peaks: the Dent Blanche, Pigne, Mont-Collon, Veisivi, and several others. Other villages have melodious names like Les Haudères, La Sage, Villa, La Forclaz, and Ferpècle. Higher up, at 6670 feet, you reach Arolla, only a stone's throw from the glaciers.

Winter sports were introduced a few years ago. At Arolla there are ski tows, and cross-country skiers like it a lot. The region is also rich in alpine flora and fauna.

Food and Lodging

Hôtel Hermitage (tel. 83-12-32) is a family-run, white-walled house with balconies set in a park area filled with pines. The inside is rustically paneled with light-grained wood. The floors are usually flagstone or newly laid parquet, while the bedrooms are freshly painted and cheerful. The Chevrier and the Gaspoz families, the owners, know everybody in town. They charge between 25F ($11.48) and 47F ($21.59) in a single and between 43F ($19.76) and 85F ($39.06) in a double, including breakfast. Half board is an additional 18F ($8.27) per person.

7. Crans-Montana

Crans and Montana-Vermala, at 4985 feet, are twin resorts accessible by good roads from Sion or the market town of Sierre (also by funicular from Sierre). They are modern and fashionable ski areas, often drawing such celebrities as Gina Lollobrigida, and they lie on a handsome plateau with air that's been called "lighter than champagne." Skiers can not only ski, but enjoy views of the valley of the Rhône. Connected to the Crans-Montana area is Aminona, at 4920 feet, still an infant resort, but rising rapidly.

Crans is made up for the most part of colonies of apartments and hotels, often in the half-timbered mountain style. Montana, the older part, is built around a lake.

One of the most spectacular ascents is to Point Plaine Morte at nearly 10,000 feet, which, even at so great a height, still has runs suitable even for the neophyte. To reach it, take the gondola at Montana-Barzettes, to the east of Montana, stopping at Les Violettes first. There's a restaurant at Plaine Morte.

Holiday-makers also like to head for the Cry d'Err at 7430 feet for its big dining room (the terrace is popular for sunbathing). A gondola—again from Montana—goes to Cry d'Err, and there's another gondola departing from Crans as well.

The Piste Nationale is known for its steep, narrow runs which attract the most experienced of skiers, although Les Violettes is for fine intermediate skiing. Mount Tubang, with its more challenging runs, is another slope only for the more skilled skier.

Another section of this cluster of resorts, Crans sur Sierre, is built to the west of Crans around a group of tiny lakes.

WHERE TO STAY: There are accommodations in all of these tiny resorts, but the following are my recommendations:

Hotels at Crans

Hôtel du Golf (tel. 41-42-42) is an attractively designed establishment with lots of windows and a flat roof which sprawls across a green area near a lake. There is, as you'd expect, a golf course and an elegant series of salons and bars, many of them with fireplaces. The decor is warmly upholstered, with deep-seated reproductions of antique chairs clustered into attractive groupings. The bedrooms are colorful and sunny, containing a balcony, mini-bar, radio, phone, and TV, and costing between 70F ($32.16) and 180F ($82.71) in a single, between 95F ($43.65) and 380F ($174.61) in a double. Half board is available for an additional 35F ($16.08).

Hôtel Beau-Séjour (tel. 41-24-46). This six-story hotel is one of the best at the resort, with an un-selfconscious decor that would have been familiar to Ike and Mamie. You might have a drink at the bar, with its modified art deco touch, or in front of the abstractly shaped fireplace in the 1920s-style barrel chairs covered in a textured maroon velvet. The gardens around the hotel are dotted with sun chairs and tables, where sometimes the resident orchestra plays before dinner. Recently the hotel completed an indoor swimming pool, large enough to go a lap in. A bar area is visible through a glass window on the other side. The Lorétan family are your congenial hosts, charging from 55F ($25.27) to 115F ($52.84) per person in a single or double room with or without private bath, according to the season. Breakfast is included, and a very good half board is offered for another 30F ($13.78) per person daily.

Hôtel de l'Étrier (tel. 41-15-15) is composed of two steeply roofed modern buildings, with prominent balconies and big windows. They're connected to one another and set at slightly different angles for an unusual effect that is particularly dramatic at night when the light filters through the different colored curtains, giving the windows almost the impression of stained glass. The swimming pool is well heated and partially covered for year-round bathing, and has a fully staffed bar operating out of one corner. The rest of the hotel is comfortable, ultramodern, and very attractive, with pleasing abstract murals color coordinated to the plants and shaggy area rugs. A 7½-acre park in front of the hotel is dotted with lawn chairs in summer. Singles range from 100F ($45.95) to 140F ($64.33), while doubles go from 90F ($41.35) to 140F ($64.33) per person, with half board included. Peter and Roland Gaulé are the owners.

Hôtel des Mélèzes (tel. 43-18-12) is an especially inviting hotel with a colorful and pleasing decor that makes you feel warm just by walking inside. The double rooms are spacious, with woven textiles serving as bedspreads. The dining room has been angled for a view which makes it hard to concentrate on your food, while a two-tiered bar area is outfitted with full-grained amber-colored paneling. The hotel is affiliated with tour agencies in France, Belgium, and Great Britain, which ensures an international clientele. Henri Lamon is the conscientious and professional director, charging between 60F ($27.57) and 90F ($41.35) per person daily, depending on the season, with half board included.

Hôtel Pensione Centrale (tel. 41-37-67) is a comfortable family-run pension in the center of town. The exterior is a solid-looking wood-and-stucco chalet with shutters and a restaurant on the ground floor. The renovated rooms have phone and radio, offering fairly personalized service. The Hürlimann and Funkenberg families maintain this 36-bed establishment, charging between 25F ($11.48) and 60F ($27.57) in a single and between 41F ($18.83) and 100F ($45.95) for a double, breakfast included. Half board costs an additional 15F ($6.89) per person daily.

Hotels at Montana-Vermala

Hôtel Curling (tel. 41-12-42). You'll have a pleasant time here even if you don't like to curl. But if you do, there's ample opportunity on the ice-skating rink near the hotel. The interior is warmly and rustically decorated with leather chairs, paneling, and flagstone floors, plus centrally placed hearths which funnel their smoke up through metallic stovepipes. The hotel is closed during May and November, but is open otherwise, charging between 75F ($34.46) and 115F ($52.84) per person daily, with half board included. Nicholas Barras is the congenial owner.

Hôtel de la Forêt (tel. 41-36-08) lies only 300 yards from the cable car of Les Viollettes–Plaine Morte. The Morard family does everything it can to set a lighthearted ambience, which is most successful during its weekly raclette parties. The view through the huge windows of the swimming pool is spectacular, and guests have a choice of three terraces for summer or midwinter sunbathing. A very large dining room serves well-prepared meals, while the pianist in a rustic piano bar often encourages people to dance. The establishment is laid out in three buildings—the main hotel, an annex, and the pool with apartments nearby. Hotel rates range between 44F ($20.22) and 98F ($45.03) in a single and between 71F ($32.62) and 162F ($74.44) in a double, with breakfast included. Half board is available for an additional 25F ($11.49).

Hôtel Mirabeau (tel. 41-39-12) is a streamlined chalet, rather large, without the ornamentation of older buildings, yet still constructed with the best materials and an ample use of stone and natural wood. The hotel houses several shops, including a bank on the ground floor, yet opens into a very cozy ambience of Christmas colors and lots of warmly rustic furniture. Each of the conservatively decorated accommodations has its own bath, as well as a balcony, phone, radio, and TV. Singles rent for between 56F ($25.73) and 139F ($63.87), while doubles cost from 92F ($42.27) to 233F ($107.06), with half board offered for another 28F ($12.86) per person daily.

Hôtel St-George (tel. 41-24-14). On a sunny summer's day, with the rock garden and swimming pool in front and the blinding white balconies stretching overhead, you'd imagine you were in the Caribbean. This illusion is quickly dispelled as soon as you see the mountains in the distance, but, all in all, this is a very pleasant hotel. The interior has enough intimate corners, conversational groupings, and coziness to make any recluse happy, along with well-decorated bedrooms with conservatively traditional furniture and good views of the mountains. Roland Grunder-Fischer is the capable owner, charging between 35F ($16.08) and 102F ($46.86) in a single and between 58F ($26.65) and 174F ($79.95) in a double, depending on the season and the plumbing. Half board is an additional 25F ($11.49) per person.

Hôtel Cisalpin (tel. 41-24-25) is a multiroofed hotel with white walls and dark wood trim at the top of a steep hill which an enterprising athlete might use as a private ski slope. It has its own mountaineering and ski school, and is close to the cable car leading to Les Violettes–Plaine Morte. The interior is filled with the kind of nooks and crannies where you can curl up with a drink (or a friend), and is almost universally paneled with light-grained pine. One of the dining rooms has an attractive format of local flagstones built into two sides of the room, with a fireplace burning against one corner. J. P. Clivaz, the owner, charges between 25F ($11.48) and 45F ($20.67) in a single and between 42F ($19.29) and 75F ($34.46) for a double, with breakfast included. Half board is available for another 15F ($6.89) per person daily.

Hotels at Crans sur Sierre

Hôtel Alpina and **Savoy** (tel. 41-21-42) is a very large hotel with rows of weather-proofed windows facing south plus an attractively updated ambience. It has a covered swimming pool where the walls and roof are fashioned of rustic wood and glass, along with a sauna, exercise room, several bar areas (one of which has a teepee-like ceiling of rough-cut branches), and a series of well-decorated and spacious bedrooms. The brick terrace looks out over vineyards with alpine ridges looming up in the distance. The bar area is ideally suited for conversations with a friend or two. The Mudry family maintain this establishment. They charge between 65F ($29.86) and 160F ($73.52) in a single and between 110F ($50.54) and 260F ($119.47) in a double, including breakfast. Prices depend on the season. Half board is another 30F ($13.78) per person daily.

RESTAURANTS IN THE AREA: **Rôtisserie de la Channe Valaisanne,** rue Centrale (tel. 41-12-58), in Crans sur Sierre, is the place to go for what is probably the best meats in the region. The bar area is so pleasantly gemütlich that many guests ask to wait a while before going to their table. Max Bagnoud and his wife Margot set the unpretentious tone of this friendly place, where conversation seems to be enhanced by the fact that many of the savory dishes are destined for two persons. You might begin your meal with a homemade pâté in puff pastry, or a plate of air-dried alpine beef, perhaps a shrimp bisque. For a follow-up, try the côte de Charolais or chateaubriand, or two kinds of fondue, even a spit-roasted lamb or chicken. Fish might appeal to you when you learn it's giant shrimp or blue trout. You'll also be interested in the wine list, which understandably places the local Fendant as the first category. The restaurant is open seven days a week from 7:30 a.m. to midnight, but closes yearly from mid-May to mid-June and for the month of November. Fixed-price meals range from 19F ($8.73) to 34F ($15.62), while à la carte dinners cost from 50F ($22.98) per person.

Restaurant Jeanne d'Arc (tel. 41-82-42). Diners have to drive to the south shore of nearby Lake Grenon to reach this citadel of fine cuisine. Once they arrive, they never seem to mind the short distance. All culinary trends are represented in the assorted list of specialties which are invariably served with tremendous flair. They include ragoût of lobster with fresh leafy vegetables and truffled butter, seawolf (meerwolf) in crab sauce, ragoût of fresh quail with goose liver toasts, a warm three-fish terrine, and a fondant of Bresse hen fourré with a superb sauce suprême. The restaurant is closed from mid-November to mid-December, but open daily otherwise from noon to 3:30 p.m. and 6:30 p.m. to midnight. Noontime fixed-price meals cost from 45F ($20.68), and evening table d'hôte gourmet dinners go as high as 110F ($50.54). À la carte dinners range from 130F ($49.54) to 140F ($64.33).

Rôtisserie de la Reine (tel. 41-18-85) is the result of the happy combination of Max Leonard and his wife, S. Marlot. They open at 8:30 a.m. and remain so until very late every day of the year, except during most of May and November. The restaurant specializes in sole meunière, sauerkraut with pork products, grilled lobster, tournedos bordelaise, and if you phone ahead, couscous. A noontime fixed-price meal is a reasonable 14F ($6.43), while more expensive evening meals cost between 19F ($8.73) and a gourmet special for around 86F ($39.51), which comes with half a bottle of champagne. In the evening, an à la carte meal will cost around 55F ($25.27).

APRÈS SKI: Most of the hotels have bars which are lively at night. Often skiers and nonskiers spend their entire evening in one of the local restaurants, enjoying pizza, fondue, or raclette, along with beer or wine. One of the most pleasant bars, drawing an attractive crowd, is the one in the **Hôtel Mirabeau,** already recommended. Valasian specialties are served here.

In Montana, the **Hotel Central** (tel. 41-36-66), run by Mr. Pedersoli-Premoselli, has the active Le Mazot, which often presents floor shows with live groups who play for dancing.

At the **Hôtel de la Forêt,** raclette evenings are offered, along with music and a pleasant bar where a pianist entertains.

The **Crans-Ambassador,** at Montana (tel. 41-52-22), draws a generally chic crowd to its Binocle, with handsome decoration and good music. It also has a rôtisserie and a grand buffet.

Many of these other clubs come and go with frightening irregularity. At the risk of quickly being out of date, I'll also suggest the following: the **Pasha**

Club for disco dancing; the **Gipsy,** underneath the Rôtisserie de la Reine, which draws a wild young crowd on many a cold night; the **Number One** disco (with few challengers); and the **Hotel Miedzor** (tel. 41-44-33), which has a good bar and restaurant with a cozy ambience if that's your idea of après-ski fun.

8. Leukerbad

At 4630 feet, this centuries-old spa is connected with Sierre and Leuk-Susten by road. Its water cure has drawn spa devotees from all over Europe, and it now complements taking the waters by offering good skiing on the slopes of the Torrent area and on the Gemmi Pass, accessible by cable cars.

It had a great heyday of fashion in the 19th century, and has spent millions of dollars trying to anticipate and adjust to the needs of modern tourists.

Called in French, Loèche-les-Bains, Leukerbad enjoys a particularly romantic site, surrounded by alpine meadows on the northern part of the upper Rhône Valley, lying on the route to the Gemmi Pass.

It has a total of ten indoor and seven outdoor thermal baths, and a host of sports activities.

FOOD AND LODGING: **Hotel Bristol** (tel. 61-18-33) is modern, divided into two almost identical balconied buildings which share a common swimming pool. They're connected by a heated underground tunnel, which makes sharing the solarium and hairdressing facilities easier. Clients who stay in Bristol I usually select full board, while guests in Bristol II have kitchenettes and usually take one of the half-board plans. The entire complex is offset by a background of rocky alpine cliffs, although the management creates its own small world with the agreeable buffet picnics they sometimes hold on the lawns in front. Bedrooms are elegantly modern, with elaborately grained trim from exotic wood. The pine-paneled public rooms are, at their best, gemütlich. The Erwin Lorétan family, the owners and conscientious hosts, charge from 80F ($36.76) to 160F ($73.52) in a single and from 137F ($62.95) to 258F ($118.55) in a double, with half board included. Full board is available for an additional 12F ($5.51) per person daily.

Hôtel des Alpes (tel. 61-26-51) is one of the few hotels in the region not designed to look like a chalet. A very large structure, it has a triangular pediment on the roofline between two symmetrical wings, both of which are painted white. It's part of the medical center of the village, which offers a wide range of message and therapy sessions under a rigidly supervised format of diet and exercise. In addition to the tennis courts and indoor pool, the hotel has a comfortable array of well-furnished public rooms, some of which are filled with 19th-century antiques. A bar area is paneled with well-oiled hardwoods, offering a restful place for an intimate drink. Singles, depending on the plumbing and the season, rent for between 80F ($36.76) and 150F ($68.93), while doubles with or without bath cost from 140F ($64.33) to 260F ($119.47), with half board included.

Hôtel Maison Blanc-Grand Bain (tel. 61-11-12) are two hotels under the same roof, with different managements but the same allegiance to the village medical center. You'll recognize it immediately because of the arched arcade on the ground floor supported by gracefully modified Corinthian columns. The interior is filled with comfortable chairs, a scattering of Oriental rugs, and an old-world service which caters to persons taking the cure at the medical facility connected to the hotel. Prices for the two establishments are the same—from

72F ($33.08) to 120F ($55.14) in a single and from 155F ($71.22) to 210F ($96.49) in a double, including half board. Prices, of course, vary according to the season and the plumbing.

Hotel Zayetta (tel. 61-16-46) is a modern hotel with four tiers of balconies angled toward the sun for maximum illumination of the attractive bedrooms. A heated swimming pool and a sauna are under the same roof, along with a host of therapy and massage facilities which include even the more exotic mudpacking techniques. The dining areas and the bar are intimately lit in a way that makes virtually anybody look good, and the salons are finished in a kind of understated elegance that usually centers on a blazing fire. All the accommodations contain private bath, costing between 78F ($35.84) and 103F ($47.32) in a single and between 128F ($58.82) and 164F ($75.35) in a double, with half board included.

Hotel Dala (tel. 61-12-13) is an angular modern building with a restaurant on the ground floor and four tiers of balconied bedrooms on top. Each of the colorful units has its own bath. On the premises is a marble-floored dancing bar, plus a warmly decorated dining room with stone detailing and a large staff. The Lorétan-Grichting family, your hosts, charge 90F ($41.35) and 120F ($55.14) for a double room, with an English breakfast included. Triples range between 140F ($64.33) and 170F ($78.11) daily.

9. Grimentz

At 5150 feet, Grimentz has much traditional allure, and is known for its alpine hospitality. Many visitors drive here just to look at its old chalets mellowed by the sun. The town has known many hard times, but has survived them nobly, and today maintains many of its old customs and traditions.

It's the starting point for several well-known walks—the lake and hut at Moity, Pas de Lona, and Cold de Torrent, with its rich alpine flora and fauna—and offers mechanical ski lifts up to the Becs de Bosson. It also has a heated closed swimming pool, two tennis courts, and an outdoor skating rink, and many cross-country trails.

FOOD AND LODGING: **Hôtel La Cordée** (tel. 65-12-46) is a well-organized hotel with many elegant touches and a thick-beamed construction which reminds you you're in the Alps. The bedrooms are outfitted with comfortable beds that neatly tuck into armoires every morning for a maximum of living space during the day. Each of the accommodations has a private balcony and bath, plus an individualized decor in warm colors, often soft reds and pinks. Francis and Andrée Fauvet prepare the food personally, which is served in the well-appointed dining room. Singles range between 47F ($21.59) and 100F ($45.95), while doubles cost from 70F ($32.17) to 125F ($57.43), including breakfast. Half board goes for an additional 19F ($8.73).

Hotel Marenda (tel. 65-11-71) is a white stucco house with blue-gray shutters and a modified mansard roof. It has a pleasant garden, a wood-trimmed extension, and cozy sitting rooms with pine paneling and prominent fireplaces. A flagstone and gravel terrace offers drink service in a spacious area surrounded by trees. Singles range from 29F ($13.32) to 58F ($26.65), while doubles cost from 47F ($21.59) to 98F ($45.03) per person daily, with half board going for another 15F ($6.89) per person.

Hôtel Moiry (tel. 65-11-44). The owner of this attractively simple establishment works as a local ski instructor and mountain guide. His name is Vital Salamin, and he manages his pleasantly pine-paneled establishment with a friendly attitude. A nearby annex provides additional bedrooms under a low-lying roof covered with thick cedar shingles, surrounded by a summertime garden. Singles range between 25F ($11.48) and 43F ($19.75), while doubles cost from 37F ($17) to 68F ($31.25), depending on the plumbing and the season. Half board is offered for another 12F ($5.51) per person daily.

10. Zermatt and the Matterhorn

Zermatt (5315 feet above sea level), a small village in the shadow of the great Matterhorn mountain (14,690 feet), made its debut as a ski resort more than 100 years ago when it was "discovered" by the British, the first major tourists of Switzerland. The spotlight of world interest was turned on the **Matterhorn** when Edward Whymper, British explorer and mountaineer, began a series of determined efforts to climb it. He made the attempt half a dozen times between 1861 and 1865, trying it from the Italian side of the Pennine Alps. By a freak accident Whymper saw the Swiss side of the great mountain, which appeared to him less formidable than he had heard it described. On July 14, 1865, he became the first man to climb the Matterhorn, reaching the summit from the Swiss side, although in the process four of the climbers of his team fell to their deaths. Whymper and two guides made it to safety and into history. Three days later an Italian guide, Jean-Antoine Carrel, successfully made the climb from the Italian side.

The Matterhorn, called Mount Cervin by the French-speaking Swiss, still lures mountain climbers, with the two most outstanding "hikes" being the climb up to the **Mettelhorn** (11,000 feet) and the hike up to the **Matterhorn Hut,** lying at the base of the peak.

Since Whymper's time, Zermatt has become a world-renowned international resort, with all the deluxe and first-class amenities you'd expect. However, in many of its little satellite hamlets you'll still find much of the original charm that put Zermatt on the tourist map long ago. From Zermatt you can look onto some of the highest peaks in Switzerland.

You can walk from one end of Zermatt to the other in about 15 minutes. Along the way from the railroad station to the parish church you'll see little except shops, hotels, and masses of tourists. Only horse-drawn carriage taxis and small battery-run vehicles are permitted in the town, but still, with carts, carriages, and milling throngs of people, there are such things as traffic jams in "traffic-free" Zermatt in peak season.

The Seiler family launched the resort concept in the mid-19th century, and the Seiler chain still owns many fine Zermatt hotels. The style the family originated is used for a number of establishments today. You'll see many Valais-style chalets as well as some *mazots,* or little barns, which are characteristic of the region.

More snow falls here than at most other winter resorts on the continent, and Zermatt boasts the best spring skiing in the Alps. There is a high season both in the peak summer months and in winter when skiers pour in, but actually the resort is fairly busy all year. Skiing lasts until late spring since the inception of the high-altitude ski tours *(Haute Route),* and it goes right through the summer at Théodul Pass.

To reach Zermatt, you can drive to **Täsch,** three miles away, and park your car there in an open lot. A rail shuttle takes you to the resort for 8.80F ($4.04) per person for a round trip. Always arrive at Zermatt with a hotel reservation, and if you let the staff know your arrival time, you'll probably be met by one of the hotel's battery-powered pickup carts which will transport you and your luggage. If you're traveling by train, take one to Visp or Brig where you can board a narrow-guage train for the ride to Zermatt. Geneva is about 3½ to 4 hours from the resort.

Zermatt has a total of 30 mountain railroads, lifts, and gondolas. There are dozens of excursion possibilities, the one with the highest popularity rating being a visit by rack railway to **Gornergrat** (10,170 feet). This is the highest open-air railroad in Europe. At **Riffelberg** you'll have a spectacular view of the Matterhorn. If you elect to go only this far, a round-trip ticket will cost you 28F ($12.87). For the entire journey to Gornergrat you'll pay 40F ($18.38) for a round-trip ticket. Once at Gornergrat, you can take a two-stage cableway to Stockhorn (11,180 feet), for another 14F ($6.43) round trip. There's an observatory at Gornergrat which looks out onto the Gorner glacier. The view takes in the **Dom,** part of the Mischabel massif, which at 14,912 feet is the highest mountain entirely within Switzerland.

A second popular visit is to the **Schwarzsee** (8480 feet), the "black lake." Magnificent vistas can be seen from the Schwarzseehotel. This much-photographed lake lies at the foot of the Matterhorn. Allow an hour to reach it. The round-trip fare on the cable car is 20F ($9.19). **Klein Matterhorn** (12,533 feet) is reached by the highest aerial cableway in Europe, with departures from 7:30 a.m. daily in front of the Schwarzsee cable-car station. A round-trip ticket to Klein Matterhorn costs 40F ($18.38). If you go via Schwarzsee, it costs 53F ($24.35) per round trip.

Helicopter rides around the Matterhorn are possible, but I advise you to go only on a clear day. You'll be flown to the top, with the copter hovering long enough for the passengers to snap pictures madly. The whirlybird then takes you around the Matterhorn pyramid before making its descent. This is a pretty frightening trip for some visitors, but it's relatively safe, and it's certainly thrilling. The cost is about $50 (U.S.) and well worth it. The rides are operated by **Air Zermatt** from the heliport (tel. 67-34-87) outside the village. The same airline is on 24-hour duty to rescue injured persons.

Zermatt has varied skiing, from wide, gentle slopes to difficult runs. At the official **ski school** (tel. 67-24-51), instruction is provided in the various classes by certified ski instructors and mountain guides. The three principal ski areas are the already-mentioned **Gornergrat–Stockhorn** site; the **Blauherd–Unter Rothorn** area, reached by underground mountain rail from the village to Sunegga and then by gondola; and the **Schwarzsee–Théodul** sector, reached on its first stage by cableways to Furi. You can even ski across Théodul Pass to Cervinia in Italy for lunch. For the cross-country skier and the touring skier, a variety of courses is offered. There's a cross-country pavilion in Furi-Schweigmatten.

Zermatt is also a popular curling center, with eight rinks all equipped with precision curling stones. There are also two natural ice-skating rinks as well as sunny, signposted paths for walking.

In such a setting, with mountains to climb and snowy peaks to view, you may not dwell on museums, but there is one, the **Alpine Museum,** charging 3F ($1.38). It's open from July 1 to the beginning of October from 10 a.m. to noon and 4 to 6 p.m.: from December to the end of June, from 4:30 to 6:30 p.m. Displayed are relics of Edward Whymper, detailing the conquest of the Matterhorn; relief models of the great mountain; and artifacts from the prehistoric and Roman eras.

PRACTICAL FACTS: To make your visit to Zermatt a happy experience, **Tourist Office Zermatt,** Am Bahnhofplatz (tel. 67-01-31), will supply information and advice.

If you need a **babysitter,** try Kinderheim Theresia (tel. 67-20-96) or Seiler's Kindergarten (tel. 66-11-21).

To get in touch with the local protectors of law and order, call: **community police** (tel. 67-38-22) or the **district police** (tel. 67-21-97).

Swissair Rescue Service is available on a 24-hour emergency basis (tel. 47-47-47).

Looking for a **drugstore?** Pharmacie International Zermatt is your answer (tel. 67-34-84).

The new **telegraph and telephone** building is situated between the post office and the Alpine Museum. Inside are 18 phone booths, one of which contains a Telex for public use and one fitted for use of handicapped persons (tel. 67-41-94). The building is open December 1 to April 15 and June 15 to September from 8 a.m. to 9 p.m. Monday through Saturday, from 9 a.m. to noon and 5 to 9 p.m. on Sunday and public holidays. In the off-season it's open from 8 a.m. to noon and 1:45 to 7 p.m. Monday through Friday, to 5 p.m. on Saturday. It's closed on Sunday and holidays in low season.

Post office hours are from 7:30 a.m. to noon and 1:45 to 6:30 p.m. Monday through Friday, from 7:30 to 11 a.m. on Saturday.

Religious services in Zermatt are held in the Roman Catholic church and at the English St. Peter Church. For information on times of worship, phone Tourist Office Zermatt, listed above.

WHERE TO STAY: The innkeepers of Zermatt have seen tourists by the thousands come and go. Many a manager started life as a 12-year-old bellboy carrying the luggage of foreign tourists. They have grown a little world weary perhaps, after so many years of service, but nevertheless, following an autumnal lull in their business, they polish their smiles and get ready to welcome an ever-increasing influx of new visitors each year.

Zermatt has something for most purses. Its hotels come in all sizes and shapes, both large and small. In all, the resort has about 100 hotels and guest houses—your first impression might be that every chalet-style building in town is a hotel. These hotel beds are backed up by a wide range of holiday apartments and private rooms.

The Upper Bracket

Seiler Mount Cervin und Seilerhaus (tel. 66-11-21) has been considered one of Zermatt's leading hotels since it was established more than 125 years ago. The interior includes many of the sunny, spacious, and well-appointed rooms you'd expect from a first-class hotel, with all of the fine craftsmanship and service that the Seiler chain is known for. The well-dressed guests dine, drink, and dance in the top-notch bar and disco, among the best known in Zermatt. In the center of town, it has one of the most luxurious pools in Zermatt, along with the usual sauna and massage facilities. In winter, a kindergarten cares for children under the supervision of a nursery school teacher. The Seilerhaus is the attractive restaurant and guest house across from the main hotel with comfortable rooms and a first-class cuisine.

The 129 units rent for between 73F ($33.54) and 185F ($85) per person, with half board included. For 8F ($3.67) additional, someone will pick you and your bags up at the hotel, in winter in a horse-drawn sleigh, in summer in an old-fashioned, horse-drawn carriage.

Grand Hotel Zermatterhof (tel. 66-11-01) seems to be one of the few hotels in town not designed to look like a chalet. Its symmetrical white facade looks vaguely Régence-style. The interior is attractive in an understated kind of well-upholstered way, with bronze-colored detailing in the intimate bar area, cane-backed French provincial chairs in the dining room, a carpeted exercise unit, and a beautifully illuminated swimming pool. The floors usually have at least one handmade rug, while the bedrooms are accented with wood paneling and vivid colors. *Per-person* prices, with half board included, range from 75F ($34.46) to 185F ($85), depending on the season and the accommodation.

Hotel Alex (tel. 67-17-26). For the many observers of chicdom in Zermatt this hotel is rising quickly as one of the poshest and most congenial places in town, with a nightlife that everyone should sample at least once. The hotel is filled with lots of rarely seen architectural details, such as a free-form swimming pool beneath a half-timbered ceiling with a round lunette window on top. The flagstoned public rooms are outfitted with elegant paneling and amusingly grotesque statues of demigods, one of whom stirs a cauldron with his trident (he happens to be standing on top of an open fireplace).

Everywhere you look you'll see original and creative statements in natural materials, beautifully crafted in an amusingly innovative way. These features have not been lost upon the Zermatt community, who flock to the dancing bar virtually every evening. In this exclusively fashionable place, the bar stools are carved into replicas of ibex torsos, with cowhide covering the padded seats.

The bedrooms usually have good views of the mountains, are beautifully appointed, and have private baths in each of them. Singles cost between 91F ($41.81) and 165F ($75.81), while doubles range from 80F ($36.76) to 180F ($82.71) per person per day, with half board included. In the hotel you'll find fitness rooms, squash courts, summertime tennis courts, community saunas, and a private sauna.

Hotel Monte Rosa (tel. 67-19-22) is the hotel which Edward Whymper, the English alpinist who first conquered the Matterhorn, recommended in the 1860s as the best hotel in Zermatt. Still renowned, the hotel is a tall, old-fashioned structure on the main street of Zermatt, with stone posts and lintels around the red-shuttered windows. The lounges inside are extraordinarily cozy, thanks to their parquet floors, thick rugs, and crackling fireplaces. The antique armchairs are beautifully upholstered in conservative stripes or more daring patterns of red and blue. The pleasant bedrooms are among the most comfortable in Zermatt, with occasional floral designs covering the walls and immaculately pressed bedcovers. Since the hotel is part of the Seiler chain, guests have free use of the swimming pool a short distance away at the Mount Cervin Hotel. Single or double units rent for between 80F ($36.76) and 160F ($73.52) per person, with half board included. Prices, of course, depend on the season, with midwinter being by far the most expensive.

Hostellerie Tenne (tel. 67-18-01) is a large, well-crafted chalet a few steps from the center of town. The architectural detailing, both inside and out, is quite beautiful, with no expense spared on the combinations of stone, thick timbers, and stucco that make a really remarkable building. Various regional antiques, illuminated by the leaded bull's-eye glass, make for a most pleasant hotel. A modern wing juts off to one side. More recent than the original building, it combines attractive loggias with chalet-style balustrades and a steep roof. The rooms inside are both cheerful and tasteful, and are reached through a modern sitting room with painted alpine scenes positioned between the beams of the ceiling. The Stöpfer family, your hosts, charge between 57F ($26.19) and

115F ($52.84) per person per day, with breakfast included. A good restaurant is on the premises (see the dining recommendations).

Hotel Schweizerhof (tel. 66-11-55) is the newest first-class hotel in town, having opened in December 1982. It's part of a nationwide Seiler chain of tastefully appointed hotels, with a conscientious management which does everything it can to make a stay here particularly pleasant. Centrally located on the main street of town, the chalet-style building has shops on its ground floor and a spacious lobby area covered with orange carpeting, designed around comfortable modern armchairs and a blazing central fireplace. Most of the sunny bedrooms are monochromatically outfitted with carved blond-wood furniture and the grays and buffs that go best with it, although some of them are done in fresh mountain springtime colors. Elegant dining facilities, a popular bar, and a funky disco complete the hotel's allure.

Each of the 104 accommodations has its own bath and costs between 95F ($43.65) and 185F ($85) per person in a single or a double, depending on the season, with half board included. The hotel is closed every year for roughly the first three weeks of May and from October 15 till December.

Hôtel Mirabeau (tel. 67-17-72) is a dramatically modern piece of architecture shaped vaguely like a chalet, with a black-and-white striped exterior and lots of balconies jutting out on all sides. The interior is simple and comfortable, with white walls, less wood paneling than older hotels, and lots of textiles. The hotel is somewhat separated from the other buildings of Zermatt, with good views of the Matterhorn. Owned by the Julen family, the rooms rent for between 65F ($29.86) and 125F ($57.43) per person in winter and between 58F ($26.65) and 95F ($43.65) per person in summer, with breakfast included. Half board is offered for an additional 12F ($5.51) per person. All units have private baths, and many contain a kitchenette.

Hotel Pollux (tel. 67-19-46) lies in a brown-and-white balconied structure on the main street of Zermatt, with several discreet signs announcing the disco and the pleasant restaurant. The interior has beautiful ceilings, lots of exposed stone, and comfortable leather chairs and sofas which will probably tempt you to have a drink in front of one of the cheerful fireplaces. The bedrooms are sunny, well upholstered, well padded, and well carpeted, with private baths and your choice of views over the busy street or toward the back of the hotel (the ones behind are slightly more expensive). Singles range from 60F ($27.57) to 90F ($41.35), while doubles cost between 52F ($23.89) and 75F ($34.46) per person, with breakfast included. Half board is offered for an additional 25F ($11.48). Children who stay in a room connected to their parents' quarters receive a 60% reduction. The restaurant is a very good choice for an evening meal (see the dining recommendations).

Hotel Walliserhof (tel. 67-11-74) lies in the center of town in a building that looks like an old Valaisian house. It has red shutters, balconies, and window boxes. A streetside café serves drinks and food. The interior has attractive groupings of stone fireplaces, masonry columns, thick walls, and flagstone floors. The carpeted bedrooms are filled with every modern comfort and pleasantly furnished with many wooden pieces. *Per-person* rates range from 65F ($29.87) to 130F ($59.74), which includes half board and lodging in either single or double rooms.

Hotels Rex and **Eden** (tel. 67-10-05 and 67-26-55) were built by two brothers (the Aufdenblattens) in 1960 in a long, balconied building with a flat roof and an equal division down the center. The hotels have separate entrances, individual collections of lawn chairs on the grassy expanse in front, and a shared swimming pool. Most of the sunny rooms face the Matterhorn. The hotels charge the same rates *per person* for single or double rooms: between

45F ($20.68) and 80F ($36.76) with private bath, including breakfast. Neither of the hotels offers a board plan. After a quick evaluation, the Eden looks slightly more luxurious and the staff is a little more friendly, although basically there is very little difference between the two. The Rex offers apartments in a separate building nearby.

Hotel Club (tel. 67-30-67) is a chalet-style building with comfortable bedrooms usually decorated in shades of brown, beige, and forest green, comfortable public rooms with new tile floors, and wood beamed ceilings. Two outdoor tennis courts and a sunny lawn are just in front of the hotel, along with a sauna and a swimming pool. Rates are between 45F ($20.67) and 85F ($39.05) per person, including breakfast.

If this is full, another hotel under the same management, called the **Tennisstar** (tel. 67-13-64), lies just behind the Club and charges from 65F ($27.27) to 125F ($57.44) per person, breakfast included. Open only in winter, this hotel looks much like its neighbor. It has several indoor tennis courts attached.

Hotel Nicoletta (tel. 66-11-51). When you enter the lobby of this modern hotel, you'll be greeted by a fireplace set beneath an exposed chimney made of burnished copper plates riveted together. The interior is carpeted, wood-trimmed, spacious, quite comfortable, and filled with deliberately contrasting designs in all the fabrics.

You'll recognize the facade of the hotel by the 18 panels set between the windows which are cleverly designed in subtle op-art patterns of two shades of brown. Near the edge of town but still within a short walk of everything, the hotel should prove pleasant in every way, especially with the panoramic swimming pool on the fourth floor, plus two nearby saunas. A pharmacy, newsstand, jewelry shop, and boutique are in the same building. The Nicoletta charges between 60F ($27.57) and 160F ($73.52) per person, with half board included. Prices depend on the season.

The Medium-Priced Range

Hotel Butterfly (tel. 67-37-21) is a modern hotel with a peaked roof and an airy facade, thanks to its large expanses of glass. The balconies have garlands of flowers in boxes during the summer. In winter the snowy expanse of the Alps serves as a backdrop. The inside is warmly rustic, with arched windows, Oriental rugs, knotty-pine furniture, and lots of exposed wood and stone. A well-stocked bar serves as an intimate rendezvous point for hotel guests and their friends. Single rooms in summer range between 73F ($33.54) and 87F ($39.98); doubles, between 67F ($30.79) and 80F ($36.76) per person. Wintertime rates go from 72F ($33.09) to 107F ($49.16) in a single, from 75F ($34.46) to 100F ($45.95) per person in a double. These prices include half board. On the premises you'll find a sauna, whirlpool, solarium, and fitness center. A. Scherer is the owner and manager.

Hotel Romantica (tel. 67-15-05). If you should look onto the roof from one of the windows of the fourth floor, you'd notice that it's made of flagstones over a superstructure built in 1962. That and other well-planned details make this a fortunate choice of hotels, particularly since the rooms, although small, are clean and efficient, and the establishment is thoughtfully staffed with capable French and Swiss employees. In summer one of the loveliest gardens in Zermatt blooms on either side of the flagstone path leading up to the hotel. You'll have somewhat of a walk up the main street of town before arriving here, although Mr. Cremonini, the third-generation owner and a local ski instructor, will come to fetch you and your bags in an electric cart if you call ahead. (You might even do this from the departure point of the cog railway leading up to

Zermatt.) Rooms rent for between 32F ($14.70) and 58F ($26.65) without private bath, for between 40F ($18.38) and 76F ($347.92) with private bath. These prices are on a *per-person* basis, and include breakfast. The hotel, by the way, has converted two small log cabins, formerly used for grain storage, into guest cottages a few paces from the front door of the main building. These might be perfect for wintertime clients with a taste for the rustic.

Hotel Darioli (tel. 7-77-48) is housed in a balconied five-story building on the main street of Zermatt not far from the train station. You'll need to climb a flight of stairs (or take the elevator) to get to the sunny reception area, where you'll probably get a friendly greeting from a member of the Darioli family. The interior is large and sunny, with a blue-and-white ceramic stove, Oriental rugs, and an attractive wood-grained bar curving around one of the corners. An antique baby's crib holds magazines in three languages. Each of the comfortable bedrooms is furnished with regional furniture, usually painted in vivid colors with floral patterns stenciled at the corners. Doubles cost between 30F ($13.78) and 65F ($29.87) per person, with breakfast, while singles range from 40F ($18.38) to 70F ($32.17).

Hotel Carina (tel. 67-17-67), lying a few minutes away from the most congested part of town, has an interior plushly covered with wood paneling and stenciled plaster, for a gemütlich ambience that is heightened by the blazing fireplaces and the masonry details. The outside is similar to dozens of other chalet-style balconied buildings in Zermatt. The Fritz Biner family, the owners, charge between 40F ($18.38) and 75F ($34.46) per person, with breakfast included, in rooms with or without private bath. A good half board is included for an additional 24F ($11.02) per person. Guests have free use of the swimming pool at another nearby hotel.

Hotel Post (tel. 67-19-32) was built in 1903, although it's gone through a startling overhaul since Karl Iversson took over 25 years ago. Its most important function in Zermatt is as a nightlife center (see "Après Ski"), but it maintains 40 beds in unusual rooms that have much of the hotel's original furniture along with modern plumbing in arrangements which sometimes put the bath into the living quarters in a somewhat risqué way. These rooms are often reserved months in advance for the winter season by regular clients whom the hotel refers to almost as "family." They rent for about 45F ($20.67) per person in summer and for anywhere between 75F ($34.46) and 95F ($43.65) per person in winter, breakfast included. A minimum stay of ten days is required in high season.

Hotel Restaurant Orion (tel. 67-16-67). The traditional facade of this cozy hotel has one continuously sloping roofline and is circled with bands of weathered shingles and white stucco. The interior is warmly decorated in a modernized rusticity which includes all the heavy timbers you'd expect, along with several skylights which illuminate the colorful tablecloths of the pleasant dining room. All the units have private baths and rent for between 50F ($22.97) and 115F ($52.84) per person, with half board available for an additional 20F ($9.19).

Hotel Alfa (tel. 67-27-84) is an attractive chalet-style building with the inevitable balconies and big windows letting light into the simply furnished public rooms. The hotel lies a few steps away from the main street of Zermatt, so you can avoid the congestion of high season. You'll find a sauna and fitness room on the premises. There's no meal service, although cold platters are available on request. Rooms cost between 31F ($14.25) and 59F ($27.11) per person, breakfast included, depending on the plumbing and the season.

Hotel Julen (tel. 67-24-81) is an attractively weathered balconied hotel across the inner-town river from the historic cemetery. You'll get a clear view of the Matterhorn from the windows of this friendly place, as well as a good meal in the main dining room with its elaborately crafted wooden ceiling and beautifully paneled walls. An indoor swimming pool is about 50 yards away. The Julen family, the owners, charge between 40F ($18.38) and 90F ($41.35) per person in summer, between 45F ($20.67) and 105F ($48.28) per person in winter. These rates apply to both single and double units with and without private bath. Half board is available for an additional 15F ($6.89) per person.

Hotel Europe (tel. 67-10-66) would be the kind of place where a skier could spend a happy winter holiday. The hotel is in a tall white structure with the kind of well-built furniture which won't break if you sit down too hard. The Europe is also well heated and weatherproof, with a sauna on the premises. Situated with a view of the Matterhorn next to the Hotel Julen and under the same management, the hotel charges between 40F ($18.38) and 75F ($34.46) per person per day in winter, and is usually closed in summer. Half board is not available.

Hotel Antika (tel. 67-21-51). Parts of this hotel are dramatically designed, including an attractive facade where each room has a covered loggia with flower boxes and wood trim. The interior is paneled with weathered slats, Oriental rugs, neutral-colored carpeting, and lots of exposed masonry, which even includes a Jacuzzi whirlpool with a covering of smooth river rocks. A large garden behind offers accommodations for quiet contemplation of the Matterhorn. While the hotel doesn't serve meals, the nearby Stockhorn restaurant, under the same management, offers good food in a rustic, mellow setting (see the dining recommendations). Rooms rent for between 35F ($16.08) and 75F ($34.46) per person, including breakfast.

Hôtel Couronne (tel. 7-76-81) is in the center of the village, next to the icy creek that runs through the town. The hotel has a flagstone roof. (If you've never seen one, it merits a careful look.) A lengthy series of balconies and a well-maintained exterior surface of white stucco complete the facade. The Couronne shelters one of Zermatt's popular restaurants on the ground floor, the Old Zermatt (see the dining recommendations), and a rustic, comfortable interior with attractively stylized murals on some of the walls. Snug bedrooms have imaginative color choices (one I saw was lavendar and red). Each of the rooms has a private bath and rents for between 50F ($22.97) and 75F ($34.46) per person per day, depending on the season. Half board is offered for an additional 15F ($6.89) to 22F ($10.11) per person.

The Budget Choices

Hotel Alphubel (tel. 67-30-03) is three minutes from the train station in a large chalet-style building with a well-constructed stone foundation. The entranceway leads up a short flight of curved stone stairs into the colorful lobby area. The Julen family, the owners, took the name from a local mountaintop. When I was last there the clientele tended to be a genteel crowd of elderly persons, but that may change in winter. The management encourages guests to take at least half board, which on a *per-person* rate costs between 55F ($25.27) and 95F ($43.65), depending on the season.

Sporthotel Riffelberg (tel. 67-22-16) was built in 1853 by a local clergyman who placed it in a dramatically desolate area at a high altitude just below the Matterhorn. It was purchased by the city of Zermatt in 1862, serving ever since as a hotel and restaurant with the kind of view, summer or winter, which people come from miles around to see. The director says that an ibex colony lives close to the nearby Riffelsee and that this location, which is farther south than Lugano, gets eight full hours of sunshine in December and even more than that in summer. The interior was recently renovated, but still maintains its rustic ambience of alpine decor. With half board (which you'd better take, since there's no place else to eat around), rooms rent for between 55F ($25.27) and 85F ($39.06) per person. Skiers find this hotel attractive as it lies at the foot of the Gornergrat cableway.

Kulmhotel Gornergrat (tel. 67-22-19). The only way to get here is to take the cable car from Riffelberg or a mountain railway from Zermatt. Because the spot is so gloriously isolated, you'd better call ahead or make reservations long in advance. The two sun terraces adjoining the hotel offer vistas of the Matterhorn's glacier with high-altitude views in almost every direction. The building itself is a fortress-like structure crafted from local stone, with what looks like an observatory in one of its towers. This is perfect in summer for guests who want to get away from urban bustle to use as a base for exploratory walks through the region. In winter it's usually a popular way station for energetic skiers, with lots of activity in the downstairs restaurant. The hotel was recently renovated and extended to include more of the simple, well-heated, weatherproof rooms. They rent from 20F ($9.19) to 50F ($22.97) per person per day. None of the units has a private bath, but the shared facilities are adequate. Half board is offered for an additional 15F ($6.89) per person.

Hotel Malva (tel. 67-30-33) is a pretty hotel built in 1936 in a chalet style with a more recent addition added later. The property of the Julen family for the past 30 years, the hotel charges between 35F ($16.08) and 47F ($21.60) per person without bath, and between 48F ($22.06) and 53F ($24.35) with private bath, breakfast included. Half board costs an additional 12F ($5.51) per person.

Hotel Touring (tel. 67-11-77) is a pleasant hotel with green shutters, wooden walls, and a chalet format with wintertime ski racks set up outside the front door. Many of the rooms have private balconies and a view of the Matterhorn. Accommodations are priced between 37F ($17.00) and 82F ($37.68) per person per day, with half board included. Wendelin Julen and his family are the owners.

Hotel Dufour (tel. 67-30-73) is another establishment owned by the Julen family, one of the town's biggest hotel owners. Four floors of weathered planking rise in a chalet style in a quiet part of the village. There are only 30 beds, so if an intimate hotel is what you want, this might be it. Accommodations rent for anywhere between 27F ($12.41) and 61F ($28.03) per person per day, with breakfast and free access to the swimming pool of another hotel nearby. No meals are served other than breakfast.

Hotel Gabelhorn (tel. 67-22-35) is an attractive chalet-style house with a flagstone roof and four stories of simple and unpretentious comfort. Mrs. Zumtaugwald, your hostess, is helpful in practically every way, particularly in giving advice on the attractions of Zermatt. She charges between 30F ($13.78) and 55F ($25.27) per person, breakfast included, in rooms with or without bath. Prices depend on the season.

EATING AROUND: Most clients are booked into a hotel in Zermatt on the half-board plan. This is the best arrangement, as it leaves you free to shop around for either lunch or dinner, while still taking advantage of the food reduction that often comes with the half-board plan. By having at least one main meal outside every day, you also don't feel "hotel bound." Zermatt is filled with many local eateries, and the discriminating visitor will want to sample the fondue and raclette at various places, not to mention rack of lamb grilled over larchwood fire. A random sampling of the leading dining choices follows:

Hostellerie Tenne (tel. 67-18-11) serves regional dishes in a well-constructed decor of Swiss antiques, thick timbers, and upholstered banquettes. Some say the Tenne has the best food in Zermatt. Specialties include leg of lamb and rack of lamb grilled on a larchwood fire, sauteed duck liver, and grilled scampi. An average meal will cost as much as 50F ($22.97). The restaurant is closed all day Monday and for lunch on Tuesday. It's open in summer from mid-June until the end of September, and in winter from December until the end of April. The Stöpfer family maintain this place, along with the attractive hotel on the same premises.

Restaurant Seilerhaus (tel. 66-11-21). The hanging lamps are made of densely leaded glass, tinted red, which vibrate musically if you touch them. You'd never expect such an unpretentious decor to house such a fine restaurant, but on the premises is a uniformed chef capable of handling most international dishes well. The upstairs is an elongated, comfortable paneled stone-walled room, with a timbered ceiling and a large expanse of glass overlooking a terrace popular in summer. However, the preferred spot to dine is the Otto Furrer Stube in the cellar, which is open only for dinner. The table d'hôte menu changes weekly, costing 70F ($32.16) for seven courses. If you skip the first two courses, the charge comes down to 58F ($26.65). Ever had grenadins de veau au citron vert? The menu translates it as veal pope's eye with green lemon, which is probably the reason non-French-speaking guests seek out the filet of rabbit with sweet basil or the rock lobster with chervil instead. You might also order guinea fowl with green lentils or John Dory with seaweed in the nouvelle cuisine style.

Old Zermatt (tel. 67-26-81) is happily inside the Hôtel Couronne on the banks of Zermatt's inner alpine river. In the restaurant's raclette stübli they specialize in two kinds of fondue, bourguignonne or chinoise, along with grilled meats on open wood fires, and of course, raclette. The place is rustic, with lots of paneling. It's open in season from 4 p.m., with meals costing from 30F ($13.78).

Restaurant Stockhorn (tel. 67-17-47) is elegantly outfitted with travertine floors, heavy beams, smoky stucco walls, an alpine wedding chest, and best of all, a blazing fire extending into the room. The establishment is directed by Emil Julen, who years ago set up this restaurant in a chalet-style building, with wooden tables and regional chairs. You'll enjoy a drink at the ski-hütte bar, followed by one of the specialties which include raclette at 4F ($1.84) a portion. Or you may prefer tournedos, piccata with spaghetti, fondue bourguignonne, pork chops, or a wide range of meats grilled over an open fire. An average meal might cost from 40F ($18.38), although less expensive items can also be ordered.

Restaurant Walliserhof (tel. 67-11-74), at the hotel of the same name, has a particularly elegant selection of hors d'oeuvres, including goose liver and caviar. Specialties include fondue bourguignonne or chinoise, along with ribs of lamb with herbs, a double veal cutlet with noodles Alfredo, and brook trout. An average à la carte meal will cost from 62F ($28.49) for two persons. A table d'hôte is attractively priced at 31F ($14.24).

Bahnhofbuffet (tel. 67-21-26) is, as its name would imply, next to the train station in the wood-paneled room which you enter through a bar/service area. The black-vested waiters serve set meals ranging from 12.50F ($5.74) to 26F ($11.94). Service is surprisingly elaborate, involving rituals with hot plates and several courses of well-prepared food. The à la carte menu offers more elaborate specialties, including veal piccata, peppersteak, fondue bourguignonne or chinoise, filet of sole with almonds, and wild game in season. The menu is in English.

Le Gitan (tel. 67-27-48) is the grill room and bar area of the Hotel Darioli. On the ground floor of a building on the busy main street of town, it serves grilled meats and raclettes from 11:30 a.m. to 11:30 p.m. The specialty here is entrecôte, along with beef filet or shrimp. If it appeals to you, you might begin your meal with a savory tomato soup spiked with gin. This cozily rustic restaurant has candlelit tables, good service, and meals from 35F ($16.08). Fondue, two types, costs 48F ($22.05) for two diners.

Arvenstube, in the Hotel Pollux (tel. 67-19-46), is divided from a less formal restaurant on the floor above by a stairwell and an open wrought-iron gate. The L-shaped room is beautifully paneled in a light-grained pine, with a bar curving invitingly around one corner. The staff is attractive and friendly, serving a tempting variety of international dishes. These might begin with assiette valaisanne, a plate of air-dried meats from the Grisons. Specialties include riz Casimir (a curry dish), entrecôte with green peppercorns, tournedos in a savory mustard sauce, or sliced veal in a mushroom cream sauce. These dishes are often served with rösti. Trout with almonds is another favorite. Meals cost from 30F ($13.79) and up.

Pizzeria Vieux-Valais (tel. 7-70-31) is a sunny and amiable kind of place, with red-checked hanging lamps, a tile floor, and a stone pizza oven in one corner. Music is often provided by recordings of the Beach Boys. A well-stocked bar serves drinks below a pine ceiling highlighted in black. The food is predominantly Italian, with some French specialties as well. Dinner for two is likely to cost from 45F ($20.68), which might include spaghetti with curry sauce or beef flavored with cognac and served with a salad. Lunch dishes cost only 8F ($3.67) apiece, and a daily special is offered for 11F ($5.05). Mine was gnocchi with a roast joint of pork with vegetables on the side, and on another day, rabbit stew with Italian corn pudding and a mixed salad. The restaurant also bakes about a dozen different pizzas, costing from 12F ($5.51) apiece.

Elsie's Place (don't ever bother to phone—just drop in and hope to find a table) lies on the main street of Zermatt, close to the Zermatterhof Hotel. In a house dating from 1879, it's not a place that overwhelms by its size, but it usually manages to pack in a big crowd, everybody seemingly showing up here for a 6 p.m. hot chocolate or Elsie's famous Irish coffee. You can also drop in during the day to order ham and eggs and hot dogs (but how did those incongruous escargots get on the menu?).

APRÈS SKI: Zermatt is known for its après-ski activities, which include tea dances, restaurants, bars, nightclubs, and discos. It has more nighttime diversions than any other resort in the Valais.

The **Hotel Post** (tel. 67-19-32), where everybody shows up after they've recovered from Elsie's Irish coffee, has a virtual monopoly on nightlife in Zermatt. After staggering out of the Hotel Post most skiers hit the sack, while the entrepreneurs of the other nightspots and bars in town often want for customers.

At the long-famous Hotel Post, below the plate glass of the lobby's reception desk, you'll see photographs of the smiling athletes, models, and good-hearted people who fall into the unusual ambience of this unusual hotel. The founder is Karl Ivarsson, an American, who for 25 years has ruled over one of the oldest hotels in Zermatt, built in 1903. He has gradually expanded it into the most complete entertainment complex in Zermatt, sheltering many nightspots and restaurants under one roof.

The **Brown Cow,** on the street level, is a rustic room with a 19th-century earth rake hanging from the ceiling (it's almost a work of art). The "Cow," as it's called, serves drinks and snacks to jukebox music. Hamburgers, BLTs, goulash soup, Beach Bun sandwiches, and salads in general cost from 5F ($2.29) to 8F ($3.68), with beer going for another 2.20F ($1.01).

A walk past the reception desk will lead you to the **Pink Elephant,** which in all its art nouveau glory is one of the most exclusive bars in Zermatt. It's a favorite with David Bowie and John Lord (Deep Purple), both of whom have entertained here. A stainless-steel dance floor is surrounded by marble tables where attractive barmaids serve drinks costing from 7F ($3.21) during happy hour from 7 to 10 p.m. and 12F ($5.51) after 10 p.m. The dress code is informal, yet many clients still manage an aura of casual chic.

When you tire of the potted palms and worldly conversations here, you can move on to **Le Village,** which is the most interesting disco in Zermatt. Opening at 9 p.m., it shows sports movies (most often skiing) from 9:30 to 10:30, which sets the pace for the sports enthusiasts attracted to this place. The action takes place in a high-ceilinged and very rustic room with an oversize model of Snoopy hanging above the dance floor. The place is fun and very crowded, but don't be afraid to move on to—

The **Spaghetti Factory,** an Italian taverna on a balcony overlooking the dance floor. You'll hear disco music, but it's soft enough that you also might hear what your companion is saying. The entire construction was at one time an alpine barn, which an engineer with a lot of imagination transformed into this gemütlich hangout. Spaghetti costs from 9.50F ($4.36).

If you prefer more elegant fare, **Zamoura (Le Bistrot)** is everything you might want in a French restaurant. In addition, the soon-to-be-completed restaurant on the top floor should have a nautical theme by the time you arrive.

Another ambience (and another restaurant) can be found in the basement. To get there, you'll pass yards of amusing original murals telling the story of the lonely tourist who looked for love in Zermatt.

The **Steakhouse** downstairs is covered with horsy artifacts and serves a porterhouse steak with a three-pepper sauce, baby rack of lamb with sage, and sirloin with roquefort sauce, preceded by a poultry terrine. There's also a salad buffet. Clients are "ski bums" and alpine cowboys who pay from 40F ($18.38) for a full meal. The entrance is through Le Village.

Finally, for the rowdiest dive of them all, the **Broken Ski Bar,** in another section of the cellar, attracts the most hardened ski bums, who listen to hard rock at very loud volumes, drink heavily, and generally raise hell. The sound amplifier on this one is below an oval wine keg in the middle of the floor. It's said that any one of a dozen dancers usually tries to cave it in. Prices here are the same as for Le Village, a 12F ($4.51) cover charge, which includes the coat check and the price of the first drink. After that, beer costs 9F ($4.14). In winter the entire complex will sometimes rock with anywhere from 700 to 800 people.

My advice is to enter once and to keep walking and exploring. You'll never know what (or who) you'll find.

All of this is watched over by the friendly, aging dog at the reception desk that everybody refers to as La Directrice (her real name is Sheba).

In the unlikely event that the action at the Hotel Post is not for you, you might try one of the following recommendations:

The **Walliserkanne Disco** (tel. 67-22-98). Upstairs you'll see the restaurant which is so popular, even in summertime. Downstairs, you enter a rustic disco on two levels designed for maximum people-watching. The upper level is modern and elegant, with a long bar against one end with the proper height for elbow-resting. There's a type of balcony design that permits the people on the upper level to see the dancers on the rustic lower level. Going down to the dance floor, should you be so inclined, you'll see a timbered decor with stucco arches and a carved dragon leering down. A large beer costs from 5F ($2.30), and there's no cover charge. The disco is open from 9 p.m. to 2 a.m. seven nights a week. It's closed annually from mid-October to mid-November.

The **Hotel Pollux disco** (tel. 67-19-46) gets very crowded in winter with everyone from local service personnel to ski instructors to visitors from Europe and America. It's open every evening in winter from 9 p.m. to 2 a.m. The disco has a glossily modern decor with a central dance floor surrounded by little tables seating from two to four persons. There's no cover charge, and drinks cost between 7F ($3.21) and 10F ($4.60).

Grill Restaurant Spycher and Scotch Corner Bar (tel. 67-20-41), is connected to the Hotel Aristella, and under the direction of Elisbeth and Manfred Perren-Lehner. Alpine carved facial masks leer above the doorway of this half-timbered restaurant, with a large weathered bar set against one wall. It usually opens November 15 when it immediately becomes popular with skiers and visitors "from everywhere." This is the perfect place for après-ski drinks. Swiss coffee, Café Normand, and French coffee all cost 8F ($3.68) each. Full meals, and very good ones at all, are also served.

11. Saas-Fee and Grächen

SAAS-FEE: In the 13th-century village of Saas-Fee you'll often hear the terms "glacier village" and "pearl of the Alps." Like Zermatt, cars are forbidden. The village is perched on a grassy plateau, and from its citadel you can enjoy unparalleled vistas of the mammoth and encircling glaciers.

Trail blazers have spread the fame of the "highwire" mountain trails along the western and eastern escarpments of the Saas Valley. Here you'll meet all those Swiss cows you've heard so much about. Occasionally you'll come across locals in traditional garb, and stumble upon places seemingly little changed since the turn of the century.

The terminus of the famous "High Route" from Verbier through the Alps, Saas-Fee lies in a valley east of Zermatt. From Saas-Fee, unlike Zermatt, you can't view the tilted pyramid of the Matterhorn, but you'll have a lot of other peaks to look at. These include the mammoth **Feegletscher** (Fee Glacier).

Saas-Fee is reached from the Rhône Valley by a good road or by postal bus from Brig, Visp, or Stalden. Cars can be parked in large garages or parking lots outside the village.

Its many facilities include two aerial cableways, three multicabin cableways, two chair lifts, 15 ski lifts, and 32 miles of well-laid-out ski runs, plus 11 tennis courts and two ice rinks.

The mountaineering school offers you several skiing tours, climbing and excursion weeks from April to October. It also has a widely spread network of 280 kilometers of footpaths, including the Gemsweg (chamois track) from Hannig to Plattjen and the geological mountain high-level trail from Felskinn to the Britannia Hut.

At the entrance to the village is a large indoor swimming pool.

Of course, visitors to Saas-Fee want to get as close to the mountains as they can. The townspeople happily oblige. You can take a gondola cable lift to **Plattjen,** enjoying a panoramic view of the Saas Valley and the artificial lake of Mattmark. Along the way you'll see many alpine flowers in spring, and if you're lucky, a chamois.

The **Felskinn** aerial cableway heaves you up to the summer skiing area of Egginer-Felskinn. Two or three ski lifts are open the whole year, but in summer only from 8:30 a.m. to 1:30 p.m. (the snow is likely to get mushy in the afternoon).

The Spielboden gondola ski lift and the Längfluh aerial cableway bring you to **Längfluh,** an oasis in the middle of the Fee Glacier. This is the starting point for the classic mountain tour and the grand glacier tour to the Brittania Hut and to Mattmark.

Another gondola cableway explores **Hannig.** You arrive at the balcony of the Saas Valley, with a scenic alpine view of 360°. Here you can go on many walking tours in a virgin area. It's the starting point to the Mischabel Hut and many alpine tours in the Mischabel massif. A special attraction of the sloping area are the chamois and ibex.

These rides, depending on how far you travel, are reasonable in price, costing from 5F ($2.30) to 22F ($10.11).

Food and Lodging

Apart Hotel Saaser Hof (tel. 57-15-51) is constructed almost entirely of weathered beams of thick wood, with an occasional flowerbox set at irregular intervals along the three tiers of balconies. The decor inside is that of a well-heeled old Valais house. The windows are crisscrossed with strips of geometrically patterned lead, and the wood paneling of the ceilings is appropriately complicated. In one of the sitting rooms a central fireplace funnels its smoke through an elaborately crafted tube of hexagonal copper. On the premises is a sauna to warm you after a winter day outside. The apartments abandon the regional flavor of the public rooms. They're decorated in contrasting patterns of geometric lines, along with modern upholstered furniture, sometimes with wood trim. Many of the accommodations are traditional hotel rooms, whereas the apartments have kitchenettes, sometimes accommodating as many as eight guests. Prices range from 80F ($36.76) to 124F ($56.98) in a single, from 75F ($34.46) to 135F ($62.03) in a double, from 64F ($29.40) to 110F ($50.54) in a triple. All of these tariffs are *per person* per day, the difference in the rates depending on the season. However, half board is included, and all units contain private baths.

Hôtel Beau-Site (tel. 57-11-22) is a very large brown-and-white building with lots of balconies and a prominent position in the center of the village. The original hotel was built during the heyday of the British tourist in 1893. In 1957 the hotel was greatly expanded and modernized, so that today a decor of masonry walls, timbers, and lots of paneling covers the inside of this family-run (third generation) house. A swimming pool with a ceiling low enough to keep it well heated is on the premises. Each of the comfortable bedrooms has a private bath. Singles cost between 90F ($41.35) and 110F ($50.54), and doubles range from 80F ($36.76) to 120F ($55.14) per person daily, with half board included. The breakfast buffet is copious, and the evening meal includes five courses. Clients who want only bed and breakfast receive a reduction of 20F ($9.19) per person daily.

Grand Hotel Saas Fee (tel. 57-10-01), in the center of the village, is an elegant establishment with lots of renovated touches which include a sauna, whirlpool, richly beamed ceilings, and a scattering of 19th-century antiques. The comfortable bedrooms are usually trimmed with pine paneling and are decorated in monochromatic earth tones. The exterior of the hotel resembles three streamlined chalets set next to one another, with balconies extending from the southern side. Ursula and Hans Hess-Zurbriggen are the English-speaking hosts. For one of their comfortably furnished rooms, all of which contain private bath, they charge between 74F ($34) and 134F ($61.57) for singles, while doubles cost between 140F ($64.33) and 260F ($119.47), with half board included.

Hotel Burgener (tel. 57-15-22), near the ski lifts, has only 30 beds. The format is chalet style, this time with a yellow trim. A low-lying building next door, called the Ski-Hütte, does a thriving business as a terrace restaurant, especially during high season. The decor of this hotel is rustic, even by alpine standards, but comfortably appropriate after a day outdoors. The Burgener family maintains the place, charging from 62F ($28.48) to 84F ($38.59) in a single and from 11OF ($50.54) to 180F ($82.71) in a double. All accommodations have private baths, and tariffs include half board.

Hotel Britannia (tel. 4-84-43) is in the center of the village on a raised site which gives especially good views of the mountains around it. Most of the rooms have balconies with eastern or southern exposure, which illuminate the comfortable bedrooms. These units are filled with brightly colored furniture which makes everything functional yet comfortable. The exterior is a wood-covered six-story chalet with a concrete extension on the back. Singles range between 42F ($19.30) and 77F ($35.38), while doubles cost from 80F ($36.76) to 145F ($66.62), with half board included.

Hotel Allalin (tel. 57-18-15) was until recently an apartment house when it was transformed in the summer of 1983 into a three-star hotel. It has all the modern amenities you'd expect, along with a sauna, elevator, bar, and two restaurants. Many of the units have private balconies as well. Close to everything, the hotel charges from 60F ($27.57) to 94F ($43.19) in a single and from 110F ($50.54) to 184F ($84.55) in a double. All accommodations have private bath and include half board in their prices.

Hôtel des Alpes (tel. 57-15-55) is a rambling chalet-style hotel with one of its wings in traditional weathered wood and another wing crafted from white stucco. Alpine-style balconies surround the entire construction on several tiers to give practically every bedroom a balcony. The decor inside is cozily informal with the kind of furniture that children don't easily demolish. The hotel is neither glossily elegant nor trendy, but provides relaxed comfort with a conscientious management by the Zurbriggen family. Singles range from 32F ($14.70) to 48F ($22.06), and doubles go from 63F (28.95) to 90F ($41.36), including breakfast. Half board costs 12F ($5.51) per person additional.

Hotel Sonnehof (tel. 57-26-93) is an intimately small, 40-bed hotel with a personalized management directed by the Josef Huber family. The decor is nothing short of vivid, with a flame-colored reception area and an extension of the orange decor throughout many of the public rooms. The views from the bedrooms are very good. Prices for this centrally located hotel, where each of the rooms has a private bath, are from 53F ($24.35) to 81F ($37.21) in a single and from 100F ($45.95) to 162F ($74.43) in a double, with half board included. Rates vary according to the season.

Waldhotel Fletschhorn (tel. 57-21-31) serves some of the best food at the resort, and even nonguests may want to stop in here for at least one meal. This establishment lies in a handsome chalet beside a footpath a 15-minute walk from the center of Saas-Fee. Irma Dütsch-Grandjean is said by many to be one of the best cooks in the region. Her menu is extremely varied, and someone will be happy to guide you through a satisfying selection if you want assistance. Your meal might include cream of snail soup or frog legs in puff pastry, perhaps fresh duck liver with endive in the nouvelle cuisine style. Among the recommendable courses are filet of red snapper grilled with walnuts and rack of lamb which has been marinated, perhaps escalope of salmon à la crème de ciboulette, or flambeed beef. At certain times of the season a consommé of quail is served. The restaurant closes for the Easter holidays and from mid-October to mid-

December. Fixed-price meals cost from 87F ($39.98) in the evening but are cheaper at noon. A la carte meals range from 30F ($13.78) to 60F ($27.57).

Après Ski

My favorite place after dark is the rustic tavern, Sans-Souci, of the four-star **Grand Hotel,** which often has live groups who play for dancing. It can pack in 300 on a big night.

If you like a cozy bar on a cold winter's night, check out the rustic one at the four-star **Beau Site.**

Action at Saas-Fee is very casual at night, nothing very formal unless a group of visitors spontaneously decide to "dress up," which is known to happen.

Try also the Yeti Bar at the **Dom Hotel** (tel. 59-11-01).

GRÄCHEN: This was just a tiny farming village which has lately realized its potential as a budding ski resort, for those looking for lower prices than traditionally found at its more famous neighbors, Saas-Fee and Zermatt. Its popularity as a ski resort has been very recent, and it attracts a lively family trade of mostly European visitors. (All the Americans, seemingly, are headed for Zermatt and the Matterhorn.)

Grächen is built on a wind-sheltered sun terrace, set against a panoramic alpine backdrop of mountain peaks. It has several ski runs, cableway, ski lifts, and trails.

At the east of the village you can take a gondola to **Hannigalp,** which has a restaurant that can seat hundreds. From this vantage point you face a total of four drag lifts. The loftiest point is **Wannihorn,** at 7530 feet.

Food and Lodging

Hotel Elite (tel. 56-16-12) is a pleasant wood-balconied chalet which is landscaped into the hillside. The interior is pleasantly rustic with white stucco between the overhead ceiling beams. Unpretentious furniture and spacious public rooms are there if you need them, although most guests will probably stay on their balconies in summer and outdoors skiing in winter. The Reynard family, your hosts, charge from 60F ($27.57) to 84F ($38.60) in a single and from 105F ($48.24) to 150F ($68.93) in a double, including half board.

Hotel Restaurant Hannigalp (tel. 56-25-55) looks like a mix between a chalet and a Mediterranean villa, with a rustic upper section and two lower floors of big-windowed terraces that extend far out on either side. The entire complex overlooks the hotel's tennis court. The interior is pleasantly decorated with a checkerboard parquet floor in the dining room and lots of paneling and patterned carpets in the bedrooms. A nearby chalet, the Christiania, accommodates the overflow from the main hotel, for a total sleeping capacity of 50. A rustically beamed bar area serves food and drink. Singles cost between 55F ($25.27) and 80F ($36.76), while doubles range between 95F ($43.65) and 140F ($64.33), with half board included.

Hotel Walliserhof (tel. 56-11-22) offers 60 beds in a six-story chalet with red shutters and lots of balconies. A dancing bar in the basement usually has live musical groups for listeners of all ages. The Walter family, your hosts, charge from 55F ($25.27) to 80F ($36.76) in a single and from 95F ($43.65) to 140F ($64.33) in a double, depending on the season. Half board is included in these prices.

Après Ski

The action, such as there is, is very subdued. The rowdy crowd heads for Zermatt or Saas-Fee, and many people turn in early in Grächen. However, not everything shuts down at night.

To get myself started, I always drop in at the **Hotel Hannigalp** for one of its Hannigalp cocktails for fortification.

After that, the best place in the village for entertainment is the **Hotel Walliserhof,** which often has dancing to a live band.

If the action seems dull there, you might go over to the **Hotels Bellevue and Romantica** (tel. 56-24-44), which have a bar with music and a good kitchen.

The **Hotels Grächerhof und Schönegg** (tel. 56-25-15) also provide dancing and a choice of bars, along with a rôtisserie. Olga and Alex Fux-Pfammatter are your friendly, obliging hosts here.

12. Brig and the Simplon Pass

Lying south of the Rhône River, Brig is a historic stopover for international travelers, both today and centuries ago. It's also the capital of the Upper Valais region, and a major railway stopover. Famed as the starting point for the great road over the **Simplon Pass,** it lies at the north end of the **Simplon tunnel,** at 12 miles the longest in the world. Work began on the first of these twin tunnels at the turn of the century.

Napoleon ordered the road over the Simplon Pass, and construction was launched in the early years of the 19th century, making it the shortest road between the Valais and the Ticino, coming up. The Swiss try to keep the pass open all year. If the pass is not open, cars can be carried by rail through the tunnel. The road, if the weather's right, is one of the most stunning views in Europe, and should be taken for sightseeing alone. Like a slide show, the views change constantly, and there are many tricky turns—so drive carefully.

Back in Brig is a sightseeing attraction all on its own, **Stockalperschloss** or Stockalper's Castle, through which guided tours are conducted May to October from 9 to 11 a.m. and 2 to 5 p.m., daily except Monday, for a 3F ($1.38) admission. It's Switzerland's largest manor house, built by Kasper von Stockalper between 1658 and 1678. He grew rich and prosperous by recognizing the benefits of trade with Italy and by exploiting trade along the Simplon Pass. However, he was chased out of his beloved home by irate citizens of the Valais, although he returned from exile in time to die here, perhaps with memories of when he'd been welcomed into some of the royal courts of Europe. The manor consists of a mammoth building with four floors and a large gateway. The three towers with their bulbous domes symbolize the Wise Men. Ever since 1948 Brig has owned the manor, and today uses it as a museum and for administrative purposes. In its heyday it was the biggest privately owned residence in all of Switzerland.

FOOD AND LODGING: **Hotel Alpina Volkshaus,** 6 Belalpstrasse (tel. 23-76-36), was completely renovated and upgraded in 1978. Only a three-minute walk from the train station, the hotel is warmly decorated with lots of paneling and an attractively simple collection of contemporary furniture. The 100 beds are housed in unpretentious rooms, half of which contain private bath. There's a parking garage in the basement, along with two restaurants and a bar. The Fux family charges from 40F ($18.38) to 120F ($55.14) in a single and from 70F ($32.17) to 120F ($55.14) in a double, with breakfast included. Rates depend on the season and the plumbing. Half board is offered for another 19F ($8.73) per person daily.

Hotel Victoria, Bahnhofplatz (tel. 23-15-03), is the kind of place where you should stay if you had your heart set on something designed like a French château. The steep roof of this corner hotel is capped with three rows of gables, sometimes trimmed in gray stone, and a pointed witch-cap of a turret. Unfortunately, not all of the interior delivers the kind of atmosphere that the outside promises, but the modern renovations are nonetheless comfortable and tasteful. Set in front of the train station, the hotel charges from 45F ($20.68) to 70F ($32.17) in a single and from 95F ($43.65) to 125F ($57.44) in a double. Breakfast is extra, and another bed can be set up in any room for an additional 30F ($13.79).

Schlosskeller, 26 Alte Simplonstrasse (tel. 23-33-52), is in a historic building in the center of town, serving filling meals in a rustic setting. The food includes a plate of air-dried alpine beef, followed by, perhaps, filets of fera with wild rice or filet of pork madeleine. Fixed-price meals cost from 19F ($8.73) to 28F ($12.86), and à la carte dinners are priced from 23F ($10.57) to 35F ($16.08). It's closed on Monday in winter and for three weeks in January. Erwin Schwery is the owner and chef.

Restaurant Channa, 5 Furkastrasse (tel. 23-65-56), is the sympathetic restaurant managed by Peter Walch, who often invites his clients to dine on the flowery terrace in warm weather. Specialties include green pepper filet steak Madagascar, frog legs in the style of Provence, and veal kidneys flambé. Fixed-price meals range from 10F ($4.60) to 35F ($16.08).

13. Grimsel Pass

Another one of the great scenic roads of Switzerland, the Grimsel Pass lies on the boundary between the canton of Berne and the canton of Valais which we are now leaving. Take it if you want to go back to the Bernese Oberland. Among its more stunning views is one of the **Gries Glacier.** The so-called **Lake of the Dead** is named to honor the soldiers who lost their lives in the battle between the French and the Austrians in 1799.

If you're exploring at all in this area, you may want to see the snowy summit of the **Galenstock,** and the **Furka Pass,** which heads toward Andermatt on the way to Lucerne and the heart of Switzerland. In the vicinity of **Gletsch,** on the road to the Furka Pass, you can stop at the **Belvedere Hotel,** one of the most scenic vistas along this trail. You can also order drinks and food.

From here you can see the celebrated **Rhône Glacier,** where the Swiss have carved an ice grotto, for which they charge an admission of 4F ($1.84). The vista of both the Alps of the Bernese Oberland and the Valais Alps is stunning.

Back in the vicinity of the Grimsel Pass, you may want to seek out food and lodging for the night.

Hotel Grimselblick (tel. 73-11-26) is set across the road from a lake in a well-maintained white building with red shutters and plenty of space for parking. The Gemmet family, your hosts, seem to take a great interest in rock crystals. They charge between 30F ($13.79) and 37F ($17) in a single and between 50F ($22.98) and 60F ($27.57) in a double, including breakfast. Rooms are simply but comfortably furnished.

Chapter VIII

LAUSANNE AND LAKE GENEVA

1. Lausanne
2. From Lausanne to Nyon
3. The Lavaux Corniche
4. Vevey
5. Montreux
6. Château-d'Oex
7. Villars
8. Les Diablerets

IN THE FOOTSTEPS of Lord Byron and Shelley, tourists for decades have embarked upon a trek to discover the scenic wonders of Lake Geneva (Lac Léman) in the southwest corner of Switzerland. Part of the lake borders France. Actually, it was native son Jean-Jacques Rousseau who caused the lake to become such a pilgrimage among the "Romantics."

Lac Léman is the largest lake in central Europe, the Lacus Lemannus of classical writers. It embraces an area of about 225 square miles, of which 134 square miles belong to the Swiss and the rest to France. The French sector takes in most of the south shore, except for Geneva in the west and Valais in the east. The Swiss-held north shore is shaped like a large arc, and is lined with vineyards which were planted on the final slopes of the Jura.

The most popular way to visit the lake is by steamer, and this has been true every since 1823. Nearly all the cities, hamlets, and towns we'll visit along the lake have schedules of these many and varied trips posted at the landing quays. Service is usually from Easter to October, when autumn winds carry too much of a bite for lake motoring. However, in this chapter I'll assume you'll be touring by car or bus, which will allow you to stop and visit the sights along the way. Railways also run along both shores.

Lake Geneva is formed by the Rhône. It consists of both a Grand Lac to the east and a Petit Lac to the west, the latter in the Genevese portions (for a description of Geneva itself and its surrounding environs, turn to Chapter IX). When the muddy Rhône enters the lake there is a turbulence, because the waters of the lake are of an unusual blue. But eventually the river-born mud sinks to the bottom and doesn't take away from the almost transparency of some of Lac Léman's waters.

The list of celebrated personages who have chosen to live on the lake is staggering: not only Edward Gibbon, but Balzac and Dumas, André Gide and Richard Wagner, Franz Liszt and George Eliot.

In more modern times, a host of international stars—none more celebrated than the late Charlie Chaplin—have chosen a home on the lake. Along with the little tramp, I'll cite just a few of the stars and celebrities who have been attracted to the lake: Yul Brynner, Audrey Hepburn, James Mason, Noël Coward, William Holden, David Niven, Sophia Loren, and Charles Lindbergh. Of course, many went there for tax reasons in days of yore.

Our exploration will begin in the "capital" of Lac Léman, the ancient city of:

1. Lausanne

Lausanne, with 135,000 inhabitants the second-largest city on Lake Geneva and the fifth-largest city in Switzerland, rises in tiers from the lake. The city is built on five hills overlooking the lake which they call Lac Léman (they deplore hearing it called Lake Geneva!). The upper and lower towns are connected by funicular.

A haunt of international celebrities who live along the lake, and celebrated for its schools, Lausanne is connected by motorway to Geneva, 38 miles away. In the opposite direction, the Great St. Bernard road tunnel is some 60 miles from Lausanne.

This university city has been inhabited since the Stone Age, and was the ancient Roman town of Lousanna. In 1803 it became the 19th canton to join the Confederation, and is today the capital of the canton of Vaud.

For centuries Lausanne has been a favorite haunt of expatriates. Figures show that in 1930 foreigners numbered 10,548 out of the city's total population of 75,915. The city has long attracted many royal families (many of them deposed), and has been associated with such personalities as Voltaire, Lord Byron, Napoleon, Goethe, and Rousseau. It particularly flourished in the Age of Enlightment.

The **Cité** or old town still evokes the Middle Ages as a nightwatchman calls the hours from 10 p.m. to 2 a.m. from the top of the cathedral's belfry.

The hub of the town's traffic, the **Place St-François,** is the shopping and business heart of Lausanne. The Church of the St. Francis, standing there from the 13th and 14th centuries, is all that remains of an old Franciscan friary. Today the square is filled with office blocks and the main post office. Regrettably, La Grotte, the villa with the terrace on which Gibbon completed his famous history in 1787, was torn down in 1896 to make room for the post office. From St. François Square you can walk up the **rue de Bourg,** one of the most typical shopping streets of Lausanne.

Or alternatively you can take the funicular down to **Ouchy,** which is now the lakefront of Lausanne. Once it was just a sleeping fishing hamlet, but no more.

ACCOMMODATIONS: In the top hotels of the city an air of luxury and elegance prevails, which long ago made the city a favorite visiting place for the English. In summer space is tight, so try to get a reservation. Lausanne is also a city of trade fairs, conferences, and conventions, so many of its better hotels are fully booked at certain times of the year, including, for example, the International Tourism Fair in March. The tourist office will help you find a

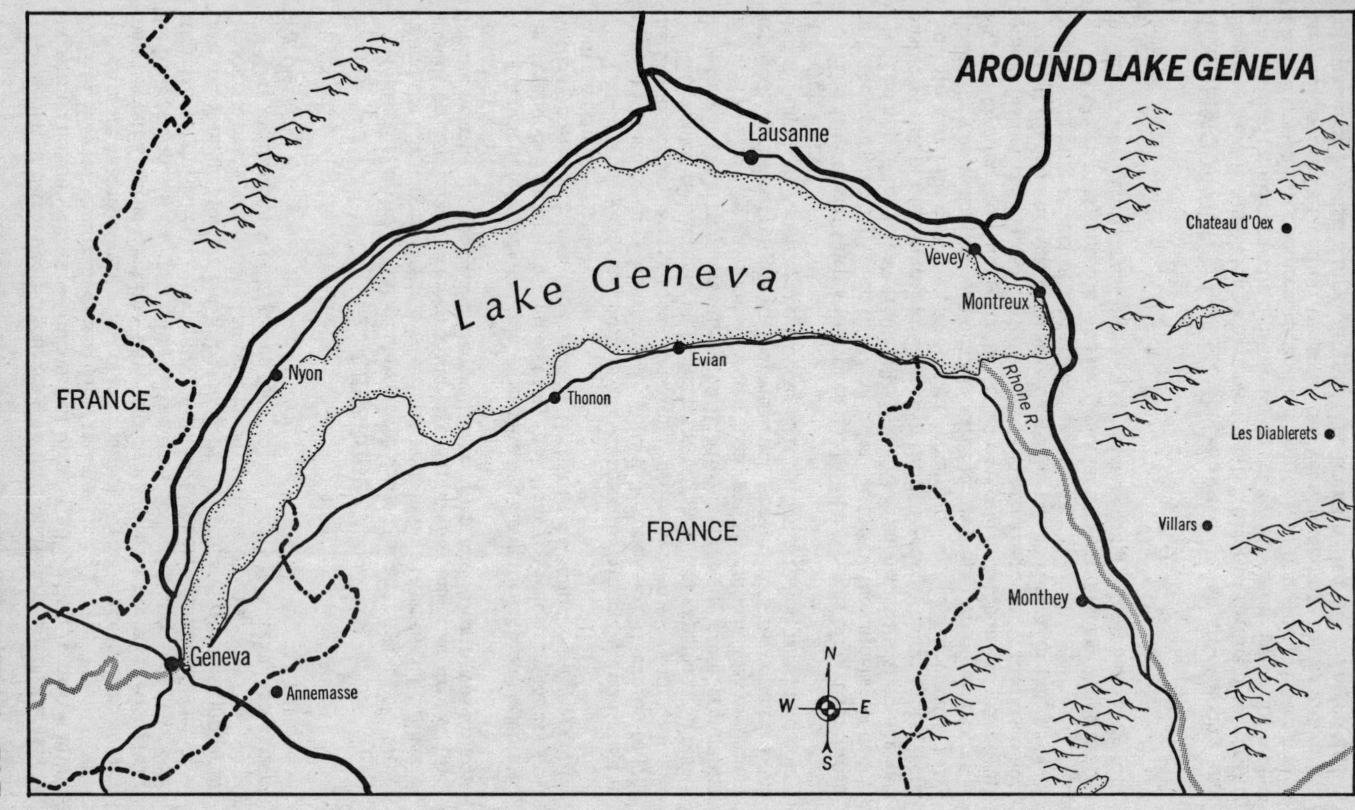
AROUND LAKE GENEVA
Lausanne
Chateau d'Oex
Vevey
Lake Geneva
Montreux
Nyon
Evian
FRANCE
Thonon
Rhone R.
Les Diablerets
FRANCE
Villars
Monthey
Geneva
N
Annemasse
W
E
S

room if you're stranded without a place to stay (or even if you aren't). They're very friendly and helpful.

If you want to be directly on the lake, seek out an accommodation in Ouchy; otherwise, you'll find many fine hotels in Lausanne proper.

The Deluxe Choices

Hôtel Beau-Rivage, Place du Général Guisan, at Ouchy (tel. 26-38-31), is set in nine acres of the most exquisitely maintained gardens in Lausanne, with cedars, many kinds of begonias, and grassy areas dotted with sculptures. All of it is a citadel of beauty and tradition, and in its some 120 years it has been host to scores of European aristocrats. The hotel dates from 1861, but another wing was added around the end of the 19th century. The Beau-Rivage is a vastly proportioned and elaborately detailed structure with a mansard roof, tall French-style windows, and miles of wrought-iron balconies. The rotunda inside is a mammoth rococo room with columns, statues of heroic deities, and a series of illuminations worthy of Vienna at its peak. Artfully lit from beneath, the room serves as one of the hotel's many public salons and is eerily empty, having no apparent purpose except to be beautiful.

In another room an exquisitely carved bar is decorated in an art nouveau style, with a restrained pianist tinkling out melodies in the corner. This is one of the last bastions of a more formal Europe, so appropriate clothing should be worn. Perhaps you'll spot an ancient Italian contessa or two. The public rooms are vast, exquisitely decorated, and very formal. On the premises you'll also find an indoor and an outdoor pool and one of the best restaurants in the canton, the Wellingtonia Room. There are tennis rooms, as well as a jogging path and an exercise room, just some of the hotel's many amenities.

Rooms are beautifully furnished and for the most part luxurious and spacious. Singles range from 120F ($55.14) to 310F ($142.45), while doubles cost from 170F ($78.12) to 350F ($160.85).

Lausanne Palace, 7-9 Grand-Chêne (tel. 20-37-11), is as grand and elegant a hotel as you'll find anywhere in Europe. Those details which are not authentically 19th century (the columns, the plaster detailing, the marble floors, and the richly oiled woodwork of the bar area) are very attractive 20th-century additions, usually in keeping with the well-maintained tradition of "The Palace," as scores of British visitors over the years have called it. The hotel is in the heart of Lausanne, with a good view of the mountains and the lake from many of its bedroom windows. Tapestries, crystal chandeliers, and gilded rococo furniture from a more ornate era fill many of the corners. The spacious bedrooms have private baths, renting for between 125F ($57.44) and 185F ($85.01) in a single and between 175F ($80.41) and 255F ($117.17) in a double, depending on the season and the accommodation.

Medium Priced and Upper Bracket Hotels

Hôtel Aulac, 4 Place de la Navigation, in Ouchy (tel. 27-14-51). The baroque yellow facade is highlighted with white trim and a Renaissance-style porch which extends up three tiers of floors between two elaborate columns. The mansard roof is inlaid with tiles set into geometric designs in brown, green, and yellow. The entire endearing structure is crowned with a tall narrow clock tower which is unmistakably Victorian. All of this sits on the water's edge with dozens of sailboats bobbing in the lake nearby. The interior has been renovated several times to include a restaurant with a nautical theme, lots of conference rooms, and well-maintained, simply furnished rooms, many quite spacious.

Singles rent for between 90F ($41.36) and 120F ($55.14), while doubles cost between 130F ($59.74) and 160F ($73.52), with breakfast included. All units contain TV, radio, phone, and mini-bar.

Le Château d'Ouchy, Place du Port, in Ouchy (tel. 26-74-51), is about the most complete retrospective of pre–20th-century architectural styles you'll find in this part of Switzerland. The central feature is a fortified tower with a black-and-red tile roof. This is surrounded by a marvelously crafted series of wings, dungeons, Renaissance-style gables, and Romanesque arches, all of it made of gray stones set intricately together. Management tells me that all of this was pieced together in the 19th century around a 12th-century core. Today it's a comfortable hotel with an impressive series of public rooms and a nightclub that's one of the most popular in town. The renovated bedrooms are furnished, in part, with Louis XIII–style pieces, at rates ranging between 90F ($41.36) and 130F ($59.74) in a single and between 130F ($59.74) and 180F ($82.71) in a double. Some of the more luxurious rooms rent for between 210F ($96.50) and 290F ($133.26). An extra bed can be set up in any room for an additional 35F ($16.08). Breakfast is included in the tariffs quoted.

Hôtel La Residence, 15 Place du Port, at Ouchy (tel. 27-77-11). Three separate buildings, all of them in the Regency style, comprise this hotel. They're separated from one another with flowered walkways, but all of them front on the lake. The entrance to the reception area has black and white diamond-shaped slabs of stone set into the floor, a massive fireplace, and an authentically beamed ceiling. This building was at one time an annex of the neighboring Beau-Rivage (it still maintains strong ties to it), and before that an offshoot of the town hall. Two of the three remaining buildings were once private villas, while the other is a convincing copy. Set on the shores of the lake in what is considered the best part of Ouchy, the hotel employs an accessible and friendly staff who appreciate the rigors of travel. Karine Schnyder, the director, charges between 110F ($50.55) and 140F ($64.33) in a single and between 140F ($64.33) and 190F ($87.31) in a double, including breakfast.

Royal Savoy, 40 avenue d'Ouchy (tel. 26-42-01), is set in a park with a swimming pool and towering trees. The building is designed château fashion, with many chimneys, a mansard roof, turrets capped by round pointed roofs, and lots of gracefully arched windows with balconies. The bedrooms are spacious and filled with carved armoires, Oriental rugs, and good reproduction antiques. The several restaurants and the bar combine very good service with an elegant decor. Singles rent for between 110F ($50.55) and 150F ($68.93), while doubles cost between 140F ($64.33) and 200F ($91.90). Half board is offered for another 30F ($13.79).

Hôtel de la Paix, 5 avenue Benjamin-Constant (tel. 20-71-71), is a sprawling 19th-century hotel with row upon row of elaborate balconies and loggias, many of them with wrought-iron detailing. The summertime awnings prevent too much sunlight from entering the rooms with southern exposure. Jacky's Bar is an intimately discreet hideaway done in an understated comfort that's easy to look at. Many of the bedrooms overlook the lake and are decorated with a streamlined elegance that's very easy to live with. Each of the rooms has a private shower and rates include a generous breakfast. Singles rent for between 105F ($48.25) and 140F ($64.33), while doubles cost between 140F ($64.33) and 200F ($91.90).

Hôtel Alpha-Palmiers, 34 Petit-Chêne (tel. 23-01-31), opened in 1970 in a modern format with radio, phone, and mini-bar in each room. This is a first-class hotel on a large-scale format popular with members of the business community. Singles rent for between 85F ($39.06) and 100F ($45.95), while doubles cost between 115F ($52.84) and 140F ($64.33), with a breakfast buffet included. Prices, of course, depend on the season.

Hotel Parking Motor Inn, 9 avenue Rond-Point (tel. 27-12-11), is a first-class hotel which opened in 1973. It's in a peaceful location, but only 300 yards from the train station. Each of its sunny accommodations has a radio, phone, and mini-bar. Two restaurants are on the premises, one of which has a replica of a 19th-century water wheel set into a masonry foundation. The facade of this one is unadorned inner-city metallic, without the ornate detailing you might have hoped for. But it's nonetheless clean and comfortable, a popular choice with business people. Singles rent for between 85F ($39.06) and 100F ($45.95), while doubles cost between 115F ($52.84) and 140F ($64.33), including a breakfast buffet.

Continental Hotel, 2 Place de la Gare (tel. 20-15-51), is very much of a downtown commercial hotel, as it's near the train station in a glass-and-concrete rectangle. The reception area is glossily outfitted with black trim and a metallic ceiling, while the comfortable bedrooms are exactly what you'd expect from such a format. Each of the accommodations has its own bath, phone, radio, TV, and mini-bar. On the premises you'll find a grill room, plus an informal restaurant, and a bar serving Russian specialties. Singles rent for between 100F ($45.95) and 140F ($64.33), while doubles cost between 140F ($64.33) and 180F ($82.71), with breakfast included. Half board can be arranged for another 25F ($11.49).

Hôtel Bellerive, 99 avenue de Cour (tel. 26-96-33), is in the center of town with a clear view from the top floors over the nearby houses and trees as far as the lake. The interior is very comfortably appointed with elegantly upholstered armchairs in autumnal colored stripes and flowery wallpaper. The bedrooms are filled with fresh colors, for the most part, and comfortable furniture. Singles rent for between 55F ($25.27) and 130F ($59.74), while doubles cost between 78F ($35.84) and 178F ($81.79), including breakfast.

Hôtel de la Navigation, Place Navigation, in Ouchy (tel. 26-20-41), is a flat-roofed hotel with gray masonry walls and a covered terrace which serves meals and drinks to a crowd of locals who enjoy the view of the sailboat port. The interior is attractively lit from pin spots and concealed sources, and outfitted with very modern furniture. The colorful bedrooms all have private bath, radio, phone, mini-bar, and TV. Singles rent for between 60F ($27.57) and 105F ($48.25), while doubles cost between 85F ($39.06) and 150F ($68.93), depending on the view, the season, and the plumbing.

Hotel Victoria, 46 avenue de la Gare (tel. 20-57-71), is a white-painted hotel with gables and a mansard roof near the train station. The renovated interior is filled with comfortably upholstered chairs and Oriental rugs. A warmly intimate bar area has padded stools, a futuristic ceiling, and in another section, some of the art nouveau vestiges of the original decor. Breakfast is included in the price, which in a single ranges between 90F ($41.36) and 115F ($52.84), between 130F ($59.74) and 160F ($73.52) in a double.

Hotel Jan, 8 avenue de Beaulieu (tel. 36-11-61), is slightly to the west of the center of Lausanne in a massive building made of concrete and glass. The hotel is close to the Palais de Beaulieu, where international congresses and sports events take place. If you're driving, you'll appreciate the garage facilities. The bedrooms are spacious and clean, as well as simply furnished with slightly dated pieces which are nonetheless comfortable. There's an unpretentious restaurant serving well-prepared food and a popular bar on the premises. All accommodations contain private bath. Singles rent for between 72F ($33.08) and 97F ($44.57), while doubles cost between 100F ($45.95) and 130F ($59.74), including breakfast.

Hotel Carlton, 4 avenue de Cour (tel. 26-32-35), looks best in summertime when a collection of electric blue awnings decorates the arched windows of the white facade. The hotel, appropriate for its position in a green park with a view of the lake, is designed almost like a Mediterranean villa, with a gently sloping red tile roof and emphatic horizontal lines. André Chollet is the competent manager, overseeing the 55 rooms, all of which contain private bath, and the garden restaurant popular in summer. Singles range from 90F ($41.36) to 130F ($59.74), while doubles cost from 130F ($59.74) to 180F ($82.71), including breakfast. Half board is an additional 30F ($13.79) per person daily.

Budget to Medium-Priced Hotels

Hôtel d'Angleterre, 9 Place du Port, in Ouchy (tel. 26-41-45), is a symmetrical four-story 19th-century building with a café on the ground floor and a position directly on the water. From the windows of the comfortable bedrooms you can see across to the mountains on the other side. The simply furnished accommodations are clean and neat. Singles rent for between 50F ($22.98) and 90F ($41.36), while doubles cost between 70F ($32.17) and 122F ($56.06), including breakfast.

Hôtel Élite, 1 avenue Sainte-Luce (tel. 20-23-61), is a five-story white hotel with a flat roof, several balconies, and a series of reproduction neoclassical details that are lost behind the large illuminated sign on the front lawn. That doesn't detract from the friendly welcome offered by hotelier M. Zufferey, who directs the establishment with style and élan. The comfortable rooms rent for between 50F ($22.98) and 90F ($41.36) in a single, between 70F ($32.17) and 120F ($55.14) in a double, including breakfast.

Hôtel AlaGare Transit, 14 rue de Simplon (tel. 27-92-52). The exterior of this friendly hotel is covered with peach-colored stucco, with summertime flowers in many of the windowboxes. It's about a block away from the train station, so owner Pierre Goy usually welcomes travel-weary clients even late into the night. A glance at the interior is enough to convince you you're in the Alps instead of in lakeside Lausanne. The public rooms and the bedrooms have lots of pine paneling stained in several different tones. On the same premises is a rustic restaurant where many local residents go for raclette and specialties of the Vaud. Half of the accommodations have private baths, while the other half use the adequate facilities in the hall. Singles range from 63F ($28.95) to 82F ($37.68), while doubles go for 84F ($38.60) to 108F ($49.63). Triples rent from 109F ($50.09) to 145F ($66.63).

Hôtel Montillier, 35 avenue de Lavaux, in Pully/Lausanne (tel. 28-75-85), is a family-run hotel on the outskirts of Lausanne, one mile from the city center. It's set in an area filled with vineyards with a view of the lake. A public bus stops frequently in front of the hotel on its way into town. The hotel presents a slightly concave glass, steel, and masonry facade to the parking lot in front. Indoors is a popular orange- and black-colored pizzera/restaurant (Le Poivrier) which serves French and Italian specialties in a vividly modern format. Singles range from 40F ($18.38) to 61F ($28.03), while doubles cost between 60F ($27.57) and 107F ($49.17), depending on the plumbing and the season. Breakfast is included in the price.

Hotel City, 5 rue Caroline (tel. 20-21-41), is a centrally located hotel just outside the old town, only 300 yards from a covered swimming pool and the parking lot of Mon Repos. There are radios, phones, and mini-bars in each accommodation, and discounts are offered for long sojourns. A comfortable hotel with few frills, the City is perfectly satisfactory if most of your time is spent sightseeing. Singles cost between 45F ($20.68) and 78F ($35.84), while doubles range from 68F ($31.25) to 103F ($47.33) with a breakfast buffet included.

Hôtel Villereuse, 23 avenue Servan, in Ouchy (tel. 26-31-91), is a small hotel run by the Strub family. Its furnishings are simple, and the format is unpretentiously satisfactory, perfectly adequate if you're on a budget. Madame Strub maintains her hotel in good working order, and is a correct and fair landlady eager to communicate if you speak a little French. Singles range from 40F ($18.38) to 74F ($34), while doubles cost between 60F ($27.57) and 95F ($43.65), including breakfast.

WHERE TO DINE: The range of restaurants in Lausanne is large, from typical Swiss places in the old town to attractive little inns on the outskirts, which are always my favorite spots, especially if they open onto Lac Léman. Many Vaudois and Swiss specialties are offered, but you also get a selection of French, Greek, Italian, and Chinese eateries as well.

If you see the Geneva lake fish omble chevalier on the menu, please order it. Trout and perch from the lake are also popular, and in autumn many restaurants feature game dishes.

The Upper Bracket

Restaurant Wellingtonia, Hôtel Beau-Rivage, Place du Général Guisan, in Ouchy (tel. 26-38-31). The decor of this restaurant and the hotel which houses it are in a quintessentially elegant setting. Before or after dinner you should see the rest of the hotel. In the meantime, while at the restaurant you can enjoy such specialties as whole sole with goose liver, lobster with whisky and cream sauce, sea bass with fennel, guinea fowl with goose liver and truffles, lobster salad with red beans and truffles, lamb cutlets in a sabayon made with very old Bordeaux, and roast rack of lamb with a sauce made with green peppercorns, followed by a selection of homemade sorbets. Several chefs are employed on a changing basis here, so it's hard to give top billing to just one. However, the food is consistently sophisticated, the service very efficient. The restaurant is open every day but Monday from 6:30 p.m. to 1 a.m. It's closed from mid-July to mid-August. Fixed-price meals range from 83F ($38.14) to 97F ($44.57), while à la carte dinners cost from 60F ($27.57).

Girardet, 1 rue d'Yverdon, Hôtel de Ville, at Crissier, near Lausanne (tel. 34-15-14). There are some who say that Fredy Girardet is the world's greatest chef. Certainly he's on every serious gourmet's gastronomic tour of Europe. This is a friendly, well-decorated restaurant, in the Crissier town hall, where daily shipments of fresh fish contribute to a menu which uses only the best possible ingredients. The restaurant, on the outskirts of Lausanne, attracts many devotees from Geneva, 38 miles away.

Chef Girardet, along with a brigade of talented assistants, prepares a delectable assortment of food which, at times, can be deceptively simple. He once told reporters that he's been known to copy some recipes from his grandmother's favorite collection. However, in the main he is greatly inspired by such famous French chefs as the Troisgros brothers, Roger Vergé, and Paul Bocuse. Monsieur Girardet, of course, is a devotee of nouvelle cuisine.

Some of his specialties (and they change all the time) include a ragoût of fresh quail with young vegetables, baby veal in lemon sauce, crayfish in caviar butter, and many seasonally adjusted dishes. Reservations are essential, and often need to be made weeks in advance. Fixed-price menus cost from 115F ($52.84), while à la carte dinners range from 110F ($50.55) to 150F ($68.93).

The restaurant is open from noon to 2 p.m. and 7 p.m. to midnight. It's closed on Sunday and Monday and for three weeks sometime in July and August and for another three weeks sometime in December and January. Surprisingly, Monsieur Girardet takes no credit cards, but then again, he doesn't have to.

Restaurant du Lac, 70 route de Lausanne, at Morgues (tel. 71-63-71), is housed in a pretty building on the quays at the edge of the lake, only 11 kilometers from Lausanne. Many residents of the bigger city make weekend excursions here to taste the unusual food prepared by one of the area's most respected kitchens. Specialties include a salad of baby lettuce with goose liver in nut oil, roast hen with a rhubarb compote, crayfish with asparagus tips in puff pastry, lobster ragoût, and an assortment of very fresh food which is adjusted seasonally, depending on what's available in the market. The cookery is very nouvelle cuisine. On warm days you'll enjoy the outdoor terrace with a view of the greenery around the lake. The restaurant is closed approximately from Christmas until the last week of January. Fixed-price meals range from 35F ($16.08) to 90F ($41.36), while à la carte dinners cost from 40F ($18.38).

Maison de Ville (tel. 87-10-07), at Grancy, is in an old farmhouse in the center of this suburb, about 15 kilometers from the center of Lausanne. The owners, Danielle Gilliéron and Florian Bürki, request that clients phone ahead for a table. They offer a delectable selection of such specialties as goose liver salad with a honey sauce, a delicate vegetable terrine, and an assorted fish plate with fennel cream sauce and young vegetables, plus roast goose in a red wine sauce with marrow. Dessert is selected from a wide and terribly fattening array. The restaurant is closed on Monday and Tuesday and for the first two weeks in January (sometimes also in the beginning of September). Fixed-price meals range from 75F ($34.46) to 95F ($43.65), while à la carte dinners cost from 50F ($22.98). Hours are from noon for lunch and from 7 p.m. for dinner.

Restaurant Mont d'Or, 1 Ch. Contigny (tel. 26-74-60), is an attractive restaurant with a growing clientele which was established by Jean-Charles Lenoir and Georges Beytrison. They do everything they can to produce a delectable array of specialties that are rich in protein and low in fat, and their cuisine is deliciously light and well flavored. Specialties include baby veal with morels in puff pastry, trout soufflé in tomato sauce, lobster salad with endive, crayfish omelet, filet of cold red snapper with baby vegetables, suprême of omble chevalier (a fish found only in Lac Léman), escalope of duck liver and apples, and a sauté of boeuf moutardier with créole rice. There's also a rich dessert selection and some very good cheese too. The restaurant is closed on Sunday, but open from 7 a.m. to midnight otherwise. A daily fixed-price luncheon menu costs a very modest 12F ($5.51), while gastronomic lunch and evening menus range from 55F ($25.27) to 65F ($29.87). À la carte dinners go from 30F ($13.79) to 65F ($29.87).

La Grappe d'Or, 3 rue Chenin de Bourg (tel. 23-07-60), is a well-decorated rôtisserie in the old city, with a luxurious decor and excellent food that attracts a well-heeled crowd of locals. Specialties include duck skewered on a brochette with orange sauce, a gratin of lobster, and seasonal produce. A lunchtime plat du jour is offered for 25F ($11.49), and this varies according to the day of the week. On Wednesday, for example, it might be pot-au-feu, or a petite marmite de poissons on Friday. Try, if featured, the medallion of sea bass or lobster in butter sauce, roast pheasant (or roebuck), or the filet of lamb with watercress. This is a Relais de Campagne member, which almost ensures a very high quality. Fixed-price meals, gourmet style, cost around 100F ($45.95), while à la carte dinners range from 37F ($17) to 57F ($26.19).

Budget to Medium-Priced Dining

La Voile d'Or, avenue de Rhodanie, at Lausanne-Vidy (tel. 27-80-11). Driving into this lakeside park evokes a scene from the French Riviera. You'll need to park your car and follow the signs on foot for a few hundred feet over lawns and through conifers before arriving at the lakeside terrace of this popular restaurant. The place is especially full on summertime weekends, when almost everyone in town seemingly comes here for a beer or glass of wine. After 9 p.m. there's dancing on the terrace. The entire establishment overlooks a marina. You can choose to eat inside or else out on the terrace. A fixed-price menu costs between 32F ($14.70) and 38F ($17.46). Specialties include scallops with mushrooms and saffron, kidneys in shallot butter, entrecôte bordelaise, and filets of perch from the lake. Wild game is featured in season. The restaurant is closed on Monday in winter and during all of January. Otherwise it's open from 9:30 a.m. to 1 a.m., although it doesn't serve warm food during all those hours.

Buffet de la Gare CFF, Place de la Gare (tel. 20-78-01), is a vast and homey place, consisting of both a low-cost brasserie, offering set meals from 9.50F ($4.37), to 11F ($5.06). I much prefer the restaurant, where you can order a table d'hôte from 15F ($6.89) to 22F ($10.11), as well as more expensive à la carte selections. You're likely to see large groups of friends dining here. There are lots of seating platforms and cubbyholes at this main railway station terminal. The chefs prepare a large choice of dishes, including vol-au-vent toulousaine, filets of sole "Uncle Charles," poached turbot in a hollandaise sauce, and mignons of pork in a cream sauce. The buffet is open daily from 5 a.m. to midnight.

Le Guet, 5 Escaliers du Marché (tel. 23-87-42), bills itself as a literary café, and if you know anything about the local artistic scene you might recognize an actor or writer from Lausanne. This establishment sits beside the famous wooden staircase leading to the belvedere of the cathedral, and might be the perfect place to eat at after seeing that part of town. The interior is a two-level collection of wooden chairs and tables, heavily beamed ceilings, stucco walls with stone detailing, and an inviting black-surfaced bar area. À la carte meals cost from 30F ($13.79), including a tempting array of local specialties: steak with mushrooms, croûte au fromage, two kinds of fondue, plus an elaborate 60F ($27.57) table d'hôte. A menu of the day costs a modest 12F ($5.51).

Café du Jorat, 1 Place de l'Ours (tel. 20-22-61), is at a busy traffic corner in a building with a trendy format of recipes such as "raclette à go-go." It's very much a local hangout in an obscure part of the city, but it's well known and respected locally for its regional cuisine. Only the adventurous diner, however, will try one of the kitchen's specialties, steak de cheval (horsemeat filet). There's a butcher shop nearby selling only horsemeat, which is highly esteemed by gourmets in the area. If you're not so adventurous, you might prefer instead the steak (that's beef) tartar, scampi flavored with anisette (a delectable combination), and tripes in tomato sauce. The chefs also prepare three kinds of fondue (au vacherin, maison, and bourguignonne). Fixed-price meals range from 30F ($13.79) to 50F ($22.98).

Il Grottino, 4 Grand-Chêne (tel. 22-76-58), is a sympathetic pizzeria open every evening until 11. However, the adjacent bar, l'Escalier, stays open until midnight. Pizzas range from 6.50F ($2.99) to 9F ($4.14), while a wide assortment of pastas cost only a little more. No one will mind if you order only a pizza and a beer. However, if you're in the mood and hungry enough, you can ask for a well-prepared meal of veal, fish, or beef, each dish costing from 19F ($8.73). The dessert menu includes divinely caloric ice cream as well as fruit dishes. The pizzeria closes at 3 p.m. on Saturday and remains closed on Sunday as well.

À la Pomme de Pin, 13 Cité Derrière (tel. 22-97-65), is in one of the most charming parts of Lausanne, on a cobblestone street in the antique district. The restaurant lies on the first floor of an early 19th-century building with shutters. This is one of my favorite little hidden-away restaurants, perched near the cathedral in the old city. Typical menu items include a wide variety of fish whose appearance is determined by their availability in the market that day. You might also prefer the chicken with morels, duck liver, sausages with leeks, and a wide variety of local dishes. Fixed-price menus range from a reasonable 30F ($13.79) to a gargantuan repast at 70F ($32.17). Hours are from 7 a.m. to midnight (however, it opens at 5 p.m. on weekends).

Restaurant Chez Pitch, 1 Chemin des Bains, at Pully-Lausanne (tel. 28-27-43), is a lakeshore restaurant near the harbor of Pully, a five-minute drive from the center of Lausanne, depending on traffic. Monsieur and Madame Gérald Ischi are the owners, serving well-prepared specialties including fera, a kind of mackerel found in the lake. They also do other fish from the lake as well, including perch, char, trout, and a salmon-trout. In addition to that, they feature excellent beef and veal plates, along with air-dried meats from the Grisons. Their selection of homemade desserts is outstanding. Count on spending from 35F ($16.08) for a meal here. The kitchen is open until 9:30 p.m., but the restaurant is closed on Tuesday and on Wednesday morning. It also shuts down in December and January.

Pinte Besson, 4 rue d'Ale (tel. 22-72-27). This entire establishment measures only about 20 by 40 feet. Half of the place is covered by a smoke-stained vault of hand-chiseled masonry, which looks as if it hasn't been touched in two centuries (it's been around since 1780). A varied collection of locals (some rather tough critters) sit shoulder to shoulder on the benches, drinking wine. You can see into part of the tiny kitchen. A glass of wine begins at 1.80F (83¢) and is also sold in carafes. The establishment is celebrated in Lausanne for its fondues. It also serves croûtes au fromage, sausages, small entrecôtes, and a steak garni. Most main courses cost around 11F ($5.06); however, a fondue for two persons with two glasses of wine will run about 28F ($12.87). The place, with sidewalk tables out front in summer, is closed on Sunday but open otherwise until midnight.

Churrasco, 51 rue de Bourg (tel. 23-14-23), is part of the Argentine steakhouse chain that has swept over all the major Swiss cities. The decor is South American and rustic, and waiters are dressed as "Saturday night gauchos." The people of Lausanne come here when they're in a festive mood, escaping their own traditions for a night on the pampas. Meals range from 30F ($13.79) and up, and include the mandatory sangría, gazpacho, as well as beefsteak grilled on a wood fire (comes in both medium and large sizes). You can select rumpsteak, entrecôte, or filet. For dessert, it's the tequila sherbet, of course.

WHAT TO SEE: The **Cathedral of Notre Dame,** focal point of the Cité, stands 500 feet above the lake, one of the finest churches in Switzerland from the Middle Ages. Begun in 1175 and consecrated in 1275, it's considered one of the most beautiful Gothic structures in the country. When Pope Gregory X came to Lausanne to consecrate the cathedral, he also crowned Rudolph of Habsburg emperor of Germany and of the Holy Roman Empire.

The doors and facade of the cathedral are luxuriantly ornamented with sculptures and bas-reliefs. The interior is relatively austere except for some

13th-century choir stalls. The beautiful rose window is from the 13th century. The cathedral is surmounted by five towers. One you can visit for a 1F (46¢) admission if you don't mind a climb up more than 230 steps. Once there, you'll be rewarded with a view of the town, the lake, and the Alps in the distance.

Viollet-le-Duc began a restoration of the cathedral in the 19th century, and it's still going on! Hours are April 1 until the end of September from 7 a.m. to 6 p.m. (till 5 p.m. in winter). On Saturday, the cathedral is open from 8 a.m. to 6 p.m. (till 5 p.m. in winter). The cathedral cannot be visited on Sunday morning because of services, but it opens in the afternoon from 2 to 6 p.m. (till 5 p.m. in winter).

The **Ancien-Evêché,** formerly the bishop's palace, at least until the beginning of the 15th century, has a 13th-century fortified tower and contains the Cathedral Museum at 2 place de la Cathédrale (tel. 22-13-68), along with a historical and iconographic collection of Old Lausanne. The latter is open in summer daily from 10 a.m. to noon and 2 to 6 p.m. except on Monday (in July and August from 10 a.m. to 6 p.m.). In winter it's open Tuesday to Friday from 2 to 5 p.m. (weekends from 10 a.m. to noon and 2 to 5 p.m.). On Thursday it's also open from 8 to 10 p.m. Admission is free. Keeping the same hours, the Cathedral Museum features a presentation of the history of the cathedral, with sculptured and painted decorations and some old stained-glass windows.

From the cathedral, head north to the end of the Cité for a visit to the **Château St-Maire,** from 1397. Built of brick and stone, it was constructed in the 14th and early 15th centuries, and was also a residence of the powerful bishops, until they were replaced by the Bernese bailiffs, who turned Lausanne into a virtual colony. It's now used for administrative offices of the canton. However, it can still be visited Monday to Friday from 8 to 11 a.m. and 2 to 5 p.m., charging no admission. It's closed on Wednesday and Friday.

In the center of town is the **Place de la Palud,** which lies to the south of the Place de la Riponne. Completely restored in the late 1970s, the **Hôtel de Ville** (town hall), from the 17th century with a Renaissance facade, sits on this square. It's the headquarters of the Communal Council, and can be visited on a guided tour daily Monday to Friday at 3 p.m. and again at 3:30 p.m. On the square is a Fountain of Justice from 1726. A clock with animated historical scenes acts out a drama every hour from 9 a.m. to 7 p.m. A traditional market is held in this square and along the side streets every Wednesday and Saturday.

From the square, the **Escaliers du Marché,** a covered flight of stairs from the Middle Ages, can be scaled if you care to visit the cathedral at this point.

The **Palais de Rumine,** on the Place de la Riponne, houses several museums, along with the university and cantonal library (with some 700,000 volumes) and the university itself, which was originally founded as an academy in 1537. The palace was built in 1906 in an Italianate style.

Chief of the city's museums is the **Musée Cantonal des Beaux-Arts** (cantonal museum of fine arts), 6 Place de la Riponne (tel. 22-83-32). This museum is largely devoted to the works of 19th-century artists who painted in western Switzerland. But it also has an impressive collection of many famous artists of the French school, including Degas, Renoir, Bonnard, Matisse, and Utrillo. Temporary exhibitions are also staged here in summer, usually costing from 2.50F ($1.15) to 3.50F ($1.61). It's open daily from 10 a.m. to noon and 2 to 5 p.m. (on Thursday evening until 8 p.m.); closed on Monday.

Other museums in this complex include the Geological Museum, the Museum of Palaeontology, the Archeological and Historical Museum, and the Zoological Museum.

On the east side of town, **Mon Repos Park** is filled with landscaped gardens and the Empire Villa where Voltaire performed *Zaïre* to an audience of friends. In the northern sector of the park stands the **Tribunal Fédéral,** constructed in the 1920s, which is today the supreme court of Switzerland.

The **Signal de Sauvabelin** (or *le signal,* as it's called), rises above the town to the north, a good 20-minute hike if you're fit. At 2125 feet, it has a restaurant and a belvedere, opening onto Lake Geneva with the Fribourg Alps in the background.

On the northwest side of town, beyond the avenue Bergières, the **Château de Beaulieu** dates from 1756. In the west wing of this castle the **Musée de l'Art Brut** (museum of the maladjusted) has been installed. A fascinating, curious mélange of art, it was collected by the famous painter Jean Dubuffet, and presented to the city. All the art, both painting and sculpture, is the work of prisoners, the mentally ill, or the criminally insane! The museum is open daily from 2 to 6 p.m., except Monday, charging an admission of 3F ($1.38).

As mentioned, **Ouchy** is the lakeside resort and bustling port city for Lausanne. Its tree-shaded quays with flower gardens stretch for almost a mile, and its small harbor contains a marina with berths for about 700 craft. As you walk along, you'll see the Savoy Alps on the opposite shore.

In the Château d'Ouchy, now a hotel and restaurant, a peace treaty was signed in 1923 among the Allies, Greece, and Turkey. The 13th-century keep of the hotel is still standing. In the Hôtel d'Angleterre (formerly the Auberge de l'Ancre) there's a plaque commemorating the stay of Lord Byron, who wrote *Prisoner of Chillon* there. In the Beau-Rivage, the Treaty of Lausanne was ratified in 1932, at the end of the conference to settle the final reparations disputes growing out of World War I.

At **Pully,** a Roman villa, the first vestiges of which were discovered in 1921, has been restored and opened to the public. It boasts a double apse and a fresco of 215 square feet, which is the most important first-century mural north of the Alps.

This **Pully Roman Villa Museum** is at Place du Prieuré (tel. 28-33-04). It shows a reconstruction of the ruins and a display of objects found on the site of the excavations. Admission free, it's open from the end of October until April 1 on Saturday and Sunday from 2 to 5 p.m. However, during the rest of the year it can be visited daily (except Monday) from 2 to 5 p.m.

A short distance north of Lausanne, you can visit the elegantly furnished **Château of Lucens** (tel. 021/95-80-32), on a hill fortified by the bishops of Lausanne in the Middle Ages to protect their town of Moudon and maintain a barrier across the valley of the little Broye River. The fortress has undergone trouble and change since it was established—destroyed in 1127, rebuilt, burned in 1190, enlarged to be the summer palace of the bishops, occupied by the Bernese, made the seat of the bailiffs of Moudon, finally becoming the property of the canton of Vaud which sold it to a private owner in 1801. By the end of the 19th century it was a boys' college and its interior architecture had been vastly changed. However, new work begun in 1921 has restored the château to its original appearance.

The present owner, Galerie Koller, an important European auction house, has decorated it with paintings, furniture, clocks, and objets d'art which are, of course, for sale but are replaced with objects of similar quality as they are purchased. Of special interest, but with no particular link to the château that I could discover, is an old Sherlock Holmes museum in one of the vaulted cellars, billed as an exact replica of the sitting room of the famous detective. Perhaps Holmes came here on a search for Moriarty!

The château is open to visitors from 10 a.m. to 6 p.m. April 1 to October 30, to 5 p.m. November 1 to December 15 and March 1 to March 30. Admission is 4.40F ($2.02) for adults, 2.20F ($1.01) for children and students.

SHOPPING: Lausanne is an interesting shopping adventure. Many first-class stores are found along the rue St-François and the rue de Bourg. In the center of town, several squares and shopping streets are earmarked for pedestrians only. Best buys are watches and jewelry, clothes, leather goods, cigarettes, and the traditional Swiss souvenirs and chocolates.

Pharmacie Bullet, 30 rue de Bourg (tel. 22-86-82), is a centrally located pharmacy which is happy to suggest over-the-counter Swiss substitutes for American medications.

Pavillon Christofle, 10 rue de Bourg (tel. 20-60-50), serves as the only distributor of Christofle crystal in the Lausanne region. Open weekdays and Saturday, the place is a showroom of glass shelves loaded with glittering objects.

Boutique Danoise, 47-49 rue de Bourg (tel. 22-01-13), is one of the best stores in Lausanne, selling an interesting variety of modern furniture, crystal, leather, and art, most of which comes from Denmark. The friendly staff speaks English.

Tabacs-Cigares Besson, 22 rue de Bourg (tel. 22-67-88), is one of the leading tobacco shops of Lausanne. The owner has a special climate-controlled room for the storage of his best cigars, many of which come from Cuba. Other merchandise includes Davidoff cigars, meerschaum pipes, and all sorts of tobacco. Alexander Senn and his attractive staff will mail certain goods back to North America for a small fee.

La Vieille Fontaine Antiquités, 9-13 Cheneau de Bourg (tel. 23-47-87), sells French 18th-century furniture, Oriental sculpture, and paintings in a building with beautifully hand-painted beams and Oriental rugs. The showrooms are comfortably crowded, so be very careful as you walk between these treasures. Ewald Oesch is the owner.

Magasin Cardas, 10 rue de Bourg (tel. 22-55-60), is an unusual store with a physical plant of skylights and crosscut tree trunks set into a white gravel floor. The establishment sells goods from 15 countries, many of them Oriental, which include ceramics, sculpture, and textiles. Before or after inspecting this shop you might stop for a coffee in the courtyard in front. There a café, **La Cour** (10 rue de Bourg), has set up three or four outdoor tables beside a modern fountain.

Lagenthal, 8 rue de Bourg (tel. 23-44-02), is directed by Mme Morard who, along with her friendly staff, sells Swiss embroideries, table linens, napkins, and crocheted potholders, as well as silk sheets.

Au Grand Maure, 12 Cité Derrière (tel. 22-05-41), is a cluttered shop on a street with many other antique stores, each selling the kind of art object difficult to find elsewhere. Ariane and Gabriel Schmid receive clients with a friendly dachshund who shyly greets visitors. They are usually open every afternoon except Sunday.

La Mirondela, 3 Ancienne Douane (tel. 22-41-59). The gracious owner, Madame Solana, speaks very little English, but is nonetheless helpful about indicating the prices of her various antiques and art objects. Many of them are reasonable in price, including a range of English and Dutch pieces as well as Swiss. The shop is not very large, and is somewhat of a walk outside the old city, but might serve as an attractive destination in an unexplored section of town.

LAUSANNE AFTER DARK: Lausanne ranks with Geneva as the focal point of intellectual life in French-speaking Switzerland. This is reflected in a rich cultural tradition.

The cultural life of the city is a four-season affair. Orchestras, famous soloists, theater, and ballet troupes from all over the world perform here. The tourist board will be helpful in giving you information on what's currently available.

In the spring an international festival brings together the world's musical elite in dance and opera; and in late June during the city festival and the Fête of Lausanne, the streets are jampacked and alive with modern troubadours who entertain free.

One of the most prestigious places for concerts, operas, and ballet is the **Beaulieu Théâtre,** 11 avenue des Bergières (tel. 21-32-11).

Likewise, the **Municipal Théâtre,** 12 avenue du Théâtre (tel. 22-64-33), also has an equally distinguished program of concert, ballets, and both classical and contemporary plays.

If you can speak French, the **Les Faux-Nez** theater, 5 rue de Bourg (tel. 22-31-72), is a boîte of chansons, with an occasional daring production.

If you want your action a little "hotter," try one of the following establishments:

The Taverne at the **Château d'Ouchy,** Place du Port, at Ouchy (tel. 26-74-51), is in one of the inner rooms of this famous hotel (see the hotel recommendations). You'll be able to see the lake from the stone-rimmed windows here, with a view of the people in the café below. The large wood-paneled room has an arched ceiling with festively parallel lines of red and blue lights. Someone has painted wall murals of the masked courtiers of Mozart's day on the dusky walls. The establishment draws an older crowd who like to come here to drink and dance to the music. The tavern opens at 9:30 p.m., and drinks average between 14F ($6.43) and 20F ($9.19).

Funny Hell, 2 Place de la Gare (tel. 20-15-51), is a disco bar with an offbeat clientele in the Hotel Continental, across from the railway station. Guests must be more than 18. The club is open daily except Tuesday from 9:30 p.m. A grinning effigy of a lighthearted hobgoblin greets you near the door, where the cover charge is 5F ($2.30) and beer costs from 12F ($5.51).

Le Paddock, Hotel Victoria, 46 avenue de la Gare (tel. 20-57-75), is a popular disco set in a framework of mirrors. An accessible DJ most often plays what you want. The management collects a 5F ($2.30) cover charge on weekends, and drinks begin at 11F ($5.06). The club is open daily except Monday from 9:30 p.m. to 4 a.m.

Tabaris Night Center, 12 bis Place St-François (tel. 22-09-33), is the not-too-elite gathering place of those who like a little erotic action. The setting is one of plush red velvet, bordello style, and gray banquettes. There's no cover charge on weekdays. A drink or a beer costs from 12F ($5.51) in the disco section, while in the adjoining cabaret they go for 15F ($6.89) and up. The cabaret has what is billed as both erotic and "semi-erotic" acts. Once you enter the front door, you can walk freely from one section to the other. The disco is open from 9:30 p.m. to 3:30 a.m., while the cabaret will entertain you from 10 p.m. to 4 a.m. daily except Sunday.

PRACTICAL FACTS: Lausanne doesn't have an airport. Most visitors fly to Cointrin at Geneva, then take a direct bus to Ouchy on the lake, the trip lasting about an hour. A train also runs from Geneva to Lausanne. In Lausanne, the office of the **Swiss Federal Railways (CFF)** is at 43 avenue de la Gare (tel. 42-11-11). Bicycles can also be hired here at the railway station at the baggage forwarding counter (tel. 42-21-62). There's also an office of the Lausanne Tourist Board in the main hall of the station (tel. 23-19-35).

However, the major **Lausanne Tourist Office** is at 60 avenue d'Ouchy (tel. 27-73-21). It's open daily from 8 a.m. to 7 p.m. from the first of June until the end of September. After that it's open from 8 a.m. to 6 p.m.

The offices of **American Express** are at 14 avenue Mon Repos (tel. 20-74-25).

Lausanne has a good **transportation** network, a funicular connecting the upper town with the railway station and the port of Ouchy down below. The **tram or bus** fare is 1.20F (56¢) regardless of the distance for a single trip completed within 60 minutes. Books of nine tickets sell for 10F ($4.60). Short trips of only one or two sections cost only .70F (33¢), and books of 11 tickets valid for these short runs cost 7F ($3.22). You buy or stamp your ticket at slot machines installed at most transport stops. A one-day season ticket is only 3.50F ($1.61), or you can have three consecutive days for 8F ($3.68).

The **underground or métro** offers rapid service: for example, six minutes between the heart of the old town to Ouchy on the lake. Departures are every 7½ minutes from 6:15 a.m. to 11:45 p.m. A ticket from the old town to Ouchy costs only .90F (47¢). There's also a shuttle service between the town center and the railway station, departing every day but Sunday from 6:30 a.m. to 8:30 p.m., costing only .50F (23¢).

For **lost property,** go to the office at 6 rue Saint-Laurent (tel. 20-70-64) weekdays from 7:30 a.m. to 11:45 a.m. and 1 to 5 p.m. (on Saturday, from 7:30 to 11:30 a.m. only).

For night and day **medical service,** including **dental care,** telephone the doctor's exchange at 32-99-32.

There are various branches of the **post office** throughout Lausanne, but the main office is at 15 Place St-François (tel. 40-38-30). It's open Monday to Friday from 7:30 a.m. to 6:30 p.m. (on Saturday, to 11 a.m. only). Telegrams can be sent at the post office (tel. 40-24-16), as can a Telex (tel. 40-24-16).

Drugstores are always open in Lausanne. A poster prominently displayed in all pharmacies indicates those that are on duty, and the local newspapers run lists of them.

The best way to get acquainted with the city is to take the **Lausanne City Tour,** with a drive through surrounding vineyards. It leaves every morning except Sunday. You'll get an overall picture and will go through the old town and later to the wine district. The tour costs 15F ($6.89) for adults and 10F ($4.60) for children.

SPORTS: As the seat of the International Olympic Committee, Lausanne has many first-rate sports facilities, and the lake itself offers not only swimming, but rowing, yachting, waterskiing, and windsurfing. You can also play tennis or golf, ride a bike, go horseback riding, or hiking.

Even in summer you can ski on the glacier of Les Diablerets (9840 feet), 38 miles from Lausanne. In winter, five covered curling rinks are active, along with two ice-skating rinks.

Winter skating: The Montchoisi Indoor Skating Rink, 30 avenue du Servan (tel. 26-10-62), is open from mid-September until the beginning of March. La Pontaise, 11 Plaines-du-Loup (tel. 36-81-63), is an open-air skating rink.

Winter curling: Ouchy Curling Link, La Nautique building, at Ouchy (tel. 27-60-31), has five playing areas active from mid-September until the end of March.

Winter tennis: This can be played at the Lausanne Tennis Association at Vidy (tel. 26-38-00), where you'll find six covered courts.

Winter swimming: This is possible at the Mon Repos indoor swimming pool, 4 avenue du Tribunal-Fédéral (tel. 23-45-66).

From spring on, **golf** is played at En Marin (tel. 91-63-18), which has an 18-hole course above Lausanne. The course, open until November, is at an altitude of 2800 feet.

Summer swimming: Bellerive Beach and its swimming pool are at 23 avenue de Rhodanie (tel. 27-81-31), and is open May to September. You'll find one Olympic-size pool and two smaller ones. There's also a public beach at Vidy, La Voile-d'Or, belonging to the restaurant (tel. 27-80-11), which is admission free. In Pully, the Municipal Swimming Pool is at the beach (tel. 28-33-20), and is open from May to September. It has both an Olympic-size pool and a pool for children.

Waterskiing: There's a stretch of water at the Ouchy promenade (near the Tour Haldimand), which attracts skiers in fair weather (tel. 26-99-11 for information).

Windsurfing: This increasingly popular sport is centered at the Bellerive Beach Windsurfing School, 47 avenue de la Harpe (tel. 27-55-22). Lessons are in English.

Tennis: From mid-April to mid-August, four covered courts are in use at 30 avenue du Servan, which is open daily from 7 a.m. to 10 p.m. (tel. 26-10-62 for more information).

Horseback riding: This sport is possible at the Chalet-à-Globet Equestrian Centre (tel. 91-64-34), which has a jumping paddock among other facilities.

2. From Lausanne to Nyon

This trip, heading west from Lausanne along the northern arch of Lac Léman, is a distance of less than 30 miles, but there's much to see along the way. You can do it in two hours, but you'll enjoy it more if you allow at least half a day.

West from Lausanne, I suggest that you detour to St. Sulpice, four miles away.

ST. SULPICE: This is an exclusive residential suburb of summer homes usually visited by those wishing to see its 12th-century Romanesque convent church. Within sight of the Savoy Alpine range and Lac Léman, the church retains its original transept and chancel. It's crowned by a cross resting on a rectangular tower. The interior is rather austere.

Back on the road again, the next stopover is in—

MORGES: With the Savoy Alps as a backdrop, Morges is a small town that's a significant headquarters for vineyards in the area. Right on the shore of the lake, the port was built on a prehistoric site inhabited by lake-dwellers. A chic international yachting set gathers here.

The **Vaud Military Museum** has been installed in the Castle of Morges, a Savoyan stronghold that was once a moated castle built by Duke Amadeus of Savoy in 1283. He wanted an imposing bastion to protect himself against the bishopric of Lausanne. In time it became the residence of a Bernese bailiff (whoever was in power at the time), from 1536 to 1798, eventually passing to the canton of Vaud which used it as an arsenal. Weapons and uniforms on display go back to the end of the 18th century and forward to modern times. It's open from the end of January until mid-December, Monday to Friday from

10 a.m. to noon and 1:30 to 5 p.m. (on weekends and holidays from 1:30 to 5 p.m. only), charging an admission of 2.50F ($1.15).

Much more interesting than the military museum is the **Alexis Forel Museum,** in Blanchenay, an old patrician house which once belonged to this engraver. It's at 54 Grand' Rue, and guided tours are conducted 2:30 to 4 p.m. (again on Thursday at 8 p.m.) for a 4F ($1.84) admission. It's closed on Sunday and Monday and on Friday in the off-season. Many of the antiques he collected date back to the 15th century, and the salons are richly decorated, with not only tapestries, paintings, and porcelain, but with some of his very special engravings. The glassware is particularly stunning.

On the last weekend in September, a riotious wine festival is staged here annually.

Continuing west for eight miles will lead to—

ROLLE: This is the center of a wine-growing district between Morges and Coppet known at La Côte. Light white wines are grown here, and apparently the yield is small because nearly all of the vintage is consumed locally.

Rolle's main street is flanked by old burghers' homes and some vintners' houses. The castle with four towers is from the 13th century, originally constructed by a prince of Savoy. At one time the castle was owned by Jean Baptiste Tavernier (1605–1689), the French traveler who was a pioneer of trade with India. His narratives on world travel have earned him a place in history.

From Rolle, you can head up in the hills to **Aubonne,** passing many little wine-growing villages such as Féchy. Aubonne is a 16th-century village where not much ever happens, and if you're as lucky as I was, you can sometimes purchase bottles of the local wine from a vintner.

Back on the main road, our next target along La Côte is—

NYON: This summer resort along Lac Léman has the by-now-familiar flower-bedecked quays where the little lakeside steamers arrive, letting off passengers and picking up new ones.

Julius Caesar established a Roman station here for his soldiers, who left behind many artifacts which have been excavated. From 1781 to 1813 Nyon became known for its porcelain.

The **Castle of Nyon** is an impressive stronghold from the Middle Ages, dating from the 13th century when it was built by the Counts of Savoy. It was burned to the ground but subsequently rebuilt. Today it's both a prison and a historical museum with many Roman remains which can be visited daily from 9 to 11 a.m. and 2 to 5 p.m. for an admission of 2F (92¢). It's closed on Monday, Sunday morning, and in January. You'll also see porcelain made in Nyon's heyday. From the belvedere there's a great view of the lake and the Alps, with Mont Blanc looming in the background.

Food and Lodging

Hôtel Beau-Rivage, 49 rue de Rive (tel. 61-32-31), is a cozily old-fashioned hotel, sitting right on the quays of the old town. Its floor plan would probably be a perfect square except for the small extension off to one side. Its wrought-iron balconies are usually covered with flowers, which you can peer over for one of the best lakeside views in Nyon. A summertime ambience usually fills the public rooms because of their aquamarine window blinds and the placement of modern paintings in bright colors in prominent places. Each of the accommodations has color TV, radio, mini-bar, and direct-dial phone.

Singles rent for between 90F ($41.36) and 120F ($55.14), while doubles cost from 120F ($55.14) and 170F ($78.12), including breakfast. Private parking is available for another 10F ($4.60) per day.

Hôtel du Clos de Sadex (tel. 61-28-31) is a dignified establishment with gables and a tile roof in its own park on the shores of the lake, one kilometer from the center of Nyon. The hotel is decorated inside with an elaborately crafted staircase, parquet floors, and 19th-century antiques, some of which were part of the original furnishings of this former private residence. You'll find only 18 bedrooms, the majority of which contain private baths. The de Tscharner family, the owners, charge from 60F ($27.57) to 130F ($59.74) in a single and between 90F ($41.36) and 190F ($87.31) in a double, according to the season and the view. Half board is offered for an additional 35F ($16.08) per person daily, and extra bed can be set up in any room for another 35F also.

Le Léman, rue de Rive (tel. 61-22-41), beside the lake, is a seafood restaurant, looking out over a jetty where the very boat that caught that day's specialty might be moored. The establishment is known for its lake fish, which head chef Claude Louboutin knows how to prepare delectably. One form is as a lakefish brochette with white wine and tarragon sauce. Other specialties include trout, sole, and perch. Try also the lobster or fish ragoût, perhaps the filet of sole with artichoke hearts or the trout with fresh mushrooms and walnut oil. Meat courses include veal, goose, beef, and chicken dishes. Fixed-price meals range from 40F ($18.38) to 65F ($29.87), while à la carte dinners could go as high as 75F ($34.46) to 95F ($43.65), the latter a banquet. The restaurant is closed in winter, but open otherwise seven days a week from June to September.

Hostellerie du XVIe Siècle, Place du Marché (tel. 61-24-41), is a pleasant restaurant where you'll at least get a taste of another era, in addition to tasting a fine cuisine emphasizing grilled meats. Beefsteak is usually embellished with four kinds of fresh vegetables. Should you want fish, try the savory fish soup, a good way to begin a meal, or perhaps the Breton-style scampi. You can easily spend 55F ($25.27) here, but it's possible to do it for less. The restaurant shuts down on Sunday.

3. The Lavaux Corniche

Back in Lausanne, we now strike out for an eastward trek along the lake, in a section of hillsides and vineyards known as the "Lavaux Corniche," or Corniche Vaudoise. The first stopover, Pully, with its Roman remains, was already previewed in the section on Lausanne.

Our final goal will be world-famed Vevey, at a distance of 17 miles, and after that, Montreux. Personally I find this section one of the loveliest in the country, and I'm not alone in that judgment. All along the way, you'll have views of the towering peaks looming at the upper end of Lake Geneva.

You'll pass the vintner's village of **Corsier,** with its 12th-century church and Romanesque tower. Charlie Chaplin, who died in 1977, is buried here.

CHEXBRES-CULLY: The road to **Cully,** some five miles east of Lausanne, will give you a fine view of Lac Léman as it takes you to the heart of the wine-growing region of Lavaux which covers the mountain slopes on the northeastern side of Geneva's lake. Cully offers swimming, fishing, and boating in the little bay on which it lies and in the lake.

If you have time, I recommend that you turn right on the Corniche (the cliff road) which will take you through thriving vineyards to the little summer resort of **Chexbres.** The drive alone is worth this short detour, as it offers stunning views. Chexbres, positioned on the Corniche, has been called "the balcony of the lake." From here, you can enjoy a stroll through the nearby vineyards and forests and perhaps a stop at one of the friendly wine cellars to taste the product of the grapevines you've passed by.

Continue along the road to **Dézaley,** which produces the light white wine favored by the Genevese.

Food and Lodging

Auberge du Raisin, Place de l'Hôtel de Ville (tel. 99-21-31), at Cully, offers hearthside dining in a very old house with a warmly rustic decor. This might more appropriately be called a tavern, where no one will mind if you only order a beer after the rush of diners is through. The village, halfway between Montreux and Lausanne, is an attractive stopping point if you're going from one to the other. Specialties include a light-textured selection of such favorites as fish salad, medallions of veal in citrus sauce, salmon with fresh chives, and crayfish or turbot in a tarragon sauce. If you go gourmet crazy, you might spend as much as 70F ($32.17), but it's possible to do it for much less.

Hôtel du Signal (tel. 56-25-25), at Chexbres, is set in 60 acres of parkland, much of it heavily forested and leading down to the lake. The hotel is a sprawling château-like building with several modern additions, including a separate building for the 25-yard indoor swimming pool and well-maintained tennis courts. The contemporary furniture in the public rooms is sometimes complemented with an Oriental rug or a grouping of Victorian furniture. At any point, you're likely to sit in front of a wide glass window giving panoramic views over the gently rolling hills of the Vaud. A French-style restaurant serves very good food for an additional 22F ($10.11) per person daily. Singles rent for between 60F ($27.57) and 95F ($43.65), while doubles cost between 110F ($50.55) and 164F ($75.36).

Hôtel Cécil (tel. 56-12-92), at Chexbres, is a modern chalet-style hotel with an elaborate series of decorative stone posts and lintels with no purpose other than to separate its gardens from the street. On the conifer-dotted lawns you'll find a swimming pool. Bernard Cachin, the owner, charges between 35F ($16.08) and 57F ($26.19) in a single and between 57F ($26.19) and 97F ($44.57) in a double, depending on the season and the plumbing. Rooms are pleasant and comfortable.

4. Vevey

The home of Nestlé chocolate, the resort of Vevey has been popular with English visitors since the 19th century. It still is.

About every 25 years Vevey stages the riotious **Fêtes des Vignerons,** a wine-growers' carnival in honor of Bacchus, the god of wine. The last celebration was in 1977, and hopefully you'll be around for the next one if you missed it.

Vevey lies at the foot of Mount Pèlerin, to which an excursion can be made. The town, dating from Roman times, was built at the mouth of the Veveyse River, and is the center of the Lavaux vineyards. In the Middle Ages it was known as an important trading post on the route from Piedmont in Italy to Burgundy in France. As such, it has long been accustomed to receiving and entertaining visitors.

You might begin your exploration on the **Grand-Place,** a mammoth market plaza fronting Lac Léman. The corn exchange on the north dates from the early 19th century. Jean-Jacques Rousseau lodged at the Auberge de la Clef in 1730, in the vicinity of the Théâtre. As you walk in this area and along the quay you'll have views of the Savoy Alps.

Vevey's antique curiosity is the **Church of St. Martin,** dating from the 12th century and standing on a belvedere overlooking the resort. A large rectangular tower with a quartet of turrets characterizes the church, from which there's a good view of Vevey.

The **Jenisch Museum** is an art gallery with some fine works by Courbet, plus some local modern Swiss-born painters. It's open from the first of May until the end of October from 10 a.m. to noon and 2 to 4 p.m. (5 p.m. on Monday). Otherwise it's open weekdays from 2 to 4 p.m. and on Sunday and holidays from 11 a.m. to noon and 2 to 4 p.m.; closed Monday.

In the château at 45 rue d'Italie, the **Old Vevey Museum** has been installed (tel. 51-07-22). If you missed the Bacchus festival, you'll see many of the costumes worn then displayed here. In addition it exhibits 18th-century antiques and mementos of the vintners. It's open from 10 a.m. to noon and 2 to 5 p.m. (opens at 11 a.m. on Sunday and closed on Monday).

The most important excursion in the area is to the **Pèlerin,** a distance of slightly more than 15 miles. As you ascend, you'll have a panoramic sweep of Lake Geneva, the Savoy Alps, and the valley of the Rhône. You can drive via Corsier or go by funicular via Corseaux.

WHERE TO STAY: **Les Trois Couronnes** (tel. 51-30-05) has such a desirable location in the center of town that even its address is merely "Au Centre." Considered the leading hotel of Vevey, it's housed in a nobly detailed building of white stucco and gray stone at the edge of the lake. The interior lobby has an elegant gallery where visitors can peer over white balustrades to the carpeted lobby three floors below. The redecorated bedrooms still retain much of their 19th-century allure, including some attractive antiques in the more expensive rooms. Singles rent for between 100F ($45.95) and 160F ($73.52), while doubles range from 190F ($87.31) to 310F ($142.49), the latter for suite-like accommodations. All tariffs include breakfast. Half board is available for another 50F ($22.98) per person daily.

Hôtel du Lac, Au Centre (tel. 51-10-41), has for years and years enthralled visitors with its lakeside view. A favorite hotel, especially with the visiting English, it has a swimming pool on its grounds and a gardenside terrace with that incomparable view. It also has an affiliation with the just-recommended Trois Couronnes, but is cheaper. The English-speaking director, Monsieur Ehrensperger, has hired a very competent staff, and the hotel is run efficiently but also in a friendly manner. Many guests prefer a resort holiday here instead of going on to nearby Montreux. Rooms are pleasantly furnished and most comfortable (some, of course, are far superior to others). Singles rent from a low of 50F ($22.98) to a high of 120F ($55.14), the latter price if you demand *that* view from your bedroom window. Likewise, doubles range from a low of 80F ($36.76) to a high of 200F ($91.90), with half board costing another 25F ($11.49) per person daily. In addition to the room with the view, the plumbing and the season also affect the price.

Hôtel Comte, 14 avenue des Alpes (tel. 54-14-41), is a baroque building with two tiers of red-tile gables, two of which are elaborately ornate and a balconied facade of yellow stucco with white trim. A blue awning identifies the elegant ground-floor restaurant, whose entrance is beneath the verdant leaves of a tree-like shrub trained to grow in a sweeping arc over the heads of many visitors. You'll be only a few paces from the lake at this pleasant spot, set in the midst of a well-maintained garden. Bedrooms rent for between 80F ($36.76) and 100F ($45.95) in a single and between 130F ($59.74) and 170F ($78.12) in a double. Half board is offered for another 25F ($11.49) per person daily.

Hôtel Touring et Gare, Place de la Gare (tel. 51-06-47), is an old-fashioned resort-style hotel with red shutters, a mansard roof, semi-baroque gables, and a popular restaurant under an awning on the ground floor. The 30 bedrooms range from 40F ($18.38) to 60F ($27.57) in a single and from 60F ($27.57) to 95F ($43.65) in a double, depending on the season and the plumbing. The rooms are slightly dated, but reasonably comfortable. Half board goes for another 15F ($6.89) per person daily.

Hôtel de Famille, 20 rue des Communaux (tel. 51-39-31), is in the very center of commercial Vevey on a series of busy streets near the railway station. The establishment is a large 19th-century building crafted in the old resort style of exterior symmetry, lots of detailing, and high ceilings. The interior has been drastically remodeled into a format of modern upholstered furniture and vividly geometric wallpaper. If you don't seek historical authenticity in decor, you'll find this a clean and comfortable hotel. A small indoor swimming pool and a rooftop terrace with chaise lounges and card tables are additional benefits. Singles range between 43F ($19.76) and 55F ($25.27), while doubles cost between 39F ($17.92) and 53F ($24.35) per person daily, including breakfast. Children who stay in their parents' room receive discounts of 50% up to age 6 and 30% from age 6 to 12.

WHERE TO DINE: Chez Pierre (Le Raisin), Place du Marché (tel. 51-10-28). The "Pierre" of the title stands for Pierre Béthaz, a former resident of Geneva who has become almost a celebrity in the subculture of European gourmet cooks. He is occasionally credited with helping to popularize nouvelle cuisine before it caught on with the mass appeal it has today. Specialties in his attractive restaurant include homemade goose liver pâté, mussels with saffron rice, rack of lamb provençal, cêpes (flap mushrooms) à la provençale, crabmeat in puff pastry with onion ringlets, and poached salmon. Fixed-price meals range from 50F ($22.98) to 120F ($55.14), while à la carte dinners cost from 100F ($45.95). The restaurant is closed Sunday evening at 4 p.m. in summer and all day Monday.

Taverne du Château, 43 rue d'Italie (tel. 51-12-10). This generously proportioned stucco building probably had a commercial use when it was constructed near the lake in 1681. Because of its hip roof and its size it looks almost like a grange, and even has a large carved beam extending out from above one of the top-floor windows, presumably for pulleying supplies upstairs. You'll identify the place by the wrought-iron and gilt sign above the pavement, representing what looks like two men and a horse fighting with one another. Aldo Ferrari is the owner of this popular place. He prepares such menu items as veal kidneys with artichokes, filet of beef in a morel sauce, carré d'agneau (lamb) with herbs from Provence, roebuck with pears and red wine, and smoked salmon. Dessert might be a soufflé glacé with Grand Marnier. Fixed-price meals begin at 60F ($27.57), climbing to 85F ($39.06), with à la carte dinners costing roughly the same. The restaurant is closed on Sunday evening and all day Monday, but open otherwise from 9 a.m. to midnight.

La Terrasse, 2 rue Chenevières (tel. 54-33-96), is in the center of town, across from the Hôtel du Lac, near the Church of Notre Dame. It offers a flowery terrace for dining, which is covered and heated when the weather requires it. The restaurant serves seven days a week from 8 a.m. to midnight, offering raclette specials every Friday and Saturday night in summer. The regular menu features dishes such as filet of fried perch, sweetbreads, sole with almonds served with fines herbes, and filet of beef with morels. Fixed-price meals range from 23F ($10.57), but you can spend far more, of course.

La Pinte de l'Hôtel de Ville, rue de l'Hôtel de Ville (tel. 52-63-43), has an ambience of puce-colored tablecloths in an unpretentious setting which is informal yet very correct. Service is good either in the main dining room or in the tree-shaded square across the quiet street where the management has set up a collection of café tables. Inside, the walls are covered with wood half-paneling and are bathed in sunlight from the large windows. This friendly place specializes in escargots prepared in different ways, including with mushrooms "from the woods." The fixed-price menu for 23F ($10.57) is likely to include terrine maison, clear oxtail soup, shredded beef with pommes soufflées, tomatoes provençales, a salad, and flan for dessert. The food is not only well prepared, but represents a bargain in expensive Vevey. À la carte meals might cost around 30F ($13.79), and could include entrecôte, prepared four different ways, or game in season. The restaurant is open every day from morning till midnight. In case you're curious, "pinte" is old French for bistro.

Brasserie Feldschlösschen, 45 rue du Simplon (tel. 51-31-67), is a working-person's brasserie on a busy commercial street in downtown Vevey. A 35-foot glass window opens in summertime onto a geranium-filled green area with a fountain. Named after a popular beer, the restaurant is a large, wood-paneled, and efficient place. One end of the room is filled with a large nickel-plated serving area and a large mural of medieval maps of Vevey. Fixed-price meals range from 25F ($11.49) and might include peppersteak, salade niçoise, Indian rice, or two types of spaghetti, along with good hams, sausages, and hors d'oeuvres. The brasserie is open every day.

White Horse Pub, 33 rue du Simplon (tel. 51-02-34), is a popular tavern, with smoky paneling, comfortable Jacobean chairs, pink lampshades, and an amplified radio station playing rock music. The clientele tends to be quite young. Whisky begins at 4.50F ($2.07), and a large local beer—referred to here as "sailor's size"—costs 3.50F ($1.61). Cheeseburgers, french fries, steaks, soups, and ice creams are the only food items, along with a plate of hors d'oeuvres. Snacks begin at 9.50F ($4.67).

5. Montreux

The queen of the Vaud Riviera, Montreux rises like an amphitheater from the shores of Lake Geneva. It's an Edwardian town with a decided French accent. Expatriates since the 19th century have lived here, reporting on its balmy climate which allows Mediterranean-type vegetation to grow. The mountains in the background protect the resort from the winds of winter, and along the shore grow walnut trees, fruit trees, cypresses, magnolias, bay trees, almonds, and even palm trees. Montreux's climate is considered the mildest on the north side of the Alps.

The city has grown and expanded greatly in this century, taking over former villages along the shoreline. One of these is Clarens, which was used by Rousseau as the setting for *La Nouvelle Héloïse.*

In summer the town is overrun with traffic from the Great St. Bernard Tunnel, linking Germany's autobahn with Italy's autostrada. It's also on the main Simplon railway line. Many mountain railways terminate here. The best known is the Montreux Oberland Bahn, taking visitors into the famous ski resorts of the Bernese Oberland.

The year-round resort, built on a curve of the great bay of Lac Léman, is also the setting for various festivals, when it's virtually impossible to get a hotel room without advance reservations.

The best known of these is the **Festival du Jazz** beginning the second Friday in July. Billed as an extravaganza, it lasts 2½ weeks. Everybody from Al Jarreau to Jackson Browne is likely to show up. Tickets begin at 18F ($8.27) for some performances, but could go as high as 75F ($34.46). For more information, write to Festival du Jazz, Case 97, CH-1820.

At the end of summer there's a classical music festival. For information on this, write to **Festival de Musique,** Case 124, CH-1820. There's also the Golden Rose TV Festival in spring, plus a Narcissus Festival in May and June.

Old Montreux is worth exploring with its typical vintage houses and narrow, crooked streets, and, later, a stroll along the promenade by the lake is in order.

EXCURSIONS IN THE ENVIRONS: Everybody seemingly heads to the **Castle of Chillon,** two miles south of Montreux. The most impressive moated castle in Switzerland, Chillon was immortalized by Lord Byron in his *The Prisoner of Chillon.* Its old section is thought to be 1000 years old; however, most of it dates from the 13th century, built under Peter II of Savoy. It's considered one of the best preserved medieval castles of Europe, and was the scene of many trials of so-called sorcerers who were horribly tortured. Its most famous prisoner, the one given literary fame by Byron, was François Bonivard, the prior of St. Victori in Geneva who supported the Reformation. This so angered the Catholic Duke of Savoy that he had him chained in the dungeon from 1530 to 1534 when he was released by the Bernese.

The castle can be visited in July and August, Monday to Saturday from 9 a.m. to 6:30 p.m. (on Sunday to 6 p.m.). April to June and in September it's open from 9 a.m. to noon and 1:30 to 6 p.m. In March and October its hours are from 10 a.m. to noon and 1:30 to 5 p.m. (November to February to 4 p.m.). Admission is 3.50F ($1.61) for adults and 1.50F (69¢) for children.

The **Rochers de Naye** at 6700 feet is one of the most popular tours along Lake Geneva. From Montreux a rail car takes visitors in less than an hour up to Rochers de Naye. The rack railway runs about seven times a day in season, with the last departure at 4:30 p.m. The return is at 5:30 p.m., and a round-trip fare is about 20F ($9.19) per person.

The train ascends the slopes over Lac Léman, passing **Glion,** a little resort on a rocky crag almost suspended between lake and mountains. You come to **Caux** at 3600 feet, lying on a natural balcony overhanging the blue bowl of the lake. Finally, the peak of Rochers de Naye rises high in the Vaudois Alps. In the distance you can see the Savoy Alps, including Mont Blanc and the Jura Alps. At the end is an alpine flower garden, the loftiest in Europe.

Skiing is possible here between December and April. There's a ski lift and a Swiss ski school, plus a hotel.

The little port town of **Villeneuve** also makes for an interesting excursion. At the end of the lake, it was here that Lord Byron wrote *The Prisoner of Chillon* in 1861. The town is used to famous visitors. Romain Rolland lived here, receiving a visit from Mahatma Gandhi. Many artists have painted the charm of the little town and countryside. The famous painter, Kokoschka, chose Villeneuve as his residence. It's within a few minutes' walk of the Castle of Chillon.

WHERE TO STAY: In addition to hotels in Montreux itself, there are also accommodations in Glion and Rochers de Naye.

In Montreux

Le Montreux Palace, 100 Grand-Rue (tel. 63-53-73), has the kind of opulent 19th-century detailing which many travelers look for whenever they're abroad. The salons and bedrooms have been exquisitely renovated in a style more or less conforming to the original plans. These include embellished ceilings, parquet floors, and crystal chandeliers. In one room, an art nouveau stained-glass skylight is set above an arched ceiling with statues of cupids and demigods. On the well-maintained lakefront grounds you'll find a very large, abstractly shaped swimming pool with nine angular sides, as well as a bar and refreshment facility housed under a modern teepee. There are also tennis courts. Everyone in towns knows "The Palace." Its dignified facade sprawls over a large area of yellow awnings and mansard-style embellishments. It even has its own parking garage, which you'll be grateful for in congested Montreux, along with an 18-hole golf course in another part of town. Many of the bedrooms, certainly the best ones, have a lot of style and room. Singles rent from 200F ($91.90), while doubles cost from 300F ($137.85).

Hyatt Continental, 97 Grand-Rue (tel. 63-51-31), is my favorite hotel in Montreux, decorated in a futuristic blend of elegant materials and unusual lighting. Huge vistas from inside the public rooms and the bedrooms face the lake. The decor is at the same time elegant and lighthearted. A piano bar on the ground floor is plushly upholstered in subtle colors, while the musical acts seem to draw residents from around the lake area. The 143 bedrooms have all the conveniences you'd expect in a luxury hotel. Because of the parking problem in Montreux there's an underground garage. Singles rent for between 145F ($66.63) and 175F ($80.41), while doubles range from 175F ($80.41) to 210F ($96.50), depending on the season. There's an indoor pool and sauna, and the lakeside location is on one of the most beautifully maintained promenades along the water.

Hôtel National, 2 Ch. du National (tel. 63-49-11), was built in 1872 to receive the flood of visitors who were beginning to discover Lake Geneva. Designed around two Victorian towers connected by a five-story middle section, it sits slightly above the lake behind dozens of yellow awnings. Its six-sided swimming pool has a Japanese-style walkway built over part of it. The interior has been tastefully renovated and is filled today with furniture, in part reminiscent of the 19th century, along with some modern pieces. Singles rent for between 90F ($41.36) and 140F ($64.33), while doubles cost from 130F ($59.74) to 210F ($96.50).

Eurotel, 81 Grand-Rue (tel. 63-49-51), is a silvery skyscraper of a hotel on the main road to Vevey, with a frontage on the lake. It has most of the facilities you'd expect from such a large hotel, including an indoor swimming pool, a piano bar, a solarium, a sauna, and lake-view balconies, along with predictably modern rooms filled with unoffensive furnishings. There's a covered garage under the building. The establishment is run with a kind of big-city efficiency, and there's usually a room available in any season—and it will be clean and comfortable. Singles cost from 90F ($41.36) to 130F ($59.74), while doubles range from 80F ($36.76) to 105F ($48.25) per person daily, with a buffet breakfast included.

Hôtel Helvétie, 32 avenue du Casino (tel. 63-25-51), is a Victorian resort hotel with an L-shaped floor plan plus a two-storied series of public rooms set into a sheltered corner. A roof garden on the seventh floor has good views of the lake, with waiter service in case you should want a drink. The public rooms are decorated with white-paneled ceilings, Oriental rugs, and a scattering of Jacobean chairs and good reading lamps. A few blocks from the lake, near the Casino, the hotel charges from 45F ($20.68) to 95F ($43.65) in a single and from 105F ($48.25) to 147F ($67.55) in a double. Half board costs an additional 20F ($9.19) per person daily. The hotel is very popular in the summertime when it's usually fully booked.

Hôtel Bon Accueil, 80 Grand-Rue (tell 63-05-51), is a concrete building with red awnings attractively located in a park with views of the lake. The format is contemporary, with extra touches like wood paneling to relieve some of the angular surfaces. Bedrooms are clean and streamlined as well as very comfortable. The best ones benefit from private balconies and views of the lake. Each of the accommodations has a mini-bar, radio, and phone. Singles range from 65F ($29.87) to 95F ($43.65), while doubles cost from 105F ($48.25) to 150F ($68.93).

Pension Villa Victoria (tel. 64-36-11), at Clarens-Montreux, is a rambling Victorian house with a red tile roof and four high-ceilinged stories of comfortable bedrooms. Another building nearby handles the overflow. The Herren family maintains the property, with the assistance of their many small children. If you're coming from the train station in Montreux, take the trolleybus in the direction of Vevey, getting off 2½ kilometers later at the Basset stop. Singles rent for between 35F ($16.08) and 50F ($22.98), while doubles range from 39F ($17.92) to 47F ($21.60) per person, with full board included. Guests are encouraged not to smoke on the premises, and no alcohol is served.

Hôtel Ermitage (tel. 64-44-11), at Clarens-Montreux, is a pleasantly situated family-run hotel with a mansard roof, three floors of comfortable rooms, and a sun terrace covered with an awning. Some of the rooms inside are spacious, opening onto views of the lake. The hotel is very comfortable, and children are welcome (chances are, they'll find plenty of playmates). Rooms range from 50F ($22.98) to 95F ($43.65) in a single and from 105F ($40.25) to 147F ($67.55) in a double.

Hôtel Tilda au Lac, Quai de Vernex (tel. 63-38-14), is a graciously proportioned, old-fashioned, and cluttered villa at the edge of the lake, next door to the Continental Hyatt. What a contrast in lifestyles! It's one of the best of the budget-priced hostelries of Montreux, and it offers beautiful views of the lake, especially from the top floor where, if you get the right chamber, you can sit on your private balcony which was erected in 1907 by the owner of the old Continental Hotel—he wanted to provide housing for his mother. His mother's name was Matilda, hence the name Hotel Tilda. The building is owned by the sensitive and intelligent Miss Brandenburger, who frequently stores the paintings of her many artist friends. She charges from 45F ($20.68) to 50F ($22.98) in a single and from 70F ($32.17) to 105F ($48.25) in a double, including breakfast. None of the rooms has a full bath, but the shared facilities are adequate. There is no private parking; you'll have to use the garage at the Continental, for which you'll be charged.

Staying at Glion

Hôtel Monte-Fleuri, route de Glion (tel. 62-38-87). Set on the side of a forested hill above Montreux, this old-fashioned hotel has spacious and well-appointed public rooms with panoramic views over the lake. Attractive walkways surround the establishment leading in all directions. Comfortably furnished singles rent for between 27F ($12.41) and 72F ($33.08), while doubles cost from 47F ($21.60) to 122F ($56.06), depending on the season, plumbing, and view. Half board is offered for an additional 15F ($6.89) per person daily.

Hotel Victoria (tel. 63-31-31) is the gracious dowager queen of Glion hotels, housed in a white-painted Victorian building with mansard roofs and yellow awnings. It's surrounded by the conifers of the forested hillside leading down to the lake, with an outdoor pool set into the grounds. Many of the high-ceilinged bedrooms are filled with 19th-century furniture, including the kind of armchair the French call "Voltaire." The public rooms are richly decorated with Oriental rugs, oil paintings, and old furniture. The terrace is filled with diners on many summertime weekends, while the warmly lit restaurant and bar area serves very good food. Singles rent for between 85F ($39.06) and 170F ($78.12), while doubles cost from 120F ($55.14) to 210F ($96.50), including breakfast. Half board is offered for another 30F ($13.79) per person daily.

A Perch at Rochers de Naye

Hôtel des Rochers de Naye (tel. 63-65-47) is a solid-looking masonry building set among the desolate upper regions of the peaks around Rochers de Naye. The site could serve as a starting point for some dramatic hillclimbing through the region, but you'd better stick to the easier paths if you're not used to the altitude. Rooms are simply furnished and functional, and usually filled with nature-lovers. Singles cost 35F ($16.08), with doubles renting for 60F ($27.57).

DINING IN AND AROUND MONTREUX: **Le Club**, Place du Debarcadère (tel. 62-04-65). From the street, you'll see what looks like a well-appointed vestibule of an expensive private home. A stairway leads you into a large room with an antique bull's eye mirror, green carpeting, and elegant settees and upholstered chairs. The entire setup looks like a formal living room at an ambassador's headquarters, with elegantly painted pink-and-green marble columns with gilded capitals and Louis XIV chairs. The room is a very good reproduction, and as such represents the best of modern comfort combined with old-style charm. A marble-topped bar against one of the walls provides drinks, which you might enjoy before being ushered into the richly appointed Victorian-style dining room. Amid the maroon velvet wall coverings, you can enjoy a terrine of sweetbreads with a mousseline of vegetables to get you going. You might follow that with an escalope of salmon with a sorrel sabayon or perhaps guina fowl with champagne, or perhaps dorade with fennel. Among the very special dishes to cite are mignons de boeuf with chanterelles and carré d'agneau (lamb) in a mustard sauce. Expect to spend from 55F ($25.27) and up for a meal here.

Le Pont de Brent (tel. 61-52-30), at Brent, is in a renovated town house in a village a short distance from the center of Montreux. Gerald Rabaey is the owner and chef, and it's rumored he can deliciously contain virtually any delicacy within an envelope of puff pastry. The decor is most tasteful. Among the nouvelle cuisine delights are crayfish, mussels with green asparagus (naturally, in puff pastry), warm goose liver with endive, and meerwolk in Pinot Noir. Fixed-price meals range from 6CF ($27.57) to 110F ($50.52), with à la carte dinners costing from 90F ($41.36). The restaurant is closed Sunday evening and all day Monday.

La Vieille Ferme (tel. 64-64-65), at Montreux-Chailly, is set in the country in a rustic stone house which has regional music playing almost every night of the week except Monday when it's closed (it is also closed from mid-January to mid-February). You'll leave Montreux for the village of Chailly, a few kilometers away. The owner, Monsieur Mabillard, welcomes you with his specialties which include ham, raclette, fondue, filet of perch, as well as snails in green peppercorns and puff pastry, and a superb homemade terrine. Perhaps you'll prefer a gratin of shrimp or beef either grilled or served Wellington style. Fixed-price meals range from 38F ($17.46), while à la carte dinners cost from 53F ($24.35). The restaurant is open from 9 a.m. to midnight except on Tuesday when it closes at 7 p.m.

Le Clos des Alpes (tel. 61-46-18), Cheaulin-sur-Montreux, is set above Montreux in an area filled with open fields and meadows. You'll have a view of the Alps from here, especially from your seat on the veranda. Much of the cookery has nouvelle cuisine overtones, including lotte with pepperoni, a goose liver terrine, and suckling veal with morels in a puff pastry. Fixed-price meals cost from 55F ($25.27), and à la carte dinners are from 60F ($27.57). The restaurant is closed on Sunday evening and all day Monday.

Brasserie Bavaria, 27 avenue du Casino (tel. 61-25-48), is a middle-class restaurant with an atmosphere somewhat like a beer hall. The walls are covered with frescoes of 19th-century equestriennes flirting with fieldhands. On busy nights the place fairly bustles with dozens of people relaxing, laughing, and enjoying their reasonably priced meals. Service is hurried but elaborate. The most popular dish on the menu is sauerkraut Bavaria (with pork products). At certain times the chef is likely to serve omble chevalier, the most celebrated fish of Lake Geneva. You might also try trout meunière or a cheese fondue with gruyere. Other recommendable main courses are the grills, perhaps sliced veal in a curry sauce with rice. When in doubt you can always order a hamburger steak. Set meals, and big ones at that, cost from 32F ($14.70), and smaller ones are served for 17F ($7.81). The brasserie takes a rest on Saturday.

MONTREUX AFTER DARK: **The Casino** (tel. 45-31-45), in the heart of the town, hugs most of the action. Since the limit of any wager is 5F ($2.30) in Switzerland, this casino, like many others, has evolved into more of an entertainment complex than a gambling hall. True, there's a green baize table and rolling balls where you can tempt Lady Chance, but the main focus is on the cabaret, disco, restaurant, two bars, music hall, and the movie theater.

Parking is well-near impossible in the area, so there's a garage with coin-operated meters in the basement. You enter the glass doors, possibly avoiding a tour bus unloading its passengers, and proceed to the cabaret down a long red staircase, with a short tunnel at the end. This club has everything from strip acts to clowns, and is open from 10 p.m. to 4 a.m. every night but Sunday. There's no cover, but drinks cost from 14F ($6.43) apiece.

Back on the main floor you can enter the American-style disco, Platinum, which has comfortable banquettes, lots of chrome, and recently released songs. Entrance is 6F ($2.76) on Friday, going up to 8F ($3.68) on Saturday. Drinks cost from 10F ($4.60) and up, and you must be at least 18. The disco opens at 9:30 p.m.

On the same floor you'll see an exposed piano bar, a "Bar du Festival," where repeat videos are shown of the performers at the most recent Montreux Jazz Festival, and a 3000-seat concert hall for a changing list of musical acts.

The restaurant has a panoramic view of the lake from your perch in one of its upholstered bentwood chairs. In summertime the swimming pool and the terrace around it are pleasant places. A movie theater and a hairdressing salon also draw a crowd.

To sum up, the Casino is something to see at least once.

Hazyland Disco (tel. 63-56-46) is on a busy street opposite the Hotel Palace at 100 Grand-Rue. The disco has big windows in an art nouveau format with fanciful wrought-iron detailing. It frequently has live acts, and when no one's playing, clients dance to disco music. You'll see a bar area to the right as you enter, and a group of trendily dressed patrons, most of whom appear to be under 25. When I was last there, a Michael Jackson look-alike sang Michael Jackson songs under a red strobe light. Beer costs 8F ($3.68) to 10F ($4.60), and there is no cover charge.

6. Château-d'Oex

The unspoiled French-speaking capital of the Pays-d'Enhaut, the upper land, Château-d'Oex (pronounced "shah-toh day") is popular with Europeans as a family resort. The village has lots of character and old-fashioned charm. Lying in a broad, sunny alpine valley above Lake Geneva, this area is just beginning to emerge as a winter sports center and a summer mountain resort, drawing vacationers who are interested more in a friendly, relaxed atmosphere than in the latest in chic.

In particular, Château-d'Oex is attuned to the needs of beginning and intermediate skiers, offering in winter an aerial cableway to take you to the heights and all types of skiing and other snow- and ice-associated sports, as well as ballooning, indoor horseback riding, and—what else?—après-ski parties.

Summer attractions in this part of the "Green Highland" of Switzerland include a heated swimming pool, hard tennis courts, horseback riding along park trails, a sightseeing cable railway to take you into the mountains, hang-gliding, trout fishing, and mini-golf.

If time is on your side, take the postal bus to **Col des Mosses,** one of the most scenic such rides in this part of Switzerland. You can also take the cableway from the heart of the resort to **Pra Perron** (4020 feet) and from there go by gondola on up to **La Braye** (5350 feet).

Château-d'Oex is halfway between Montreux and Interlaken, about 15 minutes from Gstaad.

FOOD AND LODGING: **Bon Accueil** (tel. 4-63-20) is my preferred choice. About a 12-minute stroll from the heart of the resort, it dates from 1756. It's built in the old-fashioned chalet hotel style, with sea-green shutters and beautifully weathered siding. The dowager hotel of Château-d'Oex, it has been completely updated with many modern improvements. However, it remains traditional in taste, as reflected by its cozy public rooms where a fire is likely to be blazing. There are plenty of sitting rooms, and less than a dozen of the private bedrooms contain private baths. Families like this place a lot. Half-board rates, depending on the season, range from 120F ($55.15) to 160F ($73.52), while singles, on the same arrangement, cost from 65F ($29.87) to 90F ($41.36).

Hôtel Résidence La Rocaille (tel. 4-62-15), in the northeast side of the resort, lies about seven minutes from the heart of the village. This is one of the best of the small hotels, with friendly, very helpful owners. Some of the accommodations have their own self-catering facilities. The bedrooms are well furnished and most comfortable, and it's a good choice for families who take their holidays together. Singles range from 70F ($32.17) to 105F ($48.25), while doubles cost from 110F ($50.55) to 160F ($73.52), depending on the season. These tariffs include service, tax, and breakfast. The hotel has a very attractive ambience, with much use made of wood paneling and beamed ceilings. It's one of the preferred stopovers among the après-ski crowd.

Hôtel Beau-Séjour (tel. 4-74-23) stands near the cableway terminal to La Braye just outside the heart of the resort. This is a long-established, popular hotel in a shuttered building with a Mediterranean-style roof. Many of the accommodations have been updated with modern plumbing. The spacious dining room opens onto panoramic views. The cooperative owners are the Cusinay family, who charge from 45F ($20.68) to 72F ($33.08) in a single and from 78F ($35.84) to 128F ($58.82) in a double.

Hôtel-Pension La Printanière (tel. 4-61-13) is a pleasant country house with a tranquil view and a simple but solid architectural style that could as easily be found in rural Pennsylvania as in Switzerland. Paul Thévenaz and his family close the hotel every year from sometime in mid-October, not reopening until shortly before Christmas. Their rooms are comfortably and simply furnished, costing from 30F ($13.79) in a single and from 50F ($22.98) in a double. Half-board terms begin at 40F ($18.38) in a single, rising to 76F ($34.92) in a double.

APRÈS SKI: My favorite place in town after dark is the cellar bar of the already-recommended **Bon Accueil.** You enter it by going down through a trapdoor, which only adds to the sense of adventure. There you'll find logs blazing on the open fire. Music is played for dancing, and it's one of the friendliest and most delightful spots in Château-d'Oex. It's furnished with Swiss antiques.

If you're hungry and want a gemütlich atmosphere, you might also seek out the Taverne at the **Beau-Séjour** and the restaurant at **Hôtel La Rocaille.**

7. Villars

This mountain resort (4268 feet), halfway between lake and glacier, overlooks the Rhône Valley over the vine-covered slopes around Aigle. It's considered the leading mountain resort in French-speaking Switzerland. Along with Arveyes and Chesières, Villars forms a resort area in the lower Valais (although it's still officially part of the canton of Vaud), and is far more fashionable than its companion villages.

The plateau on which the resort is situated, a true alpine balcony, has woodland slopes of the Chamossaire to the north. To the south it has a panoramic view of the French and Swiss Alps, with Dents du Midi mountain range opposite and Mont Blanc visible in the distance.

The long-established resort, in its sheltered location with a calm atmosphere seldom troubled by winds, offers craft shops, nightclubs, good restaurants and hotels, and all services you may require to make your stay here pleasant.

The principal ski area is at **Bretaye** (6050 feet), reached by mountain railroad. (You may find the cars packed at the height of the season.) From there you can take lifts in many directions. One goes to the top of **Chamossaire** (7200 feet).

You can reach the resort by electic mountain railway from Bex, the trip taking about an hour and 20 minutes.

FOOD AND LODGING: **Hôtel du Park** (tel. 35-21-21) is an excellent first-class choice, on its own well-kept grounds about 12 minutes from the heart of Villars. The grounds are a potent lure, with two ski lifts, three tennis courts, and "pitch-and-putt" golf. The hotel, which draws many repeat visitors, is pleasantly furnished, and many of the private bedrooms are generous in size (all accommodations contain private shower or bath). The majority also contain private balconies, opening onto superb views. In summer, tariffs on the full-board basis range from 110F ($50.55) to 182F ($83.63) in a single and from 110F ($50.55) to 165F ($75.82) per person in a double. Even more expensive suites are available as well. The long and well-lit dining room is among the finest in town, with a traditional atmosphere. There's an "ice bar" outside for drinks before lunch, as well as a swimming pool. A disco on the premises has a round area for dancing, the shape of which is repeated in the ceiling where an artist's depiction includes a galaxy of mythical beasts.

Eurotel (tel. 35-31-31) opened in 1976 in a sprawling seven-story format of a chalet-style establishment, with balconies and wood detailing. The interior is filled with pleasant, easily forgettable furniture plus lots of exposed wood and metal. Some of the well-furnished rooms have kitchenettes, and you'll also find a sauna and a swimming pool on the premises. Singles rent for between 74F ($34) and 124F ($56.98), while doubles range from 49F ($22.52) to 109F ($50.09) per person daily. Units with kitchenette cost an additional 10F ($4.60) per person, with an obligatory cleanup fee of 20F ($9.19) when you leave. Breakfast is another 12F ($5.51) per person daily.

Hôtel Marie-Louise (tel. 35-24-77) is the ideal country hotel, set in the midst of a large park with 90% of its bedrooms facing south. Every rustic note is sounded in its interior. The dining rooms are a combination of stucco with beams and polished paneling, and an attractively orchestrated service makes you feel at home. One of the salons is outfitted with vertically striped wallpaper and 19th-century antiques. The other salons are filled with furniture that can easily handle a guest with ski boots. This hotel is close to all the major sports facilities. On the premises are summertime tennis courts, plus a dancing bar. The owners, the Angelini family, charge from 40F ($18.38) to 88F ($40.44) in a single and from 70F ($32.17) to 160F ($73.52) in a double, depending on the season. These tariffs include breakfast, and half board is offered for another 22F ($10.11) per person daily.

Chalet Henriette (tel. 3-21-63) is a weathered chalet with cutout patterns in its balconies and light-green shutters. The interior is pierced with large windows, which illuminate the alpine furniture set off by the sunny autumnal colors used throughout the interior. Only 200 yards from the Villars–Bretayne train station, the hotel charges from 35F ($16.08) to 105F ($48.25) in a single and from 60F ($27.57) to 115F ($52.84) in a double, depending on the plumbing and the season.

APRÈS SKI: Villars has many clubs, bars, and taverns, and in the very peak season it has a lively atmosphere. Many people from Geneva like to take their holidays here.

Peppino's at the already-recommended **Eurotel** is about the most sought-after dining room in town. It not only has some of the best food, but a friendly, fun-loving atmosphere and often live entertainment.

In the bar of the **Hôtel Du Parc** you can dance to a live band in season; otherwise it's disco music. The hotel's tavern grill is also a popular place for fondue and raclette.

8. Les Diablerets

If you turn off the main Geneva–Brig highway after passing Aigle and head into the mountains, you'll find Les Diablerets, a typical resort village of chalet-style buildings set against a backdrop of towering alpine peaks. These mountains are so high that the resort gets little sun in the main part of the hamlet until about the last half of February, a fact that isn't much publicized.

This is the center of some 40 miles of ski slopes, the biggest ski area in Switzerland, with access to a mammoth lift system. It's also a good base for exploring other ski resorts.

You can visit **Glacier des Diablerets** (9835 feet at its highest station), but unless you're a skilled skier you'll probably only want to relax at the panoramic restaurant before returning to the resort. A round-trip ticket from the hamlet to the glacier tip costs about 30F ($13.79). You go by gondola for some 4½ miles to Col du Pillon-Pierres Pointe, then by aerial cable on to Cabane des Diablerets (8275 feet), and thence onward and upward to the highest station of the glacier. This route is kept in operation from February to November.

Other popular ski sites of the region are **Isenau,** where a gondola at the north of the village will take you to Palette d'Isenau (5900 feet); and the **Les Mazonts–Meillerets** area, reached by ski tow and chair lift from the hamlet of Vers l'Église. You eventually reach the peak of Meillerets (6490 feet).

Les Diablerets lies to the east of Villars and to the west of Gstaad in the Vaudoise Alps.

FOOD AND LODGING: Eurotel Les Diablerets (tel. 53-17-21) is composed of three balconied wings which angle themselves into a gentle arc that encloses a well-maintained lawn area. Many of the sunny accommodations have balconies which overlook the wintertime ice-skating rink. On the premises is an indoor swimming pool as well as two sympathetic restaurants. The bar area is comfortably outfitted with striped bucket chairs, where you can read a newspaper alone or chatter with newfound friends. The bedrooms sometimes contain kitchenettes and convert into living rooms during the day. Singles rent for between 35F ($16.08) and 115F ($52.84) while doubles range from 42F ($19.30) to 100F ($45.95) per person daily, breakfast not included.

Hôtel Ermitage and **Résidence Meurice** (tel. 53-15-51) are hotels with the same management, and they're set close to one another in an alpine setting with good views. The format for both hotels is strikingly modern, with an emphasis on gently curving balconies and big windows. There's a generous use of natural wood made on the facade of both buildings. The interiors are well upholstered and streamlined, with bedrooms that convert into living rooms thanks to a foldaway bed system. Each of the units has a private bath. The public rooms include a dancing bar, two restaurants, and an indoor swimming pool. There are also tennis courts on the grounds, and horseback riding can be arranged in summer. The *per-person* rate in a double ranges from 50F ($22.98) to 93F ($42.73), depending on the season, with a supplement of 10F ($4.60) charged for single occupancy.

Hôtel Mon Abri (tel. 53-14-81) is an attractively dark-toned chalet with red shutters standing at the entrance to the resort, about a 12-minute stroll from the center. The hotel has a modern section where each well-furnished room contains a private shower or bath. However, I still prefer the older part with lots of alpine paneling. A grill room is outfitted in the old style, and a sun terrace proves very popular in summer. Rooms are comfortably and pleasantly furnished, costing between 50F ($22.98) and 81F ($37.22) in a single, with doubles ranging from 80F ($36.76) to 142F ($65.25). Half board is an additional 18F ($8.27) per person daily.

Les Lilas (tel. 53-11-34) is a small hotel, one of the best at Les Diablerets. It's built in the chalet style, and that means lots of wood paneling and beamed ceilings. Its dining room is considered one of the most attractive at the resort (it has a carnotzet with a balcony overhead). You have a choice of bedrooms that for the most part are charming, with slanted beamed ceilings and balconies opening onto views of the mountains. The bedrooms in the old section are comfortable and cozy, and those in the newer section have beamed ceilings. The hotel is very attractively furnished, showing a respect for tradition. The basic bed-and-breakfast rate starts at 35F ($16.08) per person, plus another 25F ($11.49) charged for half board. There's also a 5F ($2.30) fee charged for single occupancy and another 10F ($4.60) assessed for those desiring a room with a private bath or shower.

APRÈS SKI: After dark, Les Diablerets is no Gstaad, but there is some activity if you're not too ambitious.

One of the leading discos in town is at the already-recommended **Eurotel,** which also has a rather formal restaurant.

You might also check out the action at the also-recommended **Mon Abri,** especially in its Au Vieux Mazot where you can dine and attend tea dances after darkness falls.

The leading nightclub in town is Le Refuge, at the **Grand Hotel,** where you can dance.

As mentioned, **Les Lilas** has the most favored and rustic restaurant in town where you can enjoy fondue and raclette. You can drink at one end, and there's also a petit dance floor.

Chapter IX

GENEVA

1. Where to Stay
2. Where to Dine
3. What to See and Do
4. Where to Shop
5. Geneva After Dark
6. Excursions from Geneva
7. Getting to Know Geneva

THE THIRD-LARGEST CITY of Switzerland, Geneva stands at the lower end of Lake Geneva, called Lac Léman. It's considered the "most international of cities" because of all the international organizations (such as the Red Cross) which have their headquarters in Geneva.

Built on the Rhône, the city lies at the extreme western tip of Switzerland. In the heart of Europe—and certainly one of the crossroads of that continent—it's called "the smallest of great capitals." Geneva is linked to the outside world by a vast network of airlines, motorways, and railways.

A lively, cosmopolitan atmosphere prevails in Geneva, and it's a city of parks and promenades. In summer it becomes a virtual garden. It's also considered one of the healthiest cities in the world—the north wind blows away any pollution. The situation, in a word, is magnificent, not only lying on one of the biggest Alpine lakes, but within view of the glorious pinnacle of Mont Blanc.

Geneva is virtually surrounded by French territory. It's connected to Switzerland only by the lake and a narrow corridor. For that and other reasons Geneva is definitely a Swiss city, but with a decided French accent. The cliché has it that if you've been to New York, you haven't seen America. Likewise, Geneva will not immediately bring to mind the Switzerland of legend. You face mansard roofs, iron balconies, sidewalk cafés, and shop signs with names such as *boulangerie.* There's even a rive gauche (left bank) and rive droite (right bank). But Geneva makes no pretense at being "another Paris."

Geneva's history is long and action-packed, its first settlements going back to the Ice Age. Over the years it's been a Gallic town, a Roman city, a Burgundian capital, and an episcopal principality, among other cloaks it has worn. After settlement by primitive tribes, Geneva was conquered by the Romans, who lasted some 500 years. Julius Caesar was the first of Geneva's legendary guests to arrive (he had the bridge over the Rhône destroyed). By the end of the 11th century Geneva was ruled by bishop-princes who, more or less, engaged in battles with the House of Savoy for 200 years.

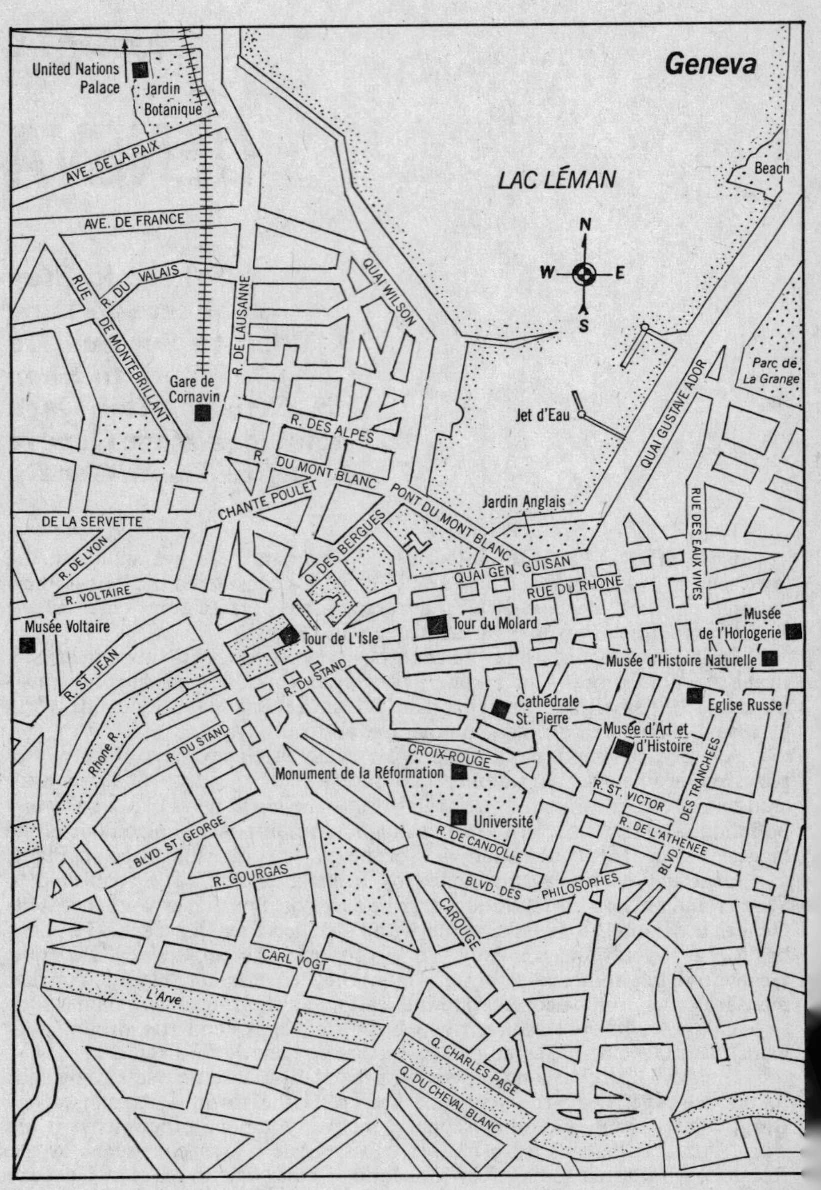
Geneva
LAC LÉMAN
N
W
E
S
United Nations Palace
Jardin Botanique
AVE. DE LA PAIX
AVE. DE FRANCE
RUE DE MONTEBRILLANT
R. DU VALAIS
R. DE LAUSANNE
QUAI WILSON
Gare de Cornavin
R. DES ALPES
R. DU MONT BLANC
CHANTE POULET
DE LA SERVETTE
PONT DU MONT BLANC
Jardin Anglais
Jet d'Eau
QUAI GUSTAVE ADOR
Beach
Parc de La Grange
RUE DES EAUX VIVES
R. DE LYON
R. VOLTAIRE
Musée Voltaire
R. ST. JEAN
Q. DES BERGUES
QUAI GEN. GUISAN
RUE DU RHONE
Tour du Molard
Tour de L'Isle
Musée de l'Horlogerie
Musée d'Histoire Naturelle
R. DU STAND
Cathédrale St. Pierre
Eglise Russe
Musée d'Art et d'Histoire
Rhone R.
R. DU STAND
CROIX-ROUGE
Monument de la Réformation
R. ST. VICTOR
BLVD. DES TRANCHEES
Université
R. DE L'ATHENEE
BLVD. ST. GEORGE
R. DE CANDOLLE
R. GOURGAS
BLVD. DES PHILOSOPHES
CAROUGE
CARL VOGT
L'Arve
Q. CHARLES PAGE
Q. DU CHEVAL BLANC

Geneva was annexed by the French in 1798 at the time of their Revolution. It stayed like an unwilling bride to France until 1814, following the collapse of Napoleon, and was admitted to the Swiss Confederation in 1815 as the capital of its own canton.

Converted by William Farel, Geneva eventually switched from Catholicism, embracing the Protestant faith (this was in 1536). The city is inevitably linked to John Calvin, a French refugee. Puritan in all ways, he ranted against theaters and dancing. He even deplored wine and food if they were partaken for enjoyment. Stern, foreboding in character, he was known for his austerity and bigotry, and the word Calvinism comes from him, of course. He even had the Spanish doctor, Miguel Serveto, burned at the stake, because he disagreed with him.

After Calvin, Geneva became such a stronghold of the Reformation that it was known in Europe as "the Rome of the Protestants." In fairness to Calvin it should be pointed out that he helped the city regain its prosperity and made it a center of French learning, welcoming refugees from all over the continent, especially from France and Italy, but also England.

By the 18th century Geneva had become one of the intellectual centers of Europe. No name was as famous as that of Jean-Jacques Rousseau, who was born here in 1712. His rival, Voltaire, came this way, as did Byron, Goethe, Victor Hugo, Chateaubriand, and a host of other luminaries.

Henri Dunant (1828–1910) had governments sign the Geneva Convention in 1863 (regrettably some of them didn't respect it). This led to the creation of the present International Red Cross.

Woodrow Wilson in 1920 proposed that Geneva be the seat of the newly formed League of Nations, and this paved the way for the city to become polyglot. It was the seat of the League until 1946. Today diplomats from all over the world flock to Geneva, to the Palais des Nations, as the city is the host to the European headquarters of the United Nations. In some respects Geneva is the very epitome of Swiss neutrality.

The name of the city is often flashed across the nightly news, including when it was the host for nuclear disarmament talks.

Much of Geneva can be explored on foot. The left bank is compact and the most colorful. The lower tower, the Rues Basses, lies between the south bank of the river and the old town. Grand-Rue is the well-preserved main street of the old town. Traffic free, it's flanked with houses dating from the 15th and 18th centuries. Rousseau was born at the simple house at no. 40.

One of the most fun times to visit Geneva is for the **Fêtes de Genève,** when the Genevese celebrate their national holiday on August 1. This is followed two weeks later by a long weekend celebration with many fireworks on the lake, street dancing, and flower-covered floats.

Another celebration on December 12 is known as **l'Escalade.** Geneva was attacked on that night in 1602 by Charles-Emmanuel, whose soldiers were unsuccessful in scaling the city ramparts. The heroine of the hour, Mère Royaume, poured a pot of boiling stew over the head of a Savoy soldier, then cracked his skull with her kettle. Citizens today stage torchlight parades through the old town, many in 17th-century costumes.

1. Where to Stay

Geneva has a lot of hotels, many of which are clustered around the main railway terminal. Because Geneva is such a city of conventions and international conferences, many of its hotels—at least the best ones in all price categories—

are often booked way in advance. The ambassadors fill up such deluxe hostelers as Richemond, the deputy assistant secretary heading for the budget hotel.

Geneva has a lot of upper-bracket hotels, in gleaming modern or old-world style. What it lacks is a sufficient number of intimate, family-run smaller hotels with atmosphere.

THE DELUXE FORTRESSES: **Le Richemond,** Jardin Brunswick (tel. 31-14-00), is unquestionably the greatest hotel in Geneva. More than a century old, it sits across from an immaculately maintained small park near the lake, with memorial columns, splashing fountains, and seasonally adjusted flowers. The hotel has been owned by the Armleder family since 1875. The travertine facade of the hotel is neoclassically severe, relieved only by the elaborately fashioned wrought-iron balustrades surrounding the balconies. You're likely to see the actual faces of people flashed across worldwide news screens here, if you can distinguish exactly who they are as they move from the shelter of their Rolls-Royces into the public rooms inside. The hotel restaurant, Gentilhomme, is reputed by many to be the finest dining establishment in Geneva (for more on this, see "Where to Dine").

In the 19th century this was, believe it or not, a relatively unpretentious guest house, but today under the direction of one of the best hôteliers in Switzerland, Jean Armleder, its public rooms look almost like a wing of an art museum, with dozens of valuable engravings and an array of furniture, some of which dates from the days of Louis XIII. The hotel, with prices on demand, has, when available, a presidential and a royal suite, both of which have been occupied by personages with those titles to justify their names. The sidewalk café, Le Jardin, is the most fashionable one in the city.

Reserve a room here early. Because of the hotel's international renown the 139 rooms fill up quickly. All accommodations have private bathrooms and a host of other luxuries. Singles rent for 120F ($55.14) to 180F ($82.71), while doubles cost from 250F ($114.88) to 300F ($137.85). Guests can request that the hotel arrange excursions for them, for which they will invariably find themselves on the backseat of a Mercedes Pullman or a Rolls-Royce Phantom V.

Hôtel Président, 47 Quai Wilson (tel. 31-10-00), lies on the lakeshore in a glistening modern building that looks more like a diplomatic headquarters of some international agency than a hotel. Each of the rooms has floor-to-ceiling sliding windows to let in as much air and light as possible, and all are beautifully furnished with a rich collection of statuary, antiques, imaginative wallpaper, and elegant upholstery. The public rooms are nothing short of opulent, many with floors that appear to be lapis-lazuli (or at least a good imitation), vintage French antiques, and velvet-covered walls. If you've always been intrigued by needlepoint, the Gobelin tapestries in one of the galleries will hold your attention for hours. Service here is impeccable, from the bell captain who will arrange for your bags to be sent to your room to the waiters in the famous Grill Room. The establishment is directed by M. R. Hasenkamp, who works for the Swissôtel chain.

The air-conditioned rooms look out over the lake and cost 192F ($88.22) in a single (it will have two beds regardless of single occupancy), 290F ($133.26) in a double. Breakfast, not included in the room price, costs an additional 18F ($8.27). Things do not come cheap here, as a quick perusal of the added charges will show you, but the world does indeed come to Geneva, and a good chunk of it chooses to bed down in style at the Président.

Hôtel Intercontinental, 7-9 Petit Saconnex (tel. 34-60-91), can be found halfway between the airport and the city center, next to the United Nations complex near the lake. The building rises high above surrounding greenery, a pleasing rectangle of steel and glass flanked by an outdoor swimming pool. The public rooms include one gourmet restaurant, Les Continents, whose Louis XV-style armchairs and polished light-grained paneling reflect the gleam of the many crystal chandeliers, and the Pergola, less formal than its companion restaurant, whose forest-green walls are meticulously covered floor to ceiling with white lattices.

The bedrooms are decorated in a wide variety of styles, many with beautifully patterned wallpaper and matching bedspreads, while the suites experiment successfully with unusual color schemes (a dusty-rose living room, for example) in an ambience which is nothing short of opulent. Singles here rent for 180F ($82.71) per day, and doubles cost 230F ($105.69) per day. Breakfast is an additional 11F ($5.06). Gerhard Schneider is the cordial front-office manager.

Noga Hilton International, 19 Quai du Mont-Blanc (tel. 31-98-11), blends traditional Hilton style with Genevese tradition to create an interesting physical plant with impeccable service. My favorite part of this hotel is the café sun terrace, where you'll be able to see the famous waterspout spewing its jet up from Lake Geneva while sipping your favorite drink. The swimming pool is open to the sunlight in summer and closed with a futuristic canopy of beams in wintertime. You'll find a casino, a restaurant, a coffeeshop with a panoramic view, and two nightclubs: one a branch of Régine's private club and another an offshoot of New Jimmy's in Paris.

Access to each of the well-appointed bedrooms is controlled by an electronic lock with an individual combination. Rooms offer air conditioning, self-dial phones, color TVs, in-house movies, radios, taped music, and minibars. Use of the fitness club and sauna come free with the rooms, which are priced at 235F ($107.98) in a double and 165F ($75.82) in a single.

The front-office manager is André Giacobino, who has helped to make the Hilton one of the "grand ladies" of the Quai du Mont-Blanc and one of the greatest of the entire chain.

Hôtel de la Paix, 11 Quai du Mont-Blanc (tel. 32-61-50). The staff of this former palace built in the 18th century still recalls the visit of Prince Rainier and the late Princess Grace of Monaco. Within the deluxe choices of Geneva, this is one of the smaller, more select establishments. Sitting directly on the lake, with a view of Mont Blanc, the hotel looks a lot like a city building in Paris, with neoclassic detailing, a gabled roofline, and a view of Brunswick Gardens. The main salon is a double-tiered arched extravaganza, with marble columns, elaborately carved Corinthian capitals, comfortably elegant furniture, and a balustraded loggia overlooking a massive crystal chandelier.

Bedrooms come in all sizes and many different decorating schemes, but they all have modern baths and all the conveniences of any deluxe hotel. Singles cost from 105F ($48.25) to 160F ($73.52); doubles range from 190F ($87.31) to 260F ($119.47). An extra bed can be set up in any room for an additional 55F ($25.27). Breakfast is included in the price.

Hôtel La Reserve, 301 route de Lausanne, Bellevue/Geneva (tel. 741-741), is an ultra-deluxe old-fashioned establishment surrounded by gardens that explode into bloom every spring with thousands of tulips, dozens of Oriental trees, and Lebanese cedars. Both the private and the public rooms are testimonials to exquisite taste. Because of its beauty, its location (only 12 minutes from both the airport and from the city center), and its extravagant luxury, the hotel draws a high percentage of repeaters. La Reserve is in fact a city landmark. Its clients are fashionably elegant, a tone encouraged by Walter Scheel, the director, who is considered one of the finest innkeepers in continental Europe. The hotel is set on eight acres of private grounds, focusing on an outdoor pool where summertime buffet lunches draw the svelte set, a lakeside terrace, four tennis courts, and a private pier which, by the way, offers motor launches for rent by hotel guests. In brief, this is a hotel of great style and charm. Its Chinese restaurant, Tse Fung, has the best Oriental food in Geneva, and the French food in the main dining room costs between 70F ($32.17) and 110F ($50.55) for a full meal, not including wine.

Single rooms rent for 175F ($80.41) on the park side, for 190F ($87.31) on the lake side. Double rooms cost 270F ($124.07) on the park side and 290F ($133.26) on the lake side, with a continental breakfast included in the charges.

Hôtel Beau-Rivage, 13 Quai du Mont-Blanc (tel. 31-02-21). If you can afford it, you really should try to stay at the former residence of the empress of Austria, which today receives my highest recommendation for traditional charm, old-world hospitality, and impeccable service. Jacques Mayer, the general manager, has employed a go-getting staff who as a team maintain a superb hotel and are to be congratulated. The hotel restaurant, Le Chat Botté (Puss in Boots), known throughout the world as one of the top one or two restaurants of Geneva, is decorated in an embroidered ambience of superior rustic wood paneling and Louis XIII–style furniture. The hotel's café terrace is known for good service and for inspired people-watching.

The bedrooms all have tiled private baths with enough counter space to lay out a warehouse of cosmetics. Attempts are made to redecorate them frequently, so you'll probably find a decor in tune with today's trends, with a good level of taste. Singles cost 185F ($85.01), while doubles go for 270F ($124.07), with breakfast included.

Hôtel du Rhône, Quai Turrettini (tel. 31-98-31), lies behind a row of verdant trees on the bank where the Rhône begins to turn into the lake. The symmetrical modern facade extends a long distance along the riverfront, with evenly spaced concrete ribs running vertically down the front of the building. Built in 1950, the hotel has had enough renovations to keep it competitive with the other deluxe palaces of Geneva, and manager Eric Glattfelder and managing director Richard Lendi do everything they can to ensure perfect service and personalized attention. The rooms are freshly decorated with attractively patterned wall-to-wall carpeting, natural colors, and classically elegant furniture, many of them with excellent views of the city. The public rooms sometimes feature a live piano player and display tapestries by contemporary artists.

The hotel has 300 rooms, plus 28 suites, all possessing bathrooms, color TVs, phones, and mini-bars, along with two restaurants, two bars, a café sun terrace, a swimming pool, and a fitness center. Singles here cost from 125F ($57.44) to 160F ($73.52), and doubles range from 195F ($89.60) to 250F ($114.88), with breakfast included. The riverside rooms, of course, are the more expensive units.

Hotel Bristol, 10 rue du Mont-Blanc (tel. 32-44-00), is 130 years old and has been one of the most sought-after hostelries in Geneva since its establishment. It sits in a beflowered public park at the lake end of a famous street leading into the Mont Blanc Bridge. The public rooms are elegantly furnished with patterned carpeting, wood paneling, and comfortable, upholstered wooden armchairs. The bedrooms are pleasingly filled with clear colors and classically tasteful antiques; some of them contain the kinds of pieces you'd expect in a provincial manor house. All units have modern baths and double-glazed windows for soundproofing. The bar is popular with Geneva's business-lunch set, and so is the graceful, lighthearted, high-ceilinged restaurant, the view from which opens onto the trees in the square behind the hotel.

Singles cost from 120F ($55.14) to 200F ($91.90); doubles range from 180F ($82.71) to 240F ($110.28). Some of the duplexes are particularly charming, priced at 280F ($128.66) to 320F ($147.04), while suites cost considerably more. Breakfast is included in the price.

Hôtel des Bergues, 33 Quai des Bergues (tel. 31-50-50), is owned by the largest hotel conglomerate in the world, Trusthouse Forte, which maintains the establishment's standards as among the best in Geneva. The frontage of the building is of a sober, classical design which has been restored to its original condition of the year it was built 150 years ago. Management has recently renovated each of the 117 bedrooms in a style quite elegant. Furniture consists in part of Louis Philippe—style dolphin-armed chairs and Empire-style tables, luxuriously upholstered in vividly sophisticated colors.

Ample use is made of marble in the lobby area, where guests register while seated at a comfortable armchair in front of a helpful staff member behind a period desk. The public rooms are lavish, with electronically sophisticated conference facilities, all decorated in a 19th-century grandeur. Reto Grass is the manager of the hotel, one of Geneva's most sophisticated hoteliers. All accommodations contain private baths along with much comfort and dozens of thoughtful extras. Singles rent for between 157F ($72.14) and 212F ($97.41), while doubles range between 254F ($116.71) and 324F ($148.88).

THE UPPER BRACKET: **Le Warwick Mediterranée,** 14 rue de Lausanne (tel. 31-62-50). The superstructure of this space-age hotel rises opposite the train station like a network of honeycombed cells placed on top of two stories of spidery, leg-like supports that shelter three restaurants, a piano bar, a gift shop, a sauna, and dozens of conference rooms with enough stenographers and private secretaries to administer the correspondence of the entire Swiss army. The lobby area is a visually striking arrangement of sweeping staircases, abstract-design loggias and balconies, hanging illuminated globes, and marble floors under a scattering of Oriental rugs.

Bedrooms are sunny, boldly patterned, and comfortable, with soundproof windows and modern plumbing. Singles cost from 110F ($50.55) for a simple room with a shower, sink, and toilet, to 250F ($114.88) in a suite. Doubles run the range from 150F ($68.93) for a standard unit to 450F ($206.78) in a suite. All rooms have TV, mini-bar, and direct-dial phone, and come with breakfast.

Cristal Hotel, 4 rue Pradier (tel. 31-34-00), is one of Geneva's newest upper-bracket hotels, having opened for business on November 1, 1982. It sits quietly on a peaceful street with lots of greenery one block south of the train station. The facade looks like a streamlined piece of poured concrete, tastefully designed, with lime-green awnings fluttering in the breeze above the discreet entrance. You'll find underground parking at the garage complex at the train station, along with most of Geneva conveniently within walking distance.

The soundproof rooms are well ventilated and come with private baths, color TVs, videos, radios, phones, and mini-bars. They are comfortably carpeted, with vivid color schemes and tasteful, interesting furniture. Breakfast is included in the daily charge of anywhere from 80F ($36.76) to 100F ($45.95) in a single, from 115F ($52.84) to 140F ($64.33) in a double. Andrea Valli is one of the managers here, and with the other workers she does everything possible to make your stay pleasant.

Hotel Ambassador, 21 Quai des Bergues (tel. 31-72-00), lies on a well-known part of Geneva's lakefront about a block away from its deluxe neighbor, the Hôtel des Bergues. The restrained facade of this establishment is graced with neoclassical detailing around the tall windows which face the Place Chevelu, with its trees and its four streams of water gushing from a single fountain. If you ask for a room on one of the top two floors you'll have a view of Mont Blanc. In summertime a pleasant café spreads itself onto the pavement in front of the hotel, whose smallish rooms are conservatively decorated in light colors and traditionally classic furnishings. A restaurant on the ground floor serves satisfying French-Swiss meals.

The tactful director and his assistant are Messers. Zamboni and Gräfe, who administer the 92 rooms with flair and style, charging from 75F ($34.46) to 100F ($45.95) in a single and from 100F ($45.95) to 140F ($64.33) in a double, with an additional fee of 30F ($13.79) if an extra bed is set up in any of the rooms. Breakfast is not included. All rooms have baths (the hotel was built in 1966) and contain phones, radios, color TVs, and refrigerators. Parking and room service are both available on the premises.

Hôtel d'Angleterre, Quai du Mont-Blanc (tel. 32-81-80). Nearly two dozen of the bedrooms of this grand old hotel of another era offer vantage points overlooking the lake. If your room has a balcony, it will usually be big enough for you and a friend to sit on for your *petit déjeuner.* Accommodations for the most part are spacious, furnished with desks, armchairs, and fine elegant furniture, and come with high ceilings and plenty of closet space. The walls are extra thick, so you can't eavesdrop (the Swiss are particularly concerned about all kinds of espionage), and the windows are double-glazed for soundproofing. The club lounge downstairs attracts visitors from the financial district who "talk turkey" over drinks, while the hotel restaurant opens onto a panoramic view of the lakeside promenade.

The uppermost rooms are the most desirable because of their view, although you'll need to reserve at least a month in advance if you want to stay in one. R. O. Bucher is a dynamic hotel manager, and in its category his hotel is one of the best values in Geneva. You'll find a private bath in each of the 66 rooms, which are priced at 135F ($62.03) in a single and at anywhere from 200F ($91.90) to 240F ($110.28) for a double, breakfast included.

Hôtel Cornavin, 33 Boulevard James-Fazy (tel. 32-21-00). The lobby of this renovated hotel 50 yards from the train station is laid out in gray-and-white marble in a circular pattern of random widths. The rest of the hotel is aggressively modern, with generous application of bright colors and vivid floral patterns in the carpeted bedrooms. Although the Cornavin is on a busy avenue in the business district the rooms are soundproofed against the traffic, and contain showers or baths along with modern plumbing accessories. Managers Hiltbrunner and Berset charge from 85F ($39.06) to 105F ($48.25) in a single and from 125F ($57.44) to 160F ($73.52) in a double, with breakfast included. There's a 30F ($13.79) additional charge if an extra bed is set up in any room.

Hotel Rex, 44 avenue Wendt (tel. 45-71-50), is five minutes away from the airport but only a few blocks away from the train station and the lake. Its streamlined entrance is tastefully simple, with the name of the hotel written in script on a black ground, surrounded by sculpted ornamental shrubs in pots serving as a framework. The rooms, tastefully furnished in restrained colors with dignified leather armchairs and containing modern baths, rent for 107F ($49.17) in a single, 150F ($68.93) in a double, breakfast included. Also on the premises you'll find an English bar, a gentlemen's drawing room, and a beautifully appointed reading room. S. Chabane is the manager.

Hotel California, 1 rue Gevray (tel. 31-55-50). The decor, as you'd expect in a hotel of this name, is imaginatively colorful, functionally modern, lighthearted, and unpretentious. Only a block from the lake, behind the Quai du

Mont-Blanc, the hotel is housed in a six-story rectangular building of aluminum, glass, and sea-green enameled panels that looks something like an office building. Bedrooms have plumbing, radios, and phones. There's one entire floor of apartments with kitchenettes available for one or two persons (prices upon request). Singles rent for 85F ($39.06) to 105F ($48.25), while doubles go for 125F ($57.44) to 165F ($75.82). Triples cost from 180F ($82.71) to 195F ($89.60), and breakfast is included in all three rates. The manager, Mr. Gaillard, is ably assisted by R. Perroud. There's no restaurant in the hotel, but you can get a drink in the rooftop bar or a drink and snacks in the downstairs bar until the wee hours of the morning. Room service is available.

Hôtel les Armures, 1 rue des Puits St-Pierre (tel. 28-91-72), is a hotel discovery in the center of the old town, one of the most charming in Geneva. It's housed in a 17th-century building which until 1981 was used as a printing factory. The public rooms have been painstakingly restored to reveal the original painted ceiling beams and a blue-and-gray fresco which management thinks is from the original building. Today the lobby is covered with Oriental rugs and several pieces of well-placed modern sculpture, which complement the suit of medieval armor standing in a corner. The hotel is housed in the same building as the oldest café in Geneva (see the restaurant recommendations, coming up). It's reached through a separate entrance on the other side of the block. Parking might be a problem here as the hotel lies deep in a maze of one-way streets. Singles range from 150F ($68.93) to 180F ($82.71), while doubles cost from 210F ($96.50) to 230F ($105.69). All the handsomely furnished bedrooms are air-conditioned, containing private bath, radio, phone, and color TV.

Hôtel l'Arbalète, 3 Tour-Maîtresse (tel. 28-41-55), offers the kind of rustic and elegant charm many visitors seek on trips to Europe. The 33 bedrooms are all different from one another, usually appointed with antiques and gracefully outfitted with heavily beamed ceilings or exposed timbers. One of the accommodations has a two-level format of light-grained wood and flowery wallpaper. A pub next door to the hotel is an English-style paneled room, with inviting chairs and a gently curved bar. This establishment is about two blocks from the Jardin Anglais in a complicated series of one-way streets. Be forewarned if you're driving that parking might be a problem. Singles range from 180F ($82.71) to 190F ($87.31), while doubles cost from 230F ($105.69) to 240F ($110.28). All units are air-conditioned, with private baths and all the conveniences.

THE MEDIUM PRICE RANGE: **Hotel Excelsior,** 34 rue Rousseau (tel. 32-09-45), can be identified in summer by the kind of sidewalk café where you'll want to stop and have coffee before returning to the onslaught of Geneva. A ground-floor restaurant, La Brocherie, which you can view through an arched picture window, serves French-Swiss food, while the rooms upstairs are comfortable and brightly decorated, with modern plumbing. They rent for 70F ($32.17) to 90F ($41.36) in a single and for 105F ($48.25) to 125F ($57.44) in a double, breakfast included. V. Buhlmann is the manager.

Hôtel Moderne, 1 rue de Berne (tel. 32-81-00), is close to the train station which, as you will find, is not far from the lake. The building itself is a seven-story symmetrical rectangle painted white, with a low-lying glass-walled restaurant housed in an extension of the main building. The entrance is an unpretentious aperture with a glass door marked by about six large decals identifying the many touring companies which have given their endorsement. The public rooms, as the name of the hotel implies, are very *moderne,* with lots of Nordic tripod tables, molded plywood chairs, and best of all, a free-form unframed mirror shaped like a silvery protoplasm stretching eight feet across one of the walls.

The bedrooms are predictably furnished, clean, comfortable, and sunny. They rent for 38F ($17.46) to 75F ($34.46) in a single, from 80F ($36.76) to 105F ($48.25) in a double, and include breakfast. Prices are slightly higher in summertime, and not all of the rooms have private baths, so be sure to know before you commit yourself. An extra bed can be set up in any room for an additional 20F ($9.19). The management speaks five languages, so communication shouldn't be a problem. The owners are the Wilhelm family.

Hôtel Suisse, 10 Place Cornavin (tel. 32-66-30), is directly opposite the railroad station, in a modern building with pleasing proportions and oversize soundproof windows. Recent renovations include an almost complete facelift of the interior, leaving behind an ambience of warm-hued tastefulness, comfortable leather chairs, an inviting lobby with russet walls, lots of paintings, and a dramatic sweeping staircase. The bedrooms all have private baths, telephones, color TVs, radios, and mini-bars, and are inviting in pleasing shades of tea green, blue-gray, and creams. Single rooms cost between 80F ($36.76) and 90F ($41.36), and doubles rent for between 95F ($43.65) and 130F ($59.74), with breakfast included. A fixed-price lunch is available for 15F ($6.89).

Hôtel Mon-Repos, 131 rue de Lausanne (tel. 32-80-10). A long expanse of green lawn is what you'll see from the lakeside windows of this hotel, on the right bank of Lake Geneva. If the day is clear you'll even see Mont Blanc off in the distance. The hotel curves gently around a corner, alternating recessed balconies with elegantly detailed windows on the sandstone facade. All the comfortable bedrooms are equipped with telephone, radio, and modicum of utilitarian furniture. You'll find a restaurant and a modern bar area with warm-hued ceiling fashioned from wooden slats. Singles and doubles without bath are priced at 55F ($25.27) and 75F ($34.46), respectively, while rooms with bath or shower rent for 75F ($34.46) in a single, 110F ($50.55) in a double, breakfast included. The hotel is owned by the Keller family, who also offer apartments with kitchenettes for guests who plan to stay for longer periods.

Hôtel Le Chandelier, 23 Grand-Rue (tel. 21-56-88) offers two dozen recently renovated bedchambers. My favorites are the ones on the top floor with sloping ceiling and gabled windows opening on views out over the rooftops of the old town. The place reeks with atmosphere and is considered one of the special hotels of Geneva, particularly since parts of the building date from the 14th century. The hotel lies on a cobblestone street in the old quarter a few minutes' walk from the lake. In spite of the rather narrow lobby, the rooms are good-sized, with bathrooms that have been called "baronial." If you're planning an extended day in town, about half a dozen studios come with kitchens, making this one of the special treasures of Geneva. A restaurant on the ground floor is under different management. Interestingly enough, the street in front of the hotel is closed to traffic from 11 p.m. to 6 a.m. the next day. All of the rooms have baths or showers, toilets, phones, and radios, and some of the larger ones have color TVs. Singles cost anywhere from 60F ($27.57) to 88F ($40.44), while doubles range from 90F ($41.36) to 108F ($49.63). An extra bed or a crib can be set up in any of the units for an additional 22F ($10.11).

Hôtel du Midi, Place Chevelu (tel. 31-78-00), is on the same tree-lined square as the Hotel Ambassador, a location ideal for sightseeing in Geneva. The building rises like a California apartment house eight stories into the air, its salmon-colored panels alternating with the big windows and the visible parts of the concrete superstructure. The hotel is much better than it looks from the outside. The windows are double-glazed to keep out the noise, and there's wall-to-wall carpeting in every room. The hotel is loaded with thoughtful extras, such as warming racks for towels, tiny refrigerators in the rooms, even built-in safes for your valuables. You'll find a tavern on the ground floor, serving drinks and snacks, a street-level brasserie decorated with red wallpaper and hanging lamps, and a popular sidewalk café in front of the splashing fountain in the Place Chevelu in summer. Doubles cost anywhere from 110F ($50.55) to 130F ($59.74), and singles rent for 90F ($41.36) to 100F ($45.95). B. G. Zamboni, the manager, administers the 84 rooms with a quiet efficiency, making efforts to be helpful in every way.

Hôtel/Motel La Tourelle, 26 route d'Hermance, Genève-Vésenaz (tel. 52-16-28), offers more than two dozen attractively styled and comfortably furnished bedrooms in what used to be a private villa in a suburb to the northeast of Geneva. The hotel is closed in December and January. Many of the bedchambers offer views of the lake beyond the well-maintained grounds of clipped grass and ornamental trees. The suburb of Vésenaz is rather exclusive, so you'll get a glimpse of what the Swiss consider a wealthy residential area during your treks back and forth to the city, only 12 minutes away by car or bus. Victor Frenkel, the English-speaking owner, charges 70F ($32.17) in a single with bath, 45F ($20.68) in a single without bath, and between 95F ($43.65) and 105F ($48.25) for a double with bath or shower. Breakfast is included.

Penta-Hotel, 75-77 avenue Louis-Casaï, Cointrin/Genève (tel. 98-47-00), lies close to the Geneva airport offering clean and comfortable rooms, all of them soundproof, with air conditioning, bathrooms, radios, phones, color TVs with in-house movies, and mini-bars. The building is sleek and modern, with lots of exposed glass, and offers two restaurants, a bar, a fitness center, a sauna, and lots of convenient boutiques, newsstands, and a car-rental agency. You'll find a hotel shuttle bus making regular runs to the airport, and public buses making frequent trips to Geneva from a bus stop in front of the hotel. Many of the conference rooms and some of the public lounges are decorated with a pattern of carpeting designed to rivet your attention to its random op-art patterns of bright green on black. The bedrooms are more conservatively furnished, renting for anywhere from 97F ($44.57) to 119F ($54.68) in a single, from 127F ($58.36) to 149F ($68.47) in a double. Breakfast costs an additional 13.50F ($6.20), while an extra bed can be set up in your room for another 15F ($6.89).

Hôtel Époque, 10 rue Voltaire, (tel. 45-25-50), is only 400 yards from the railroad station, within walking distance of the center of town. Its sober facade of concrete, glass, and aluminum shelters 54 rooms, furnished comfortably if somewhat sparsely, each with bath or shower and toilet, radio, and phone. Some of the rooms have television. Jean-Pierre and Ursula Fahrny, the proprietors, charge 60F ($27.57) to 75F ($34.46) in a single, 88F ($40.44) to 120F ($55.14) in a double, breakfast included. Half- and full-board plans are available for 18F ($8.27) and 36F ($16.54) extra, respectively.

Hôtel Touring Balance, Place Longemalle (tel. 28-71-22), about two blocks east of the lake and just off the street that runs into the Pont du Mont-Blanc, is a friendly and personalized hotel which represents the union of what used to be a Hotel Touring and a Hotel Balance. The team effort you can see today has proved to be a successful facility which attracts a clientele returning frequently. The interior at its best seems to represent a kind of updated Victorian, with an appealing highlighting of many of the original architectural details with different colors of paint, along with some interesting original modern paintings. The restaurant is a bright, sunny room, painted in cream and coffee-colored hues, with a high ceiling and tasteful light art nouveau chairs and serving trolleys. Singles rent for 85F ($39.06) to 95F ($43.65) and doubles cost anywhere from 120F ($55.14) to 135F ($62.03), breakfast included.

Hôtel Amat-Carlton, 22 rue Amat (tel. 31-68-50), is about seven city blocks east of the railroad station, on a quiet street some 300 yards from the Quai Wilson. The facade is an attractive combination of weathered vertical slats and smooth stones decoratively cemented into rectangular patterns below the modern windows. The interior is warmly decorated in browns, beiges, and wood tones, with pin lighting in the reception area. All rooms have baths and phones. Apartments and "super studios" (with kitchens and terraces) are available for longer stays. Rental price by the day is from 93F ($42.73) to 110F $50.55) in a single, from 123F ($56.52) to 140F ($64.33) in a double. Prices include breakfast but do not allow use of the kitchen. G. Grutter, the director, will provide monthly rates on request.

Hôtel Grand-Pré, 35 rue du Grand-Pré (tel. 33-91-50), can be considered a real discovery for visitors to Geneva. It's owned by Jean Armleder of the famous hotel family which owns Le Richemond, the best hotel in town, and is run with the same attention to detail but at much more reasonable prices. The manager is Eberhard Graf, a skilled hotelier who sees personally that each problem of his guests (within reason) is solved satisfactorily. The Armleder family is to be applauded for recognizing and catering to the needs of the middle-income traveler and not just the petrodollar crowd. The carefully selected staff will give directions to the airport or the center of Geneva, both of which are within easy reach. No restaurant is connected to the hotel, although the rooms are well styled, comfortable, and attractively decorated, with maintenance on a very high level. Singles in this modern hostelry go for 85F ($39.06) to 100F ($45.95), from 125F ($57.44) to 150F ($68.93) in a double, breakfast included. All units contain private baths, color TVs, radios, and refrigerators. Special terms are available for families and for long stays.

Hotel International & Terminus, 20 rue des Alpes (tel. 32-80-95), is run by the Cottier family with the assistance of the dedicated manager, A. Perucchi. It's midway between the railroad station and the lake, about a ten-minute walk to either one. A telephone and radio are to be found in every room, although some are not equipped with baths. However, there's a sink in each room, and breakfast is provided free. Singles rent for anywhere from 35F ($16.08) to 80F ($36.76), and doubles range between 58F ($25.65) and 105F ($48.25). The public rooms are decorated with reproduction Louis XIII–style chairs, Oriental rugs, and a bombé pendulum clock reaching almost to the ceiling. *Plats du Jour* in the attached restaurant cost a reasonable 8.50F ($3.91).

Hostellerie de la Vendée, 28 chemin de la Vendée, Geneva/Petit-Lancy (tel. 92-04-11). The terrace of this country inn a few miles from the center of Geneva is covered with a bright-orange awning beneath which guests sip drinks or coffee and listen to the birds sing. The Righetto family are your hosts, welcoming you to the semi-rural ambience of this modern hostelry which is for the most part attractively decorated in rustic Swiss fashion. You'll find a bar, a restaurant, and probably a local wedding reception in one of the conference rooms. Singles rent for 72F ($33.08) to 92F ($42.27), while doubles cost from 95F ($43.65) to 135F ($62.03). Additional beds can be set up for 30F ($13.79) apiece. Breakfast is included.

Hotel Eden, 135 rue de Lausanne (tel. 32-65-40), housed in a building close to the Quai du Mont-Blanc, looks a lot like a superbly constructed seven-story stone-and-stucco fortress with many art deco influences. A generously proportioned set of steps takes you into the lobby where you register after passing below the pleasingly curved and indented two-tone facade. Bedrooms are spacious and high-ceilinged, administered through the diligent efforts of F.

Gulje, who charges from 75F ($34.46) to 95F ($43.65) in a single and from 100F ($45.95) to 130F ($59.74) in a double. Breakfast is included, and lunches or dinners can be ordered for 19F ($8.73) to 23F ($10.57) each. An extra bed can be set up in any room for an additional 20F ($9.19).

Savoy Hotel, 8 Place Cornavin (tel. 31-12-52). A quick glance at a city map will tell you that this hotel is across the square from the main railroad station. It's decorated in a tasteful, streamlined kind of way, with Directoire armchairs in the lobby next to the reception desk which is painstakingly inlaid with a geometric pattern of different kinds of hardwoods. Bedrooms are air-conditioned and soundproof, each with telephone, radio, and a color TV (usually placed out of the way on a shelf near the ceiling). The rooms I saw were tastefully furnished with pink-and-white floral draperies and olive-green wall-to-wall carpeting. Singles with bath cost 90F ($41.36), while doubles rent for 140F ($64.33). You'll find a restaurant and bar on the premises.

Hôtel Athénée, 6 route de Malagnou (tel. 46-39-33), is an elegantly appointed eight-story hotel with a white rectangular facade whose evenly spaced windows are decorated with prominent posts and lintels. The gardens around this establishment are several blocks off the south bank of the lake, about six blocks southeast of the English Garden. Parts of the interior are decorated like an 18th-century pleasure palace, with gray and white marble floors, dark scarlet wallpaper with white trim, Louis XIII–style gilded furniture, and in the dining room, skillfully fashioned Ionic half-columns supporting the elaborately molded ceilings. The hotel offers 90 beds in rooms with and without private baths. Singles rent for anywhere from 40F ($18.38) to 85F ($39.06), while doubles range from 65F ($29.87) to 140F ($64.33). All rooms have radios and telephones. You can get here from anywhere in Geneva by taking city bus no. 1, 11, 5, or 8.

Hôtel Century Genève, 24 avenue de Frontenex (tel. 36-80-95), is striking with its use of burnished copper and polished hardwoods in the lobby area. In the restaurant/bar, a copper chimney divided into rectangles almost like a Mondrian painting descends from the ceiling to catch the smoke from the fireplace in the center of the room. Black marble and russet Oriental rugs abound, creating an ambience that is warm, comfortable, and inviting. The hotel is within walking distance of both the Rhône and the lake. The 150 rooms are comfortably decorated, with generous use of pure white and scarlet in the bedroom fabrics. All units have baths. The hotel manager, Renzo Zanon, charges from 55F ($25.27) to 102F ($46.87) in a single and from 75F ($34.46) to 160F ($73.52) in a double, breakfast included.

Hôtel de Berne, 26 rue de Berne (tel. 31-60-00). Modern and boxy, with maroon racing stripes spanning the facade horizontally, this centrally located hotel, directed by S. di Mare, offers 80 soundproof rooms with bath, phone, radio, and TV. The lobby is a high-ceilinged expanse of chrome columns and scarlet-patterned carpeting. Bedrooms are functionally decorated in simple furnishings and vivid colors. Singles cost from 85F ($39.06) to 110F ($50.55), while doubles range from 120F ($55.14) to 145F ($66.63), breakfast included. A restaurant and bar are on the premises.

Hôtel Edelweiss, 2 Place de la Navigation (tel. 31-36-58). My favorite rooms here are the ones furnished with naïvely provincial pine reproductions, probably from the mountain regions of Switzerland. The hotel facade rises eight stories above its neighbors near the Quai Wilson. It looks something like a stack of pale-green and white building blocks piled four across and eight high, with prominent windows set in the concrete superstructure. Whoever decorated the lobby seems to have tried to recreate some alpine grange, with a reception desk fashioned something like an agrarian well somewhere in the country. All of this aside, the rooms are comfortable, clean, and cozy, costing 96F ($44.11) in a single and 125F ($57.44) in a double, breakfast included.

Hôtel Epsom, 18 rue Richemont (tel. 32-08-33), offering 330 beds in two modern buildings joined by an interconnecting lobby, is within walking distance of the railroad station, the lake, and everything of note in Geneva. The management displays two flags over the entrance, one for Switzerland, one for the city of Geneva. The lobby features an elongated marble reception desk and a marble floor protected by an almost never-ending row of blue, red, and black Oriental rugs in bold geometric patterns. Singles here rent for 115F ($52.84), while doubles cost 150F ($68.93), breakfast included. Rooms are comfortably furnished in striped bedcovers and armchairs. You'll find a restaurant and bar on the premises.

Hôtel Maroli, 15 rue Jean-Violette (tel. 20-45-75), lies four tram stops from the center of Geneva (take tram 12 or bus 11). Entirely renovated in 1977, the hotel, under the direction of the Rostan family, offers comfortably furnished rooms, costing 85F ($39.06) in a single, 110F ($50.55) in a double, and 130F ($59.74) in a triple. All units have private baths, except for a few singles that have showers but no toilets, renting for only 70F ($32.17). You'll find a restaurant and a bar on the premises, along with public rooms warmly decorated in brightly patterned carpets and deep, armless chairs.

THE BUDGET CATEGORY: **Hôtel le Grinil,** 7 avenue de Sainte-Clothilde (tel. 28-30-55), rises futuristically on a plot of land between the junction of the Rhône and the Arve (not far from the rue des Deux Ponts). Besides the many conference facilities, the hotel offers 50 rooms, many with showers but no toilets. Affiliated with the YMCA, it's only a short distance from the center of town and is said to be one of the "best for value" candidates in Geneva. Everything is streamlined, modern, and warmly decorated. Although the rooms are smallish, they're sunny and clean, costing from 41F ($18.84) to 66F ($30.33) in a single, from 59F ($27.11) to 90F ($41.36) in a double, from 69F ($31.71) to 90F ($41.36) in a triple, and from 80F ($36.76) to 100F ($45.95) in a family room, which has four beds. Breakfast is included for all registered guests in any room, and the hotel has complete facilities for handicapped patrons. The director is Harry van Dongen.

Genève Hôtel Lido, rue Chantepoulet (tel. 31-55-30), lies two blocks from the train station and offers sunny, soundproof rooms with views over the city. The hotel is small enough to offer personalized service, with 32 rooms decorated in modern colors and comfortable beds. The Rossier family are your hosts, charging from 32F ($14.70) to 45F ($20.68) in a single, from 50F ($22.98) to 85F ($39.06) in a double. Breakfast is included. Not all the rooms have private baths, so know what you're getting before you commit yourself.

Hôtel Bernina, 22 Place Cornavin (tel. 31-49-50), is a hotel which someone once described as "elderly but not creaky." It sits on the square opposite the train station in an old-fashioned rectangular building, with iron balustrades on the balconies and neoclassical detailing around the windows. The hotel offers 76 rooms on six floors, and if you're kept awake at night by street noise you should ask for a nest near the top. Inside you'll find a large, rambling, split-level lobby with a black-and-white tile floor and a sweeping red-carpeted staircase. Bedrooms are spacious, and the closets are big enough to store trunks in. Paul à Porta, the English-speaking manager, charges from 44F ($20.22) to 63F ($28.95) in a single, from 70F ($32.17) to 90F ($41.36) in a double, and from 96F ($44.11) to 125F ($57.44) in a triple, breakfast included.

Hotel Windsor, 31 rue de Berne (tel. 31-71-30), lies four blocks from the Quai Wilson and three blocks from the train station. Rooms are small and a little run-down, yet for the price—70F ($22.17) in a single, from 85F ($39.06) to 100F ($45.95) in a double—you might want to make it your address in Geneva for a night. Breakfast is included. The lobby is focused around a large masonry fireplace and is vividly decorated in shades of blue and red. Each unit has a private bath or shower, phone, radio, and TV. There's a total of 100 beds.

Rivoli Hotel, 6 rue des Paquis (tel. 31-85-50), is centrally located, three minutes from both the train station and the lake. The rooms are small, predictably furnished with slightly run-down furnishings, but comfortable. Breakfast is included in the price of 90F ($41.36) in a double, from 60F ($27.57) to 70F ($32.17) in a single. All units contain showers, although the occupants of the cheapest singles must use the toilet in the hall.

Hôtel Paquis-Fleuri, 23 rue des Paquis (tel. 31-34-52), lies only two blocks from the prestigious hotels on the Quai du Mont-Blanc but is considerably cheaper. In fact it's one of the best hotel buys in town. It contains only a dozen rooms (and are they scrubbed!), which are for the most part pleasantly furnished, contain telephones, and can be reached by elevator from the lobby. Some of the units face a tranquil courtyard. A generous breakfast is included in the price of the rooms. With showers, singles cost 50F ($22.98); doubles, 80F ($36.76). Without showers, singles rent for 40F ($18.38); doubles, 60F ($27.57).

Hôtel Dumas, 17 avenue Dumas (tel. 46-39-67), lies in a residential section, the Champel, where the university is located and where many chic Geneva residents have chosen to live. The establishment is casual, with an attractive lobby and public rooms in various shades of brown. The bedrooms are a mixed bag. Some are brightly lit, well kept, and attractively furnished; others could use some sprucing up. There are only 16 units in all, which share a quartet of bathrooms. The hotel is well recommended, however, to budgeteers, especially those planning to be in Geneva for a while. Singles cost 38F ($17.46), while doubles rent for 55F ($27.27) a night, breakfast included. Take bus no. 3 or 33 from tne main railroad station.

Hôtel des Tourelles, 2 boulevard James-Fazy (tel. 32-44-23). Not to be confused with a hotel previously recommended, La Tourelle, this family-run establishment (the Meier family) offers about two dozen rooms with good views of the river. None of the rooms has a private bath, although the corridor facilities are perfectly adequate. The hotel stands next to the Hôtel du Rhône, at the place where the river becomes Lake Geneva. Not stylish, the rooms are nevertheless pleasantly furnished and comfortable. Singles cost 42F ($19.30), while doubles rent for 55F ($25.27), with breakfast included.

Hôtel Rousseau, 13 rue J-J Rousseau (tel. 31-55-70), honors the French author and political theorist who was born in Geneva in 1712. The hotel is well located, not far from the river-fronting Quai des Bergues, on a busy commercial street. The establishment is best known for its restaurant on the second floor, but it also offers about a dozen bedrooms with personalized service from the family which runs it. A typical unit is well lit, carpeted, and decorated with comfortable furniture. Singles rent for 65F ($29.87) to 69F ($31.71) and doubles range anywhere from 95F ($43.65) to 99F ($45.49), breakfast included. You may not be able to get a room without a reservation, as the hotel is popular with travelers.

Hôtel le Clos Voltaire, 49 rue de Lyon (tel. 44-70-14), receives the highest recommendation in its category, especially for the history buff who'll want to know how this house was connected with Voltaire. Set in a floral park, the suburban location is nothing short of being totally relaxing. Covered with vines, the house is on the main road to Lyon, offering parking in front and an attractive garden. Of the 40 accommodations, only eight have some sort of private plumbing; for the rest, there are adequate facilities in the hallways. This hotel is ideal if you have a private car. Singles rent for 45F ($20.68) without bath, 60F ($27.57) with bath; doubles cost 60F ($27.57) without bath, 80F ($36.76) with bath. Breakfast is included in the tariffs.

Hôtel le Montbrillant, 2 rue Montbrillant (tel. 33-77-84). Forget about the exterior of this building when you see it up close. The owners inside will warm it up during your stay here, and some of the best rates in super-expensive Geneva will put you in a more forgiving mood. Singles rent for 45F ($20.68) and doubles for 60F ($27.57) to 75F ($34.46), breakfast included. The hard-working chambermaids do what they can to scrub things up, but the rooms are nevertheless a little drab. Despite that, this hotel represents very good value for the money. In the vicinity of the station, this is recommended as a clean, safe, and reasonably comfortable choice. The owners are Mr. and Mrs. Reto Decurtins.

Hôtel Beau-Site, 3 Place du Cirque (tel. 28-10-08). The elevator lifts you to the reception desk of this elaborately embellished hotel near the university. It offers 55 beds in rooms that are not lavishly furnished but which are improved by occasional use of autumnal colors. The place is well kept. It's obvious that the English-speaking management has expended a lot of elbow grease here. Recent renovations have improved the public rooms too. The units offer a range of plumbing possibilities, but you'll find that singles go between 40F ($18.38) and 45F ($20.68), while doubles cost from 60F ($27.57) to 65F ($29.87), breakfast included. Nonworking marble fireplaces are in some of the bedrooms, and oversize, heavily carved sideboards in the dining room.

2. Where to Dine

Geneva is one of the gastronomical centers of Europe, with a decided French influence, as would be expected. None of the Genevese today seems to heed Calvin's warnings against "the pleasures of the table." Eating well in Geneva is practiced with consummate flair and style, and meals, often in dramatic lakeside settings, are often long, drawn-out affairs.

Despite its position as one of the international hubs of the world, there aren't as many different cuisines as you might have anticipated (although it has the greatest Chinese restaurant in all of Europe).

Geneva naturally serves all the typically Swiss dishes, such as filets of perch from Lake Geneva and fricassée of pork. In season, many of its restaurants offer a marvelous vegetable that has some of the taste of an artichoke. It's called cardon and is usually served au gratin. By all means try the Genevese sausage, longeole. From Lac Léman emerges one of the great fishes found in any alpine lake, omble chevalier, like a grayling. Some gourmets have compared it to salmon.

Cheese is also important on the Genevese table, including such Swiss cheese as tomme and gruyère, plus, in season, the celebrated vacherin from the Joux Valley. Naturally, everything will taste better with Perlan (white wine) and Gamay (red wine) from Geneva's own vineyards.

Now, the bad news. Geneva is one of the most expensive cities in Europe for dining out.

SOME DELUXE CHOICES: Restaurant du Parc des Eaux-Vives, 82 Quai Gustave-Ador (tel. 35-41-44). You'll pass by a series of architectural details that are baronial (a wrought-iron gate, immaculately maintained grounds, a winding driveway). Eventually you'll be seated in the dining room of a pinkish-gray stone château owned by the city of Geneva. By almost everyone's vote, the restaurant lies in the most beautiful part of Geneva (a section of it reserved for the Geneva Tennis Club). The chefs adjust the menu according to the produce of the season, but tend to concentrate on the time-honored recipes of classical French cuisine, which is probably what the conservative patrons of this restaurant prefer. The local trout is superb, and the menu offers many game dishes in autumn. Of course everything tastes better with truffles, including the lobster salad, the foie gras, and the suprême of sea perch with green lettuce and champagne sauce or the breast of duck with olives or cherries. The restaurant shuts down on Monday and from January until mid-February. Dinners cost around 85F ($39.06), but lunchtime meals are slightly less expensive, 50F ($22.98). The restaurant serves from noon to 2 p.m. and from 7:30 p.m. in summer (from 7 p.m. in winter).

Restaurant Amphitryon, 33 Quai des Bergues (tel. 31-50-50). At one of the most prestigious hotels of Geneva (the Hôtel des Bergues), you'll dine in an ambience like that of a palace. The chefs, supervised by Albert Felli, produce a blend of classical and nouvelle cuisine that the Genevois find most alluring. Amphitryon, by the way, means "host" in 19th-century French. The staff today provides the impeccable service worthy of that distinction.

You might enjoy a simple lunch here, which could include slices of duck breast with horseradish sauce followed by shoulder of lamb with spinach and sauteed potatoes lightly seasoned with garlic, climaxed by cheese or dessert, all for 38F ($17.46). Or you could select a more elaborate meal, which might include lobster broth with fresh herbs, a cassoulet of fresh snails forestière, a "trilogy" of three kinds of steamed fish with white butter, or duck breast with honey and lime. The choice here is so wide that à la carte meals could range from 50F ($22.98) to 125F ($57.44). The restaurant is open daily from noon to 3 p.m. and 7 to 11 p.m.

Another restaurant in the same hotel, **Le Pavillon,** is less formal, less expensive, costing around 50F ($22.98) for an à la carte dinner, with fixed-price meals costing from 21F ($9.65). The menu is very attractively varied and contains such elegant items as poached or grilled salmon with hollandaise, broiled turbot with mustard sauce, veal cutlet with sage, or veal piccata with morels. There's an unpretentious wine list (why not try the local Fendant?).

Le Chat Botté, 13 Quai du Mont-Blanc (tel. 31-02-21), represents a sophisticated partnership between entrepreneur Fred Mayer and his star-rated head chef, Jean-Marie Coibrie, who used to work at some of the best restaurants in Paris and the Côte d'Azur, including Prunier and Ledoyen. Le Chat Botté gracefully serves Geneva just about the best food available in an elegantly decorated format of tapestries and sculpture. Cuisine is of the great classical French school. Some dishes have been virtually unchanged from recipes a hundred years old. From a large selection, you might compose a meal of filets of Saint-Pierre in a red wine sauce or a rack of lamb with a sauce made from old port, medallions of roebuck with ginger and marrow, or a fricassée of suckling veal with basil. You might also try the salmon Janine. A wine list will open one of the finest cellars in Geneva to you. Your meal might also be served on the terrace. None of this comes inexpensively, but many satisfied diners agree that the price is worth it. Fixed-price meals range from 67F ($30.79) to 97F ($44.57), while à la carte dinners cost from 65F ($29.87) to 94F ($43.19). Reservations are important. The restaurant is open daily from noon to 2:15 p.m. and 7 to 10:15 p.m. which means you should get there before 9:30 p.m. The restaurant is in the Hôtel Beau-Rivage.

Le Gentilhomme, Hôtel Richemond, Jardin Brunswick (tel. 31-14-00). To have a rendezvous at the Richemond was—and *is*—one of the chicest invitations you can extend or receive in Geneva. This is the Maxim's of Geneva, and you should arrive there before 11:30 p.m. and expect to spend from 85F ($39.06) and up for a gourmet meal impeccably served in a 19th-century cadre of crimson silk and glittering crystal. Set meals range from 75F ($34.46) to 105F ($48.25). Specialties prepared by chefs Bagnoud and Yvelin include filet of turbot with violets, a seafish terrine with chive sauce, crabmeat in puff pastry, cucumber soup with fresh dill, and roast duck with a candied lemon zest. The wines are among the best in the city, and service is every day. Don't dress informally.

THE UPPER BRACKET: **La Perle du Lac,** 128 rue de Lausanne (tel. 31-35-04), is a very well-known restaurant which has been around forever and which is owned and maintained by the city of Geneva under the direction of André Hauri. In fashionable Mon Repos park, not far from the United Nations complex, the restaurant has bay windows which look out over ancient trees and elaborately manicured lawns. The interior is lovely, with warm wintertime candlelight, but in summer you may want to reserve a table on the al fresco terrace. A supremely talented French chef, Daniel Grenard, does a marvelous fricassée of frog legs. Other specialties include perch, omble chevalier, trout, a mixed grill, and a sea bass with mint sabayon, perhaps filet mignon of veal with mushroom mousse and basil, or else a ragoût of baby turbot and lobster. His sorbets (ask for a mixture) are superb. This is the only restaurant in Geneva that opens directly onto the lakefront. A meal without wine will cost from 75F ($34.46). The restaurant is closed on Monday and from around Christmas until the beginning of February. Always reserve ahead and arrive before 9:30 p.m.

Le Béarn, 4 Quai de la Poste (tel. 21-00-28), is a well-established culinary monument with an impressive list of clients which include some of the world's leading bankers, the Aga Khan, the Baron de Rothschild, and a host of international celebrities. The recently renovated interior is filled with Empire furniture. Jean-Paul and his wife Denise have elevated this restaurant to what might be the best dining room in the business center of Geneva. You might enjoy their goose liver salad with crabmeat and asparagus or a ragoût of lotte with lobster, perhaps a plate called les trois gourmandises—smoked salmon, lobster, and shrimp on the same platter. You might further try a ragoût of quail breast with baby lettuce leaves or a classic barbary goose in wine sauce. Fixed-price meals range from 58F ($26.65) to 110F ($50.55) while à la carte dinners cost from 80F ($36.76). The restaurant is closed on Saturday at lunch, all day Sunday, and from mid-July to mid-August. Go before 9:30 p.m.

Mère Royaume, 9 rue des Corps-Saints (tel. 32-70-08), is named after the heroine of 1602 referred to in the introduction, the hearty lass who poured boiling stew over a soldier's head and cracked his skull with her kettle. After all that you'd expect robust regional fare here. What you get instead is delicately cooked French specialties. The head chef, Monsieur Bertrand, is a sophisticated artist in the kitchen, as reflected by his omble from Lake Geneva and by such dishes as eggs au Bouzy. He offers meerwolf in puff pastry with spinach, breast of hen with cider vinegar, and goose liver with raspberry vinegar, very nouvelle cuisine. The trout, in the word of one diner, is "divine." The decor is wood paneled in the old style. The restaurant is closed on Saturday for lunch and all day Sunday, and its last orders go in at 10 p.m. Always call for a reservation, and count on spending from 75F ($34.46) for a fine meal here. In the same house you'll find a less expensive brasserie and an attractively planted terrace. The bar is named after that epic battle of 1602.

Restaurant Curling, 9 bis Chemin du Fief-du-Chapître (tel. 93-62-44), at Petit-Lancy. If you've never tried curling, you'll meet plenty of people here who have. Many of them have even adopted the first room of this establishment as their favorite meeting place. You should head, however, through the brasserie to the main dining room, which has gained an enviable reputation for the excellent cookery of Daniel Ficht. He's one of the finest chefs of Geneva, preparing such dishes as poached sole, a gratin of shrimp and lobster, or duckling suprême with colbert butter. His foie gras is velvet. Service here is unhurried, so be prepared for a leisurely meal and count on spending some 85F ($39.06) for the privilege. Lunch is less expensive. The restaurant is open from 8 a.m. to midnight, but is closed all day Sunday and for lunch on Monday. Vacation time is from mid-July to mid-August.

Au Fin Bec, 55 rue de Berne (tel. 32-29-19), has been around for a long time. It's known for its game dishes, although a glance at the menu will reveal about 30 items, any one of which would be palate-tempting. If you're on an eating binge you can order the menu gourmande at 90F ($41.36), providing you with six deliciously filling courses including both meat and fish. In winter you'll have a trio of dining rooms to chose from, while in summer you surely will prefer the shaded terrace. Cardon is a specialty in autumn, while other dishes include a fricassée of crabmeat with young vegetables or a salad of fresh lotte with avocado. Some of the desserts, such as the hot strawberry soufflé, are so elaborate they have to be ordered at the beginning of the meal. The format here is intimate, cozy, and comfortable. If you order à la carte you could spend as much as 85F ($39.06). The restaurant is open weekdays, but on Saturday for dinner only (closed Sunday and every August).

Le Duc, 7 Quai du Mont-Blanc (tel. 31-73-30), is an uncompromisingly excellent restaurant which has built up a faithful clientele by serving the same superbly flavored fish dishes since it opened in 1976. Part of its success is because director Pietro Saverioni works hard at welcoming each guest with sincerity and charm. The decor is discreetly elegant, the perfect setting for seafood prepared with finesse by the Minchelli brothers. Daily shipments of fish arrive from Rungis, the wholesale market of Paris. Standards are so high that the brothers once closed the restaurant for a day during a French strike rather than serve day-old fish. Specialties include virtually everything with gills, but some meat dishes are offered too. Try the red mullet in butter sauce or the fish and crustacean stew, perhaps the crayfish soufflé. Other recommendable main courses include John Dory in butter sauce, loup with lemon, or lobster in orange sauce. Count on spending from 55F ($25.27) to 80F ($36.76) for a meal here. Reservations are suggested. It's closed on Sunday and Monday, but open every other day from 12:15 to 3 p.m. and 7:30 to 10:30 p.m.

Hostellerie de la Vendée (Restaurant du Pont Rouge), 28 Chemin de la Vendée (tel. 92-04-11), at Petit-Lancy, has an austere, albeit expensive "Calvinist" interior, but the reformer would have been shocked at the devotion to food and service. You'll drive into a countryside district known for its outstanding restaurants. Run by the Righetto brothers, the restaurant is chic and known for its seasonal specialties and location at the edge of Geneva. Go before 9 p.m. (it opens at 7 p.m.) for dinner, or for lunch from noon to 1:45 p.m. It's closed on Sunday and takes a long Christmas holiday. You'll enjoy the foie gras prepared many different ways by the chef, Monsieur Bonneau. Try also his filet of sea bass or his duckling with peaches. Dessert might be a soufflé Grand Marnier. You'll spend about 75F ($34.46) for a meal here. The terrace is shaded in summertime.

Restaurant L'Arlequin, 34 Quai du Général-Guisan (tel. 21-13-44), is part of the Hôtel Métropole. The large room is outfitted with clear colors, a classical decor, and lots of flowers. According to the day's shopping, chef Alain Jennings offers omble, trout, sea bass, and turbot, as as well as lobster terrine, mussels with saffron, warm salmon sausage with white butter, and steamed sea bass with tomatoes, along with veal kidneys flambé, mousseline of frog legs with a warm crayfish sauce, and côte de boeuf bourguignon. The menu gastronomique costs from 80F ($36.76) to 95F ($43.65), and fixed-price evening meals are from 60F ($27.57). The restaurant is open every day, and reservations are suggested.

Via Veneto, 10 rue de la Tour Maîtresse (tel. 21-65-93), is a small restaurant in the center of town, known for its rich continental fare. The food is consistently good, and is under the supervision of chef Alain Lavergnats who, before coming here, worked in three prestigious restaurants of France. The excellent service is directed by Gil Castrucci, the owner. The restaurant closes on Sunday and from mid-July to mid-August. Reservations are suggested. Fixed-price meals cost from 65F ($29.87) to 81F ($37.22), and à la carte dinners begin at 60F ($27.57). You might enjoy the pheasant salad in its own mousse or a lobster and mushroom salad, followed by a mixture of truffles, wild mushrooms, and a fondant of foie gras in puff pastry or a mousse of snails in a green butter sauce. Elegant desserts follow if you're up to it.

THE MIDDLE BRACKET: Chez Valentino, 63 route de Thonon (tel. 52-14-40), Vésenaz-Genève, is an Italian restaurant with great antipasti and lots of atmosphere. Valentino Peloso, the hard-working owner, prepares many of the specialties himself. His restaurant lies in a suburb about three miles from the heart of the city. No lunch is served on Monday and Tuesday, and the restaurant is shut down for much of the month of August. The moderately priced meals include minestrone, followed by gnocchi alla piemontese, tagliatelle with gorgonzola or eggplant gorgonzola. The antipasti contain a selection of everything's that's wonderful in the kitchen, while the carpaccio or Parma ham is also very good. Main courses might feature frog legs provençal, curried scampi, pigeon, or côte de veal Valentino. Other items run the gamut from fish to beef to lamb and chicken. À la carte meals begin at 25F ($11.49), but you'll spend far more, or course, if you order a meat dish.

Restaurant Tse-Fung, 301 route de Lausanne (tel. 74-17-36), is considered one of the finest Oriental restaurants in Europe. It's Chinese, expensive, and located inside the Hôtel La Réserve. Specialties include marmite mongole, lacquered duck, and other Cantonese, Peking, and Shanghai recipes. À la carte meals range from 18F ($8.27) to 32F ($14.70), and a fixed-price meal begins at 60F ($27.57). There is a bar and a terrace.

Le Chandelier, 23 Grand-Rue (tel. 28-11-88), nostalgically basks in its fame from the novel *Goldfinger.* This restaurant, in a hotel of the same name, was an old stamping ground of the late Ian Fleming. He always wanted to sit by the table right at the door to the kitchen. In the old town, the restaurant has a mellow glow, as it's been around for some time. It offers excellent grills and many specialties such as feuilletes de veau with three kinds of mustard in its sauce, entrecôte bordelaise, tornedos with morels, and carré d'agneau (lamb) flavored with thyme. Its main specialty, however, is fondue bourguignonne, but the chef also does scampi curry and trout with almonds very well. To open your meal you might try either the lobster bisque or the real turtle soup. Monsieur Zufferey is the director. Count on spending from 55F ($25.27) for an excellent meal here.

A l'Olivier de Provence, 13 rue Jacques-Dalphin (tel. 42-04-50), at Carouge, is one of the best restaurants on the outskirts of Geneva. It has a lovely summer garden where you'll dine under shade trees. Prices are moderate, ranging from 18F ($8.27) to 22F ($10.11) for a fixed-price meal and from 22F ($10.11) to 40F ($18.38) for an à la carte dinner. Many of the most savory dishes from Provence are offered here, including loup de mer (sea bass) flambé. A fixed-price gourmet meal is offered for 60F ($27.57).

La Louisiane, 21 rue du Rhône (tèl. 28-29-25), is an elegant tearoom which serves pastries, small sandwiches, and light meals to a crowd of well-dressed shoppers. Outfitted with bamboo and wicker chairs, along with lots of plants, the establishment is open from 8 a.m. to 7:30 p.m. every day but Sunday. You can drop in for coffee and delicate sandwiches anytime, but hot meals are served only between 11:45 a.m. and 3 p.m. Caviar blinis at 33F ($15.16) are the most expensive item on the menu, followed by an array of pastas with foie gras and truffles, smoked salmon, morels, or crabmeat, all costing from 14F ($6.43) to 20F ($9.19). An imaginative array of omelets with homemade pasta are served for 17F ($7.81). All are named after 20th-century celebrities (the James Dean version is made with truffles). Salads are varied and interesting too.

THE BUDGET RANGE: **Taverne de la Madeleine,** 20 rue Toutes Âmes (tel. 28-40-32), is set against the old city wall to the side of the Église de la Madeleine. If you get confused while looking for it, just circle the church until you see it on higher ground at the corner of rue des Barrières. Inside an old three-story house you'll find a very good restaurant with brusquely efficient service which caters to many of the local business community, especially at lunch. The establishment serves no alcohol (but does offer alcohol-free beer, however). A wall sign advertises eight kinds of tea. At red café chairs pulled up to small bistro-style tables, you can order a variety of simple and well-prepared dishes from overworked motherly waitresses who carry enormous loads of plates from one end of the restaurant to the other. Specials include two types of spaghetti, vegetarian sandwiches, and such hearty fare as a big plate of ossobuco with pommes frites. An escalope de veau with potatoes and salad costs 12F ($5.51), while an average à la carte meal goes for 16F ($7.35). The restaurant is open weekdays until 7 p.m. and is closed Sunday.

Café de la Cité, 27 rue de la Cité (tel. 21-30-60). You'll stumble upon a small art nouveau facade in beautifully grained wood with stylized violets in the corners. The handcrafted tables have been refinished to show woods more suitable for 19th-century antiques than for a café table in a working-class bistro. This is a family-operated, inexpensive hideaway on a street filled with antique stores. When I was last there someone was incongruously playing honky-tonk country music (Hank Williams, no less!). A menu of the day is offered for only 10F ($4.60), and the chef's specials are likely to include fondue with mushrooms or morels, escargots, frog legs provençal, scallops, and good spaghetti. An à la carte meal will cost from 25F ($11.49). No one will care if you drop in for a beer or some wine during nonlunch hours. The café shuts down every evening at 11.

Restaurant du Palais de Justice, 8 Place Bourg-de-Four (tel. 20-42-54), is a simple little place with lots of atmosphere in spite of its pretentious name. You'll find it in the old town on a colorful square with lots of other attractive establishments around it. Across from the Palais de Justice, the restaurant offers three different places at which to dine, with separate menus for each. The Restaurant is one flight up from the street level, and the most expensive of the trio. It offers attractively served and well-prepared meals from 31F ($14.25), which might include terrine maison, turbot mousse, and a savory array of beef dishes as well as osso buco. La Taverne serves six different kinds of pizza from 6.50F ($2.99) to 8.50F ($3.91), and three kinds of fondue from 20F ($9.19). Finally, the Restaurant du Rez-de-Chaussée serves basically the same dishes as La Taverne (pizza and fondue). It has a street-level format of rustic wood, white stucco, and exposed masonry, along with a rattan ceiling. The trio is closed Sunday and for lunch on Monday.

Restaurant les Armures, 1 rue du Puits-St-Pierre (tel. 28-91-72), couldn't be in a more colorful part of the old town, across a cobblestone street from a medieval arsenal. The chiseled stone facade has seen many owners, but this is still the oldest café in Geneva, with a clientele which drops in for coffee or cheese fondue whenever they're in that part of the city. The fondue is considered the best in town, and the setting is rustic enough to allow you to appreciate that recipe's mountain origins. The establishment prepares three types, priced from 14F ($6.43) to 17.50F ($8.04), along with raclette, costing from 4F ($1.84) per portion. Many Genevese make a meal out of the hash-brown potato dish, rösti, at 5F ($2.30) a portion. Other specialties include eight types of pizza, along with hamburgers, french fries, five pasta courses, and good sausages with potato salad, all of them priced from 9F ($4.14). The sauerkraut garni at 15F ($6.89) is a savory meal in itself. The restaurant is closed all day Sunday and for lunch on Monday.

La Potinière, Jardin Anglais (tel. 21-71-62), could provide the kind of setting for a lovely summertime lunch where you'll probably dawdle over coffee with a friend. There's no real indoor area around here, but you'll be protected from the rushing traffic on the nearby quays by an expanse of lawn and a low wall of flowers. Guests sit on a flagstone terrace on blue folding chairs with a canopy as a protection against sudden cloudbursts. Black-vested waiters serve lunches to dozens of local residents, from officeworkers to members of the well-heeled gentry. A weekly fixed-price menu in English (after all, this is the Jardin Anglais) costs from 21F ($9.65), and might include both Swiss and continental dishes from cold roast beef to entrecôte. Fondue bourguignonne is a specialty. The restaurant is open from 11 a.m. to 10:30 p.m. in summer only (closed from October to March).

Café du Centre, 5 Place du Moulard (tel. 21-85-86). The square where this establishment is located is separated from the busy quays by a clock tower of chiseled stone. The square has very little traffic and lots of flower stalls, and in summer, many café tables. It's like some giant living room. Many of these tables belong to this old-fashioned brasserie. A more expensive upstairs room, when it's open, is decorated with 17th-century stained glass. But most of the business takes place outdoors in summer or on the ground-floor café level. This rooms opens pleasantly onto the square, in a long narrow vista of symmetrically placed tables, with wood covering the walls and ceiling. Someone will bring you a thick menu with more than 120 food items. A fixed-price lunch with wine costs from 18F ($8.27) to 25F ($11.49) if you include dessert. The menu is in English. Vegetarian meals are also offered. Irish coffee might be an attractive midday beverage.

Edelweiss, 2 Place de la Navigation (tel. 31-49-40), in a hotel previously recommended, looks like an alpine fantasy of rustic wood, geraniums, and folkloric music. Flags from many nations hang near the ceiling. You can go here, dine on Swiss specialties such as fondue, listen to the music, and even dance, all for a relatively moderate price of about 35F ($16.08) per person. It's economical when you consider that you get both food and entertainment, and you can make an evening of it. Go anytime between 7 p.m. and midnight.

Yankee Clipper, 3 rue Chaponière (tel. 32-21-31). In some parts of Geneva, to go American is chic, and the Yankee Clipper is the principal devotee of that trend. If you like your beer from Milwaukee and your wine from the vinevards of California, then this is your resting place for the night. You can also go for lunch from noon to 2 p.m. (dinner, drinks, light meals, whatever, are served from 6 to 11 p.m.). The French call it cuisine américaine, and is the typical European cliché of Stateside food that means hamburgers, U.S. beef, and barbecue. The salad bar is a worthy accompaniment to most main dishes. You can spend all sorts of money here, depending on what you order to drink, but you can easily get by for 30F ($13.79).

Au Pied de Cochon, 4 Place du Bourg-de-Four (tel. 20-47-97), which has a namesake in Paris, is the best place to go in Geneva for hearty Lyonnaise fare. The place is very popular with young people, who like to order the pig feet. The motto around here is practically "le cochon est roi" (pig is king). The setting is fin-de-siècle, and most of the meat and poultry dishes, especially the pork, are excellent, yet the cost for a meal begins at 25F ($11.49). A plat du jour is usually featured for 12F ($5.51). Hours are from noon to 2:30 p.m. and 7 to 11 p.m.

3. What to See and Do

If you arrive in Geneva in summer, as most tourists will, you might begin your discovery of the city by a long promenade along the **"Quays of Geneva."** The one sight you can't miss—even if you tried!—is the **Jet d'Eau,** the famous fountain that is the trademark of the city. Visible for miles around from April to September, it throws water 460 feet into the air above the lake. The *bise* (wind) blows the spume into a feathery, fluttery fan, often wetting those below who stand too close. The Genevese call the fountain the "jeddo." It dates from 1891, but was much improved in 1951. Many cities have sent engineers to Geneva to discover the workings of the fountain, but it remains a state secret, carefully guarded. It pumps 132 gallons of water at 125 miles per hour.

Then you'll be ready to explore the quays, with their luxuriantly planted flower gardens, dotted with ancient buildings. The aquatic population consists of seagulls, ducks, and swans. A fleet of small boats, called *Mouettes genevoises,* shuttles visitors from one quay to another from spring until autumn's blasts become too chilly.

Like the water jet, the **Flower Clock** in the **Jardin Anglais** is another Geneva trademark. Its face is made of flowers, and it keeps perfect time (but what else in this world-famed center of watchmaking?). The Jardin Anglais is at the foot of the Mont Blanc Bridge, which spans the river at the point where the Rhône leaves Lake Geneva. It was rebuilt in 1969.

After leaving the garden you can walk along the Quai des Bergues as far as the bridge, called the Pont des Bergues. If you cross this bridge you'll come to **Île Rousseau,** with a statue of Geneva's most famous son done by Pradier in 1834. This island, the former stamping ground of the philosopher, is home to any number of ducks, swans, and other aquatic fowl such as grebes. In the middle of the Rhône, it was once a bulwark of Geneva's river defenses.

You can continue crossing the bridge and can then follow the Besançon Hugues quay until you reach **Tour-de-'Île,** farther downstream. Built in 1219, a château which once stood here was used as a prison by the Counts of Savoy. A wall plaque commemorates the visit of Caesar in 58 B.C. The tower is all that remains from the 13th-century castle. It was here that freedom fighter Philibert Berthelier was decapitated in 1519. Nowadays the Geneva Tourist

Office is located on the island. You can also explore the old markets where often there are exhibitions of the works of contemporary Genevese artists.

If you walk east along the Quai des Bergues you'll return to the Pont du Mont-Blanc. To the left, facing the lake, is the **Brunswick Monument,** the tomb of Charles II of Brunswick who died in Geneva in 1873. The duke left his fortune to the city provided it built a monument to him. Geneva accepted the fortune and modeled the tomb after the Scaglieri tombs in Verona.

THE SIGHTS OF VIEILLE VILLE: "Old Town" in Geneva is one of the most remarkable in Switzerland. It stands on the left bank, where the cultural life of Geneva flourishes.

The old quarter is dominated by the **Cathedral of St. Pierre,** originally built between the 10th and 13th centuries and partially reconstructed in the 15th century. The church looks out over Geneva from its hilltop perch. It became Protestant in 1536. The interior is austere, just the way Calvin preferred it (his seat is on the north side). The church has seen much recent renovation, and it has a modern organ with 6000 pipes. If you don't mind some 145 steps, you can climb to the north tower for a splendid vista of the city, its lake, the Alps, and the Jura mountains. Admission is 2F (92¢). The cathedral is open from 9 a.m. to noon and 2 to 5 p.m. (stays open until 6 p.m. in October). However, in summer its afternoon hours are different, from 1:30 to 7 p.m.

Adjoining the southwest corner of the cathedral, the **Chapelle des Macchabées** was built in 1406 but much restored during World War II. It's in the High Gothic style, extravagantly ornate.

Next door to the cathedral is the **Temple de l'Auditoire,** or Calvin auditorium, a Gothic church were Knox and Calvin preached. It was restored in 1959 in time for Calvin's 450th anniversary.

After leaving the cathedral, strike out across the Cour St-Pierre, turning left onto the rue St-Pierre, where at no. 4 you'll encounter **Maison Tavel,** the oldest house in Geneva. First built in 1303, according to dim records, it was apparently rebuilt in 1334. It's decorated with amusing carved heads and a fine turret, and has a 12th-century cellar, which predates the original building.

The **Hôtel de Ville** (city hall), a short walk from the cathedral, dates from the 16th and 17th centuries. It has a cobbled ramp instead of a staircase. The Salle d'Alabama is the salon where arbitration between America and England in 1872 was peacefully resolved. Its Baudet Tower was constructed in 1455. Incidentally, the Red Cross originated here in 1864.

Across from the city hall is the **Arsenal,** an arcaded structure dating from 1634. In the courtyard of the building is a cannon cast in 1683.

Still in this general complex, the **Place du Bourg-de-Four** is an irregular square dating from the Middle Ages, although long before that it was a Roman forum. The Palais de Justice here was built in 1707, and has housed courts of law since 1860. You'll find many antiquaries' shops, art galleries, and a flower-bedecked fountain.

Another pride of Geneva is the **Reformation Monument,** beneath the walls of the old town on the Promenade des Bastions. One hundred yards long, it was constructed against a 16th-century rampart. In the austere style so beloved by Calvin himself, it's a bit drab, but an enduring landmark nevertheless. Erected in 1917, it depicts big statues of a quartet of Genevese reformers, including Knox, Calvin, Bèze, and Farel. On each end are memorials to Luther and Zwingli. Oliver Cromwell and even the Pilgrim Fathers get in on the act.

Also in the old town, a short walk from the cathedral is **Église St-Germain,** the Church of St. Germain, which was built on the site of an early

Christian church, perhaps from the fourth and fifth centuries. Restored in 1959, it has the remains of a 14th-century altar, the time of the building's construction. It saw more work in the 15th century. The stained-glass windows are contemporary.

MORE PARKS, GARDENS, AND SQUARES: Below the old quarter, to the southwest, is the **Place Neuve,** with its equestrian statue of General Dufour, one of the cofounders of the Red Cross. It's considered the cultural heart of Geneva as it's ringed by the Grand Théâtre, the Conservatory of Music, and the Rath Museum. The Grand Théâtre (opera house) was built in 1874 and will be visited in our after-dark wanderings. The Conservatoire de Musique is from 1858. The **Rath Museum,** Place Neuve (tel. 28-56-16), reached by tram 12, has temporary exhibitions of paintings and sculpture, and is open Tuesday to Sunday from 10 a.m. to noon and 2 to 6 p.m. (on Monday, only from 2 to 6 p.m.).

If you walk along the quays, heading north as if to Lausanne, you'll come to some of the most beautiful parks in Geneva. Off the Avenue de France looms the **Parc Mon Repos,** and off the rue de Lausanne lies **La Perle du Lac,** both stunning lakeside parks. Directly to the right is the **Jardin Botanique** (botanical garden), established in 1902. It has a small alpine garden and a little zoo, and can be visited from 7 a.m. to 6:30 p.m. in summer (otherwise from 8 a.m. to 5 p.m.).

Back at the lakeside, you can take a boat to the other side of the lake, getting off at Gustave Ador quay. From there you can explore two more lakeside parks, **Parc de la Grange,** which has the most extravagant rose garden in Switzerland (at its best in June), and next to it, the equally beautiful **Parc des Eaux-Vives.**

Or alternatively, when you leave the Botanical Garden on the left bank, you can head west along Avenue de la Paix to the—

Place des Nations, the former home of the League of Nations and the present headquarters of the United Nations in Europe. The location is about a mile north from the Mont Blanc Bridge. Up to 1936 the League met at the Palais Wilson. However, in 1936 the headquarters was transferred to the Palais des Nations. The Aga Khan inaugurated the Palais, but its days were numbered. After excluding Russia in 1940 it saw its influence decline, although minor operations continued through the war years until it was dissolved in 1946, as the new United Nations met in San Francisco. The complex of buildings here is the second largest in Europe after Versailles. The palace can be visited from 9:15 a.m. to noon and 2 to 5:15 p.m. in summer. From the first of October to mid-May, hours are from 9:15 a.m. to noon and 2 to 5:15 p.m. Conducted tours form at entrance no. 7, leaving every hour daily in summer. Admission is 3.50F ($1.61) for adults and 2.50F ($1.15) for students. Children are admitted free. Inside is a philatelic museum and a small museum of diplomatic history, but it's the building itself that's of interest.

THE LEADING MUSEUMS: **Musée d'Art et Histoire** (museum of art and history), 2 rue Charles-Galland (tel. 29-00-11), is the most important museum in Geneva. It lies between the Boulevard Jacques-Dalcroze and the Boulevard Helvétique, and is open from 10 a.m. to noon and 2 to 6 p.m. (closed Monday morning). Seemingly, it has a little bit of everything, going back to relics of the prehistoric people who lived in pile dwellings. Over the centuries came the Egyptians, of which the museum has many relics, along with Greek vases, medieval stained glass, 12th-century armory, and many paintings of the Flemish and Italian schools. The Etruscan pottery is impressive, as is the medieval furniture. See the altarpiece by Konrad Witz from 1444, showing the "miraculous" draught of fishes. Swiss timepieces are duly honored, and many galleries contain works by such world-famed artists as Dufy, Chagall, and Van Gogh. The collection of impressionists is exceptional. In the basement you can see a model of Geneva as it was in 1850.

To the west of the Palais des Nations, the **Musée de l'Ariana,** 10 avenue de la Paix (tel. 33-39-44), is open Tuesday to Sunday from 10 a.m. to 5 p.m., April to October only. The building itself is in the Italian Renaissance style, built in 1877 for P. F. Revilliod, the 19th-century Genevese writer who began the collection. Today it's one of the top three museums in Europe devoted to porcelain and pottery. Here you'll see Sèvres at its best, along with the celebrated Delft porcelain and that of Meissen. It's also the headquarters of the international academy of ceramics. The collection doesn't overlook the Orient either, with many superb pieces from Japan and China.

Musée du Petit Palais, 2 Terrasse Saint-Victori (tel. 46-14-33), is sheltered in a 17th-century town house, displaying artwork from 1890 until the present day. It's known chiefly for its collection of impressionists and postimpressionists, although the Pointillists and Fauve artists are also represented. This private museum is like a course in art history, as you note such outstanding artists as Chagall, Utrillo, and Rousseau. Admission is 5F ($2.30) for adults and 3.50F ($1.61) for students. Visit from 10 a.m. to noon and 2 to 6 p.m., except on Monday morning.

The **Musée d'Histoire Naturelle** (natural history museum), 11 route de Malagnou (tel. 35-91-30), is the most important such museum in Europe. It awes with its vivariums and aquariums, its displays of local fauna, but also tropical mammals and birds. It's open from 10 a.m. to noon and 2 to 5 p.m. (closed Monday).

At the rue du Mont-Blanc you can take bus no. 6 to the **Institut et Musée Voltaire,** 25 rue des Délices (tel. 44-71-33). Voltaire lived here during his period of exile from 1755 to 1765. The museum displays furniture, manuscripts, and letters of the great philosopher, along with portraits, plus a terracotta model of the philosopher's statue by Houdon. The museum is open Monday to Friday from 2 to 5 p.m., charging 1F (46¢) admission for adults (free for students).

The **Musée de l'Horlogerie** (watch museum), 15 route de Malagnou (tel. 36-74-12), is in a town house on its own grounds. The history of watches and clocks from the 16th century is traced in this museum, open from 10 a.m. to noon and 2 to 6 p.m. (closed Monday morning). It displays everything from sand-timers to sundials, although most of the exhibits are concerned with the watches of Geneva, usually from the 17th and 18th centuries. The enameled watches of the 19th century are particularly outstanding (many have chimes that play when you open them).

The **Baur Collections,** 8 rue Munier-Romilly (tel. 46-17-29), in the 19th-century home of the original owner, with a tiny garden, is a private exhibit of Japanese and Chinese porcelain and ceramics. Jade, porcelain, and much delicate work are displayed here, including some 17th-century Japanese art. It's open in the afternoon only, from 2 to 6 p.m., charging an admission of 3F ($1.38).

The **Musée d'Instruments Anciens de Musique** (museum of antique musical instruments), 23 rue Lefort (tel. 46-95-65), displays a private collection that was purchased by the city of Geneva. The original owner is still the curator. Many of the instruments are still in working order, and are occasionally played.

The museum is open Tuesday from 3 to 6 p.m.; Thursday from 10 a.m. to noon and from 3 to 6 p.m., and on Friday from 8 to 10 p.m. Admission is only 1F (46¢).

The **Musée de l'Histoire des Sciences** (museum of the history of science), at Villa Bartholoni, 128 rue de Lausanne (tel. 31-69-85), contains mementos of Swiss scientists showing how they've excelled in medicine, astronomy, physics, and mathematics. It's open April to October daily from 2 to 6 p.m.

The **Library of Geneva** contains two museums. It lies on the south side of the Promenade des Bastions, and has been there since 1873. Originally it was a Calvin-founded academy in 1559, and reformed theologians were trained here. The east wing of the library dates from the 15th century and has some 1.2 million volumes.

In the Salle Lullin of the library, the **Jean-Jacques Rousseau Museum,** Promenade des Bastions (tel. 20-82-66), contains manuscripts, correspondence, prints, a bust by Houdon, and the death mask of the famous philosopher. Charging no admission, it's open from 9 a.m. to noon and 2 to 5 p.m. (closed Sunday and Saturday afternoon).

The other museum is the **Musée Historique de la Reformation,** also in the Bibliothèque Publique at the university on the Promenade des Bastions. It will be of particular interest to those interested in Knox and Calvin. It's open Monday to Friday from 9 a.m. to noon and 2 to 6 p.m. (on Saturday, only from 9 a.m. to noon), charging no admission.

4. Where to Shop

From boutiques to department stores, Geneva is a shopping parade. Everybody knows that it's a world center of watchmaking and jewelry, but you can also pick up excellent items such as embroidered blouses or music boxes made by peasants in the Jura during the long winter months.

A host of merchandise is sold, ranging from cuckoos from German Switzerland to cigars from Havana. Supplies of chocolate are always a temptation, and the city also is a place to buy the famous multiblade knives of the Swiss army. These knives are even favored by astronauts.

Geneva, of course, practically invented the wristwatch, not to mention the self-winding watch, the waterproof watch, etc. Watchmaking in the city dates from the 16th century. Avoid purchasing a Swiss watch in one of the souvenir stores. If a jeweler is legitimate, he or she will display a symbol of the Geneva Association of Watchmakers and Jewelers. All the fine names are sold here: Constantin, Longines, Omega.

The city has luxury merchandise from all over the world—and not just watches and jewelery. Sometimes you'll find discounts on such items as cameras.

Nearly all the sales personnel I've encountered spoke English and were always most helpful.

Shopping might begin, as it has for centuries, at the **Place du Molard.** Once this was the harbor of Geneva, but then the water receded. Before it was killed by French intervention and competition from Lyon in France, merchants from all over Europe brought their merchandise such as rich silks here to sell and display at the once-famous trade fairs of Geneva.

Or alternatively, if you're walking along the world-famous **rue du Rhône,** and are put off by the prices, go one block south to the **rue du Marché,** which in various sections becomes the rue Croix d'Or and the rue de Rive. Don't be afraid to comparison-shop in Geneva. Some local residents tell me that many of the major shops on the rue du Rhône price their goods so high "that only wealthy foreign buyers can afford them."

Bucherer, 45 rue du Rhône (tel. 21-62-66). The thing to remember about this store is not to be intimidated by the dignified facade and the elegantly futuristic ground floor. Naturally the store sells expensive watches and diamonds in a chrome-and-crystal format of great beauty. But what many visitors don't realize is that its white-carpeted third floor is filled with relatively inexpensive watches costing from 220F ($101.09). Once you're on that floor, you'll also find a large selection of cuckoo clocks, music boxes, embroideries, and souvenirs, as well as charming gift items such as porcelain pill boxes beginning at 50F ($22.98).

Bruno Magli, 47 rue du Rhône (tel. 21-53-77), is one of the most complete shoestores in Geneva, selling an elegant variety of shoes, purses, and accessories, all made in Italy, beginning at 200F ($91.90). The shop is owned by the friendly and sophisticated Henri Zeitoun, who employs a staff eager to be of assistance.

Hermès, 43 rue du Rhône (tel. 21-76-77), sells purses, a few suitcases, women's coats, skirts, and accessories in the well-known conservative style that has made Hermès such a famous name around the world. You'll also find watches with the distinctive Hermès leather bracelet. Naturally, the famous Hermès scarf, beginning at 175F ($80.41), is on sale.

Gübelin Jewellers, 1 Place du Molard or 60 rue du Rhône (tel. 28-86-55), is known mainly for watches, but you can buy a 10-karat emerald here if it suits your fancy and your pocketbook. You'll see two perpetual clocks in the windows, giving chronological as well as astrological time, with fanciful notations of the different time zones around the world in colored enamel. The watches are among the best names in Switzerland, although you can also buy gift items for as little as 140F ($64.33), which might include pen and pencil sets. The store is closed from noon to 2 p.m., but otherwise open every day except Sunday from 8 a.m. to 5 p.m.

L. Scherrer, 29 rue du Rhône (tel. 21-70-96), sells a good selection of watches, diamonds, and gems from an elegant storefront on the most prestigious street in Geneva. The very polite staff caters to an elite clientele who are mainly interested in the eight brands of Swiss watches sold here.

Celine, 23 rue du Rhône (tel. 21-14-03), sells all the clothing and accessories that any horsewoman or would-be equestrienne could use, as well as a selection of fashionably conservative skirts, blouses, and purses. Items are very expensive in a shop dedicated to preserving the allure of its name.

For simpler items, you might try the **Boutique du Fumeur,** 2 Place du Molard (tel. 28-75-38), which sells a wide selection of tobacco, pipes, and cigars, many from Havana. The owners are two sisters-in-law, Madames Maurer and Adair. But for more complicated items you should go to—

Davidoff, 2 rue de Rive (tel. 28-90-41), the most famous tobacco store in the world. It sells the best cigars in all of Europe. The staff grades and sorts Cuban cigars like vintages of very old wines. A massive climate-controlled storage room in the basement holds dozens of Cuban cigars never imported into America. Russian exile Zino Davidoff (born in 1906) set up a revolutionary system of mixing grades of tobacco from his shop in Geneva, where Lenin and other exiles gathered to ponder the fate of their mother country. Today you'll see some of the world's greatest cigar boxes and all kinds of smoking paraphernalia. The shop is open every day but Sunday.

Confiserie Rohr, 3 Place du Molard (tel. 21-63-03), and 42 rue du Rhône (tel. 21-68-76), sells the kinds of chocolates you can smell from the street. They fairly pull you into the store where, displayed behind glass countertops, you'll see my personal favorite, chocolate-covered truffles. As a novelty you might also try the poubelles au chocolat (chocolate "garbage pails"). Most candies sell for about $10 (U.S.) per pound, and the shop is open daily except Sunday until 6:45 p.m.

Art et Style, 10 Grand-Rue (tel. 21-45-97), is the kind of antique store that looks and feels more like a museum than a commercial enterprise. The high-ceilinged room is packed with 17th-century sculpture and enough furniture to fill a large and very elegant house. Henry Perey is the buyer and owner, and his staff is eager to explain origins and prices.

Grand Passage, 13-15 rue du Marché (tel. 20-66-11), has just about everything, ranging from a travel bureau to an agency selling theater tickets, as well as a hairdresser, a newspaper kiosk, and a handful of boutiques, plus a restaurant and a shop selling sandwiches to go. The latter might make an inexpensive snack or a complete lunch if you're watching your centimes.

Jouets Weber (Franz Carl Weber), 12 rue de la Croix d'Or (tel. 28-42-55), sells children's toys of all kinds, from slide shows to cartoon characters, as well as dolls and sports equipment. Lying at the corner of rue de la Fontaine, it's the best in the city.

Pharmacie Principale, Grand Passage, 11 rue du Marché (tel. 21-31-30). Between the glamorous rue du Rhône and the less expensive rue du Marché you'll find one of the world's biggest drugstores, specializing not only in medicines, but in fashions, perfumes, optical equipment, cameras, and photo supplies. If your glasses need adjusting, you can take them to the optometrist on the second floor.

Bon Génie, 34 rue du Marché (tel. 28-82-22), is a department store emporium on the Place du Molard which sells high-fashion items, mainly for women. It's storefront windows have cleverly assembled art objects from local museums, which are displayed alongside designer clothes. There's also a limited selection of men's clothing too.

Aux Arts du Feu, 18 Quai Général-Guisan (tel. 21-35-21), is a waterside store with big windows and lots of brass trim, selling expensive objects of crystal, porcelain, china, silver, and decorative objects from around the world.

Pharmacie de Saint-Gervais, 1 Tour de l'Île (tel. 21-30-05), might be the most centrally located pharmacy of all of Geneva, as it stands next door to the main tourist office. It's open weekdays from 8:30 a.m. to 12:30 p.m. and 1:30 to 6:30 p.m. (on Saturday, from 8:30 a.m. to 12:30 p.m. only).

E. Schmitt and Co. Antiquités, 3 rue de l'Hôtel de Ville (tel. 28-35-40), is the kind of antique store where you'll want to know the price of everything. Many of the pieces are English, and they're beautifully displayed in the ground-floor rooms of an 18th-century private house. Be sure to ask the director, Madame Guichard, to take you across the cobblestone courtyard to see the other beautifully illuminated showrooms.

5. Geneva After Dark

Geneva has more nightlife than any other city in Switzerland, and if you get bored in this former city of Calvin, you can always drive in a short time across the border into France. For example, there's gambling at Divonne in France, 12½ miles away, which draws many of the Genevois since Switzerland limits bets to 5F ($2.30).

On a cultural note, the **Grand Théâtre,** Place Neuve (tel. 21-23-11), is one of the most opulent opera houses in Europe, modeled after the Paris Opéra. It was constructed in the 1880s, but burned in 1951. However, it has been rebuilt in the grand manner, with velvet draperies, crystal chandeliers, mammoth paintings, and marble. From October to May it presents one of the most distinguished opera seasons in Europe.

Victoria Hall, rue Hornung (tel. 28-33-80), is the home of the celebrated Orchestre de la Suisse Romande, but it may be difficult to obtain tickets.

The best place for jazz sessions is the **Café des Négociants,** Place du Molard (tel. 28-22-10), which are presented mainly on Friday and Saturday nights.

Most Geneva nightlife centers around the Place Bourg-de-Four, a former stagecoach stop during the 19th century. In the old town there are lots of outdoor cafés in summer, attracting a chic crowd of the affluent and semi-affluent Genevois.

Maxim's Cabaret, 2 rue Thalberg (tel. 32-99-00), is a small Lido-style cabaret and music hall owned by Bob Azzam, the conductor and composer (he's known for the famous *Mustapha*). The club is open nightly from 9:30 to dawn, with two different shows at 11:30 p.m. and again at 1:30 a.m. It's a lovely spot, much favored by visitors, and with some very good acts. There's a cover charge of 10F ($4.60), and most drinks cost from 20F ($9.19). A small restaurant serves a fixed-price dinner with smoked salmon and foie gras for 70F ($32.17).

Griffin's Club, 36 Boulevard Helvétique (tel. 35-12-18), is considered the best, the most fun, and the chicest club in Geneva. But technically it's private and you may or may not get in, depending on the mood of the management at the time of your particular visit. The popularity of nightclubs comes and goes, but the collection of celebrities who have traipsed in here reads like a who's who from the tabloids. Jackets are required for men. The club opens at 10 p.m., and an attached restaurant starts doing business at 8. Drinks cost from 20F ($9.19) to 26F ($11.95), and dinner goes from 110F ($50.55) per person. The owner and manager, Bernard Grobet, is a local celebrity.

Club de la Tour, 6 rue de la Tour de Boël (tel. 21-00-33), is a difficult-to-locate club on one of Geneva's most charming squares in the old town. It's in a building owned at one time by the Genevois patriot, Besonçon Hughes (1482–1532). The club has chiseled stone and stucco walls with a wrought-iron dragon sticking out over the street. Inside, three levels of balconies overlook the central dance and performance area. Musical groups play rock and mild punk, alternating with disco from 10 p.m. to 4 a.m. No jeans or sneakers are permitted. There's a 10F ($4.60) cover charge on weekends only, with drinks costing from 18F ($8.27) apiece. The club is closed on Sunday, and it has a small restaurant inside.

Velvet Club, 7 rue du Jeu de l'Arc (tel. 35-00-00), still attracts a few loyal devotees who enjoy the *danseuses modernes* at the 10:30 p.m. show (the club opens at 9:30). There's no cover charge for women, but a 10F ($4.60) cover for men on weekends, plus a 20F ($9.19) cover charge in December. Jackets are required for men. There's disco between cabaret acts, and drinks cost from 16F ($7.35). A small restaurant is also on the premises.

Club 58, 15 Glacis de Rive (tel. 35-15-15), requires a jacket for men, plus a cover charge of 30F ($13.79) for men. However, women enter free. Cabaret shows begin at 12:30 a.m. and again at 2 a.m., with disco in between shows. Drinks cost from 18F ($8.27) to 25F ($11.49). There's a restaurant attached.

Pussy Cat Saloon, 15 Glacis de Rive (tel. 35-15-15), in the same building as Club 58, is a cabaret/music hall/striptease joint where "ballets" (that's what they're called) begin at 11 p.m. and again at 1 a.m. The cover charge is 10F ($4.60), with drinks costing from 18F ($8.27) to 24F ($11.03). Dinner is usually arranged at Club 58, and men are required to wear jackets to watch performers sans apparel. The club opens at 10 p.m.

Ba-Ta-Clan, 15 rue de la Fontaine (tel. 29-64-98), is the other leading strip joint of Geneva. In fact many prefer it. There's a 10F ($4.60) cover on weekdays, rising to 20F ($9.19) on weekends. A jacket and tie are obligatory for men. There's disco music between shows, which are at 10 p.m. and again at 1 a.m. Drinks cost from 18F ($8.27) and up.

La Garçonnière, 22 Place Bémont (tel. 28-21-61), features transvestite acts, drawing both a straight and a gay crowd. It has a disco-cabaret format, featuring burlesque acts. Two nightly shows are presented at 11:30 and at 1:30. It's open every night from 10 p.m. to 4 a.m. (until 5 a.m. on weekends). The charge is 7F ($3.22) as a cover on weekdays, rising to 10F ($4.60) on weekends. Drinks cost from 15F ($6.89) to 19F ($8.73). A small restaurant is attached, with dinner reservations accepted after 10 p.m.

New Bar à Whiskey, 9-11 rue du Prince (tel. 28-14-28), is a disco with an occasional cover charge, but with free entrance to women. It's open from 10 p.m. till dawn, charging 10F ($4.60) for a drink. Jackets are requested for men.

Pub Clémence, Place Bourg-de-Four (tel. 20-10-96). You'll see an unpretentious green facade facing the cobblestones of one of Geneva's oldest squares. From one direction you can't even see the establishment's name, but all Genevois know about it—it's the city's most famous pub. An occasional guitarist will provide music, but more frequently you'll see an under-35 crowd who come to see and be seen in the informal ambience. The second floor is reached by a very narrow wooden staircase. Coffee costs 3.20F ($1.48) for two persons.

Mr. Pickwick Pub, 80 rue Lausanne (tel. 31-67-95), serves simple, English-style meals, but mostly the patrons come here to drink. The paneled rooms are filled in the evening with an attractive young crowd, who enjoy the dimly lit, friendly ambience. The place gets very crowded, and can be quite fun. Irish coffee is a specialty, but most visitors order beer at 2.50F ($1.15) a mug. The decor is naturally inspired by Britain, as the name would suggest, but the music on the jukebox is likely to be from the States. In Geneva, the pub is sometimes called the "Tower of Babble" because of all the polygot tongues spoken (many employees from the United Nations hang out here). It's open from 10 a.m. to 1 a.m. on weekdays and until 2 a.m. on Saturday. Naturally you can order steak-and-kidney pie. The cost is 9F ($4.14) for a good-size plate.

A lot of the nightlife takes place on the outskirts. My favorite is **Au Chaudron,** 14 rue Jacques-Dalphini (tel. 42-77-98), in the conveniently reached suburb of Carouge. The club shuts down on Sunday but is open every other night. Some people refer to it as a kind of "catch-a-rising-star" nitery. That is, it often provides a forum for those who can sing, or think they can sing. There's dancing to live music, in this huge barrack-like complex. It's very casual. Drinks begin at 8F ($3.68).

6. Excursions from Geneva

The region around Geneva is rich in attractions. Many of the most popular places—at least around the lake—have been covered in Chapter VIII on Lausanne and Lake Geneva. Refer to that chapter for highlights around the lake itself.

However, a few attractions are practically at the doorstep of the city itself, and we'll survey these in this section.

The limestone ridge of **Mount Salève** ("house mountain") lies four miles south of Geneva. Its peak is 4000 feet high, but you'll need a passport to reach it, as it lies in France. If you have a car, you'll find that a good road goes up this mountain which is popular with rock-climbers.

Bus no. 8 or an auto will take you to **Veyrier,** on the French frontier with a passport and Customs control. There you'll find the lower station of a cable car which will take you in six minutes to a height of 3750 feet on Mount Salève. From the top you'll have a panoramic sweep of the Valley of the Arve, with Geneva and Mont Blanc in the background.

Carouge, a suburb of Geneva, is a bit of European nostalgia. It dates mainly from the 18th century, when it was built by the king of Sardinia as a rival of Geneva. Architects from Turin supplied the Pietmontese charm.

At the 1815 Congress of Vienna, Carouge was annexed to the canton of Geneva. Once Carouge was the playground of smugglers and gold-washers who panned for the precious metal in the Arve. The Genevese themselves—at least those who wanted to escape from the puritanical city—fled here, seeking the company of prostitutes and the "low life."

Switzerland now considers Carouge a national landmark because of its architecture. Begin your exploration in the Market Square with its old fountain, plane trees, and markets. A Roman stone was imbedded in the Church of the Holy Cross. As you walk about, you'll pass the Court of the Palace of the Count of Veyrier, dating from 1783, the Place du Temple with a fountain from 1857, and a Louis XVI–carved door at 18 rue Saint-Victor. Many bars and cafés in the town serve excellent white wine from the Genevese vineyards.

Lord Byron and Shelley both lived in the residential suburb of **Cologny,** which is reached by bus A from Geneva. It lies nine miles to the northeast. From here you'll have a panoramic view of the lake and Geneva, with its Palais des Nations. The view is especially good from the "Byron Stone" on the Chemin de Ruth ("Ruth's Path") leading to the Byron fields. In 1816 Byron stayed at the Villa Diodati, where he met Shelley.

The best time to go to Cologny is on a Thursday afternoon when you can visit the **Bodmeriana Library,** Chemin du Guignard (tel. 36-23-70), the posh villa of Martin Bodmer, Zurich millionaire. At that time his private collection of first editions, rare manuscripts, and objets d'art are on display.

If you'd like to do what the Genevese themselves do on a good day, take bus C, departing from Rond-Point de Rive in Geneva, heading for **Jussy,** a charming village in a rural setting, from which you can ramble through the woods and explore the countryside around Geneva on foot.

On the lake, **Hermance,** a mellow old fishermen's village, is reached by taking bus no. 9 from Rond-Point de Rive in Geneva. The village, founded in 1245, has been restored attractively, and in summer it's in virtual bloom there are so many flowers. The town is "crowned" by a tower dating from the Middle Ages, and its Chapel of St. Catherine is from the 15th century. The Genevese come here to browse through the art galleries, later enjoying drinks and food in several café-restaurants surrounded by gardens. Before heading back, I suggest a walk along the lake.

If you'd like to see some of the vineyards of Geneva, you can visit **Russin** and **Dardagny,** taking a train from the Gare Cornavin in Geneva. In about ten minutes you'll reach Russin, in the center of a wine-growing region. Later on you can go on to Dardagny, a landmark village with a castle by the Valley of the Allondon. Take the Donzelle route, through vineyards, where you'll eventually get a train to take you back to Geneva.

One of the most interesting day trips in the region is a bit farther afield at **Coppet,** a little town on the western shore of Lake Geneva, a distance of nine miles, lying in the canton of Vaud.

The **Château de Coppet** (tel. 76-10-28) attracted some of the greatest minds of the 18th and 19th centuries. Lying on the lake, this seignorial château, between Lausanne and Geneva, was purchased in 1784 by Jacques Necker, the finance minister of Louis XVI. His daughter became the legendary Madame de Staël, the great French woman of letters. Her opposition to Napoleon sent her into exile, but she continued to receive many famous visitors. Her granddaughter married the Comte d'Haussonville, and the château has remained in the possession of Necker's direct descendants. In its museum are mementos of Madame de Staël. It's open March to October daily except Monday from 10 a.m. to noon and 2 to 5:30 p.m., charging 3.50F ($1.61) admission. Guided tours are conducted.

7. Getting to Know Geneva

PRACTICAL FACTS: Many visitors from the continent arrive at the Gare Cornavin, where the CFF railway office is situated. The **Bureau de Logement,** or accommodation bureau (tel. 32-53-40), is open at the station to make hotel reservations for you from June to September only. Hours are from 9:30 a.m. to 10 p.m. daily.

The **Office du Tourisme de Genève** (main tourist office), 1 Tour-de-l'Île (tel. 28-72-33), is open Monday to Friday from 8:15 a.m. to 6 p.m. and on Saturday from 9 a.m. to 5 p.m. In July and August it's also open on Sunday from 10 a.m. to noon and 2 to 10 p.m. The entrance to the office, on the island in the middle of the Rhône, is actually on rue des Moulins.

American Express, 7 rue du Mont-Blanc (tel. 32-65-80), is open Monday to Friday from 8:30 a.m. to 5:30 p.m. and from 9 a.m. to noon on Saturday.

The **U.S. Consulate** is at 11 route Pregny (tel. 99-02-11).

The **post office** at Gare Cornavin, 11 rue de Lausanne, is open Monday to Saturday from 6 a.m. to 10:30 p.m. and from 8 a.m. to 10:30 p.m. on Sunday.

The **money exchange,** also at Gare Cornavin, is open weekdays from 5:30 a.m. to 10:30 p.m. and on Saturday and Sunday until 8:30 p.m.

For banking, the **Société de Banque Suisse** (Swiss Bank Corporation) is at 2 rue de la Confédération (tel. 22-41-11).

The **American Library,** 2 rue de Monthoux (tel. 32-80-97), has a subscription service open to those looking for a wide variety of English-language books. A subscription must be for at least a month.

Radio Pays de Gex plays the American Top Ten songs with comment and introduction by an American disc jockey. This program is on daily from 8 to 9 a.m. and on Saturday at 8:30 p.m.

In an **emergency,** dial 117 for firefighters, ambulance, or police.

SPORTS: In health-conscious Switzerland, this is a big item, and Geneva has many facilities to help you get and keep fit.

Golfers will enjoy the 18-hole **Golf Club of Geneva** at Cologny. **Tennis** can be played at several clubs, among them the Geneva Tennis Club at Parc des Eaux-Vives.

Water sports include **sailing,** which is easily available along the quays, especially Mont-Blanc and Wilson. Swimmers will find fine **beaches** along the lake for use in summer. The most popular is Geneva Beach (Genève Plage), where you can enjoy the water from 9 a.m. to 7 p.m. for 5F ($2.30). You can also swim in the lake at Bains des Pâquis, Quai du Mont-Blanc in summer for only .50F (23¢).

TRANSPORT: For the most part, transportation originates at **Place Cornavin,** fronting the main railroad station. From here, you can take bus O or F to the Palais des Nations. The **Swissair shuttle bus** runs between Cointrin Airport, about three miles from the heart of town, and Gare Cornavin, leaving every 20 minutes from 7 a.m. to 11:15 p.m. The fare is 5F ($2.30) per person, and the trip takes about 15 to 20 minutes.

You'll often find French-speaking women in the drivers' seats on the **Transports Publics Genevois (TPG)** vehicles. No tickets are sold inside buses or trams. Likewise, no tickets can be validated inside the vehicles. Every transaction must take place at one of the coin-operated vending machines placed at each stop. Types of tickets include:

1. Free circulation for one hour, with as many changes as you wish, which could include a return on a different vehicle. Cost of this ticket is 1.20F (55¢).

2. A trip limited to three stops without changing vehicles at a cost of .70F (32¢).

3. Half-price tickets which permit rides for one hour only, for children ages 6 to 12; cost, .60F (28¢).

If you plan on using the system frequently, you can save a small amount of money by purchasing the above tickets from a specialized distributor who sells them in packets of six or seven tickets. Each of these tickets must be validated at the machine before entering the vahicle. Tariffs for these packets are 6.50F ($2.99), 4.50F ($2.07), and 3.50F ($1.61), respectively.

Children under 6 ride free, with a limit of two children per adult. For a child in a baby carriage, full adult fare is charged.

Certain lines in the TBG system extend far into the country. These are marked "Reseau de Campagne" or "Lignes de Campagne." Tickets for long distances are sold by the conductor of each car, with the price determined by the distance the passenger wants to travel.

Most tourists will be interested in an all-day ticket good on any line, costing 5F ($2.30). Similar tickets for children ages 6 to 12 are sold for half price. These tickets may be purchased at the agents whose addresses are listed on each of the validation machines or by the conductors of the cars marked "Reseau de Campagne." Special commuter cards are also sold for periods of 10, 20, 30, or 365 days, with a complicated rate base determined at the addresses indicated on each vending machine.

TOURS: A two-hour City Tour is operated daily all year by **Key Tours S.A.,** 7 rue des Alpes, Place Mont-Blanc (tel. 31-41-40). The tour starts from the Gare Routière, Place Dorcière, the bus station near the Key Tours office. In December and January tours begin at 2 p.m.; in February, March, April, and November at 10 a.m. and 2 p.m.; in May, June, and October at 10 a.m. and at 2 and 2:30 p.m.; and in July, August, and September at 9:30 and 10 a.m. and at 2 and 2:30 p.m. A bus will drive you through the city and you'll see famous sites, monuments, and landmarks of Geneva and the lake promenades. In the old town you take a walk down to the Bastions Park where you'll see the Reformation Wall. After a stop at the International Center, at which, among other organizations, you'll be shown the headquarters of the International Red Cross, the bus returns to its starting place. Adults are charged 16F ($7.35); children 4 to 12 accompanied by an adult, 8F ($3.68).

Many other excursions are offered, including a 2½-hour boat trip on the Rhône aboard the *Bâteau du Rhône,* with commentary in English. The trip takes you from Geneva to the Verdois dam and back. Departure, opposite the Hôtel du Rhône, takes place at 2:30 p.m. daily from April 1 to October 30 and also at 10:30 a.m. on Thursday, Saturday, and Sunday. The boat trip costs 14F ($6.43) for adults, 8F ($3.68) for children 6 to 12 years of age.

Lake cruises may be taken from May 29 to September 24, the trips including only first-class boat transportation (no guides and no meals).

An **all-day cruise** will take you on a complete tour of the lake, leaving from Jardin Anglais pier at 8 and 10:15 a.m. daily and from Mont Blanc pier at 9:15 a.m. (only on Sunday in May, June, and September) and returning at from 6:45 to 8:50 p.m. The cost of the cruise, which takes you past Nyon, Lausanne, Vevey, Montreux, Evian, and Thonon, is 42F ($19.30) for adults, half price for children 6 to 16.

You can go to Montreux and Chillon on a **Castle Cruise** by boat, returning by train. The boat leaves from Mont Blanc pier daily at 9:15 a.m., arriving at Chillon at 2:15 p.m., or you can embark at Jardin Anglais pier at 10:45 a.m. and arrive at Chillon at 3:42 p.m. Trains for the one-hour round trip make the run every hour. Cost of the excursion is 45F ($20.68) for adults, half price for children 6 to 16. Entrance to the Château de Chillon costs 4F ($1.84).

A shorter cruise takes you around the lower part of the lake in half a day, taking you past Nyon and Yvoire. You can depart from Mont-Blanc pier at 9:15 a.m., returning at 2:05 p.m.; or from Jardin Anglais pier at 2:30 p.m., returning at 6 p.m. This trip costs adults 22F ($10.11); children from 6 to 16, 11F ($5.06).

If you have time, I highly recommend a **Mont Blanc excursion,** an all-day trip to Chamonix by bus and a cable-car ride to the summit of the Aiguille du Midi, (12,610 feet) for a memorable alpine panorama. The tour is offered daily all year, leaving Geneva at 8:30 a.m. and returning at 5:30 p.m. from October to April and at 6:30 p.m. from May to September. Buses leave from the station, Gare Routière. You must take your passport with you.

If you choose, you may make other ascents on this tour, to Vallée Blanche by telecabin, an extension of the Aiguille du Midi climb, from April to October; to Mer de Glace via electric rack railway to the edge of the glacier from which you may descend to the ice grotto (not available in winter); and/or to Le Brévent, an ascent by cable car to a rocky belvedere at 7900 feet, facing the Mont Blanc range.

Prices for a complete trip vary according to which of the options you prefer after reaching Chamonix. With lunch, adults pay 90F ($41.36) and children 4 to 12 pay 55F ($25.27) to ascend Aiguille du Midi; adults pay 112F ($51.46) and children pay 66F ($30.33) for the Aiguille du Midi–Vallée Blanche trek; adults are charged 106F ($48.71) and children pay 63F ($28.95) to go to Aiguille du Midi and Mer de Glace or Le Brévent; adults pay 128F, ($58.82) and children are charged 74F ($34) to go to Aiguille du Midi–Vallée Blanche–Mer de Glace or Aiguille du Midi–Vallée Blanche–Le Brévent. Adults are charged 78F ($35.84) and children pay 49F ($22.52) to go from Chamonix to either Mer de Glace or Le Brévent, and it costs 94F ($43.19) for adults and 57F ($26.19) for children to go to Chamonix and then to Mer de Glace and Le Brévent.

An adult who chooses to spend the entire day in Chamonix will be charged 62F ($28.49) for the trip, while children pay 41F ($18.84), if lunch is included. Without lunch, subtract 20F ($9.19) from each of the prices given.

An English-speaking guide will accompany your bus tour. Key Tours S.A., operators of the excursion, require a minimum of eight persons per trip.

Chapter X

LUCERNE AND CENTRAL SWITZERLAND

1. Zug
2. Lucerne
3. Lake Lucerne, North and East
4. From Schwyz to St. Gotthard
5. Lake Lucerne, West and South

THE MOUNTAINTOPS of the "heartland" of Switzerland have what is called "eternal snow." The flanks are lined with glacier ice.

Paddle-steamers across the lakes in the region lead to lidos or summer bathing beaches. You'll make much use of railways and cable cars as you climb skyward in bright alpine sun to see for yourself what the charms of Rigi or Pilatus are all about. In winter, skating and curling rinks, cross-country ski tracks, toboggan runs, indoor swimming pools, and skiing in the mountains lure the visitor.

Lucerne and its lake are part of William Tell country, where the seeds that led to the Confederation were sown. For many Americans it's all they'll ever see of Switzerland. That's a shame, as the country has so much more to offer. But if the area in and around Lucerne is all that can be seen, then it's a worthy choice, for there's much to learn of the Swiss people here.

As one local Swiss official told me, "We just call it Lake Lucerne, because that way the foreigners understand better." Actually, the lake in German is known as Vierwaldstättersee, or in French as Lac des Quatre Cantons, the lake of the four cantons, which are comprised not only of Lucerne, but also Uri, Unterwalden, and Schwyz (Switzerland gets its name from Schwyz canton).

The lake lies between the steep limestone mountains, Rigi in the north and Pilatus in the southwest. Bürgenstock, a promontory that thrusts itself into the lake, is now a world-famous hotel citadel. Seelisberg, a promontory to the south, is also well known. All this irregular geography gives the lake a romantic look. The lake itself is a prehistoric terminal basin of a glacier.

It was near Brunnen that the "Everlasting league" of 1315 was made, in the meadow of Rütli, which undoubtedly will be pointed out to you as you travel along in a lake steamer. Of course many of the sights in the area have to do with Tell and the legendary Gessler, both of which characters were supposedly fictional.

Lucerne is the only major city, and most Americans will want to settle in there. However, if you prefer one of the secluded resorts around the lake, I've included some hotel selections for you as well.

The lake is about 24 miles long, and at its broadest point is two miles wide. It's the fourth largest of the lakes of Switzerland, and one of the most frequented tourist areas in all of Europe.

However, your actual gateway to central Switzerland will not be Lucerne, but Zug, immediately following.

1. Zug

The town of Zug, called the gateway to central Switzerland, stands on the northeast shore of Lake Zug, or Zugersee if you prefer the Swiss name for this second-largest lake in the region. Some 9 miles long and 2½ miles wide, the lake lies to the north of Lake Lucerne, more than a mile from that lake's Küssnacht arm.

Zug, beautifully placed in a setting of orchards and gardens, is the capital of the canton of Zug, the smallest state in the country, sometimes called "the Rhode Island of Switzerland." It joined the Confederation in 1352, with its government affairs being contained within the old walled city.

Zug is still medieval in some parts, with many fountains and old burghers' houses. Building of the **Church of St. Oswald,** of late Gothic style lavishly embellished inside, was started in 1478 and completed early in the following century. The **Rathaus** (town hall) was ready for use in 1505. Relics of the ancient fortifications that used to protect the town may still be seen. In the old town, seek out in particular the **Fischmarkt,** with its mellow old houses, some with overhanging balconies and painted gables.

Zugerberg, a flat-topped mountain (3255 feet), overlooks Zug from the southeast. To ascend the mountain, take a steep road up for six miles or board the funicular at Schönegg. From a belvedere on the mountain you overlook the town, the canton, and the lake, as well as viewing the towering peaks of such mountains as the Jungfrau, the Eiger, the Pilatus, and the Rigi. In case you don't go up the Zugerberg, you can enjoy a good view of these peaks from a lakeside promenade in the town.

While you're in Zug, sample its renowned drink, Zuger kirschwasser, made from the juice of cherries grown in the local orchards.

FOOD AND LODGING: **Hotel Rosenberg,** 33 Rosenbergstrasse (tel. 21-43-43), is a very modern building constructed in a series of glass-walled rectangles that would look appropriate on the campus of an American university. The interior, however, is far more elegant than any college dormitory. It has Oriental rugs, lots of paneling, and sunny, well-furnished bedrooms with lots of light from big windows. Singles rent for between 70F ($32.17) and 95F ($43.65), while doubles cost from 105F ($48.25) to 135F ($62.03), including breakfast.

Hotel Löwen am See (tel. 21-77-22) is a 19th-century stone building with white walls and neoclassical detailing under its brown tile roof. The ceilings of the two restaurants inside are elaborately paneled and beamed. The rather stark bedrooms are unadorned with anything except the essential furniture, but are rather comfortable. Singles range from 43F ($19.76) to 60F ($27.57), while doubles cost from 73F ($33.54) to 100F ($45.95), with breakfast included.

Aklin, Am Zytturm (tel. 21-18-66), a deluxe place at which to dine, is housed in the building of the old city where the bakers' guild used to meet. The locale has been attractively renovated by Margrit Riegger-Aklin, the owner, who with her chef, Herr Kleinmann, prepare such specialties as rack of lamb with provençal herbs, "seawolf" with mustard sauce, fresh salmon with two kinds of pepper, beef with sherry, and lamb stew with young vegetables. You might begin your meal with goose liver pâté with pears. The cookery is called *cuisine du marché.* The restaurant is open from 11 a.m. till midnight every day except Christmas, offering fixed-price meals from 74F ($34) to 105F ($48.25), with à la carte dinners priced at a more modest 45F ($20.68).

Schiff, 2 Graben (tel. 21-00-55). The decor is elegantly decorated with shades of white and dark burgundy, as well as with beautifully grained old furniture, parquet floors, and an occasional ornamental plant. You'll probably want to have a drink at the colorful hors d'oeuvres bar before looking over the handwritten menu. Chef Benjamin Böckli specializes in seafood and everything good that usually accompanies it. Some of his products include freshwater crabs Dalmatian style, fresh salmon, and homemade terrine, each dish served with style. The restaurant is closed on Monday and from Christmas until the end of January. Fixed-price meals range from 13F ($5.97) to 21F ($9.65), while à la carte dinners cost from 17F ($7.81) to 50F ($22.98). The restaurant is on the first floor of an old house on the lake, and reservations are suggested.

2. Lucerne

At the north end of Lake Lucerne, Lucerne (Luzern in German) always seems to be a favorite of visiting Americans, because it lives up to a cliché image of a Swiss town. That is, it has narrow, old cobblestone streets in its medieval quarter, slender spires and turrets, covered bridges, promenades, and plazas dominated by fountains, as well as frescoed houses. You have both lake and mountains here. As the people of Lucerne will tell you, "you're never very far from the snow."

When you finish exploring the city itself, you can take literally dozens of half- or full-day excursions, so many visitors wisely allow at least five days for Lucerne on their jampacked itineraries. Since it's a real tourist town, especially in summer, the sights and excursions are well organized. You can do everything from take a cruise in an old paddle-wheel steamer to explore an eerie petrified world of a glacier garden dating back millions of years.

Lucerne's gate to the south is formed by two mountain giants, Rigi and Pilatus, with a backdrop of the snow-capped Alps. Its history has long been tied to the St. Gotthard pass. In the 13th century this was a mule path, becoming a carriage route in 1820. By 1882 it had a rail tunnel.

Lucerne is easily reached, not only by motorway (either bus or car), but by international express trains from both north and south. The international airport at Zurich is only an hour away.

Once a vassal city of the Habsburgs, Lucerne became the first city to join the Swiss Confederation in 1332. The Reformation didn't take over in Lucerne, as it did in such cities as Geneva and Zurich, and Lucerne today remains a stronghold of Catholicism.

Lucerne is at its best on Tuesday and Saturday mornings when it becomes a lively market town. The markets—sheltered under stately arcades—overflow onto both the right and left banks of the River Reuss. It's also a city of folk festivals and culture, as well as the center of several sporting events.

Arturo Toscanini was one of the founders of the **Lucerne International Festival of Music,** which takes place in mid-August and is one of the most important such events in Europe, attracting some of the world's best soloists and orchestras. Richard Wagner, in fact, was an early guest and performer (a museum devoted to the great maestro lies on the outskirts of Lucerne). For

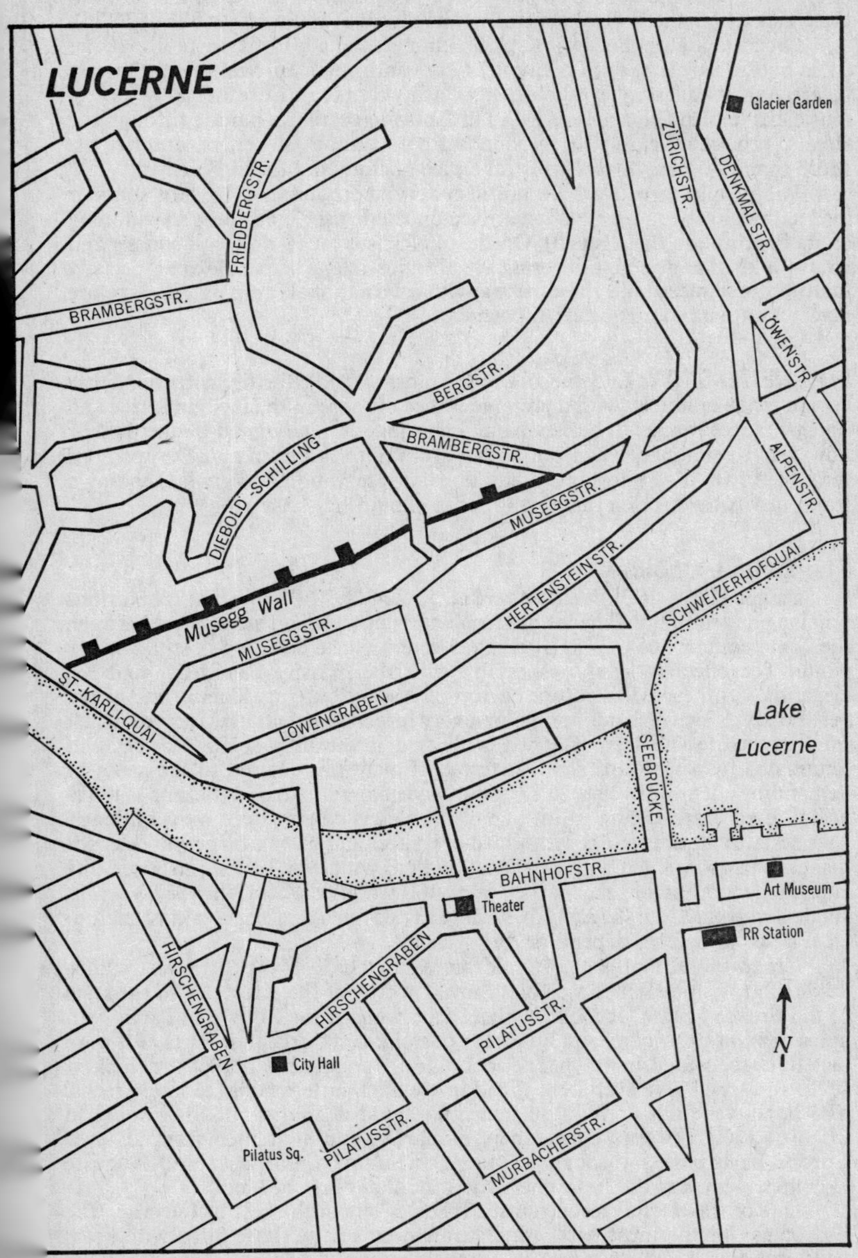
LUCERNE
Glacier Garden
FRIEDBERGSTR.
ZÜRICHSTR.
DENKMALSTR.
BRAMBERGSTR.
LÖWENSTR.
BERGSTR.
BRAMBERGSTR.
DIEBOLD-SCHILLING
ALPENSTR.
MUSEGGSTR.
HERTENSTEINSTR.
SCHWEIZERHOFQUAI
Musegg Wall
MUSEGGSTR.
ST.-KARLI-QUAI
LOWENGRABEN
Lake Lucerne
SEEBRÜCKE
BAHNHOFSTR.
Art Museum
Theater
RR Station
HIRSCHENGRABEN
HIRSCHENGRABEN
PILATUSSTR.
N
City Hall
PILATUSSTR.
MURBACHERSTR.
Pilatus Sq.

information, call the central booking office in Lucerne at 23-52-72 for information. Tickets for the festival generally range from 10F ($4.60) to 80F ($36.76).

Lucerne is also the setting for a summer night festival, a tradition that dates back 250 years, with many fireworks and much entertainment. Shortly before Ash Wednesday every year it's Carnival time in Lucerne, as groups of musicians (called *Guuggenmusigen*) in fantastic costumes parade through the streets, producing ear-splitting sounds from trumphets, kettles, and drums. More than 400 fancy-dress balls take place before and during carnival!

The people who live here are also very sports-oriented. Every summer international rowing regattas take place on the Rotsee, and there's swimming on its famous lido (lake beach). On the outskirts is an 18-hole golf course, and tennis, hiking, and mountaineering are also possible. The people are especially fond of horse races, and these, along with international jumping contests, are marked on many an equestrian calendar.

WHERE TO STAY: Lucerne, one of the most-visited cities of Switzerland, has a wide range of hotels, with a preponderance of those in the medium-price and upper-bracket ranges. It suffers from a shortage of really good budget hotels, however. In summer, when the hordes from both America and Europe pour into this town, it's important to nail down a reservation. Otherwise, finding a room in whatever price range you desire should not be a problem.

The Deluxe Choices

Palace Hotel, 10 Haldenstrasse (tel. 50-22-22). The lobby of this luxurious hotel is painted in light shades of green and yellow, which are applied between the Ionic columns of the high-ceilinged room whose detailing is still a starry white. The effect is lovely, especially with the massive chandelier and the elegantly lighthearted furniture on top of a sea-green rug. This is one of the best hotels in Switzerland, housed in a very large 19th-century structure which rambles beside the lake. Capped with two interesting-looking towers and dominated by a mansard roof, the establishment has catered to the needs of demanding clients for years. A Victorian-style bar with globe lights and leather-upholstered barrel chairs is just one of the rooms where you'll want to linger. Two restaurants are staffed with a host of waiters and chefs who prepare elegant dishes for a room filled with tapestries and tall windows. Jürg Reinshagen, the capable general manager, charges from 100F ($45.95) to 190F ($87.31) in a single and from 160F ($73.52) to 300F ($137.85) in a double, breakfast included. Prices, of course, depend on the season.

Grand Hotel National, 4 Haldenstrasse (tel. 50-11-11), is a vast edifice made of gray stone which was built, in the words of the director, "in the style of the French kings." It looks almost like a wing of the Louvre in Paris, with acres of mansard roofing and hundreds of stone-flanked gables. Parts of it were tastefully renovated in 1978. The lobby, for example, has one of the thickest sculpted carpets I've ever seen, tinted in abstract patterns of blues and greens. The hotel was built in 1870, to house the flood of tourists just beginning to discover Lake Lucerne. Since then, monarchs and statesmen from all over Europe have passed through its doors, including César Ritz and Auguste Escoffier, who was the head chef when the hotel first opened.

One of the elegant restaurants, Pfyffer, is one of the best in Lucerne. The bedrooms, for the most part, are charming, especially those filled with brass beds and gilded wall sconces. An indoor swimming pool is on the premises, along with massage facilities, while an 18-hole golf course is a few minutes away by car. The more expensive units face the lake, but all of them are equipped with private bath, TV, radio, and phone. Singles range from 100F ($45.95) to 190F ($87.31), while doubles cost between 180F ($82.71) and 300F ($137.85), depending on the season. Breakfast is included in the price.

Carlton Hotel Tivoli, 57 Haldenstrasse (tel. 51-30-51), is on the tree-lined promenade on the north side of the lake in a region filled with resort hotels and private homes. It has its own lakeside tennis courts and a marina built out into the lake. The ambience is one of clear open space and unobtrusive modern furniture. Because of the high ceilings, the light furniture, and the big windows, one has a feeling of being outdoors most of the time. A terrace restaurant serves good food, while a piano bar often features live music. The 100 accommodations all have private baths, renting for between 100F ($45.95) and 145F ($66.63) in a single, from 155F ($71.22) to 252F ($115.80) in a double. An extra bed can be set up in any room for another 50F ($22.98), while arrangements can also be made for connecting a single and a double room. Breakfast is included.

Schweizerhof Lucerne, 3 Schweizerhofquai (tel. 50-22-11), has been under the ownership of the Hauser family since 1861. It's truly a 19th-century palace-style hotel, with pink marble columns and pilasters in the lobby which support the plaster detailing on the cream-colored ceilings. An American-style bar is outfitted with rich woods, Louis XV–style armchairs, and leather bar stools. The bedrooms are the kind of spacious, well-furnished places where you could safely send your favorite nephew on his honeymoon. This hotel is a rigidly symmetrical and very pleasing collection of three evenly spaced white buildings connected by arched passageways. They ramble along the lakefront for at least two full blocks, giving a strong impression of an architectural style whose grandeur may never be repeated. Singles rent for between 70F ($32.17) and 165F ($75.82), while doubles cost from 105F ($48.25) to 275F ($126.35), depending on the plumbing and the season.

The Upper Bracket

Hotel Monopol, 1 Pilatusstrasse (tel. 23-08-66), lies behind a very grand facade of carved limestone, wrought-iron balconies, and elaborately detailed windows and half-columns. Built in 1898, the hotel has individually furnished rooms, some of them very up-to-date, and others in a cozily paneled format of alcove beds and chalet chairs. A tavern within the hotel looks like an inviting forest of rustic vertical beams, with a live pianist every evening from 7 to 11. A more formal French restaurant, the Arbalète, serves classic meals in a lighthearted decor of crimson walls and modern chandeliers. Each of the accommodations has a private bath, with radio, phone, and mini-bar. Singles range from 85F ($39.06) to 107F ($49.17), while doubles go from 138F ($63.41) to 182F ($83.63), with breakfast included. Oldtime residents of Lucerne, by the way, sometimes refer to this place as the Hotel Monopol and Métropole, but the management tells me it's comfortable just calling it "the Monopol."

Hotel Schiller, 15 Pilatusstrasse (tel. 23-51-55). The entrance is indicated by a yellow awning above a busy commercial street. You'll be surrounded by other antique buildings, although this one might stand out more because of its 19th-century detailing. A sidewalk café serves drinks and food beneath the bedroom windows, which are usually decorated with summertime flower boxes. Inside, a decorator has added dramatic touches, such as dark-green walls with attractively framed prints and an occasional bronze statue. A rustic restaurant has the kind of heavy beams overhead you've come to expect in the Alps, as well as an open hearth where a black-vested staff member grills savory steaks.

Many of the accommodations have been modernized into a streamlined format of angular furniture and comfortable beds, with modern baths, phones, and, in some cases, TVs and mini-bars. You'll be only a five-minute walk from the train station. Singles range from 62F ($28.49) to 91F ($41.82), while doubles cost from 94F ($43.19) to 152F ($69.84), depending on the size, the plumbing, and the season.

Hotel zum Rebstock, Sankt Leodegar Platz (tel. 51-35-81), is one of the most charming hotels in its price range in Lucerne. It's housed in a half-timbered green-shuttered house with a brown tile roof which visitors can see on their way down the hill from the nearby Hofkirche. It used to be the headquarters of the wine-growers guild (1443), and was later used as a recruitment center for the tough Swiss mercenaries who came from this region (the pope was one of the main recruiters). Bedrooms inside tend to be smaller than you may be used to, but are charmingly decorated in shades of blue and white, sometimes pink and green. The better ones usually have at least one unpretentious antique, while some of the others are more modern. If you're interested in a daytime hill-climbing expedition, the management will pack you a trail lunch. Otherwise, you might choose to eat in the thick-walled restaurant or on the garden terrace. Singles rent for between 65F ($29.87) and 95F ($43.65), while doubles range from 100F ($45.95) to 150F ($68.93). Triples cost between 115F ($52.84) and 170F ($78.12), including breakfast.

Hotel Union, 16 Löwenstrasse (tel. 51-36-51). You can tell that this was once a very grand hotel, and it still does everything possible to maintain high standards of comfort and service. The lobby is outfitted with conservatively modern decor which includes massive columns of reddish stone holding up a high ceiling. In the stairwell leading to the breakfast room and the bedrooms you'll see a massive chandelier which was skillfully designed for this space. Public rooms include a very attractive bar, two restaurants, and a ballroom which you should at least have a look at. Don't be put off by the imposing facade of this place: it gives clean and comfortable accommodations for less than you'd think. There are adequate showers on each floor for the residents of the bathless chambers. Singles range from 48F ($22.06) to 100F ($45.95), while doubles cost from 72F ($33.08) to 166F ($76.30), breakfast included. Parking is a few blocks away at a garage.

Romantik-Hotel Wilden Mann, 5 Freigerichstrasse (tel. 23-16-66). If you pay for half board here, you can take your meals at two other hotels owned by the same management (the Château Gütsch and the Carlton Tivoli). Chances are, however, you'll choose to eat in the Swiss-style paneled dining room with the vaulted arches and heraldic designs. This hotel is set in the middle of the old town, in a building with lots of flowerboxes, carved stone detailing, and elegant furniture. Each of the bedrooms is different, usually more modern than the public rooms downstairs, although attractive and one-of-a-kind. Singles range from 49F ($22.52) to 105F ($48.25), while doubles cost from 70F ($32.17) to 170F ($78.12), with breakfast included. Prices, of course, depend on the season and the plumbing. Half board is available for an additional 27F ($12.41) per person daily.

Grand Hotel Europe, 59 Haldenstrasse (tel. 30-11-11), is an elegant 19th-century hotel one block away from the north shore of the lake. It has neoclassical pediments above the windows of its white facade, and a row of red awnings sheltering the public rooms from the sunshine in the garden. Some of the sitting rooms are decorated with very large tapestries, Oriental rugs, and comfortably upholstered couches and easy chairs. The bedrooms are usually spacious and well furnished. The hotel is open from the first of April until the end of October. Singles cost from 95F ($43.65) to 113F ($51.92), while doubles range from

160F ($73.52) to 196F ($90.06). Half board is an additional 20F ($9.19) per person daily.

Hotel Astoria, 29 Pilatusstrasse (tel. 23-53-23), is in the center of Lucerne in a modern block-shaped building with prominent horizontal rows of windows. The interior is attractively subdued, with metal and stucco detailing, along with glistening accents and enameled metal. In the popular bar area the walls are upholstered in soft green, with a metallic ceiling reflecting the flames from the central tubular fireplace. The 110 well-furnished rooms each have private bath, radio, and phone, and some of them also have a TV. Singles range from 67F ($30.79) to 92F ($42.27), while doubles cost from 87F ($39.98) to 157F ($72.14), with breakfast included.

Hotel Montana, 22 Adlingenswilerstrasse (tel. 51-65-65), is a beautifully detailed 19th-century hotel set slightly above lake level on a quiet hillside. The hotel maintains its own private cable car so that its guests can ride in comfort down to the lakeside promenades. The interior is filled with the kind of old-fashioned grandeur that you might be looking for, including a lobby area with a contrasting series of Oriental rugs, brocaded antique chairs and settees, and polished paneling stretching up to the ornamented ceilings. A sympathetic curved bar area and terrace with a panoramic view over the lake are very pleasant stopping points. Singles rent for between 88F ($40.44) and 155F ($70.76), while doubles cost from 152F ($69.84) to 206F ($94.86), with breakfast included. An extra bed can be set up in any room for an additional 40F ($18.38). All units contain a private bath, and the hotel is closed every year from November to March.

Hotel Flora, 5 Seidenhofstrasse (tel. 24-44-44), has the kind of modern decor that is warmly fashioned from wood and metal into a pleasing angularity, but which adds folkloric touches in key places to remind you that you are in Switzerland. A disco on the premises is a fantasy of comfortable banquettes and hanging pin lights, while the bars provide comfortable and up-to-date places for an intimate drink. You'll be near the railway station in a large hotel with 145 rooms and a strong dedication to good service. One of the restaurants has a folkloric musical show about every evening, with yodelers and alpine horns. If you didn't have your heart set on an old-fashioned hotel, this is a good choice. Each of the comfortable rooms has a private bath, along with TV, radio, and phone. Breakfast is included in the price, which ranges from 78F ($35.84) to 100F ($45.95) in a single, with doubles costing from 128F ($58.82) to 175F ($80.41), depending on the season.

Hotel Château Gütsch, Kanonenstrasse (tel. 22-02-72). If you've ever dreamed of ruling over part of your own castle, this could be your chance. The outrageously ornate tower on top of this château could have been designed by Mad King Ludwig himself. The rest of the building, lying above the city, is crafted of gray stone and red tiles, sometimes with half timbering, and always surrounded by mountain paths and pleasant lawns. A swimming pool with a view of the lake is separated from the main building by a copse of trees. Inside you'll find dozens of antiques unlike any you may have seen before, some of them a cross between Louis XV and art nouveau. A rustic bar and wine cellar are outfitted with huge oval wine barrels set into the masonry walls, with wagon-wheel chandeliers illuminating the polished woodwork. Comfortably furnished singles range from 75F ($34.46) to 107F ($49.17), while doubles cost between 115F ($52.84) and 180F ($82.71), depending on the season. Breakfast is included.

Hotel Balances and **Bellevue,** Weinmarkt (tel. 51-18-51), is a quiet hotel with a desirable location on the River Reuss. The riverside frontage is elaborately crafted of gray stone with lots of curlicue wrought-iron balconies, and fire-engine-red awnings. A waterside café does a thriving business on a hot day, especially since most of the town on the other side of the river will be spread out for viewing. When you exit from the front door you'll be in the most colorful square in town, opposite a building with frescoes all over the facade. Inside the hotel you'll find a pleasing blend of Oriental rugs and high ceilings. Some of the rooms have been updated in a contemporary style, but all are usually tasteful and pleasing. Clients are authorized to drive to the hotel, even if the barricades have temporarily turned the inner city into a pedestrian zone. Accommodations on the river side are understandably more in price. Singles range from 82F ($37.68) to 102F ($46.87), while doubles cost between 135F ($62.03) and 200F ($91.90). Triples are tabbed in the range of 180F ($82.71) to 230F ($105.69). Each of the units has its own bath and comes with a light breakfast. American breakfasts are available for another 12F ($5.51).

Luzernerhof, 3 Alpenstrasse (tel. 51-46-46), is a centrally located silvery rectangle of a building with brick detailing around its corners and a streetside café. Each of its spacious, well-furnished bedrooms has a private bath and a modern format of geometric carpeting and Scandinavian chairs. You'll find a restaurant, a grill room, and a bar open until late at night. Accommodations in single or double rooms range from 53F ($24.35) to 83F ($38.14) per person daily, with breakfast included.

The Middle Bracket

Hotel Schiff, 8 Unter der Egg (tel. 51-38-51), is an attractively styled, aged yellow stucco building with a gabled roof made of weathered tiles. Except for its color it blends into the neighboring buildings on either side, one of which has almost the same shape and size. The building is separated from the Reuss only by a short pedestrian walkway, where someone has set up café tables below the chestnut trees lining the banks of the river. Inside, the bedrooms are filled with inexpensive modern furniture, yet have all the character that automatically comes from exposed timbers, thick stucco walls, and an occasional sloped ceiling. A restaurant on the premises serves meals either inside or on the balcony. All the singles are bathless, renting for between 37F ($17) and 47F ($21.60), while doubles cost from 60F ($27.57) to 135F ($62.03), depending on the season, the exposure, and (for the double rooms only) the plumbing.

Hôtel des Alpes, 5 Rathausquai (tel. 51-58-25), has an elegantly tall and narrow facade with lots of restrained detailing that leans a little toward the baroque. A riverside restaurant and café serves meals on the terrace just above the Reuss, which has a frontal view of Lucerne's famous covered bridge. Inside, the public rooms still retain some of their old-fashioned detailing, although the bedrooms are usually streamlined, modernized, and filled with functional pieces. Parking facilities are across the river at the nearby train station. Each of the bedrooms has its own private bath, costing from 55F ($25.27) to 77F ($35.38) in a single and from 85F ($39.06) to 130F ($59.74) in a double, depending on the exposure and the season. Breakfast is included.

Hotel Johanniter, 18 Bundesplatz (tel. 23-18-55). The paneling around the inside of this pleasing hotel has the kind of light-grained patina any of us would like to reproduce in our own home. The bedrooms have carved alpine head- and footboards and wood trim around the doors. The overall effect is comfortable, warm, and attractive. Even the modern leatherette chairs in the lobby look attractively in place next to their modern paintings. The hotel is behind the railway station about six blocks from the lake. Gerhard Fahrni, your host, charges from 45F ($20.68) to 60F ($27.57) in a single and from 38F ($17.46) to 54F ($24.81) per person in a double, with breakfast included. These prices depend on the season and the plumbing. Modern showers have been installed on each floor.

Hotel Alpina, 6 Frankenstrasse (tel. 23-00-77), is a one-minute walk from the train station. Its interior is attractively and comfortably furnished with plush carpeting in rich colors and several pieces of painted alpine furniture. The bedrooms are spacious and often high ceilinged, and are outfitted with conservative furniture. An attached restaurant is rustic, wood beamed, and clean. Singles range from 46F ($21.14) to 65F ($29.87), while doubles cost from 72F ($33.08) to 109F ($50.09).

Hotel Kolping, 8 Friedenstrasse (tel. 51-23-51), has a restrained facade of gray stone and stucco near the lion statue. It sometimes accepts large tour groups, so you may not be able to get a room here in high season. The interior is usually outfitted in a pastiche of modern and newly installed rustic furniture, although the overall effect is pleasing and comfortable. A chalet-style restaurant is covered with blond paneling from top to bottom. The hotel is a pleasant and unpretentious establishment which tries to please. Singles range from 40F ($18.38) to 65F ($29.87), while doubles cost from 61F ($28.03) to 109F ($50.09), depending on the season and the plumbing.

Hôtel de la Paix, 2 Museggstrasse (tel. 51-52-53), can be found between the Lion monument and the lake. The facade is constructed in a pastiche of styles that includes Renaissance bay windows, Italianate painted panels, and Victorian gables. All of it is incongruously capped with a baroque tower, which, considering the rest of the building, doesn't look at all out of place. The interior has two rustic restaurants, a sauna, and a small wood-ceilinged swimming pool. City parking is close to the hotel. Singles cost from 42F ($19.30) to 72F ($33.08), while doubles range from 63F ($28.95) to 123F ($56.52), depending on the season and plumbing. Breakfast is included in the price.

Hotel Hermitage, Luzern-Seeburg (tel. 31-37-37). Technically this hotel is in Lucerne, although you'll need to get there on a bus which leaves from the main station or on a boat that departs from the city docks. One part of the hotel is an attractive older house, painted white, with a modern extension off to one side. Guests are invited to sit on a lakeside terrace for meals or coffee, or to sun themselves on the grassy lawns. A nearby annex holds the overflow from the main hotel. Singles range from 39F ($17.92) to 50F ($22.98) and doubles cost from 50F ($22.98) to 63F ($28.95) per person, with breakfast included. Prices, of course, depend on the season and the view.

Hotel Eden, 47 Haldenstrasse (tel. 51-38-06), is an old-fashioned hotel with the kind of fussy detailing that only the late 19th century provided. It has a pleasant location near the lakeside promenade. Clients enjoy a wide vista of the lake and mountains from the windows of their bedrooms, some of which have flowery wallpaper and molded ceilings. The attractively unglossy bar area has an octagonal pattern sculptured from plaster set into its high ceiling, with antique tables made from elegant headboards. The Fioretti family charges from 45F ($20.68) to 78F ($35.84) in a single and from 65F ($29.87) to 130F ($59.74) in a double, depending on the season and the plumbing.

Hotels Continental and **Park,** 4–13 Morgartenstrasse (tel. 23-75-66), have an attractive facade of gray masonry and darker gray detailing. A row of evenly spaced gables juts out from the sixth-floor roofline, while the exterior of the ground-floor restaurant is framed in black. Near the train station, these hotels offer their comfortable rooms to visitors who pay between 56F ($25.73) and 89F ($40.90) in a single and between 89F ($40.90) and 130F ($59.74) in a double, with breakfast included.

Hotel Rothaus, 4 Klosterstrasse (tel. 22-45-22), is a newly built hotel in the center of town. The angular modern facade is relieved by the placement of red shutters near the weatherproof windows. The interior has a pleasant sitting room with upholstered chairs, contrasting Oriental rugs, and an oversize armoire in reddish carved wood dominating one wall. The other public rooms are paneled and beamed, with wood furniture and wrought-iron lighting fixtures. Singles rent for between 40F ($18.38) and 66F ($30.33), while doubles cost from 64F ($29.41) to 117F ($53.76), depending on the season. Breakfast is included.

The Budget Range

Hôtel le Cachet, 6 Falkengasse (tel. 51-55-46), is a modern hotel in the center of the old town, a five-minute walk from the train station. Each of the rooms has a private bath, phone, and radio. A pleasant bistro and snackbar under the same management is outfitted with Victorian globe lights and a colorful decor of red and green with plenty of wood accents. Singles range from 45F ($20.68) to 52F ($23.89), and doubles cost from 77F ($35.38) to 97F ($44.57), depending on the season and the plumbing. Ernest and Blanka Kubesch are the owners.

Touristenhotel, 12 St. Karliquai (tel. 51-24-74), is an attractive choice for a budget hotel in Lucerne, with sometimes as many as four beds in a room and a simple but pleasant decor of hanging wicker lamps and angular chairs. You'll recognize the hotel by its lime-green facade on the water, lying a few minutes from the train station. None of the bedrooms has a private bath, but you'll find adequate shower facilities on each floor. The dining hall serves meals, including the breakfast that is included in the room price. Singles range from 33F ($15.16) to 42F ($19.30), while doubles cost from 49F ($22.52) to 70F ($32.17), depending on the season.

Pension Villa Maria, 36 Haldenstrasse (tel. 31-21-19), is a family-run pension in a three-story private home on the north shore of the lake. The public rooms are decorated like someone's comfortably cluttered living room, in shades of gold, pink, and red, while the bedrooms are spacious, clean, and comfortable. The Winkler family is happy to help guests in any way it can. Bathless singles range from 32F ($14.70) to 45F ($20.68), while doubles cost between 51F ($23.44) and 93F ($42.73), with breakfast included. The prices, of course, depend on the season.

READER'S GUEST HOUSE SELECTION (MEGGEN): "Purely by luck, my sister and I happened on a small guest house just five minutes from Lucerne, the **Clarida** in Meggen (tel. 37-12-87). The house is in a quiet area, but what made our stay so outstanding was the food. The first night, we were served dinner on an open patio, and the veal dish we chose was superbly prepared and served. The second night we had calf liver, which was delicious. It seems that on any trip there is at least one place which lingers in your memory, and this one is well worth making a five-minute jog in your travels. Prices are around 45F ($20.68) for a double bedroom" (Kathleen Rice, Cheshire, Conn.).

WHERE TO DINE: Lucerne is blessed with some of the finest restaurants in Switzerland, in a wide category of price. So you definitely won't be confined to your hotel dining room when it comes time to eat. Prices, in the main, are fairly reasonable.

The Upper Bracket

Chez Marianne (Restaurant zum Raben), 5 Am Kornmarkt (tel. 51-51-35), is the personal statement of Marianne Kaltenbach, a celebrity in Switzerland because of her well-known cookbooks. In the heart of the old town, the building dates from the Middle Ages. The restaurant is divided into four elegant rooms, usually with wood panels, alpine chairs, and chandeliers of deer antlers carved into human figures, plus lots of 80-year-old photographs of a thriving Lucerne. An inner room is my personal favorite. It has exquisitely crafted Louis-Philippe chairs in glowing hardwoods, built-in floor-to-ceiling Gothic revival cupboards, mirrors, modern paintings, and views of the river. Swiss menus are offered from 25F ($11.49) to 39F ($17.92). Specialties include filet of pike with a saffron cream sauce, venison pâté with nuts and bitter orange sauce, and boiled beef with horseradish. Reservations are suggested. The restaurant is closed on Monday, but open otherwise from 11:30 a.m. for lunch, serving dinner until 9:30 p.m.

Old Swiss House, 4 Löwenplatz (tel. 51-61-71), is housed in such a charming half-timbered building that Anheuser-Busch built an enlarged replica of it in Busch Gardens in Tampa, Florida, in 1964. The Lucerne restaurant is famous, with a series of antique-filled upper floors usually reserved for private parties, and a ground-floor restaurant decorated mostly with objects from the 17th century. You'll enter through an oak door with wrought-iron embellishments and be face to face with a long bar. Waitresses in regional dress hurry about, serving the tables. Your own table will probably be close to one of the leaded-glass windows in one of the heavily timbered dining rooms. The Buholzer family has owned this place for many years. A city parking lot is a few hundred yards away, although there are a few parking places with meters nearby if you can find a slot. The restaurant is open daily from 9 a.m. to midnight. Specialties include homemade cheese croquettes, onion soup, a local fish caught fresh every day from Lake Lucerne, veal prepared at your table, and a deluxe wienerschnitzel (like you've never tasted before!), plus veal escalope topped with ham and cheese in a velvety-smooth cream sauce. From 11 a.m. to 6 p.m. a light luncheon menu ranges in price from 10F ($4.60) to 20F ($9.19). A large five-course menu costs from 33F ($15.16) to 59F ($27.11).

Le Manoir, 9 Bundesplatz (tel. 23-23-48). Roman Stübinger and his wife Elke achieved local fame and lots of international attention when they renovated a terraced building next to the train station a few years ago. They brought nouvelle cuisine in full force to Lucerne and, it's rumored, did more to change local tastes than any other restaurant. Blessed with what appears to be enormous energy, the Austrian-born owner grows many of his own vegetables and personally writes out the day's menu by hand. He also prepares a constantly changing series of impeccably flavored delicacies. Everything is cuisine du marché in the freshest sense of that expression. Elke presides over the dining room with great poise, sometimes suggesting a three-course business lunch at 30F ($13.79) for clients who don't want to dawdle. More elaborate dishes include filets of turbot with sage, asparagus tips served with chive sabayon, fresh duckling, lake trout with leeks in champagne sauce, or fricassée of rabbit with prunes and old Bordeaux. The restaurant is closed on Monday. Fixed-price meals range from 65F ($29.87) to 100F ($45.95), with à la carte dinners costing from 30F ($13.79) to 90F ($41.36).

Arbalète, Hotel Monopole, 1 Pilatusstrasse (tel. 23-08-66), is an elegantly decorated restaurant with crimson walls and modern chandeliers in the first floor of this hotel. Specialties include a clear bouillon of lobster, a gratin of veal kidneys, turbot with anise sauce, and rolled filet of sole stuffed with shrimp. You also might be served Breton crêpes, chicken à la king (but not the type usually presented at Kiwanis Club suppers), or chipped veal in cream sauce, with rösti, Zuricher style. The restaurant, whose name means crossbow, is open from 6 a.m. to 12:30 a.m. Set meals range from 30F to 85F ($39.06), with à la carte dinners costing from 30F ($13.79) to 70F ($32.17).

Von Pfyffer-Stube, Hotel National, 4 Haldenstrasse (tel. 50-11-11). The menu and staff have changed since Escoffier worked in the kitchen here in 1870. However, many of the same valuable paintings still hang on the elegantly decorated walls. Despite the Teutonic name, the restaurant is undeniably French in its cuisine, serving elaborately presented specialties which include filet of burbot, crayfish and foie gras salad in walnut oil, mussels with chives, and several deliciously prepared veal dishes, ranging from the regional specialty in cream sauce with rösti to a special recipe "von Pfyffer." The restaurant is open from 11:30 a.m. to 2 p.m. and 6 p.m. to midnight every day of the year. Fixed-price menus range from 65F ($29.87), with à la carte dinners costing from 36F ($16.54) to 72F ($33.08).

The Middle Bracket

Restaurant Wilden Mann, 30 Bahnhofstrasse (tel. 23-16-66), has vaulted smoky ceilings and lots of paneling, the kind of well-maintained rustic ambience you normally associate with the Alps. It's been owned by the same family for the last 130 years, and today is one of the better known restaurants in the old town. A five-course fixed-price menu might offer a ragoût of fresh mushrooms and chanterelles with sage, a cutting from a side of beef with mustard sauce, or medallions of veal with leeks, perhaps shrimp bisque, followed by filet of sole with lime sauce. Table d'hôte meals cost from 25F ($11.49) to 42F ($19.30), while à la carte dinners range from 32F ($14.70) to 53F ($24.35). The restaurant is open every day.

Restaurant Lapin, Hôtel de la Paix, 2 Museggstrasse (tel. 51-52-53). This restaurant is attractively angled so that it opens like a fan from the entrance. The format is light-grained and rustic, with a separate bar area overlooking a picture window and a few comfortable banquettes near hanging parchment lamps. One wall is made of exposed stone. Please note that the restaurant is at the corner of the Alpenstrasse, because if you begin your search at the wrong end of the street, you'll have a very long walk up some steep hills. The establishment is run by Mr. Zehnder-Real. Specialties include international fare such as sirloin steak Café de Paris and veal piccata, as well as excellent fish dishes such as sole. To honor its namesake, lapin (rabbit), the chef prepares a terrine made with rabbit. He also does a fine chicken curry with rice. You can also order the classic Swiss dish, sausage and rösti. Meals cost from 40F ($18.38).

Schwanen Restaurants, 4 Schwanenplatz (tel. 51-11-77). Under the same roof are two distinctly different restaurants, both of them well suited for a sympathetic dinner with a friend. Le Bec Rouge is the more elegant—and expensive—of the two. It lies on the upper floor, with good views of the lake. In the bar area you'll see a four-foot model of the Italian vessel, *Raphaello,* behind a Plexiglas case. A large photograph of the main mast of what is probably the same ship graces five feet of one of the walls. The restaurant is in a separate area, in a room with windows on three sides and a decor like that of an old steamship. It has soft pink lampshades, wooden ceilings, and an attractive staff. The tables are spacious, the lighting intimate, and the service elegant. The chef prepares excellent fish dishes, many from the lake, including trout and perch. Main courses include some excellent U.S. beef and fondue bourguignonne (served only for two persons), as well as veal steak with fresh mushrooms and cream sauce. Dessert selections are made from the trolley. Dinners begin at 30F ($13.79), but you'll more likely spend from 45F ($20.22) to 60F ($27.57).

The second part of this swan has a very different ambience and menu, and is cheaper. The Trattoria al Lago, on the ground floor, is less formal. It has many seating areas, all filled with hanging lamps, stone floors, and many small series of stairs leading from one part to another. In the innermost recess of this labyrinthine restaurant you'll find the kind of bar where you'll be able to sit for a good long time with an end-of-the-day drink. Both Swiss and Italian specialties are prepared by the kitchen, ranging from homemade pizza, tortellini, spaghetti, tripe soup with vegetables, boiled farm hams, raclette Valaisanne, and such standards as sausage with sauerkraut and potatoes. Count on spending from 22F ($10.11).

China Restaurant Li-Tai-Pe, 14 Furrengasse (tel. 51-10-23), is the best Chinese restaurant in Lucerne, run by Robert and Margaret Chi Tsun. (He was an assistant to Gen. Chiang Kai-shek for a short period.) On a narrow street in the old town, the restaurant is somberly lit and decorated with Oriental artifacts. The cuisine is Peking style, and includes crispy fried boneless chicken, "eight treasures" fried rice, beef in oyster oil, abalone with bamboo shoots, crispy fried wonton, sweet-and-sour spare ribs, diced duck with almonds, and pork with soya noodles. The major specialty, which must be ordered a day in advance is a chrysanthemum pot. Meals cost from 40F ($18.38), and service is from 11:30 a.m. to 2:30 p.m. and 6:30 to 11 p.m. It's closed on Monday.

Hofstube, Hotel Rebstock, 3 St. Leodegar Strasse (tel. 51-35-81), is the restaurant attached to the Hotel Zum Rebstock (see the hotel recommendations). Next to a building used as a guildhall for Lucerne wine growers in the Middle Ages, the site is rich in history. Today a 1920s-style entrance hall is filled with valuable art deco and an extravagant bouquet of flowers. Claudia Moser is the auburn-haired owner who three years ago established this flourishing restaurant, which is spread out into two gemütlich rooms, one with carved timbers. A big green courtyard is behind the hotel, and it's lit with spotlights. A table here is preferred on a warm evening. The friendly staff serves classical specialties, including an impressive list of terrines, an elixir of morels, lake trout, tournedos 1900 style, a rack of lamb, or duckling in orange sauce. You might be more adventurous and order pig feet with morels or suckling veal with leafy spinach. Desserts are very good as well ("cool hits for hot dates"). Fixed-price meals range from 12F ($5.51) to 37F ($17), while à la carte dinners cost from 25F ($11.49) to 65F ($29.87).

Eichhof, 106 Obergrundstrasse (tel. 41-11-74), bears the name of a well-known local beer which, not surprisingly, is used in the house recipe for pig feet and pork shoulder. Many of the relaxed patrons will be drinking this same brew from large steins, and will usually be on the summertime terrace if weather permits. Heinzpeter Meier and his wife Maria, the owners, often serve an extensive menu of wild game, along with other specialties such as duckling in green peppercorns with cream sauce or rack of lamb provençal. The restaurant is closed on Sunday evening, all day Monday, and for the month of February. À la carte meals range from 21F ($9.65) to 37F ($17), with fixed-price dinners costing between 20F ($9.19) and 35F ($16.08).

The Budget Range

Kunst and **Kongresshaus Restaurants,** at the Bahnhof (tel. 23-181-16), is connected with the largest convention hall in Lucerne. Next to the train station in a modern metallic building with an equestrian statue in front, the establishments are surrounded by flowering, well-maintained parks. Three different restaurants inside (the Tell stube, the saloon, and the bistro/bar) offer well-prepared food with lunches costing from 8F ($3.68) to 27F ($12.41). In summer a terrace area has self-serve sausages and barbecues, starting at 3.50F ($1.61).

Pinocchio, Hirschenplatz (tel. 51-10-96). The most interesting feature of the simple upstairs bar (which is where most of the action is at night) is the medieval "safe" door placed into a decorative alcove. The rest of the establishment is predictably furnished with wood ceilings and very small tables with chairs. The ground floor holds only six indoor tables, although many more than that are set up on the cobblestone square in front. Inexpensive Italian specialties are served, including lasagne verdi, Neapolitan pizza, alpine dishes, as well as the more prosaic cheeseburger and french fries. Meals cost from 20F ($9.19).

Wienerwald, Hirschenplatz (tel. 51-30-14), is part of the European chain so popular with Swiss families and their children. It could perhaps be called the Howard Johnson of Switzerland, except it specializes in chicken instead of ice cream. The format, in the typical Wienerwald style, is rustic and attractively outfitted with beams and timbers. It's open from 11 a.m. to 2 p.m. and 6 to 11 p.m. Meals range upward from 10F ($4.60) and almost invariably include half a grilled chicken. The kitchen also prepares a variety of beef, pork, and veal dishes.

Bristol Vegetarian Restaurant, 3 Obergrund (tel. 23-68-66), is a sunny, wood-paneled restaurant with lots of brickwork, modern textiles, hanging orange lamps, and bas-relief designs centered around nature themes (a harpist feeding birds, etc.). The service is quick and efficient. Many older persons will probably be there at lunch, reading the periodicals provided by the Sauter family. Near the Pilatusplatz, the establishment serves fish, raclette with potatoes, whole-meal spaghetti, a large vegetable spinach ravioli, sliced tofu, and a salad platter with eight different varieties, including egg and asparagus tips. The salads are prepared fresh every day and are served for 1.50F (69¢) a portion. Meals range from 11F ($5.06), and include one of the best items on the menu, rösti with melted cheese. The restaurant is open Monday to Saturday from 8 a.m. to 9:30 p.m., and a breakfast here costs from 3.50F ($1.61).

Schiffrestaurant Wilhelm Tell, 9 Landungsbrucke (tel. 51-23-30). When it was built in 1908 this lake cruiser sailed boatloads of happy visitors from one end of Lake Lucerne to the other. Unfortunately ships, like people, must eventually retire. Twelve years ago, Eduard Raber-Eberle transformed this one into one of the most unusual restaurants in Lucerne. The bow area (they call it the "second-class section") serves drinks and snacks on café tables under the open sky or on banquettes in the area where the steering wheel used to be. In the aft section you'll find a charming, low-ceilinged restaurant in green and white where better class food is sérved with alert attention worthy of a crew on the high seas. The engine room has been ripped off to expose the best polished boat engine in Switzerland. You can have a beer in the bow area anytime (where you'll probably want to drop bread chunks to the hungry swans). You can also dine here at prices ranging from 10F ($4.60) to 14F ($6.43). Meals might include fried perch filets, sole filets served seaman style, and good soups such as lobster cream. À la carte meals cost from 35F ($16.08). The restaurant only sails from April to October.

Peppino, 7 Theaterstrasse (tel. 23-77-71). There's nothing antique about this place, other than some painted and carved wagon wheels from the 19th century. Yet there is nonetheless an atmosphere of good taste and solidity. You might choose simply to have a drink in the stucco bar area, with its modern rustic beams and timbers and pleasantly spartan format, or you might go off to the dining room on the left. This room has an olive-tinted ceiling and a spacious, sunny format which is elegantly Italian. The unpretentious menu offers simple lunches from 9F ($4.14) to 10F ($4.60) which might include pizza, pasta, and a list of such fish specialties as a savory kettle of mussels. The veal dishes are also very good. A pasta specialty is rigatoni all'Emiliana. À la carte meals might range as high as 40F ($18.38) and up.

Galliker, Kasernenplatz (tel. 22-10-02), is a large, friendly kind of place which serves generous portions of unpretentious, well-prepared food to a stream of summertime visitors and to a loyal body of regular clients too. The decor is rustic. Many regional specialties are served, including calf head vinaigrette with rösti, "just like your grandmother used to make." They also offer fixed-price specials which change according to the day of the week. On Tuesday, Thursday, and Saturday it's pot-au-feu. Farmer-style bratwurst seasoned with caraway seed is also popular, and there are good fruited desserts as well. The restaurant is closed for three weeks in summer and on Sunday. The pot-au-feu costs $18F ($8.27), while à la carte meals range from 18F ($8.27) to 39F ($17.92).

WHAT TO SEE: The very symbol of Lucerne is the **Kappellbrücke** (Chapel Bridge), the covered wooden footbridge that crosses the River Reuss diagonally. Built in 1333 as part of the city's defenses, the bridge is about 560 feet long. One of the best preserved wooden bridges in Switzerland, the structure also has a Wasserturm (water tower), octagonal in shape, once used as a prison and torture chamber and later as a storehouse for the town's archives. The bridge has more than a hundred paintings, some done in 1599 by Heinrich Wägmann, showing the life and costumes of the people.

Farther downstream is the other famous covered wooden bridge, the **Spreuerbrücke,** also known as the "Mills Bridge." This bridge was built in 1407, spanning an arm of the Reuss, and it was restored in the 19th century. Painted gables portray a *Dance of Death.* These are from the 17th century by Kaspar Meglinger, commemorating a plague that had infected the city.

On the right bank of the Reuss, **Old Town** still contains many burghers' houses with oriel windows and old squares with fountains.

From **Schwanenplatz** (Swan Square), filled with many shops, you can walk to Kapellplatz, on which stands **St. Peter's Chapel** from 1178, the oldest church in Lucerne. In the center of this piazza is a fountain honoring carnival.

Kappellgasse, flanked by shops, will take you to the **Kornmarkt** (grain exchange), on which stands the **Altes Rathaus** (old town hall), a Renaissance building from 1602 with impressive masonry and a tremendous roof. It's crowned by a tall rectangular tower, looking down on the market-day crowds under the arcades on Tuesday and Saturday morning.

To the east of city hall, entered on Furrengasse, is the 17th-century **Am Rhyn-Haus,** which houses a small but choice collection of the works of Pablo Picasso. This collection was composed of works from the last 20 years of the artist's life. It's open May to September from 10 a.m. to noon and 3 to 6 p.m. However, it shuts down on Monday. From October to April it's open only on Friday, Saturday, and Sunday from 11 a.m. to noon and 3 to 5 p.m. Visits at other hours can be arranged by telephone: 51-17-73.

To the west of the Kornmarkt stands the **Weinmarkt,** a lovely old square with a splendid fountain which is a reproduction of a famous one that stood there. Long ago, the mystery play *Confraternity of the Crown of Thorns* was performed here. Among the colorful old dwellings on the square is the Müllersche Apotheke, a "drugstore" from 1530.

At some point in your journey of discovery you'll want to see Lucerne from one of the lookout towers. They're part of the old fortifications built along the north side of the medieval sector between 1350 and 1408, with a total of nine towers, each one in a different style. At twilight they stand in dramatic silhouette against the sky. Known as the **Museggtürme,** these ramparts are open to the public from 8 a.m. to 8 p.m. for a summer walk. The Schirmerturm tower is among those open to those who would like to climb nearly 100 steps for a view of the city and its spires.

Your eye may be drawn to the **Quays of Lucerne,** along the northern rim of the lake. Planted with trees, these quays make for a satisfying promenade, and they're lined with hotels and shops. They also have beautiful views not only of Lucerne and its lake, but the not-so-distant Alps, which stretch from the Rigi to the Pilatus which we'll view later. The quays lead to Lido beach, Lucerne's "Riviera," which is popular in the summer. Incidentally the Kursaal, with a restaurant and gaming rooms, lies at the Kurplatz on Nationalquai.

Rising above Nationalquai, the twin towers of the Catholic **Hofkirche** come into view. This is the major church of the city, known as the Collegiate Church of St. Leodegar, named after the patron saint of Lucerne. Once this was a monastery, but the present Gothic-Renaissance building dates from the 17th century. The interior has rich wrought-iron work and carvings, and a celebrated organ from 1640 which has 4950 pipes (concerts are given on it in summer). The church also has a beautiful courtyard with arcades, containing tombs of patrician families.

After leaving Kurplatz, head down Löwenstrasse to the Löwenplatz, where you can view the **Panorama of the City,** anytime from mid-March to mid-November, from 8 a.m. to noon and 12:30 to 6 p.m. (in July and August it's open all day from 8 a.m. to 6 p.m.), charging an admission of 2F (92¢). The artist Castres, working with others, depicted the retreat of the French army into Switzerland during the 1870–1871 Franco-German war. The canvas covers 11,836 square feet!

Nearby stands the landmark **Löwendenkmal,** or Lion Monument. Designed by Thorwaldsen, it was dedicated in 1821. It commemorates the heroic struggle of the Swiss Guards who died at the Tuileries in 1792 trying to save the life of Marie Antoinette. One of Europe's best known monuments, it was hewn out of sandstone. When Mark Twain on his grand tour of Europe saw the *Dying Lion of Lucerne,* he called it "the saddest and most poignant piece of rock in the world."

Rising above the monument, the **Gletschergarten** (glacier garden) dates from the Ice Age when glaciers covered Lake Lucerne. It's a series of potholes worn in a sandstone rock bed of an ancient glacier. In all, there are 32 "potholes," which were excavated in 1872. One of them is nearly 30 feet deep and 26 feet wide. A museum at the site contains a famous relief map of the Alps from the 18th century, along with prehistoric remains of plant and animal life, as well as a Swiss homeland museum. The gardens are open from the first of March until the end of April from 9 a.m. to 5 p.m. From the first of May until mid-October they can be visited from 8 a.m. to 6 p.m. From mid-October to mid-November they receive visitors from 9 a.m. to 5 p.m., and from mid-November until the end of February they're open only from 10:30 a.m. to 4:30 p.m. They're closed on Monday in winter, and always charge 3.50F ($1.61) for admission.

On the south bank of the Reuss, the Bahnhofplatz contains the railway station and the nearby docks, from which you can take tours of Lake Lucerne. At the end of the large square, near the station, is the Kunst- und Kongresshaus from 1932. It contains not only the concert hall, but the **Kunstmuseum** (fine arts museum), open from 10 a.m. to noon and 2 to 5 p.m. October to June. It's closed on Monday. Its regular admission is 3.50F ($1.61), which usually rises to 5F ($2.30) for special exhibitions. Many paintings by Swiss artists, dating from the 16th century and going up to the present, are displayed. Naturally,

Holder gets in on the act. Many famous names decorate the walls, including Dufy and Utrillo.

West of the Hauptbahnhof on the left bank of the Reuss stands the **Jesuitenkirche** or Jesuits' church, a baroque structure from 1666 with a 1750 rococo interior. It's quite a confection, with its pink porphyry and frescoes.

To the right of the church, Bahnhofsstrasse will lead to the **Regierungsgebäude** (government palace). Built in an opulent Renaissance style from 1556, the building was once the home of Lukas Ritter, the local bailiff. The cantonal government took it over in 1804. The original fountain that stood for years on Weinmarkt is preserved here in a covered courtyard. It dates from 1481.

To the southwest of the government building stands the **Franziskanerkirche** or Franciscan church, which was built in the 13th century but has had so many builders over the centuries you wouldn't know it. The wooden pulpit is from 1628, the choir stalls from 1647.

Europe's number one transport museum, the **Verkehrshaus des Schweiz** (Swiss Transport Museum), lies on the Lidostrasse, beyond the Haldenstrasse cable-car station. This is one of the top drawing museums in the country, very popular with Americans. The old and the new in transport are combined here—everything from railway cars, airplanes, automobiles, ships, even spaceships!

The *Rigi,* the oldest ship in the country, an 1847 steamboat, has found a permanent retirement base here (it's been converted into a restaurant). The most popular exhibition is a scale model of a Swiss railway crossing the Gotthard (a dozen trains move simultaneously).

Part of the Swiss Transport Museum, the **Longines Planetarium** can be entered at the eastern end of the complex. It's the only planetarium in Switzerland and one of the most modern in Europe. Here you can experience the composition of the firmament and the movement of the constellations as well as see an eclipse of the sun and the moon. You'll see what the astronauts saw in space travel.

Also connected with the museum, the **Hans Erni House** contains artwork by this well-known native-born son.

The museum complex is open from the first of March until the end of October from 9 a.m. to 6 p.m. Otherwise it's open Monday to Saturday from 10 a.m. to 4 p.m., on Sunday to 5 p.m., charging an admission of 6F ($2.76).

Another museum of note is the **Trachtenmuseum** (national costume museum), housed in a former private villa in parklike grounds on the outskirts of Lucerne. Here are displayed folk costumes from each canton in the Confederation. Some of the costumes are from other countries in Europe as well. To reach the museum, leave Lucerne on the Dreilindenstrasse, taking the highway for about half a mile. At the junction, turn left off the road to Basle, swinging onto the Utenberg route. Visits are possible from 9 a.m. to 5:30 p.m. anytime from Easter Sunday until the end of October for a 2.50F ($1.15) admission.

The major museum in the environs is the **Richard Wagner Museum** in the suburb of Tribschen, about two miles from the city. Wagner lived here from 1866 to 1872 and composed *Die Meistersinger,* among other works. The museum displays some original scores of the maestro, along with much memorabilia, including letters and pictures. In one section a collection of antique musical instruments is displayed. The museum is open from 9 a.m. to noon and 2 to 6 p.m., on Sunday from 10:30 a.m. to 5:30 p.m. (it's closed Monday, Wednesday, and Friday from mid-September to mid-April). Admission is 3F ($1.38). To reach the museum, you can go by motorboat, which leaves every hour from in front of the railway station (rail passes are valid for this trip). You can also go by bus no. 6 or 7 to Wartegg.

TOURS: From Lucerne, the lake, or Vierwaldstättersee, winds along 23 miles deep into the alpine ranges of the heart of Switzerland. The **Lake Lucerne Navigation Company** has 17 boats, of which five are paddle-steamers, to service this area. In season, boats depart Lucerne approximately every hour, a tour of the lake usually taking 6½ hours and costing from 25F ($11.49) per person. You can board the vessel and buy your ticket at the landing station opposite the Hauptbahnhof in Lucerne.

On these steamers you get waterscape with majestic mountains in the background. Many half- or full-day excursions are offered, actually an overwhelming choice if you have little time for central Switzerland. Many of these excursions can be combined with a trip to the top of a mountain by cable car or funicular. All of the main steamer services have a restaurant on board.

WHERE TO SHOP: Lucerne is an excellent shopping center if you can wade through the junk and souvenir shops. Of course, many visitors come here to purchase a watch. Some make a day excursion from Zurich on the train to do just that!

Bucherer, Schwanenplatz (tel. 50-99-50), is the most mammoth watch retailer on earth, with headquarters in Lucerne. At this major outlet they sell more than 10,000 gift items, including not only a wide range of watches, but clocks, souvenirs, and jewelry. They specialize in Rolex watches.

O. & I. Lauener, 9 Haldenstrasse (tel. 51-34-32), sells more than 100 models of cuckoo clocks, as well as 400-day clocks (that's right—you don't wind them for a year), wristwatches, and virtually everything else that ticks. If you've always wanted to buy a music box, this place has 85 different models, from both the Black Forest and Switzerland, playing just about every kind of melody. Prices begin at 85F ($39.05). You'll also see the flattest watch on earth, as well as an English pocket watch made in 1850 for a maharajah. The majority of the wristwatches are relatively inexpensive. The famous Swiss army knife is also sold here. The staff is charming, intelligent, and helpful in every way.

A. Hurter, 11 Löwenstrasse (tel. 22-24-79), sells a complete line of medium-priced and relatively inexpensive watches. He specializes in Itraco and Hudson brands, all made in Switzerland. One popular item he sells is a woman's watch whose jeweled insets match the semiprecious stones of the jewelry that goes with it.

Chalet Swiss Souvenirs, 23 Haldenstrasse (tel. 51-31-12), across from the Hotel National, is the biggest and most complete souvenir shop in the area. Hans Peter Hunziker and his pretty wife Ida sell the famous Swiss army knife, which they'll engrave for you on the spot for no extra charge. Music boxes usually have Reuge mechanisms inside, which, I'm told, are among the best in the country. They begin at 210F ($96.50). Beer steins, however, cost from 5F ($2.30), and cuckoo clocks begin at 55F ($25.27). In summer the shop is open from 8 a.m. to 10:30 p.m., closing on Saturday at 5 p.m.

Bollina-Schneider, 11 Haldenstrasse (tel. 51-33-66), is a small, somewhat cramped shop that sells Swiss souvenir-type items such as cards, beer steins, woodcarvings, Hummel figurines, cowbells, etchings, music boxes, Christmas cards, and Swiss army knives. Here, as in any shop like this, you'll see a lot of dust-gatherers, but there are nevertheless several good Swiss mementos. Piero Bollina is the articulate owner.

Sturzenneger, 7 Schwanenplatz (tel. 51-19-58), was established more than 100 years ago as one of the finest embroidery shops in Lucerne. It's carriage-trade clientele appreciates the high quality of virtually everything sold here, which includes women's lingerie, monogrammed handkerchiefs, petit-point embroidered purses, some folkloric items, and even a few pieces of ready-to-wear clothes.

Tefora, 8 Grendel (tel. 51-12-76), is a large, conveniently located outlet for Kodak film, as well as cameras, movie equipment, and accessories. They'll develop your pictures fast too.

Fritz Genhart Sport, 14 Löwenstrasse (tel. 51-36-41), sells everything you'd need for almost any sport you can think of, including skiing and cliff-climbing. They also have a complete line of wool coats, sneakers, and leather shorts. If you're a T-shirt devotee, you'll see three or four emblazoned with the name of your host city of the moment. The location is near the Hotel Union. They'll mail your purchases home if you wish.

AFTER DARK: Lucerne is not famous for its nightlife, but there is some. In summer one of the most popular noctural outings is to take the **Evening Cruise,** leaving from Pier No. 1, opposite the train station. For information, telephone 23-55-72. The cruise leaves every night from May till August at 8:45 p.m. The trip is timed so that night falls shortly after departure. That way, riders can see the surrounding mountains from their mid-lake position in both day and night. A folkloric orchestra puts on a show with flügelhorns and yodeling, so you might want to take pictures. There's dancing afterward. Reserve tickets in advance with a travel agent or with the concierge of the larger hotels. You can ride the boat and not see the show for 26F ($11.95). But if you want the entertainment too, it will cost 31F ($14.25), including one free drink. If you want to dine as well, you'll pay from 42F ($19.30) to 64F ($29.41), the cuisine ranging from a bowl of fondue to a simple dinner. If you're a heavy drinker (and need a few to get into the spirit of the occasion), you can end up spending considerably more. The cruise ends at approximately 11 p.m.

After that, it's off to the **Casino,** 6 Haldenstrasse (tel. 51-27-51). As with other casinos in Switzerland, the biggest wager allowed by law is 5F ($2.30). Therefore the entrepreneurs behind this establishment have expanded it into an entertainment complex of cabarets, discos, and restaurants. Part of your evening might be spent in the rectangular room with eerie lighting reserved strictly for gambling. But if betting doesn't flow in your veins, chances are you'll wander off to the Casino's other diversions. They include the following:

The **Red Rose Cabaret,** a strip club with show times at 10:30 p.m. and again at 12:15 a.m. Entrance is from the sidewalk. The cover charge is only 6F ($2.76), with beer costing a minimum of 15F ($6.89). The wallpaper is, as you might expect, bordello red, and there's a very correct currency exchange booth in the lobby.

The **Black Jack Club** is a disco, playing American and British music, for the most part. It's open from 9 p.m. to 2 a.m., and there's occasional live music on the raised stage area. The cover charge is 5.50F ($2.53).

The **Chalet** is a vast room with a heavily timbered format of alpine rusticity. You'll often find a program of folkloric music, usually on Monday and Thursday. That means all the yodeling, flag-throwing, and flügelhorns you've come to expect. It costs 25F ($11.49) without dinner and from 35F ($16.08) to 55F ($25.27) with dinner. When you enter after paying the cover charge, don't be surprised by the blast of music and the sight of thousands of locals swaying rhythmically to the "evergreen music."

The **Roulette Bar** is elegantly decorated with beige-colored marble and small café tables, art nouveau style. Drinks cost half price from 5 to 8 p.m. From 8 on, meals are served from a menu specializing in grilled meats. Beer costs from 6F ($2.76); whisky, from 8F ($3.68).

Finally, the **Seegarten** serves meals with a view of the lake. On a summer afternoon the terrace is usually filled.

All these establishments are connected with a glittering series of public rooms covered with green chevroned carpeting. If you want to take a breather from the activity inside, you might stroll around the gardens for a look at one of the most famous flower clocks in Switzerland.

Hazyland, 21 Haldenstrasse (tel. 63-56-46), is one of a chain of discos that stretches across Switzerland. Almost every weekend you'll find a different live band, ranging from pop/rock to punk. Inside this one is a red-velvet ambience of strobe lights and underweight young people whose average age is 22. A medium-size dance floor is open from 9 p.m. to 2 a.m. seven nights a week. There's no cover charge, and beer costs from 9F ($4.14). The club is opposite the Hotel National.

Restaurant Stadtkeller, 3 Sternenplatz (tel. 51-47-33). The Swiss folklore show here is considered a must on every first-timer's agenda. Admission is only 5F ($2.30), and you'll probably want a few beers once you go inside. The music starts at 8 p.m., and includes flügelhorns, yodelers, and accordions, all the players in regional garb. Someone will invariably wave a Swiss flag before the end of the show in a happy kind of patriotism. The restaurant is in the old town, in the basement of a building covered with extravagant stenciling and trompe l'oeil.

Barstube zur Gerbern, 7 Sternenplatz (tel. 51-55-50), has been called by the press "a little bit of San Francisco in Lucerne." Tony Trefny is the entrepreneur who established this up-to-date place a few years ago. It's become a very popular bar, with a video disco in a backroom. This is about the only such establishment in town with a large gay element, which becomes more visible later in the evening. The owner estimated to the press that his club was about 70% gay, but who knows? It's open Monday through Saturday from 3 p.m. to 2 a.m. and on Sunday from 6 p.m. to 2 a.m.

PRACTICAL FACTS: The city has a good **transportation** network of trams and buses, costing from .60F (28¢) to 2.60F ($1.20), depending on the mileage traversed. Before boarding, purchase your tickets at automatic vending machines.

The **railway station** can answer a lot of your practical needs. You can even rent a bicycle there for 9F ($4.14). You can make telephone calls there at an office open Monday to Friday from 6 a.m. to 11 p.m., on Saturday from 6:30 a.m. to 8 p.m., and on Sunday from 9 a.m. to noon and 3 to 8 p.m. Money can also be exchanged at the railway station from 7:30 a.m. to 9 p.m. weekdays, to 6:30 p.m. on weekends.

Next to the rail station, the **post office** on Bahnhofstrasse is open Monday to Friday from 7:30 a.m. to 5:30 p.m., on Saturday 11 a.m. However, the branch inside the railway station is open weekdays until 11 p.m. and on Saturday until 8 p.m. It's also open on Sunday from 9 a.m. to noon and 3 to 8 p.m.

The **American Express** office, 4 Schweizerhofquai (tel. 50-11-77), is open Monday to Friday from 8:30 a.m. to noon and 2 to 6 p.m. (no checks are cashed after 5 p.m., however).

The **U.S. Consulate** is at 141 Zollikerstrasse (tel. 55-25-66).

The **Lucerne Tourist Office** is at 14 Pilatusstrasse (tel. 28-52-52), near the train station. It's open Monday to Friday from 8 a.m. to noon and 2 to 6 p.m. (on Saturday from 9 a.m. to noon).

3. Lake Lucerne, North and East

The scenery around Lucerne is a blend of water, sky, and mountains. It's earned the praise of poets over the years.

Your hotel room might, for example, open onto Lake Lucerne, which locals call Vierwaldstättersee (lake of the four forest cantons). If you have either the Eurail or InterRail pass, the boat cruises are "free." The lake has many old-world villages. In addition to that, mountain railways can whisk you to elevations of 10,000 or more feet in a very short time.

For one of the best views of Lucerne and its lake, you can board a cable car at its bottom station in Lucerne on Haldenstrasse, which will take you to **Dietschiberg** at at 2065 feet. The trip takes about half an hour. You can see Pilatus and Rigi from a belvedere platform.

Another excursion will take you to **Güsch**, at 1715 feet. You can board a funicular on Baselstrasse. for the six-minute ride. At the top is a belvedere platform at the Gütsch Castle Hotel, which takes in the city and the lake, with the snow-capped Alps as a backdrop. Service in season is about every ten minutes. From May to September this funicular operates from 8:30 a.m. to 12:30 p.m., 1:15 to 7:30 p.m., and 8 to 11:30 p.m. From November to March it operates from 10 a.m. to 12:30 p.m., 1:15 to 2 p.m., and 4 to 8 p.m. (on weekends, from 10 a.m. to 8 p.m.). In April and October it operates from 9 a.m. to 3 p.m. and 4 to 9 p.m. weekdays (on weekends, from 9 a.m. to 9 p.m.). A round-trip fare costs only 3F ($1.38).

These excursions are only for those wanting good views from hilltop belvederes. The three-star mountain excursions from Lucerne are to Rigi and Pilatus (for data on Pilatus, refer to "Lake Lucerne, West and South").

The attractions of **Mount Rigi** have been extolled for centuries. Hopefully, you'll be blessed with a clear day; otherwise you're likely to be disappointed. The view from Rigi is different from that atop Mount Pilatus, so if you see both you won't be repeating your experience exactly.

Rigi, at 5900 feet, is in fact considered the most celebrated mountain view in the country. It's reached by two cog railways and a cableway. Of course, at Rigi you can't see such a wide-sweeping panoramic vista as you can from Pilatus, but the lookout from Rigi is, in my opinion, more beautiful.

Rigi is called the "island mountain," because it's seemingly isolated by the lake waters of not only Lucerne, but Zug and Lauerz. The most diehard and enthusiastic of the Victorians who made the "Grand Tour" at the turn of the century spent the night at Rigi-Kulm to see the sun rise over the Alps. The fashion began in the 18th century. This attraction, even today, is considered one of nature's loveliest offerings in all of Europe. For those wanting to partake of that long-ago tradition, many altitudinous hotels are perched along the mountainside. Victor Hugo called it "an incredible horizon." He also added, "that chaos of absurd exaggerations and scary diminutions." Mark Twain, as he relates in *A Tramp Abroad,* also climbed up to the top to see the sun rise across the Alps. But he claimed he was so exhausted that he collapsed into sleep, from which he didn't wake until the sunset. Not realizing that he had slept all day, he at first recoiled in horror believing that the sun had switched its direction and was actually rising in the west!

One way to reach the mountain is to take a lake steamer from Lucerne to Vitznau, a small resort on the northern shore of the lake. The other way to go is from Arth-Goldau, which lies on the southern part of Zug Lake. The rack railway from Vitznau to Rigi-Kulm was the first such cog railway in Europe. It dates from 1871, but the Swiss electrified it in 1937. The Arth-Goldau cog railway to Rigi-Kulm opened five years later (it lost the race to its competitor);

however, it was electrified as early as 1906. Its maximum gradient is 21%, which hardly puts it in the same league as the railway to Pilatus at 48%!

The climb from either point of departure takes slightly more than half an hour. It's possible to go up one way and come back the other if you want to see both sides of the mountain. A one-way fare costs about 22F ($10.11). Both lines in peak season make about a dozen runs a day.

WEGGIS: Nestling at the foot of Rigi mountain, 18½ miles from Lucerne, is the lakeside resort of Weggis, one of a trio of holiday centers sharing the sunshine and mild climate. The sunny side of the Rigi, where these resorts (Weggis, Vitznau, and Gersau) lie, has been likened to favored parts of Italy and indeed has for many years attracted visitors to its beautiful countryside. Mark Twain stayed here in 1897.

Weggis is usually the first port of call for steamers from Lucerne and is also easily accessible from the international St. Gotthard railway line, although it's not on the main traffic route. People wishing to take excursions into nearby mountains flock to the area from early spring to late autumn, many taking the aerial cableway up to Rigi-Kaltbad (4756 feet) in back of Weggis, where a mountain health resort is maintained.

Weggis and its sister resorts are about an hour's walk (or a five-minute drive) apart. You can also make a trip from here on a Lake Lucerne steamer or on the mountain transport of the Rigi Railways.

Food and Lodging

Hotel Albana (tel. 93-21-41). One of the public rooms of this family-run hotel looks almost baronial. The black sheen of the grand piano contrasts with the shiny cream color of the ten-foot ceramic stove. Heavy brass chandeliers hang from the frescoed ceiling, and very large mirrors in rococo gilt reflect the mellow patina of the wood paneling. The bedrooms are far more simple, although the head- and footboards are usually crafted of knotty pine. The windows afford good views of the nearby lake. The attractive restaurant was designed around the panoramic windows, and a terrace seems to command the entire lake, owing to its position raised up above the water. The hotel closes from November to March. When it's open, singles range from 57F ($26.19) to 115F ($52.84), while doubles cost between 102F ($46.87) and 204F ($93.74), with half board included. The Wolf family are flexible about board plans, allowing you to tell them at the beginning of each day of your stay whether you'll be on half, full, or no board for that particular day.

Hotel Alexander (tel. 93-22-22) is a very large flat-roofed building with a private loggia attached to every room, and a pleasant swimming pool below the glass wall of one of the sitting rooms. The public rooms are conservatively decorated in Oriental rugs and comfortable upholstered chairs. Another pool is found inside, along with an attractive dining room. Each of the bedrooms faces south, containing a private bath, phone, radio, and TV. Singles with half board range from 68F ($31.25) to 115F ($52.84), while doubles with half board cost between 130F ($59.74) and 204F ($94.86).

Hôtel Beau-Rivage (tel. 93-14-22). There are many assets to this hotel, but one of the best is the lawn which has been extended, thanks to a masonry retaining wall, right down to the lake. The view of the mountains from here is exhilarating. The hotel itself is a symmetrical yellow building with a series of wrought-iron balconies, a prominent nameplate in red letters, and a Swiss flag. From your windows you'll look down onto the flagstone borders of the swimming pool. The inside is pleasantly paneled and wallpapered, with a wood-paneled restaurant and a comfortable bar. Singles range from 75F ($34.46) to 110F ($50.55), while doubles cost between 134F ($61.57) and 230F ($105.69), with half board included. Prices, of course, depend on the season and the plumbing.

Hotel Central am See (tel. 93-13-17) is an old-fashioned resort hotel with at least six gables, and many more if you count the smaller ones. It sits on a shady peninsula jutting out into the lake. The hotel swimming pool comes very close to the water's edge, and if you happen to be floating on its heated waters, you'll be in a good position to watch the steamers sailing up and down the lake. The interior is outfitted with a fancy collection of comfortable furniture. An elevator will take you to your simple and comfortable bedroom, which will cost between 40F ($18.38) and 73F ($33.54) per person per day, breakfast included, with a singles supplement of between 3F ($1.38) and 6F ($2.76), depending on the season.

Hotel Waldstaetten (tel. 93-13-41) is a recently constructed three-story hotel surrounded by a well-planned garden with lots of red leafy trees. The bedrooms all contain private baths and have low-slung beds, contrasting solid colors, and phone and radio. Some of the accommodations open onto balconies with views of the lake. With breakfast included, singles range between 56F ($25.73) and 100F ($45.95), while doubles cost between 100F ($45.95) and 174F ($79.95).

Hotel Rössli (tel. 93-11-06) has a very narrow medieval-looking turret extending upward from its exposed corner and a mansard roof decorated in alternating shades of gray slate. The inside has been renovated into a comfortable and modern format of wrought iron, wicker chairs, and hanging lamps. The Nölly family has set up a sidewalk café behind the flowers, statues, and fountain of the square on which the hotel sits. The hotel lies on the lakeside road in a tranquil position near the center of the village. Depending on the season, the half-board rate in a single ranges from 52F ($23.89) to 68F ($31.25), and in a double from 48F ($22.06) to 60F ($27.57) per person.

VITZNAU: On around Lake Lucerne in another bay at the foot of the Rigi, Vitznau (1446 feet) enjoys the same salubrious climate as does Weggis. You can reach this spot, where an alpine panorama is mirrored in the waters of the lake, in about an hour's trip from Zurich on the motorway. A lake steamer will bring you here from Lucerne in about the same length of time, or you can drive from that city in approximately 30 minutes if you don't stop too often to drink in the scenic beauty.

From April to October Vitznau is ideal for an active holiday, offering bathing in the lake or in one of the indoor or outdoor pools, tennis, and inviting walks through meadows, woodlands, and mountains. It's at the lower terminal of the Rigi cog-wheel railway line, which causes many visitors just to pass through and therefore miss the beauty of the resort—an unfortunate oversight.

Food and Lodging

Park Hotel (tel. 83-13-22) is a luxurious summertime hotel designed like a castle. It has a central tower that you can easily imagine as part of a medieval fortification, plus a steep roof made of blue-gray slate. A newly constructed swimming pool is separated from the hotel by a sun terrace with parasols. Two tennis courts, sailing and waterskiing facilities, and miles of forested walkways give guests plenty to do. The public rooms inside are as grandly high-ceilinged as you could hope for, while the carpeted, well-furnished bedrooms each contain a private bath and an attractive assortment of conservative furniture. Singles range from 105F ($48.25) to 160F ($73.52), while doubles cost between 195F ($89.60) and 280F ($128.66), depending on the accommodation and the season.

Hotel Vitznauerhof (tel 83-13-15) is a pleasant resort-style hotel with five rambling floors and a gabled hip roof covered with red tiles. In summer you'll often see orange awnings on some of the windows below the half-timbering. A tennis court and a grassy beach area lie close to the lake. The bedrooms are attractively simple, with big windows occasionally leading out onto a balcony. Singles range from 45F ($20.68) to 83F ($38.14), while doubles cost between 104F ($47.79) and 150F ($68.93), with breakfast included. Prices, of course, depend on the size, plumbing, exposure, and season. The hotel closes in winter.

Hotel Schiff (tel. 83-13-57). Parts of the interior are designed like a pub in a harborside city. The hotel has plenty of brass fittings and some engine controls from an old-fashioned boat. You'll know you're going to get a strong dose of seaside nostalgia as you approach the house, because the Zimmermann family has landscaped a facsimile of the front of a lake cruiser into the sloping side of their garden. A very pleasant terrace gives a shaded waterside view which is as good as that from many bigger establishments. There are only 20 beds in the hotel. None of the rooms has a private bath, but the facilities on each floor are perfectly adequate. Singles rent for about 41F ($18.84) per night, with doubles costing about 36F ($16.54) per person nightly, with breakfast included.

RIGI: On the south side of Mt. Rigi, the Vitznau-Rigi railway starts from Vitznau on Lake Lucerne, and heads for Kulm peak, after passing through the mountain stations of Rigi-Kaltbad–First, Rigi Staffelhoehe, and Rigi Staffel. In summer there are also nostalgic steam trains traveling on this stretch of electric rack-and-pinion railway. Running every 30 minutes, an aerial cableway with large cabins connects Weggis, also on Lake Lucerne, with the little mountain village of Rigi Kaltbad.

I have already extolled the scenic excitement of Rigi in this section. If you'd like to do something adventurous—far removed from traffic—you might consider a mountain top hotel in this most fascinating section of central Switzerland. Some recommendations follow:

Food and Lodging

Hostellerie Rigi, at Rigi-Kaltbad (tel. 83-16-16), is a strikingly contemporary building, with wide expanses of almost unbroken glass topped with an abstract roofline that seems to fold down shelteringly above it. The inside is very attractive and unusual, with ample use of natural-grain wood, stone detailing, sloped ceilings, sunny vistas, and lots of space. A desirable collection of voluptuously curved 19th-century furniture gives an attractive contrast to the dramatic angularity of some of the public rooms. A beautiful indoor swimming pool, sauna, fitness room, bowling alley, kindergarten with monitor, and a beauty salon are all part of the facilities. I especially like the darkly lit bar area, which seems to encourage a good time. Singles rent for between 62F ($28.49) and 97F ($44.57), while doubles cost from 58F ($26.65) to 91F ($41.82).

Hotel Bellevue, at Rigi-Kaltbad (tel. 83-13-51). If you've just been married, or if you feel a little reckless, the hotel has a newlywed suite with an old-fashioned bed and a double bathtub. Chances are, however, that no matter what your relationship is like, you'll eventually end up in one of the beautifully paneled public rooms or on the panoramic terrace. Almost everything about this lofty hotel is attractive and comfortable, with a view from almost every room that is magnificent. No two of the bedrooms are exactly alike, but overall they're very satisfactory. Singles rent for between 55F ($25.27) and 85F ($39.06), while doubles cost from 55F ($25.27) to 75F ($34.46) per person daily, with breakfast included. Prices, of course, depend on the season and the accommodations. Each of the units has a private bath.

Hotel Rigi Kulm, at the summit (tel. 83-13-12), is connected by an underground tunnel to the terminus of the cog railway leading into the village. In summertime, however, you might prefer to walk above ground to reach the large simple building with its gray stone detailing that looks as though it could withstand any winter storm. The interior is high-ceilinged, very elegant, and filled with tasteful furniture which includes a good selection of antiques. From the hotel's sun terrace, where the lunch tables are covered with red cloths, you'll see the weather patterns literally change before your eyes in the valley below. The overflow from the main house is lodged in an annex nearby, which also is connected by underground tunnel to the main hotel. The Käppeli family charges between 40F ($18.38) and 50F ($22.98) in a single and between 70F ($32.17) and 90F ($41.36) for a double. Half board is offered for an additional 15F ($6.89) per person daily.

GERSAU: The most tranquil and least frequented of the trio of lakeside resorts along the northern rim of the eastern leg of Lake Lucerne is Gersau (1450 feet), where laurels, chestnuts, and fig trees grow in the mild climate just as they do in Weggis and Vitznau. From April to October, Gersau makes a convenient base for exploring the Rigi. You have a good view of the Alps from this bayfront resort, and I've found it an ideal stopover when I go south on the lake road to St. Gotthard.

Gersau is the oldest health resort of Lake Lucerne. From 1332 to 1798 it had the distinction of being the smallest independent republic in the world, giving up its independence when it joined the growing confederation of Swiss towns and cantons for safety's sake.

Food and Lodging

Hôtel Beau-Rivage (tel. 84-12-23) is a flat-roofed, balconied building on an attractively small scale bordering the lake. The facade is painted sea green and white, with orange awnings protecting the pleasant bedrooms from the waterside glare. The public rooms are outfitted with lots of plants and contemporary furniture. In summer an orchestra plays before and during dinner. There's an outdoor swimming pool, plus an elevator and table tennis available. Single or double accommodations rent for between 42F ($19.30) and 57F ($26.19) per person daily, with breakfast included.

BRUNNEN: At Brunnen, a health and holiday resort in a beautiful inlet on the southern part of Lake Lucerne, I never miss going to the lakeside quays to enjoy the fine views of the meeting of lakes and Alps. Brunnen (about 1300 feet), at the foot of Frohnalpstock, is probably the most popular resort in the canton of Schwyz, on Lake Uri in the very heart of Switzerland. It was in this area that the Confederation was born, and you'll find many reminders of the country's historic past, including archives in Schwyz where the Confederation documents are displayed and the **Federal Chapel** in Brunnen.

This is William Tell country. Around the year 1250 several families left Raron in the Valais and crossed the Alps to establish new homes in Schächental/Uri, until then uninhabited. Records show that among the families were the Tells. William Tell enters folk history as the hero of a decisive battle in 1315, who reportedly died in 1350, though historians have no authentication of such an individual heroic figure. The man who calmly and safely shot an apple off the head of his brave young son with a bow and arrow in a test of prowess is honored by the Swiss with the **Tell Monument.** In Sisikon, just south of Brunnen, stands the **Tell Chapel,** restored in 1881. Records of the chapel date from the dawn of the 16th century. The paintings in the chapel are by Stückelberg. Many people visit it on excusions from Brunnen.

Brunnen is the starting point of the **Axenstrasse,** the stunning panoramic road leading south toward the St. Gotthard Pass. It goes above the rim of Lake Uri (or Urnersee) in and out of subterranean passageways or galleries that were carved out of the mountain rock. The resort is a starting place for exploratory trips by ship, mountain railway, bus, or train to all points around Lake Lucerne. International express trains on the Gotthard line stop at Brunnen, and it can also be reached by road. It's about an hour's drive from Zurich's Kloten international airport.

Food and Lodging

Park Hotel (tel. 31-16-81) is a large château with gray shutters and a hipped roof that encompasses the top two floors. The interior is an attractive mixture of white walls and full-grained wood. The hotel is surrounded with pleasant lawns and very old trees. On the premises is a tennis court. The hotel has been renovated several times since its construction (the last time was in 1981). Well-furnished singles range from 59F ($27.11) to 79F ($36.30), while doubles cost between 96F ($44.11) and 136F ($62.49), breakfast included.

Seehotel Waldstätterhof (tel. 33-11-33) is an elegantly proportioned building which might look its best from a boat a few hundred yards out on the lake. The symmetrical white facade is capped with a modified mansard roof, while a series of well-proportioned balconies allows summertime guests to enjoy the lakeside air. The hotel opened in 1870, although the continuing renovations (the last one in 1975) have kept it in the mainstream of modern comfort. The grounds are on an extensively planted peninsula extending into the lake. You'll find tennis courts, an outdoor pool, an indoor pool, a sailing school, and very close to the hotel, the landing stage for the Lake Lucerne steamer trips. The public rooms are as grand as you'd expect (be sure to notice the fanciful chandeliers in the dining room). The dancing bar within the hotel might be one of the most attractive nightspots in the resort. Singles range from 80F ($36.76) to 120F ($55.14), while doubles cost between 130F ($59.74) and 190F ($87.31), depending on the accommodation and season. Breakfast is included, and for another 25F ($11.49) per person daily you can have half board.

Hotel Bellevue (tel. 31-13-19), a first-class choice, is a pleasantly renovated hotel on the edge of the lake with a café and sun terrace that many of the locals use as their own. The freshly painted bedrooms are usually carpeted, and always have private bath. Werner Achermann and his family welcome guests, charging them from 59F ($27.11) to 79F ($36.30) in a single and from 96F ($44.11) to 136F ($62.49) in a double, including breakfast. With its Tropicana Bar and Casino, the hotel is also the center of nightlife for the town. In addition to the gambling room, there's dancing to an orchestra. Other facilities include a reading and TV room, a restaurant with a view, and private parking.

Hôtel du Lac-Hirschen (tel. 31-13-15) is a beautifully symmetrical 19th-century building of a design that might be neoclassical French or Italian. It sits at the edge of the lake, with a rustic interior. Comfortably furnished rooms go for between 42F ($19.30) and 60F ($27.57) per person in a double, with an additional supplement of 8F ($3.68) for residents of single accommodations. A nearby hotel with the same management charges similar rates. In a boxy rectangular format with a flat roof and lots of balconies, it's called the Hotel Alfa (same phone).

Hotel Elite-Aurora (tel. 31-10-24) is a lakeside hotel built in a beige wood and buff-colored format of big windows and prominent balconies. Many guests spend part of the afternoon on the waterside terrace under shade trees. The 80 rooms are simply and attractively decorated in earth tones, with comfortable beds. The public rooms are dignified and modern, and filled partly with cream-colored sofas. Doubles cost from 40F ($18.38) to 55F ($25.27) per person daily, depending on the plumbing and the season. Singles are usually housed in the hotel annex a short distance away, at rates just slightly higher than the per-person rate in a double.

Hotel Alpina (tel. 31-18-13) is housed in a very pleasant gabled building with a second-floor veranda and buff-colored shutters. The Geisseler family, the English-speaking owners, do everything they can to be of help. Their bedrooms are simple, clean, and comfortable, while the unpretentious dining hall has sunny windows and well-prepared food. Singles range from 35F ($16.08) to 55F ($25.27), while doubles cost between 60F ($27.57) and 100F ($45.95), with breakfast included. Half board is an additional 14F ($6.43) per person. Prices, of course, depend on the plumbing and season.

After Brunnen, we continue south as far as the little port and holiday resort of:

FLÜELEN: The resort lies on a delta at the head of the Reuss River. Many motorists prefer a stopover here before going on to the St. Gotthard Pass. If you're like them, here are some recommendations:

Food and Lodging

Hostellerie Sternen (tel. 2-18-35) has a gold star positioned above the curved entrance at the corner of the building. You'll enter a sympathetic ambience of good food (see the separate restaurant recommendation) and modernized rusticity. Some of the bedrooms have wood ceilings, tile floors, and colored timbers set in central positions near the comfortable beds. Singles range from 40F ($18.38) to 50F ($22.98) while doubles cost from 75F ($34.46) to 95F ($43.65), breakfast included. All accommodations contain private baths.

Hotel Flüelerhof (tel. 2-11-49) is a tasteful hotel built in 1981, with a modern design. It's studded with flowered balconies, big windows, and lots of comfort. Bathrooms and bedrooms are very attractive, while the public rooms are filled with brick and wood detailing along with rustic touches. On the premises you'll find a grill room, a restaurant, an indoor and outdoor café, and a well-maintained garden. Singles range from 40F ($18.38) to 55F ($25.27), while doubles cost between 65F ($29.87) and 95F ($43.65), with breakfast included. Prices depend on the season, plumbing, and room assignment.

Hotel Tourist (tel. 2-15-91) is a chalet hotel with two frontal balconies, wood shutters, and darker wood clapboards. The ground floor is made of white stucco, with a sun terrace and café set above the road in front. The Arndt family charges between 40F ($18.38) and 50F ($22.98) in a single and between 60F ($27.57) and 80F ($36.76) in a double, with breakfast included. The hotel is open only from May to October.

Rôtisserie Sternen (tel. 2-18-35), in the hotel of the same name, has been in the hands of the Sigrist family since 1870. Four generations since its establishment, it's become one of the best dining rooms in the region. Today the impeccably uniformed staff, headed by Jost Sigrist, turns out an array of light-textured dishes that compare favorably with delicacies in far more sophisticated resorts. The dining room is unpretentiously dignified, in a contemporary format with lots of warmth and visual interest. A nine-course gourmet meal is the house specialty, although you can order fewer courses if you want to. They might include pig feet with cabbage and morels stuffed with curds or a variety of less exotic food which you'll probably find delectable. Fixed-price meals range from 20F ($9.19) to 70F ($32.17), while à la carte dinners cost from 24F ($11.03) to 48F ($22.06). The rôtisserie is open every day except from New Year's until mid-February.

4. From Schwyz to St. Gotthard

From the "birthplace" of the Confederation to the St. Gotthard Pass is one of the most historic and most frequented routes in Switzerland, taking in the William Tell country.

Except for the first part of this trip, we leave the shores of Lake Lucerne, stopping off at the resorts and towns of Altdorf, Amsteg, and Andermatt before crossing the St. Gotthard Pass itself.

In the 18th and 19th centuries, roadbuilders began the long, tedious, and dangerous task of opening the pass to traffic, thus making for the shortest route from north to south.

The railway tunnel, stretching for some nine miles, goes under the towering peak of the St. Gotthard massif which reaches a height of 3790 feet. The toll-free St. Gotthard road tunnel opened in 1980 and was hailed at its inauguration as the longest road tunnel on earth, traversing a distance of some ten miles. It is, of course, open all year.

The St. Gotthard Pass, at 6920 feet, provides a link between the Grisons and the Valais Alps. It's one of the most stunning and scenic passes in Switzerland.

We'll begin our trip at:

SCHWYZ: At the "core of Helvetia," this pleasant little town—set in the midst of orchards on a mountain terrace—lent its name and flag to the whole country. Lying under the towering twin horns of the Gross Mythen, it is also the repository of the country's most treasured archives. The location is between Lake Lucerne and Lake Lauerz. Its mountain "annex" is the little resort of Stoos, at 4250 feet.

Since the 16th century, when foreign powers such as France needed mercenaries, they were often recruited here. The men of Schwyz were known for their prowess and courage. Those who lived returned to build the sturdy and often quite opulent homes you can still see today.

Schwyz was in the vanguard of the eventual Confederation when it joined with the neighboring districts of Uri and Unterwalden to create an "everlasting league" on August 1, 1291. Since then its name in a dialectical form (Schweiz) was applied by foreigners from the 14th century on to label the country.

The **Bundesbriefarchiv** (archives of the federal charters) was erected in 1936 to house the original documents of the Swiss Confederation. It can be visited from 9:30 to 11:30 a.m. and 2 to 5 p.m. for an admission of 1F (46¢). This rather simple concrete structure, with a frescoed facade, stands on Bahnhofstrasse, and contains the original deed of the Confederation. Many other historical documents and mementos are displayed.

The parish **Church of St. Martin,** built in 1774, is richly embellished in the flamboyant baroque style. In the nave are many frescoes.

The only other building of note is the **Rathaus** (town hall), dating from 1642, its facade handsomely decorated with frescoes better than those at the national archives building. These murals recall epic moments in Swiss history. To gain entrance, apply to the concierge. In a museum tower south of the town hall is a cantonal historical museum, of interest only if you're a Swiss historian.

From Schwyz you can take the road through the Muota valley to Schlatti, a distance of only two miles. It's also possible to go by bus, a 12-minute run. There the steepest funicular in Switzerland, with a gradient up to nearly 78%, will take you in eight minutes up the treacherously steep wooded slope to **Stoos,** a hamlet clinging to a mountain plateau. Stoos is a relatively undiscovered winter ski resort. If you visit in summer, know that you'll be safe and secure in a hideaway where no one will ever find you! It has no traffic, as there are no roads. You also lose yourself among the cows in the alpine meadows with their beautiful wildflowers, which live for such a short time if you dare pick one.

Back in the valley, you migh consider a trip to the mammoth **Hölloch Caves** even more intriguing. Take the Muotathal road southeast of Schwyz for about nine miles. The Höllochgrotte, the largest grotto in Europe, is a geological phenomenon known all over the world. The total length of the passages is just under 60 miles, of which only about half a mile is open to visitors.

Of course, you should only strike out here if the weather is fair. Telephone the guide at 47-12-08 before making the trip, and allow about an hour for exploration, which will cost 3.50F ($1.61).

Virtually unknown at the turn of the century, the grotto has been much explored in the postwar years, especially in the 1950s. Of course you'll see stalagmites and stalactites, which you'd expect. But more than that, you'll also get to view other eerie underworld formations, which reach their zenith at the "grosse pagoda."

Food and Lodging in and Around Schwyz

Hotel Wysses Rössli (tel. 21-19-22), in the center of Schwyz, is a green-shuttered building on a cobblestone square. The management tells me that the hotel is newly built, yet some of its banqueting rooms were removed intact from an 18th-century baroque house. The part you'll see is attractively rustic, with contemporary bedrooms outfitted with an occasional leather chair. There's also a warmly intimate bar area in shades of cream, terracotta, and brown. Singles range from 70F ($32.17) to 80F ($36.76), while doubles cost from 65F ($29.87) to 80F ($36.76) per person. All accommodations have private bath, phone, radio, and mini-bar.

Hotel Kristall, 172 Bahnhofstrasse (tel. 21-34-74), on the outskirts at Seewen-Schwyz, is a 50-bed hotel in a flat-roofed format of white concrete with blue trim that looks vaguely like a hospital. The management does everything it can to make your stay comfortable. The hotel has both an à la carte restaurant and a snackbar for those who want their meals in a hurry. There's also a garden restaurant. The rooms are cozy and comfortable, often with small personal touches. Each accommodation has a private bath or shower, as well as phone and radio. To stay here on half-board terms costs 38F ($17.46) in a single and 76F ($34.92) in a double, a real bargain.

Food and Lodging at Stoos

Sporthotel Stoos (tel. 21-15-05). If you'd look at this sprawling building from one angle, you'd swear it was designed around a giant hexagon. A short walk around it, however, will change that impression, particularly from the rear where it appears more like a balconied rectangle. More surprises await you inside, including enough rustically appointed niches to make any recluse happy. You'll find an intimately lit, wood-paneled bar, another bar for dancing, a children's playroom, an indoor swimming pool, and a comfortable restaurant with discreet tartan patterns in the warmly tinted curtains. The 120 beds usually fold away during the day, which transforms your room into a salon. Many of the accommodations have kitchenettes. Tennis courts are open in summer. Singles rent for between 64F ($29.41) and 87F ($39.98), while doubles range from 49F ($22.52) to 89F ($40.90) per person, with breakfast included. Prices, of course, change with the season. All accommodations contain private baths.

Before continuing our journey south to the St. Gotthard Pass, you may want to make the following detour:

A Side Trip to Einsiedeln

Ever since the Middle Ages Einsiedeln has been known as a place of pilgrimage. The venerated statue of the "Black Virgin" in the Holy Chapel of the **Klosterkirche** (abbey church) is the lure.

The thousand-year-old Benedictine abbey, a magnificent group of monastery buildings erected from 1704 to 1770, is considered the finest example of Vorarlberg baroque architecture in Switzerland.

The town, only 18 miles from our last stopover at Schwyz, is a resort in both winter and summer, perched in a high valley of the "pre-Alps." The town is without fog for most of the year. In summer water sports are possible on Lake Sihl, and walking and mountain climbing are avidly practiced.

But it's as a pilgrimage site that the town is known, and it draws lots of the devout who come here to attend liturgical revival and ecumenical conferences.

On September 14 the annual festival of the "Miracle Dedication" takes place, and there are torch-lit marches throughout the resort. Every five years (next show, 1985), the town stages performances of *The Great Theatre of the World,* an ecclesiastical drama written by Don Pedro Calderón, first performed at the court of Spain in 1685.

The abbey itself was founded in 934, embracing a band of hermits. The monastery was erected over the grave of Meinrad, who was murdered in 861 by men thinking he was hiding gold. As the story goes, ravens followed the slayers to Zurich, where they called attention to the killers who were subsequently punished.

On five different occasions the monastery was destroyed by fire, but each time it was rebuilt. French Revolutionaries at one point stormed the church, hoping to capture the "Black Madonna," but she had already been carted off to Austria.

The church has twin towers and contains, among other art and architectural curiosities, the largest fresco in the country. Its wrought-iron choir screen is from 1684. A lot of the decoration is from two brothers from Bavaria, the Asam family.

From the south side of the building complex, you can go into the **Princes' Hall** (also known as the Grosser Saal or "abbey great hall"), where special exhibitions are staged, coming from the monastery's diverse and acclaimed art collections. The stucco decoration in the hall is from the early 18th century. It's open from 9 to 11:30 a.m. and 1:30 to 6 p.m. weekdays; closed Sunday. Admission is only .50F (23¢).

After surveying the food and lodging scene here, we'll pick up the trail again and head out from Schwyz on the route south.

Hotel Drei Könige (tel. 53-39-83) has a dramatically modern design which features a double tier of glass-walled public rooms extending toward the baroque monastery across the square. Another three floors of cubical balconies rise above the public rooms, with a similar wing stretching toward the rear. The lobby is paved with beautifully striated brown-and-white marble beneath a timbered ceiling and leather armchairs. The comfortable bedrooms are spacious and filled with simple, dignified furniture. This is one of the newest hotels in town. There's a grill room on the premises, plus a dancing bar. The 51 accommodations all have private bath, renting for between 60F ($27.57) and 65F ($29.87) in a single and between 94F ($43.19) and 130F ($59.74) in a double. Triples cost 128F ($58.82), and breakfast is included in all rates.

Hotel St. Georg (tel. 53-24-51) is close to the cloisters in a neoclassical town house with a modernized ground floor (they've added a picture window) and a contemporary addition to one side. The public rooms are filled with black leatherette chairs and neutral colors. Comfortably furnished singles rent for between 35F ($16.08) and 52F ($23.89), while doubles cost between 63F ($28.95) and 100F ($45.95), with breakfast included. Prices depend on the season. Under the same management, you'll also find:

Hotel zum Storchen (tel. 53-37-60), which in summertime has a cascade of flowers. A Renaissance-style bay window looks out from the second floor. Across the street from the Hotel St. Georg, it has a decor which is slightly more appealing than that of its neighbor, with lots of paneling and spacious bedrooms filled with simple furniture. Singles rent for between 45F ($20.68) and 51F ($23.44), while doubles cost from 61F ($28.03) to 97F ($44.57). All accommodations have private bath, unlike its neighbor across the street.

Hotel Katharinahof (tel. 53-25-08) is an attractively old-fashioned building on a quiet street facing the abbey. The establishment is run by the Koch family, who have installed an elevator and added private baths to each of the comfortable bedrooms. A sauna and a billiard room are on the premises. Singles range from 40F ($18.38) to 52F ($23.89), while doubles cost from 66F ($30.33) to 102F ($46.87), with breakfast included.

ALTDORF: As a respite from mountain climbing, you may want to explore sights closer to the ground. Of all the folk heroes to emerge from the heartland of Switzerland, none is more famous than William Tell. The legend of William Tell's skill in shooting at and striking the apple placed on the head of his little son by order of Gessler, the tyrannical Austrian bailiff of Uri, needs no recounting here.

The Tell story, first found in a ballad, dates back to the 15th century. Over the years the tale has become closely bound up with the legendary history of the origin of the Swiss Confederation itself. The story has appeared in many versions, reaching world renown in 1804 in a play by Friedrich von Schiller who, after Goethe, was the greatest name in German literature. It really doesn't matter that William Tell didn't exist. It's a fit allegory to describe the tenacity and the independence of the Swiss people in their fight and struggle for freedom against oppression.

Altdorf is the key to the St. Gotthard Pass, lying on the north side of the Alps, and the capital of the canton of Uri, lying two miles south of the outflow of the Reuss River into Lake Uri. It's the starting point of the road over the Klausen Pass.

Altdorf is also the town in which William Tell is alleged to have shot the apple off his son's head. The statue of this legendary archer stands in the main square of town, in front of the early-19th-century town hall and a tower dating from the Middle Ages. The monument was by Richard Kissling in 1895, and it was this image, engraved on the postage stamp, that has become familiar to people all over the globe.

The road to the Klausen Pass leads to **Bürglen,** a small hamlet that is one of the oldest in Uri. (Incidentally, snowdrifts block this pass from October to May.) Bürglen was the alleged birthplace of William Tell, and the village has set up the **Tell Museum,** open from the first of June until the end of October, from 9:30 to 11:30 a.m. and 2 to 5 p.m., charging an admission of 2F (92¢). The museum contains documents and mementos relating to that period of early Swiss history in which Tell supposedly lived. The museum is in a Romanesque tower adjacent to the parish church.

The most charming way to go to Altdorf from Lucerne is by lake steamer. Take the vessel to Flüelen at the far end of the lake and allow some three hours. From Flüelen, you can make a bus connection for the short run to Altdorf.

Food and Lodging

Hotel Bahnhof (tel. 2-10-32). The cheaper rooms tend to be rather small, although they're pleasantly paneled and comfortable, while the more expensive units are most spacious. This is a well-established tourist hotel, with pleasantly dated furniture in some of the public rooms. Rather than being a detriment, it all contributes to a kind of lighthearted kitsch, which is encouraged by the friendly attention of Mrs. Anna Niederberger and her family. It's located, to judge by its name, near the train station in what looks like a former private house with a modern addition in front. Singles cost between 28F ($12.87) and 32F ($14.70), while doubles range from 51F ($23.44) to 55F ($25.27). None of the accommodations has a private bath, but there's a sink in every room and shared facilities off the hallways.

AMSTEG: This is a traditional stop on the St. Gotthard route, and the starting point for car drivers over the passes. It's also a good center for walks and mountain excursions. The resort lies at the mouth of the Maderanertal. In the distance you can see a tall viaduct which holds the tracks of the St. Gotthard railway.

Food and Lodging

Hotel Stern und Post (tel. 6-44-40) is a former post house with lots of atmosphere, a steep tile roof with gently curving eaves, and long rows of small-paned windows with flowerboxes. For the past 150 years there's been a hotel operating out of this charming building, which is today managed by the Tresch family. The interior is elegantly furnished with a combination of 19th-century parlor antiques and chalet chairs. If you decide to dine in (and the cuisine is certainly worth it), you'll be shown a table in the high-ceilinged dining room with fern-green walls and big windows. The very excellent trout comes from regional streams, and arrives in more than half a dozen different varieties. Many of the other specialties are written tongue-in-cheek in regional dialect, so you may need a staff member to assist you. These include pork with potatoes and chestnuts, and a variety of other delicacies. Prices begin at 35F ($16.08). Some of the bedrooms are furnished with Victorian beds and lots of gingerbread. A word of caution: If you're uncomfortable in too short a bed, these particular chambers might not be for you. Singles range from 37F ($17) to 75F ($34.46), while doubles cost from 60F ($27.57) to 133F ($61.11), with breakfast included. Prices depend on the season and plumbing.

ANDERMATT: At the crossroads of the Alps, Andermatt is known for its many days of sunshine in winter and is a major sports center. In the Urseren Valley, it's at the junction of four alpine roads. The St. Gotthard highway crosses the road to Oberalp and Furka at Andermatt.

In summer it attracts those wanting to get away from it all. Excursions and hikes across the mountain passes are possible. In winter it draws skiers to its trails, runs, and tracks down the Gemsstock, the Nätschen, the Oberalp, and the Winterhorn. There's also a 12½-mile-long cross-country ski track open from November to May, which has safety devices against snowdrifts and avalanches.

Other sporting facilities include a Swiss ski school, an ice-skating rink with curling equipment, sleigh runs, and squash tennis in winter. There's also an indoor swimming pool.

Food and Lodging

Hotel Drei Könige und Post (tel. 6-72-03) is a white-walled chalet with buttressed eaves and brown shutters. A café terrace serves drinks and food in front, repeating a tradition established as early as 1234 for an inn on this site. This family-run hotel is much more recent than that, and was renovated in 1977 in a format of comfortably paneled bedrooms with balconies, panoramic views, and private baths. The Renner family charges between 45F ($20.68) and 69F ($31.71) per person daily, with breakfast included. Prices depend on the season and your room assignment.

5. Lake Lucerne, West and South

Back at Lucerne, we set out this time to the west and to the south, heading first for a major mountain excursion to **Mt. Pilatus,** a 7000-foot summit overlooking Lucerne, and dominating the western sector of Lake Lucerne. The name probably comes from a Latin word meaning "covered with clouds," but legend ascribes it to Pontius Pilate.

There are two ways of reaching Pilatus, which is one of the most popular excursions in central Switzerland. First, you can take a lake steamer to Alpnachstad. Rail passes are valid on lake steamers; otherwise, you must pay 8F ($3.68). From the end of April until the first of November the famous electric Pilatus railway climbs the mountain from Alpnachstad to Pilatus-Kulm. This is considered the steepest cog-wheel railroad in the world, with a 48% gradient.

In summer service is about every 45 minutes, and a round-trip ticket costs about 30F ($13.79). At the upper platform when you get off, you'll find two mountain hotels. From the belvedere, an alpine vista will unfold for you, taking in not only the lake, but Rigi and Bürgenstock. If you don't want to go back on the railway, you can return by cable car to Kriens, where a trolley (no. 1) will deliver you back to Lucerne at a cost of 8F ($3.68) per person.

Alternatively, you can reach Mt. Pilatus by taking the trolley out to Kriens (a suburb of Lucerne), and there get a ride in a four-seater cabin of a cable car which glides over meadows and forests to Fräkmüntegg. This trip takes about half an hour, and you arrive at an elevation of 4600 feet. At Fräkmüntegg you switch to an aerial cableway, really a stunning feat of advanced engineering, swinging alongside the cliff up to the very peak, in both summer and winter.

Once there, you'll find that no one believes the legend about Pontius Pilate anymore. But for centuries many men in Switzerland would not climb the mountain out of fear that it was haunted by the ghost of Pilate, who would bring havoc to the weather, causing fearful storms. In fact the city fathers of Lucerne, who took this legend seriously, banned travel up the mountain until the very end of medieval times. But after that it drew a steady stream of curiosity-seekers, even, according to reports, Queen Victoria in 1868.

HERGISWIL: Five miles from Lucerne, right on the lake, this idyllic little holiday resort can be reached from the city in ten minutes by train or car. This is a peaceful vacation spot away from the motorway, offering excursions by train, boat, mountain railway, cable car, or bus as well as fine walks along the shores of the "Lake of the Four Cantons" (Lucerne, Nidwalden, Uri, and Schwyz) and hiking in the area of Mt. Pilatus.

You'll find tennis courts, a lake beach, indoor swimming, and other activities if you're energetic. If you're like me, you may want to spend time just sitting on a bench and watching the steamers plying their way on Lake Lucerne or enjoying the folk entertainment offered in the evening.

Food and Lodging

Seehotel Pilatus (tel. 95-15-55). My favorite part of this lakeside hotel is the half-timbered sitting room with red bricks filling the gaps between the beams. You'll usually see a fireplace blazing, with formats ranging from a traditional walled fireplace to a red-tile central chimney in the middle of the contemporary bar area. The indoor swimming pool is surrounded with glass walls and green plants, while a dance bar often has live music. The bedrooms are romantically charming, with multicolored spreads, wood slats, and panoramic balconies with alpine patterns cut into the bannisters. Part of the exterior is chalet style, with two modern extension annexes nearby in a more up-to-date style. Singles range from 55F ($25.27) to 95F ($43.65), while doubles cost from 95F ($46.65) to 165F ($75.82), with breakfast included. Prices depend on the season.

Hotel Belvedere (tel. 95-11-35). There are many attractive parts of this hotel, including its lakeside location next to a baroque church and the marina whose boats moor almost in front of the hotel restaurant. It's neo-chalet in style, with white stucco and weathered wood. Many of the guests choose to spend part of their morning relaxing on the sunny terrace. The restaurant serves consistently good food, in a rural setting with attractively placed copper pots hanging on the cream-colored walls. Singles range from 58F ($26.68) to

80F ($36.76), while doubles cost between 86F ($39.52) and 130F ($59.74). Half board costs an additional 20F ($9.19) per person.

BÜRGENSTOCK: The choicest place along Lake Lucerne, Bürgenstock is both a six-mile limestone ridge and a hotel colony that is virtually a deluxe citadel. Many celebrities (like Audrey Hepburn and Sophia Loren) who have chosen to live here have only added to its international reputation.

Don't go here for heights: you've already had those, especially if you made the trek up Mt. Pilatus. At its highest point, Bürgenstock rises only 1640 feet on its northern side. The southern side gently drops in slopes, often with contented cows, to the Stans Valley.

You can drive to Bürgenstock, about ten miles south of Lucerne, by going first to Stansstad. From there, a three-mile road is steep and narrow and recommended only to the most skilled of drivers.

However, I prefer to take a half-hour steamer trip from Lucerne to the landing platform at Kehrsiten. At Kehrsiten, a funicular will whisk you to Bürgenstock in about eight minutes. The funicular has a gradient of 45%. At the upper stations of the platform you'll encounter one of the poshest spots of luxury in all Switzerland.

Once there, you can walk along the Felsenweg, a cliff path along the Hammetschwand. At the Hammetschwand elevator you can go to the upper station at 3580 feet. At the summit, you'll have a vista of the lakes of the heart of Switzerland and the Bernese Alps.

Food and Lodging

The **Bürgenstock Hotel Estate** (tel. 64-13-31). If you didn't bring your evening clothes, don't assume that the management will let you in to dinner. This is one of the most exclusive hotels in Europe, certainly one that will make you feel privileged to be there. It's the largest privately owned hotel estate in Switzerland. The public rooms are almost awash with priceless art treasures (especially Rubens, but also van Dyck, Tintoretto, and Brueghel) collected by the father of the present owner, Fritz Frey. Even the furniture inside is worthy of a modern-day Versailles.

The estate is actually a complex of three buildings, the Grand, the Palace, and the less exclusive residence, the Park. On the grounds you'll be surrounded by a verdant natural greenery which has been cultivated and trained into one of the most beautiful spots in the Alps. Facilities include a free-form outdoor swimming pool, a tavern, a rustically beamed nightclub, a golf course, and lots of open fireplaces. A resident of the hotel told me that everything about this place is idyllic except for the occasional lack of sunny weather (which all the money in the world can't guarantee) and the infrequent groups of curious nonresidents who want to promenade through the hotel grounds.

Rates at the Palace range from 170F ($78.12) to 215F ($98.79) in a single and from 145F ($66.63) to 170F ($78.12) per person in a double, with half board included. Rates at the Grand range from 215F ($98.79) to 250F ($114.88) in a single and from 175F ($80.41) to 225F ($103.39) per person in a double, including breakfast but no meals. Rates at the Park range from 100F ($45.95) to 145F ($66.63) in a single and from 85F ($39.06) to 120F ($55.15) per person in a double, depending on the plumbing (some bathless rooms are available). Breakfast but no meals are included at the Park. All three hotels are open from April till October.

Want something far less expensive than such a deluxe citadel? Try one of the following recommendations:

Hotel Fürigen (tel. 61-12-54) is a very large resort hotel with white walls and a red tile roof divided into gables and an occasional tower. It's set on a wooded hillside high above the lake, although a private beach is connected to the hotel by a private cog railway. The comfortable bedrooms offer good views of the lake. Guests usually relax on the terraces, in the dancing bar, or in the pleasant restaurant. Singles range from 56F ($27.53) to 69F ($31.71), while doubles cost from 56F ($25.73) to 62F ($28.49) per person daily, depending on the season, with breakfast included.

Hotel Waldeim (tel 64-13-06) is a stone-flanked modern hotel with a swimming pool a few dozen yards from the main building and a series of comfortable rooms with private baths. One of the public rooms has molded plastic chairs and sliding glass doors that are usually opened in summer onto a panoramic terrace. *Per-person* rates range between 40F ($18.38) and 60F ($27.57), depending on the accommodation and exposure.

STANSSTAD: From Lucerne, it's only an eight-minute drive here by the N2 motorway. By rail or lake steamer, allow anywhere from 20 minutes to half an hour. Stansstad is a good center for exploring the chic Bürgenstock area, just recommended. However, it's much cheaper. In summer you can bathe and fish in Lake Lucerne, and there are many possibilities for sailing, waterskiing, and rowing, along with riding, hiking, and summer skiing on the Titlis.

Food and Lodging

Hotel Schützen (tel. 61-13-55). The owners of this sprawling hotel began with a 19th-century house which they expanded into a modern complex of flat roofs and loggias. The entire complex is painted a baroque yellow and surrounded by a very pretty flower garden. The color scheme of the public rooms is a flowery red-and-violet combination, which will certainly capture your attention. The bedrooms are up-to-date, comfortable, and simply furnished with angular functional furniture. Singles range from 43F ($19.76) to 85F ($39.06), while doubles cost between 75F ($34.46) and 150F ($68.93), depending on the season and the plumbing.

STANS: Stans, to the south of Bürgenstock, attracts relatively few American visitors, but it's a good center if you plan to tour yet another mountain, the **Stanserhorn.**

The town is of much more interest to the Swiss because of its connections with some of the country's major heroes: Arnold von Winkelried (a martyr of the Battle of Sempach in 1386 against the Austrians), Nikolaus von Flüe (a hermit who saved the Confederation through peaceful arbitration), and Heinrich Pestalozzi (1746–1827), the famous Swiss educator, who is revered in the country because of his tireless efforts to aid poor, orphaned, and helpless children.

The capital of the half-canton of Nidwalden, Stans is a little market town set in the midst of many orchards. Its parish church, in the baroque style, dates from the 1640s, and there's a monument to von Winkelried.

To reach Stans from Lucerne, you can drive there in your own car or else go via the Engelberg railway.

At the lower station of the Stanserhorn funicular, you can board for a combined funicular and cable-car ride to the top of the Stanserhorn at 6235 feet. The ascent to the panoramic restaurant of Stanserhorn-Kulm takes about half an hour. Once at the summit you'll have a majestic view of the Bernese Alps and Lake Lucerne.

Food and Lodging

Hotel Regina (tel. 61-31-73) is a four-story concrete building on Bahnhofstrasse with balconies which curve around its exposed corner. The interior is about as simple as you can get without being spartan, yet nonetheless it's comfortable, clean, and attractive. Bedrooms are carpeted in neutral colors, with chrome-based chairs and colorful furniture. Singles range from 35F ($16.08) to 45F ($20.68), while doubles cost between 65F ($29.87) and 80F ($36.76), including breakfast. There's no restaurant in the hotel. Regina Gerig is both the owner and the namesake of the hotel.

Hotel Stanserhof (tel. 61-41-22). My favorite room in this family-run hotel is the restaurant/café area with the thick colored glass set into irregular squares that look like a Mondrian painting. The rest of the hotel is well maintained, often paneled, and very comfortable. The smallish bedrooms are predictably furnished in forgettable furniture, yet are usually sunny and clean. Singles range from 34F ($15.62) to 42F ($19.30), with doubles costing between 58F ($26.65) and 74F ($34), including breakfast. Prices depend on the season and the plumbing.

ENGELBERG: A 20-minute car ride from Lucerne will deliver you to Engelberg, a popular summer and winter resort in an alpine valley that "glistens with perpetual snow," in the words of one Swiss poet. Many international skiing tournaments take place here, but mainly the village is visited because it's an excursion center for exploring **Mt. Titlis** at 10,627 feet.

The town is well equipped to receive visitors, with ski runs in the heights where the snow can still fly from your skis even when it's springtime in the valley. It has eight mountain track and cable railways, plus 14 ski tows and chair lifts. Other attractions include cross-country ski trails, an extensive sled run, ice skating, curling, a Swiss ski school, more than 20 miles of level walking and hiking paths, indoor swimming pools, a casino, and sports activities planned especially for children.

The **Benedictine abbey** in town was founded about 1120, and the entire valley was ruled from here until the French invasion of 1798. Much of the complex, certainly the church, can be visited by the public, although parts of it are now a religious college. The church, incidentally, contains one of the largest organs in the country.

But you may not want to linger long, as Mt. Titlis is a powerful lure. Titlis is always covered by snow and ice, and it's the highest elevation in the heart of Switzerland which you can visit for a panorama of the Alps, including an "ice cave" and a glacier trail.

It will take a funicular and three cable cars to enable you to reach the highest belvedere, at 9900 feet. But once there, it will be worth it, for you'll have a view of not only the Jungfrau and the Matterhorn, but on a clear day you can see as far as Zurich and Basle. Incidentally, the last stage of the cable-car trip is the most spectacular, because you are taken right over the glacier. Visitors with respiratory problems may want to forgo this trip because of the thinness of the air at this elevation.

The trip from Engelberg to Titlis takes only 45 minutes. There's a summit terminal with an observation lounge and a large sun terrace. In summer there's also a ski run with a ski lift. You'll find two restaurants, the Panorama Restaurant Titlis at 10,000 feet and the Gletscher-Restaurant Stand at 8040 feet. Figure on about 3½ hours if you plan to make this trip. Usually there is service about every half hour, and a round-trip ticket sells for about 40F ($18.38).

Food and Lodging

Ring Hotel (tel. 94-18-22) is a modern concrete rectangle that sits in a pleasant green area with a good view. From one side you'll see a blank cement wall, but from two of the others the view improves, with evenly spaced rows of wood-trimmed loggias. A sun terrace is thoughtfully placed for a maximum view of the valley below. Bedrooms are comfortable and modern, with brightly colored curtains to keep out the morning light. A dance band plays every night in winter, and a hotel bus provides a frequent link to the center of the village. Each of the accommodations has a private bath, balcony, radio, and phone. Doubles rent for between 70F ($32.17) and 105F ($48.25) per person daily; with half board included, depending on the floor and the season. A surcharge of between 9F ($4.14) and 23F ($10.57) is added to the above rates for single occupancy.

Hotel Bellevue-Terminus (tel. 94-12-13) is a Victorian elephant of a building, with lots of different architectural features that seem to be connected only by a complicated roofline with lots of gables and curves. The overall effect is authentically 19th century. The surrounding gardens are thoughtfully planned around curved walkways and flowering shrubs. The interior has some uncluttered rustic sections and a few modern touches from the '60s (especially the bedrooms). But the lobby area is the real prize. It's supported by white marble columns and bedecked with contrasting Oriental rugs, deep leather chairs, and huge windows. Tennis courts are on the premises. The 45 rooms range from 43F ($19.76) to 72F ($33.08) in a single and from 76F ($34.92) to 134F ($61.57) in a double, with breakfast included. Prices depend on the season and the plumbing.

Restaurant Hess (tel. 94-13-66) is one of the most charming restaurants in the area. Located in a 100-year-old hotel with rustic paneling and plenty of evening candlelight, it serves local specialties, often accompanied by rösti. You might start off with cream of broccoli soup or a terrine of wild game (in season). Another good dish is filet of goose with leeks. The house specialty is "Hesstopf" (ask the waiter to explain). An attractive bar area with a live pianist is a popular place to relax either before or after a meal. The restaurant is closed the first two weeks in May and from mid-October to mid-December. The Hess family offers comfortably renovated rooms in their hotel for between 50F ($22.98) and 100F ($45.95) in a single, between 80F ($36.76) and 166F ($76.30) in a double, including breakfast. Prices depend on the season. There are tennis courts on the premises.

BECKENRIED/KLEWENALP: Some 12½ miles from Lucerne along the N2 motorway in one of the most beautiful sections of the heartland of Switzerland lies this center for both winter and summer sports. The peaceful atmosphere and mild climate of **Beckenried** invite you to forget the stresses of everyday life back home and enjoy the many recreational activities offered here: excursions on the lake and into the mountains, swimming, boating, fishing, and walking through the verdant meadows and woods.

Klewenalp (5200 feet), above Beckenried, is a sun terrace overlooking Lake Lucerne. Besides summer pleasures, the resort is a joy to skiers in winter, with fine slopes and runs, five ski lifts, a ski school, and lots of sunshine.

Beckenried is easily accessible by car via the Germany–Basle–Italy motorway, by car ferry from Gersau, or by lake steamer, train, or bus. An aerial cableway, one of the largest in the lake area, takes you rapidly up to Klewenalp.

Food and Lodging

Sternen Hotel am See, at Beckenried (tel. 64-11-07), is the best known lakeside hotel, standing on its own grounds. The bowling alley inside is a Teutonic version, with a heavily timbered ceiling, four lanes, and a collection of chalet chairs and cloth-covered tables off to the side. The public rooms have elaborately carved cupboards, lots of paneling, and a mildly heraldic decor. The hotel offers balconies off every room, plus a café terrace angled for maximum exposure to the sunlight. *Per-person* rates in a double range from 54F ($24.81) to 73F ($33.54), including breakfast. Singles require an additional charge of around 12F ($5.51). Prices depend on the season, and all the accommodations contain private bath, radio, and phone.

Hotel Edelweiss, at Beckenried (tel. 64-12-52), is a roadside hotel with a Victorian-style octagonal tower rising above the main lobby. The sitting room has a wintertime fireplace and a slate floor. The dining room has big-windowed views of the lake. The renovated bedrooms are somewhat on the small side, but are comfortable and simply furnished with modern furniture. Singles cost from 46F ($21.14) to 61F ($28.03), while doubles range from 36F ($16.54) to 56F ($25.73), including breakfast. Prices depend on the plumbing, the view, and the season.

Inter-Hotel Klewenalp, at Klewenalp (tel. 64-29-22), sits on an isolated bluff looking down at the lake and the Alps which surround it. It's a solid-looking balconied building, with a simple roof and a series of glass-walled public rooms. The inside is comfortably carpeted, filled with padded contoured chairs and prominently placed fireplaces. The hotel has its own ski school, a terraced restaurant, and a bowling alley. The 30 bedrooms rent for between 55F ($25.27) and 85F ($39.06) per person daily, with half board included. A nearby guest house, Chalet Guggeregg, is owned by the same management. More rustic in format, it charges between 50F ($22.98) and 60F ($27.57) per person daily in a double, with half board included. There's an additional charge of 10F ($4.60) in mid and high season for occupants of a single.

MELCHSEE-FRUTT: This well-known mountain holiday center, at an altitude of 6300 feet, draws vacationers in both summer and winter. Lying in a beautiful valley on the shore of an alpine lake, the Melch See, the resort enjoys an invigorating, high-altitude climate with strong sunshine in which visitors may participate in summer activities such as walking along signposted paths, going on excursions amid the alpine flowers and wooded areas, trout fishing, bicycling, indoor swimming, or just relaxing with excellent views of the Titlis mountain chain to look at.

Winter brings ample snow from December to the end of April, with good facilities for skiers from the ranks of beginners up to experts. You can leave the smallfry under capable supervision at a day nursery while you take ski lessons, try curling or ice skating on the rinks, or enjoy other winter activities. The road up to nearby Stöckalp is open throughout the winter, with ample free parking for your car, and a snow taxi will take you on to the resort.

Melchsee-Frutt is in the canton of Obwalden in central Switzerland.

Food and Lodging

Sporthotel Kurhaus Frutt (tel. 67-12-12) is a flat-roofed, three-story building with wooden balconies and a position in an alpine meadow. A few cows graze on the lawns some distance away, while the views are very good of the snow-covered mountains in the distance. The bedrooms are usually paneled and tasteful. On the premises you'll find a whirlpool, a sauna, and an exercise room, plus a bowling alley, a rustic restaurant, and a dance bar. Sepp Durrer and his family are your hosts. They charge between 65F ($29.87) and 84F ($38.60) in a single and between 92F ($42.27) and 150F ($68.93) in a double. These prices include half board, and the difference in tariffs depends on the season.

Hotel Reinhard (tel. 67-12-25) has a brightly colored interior filled with a few antiques and an attractive detailing made of masonry walls and heavy timbers. There's a comfortable restaurant, and the bedrooms are streamlined with patterned carpeting and autumnal colors. *Per-person* rates in doubles with half board range from 65F ($29.87) to 95F ($43.65), depending on the season. A single supplement with half board costs an additional 10F ($4.60) per day.

SACHSELN: Heading south from Lake Lucerne, en route to Interlaken, you may want to consider a stopover at Sachseln, a tiny resort where the lake, plains, and mountains form a landscape of rare harmony. This lakeside village is particularly popular in the summer months, drawing a lively family trade, mostly Europeans. Sachseln lies in the half-canton of Obwalden, which takes in the beautiful Sarner See. Also in summer there is much tourist traffic from Lucerne to Interlaken over the Brünig Pass. This pass goes to Brienz which is studded with lakeside resorts.

Food and Lodging

Hotel Kreuz (tel. 66-14-66). Since parts of the walls and foundations date from the Middle Ages, the management has understandly tried to blend the architectural styles of the annexes into the spirit of the main building. Most of the bedrooms are in the newer sections, and they're filled with a scattering of old furniture and wall-to-wall carpeting. The main house has wood-paneled public rooms filled with 19th-century antiques, and some stained glass from 1656. Among the many celebrities who have stayed here are Pablo Casals, Konrad Adenauer, and the future Pope VI (called Cardinal Montini at the time), along with Zita, the empress of Austria. All accommodations contain private bath, renting for 55F ($25.27) to 75F ($34.46) in a single and from 90F ($41.36) to 120F ($55.14) in a double.

Chapter XI

THE GRISONS AND THE ENGADINE

1. Chur
2. Arosa
3. Klosters
4. Davos
5. Scuol/Tarasp/Vulpera
6. S-chanf and Zuoz
7. Samedan and Celerina
8. St. Moritz
9. Pontresina
10. Silvaplana
11. Sils Maria (Baselgia)
12. Flims (Laax)
13. Splügen
14. Valbella/Lenzerheide
15. Savognin

THE GRISONS by any other name is still the largest, most easterly, and least developed of all the Swiss cantons. Its German name is Graubünden; to the Romansh-speaking population it's Grischun; and the Italians call it Grigioni. We'll stick with Grisons, its French name, which is usually used by English-speaking people. Adding to this somewhat puzzling situation is the fact that French is not generally spoken in this canton.

This sparsely settled region is quite mountainous, with some 140 square miles of glaciers. Forests cover one-fifth of the canton's total area. Juf, nearly 7000 feet above sea level, is the highest permanently inhabited village in the Alps. Even the 150 or so valleys of the Grisons are high, between 2953 and 6562 feet, and the highest peak, Bernina, reaches 13,285 feet. The alpine scenery here differs from that of other areas of Switzerland because of the altitude and topography, and the air is clear and invigorating, which has led to the establishment of many health centers in the Grisons. The height makes it cooler at night in summer, but it enjoys the extra daytime warmth of other southern cantons.

The Grisons contain the sources of the Rhine, which is served by many tributaries, and of the Inn (En in Romansh) Rivers, whose upper stretches form the major valleys of the canton.

The territory of the Grisons was once a part of Rhaetia, peopled by Celtic tribes in pre-Christian times. In 15 B.C. the Romans conquered the Rhaetians, began colonization, and built alpine roads, some along courses which have not till now been much changed. The Franks, a West Germanic people, entered the Roman provinces in the third century and established themselves along the Rhine. They and their fellow Germanic successors, the Ostrogoths, largely Teutonized the Roman territories they seized, gradually changing the language of the inhabitants to Germanic dialects, especially in the northern regions. German is spoken today by about half of the Grisons population, mainly around Davos and Chur, the capital of the canton. About a sixth of the people of the Grisons, those living in the southern portion, speak the language of their next-door neighbor, Italy.

The people of the upper valleys of the Rhine and the Inn were protected from Germanization by the seclusion of their habitation, and today they still cling to their ancestral tongue, called Romansh, the language of a third of the Swiss living in the Grisons. Both the dialect spoken in the Engadine, Ladin, and that of the Vorderrhein (front or upper Rhine) Valley, Surveltisch, are direct descendents of the Latin spoken in the Roman province of Rhaetia. The centuries have altered it, until to me it sounds like Spanish spoken by a person with a cleft palate and a heavy German accent. This stubborn persistence in retaining the tongue of their ancestors led to the recognition in 1938 of Romansh as the fourth Swiss national language.

From the time of the Romans through the Middle Ages you could take the High Road, the *Obere Strasse* which used the Juli Julier and the Septimer Passes, and I could take the Low Road, the *Untere Strasse* via Splügen Pass, and we would have had lots of company. These roads gave Rhaetia a monopoly on almost all transalpine traffic through the territory then, and even today the route of the Low Road is still used. The Septimer Pass fell into disuse following the building of a more car-worthy road running through the San Bernardino Pass, which now has a tunnel, allowing use of the north-south route all year.

It seems reasonable to say that the roads in the Grisons, many of which were repaired and linked with a network in the early 19th century, owe at least part of their survival to the fact that until 1927 the citizens of this canton did not allow motor vehicles on their roads. Even today it's illegal to drive cars in Arosa after nightfall.

This ban on use of roads by motor cars made popular the Rhaetian railway, with its narrow-gauge trains running on a track along hairpin curves and through tunnels. This ride is still a pleasant and thrilling journey through the Grisons. Or you can embark on excursions via postal buses to take you to the high passes.

The peasants of this canton banded together in 1395 to form the Ligue Grise (Gray League), from which the name Grisons is derived. Two other such leagues were formed in the area, all joining to oppose Habsburg domination. In 1803 the three leagues formed a single canton which joined the Swiss Confederation. The Reformation was adopted by only part of the canton.

Much of the population of the Grisons today earns its living by catering to tourists, who find this like a separate world with major ski resorts and small settlements waiting to help them have happy holidays. If you always like to drink the "spirit of the land" when you travel, add to your happiness by trying the local wine, veltliner. Chances are it will be red, but you may be fortunate enough to taste the rare "green" veltliner.

While you're in the Grisons, be on the lookout for embroidery done by the women of the canton during the long winter evenings. It's exquisite. You can also purchase hand-woven linens.

THE ENGADINE: The Valley of the Inn (or the En, as the locals call it in Romansh) stretches for 60 miles, from the Maloja plateau (5955 feet) to Finstermünz, with all villages except Sils lying at a higher altitude than the plateau. The highest is St. Moritz, at 6036 feet.

Lower Engadine is reached from Davos over the Fluëla Pass (7818 feet) and by the Ofen Pass (7050 feet). Four major passes lead into the **Upper Engadine:** Maloja (5955 feet), Julier (7493 feet), Albula (7585 feet), and Bernina (7621 feet). The upper valley contains several lakes, including the St. Moritz.

The Engadine is enclosed by great mountain ranges with alpine meadows and forests on the steep hillsides. The villages are built of stone, originally as a protection against fires that swept the narrow windy valleys. The whitewashed houses in the villages, known for their *chaminades* or larders, often have *sgraffito* decoration with mottos and heraldic devices, and you'll see many a *balcun tort* (oriel). The population is of Rhaeto-Romanic heritage and is mostly Protestant.

From the Majola Pass the road runs northeast through the Upper Engadine, where the clear mountain skies and dry, light breezes make the area popular both in summer and in winter, despite its somewhat stark scenery. Since the 19th century when Upper Engadine became fashionable for its "air cure," it has developed into a primarily winter sports center, highlighted by St. Moritz.

In the Lower Engadine, where the valley is narrower and more forested, and two major attractions are the mineral springs of Scuol and the Swiss National Park, a wildlife sanctuary stretching for some 55 miles. Here you'll find the true alpine flora and fauna.

Some of Engadine's ancient customs have died out, but two which are upheld throughout the area are the Chalanda Marz (the first of March) and the Schlitteda.

The **Chalanda Marz,** celebrated by the youth of Engadine, descended from the old Roman New Year festival and has been observed since the time when the Rhaetian valleys were under Roman rule. Early on the morning of March 1 schoolboys congregate at the center meeting place of each Engadine village. With bells large and small, the boys create a hullabaloo to frighten the winter monster and lure spring out from its snowy bed. The boys are divided into "herds" which go from house to house soliciting goodies such as fruit, sweets, and chestnuts. Romanic songs of spring are sung, in which the girls of the village are requested to join. Money is accepted from visitors and locals in lieu of edible goodies, with the proceeds usually being used for school trips.

An especially beautiful custom is the observance of **Schlitteda,** a romantic horse-drawn sleigh ride in January, participated in by the unmarried youth of the villages. The couples dress in the colorful traditional costume of the region, *schlittunza,* a scarlet festive garb. In a decorated sleigh, they set out for a nearby village on a ride which usually takes about two hours. When they reach their goal they're served a hot spiced wine drink and pastries to strengthen them for their trip home after music and dancing. Back home after a romantic ride through the Engadine night, the couple dines at the girl's home. Visitors enjoy the sight of the brightly dressed pairs backgrounded by snowy fields and mountains and the festivities which take place in village squares as the sleigh rides get under way, with outriders in three-cornered hats and jabots arranging the procession. Musicians in traditional costumes accompany the young couples in another sleigh and are greeted in the villages they pass through by townspeople dancing in the square.

In summer, music lovers are drawn to the Engadine Concert Weeks during which chamber music concerts are given throughout the area, arranged by the Upper Engadine Tourist Office.

1. Chur

The capital of the Grisons, Chur is the oldest town in Switzerland, dating back, according to recent excavations, to 3000 B.C. The Romans founded a settlement here in 15th B.C., calling it Curia Rhaetorum. At an elevation of 1955 feet, it lies in the Rhine Valley, surrounded by towering mountains. The River Plessur flows through it on its way to the Rhine.

Chur is a meeting point for routes from Italy over the Alpine passes, and as such it combines both Rhaetian and Italian influences. This mountain town is a tourist favorite, but also the largest trading center between Zurich and Milan. Incidentally, Chur lies 75 miles from Zurich, which is reached in about 90 minutes.

The town is also an important rail center, the terminus of some international lines such as the standard-gauge railway from Sargans. It's also the starting point for the narrow-gauge line to St. Moritz, known as the Rhätische Bahn. The Chur–Arosa line and the *Glacier Express* also start here.

In 450 Chur became the see of a bishop, and much of its history has been tied up with that position. It still has a bishop, but he no longer has the power, of course, that his predecessors did. These bishops virtually ruled the town until 1526.

Because of its position as a transportation network, Chur is a good center for exploring the Grisons. The commute is easy to more expensive Arosa and Davos, as well as the Engadine. At the **tourist office** on Bahnhofplatz (tel. 22-18-18), you'll be told how to reach as many as 20 castle ruins in the Domleschg on a 6½-mile trip. Another excursion which will be outlined for you is to Splügen, which is said to have the prettiest mountain-pass village in the Tamina ravine.

Many possibilities for sports also exist—in both summer and winter. In summer you can hike on marked trails and go skiing at 9000 feet (only 1¼ hours away), as well as participate in swimming and riding. In winter Chur is the starting point for 20 top ski areas.

You'll also want to spend as much time as possible in Chur, as it offers many attractions. Emperors and kings, armies and traders, have marched through Chur, and many have left their legacies. City officials have made it easy for you to go on a self-guided tour of the medieval sector (green and red footprints are painted on the sidewalks). You'll come across colorful squares with flower-bedecked fountains and narrow streets, along with elegant houses and many towers.

The **cathedral** was erected from 1178 to 1282, although it has seen much rebuilding, one as recent as the 19th century. It was constructed on the site of an even older building. Inside it displays a 15th-century triptych in gilded wood at the high altar. This is the largest Gothic triptych in Switzerland. To visit the Dom Treasury, you'll have to apply to the sacristan at building no. 2 on the square. For a cost of 1.50F (69¢) he'll show you many medieval reliquaries, among other treasures, including the relics of St. Lucius of the second century.

Close to the cathedral, the **Bishop's Palace,** still the residence of a bishop, was begun in 1732 in the baroque style. The palace opens onto the Hofplatz—the site of a Roman fort—and in its cellar you can order food and drink (see below).

The town has at least two museums worthy of your attention, including the Rhaetic Museum **(Rätisches Museum),** open from 10 a.m. to noon and 2 to 5 p.m. except Monday, charging an admission of 1F (46¢). It's installed in the Buolsches Haus, which was constructed from 1674 to 1680. The museum presents exhibits illustrating the folklore of the canon and has a prehistoric collection as well.

The **Kunstmuseum** (fine arts museum) stands on Bahnhofstrasse. Charging 1F (46¢) for admission, it's open from 10 a.m. to noon and 2 to 5 p.m. except Monday. It displays paintings and sculptures from many artists who earned acclaim in the Grisons. Some of its works are by such world-famed artists as Giovanni, Angelica Kauffmann, and Segantini, as well as Alberto and Augusto Giacometti. But I always make a special pilgrimage to it to see the largest collection in the world of one of my all-time favorite artists, the incomparable Ernst Ludwig Kirchner (1880–1938), the German painter and leader of the "Bridge" school of expressionists. His figures are distorted, his pictures sharply patterned and colored. The Nazis destroyed many of his works, finding them decadent, and he subsequently committed suicide before the outbreak of World War II.

WHERE TO STAY: **Duc de Rohan,** 44 Masanerstrasse (tel. 22-10-22), is a white-walled, flat-roofed hotel five minutes from the train station at the north end of town. It was built a few years ago and is known locally for its conference facilities. The inside has a large indoor swimming pool, a sauna, massage facilities, and a fitness club. Many of the public rooms have been elegantly outfitted with rococo and 19th-century antiques, grouped into pastel-colored conversation areas. A vaulted bar has its own share of hunting trophies, while a high-ceilinged restaurant is beamed with wrought-iron lighting fixtures, along with baronial chairs covered with red and black tartans. Well-furnished singles range from 58F ($26.65) to 75F ($34.46), while doubles cost from 100F ($45.95) to 118F ($54.22), breakfast included.

Hotel Chur, 2 Welschdörfli (tel. 22-21-61), has an imposing facade of tall windows, arched ground-floor windows, and fifth-floor gables. The interior has been renovated into an attractive format of three restaurants and comfortably updated bedrooms, each of which has a private bath, phone, mini-bar, radio, and on occasion a well-placed reproduction of a Queen Anne chair. The Cava Grischa is an informal cellar room with black-vested waiters, rustic paneling, and nighttime folkloric or modern music with dancing. The Bistro is an art nouveau fantasy of wrought iron and bentwood chairs, with crêpes and light snacks offered. Finally, the Welschdörfli is an elegant dining room, serving nouvelle cuisine and Grisons-style cookery. Singles range between 60F ($27.57) and 78F ($35.84), while doubles cost from 100F ($45.95) to 117F ($53.76), breakfast included.

Hotel Stern, 11 Reichsgasse (tel. 22-35-55), is one of Switzerland's "romantic hotels," which usually means a greater-than-usual level of antique authenticity and charm. The outside looks like a giant strawberry mousse, painted a vivid pink with white shutters. Management will meet you at the train station if you call ahead; however, it's only a seven-minute walk. The staff wears regional costumes, and many of the walls are covered with pine paneling, some of it dating from 1646. The ceilings often are vaulted or timbered. The bedrooms are usually more up-to-date, but with a wood-grained format that corresponds well with the antiques and wrought iron used in the public rooms. Emil Pfister, the owner, charges from 65F ($29.87) to 70F ($32.17) in a single and from 96F ($44.11) to 106F ($48.71) in a double, breakfast included. There is free parking.

Hotel Freieck, 50 Reichsgasse (tel. 22-63-22), is a tall, neutral-colored building with gray shutters, an uncomplicated roofline, and a series of black line drawings representing grape vines, a sundial, and two friendly lions. The establishment is about five minutes on foot from the rail station. The bedrooms have obviously been renovated into a streamlined format of simple furniture and comfortable low beds. The emphasis of the establishment, however, seems to be on the restaurants inside, which range from a rustic stucco room with massive beams stretching just below the vaulting to a paneled contemporary room with simple tables and white napery. The Maurer family, your hosts, charge from 44F ($20.22) to 63F ($28.95) in a single and from 70F ($32.17) to 102F ($46.87) in a double, with breakfast included.

Hotel Zunfthaus zur Rebleuten, Pfisterplatz (tel. 22-17-13), was built in 1483 in the middle of the old town. It sits in front of a fountain behind blue shutters and a beautiful type of ground-floor window ornamentation I've never seen on any other building. The inside is carefully paneled, with elaborate chandeliers, leaded-glass windows, and hunting trophies. The bedrooms sometimes have exposed timbers between the white stucco, along with comfortable beds with pine head- and footboards. Ralph Cottiati, the owner, charges from 42F ($19.30) to 56F ($25.73) in a single and from 68F ($31.25) to 92F ($42.27) in a double, with breakfast included.

Posthotel, 11 Poststrasse (tel. 22-68-44), is a straightforward hotel in a five-story rectangular building with a flat roof and a series of privately run shops behind the glass windows of part of the ground floor. The inside is functionally modern, with bright colors and predictable functional furnishings. The Huber family, your hosts, charge, with breakfast included, from 46F ($21.14) to 70F ($32.17) in a single and from 72F ($33.08) to 106F ($48.71) in a double. Prices depend on the season and the plumbing.

Hotel Drei Könige, 18 Reichsgasse (tel. 22-17-25), is at the entrance to the old city, a five-minute walk from the beginning of the Brambrüesch chair lift. The Schällibaum family has run this old-fashioned hotel since 1911. It has an alpine format of lots of paneling and chalet chairs in an updated series of public rooms and comfortable bedrooms. The weinstube is popular with locals. Singles range from 42F ($19.30) to 54F ($24.81), and doubles cost from 70F ($32.17) to 88F ($40.44), with breakfast included, the prices depending on the season and the plumbing.

WHERE TO DINE: **Pestalozza** (tel. 22-24-58). If you're an art lover as well as a gourmet, you'll appreciate this friendly Italian restaurant, with its white walls and vaulted ceilings. The decor is more modern than you'd expect from a restaurant located in the old town, but much of it is decorated with the paintings of the Italian-Swiss artist Mario Comensoli. The well-prepared and moderately priced menus include white and green homemade pasta with gorgonzola, a brochette of lobster and salmon, rolled filet of veal stuffed with ham, and a gratinée of fennel. Tasty and light-textured desserts include vanilla ice cream with a deliciously fermented sauce. Fixed-price meals range from 16F ($7.35) to 60F ($27.57), while à la carte dinners cost from 25F ($11.49) to 45F ($20.68).

Zunfthaus zur Rebleuten, Pfisterplatz (tel. 22-17-13). You'll certainly get a sense of history from the walls of this second-floor restaurant. Some of the decoration was painstakingly inlaid with darker woods, making the wall coverings more like furniture than paneling. The building dates from 1483, but the recipes served within are far more contemporary. They include a savory consommé flavored, Teutonic style, with marrow, delicately sauteed frog legs, and a specialty unique to the region, a "Chur hot-pot," which consists of a savory filet of pork with homemade spätzli in a pot. Reservations are suggested. Fixed-price meals range from 20F ($9.19) to 50F ($22.98) while à la carte dinners cost from 25F ($11.49) to 43F ($19.76).

Duc du Rohan, 44 Masanerstrasse (tel. 22-10-22). The chef, Herr Elvedi, is known for preparing a wide variety of dishes, usually with imagination and flair. They might include fresh grilled shrimp, salmon, veal scaloppine with Marsala, sweetbreads with morels, and in autumn, game specialties. You might also enjoy the seafood specialties (in season), or smoked roast pork in a red wine sauce, home-grown asparagus, and a gratin of shrimp. Meals range from 23F ($10.57) to 85F ($39.06) on the à la carte. The restaurant, part of the hotel already recommended, is open for lunch and dinner (until midnight). The dining room is in one of Chur's newest first-class hotels on the north side of town, a few minutes on foot from the train station.

The **Hofkellerei,** 1 Hofplatz (tel. 23-32-30), is a cellar pub in the Bishop's Palace, already previewed as a sightseeing attraction. I always go here for two specialties of the region, Bündnerfleisch (air-dried beef) and Valtelline wine. Service is friendly and efficient, and the alpine food is very good. Regional furniture enhances the mellow atmosphere even more. Count on spending some 30F ($13.79) for a meal.

2. Arosa

One of the highest of the alpine resorts, Arosa (6000 feet) lies in a sheltered basin at the top of the Schanfigg Valley, off the main road but easily reached from Chur. The village has existed since the 14th century. Arosa is known for its pure mountain air and a certain unaffected ambience, set against a backdrop of pine- and larch-studded hills. There are many small lakes in the area also. If St. Moritz is too ultra-chic for you, Arosa may be your answer. In other words, you don't have to pack a formal gown or a dinner jacket if you like to spend your vacation at a ski resort. Arosa lures family trade through such attractions as kindergartens for the smaller visitors.

To make the 19-mile drive from Chur in good weather, allow at least an hour as the road is steep and winding. As for making the drive in icy weather, my advice is to forget it! Instead, take the narrow-gauge railway which has been in operation since the first year of World War I. Even if you make the trip by car, you'll have to make other arrangements if you want to circulate at night, because, as I mentioned earlier, it's illegal to drive in Arosa once night falls.

The village consists of one main street, lined with hotels, as this is the most popular resort in the Grisons after Davos and St. Moritz. As a ski center, it enjoys world repute, drawing an international crowd to its slopes. Arosa does a thriving summer business, but it's mostly in winter that the crowds pour in. It offers some of the best ski runs in the Grisons, some 15 miles of them, plus one of the best ski schools in Switzerland, with some 100 instructors.

Skiing is popular in the Obersee area at the eastern edge of the resort, reached by cable car to Weisshorn (8700 feet). To the west, skiers take the Hörnli gondola, reaching Hörnligrat (8180 feet) in about 16 minutes. Drag lifts at Hörnligrat fan out, taking skiers to their destinations. Cross-country skiers gravitate to Arosa. However, it's estimated that one out of every two winter guests comes to Arosa not to ski but to enjoy the activity of the place, especially après-ski.

Curling, Bavarian style, is popular in Arosa, as are ice skating and hockey. Horseracing on the ice and snow is another sport to follow.

Summer visitors find many pursuits, including tennis and golf on a nine-hole course. Fishing is also possible in the cold lake water, or you can go up to Hörnligrat, the starting point for many walks in the mountains.

WHERE TO STAY: Arosa hotels, for the most part, are modern or at least up-to-date. In the peak season months reservations are imperative—that is, in winter. In summer it's much easier to find accommodations. The only problem is that Arosa is generously endowed with expensive and upper-bracket hotels, whereas the pickings in the budget category are slim indeed.

The Deluxe Category

Alexandra Palace (tel. 31-01-11) is designed in a semicircular curve of balconied rooms layered on top of one another, with oversize windows and a view over Arosa and the snow-covered mountains in the distance. Inside you'll find a heated swimming pool, a sauna, a disco, an invitingly attractive restaurant, and a tavern. The hotel offers 150 panoramic rooms for sports enthusiasts, who usually spend their days skiing or hiking through the neighboring hills. Free bus transportation is provided by the hotel to key points in the area, although most guests choose to walk the 500 yards to the nearby ski lifts. The hotel often stages an evening entertainment program to amuse guests. Examples of this might include a fondue party with folkloric music, a candlelight buffet, a bowling tournament, or a sleigh ride.

High season here is from mid-November until mid-March, at which time doubles range from 135F ($62.03) to 150F ($68.93), and singles go for 150F ($68.93), the same as a double. Off-season, however, tariffs in a double are from 105F ($48.25) to 115F ($52.84), with a single paying the 115F price tag too. Rates shoot up at least 50F ($22.98) per room from December 20 through New Year's.

Arosa Kulm Hotel (tel. 31-01-31). The modern hotel with the wide glass windows that you see on this site is only the most recent reincarnation of a series of hotels, all with the same name, which have been built, destroyed, and rebuilt on this site since the first establishment was erected as a simple guest house in 1882. During summer you'll find outdoor tennis courts competing for your attention with the nearby rushing streams and hill walks that the region provides. A heated swimming pool with glass walls opening to the mountains is available all year round, along with a wide range of fitness, massage, and cosmetic programs. The array of public rooms includes rustically attractive restaurants, a weinstube, and nightclubs with a sophisticated clientele that should provide whatever it is you're looking for.

The bedrooms frequently afford panoramic views from behind large windows. Their decor is often a combination of warmly tinted fabrics, pine paneling, and comfortable furnishings. In high season singles range between 195F ($89.60) and 275F ($126.35), dropping to 165F ($75.82) and 215F ($98.79) otherwise. Doubles go for a peak 150F ($68.93) to 225F ($103.39) per person from the first week of February until mid-March, reduced to 120F ($55.14) to 175F ($80.41) per person at other times. Rates soar even higher over the Christmas holidays.

Tschuggen Grand Hotel (tel. 31-02-21). The literature distributed by this hotel reads almost like an invitation to a private party. The facade is high rise and modern, and the interior is enhanced by decorating devices seemingly from the pages of *Architectural Digest:* potted palms, distressed tortoise-shell wallpaper, and geometric brass frames surrounding lots of mirrors. In fact the hotel is one of the most glamorous choices in the Swiss Alps, attracting a clientele appropriate to its setting.

In the basement you'll find a ski shop that will fully equip you in the latest winter slope fashion. At night the place is lively with a disco and bowling center, plus a handsome, intimate stube where everybody seems in a festive mood on a snowy night. Dining is in a panoramic roof garden restaurant or in the Restaurant Français. There's also a dancing room with an orchestra.

The penthouse indoor swimming pool is dramatic, as is the view from the open-air terrace. Many fitness facilities are contained within the premises, including a sauna, massage parlor (even an underwater massage!), sun-ray treatment, a hairdressing salon, beauty parlor, and a kindergarten with a nurse.

The rooms are handsomely decorated and beautifully kept. The highest tariffs are charged from mid-February until mid-March. Singles on half board, depending on the season, pay from a low of 142F ($65.25) to a high of 325F ($149.34), the latter rate charged over the Christmas season for the most deluxe chambers. Doubles on half board are charged from a low of 117F ($53.76) per person to a high of 310F ($142.45) per person. Each week there are two *soirées élégantes* for which evening dress is compulsory. Winter season begins November 26, with Arosa's traditional ski weeks, closing on the first of April.

Hotel Park (tel. 31-01-65) is housed in a modern building shaped like an elongated rectangle which sprawls over an extended distance behind the front-yard parking lot. The interior is richly decorated, with ample use of leather, intimate lighting, brown velvets, and everywhere the aura of a complacent comfort coming after an invigorating day outdoors. On the premises you'll find a bowling alley, pinball machines, a disco, an intimately lit bar, and several restaurants which seem to share one thing in common—warmth. Insofar as fitness is concerned, the hotel provides one indoor tennis court, two squash courts, and a swimming pool illuminated by natural light from a panoramic window view of the Alps. In winter, with the snow outside, you'll find the juxtaposition most unusual. There are also two saunas, a whirlpool, and a thorough regime of massage and cosmetic treatments.

Bedrooms, offering views of the gradually changing seasons, are richly upholstered in corduroys, velvets, and brocades. Room prices include free parking and free transportation by hotel bus to the ski lifts. H. R. Sterchi is the director, dividing his yearly season into summer and winter tariffs. In summer the rate for half board ranges from a low of 45F ($20.68) to a high of 100F ($45.95) per person. Winter tariffs go from a low of 115F ($52.84) to a high of 210F ($96.50) per person for half board.

Hof Maran (tel. 31-01-85) is an attractive hotel that looks like a full-scale mountain chalet, particularly since it sits high in an alpine meadow away from the congestion of downtown Arosa. In winter you'll notice the narrow tracks made by the dozens of cross-country skiers who pass by on one of their routes through the hills. Many of the bedrooms have balconies with enough sunlight to afford a tan even in winter. The public rooms are rustically decorated with heavy beamed ceilings, carpeting in autumnal colors, and comfortable armchairs ideal for sinking into after a day spent outdoors.

Two tennis courts with an on-the-spot tennis pro are for the sole use of hotel guests, while many scenic and well-marked mountain trails begin and end at the hotel. There's a skating rink which is well maintained in the winter, a hotel bus that takes guests at regular intervals to the town center and to the ski lifts, and nightly dancing with live music. There's also a nine-hole golf course nearby. E. Traber is the director of this complex.

All accommodations have radios and phones. In summer, a single on the half-board plan ranges from 70F ($32.17) to 115F ($52.84) a night; a double costs from 140F ($64.33) to 250F ($114.88). Guests are booked in winter on the half-board plan, which can range from a low of 65F ($29.87) to a high of 175F ($80.41) per person.

The Upper Bracket

Waldhotel-National Hotel (tel. 31-13-51). The reception room of this large, symmetrical hotel set into a forest has apricot-colored stencils decorating the arched ceiling and a beautifully carved and painted booth that looks almost like part of a pulpit of some regional church. Willy and Elisabeth Huber are the owners of this sprawling hotel designed with two wings on either side of a central core. A wood-paneled restaurant has a Swiss tile oven at one end and a quality of craftsmanship that is outstanding. The management offers a weekly gala dinner by candlelight, a breakfast buffet which is by any comparison copious, and a heated swimming pool with a wide range of massage and stress-reduction treatments.

Skiers will be glad to know that it's possible for them to begin and end a day of skiing from the hotel without (unless they fall) removing their skis. A chair lift and a cable car begin at a point just below the hotel. Accommodations are available from December until Easter and from June until September.

Half-board rates range from a low of 84F ($38.60) to a high of 180F ($82.71) per person in winter. In summer rates are reduced, from a low of 40F ($18.38) to 92F ($42.27) per person per day with half-board. The price difference is determined by the view from the room, the exposure, and the plumbing.

Hotel Excelsior (tel. 31-16-61) can be found in a quiet place in the center of town. It blends attractively into the conifer-dotted lawn around it, with a series of cantilevered balconies over wall-size panoramic windows. Bedrooms are invitingly decorated in comfortable furniture, although your gaze will usually be drawn to the mountain vista beyond your terrace. The hotel has a cleverly decorated swimming pool, where depictions of stylized fish seem to splash in and out of the water. A host of public rooms includes a cozily rustic weinstube and an inviting series of lounges, plus a restaurant and a bar with a dance floor and live music. Oscar Rederer, the owner, directs that Tuesday be reserved for a farmer's buffet and Thursday be held for the weekly gala dinner, which guests at this lively hostelry seem to enjoy greatly. The Bündnerstübli serves à la carte Swiss specialties to guests who want to break their dependence on the board plan.

Half-board rates in a double range between 90F ($41.36) and 160F ($73.52) per person per day, with the most expensive rates being charged over Christmas and New Year's, when a minimum stay of 14 days is required. All accommodations have private baths, although you'll find a wide price difference between rooms with and without southern exposure and balconies. Full board is available for an additional 15F ($5.89) per person per day.

Hotel Eden (tel. 31-18-77) is surrounded by pine trees in the center of Arosa near the cable car and ski lift. The hotel is pleasingly proportioned, with five tiers of weathered balconies and a gridwork design of sunstreaked planking over white walls. A covered skating rink and a Swiss-style ski school are connected to the hotel, which is ably directed by Monique Kühne. Each of the spacious units has its own private bath, radio, and telephone, and all rooms with southern exposure have their own balconies. Inside you'll find a heated whirlpool, fitness room, children's playroom, and a piano bar with live music. The public rooms are accented with marble floors, several Oriental rugs, hanging lamps, and wall-to-wall carpeting.

Prices are always quoted with half-board plans attached, and vary according to the season, the room's exposure, and whether or not it has a balcony. The cost on a *per-person* basis is 90F ($41.36) to 150F ($68.93) per day in winter, with prices at Christmas rising to between 140F ($64.33) and 170F ($78.12). The hotel, by the way, offers ski vacations with *per-person* rates of 720F ($330.84) to 750F ($344.63) weekly in a double and 765F ($351.52) to 795F ($365.30) weekly in a single, including breakfast and evening meals, taxes, services, use of the ski lift and cable car, and 12 half-day sessions at a Swiss ski school. Write for reservations long in advance.

Hohe Promenade (tel. 31-26-51). The views from the terrace of this eight-story balconied hotel look down a hillside into a valley surrounded by jagged mountains. If you have vertigo, you'll want to keep the curtains of your bedroom closed because in any season the mountains seem to loom up into the carpeted space of your private quarters. All the pleasant bedrooms have tiled bathrooms, radios, and phones, while the restaurant is attractively beamed and timbered, with country-red curtains and forest-green upholstery. The center of Arosa is five minutes away by foot, but some of the ski lifts are even closer. The Ackermann family are the owners.

Winter rates are between 65F ($29.87) and 105F ($48.25) in a single. With half board, singles cost between 85F ($39.06) and 130F ($59.74). Doubles go for between 60F ($27.57) and 115F ($52.84) per person; with half board, from 80F ($39.06) to 140F ($64.33) per person. The highest prices are charged at Christmas. Summer rates are 45F ($20.68) to 60F ($27.57) in a single; with half board, 65F ($29.87) to 80F ($36.76). Doubles cost from 40F ($18.38) to 65F ($29.87) per person, with half board going for between 60F ($27.57) and 85F ($39.06) per person.

Sporthotel Valsana (tel. 31-02-75) was recently renovated to offer even more personalized service to the many guests who stay here. The building has five tiers of balconies above a row of high arched windows which direct sunlight into the public rooms. An intimately lit bar area is crowned with an intricate coffered ceiling which rests on top of the beveled pine walls. You'll find four tennis courts on the premises, both an outdoor and indoor pool, sauna and massage facilities, a playground for children, an attractive restaurant, and a weinstube with roughly hewn walls. The dancing-bar area often engages live musicians. The hotel is conveniently located for cross-country skiers and downhill racers and hikers. A kindergarten provides supervised activities for children. J. Kuhn is the director.

Single rooms rent for between 110F ($50.55) and 160F ($73.52), while doubles cost 105F ($48.25) to 145F ($66.63) per person, which includes a rich breakfast buffet and substantial discounts for children (50% if they're under 12). Each room has a toilet and shower or bath, as well as phone, TV connection, radio, mini-bar, and safe-deposit box. The upper regions of the price scale are activated only at Christmas and New Year's.

Hotel Raetia (tel. 31-02-41) is housed in a complex of chalet-style buildings on a pine-covered hillside with its own parking facilities. The decor is at the same time tasteful and rustically inviting, particularly in the intricately paneled Bündnerstube, which, with its thick walls and smallish proportions, looks like something taken piece by piece out of a 300-year-old mountain village. The main salon has the kind of wooden ceiling you'd like to install in your own home, and warmly tinted carpeting leads up to the panoramic windows which look out over the Alps. There are also a Roman Grill, a barbecue room, and a dancing bar with a red tile floor where guests can whirl away their problems. The Hasler-Hofer family are the hosts in this attractively laid-out complex, and their son is employed as the head chef.

Singles in wintertime range from 82F ($37.68) to 95F ($43.65) with half board, and doubles cost from 110F ($50.55) to 150F ($68.93) per person, with half board included, although summer rates are much lower—from 45F ($20.68) to 85F ($39.06) per person regardless of whether it's in a single or a double, with half board. The rooms at the cheaper end of the scale are without private bath.

Hotel Cristallo (tel. 31-22-61). Starting points of many of the excursions to the hills around Arosa are within easy reach of this centrally located hotel. In front, the hotel faces a street in Arosa, but in back it's braced and buttressed against the forces of gravity which threaten to pull it into the alpine meadow below. In fact the building is probably three stories taller from the rear than it is from the front because of its landscaping, although this affords good views from the windows of the rooms. Each of the units has its own bath, radio, TV hookup, and phone. A bar inside often has live music.

In winter this hotel, owned by the Twietmeyer family, charges from 90F ($41.36) to 115F ($52.84) in a single, from 170F ($78.12) to 240F ($110.28) in a double. Prices include half board for each of its occupants. In summer, rates are much lower. With half board, singles cost between 40F ($18.38) and 65F ($29.87), while doubles range from 50F ($22.98) to 60F ($27.57) per person per day.

The Middle Bracket

Hotel Belri (tel. 31-12-37). A first-time visitor to Arosa might consider one end of the village to be a collection of chalets strung out along pathways carved into the alpine meadows. One of these outlying buildings in Arosa doesn't look that much different from its neighbors, except that the Belri is the domain of Fraulein Ly Leonhard, who personally supervises almost everything that happens in her gemütlich hotel. From the outside the establishment looks like an extremely well-maintained fieldstone and varnished-pine oversize cottage, with balconies and blue shutters.

Inside you'll see a fantasy of carved, beveled, turned, and polished knotty pine, fashioned into, for example, baroque corkscrew columns, geometrically patterned ceilings, light-grained wall paneling, and in one of the bedrooms, refreshingly provincial twin beds joined by a double canopy of green-and-white fabric. Some of the bedrooms in the new annex are not as carefully handcrafted, but they nonetheless have more than enough pine paneling and cozy comfort to keep practically anyone in good spirits for his or her holiday. During the winter singles with showers (but without private toilet) rent for between 75F ($34.46) and 80F ($36.76) with half board. Doubles with full baths and half board cost 80F ($36.76) to 95F ($43.65), depending on the exposure. Children receive deductions of up to 50%.

Hotel Central (tel. 31-15-13) is housed in an unpretentious building a few minutes from the train station. The entrance is at one end of the large, recently built complex, designed like a well-proportioned addition to a much larger house. Many of the units have weathered wooden balconies and baths, radios, TV outlets, phones, and mini-bars, and are attractively furnished with a simple collection of upholstered settees and wooden chalet chairs. You'll notice a collection of antique pewter on a shelf near the ceiling of the wood-paneled restaurant, and in summer you'll enjoy the view from the terrace. A fitness center with exercise machines, whirlpool, and sauna offers comfortable relaxation to guests who come here to climb hills, ski, or collect their thoughts. In fine weather, Andy Abplanalp, Jr., the friendly owner, often organizes mountain picnics and excursions through the region for interested guests.

In summer, on half board, singles rent for around 53F ($24.35), doubles for 49F ($22.52) per person. In winter the half-board rate for singles and doubles is from 63F ($28.95) to 113F ($51.92) per person. The highest prices apply only at Christmastime.

Hotel Merkur (tel. 31-16-66). On a quiet winter's night you're likely to hear sleigh bells jingling outside the window of your room, especially since the Merkur is on a quiet street in the middle of the village. From the sidewalk, you climb 12 short steps to arrive in the central lobby of this gemütlich hotel run by Hans Herwig and his family. The pine-covered dining room is accented with highlights of forest green and red, while evening music will usually send many of the guests onto the parquet floor of the rustic dance hall. In the bar, a pianist often performs.

The bedrooms are sometimes covered floor to ceiling with lightly finished white pine boards, with the main color coming from the blue-green mountains you'll see through the window. Many accommodations have balconies and telephones, and there's a wide range of plumbing options, the simpler of which, of course, will make your room cost less. Summer rates are from 34F ($15.62) to 55F ($25.27) in a single, from 32F ($14.70) to 49F ($22.52) per person in a double or triple. Breakfast is included in these rates. The half-board plan costs 14F ($6.43) extra per person per day. In winter, a cheap single without private bath rents for between 43F ($19.76) and 55F ($25.27), depending on the date, while a single with bath rises to 72F ($33.08) in low season and is simply not offered during high season. Doubles cost, on a *per-person* basis, between 40F ($18.38) and 52F ($23.89) without bath, between 64F ($29.41) and 81F ($37.22) with bath, toilet, and balcony or loggia. Half board for persons staying in singles or doubles costs an additional 15F ($6.89) per person per day.

Hotel Streiff (tel. 31-11-17) is separated from the road by a narrow but attractive series of terraced gardens. The hotel is housed in two rectangular buildings which open their many recessed balconies toward the mountains in the distance. Erich Streiff and his family usually have a Swiss flag flying from the flattened rooftop, welcoming guests into their hotel with genuine concern for their comfort. They encourage tourists to take full board here, although a reduction of 8F ($3.68) per person is made to visitors who prefer only half board. Full board per person in winter in a unit with private bath ranges from 72F ($33.08) to 112F ($51.46); in a room without private bath, from 56F ($25.73) to 88F ($40.44). The periods over Christmas/New Year's and from early February to mid-March are the most expensive. Summer rates are cheaper. In July and August, with half board a room with bath costs from 62F ($28.49) to 72F ($33.08) per person; without bath, from 50F ($22.98) to 60F ($27.57) per person.

Hotel Alpensonne (tel. 31-15-47). Five floors of well-proportioned, chalet-style comfort make this small hotel worth trying. Containing only 56 beds, the establishment is in the middle of Arosa, near the ski lifts. The dining room and many of the bedrooms afford panoramic views of the Alps that are simply magnificent. The bedrooms are clean and attractively simple, with highlights of vivid color against pure white walls. Many of the walls are paneled with the knotty pine you'll either come to love or hate by the time you leave Arosa, but the overall effect is very pleasant. In summer, for half board the cost is from 45F ($20.68) to 60F ($27.57) in a single, from 40F ($18.38) to 60F ($27.57) per person in a double. In winter, half board for singles costs anywhere between

74F ($34.00) and 110F ($50.55), while doubles run the range from 64F ($29.41) to 104F ($47.79) per person, depending on the season and the plumbing in your room. The Bareit family are your hosts.

Hotel Belvedere-Tanneck (tel. 31-13-35). The terrace in front of this boxy hotel looks over a ten-foot stone wall to the street below, which despite its route through Arosa gets very little traffic. Don't be misled by the similarities to a concrete bunker with windows: the inside is more comfortable than you'd think, much of it covered with wood detailing and many green plants. The bedrooms, naturally, have incredible views, wall-to-wall carpeting, and wooden ceilings, with curtains you can draw to shut out the southern light if you want to sleep late.

In summer single and double rooms are priced on a *per-person* basis of anywhere from 30F ($13.79) to 42F ($19.30), which includes breakfast. Half board is offered for an additional 13F ($5.97) per person. In winter the price difference widens. Visitors, whether staying in single or double rooms, pay from 45F ($20.68) per person in a bathless, balcony-less room in low season to a high of 115F ($52.84) per person in the best room in the hotel at Christmastime. Half-board plans are available all winter, at an additional 15F ($5.89) to 23F ($10.57) per person, depending on the season. All rooms have radios, phones, and TV outlets.

The Budget Range

Hotel-Pension Vetter (tel. 31-17-02) is a conglomeration of glassed-in verandas, open porches, and wooden balconies all set up over a concrete base, looking a lot like a cube with window apertures. The interior is a cozy blending of wrought iron, heavy timbers set between stucco ceilings, half-round logs with the original bark set up vertically as partitions, and pithy bits of wisdom stenciled in German above a masonry fireplace. A television lounge looks a bit like the waiting room at your family dentist, but everything is clean and comfortable, and in winter in Arosa after a day outdoors that means a lot.

For half board, the bedrooms cost 90F ($41.36) per person in a double with heat, private bath, and toilet. A double with heat but no private bath costs 70F ($32.17) per person. A bathless single goes for 57F ($26.19) a day on the half-board plan. Frau Gritli Vetter, the manager/owner, does everything she can to help her guests. The Vetter is in the middle of town, a few steps from the railroad station.

Hotel Alpina (tel. 31-16-58). Finally, I found in Arosa a budget hotel that looks from the outside like the type of chalet one fantasizes about. There's a lot of hand-carving around the balconies and trim of the steep-roofed hotel with the terraced garden and the ubiquitous Swiss flag on a pole by the entrance. My favorite room is up under the eaves with sloping ceilings on two of the sides and a double window on the third. The walls are covered in flowered wallpaper. The public rooms are accented with various antiques, from a Voltaire couch (just picture a Voltaire chair expanded to seat two) to a baroque clock to painted chests and cupboards. Everything gives off, thanks partially to the efforts of Hans Eberhard, the owner, a contented aura of well-being. You'll be less than 600 feet from the Bahnhof here.

Single and double rooms, with half board, go anywhere from 45F ($20.68) to 65F ($29.87) per person in summer. Winter half-board rates range from 45F ($20.68) to 95F ($43.65) in a single, from 45F ($20.68) to 98F ($45.03) per person in a double. Since the hotel only contains 25 rooms, you'll get a sense of intimacy here, together with your views over the mountains.

WHERE TO DINE: Most guests book into the Arosa resort hotels on the board basis. Nearly all the major restaurants are in hotels—hence the shortage of any well-known independent dining spots. However, if you can break away for one main meal (and assuming you're not already a guest), you may want to try the cuisine at the following highly rated establishment:

The **Hotel Central** (tel. 31-51-13), already recommended, contains one of the better restaurants of Arosa, often attracting guests from the deluxe hotels. It's right in the center of town, serving attractive variations on regional recipes. It's very popular, thanks to such specialties as local trout, a very tasty steak tartare, rack of lamb, scampi maison, tournedos, and frog legs provençal, along with creamed schnitzel with noodles. Fixed-price meals range from 22F ($10.11) to 28F ($12.87), with à la carte dinners costing from 28F ($12.87) to 68F ($31.25). Meals are less expensive at lunchtime.

APRÈS SKI: Since many guests nowadays come to Arosa only for the après-ski activities, the action often continues until the morning hours. As the party-goers are making their way back to their hotels or chalets for much-needed sleep, serious skiers are just getting up for an early run on the slopes.

Several of the hotels, as mentioned, stage special events, and if you call in advance you can sometimes attend if a hotel's own guests haven't taken up all the seating.

Arosa has the usual run of taverns, bars, and gemütlich restaurants. However, the most exciting event, in my opinion, is to take a **sleigh ride** along the famous Arlenwald Road (ask at the tourist office for current details about this ride).

The most popular place in town is the all-around **Kursaal,** which has not only a casino (you can only bet 5F, however), but a Cava Bar for disco dancing, along with a bierstube, movie theater, and coffee bar. It's also the place to drop in for a midnight fondue dinner for two.

Otherwise, one of the most frequented bars in town is at the **Arosa Kulm Hotel,** already recommended. The location is near the Hörnli cableway. The bar, in the management's own words, "brims with nostalgia." The reason for this is that there have been three versions of this hotel—1882, 1914, and 1929—all of which were torn down to make way for the present 1975 version. However, the old bar was rescued and transplanted into the new facility.

The choicest disco in town is at the **Tschuggen Hotel,** which also has a ballroom where an orchestra occasionally plays for more traditional dancing.

The **Hotel Park** in peak season is another lively spot, with an active disco (where a live band often plays), along with pinball machines and a bowling alley.

And if you want something really intimate and cozy, you'll find many quiet hotel bars in town, often with a pianist to put her or him in a dreamy mood. Two hotels that especially welcome nonguests in the evening are Monique Kühne's already-recommended **Hotel Eden,** which most often has live music for dancing, and the **Hotel Carmenna** (tel. 31-17-67).

3. Klosters

Life at this 4000-foot-high village has changed greatly from the time a cloister was founded here in 1222. Today only the name remains to remind us of the previous life of this winter and summer resort lying in the wide Prättigau Valley. Many discriminating winter visitors tell me they prefer Klosters to Davos, finding its smaller size and more intimate ambience attractive, especially to a younger crowd. Also, many people find the Klosters innkeepers more hospitable than those in Davos. The local residents claim that the popular sport of tobogganing originated here.

The main road to Davos runs right through Klosters, which is some eight miles from St. Moritz and has been called a "paradigm of Swiss resorts." The village has few if any ugly structures. All of its buildings are constructed in the chalet style, providing architectural harmony, far prettier than the ugly, eyesore edifices of St. Moritz. Famous visitors of the past have included Sir Arthur Conan Doyle and Robert Louis Stevenson, who is said to have finished *Treasure Island* here, writing about tropical chicanery while surrounded by alpine beauty. In the heyday of tax benefits (earned by stars living abroad) Klosters became known as "Hollywood on the rocks." It still attracts an international crowd, likely to include Gore Vidal, Irwin Shaw, Gene Kelly, and Kirk Douglas.

You'll find some of the finest downhill skiing in the world here, with slopes for beginners as well as for the most advanced skiers. A kindergarten will look after the very young while you hit the slopes. The main part of the village is called Klosters Platz; the smaller, Dorf, site of a superb ski school, is about a mile away. Expert skiers can make the run from St. Moritz to here in just 20 minutes.

Of the two principal areas for skiing, the most popular is the **Gotschna/Parsenn.** You board the Gotschnagrat cableway in Klosters Platz, riding in a car that will carry more than 50 skiers up to the 7545-foot Gotschnagrat elevation. In the peak season, especially around February, expect lines of passengers awaiting transport up. A series of cableways, a chair lift, and 18 ski lifts hook up with the Davos Parsenn skiing areas, where your highest point will be Weissfluhgipfel (9260 feet). The Parsenn area enjoys world renown among skiers and has some of the longest runs in Europe. It offers a variety of more than 14 different cableways and ski lifts, plus more than 85 miles of well-kept runs. A ticket for a whole day for Gotschna costs 25F ($11.49) for adults, 20F ($9.19) for children. To go to the Parsenn area the charge is 34F ($15.62) for adults, 26F ($11.95) for children.

The other major area, **Madrisa,** dates from 1960s. To reach it, you go to Dorf via bus which leaves from Klosters Platz every 30 minutes. From Dorf, the Klosters-Albeina gondola will take you to a height of 6323 feet. Then by drag lift, known as the Schaffüggli, you rise to 7850 feet. The Madrisa ticket for a whole day costs 28F ($12.87) for adults, 20F ($9.19) for children.

Nontransferable Rega (season) tickets are priced according to the number of days you plan to ski.

Horse sleighing, curling, and skating are popular sports for those who don't ski.

In summer you'll find that Klosters is in the center of fine hiking grounds. The Madrisa and Gotschna/Parsenn cable cars will carry you to starting points on both sides of the valley for hikes on well-marked trails through woods and alpine meadows. In Klosters you can enjoy tennis, squash, and swimming in a heated pool.

WHERE TO STAY: **Hotel Pardenn** (tel. 4-11-41) is a rambling modern structure with a flat roof, lots of wood trim, and a low-lying extension containing a tiled indoor swimming pool. A popular sun terrace overlooks the well-landscaped lawn, and in summer vivid flowerbeds bloom between the flagstone walks. Guests reach their comfortable rooms via the green-marble circular staircase. Many of the accommodations are accented with pine paneling, while others contain flowery carpets and Louis XV–style armchairs. Within the establishment are an elevator, sauna, and massage facilities. My favorite bit of the restaurant is the central grill whose smoke is funneled through an inverted copper funnel. You can watch the uniformed chef as he prepares your meal. The 130 well-appointed accommodations rent for between 87F ($39.98) and 182F ($83.63) in a single and between 167F ($76.74) in a double, with half board included. Prices depend on the season and the plumbing.

Hotel Silvretta (tel. 4-13-53) is one of the most elegant hotels in town, housed in an imposing buff-colored building with wrought-iron balconies and pleasingly symmetrical windows. It has a stringently maintained air of the ancien régime. The interior is beautifully wallpapered in rich shades of scarlet, which complement the well-polished woodwork and the white detailing. One of the sitting rooms has a baronial fireplace covered with stone carving, with regional designs in gray and white embellishing its upper half. You'll find comfortable corners here, as well as a warmly decorated bar area with occasional live dance music. Handsomely furnished singles range from 105F ($48.25) to 167F ($76.74), while doubles cost from 175F ($80.41) to 300F ($137.85), with breakfast included.

Chesa Grischuna (tel. 4-22-22) is a very beautiful chalet worthy of the designation of "romantic hotel." A historic building with a four-star rating, it combines a collection of rustic antiques with modern facilities which usually include oversize baths and all the 20th-century comforts you've come to expect. You'll notice lots of original lithgraphs decorating the paneled walls. The overflow from the main house is lodged in a nearby annex. The hotel is closed every year from mid-April until the beginning of June. The Guler family charges from 90F ($41.36) to 165F ($75.82) in a single, while doubles cost between 170F ($78.12) and 320F ($147.04), with half board included.

Hotel Vereina (tel. 4-11-61) is my favorite hotel in Klosters, thanks partly to the attentive efforts of Eva and Stephan Diethelm, the attractive owners. The crowning feature of the exterior is the baroque dome which sits close to the main entrance. Many of the second-floor windows are grandly arched and multipaned, with at least five stories of well-maintained rooms rising above them. Much of the establishment is sheltered with a mansard roof that extends over either one or two floors, depending on which section you look at. Inside you'll find a glass-walled swimming pool and a sympathetic series of public rooms. Something always seems to be happening in the darkly paneled pub, the piano bar, or the dancing bar. The decorator understood the romantic appeal of warmly tinted chintzes and ceiling beams. An elegant restaurant serves good wines and fine food in an intimate ambience of soft lights and aristocratic decor. The entire facility is surrounded by a two-acre park containing fountains, tennis courts, Ping-Pong tables, and a children's playground. The hotel is close to nearly every sports facility in town, and only a few minutes' walk from the railway station. Singles range from 120F ($55.14) to 165F ($75.82), while doubles cost between 90F ($41.36) and 215F ($98.79) per person, with half board included. Prices depend on the exposure of the room, the plumbing, and the season.

Bad Sernens Kur- und Sporthotel (tel. 4-14-44) is a beautifully located yellow house with a solid-looking facade painted in a baroque yellow with black shutters. On the premises you'll find a very attractive swimming pool with big glass windows and a covered loggia above one side. The public rooms are attractively beamed, with clean white walls and regional style gray stenciling. A fireplace blazes in winter. The bedrooms are filled with pine furniture, including generously sized armoires and warmly tinted fabrics. Sauna and massage facilities are on the premises. Since the hotel is set behind a meadow filled with flowers, you'll have lots of opportunities for safely chosen nature walks in summer. The nearby mineral springs are popular for their alleged healing properties. With half board included, *per-person* rates range from 65F ($29.87) to 92F ($42.27), depending on the season, the plumbing, and the exposure.

Hotel-Pension Silvaplana, Klosters-Dorf (tel. 4-14-68), is a very pleasant chalet-style building with reddish shutters only a few color shades different from the weathered wood of the facade. The contrast is attractive, as are many of the other comfortably rustic details about the inside. The hotel is close to the railway station and the Klosters-Madrisa funicular. Tennis courts are a few steps away. Singles range from 48F ($22.06) to 75F ($34.46), while doubles cost from 74F ($34) to 128F ($58.82), with half board included.

Pension Büel, at Klosters-Dorf (tel. 4-26-69), is a small, family-run, L-shaped building with lots of stucco walls, brown trim, and chalet-style balconies. The inside is simple, clean, and rustic. The dining room has a knotty-pine ceiling and chalet chairs, while one of the sitting rooms has a cozy fireplace rimmed with stone and a flagstone floor. The 12 rooms rent for between 52F ($23.89) and 85F ($39.06) in a single and between 76F ($34.92) and 130F ($59.74) in a double, with half board included.

WHERE TO DINE: **Hotel Rufinis,** at Klosters-Dorf (tel. 4-13-71), is a rustic restaurant in a modern chalet near the train station. Inside you'll find a large salad buffet, French cookery, and a grill area that prepares well-presented regional specialties. A garden terrace might be your choice if you're here on a summer day, since the establishment is also billed as a tearoom with excellent ice creams and pastries. A dancing bar contributes to the area's nightlife, charging between 7F ($3.22) and 13F ($5.97) for a drink. While the hotel stays open all year, the disco closes in May, October, and November. The restaurant is as charmingly handcrafted as you'd expect, with waitresses in regional costume. There's enough exposed wood and stone to make you feel safe and cozy. Specialties include a platter of three kinds of grilled meat (veal, pork, and beef), Hawaiian pork (served with a champagne cream sauce and pineapple segments), filet of beef Café de Paris or with green peppercorns, filet of pork in a whisky cream sauce, and several kinds of spaghetti, along with the inevitable raclette and fondue. This attractive establishment is the creation of Thomas Jost and Peter Ruch. À la carte meals range from 25F ($11.49) to 83F ($38.14).

Chesa Grischuna (tel. 4-22-22) is one of Kloster's most popular restaurants, where regular clients return every year at ski season. The walls are decorated with primitive art, regional style. The cookery might be called well-prepared gutbürgerlicht, with such menu items as veal sauteed in a light cabbage broth, omble chevalier (the famous fish from Lake Geneva), and the Zuricher specialty of chipped veal with cream sauce. Among the delectable collection of desserts are apricot mousse with a cold sabayon sauce. Fixed-price meals range from 30F ($13.79) to 45F ($20.68), while à la carte dinners cost from 27F ($12.41) to 67F ($30.79). Reservations are suggested. The restaurant is closed from mid-April to the beginning of June.

Restaurant Alte Post (tel. 4-17-16) is a popular restaurant staffed with friendly locals selected by owner J. Ehrat. Specialties include rack of local lamb with herbs, beef sliced julienne style and served in the Japanese way, and regional veal, pork, and beef dishes. The menu changes with the season but usually costs a pricey 68F ($31.25). In summer the restaurant is closed on Wednesday and during the month of July.

APRÈS SKI: It's quite customary for many guests of the hotels in Klosters to head to nearby Davos for nightlife. Others prefer the more subdued nighttime fun in Klosters itself. Klosters has a good sampling of bars, taverns, restaurants, and a few nightclubs that stir to life when the season comes and snowflakes fill the air.

In fact some people from Davos come to Klosters, heading for such places as the already-recommended **Silvretta Hotel.** Its grill room is one of the best in town, and there's usually a live band playing for dancing in the bar. People often dress up a bit in the evening for this, but nothing too formal. A cozy rendezvous is the cellar bar, called "The Five to Five Club."

Another good hotel choice for dancing in a cellar bar is the **Vereina** (tel. 4-11-61), where Stephan Diethelm is your host. You might also enjoy the drinks, the company, and the piano in its scotch bar.

Perhaps the most favored after-dark gathering place is the **Hotel Chesa Grischuna** (tel. 4-22-22), run by the Guler family. However, it's necessary to make a reservation here for dinner. This beautifully furnished Grisons hotel, in the chalet style, also has dancing.

4. Davos

Davos, a premier Swiss resort, has some of the finest sports facilities in the world, as well as a diversified choice of après-ski life and entertainment such as cabaret, which make it a favorite holiday spot for the chic, the wealthy, and/or the famous.

Its two sections, **Davos-Dorf** (5128 feet) and **Davos-Platz** (5118 feet), are linked by a boulevard flanked with fashionable boutiques, shops, hotels, and cafés. The two sections were once separate entities, but in the last two decades buildings on the land between have obliterated any difference, making Davos today a small city somewhat larger than St. Moritz.

The canton of Davos, a high valley, is the second largest in Switzerland. It's surrounded by forest-covered mountains which shelter it from rough winds, giving it the pleasant, bracing climate that led to its becoming a celebrated summer and winter resort. Davos first entered the world limelight as a health resort when Dr. Alexander Spengler prescribed mountain air for his tuberculosis patients. He brought the first summer visitors here in 1860 and the first winter ones in 1865. There are still several sanatoriums in the general area. Thomas Mann used Davos, lying at the foot of the Zauberberg, as the setting for his book, *The Magic Mountain.* Robert Louis Stevenson was another visitor.

The name Davos (first Tavauns, later Dafaas) entered written history in 1160 in a document in the episcopal archives of Chur, and in 1289 a group of families from the Valais established homes here. In 1649 Davos bought its freedom from Austria. Among the old buildings to be seen in Davos-Platz are the parish **Church of St. John the Baptist,** with a nave dating from 1280–1285 and the remainder, now restored, completed in 1481. A window in the choir is by Augusto Giacometti. The adjoining **Rathaus** (town hall) has been restored. Its paneled Great Chamber (Grosse Stube) dates from 1564. In Davos-Dorf, you can see the 14th-century **Church of St. Theodulus,** and at 1 Museumstrasse is the **Old Prebend House** (Altes Pfrundhaus), the only surviving example of an old burgher's house, now sheltering a local museum.

Skiing for fun was launched here in 1888, but Davos began to appear on the world sports stage in 1899 when a large ice rink was opened for the world figure-skating and the European speed-skating championship competitions. In the same year the Davos–Schatzalp funicular and the Schatzalp toboggan run were inaugurated. Now Davos is considered one of the best ski regions in the world.

On both sides of the valley you're faced with five large ski areas, of which the most noted is the **Parsenn-Weissfluh.** To reach it, you take the Parsennbahn (railway) from Davos-Dorf to Weissfluhjoch (8740 feet), the gateway to the major ski area, with a huge number of runs in every category, especially a few descents leading back to Davos that are suitable for only the most skilled skiers. Round-trip fare on the Parsennbahn to Weissfluhjoch is 22F ($10.11).

From Weissfluhjoch, where there is a restaurant, take the cableway to Weissfluhgipfel (9260 feet). It takes about 2½ hours to reach here from Davos-Dorf. From here you can reach the celebrated Küblis run to the north. The opening of the Parsenn funicular in 1931 opened up the greatest snow fields in Switzerland.

Davos shares its snow with Klosters, which can be a skiing goal for you if you wish, but cable cars and T-bar lift service may keep you happy with the ski opportunities nearer to Davos. Beginners are advised to stick to Rinerhorn, the Strela slopes, or perhaps Pischa, where, if you're graded "intermediate" by your ski school instructor, you may be directed to Jakobshorn.

But Davos isn't only for winter holiday crowds. In summer it becomes a green lure, with first-class tennis courts, sailing and windsurfing on Lake Davos, swimming, and horseback riding. The wide mountain valleys offer opportunities for walking on about 200 miles of signposted paths. There's an 18-hole golf course, and a large indoor ice rink if you want to keep your skills and your skates sharp during the summer months.

You don't come to Davos to visit museums, but there is an interesting one on the top floor of the post office, devoted to **Ernst Ludwig Kirchner,** who lived for a while in this part of Switzerland. This leader of the "Bridge" group of expressionists who gathered in Dresden in 1905 committed suicide in 1938. Entrance to the museum is 3F ($1.38) for adults, 1F (46¢) for children. Hours are from 4 to 7 p.m. daily in July and August, 5 to 7 p.m. on Wednesday, Saturday, and Sunday from September to November, 5 to 7 p.m. daily from Easter to June and on Tuesday, Wednesday, Saturday, and Sunday from December to Easter.

WHERE TO STAY: Davos has more than 20,000 beds for visitors in more than 100 hotels of all categories, including holiday flats, private houses, and health clinics. My personal favorites in a wide price range follow. You can stay either in Davos-Platz or Davos-Dorf. If you're looking for a bargain, read from the bottom of the list.

Staying in Davos-Platz

Steigenberger Hotel Belvedere (tel. 2-12-81) is one of the grandest hotels in the Alps, with fabulously detailed construction in virtually every corner. It sits on the main road of Davos-Platz, in a light-gray classical-style building that seems to go on forever. The vast lobby area has an almost labyrinthine collection of beautifully decorated rooms, usually covered with royal blue and white carpeting. You'll see an intricately carved, pleasingly scaled fireplace that looks baronial, ornate plaster ceilings, a well-polished bar area made of glowing hardwoods, and a collection of well-upholstered armchairs which range in style from the gracefully curving contemporary to 19th-century Victorian.

The hotel was one of the world-famous resort hotels that originated in the last century, dating from around 1875. It was purchased in the 1980s by the

Steigenberger chain, one of the most prestigious in Europe. Today a member of the impeccably suited reception staff will assign you to one of the 150 accommodations which will be, at your preference, designed in either a conservatively modern format of plushly upholstered mahogany, belle époque, or Swiss regional style with pieces made from a local wood called arvenholz.

Even if you're not a swimmer, you should promenade down to the indoor pool, where a collection of massage and sauna facilities awaits you, as well as one of the most beautiful murals I've ever seen. A Tahitian lagoon with flamingos and lifelike jungle plants sway in the imaginary breeze, and seem to grow right out of the waters of the swimming pool. The illusion is helped by the fact that the entire room is well heated. Sports facilities include the three clay tennis courts across the road (for the use of hotel guests only). A band plays every night till 2 a.m. in the dancing bar, and guests have a choice of dining in two restaurants. Singles range from 60F ($27.57) to 185F ($85.01), while doubles cost between 110F ($50.55) and 355F ($163.12), breakfast included. Half board is another 35F ($16.08) per person. Prices differ according to the season.

Hotel Europe (tel. 3-59-21) is a centrally located modern hotel close to the tourist office and the Schatzalp/Strela funicular. It's built in a flat-roofed format of white stucco with horizontal rows of wood trim, which usually correspond to the rustic balconies. The interior is more formal than you'd expect, with an attractive selection of Oriental rugs below the upholstered chairs and the textured ceilings of the main sitting room. The dining room has lots of character thanks to the polished paneling and the many hunting trophies. On the premises you'll find a dancing bar with pink spotlights and live music, a casino, an indoor swimming pool, a fitness room, a sauna, and outdoor tennis courts. The bedrooms are extremely well furnished, often with French furniture and upholstered bedboards. All of them contain private bath, costing between 70F ($32.17) and 165F ($75.82) in a single and between 125F ($57.44) and 315F ($144.74) in a single, including half board. Prices depend on the season and the accommodation you're assigned.

Morosani Posthotel (tel. 211-61-64) is a flat-roofed hotel with a facade that has different balcony-filled indentations, arched windows, and stone corner mullions. The interior is paneled over much of its surface, comfortably carpeted, and filled with rustic touches. A children's playground, an indoor swimming pool, a sauna, and a very appealing bar area are all part of the facilities. Live music is performed in high season. Two nearby hotels under the same management accommodate the overflow from the main building, at roughly the same prices. Singles range from 87F ($39.98) to 185F ($85.01), while doubles cost between 81F ($37.22) and 195F ($89.60) per person daily, with half board included, depending on the season, the plumbing, and the room assignment.

Central Sporthotel (tel. 3-65-22) is a rambling 19th-century hotel built in what looks like many different sections and several different styles, all painted white and gray, and all connected by a ground-floor row of widely arched windows. Many of the accommodations have wooden balconies, as well as big sunny windows and lots of space. Some of them are filled with cambriole-legged armchairs and settees. On the premises you'll find a wood-ceilinged room with a well-lit swimming pool, a sauna, an elegant series of public rooms with occasional live music in the piano bar, and one of the liveliest discos in town. This is in a darkish wood-covered room where many of the vertical timbers are carved into regional designs. With half board included, singles rent for between 65F ($29.87) and 180F ($82.71), while doubles range from 115F ($52.84) to 340F ($156.23), depending on the season and the room assignment.

Sunstar Park Hotel (tel. 3-67-41) is a modern, flat-roofed building with brown-and-white detailing and lots of individual balconies. The structure is set in the middle of a forest of conifers, which pleasantly break some of the angular lines of the exterior. My favorite room inside is the bar area, which has a complicated series of overhead beams and timbers bolted into a modern arrangement in a circular pattern. You'll also find a rustic restaurant, a squash court, a sauna, a swimming pool, a solarium, a beauty parlor, a children's playroom, a dancing bar, and a pool room with video games. Each of the modern bedrooms has a private bath, at rates ranging from 78F ($35.84) to 170F ($78.12) in a single and from 126F ($47.90) to 306F ($140.61) in a double, with half board included.

Sunstar Hotel (tel. 54-54-17) is owned by the same management as the Sunstar Park (see above). The format is much the same, both inside and out, as its bigger sister, only it has fewer sports facilities. Rooms here are cheaper, however. Doubles range from 115F ($52.84) to 250F ($114.88), with half board included. Singles are not offered except in low season, when they range from 68F ($31.25) to 82F ($37.68), with half board included.

Kongress Hotel (tel. 6-11-81) is one of the newest first-class hotels to open in Davos, having made its première in 1982. Its bedrooms are fashioned of blond wood and a collection of fabrics whose colors blend with it beautifully. You'll be just a little bit removed from the center of the village, but many of its enthusiastic clients seem to prefer that, especially since the view from the public rooms includes a wide swathe of greenery just outside the windows. This hotel is inside the Convention Center of Davos, in the same building as the indoor swimming pool complex. Virtually all the sports facilities of Davos are close by. In addition, a public bus stops in front of the hotel for frequent rides to the ski runs. Each of the bedrooms has a private bath, radio, and phone. A sauna is available, and there's also a car park. Singles range from 81F ($37.22) to 145F ($66.63), while doubles cost from 138F ($63.41) to 260F ($119.47), with half board included. The Frey family, the attentive managers, do everything they can to be of help.

Hotel Davoserhof (tel. 3-68-17) is in the center of Davos-Platz, a short distance off the main road. It's a conservative-looking building with four floors of weatherproof windows and stone detailing on the exposed corners. The rendezvous points on the inside (that is, the dancing bar, the two restaurants, and the sun terrace) are all attractively decorated in rustically finished paneling, with lots of atmosphere and even a few antiques. My favorite bedrooms are the ones with the forest-green curtains and the glowing wood on the ceiling and all sides. Paul Petzold and his family, the owners, charge from 62F ($28.49) to 130F ($59.74) in a single and from 108F ($49.63) to 230F ($105.69) in a double, with half board included. Prices depend on the season.

Hotel Ochsen (tel. 3-52-22) is housed in a russet-colored building with recessed loggias that in summer burst into bloom with flowers. It's only a few minutes on foot from the railway station. The lobby area is tasteful, uncluttered, and filled with leather and wood tones brightened by the colors of the Oriental rug that sits on top of the chocolate-covered wall-to-wall carpeting. The restaurant is covered with knotty pine and filled with chalet chairs. The bedrooms repeat the russet theme of the outside, with colorful draperies and upholstery, along with white walls. It's a very attractive hotel, with parking on the premises. The charges are from 47F ($21.60) to 92F ($42.27) in a single and from 47F ($21.60) to 102F ($46.87) per person in a double, breakfast included. Half board costs an additional 20F ($9.19) per person daily.

Hotel Alte Post (tel. 2-54-03) is a simple white building near the Postplatz in the center of the village. You'll quickly notice that someone worked hard to carve intricate designs into each of the overhead beams in the paneled dining room, which otherwise is filled with rustic chalet chairs. There are only 25 beds in the hotel, all of them with private shower although some don't have toilets. Doubles rent for between 35F ($16.08) and 55F ($25.27) per person, with breakfast included. Half board costs an additional 14F ($6.43) to 18F ($8.27) per person daily, depending on the season.

Sporthotel Albana (tel. 3-58-41). Although the outside of this hotel might look a little bleak when snows surround it, the inside opens into a cozy series of wood-paneled rooms where you can get a good meal and a good night's rest. The establishment contains a restaurant and a less formal pizzeria. All of this is about five minutes from the train station. Silvia Ghidoni, the owner, charges from 40F ($18.38) to 71F ($32.62) in a single and from 68F ($31.25) to 120F ($55.14) in a double, with breakfast included. Prices depend on the season and the plumbing.

Staying in Davos-Dorf

Flüela Hotel (tel. 6-12-21). More than 110 years after its opening this comfortable hotel is still in the hands of the Gredig family. The current owners are Andreas and Ruth Gredig, who oversee the maintenance of the establishment with great style. Next to the train station, the hotel is a tall white structure with neon signs on the ground floor, indicating the entrance to the elegant restaurant and timbered grill. A dance bar here is very popular on a winter evening. The bedrooms are well furnished in either attractively formal furniture or cozy and rustic pieces that complement the wood paneling. Other hotel institutions include the informa stubl, which serves raclette and fondue, and the piano bar. Horseback-riding facilities are nearby. Singles range from 120F ($55.14) to 225F ($103.39), and doubles cost from 225F ($103.39) to 435F ($199.89) daily, with half board included.

Derby Hotel (tel. 6-11-66) is a rambling hotel with wood-trimmed balconies facing south over a curling and ice-skating rink. You'll know you're in an elegant hotel as soon as you cross through the grandly arched wrought-iron front door. Construction details include the usual wood-working, polished to a glossy luster, as well as a series of attractive antiques, such as the lyre-backed Empire chairs in one of the sitting rooms. A pianist is often on duty in one of the public rooms. A restaurant is intimately lit and gemütlich, and the rustic, high-ceilinged bar area often has dancing. Bedrooms are modern and balconied, often with separate sleeping alcoves apart from the main part of the accommodation (curtained off). Facilities include two restaurants, a fitness room, a sauna, an indoor swimming pool, massage facilities, a children's playroom, curling, and summertime tennis. The sun terrace is tastefully set under the arcades of the second floor. The Palüda Grill is an elegant rendezvous point with evening dancing. This hotel has been in the Walsoe family for many generations. A single or a double without bath ranges from 80F ($36.76) to 130F ($59.74). A single with bath or shower goes for 110F ($50.55) to 155F ($71.22). Doubles with bath or shower begin at 120F ($55.14), climbing to 170F ($78.12). Rates depend on the season and the quality of the room, the most superior having balconies with southern exposures and a mini-bar.

Seehof Hotel (tel. 6-12-10). A medieval historian mentioned a hotel on this site in the 14th century. Today the establishment is grandly designed around a white-and-gray stone facade to which long rows of wooden balconies have been added. The hotel has a gabled and turreted slate roof. The interior has many of the charming regional wall designs you've probably come to appreciate, especially the vaulted ceiling of the dancing bar area. The bedrooms are sometimes elaborately crafted in a constantly differing set of regional decor. The twin beds, for example, are sometimes set head to toe, railroad style, in hand-painted alcoves. The double beds, on the other hand, often have elaborately carved headboards. Rooms range from 85F ($39.06) to 195F ($89.60) per person daily, with half board included. Singles require a supplement of 10F ($4.60) per day. The hotel arranges a series of special evening events, which are included in these half-board tariffs. On Tuesday it's a gala dinner night; on Thursday, a fondue and raclette evening; and on Sunday, a farmer's buffet.

Sporthotel Meierhof (tel. 6-12-85). The covered balconies of this family-run hotel overwhelm the 19th-century roof peeking out from above them. Much of the outside is covered with greenery, overlooking a pleasant sun terrace set into the grassy lawns. Inside you'll find an occasional antique amid the more modern furniture of the bar and other public rooms. One of the restaurants (there are two) has beautiful paneling, including tall columns fashioned from the same kind of wood as that covering part of the walls and ceiling. Singles range from 80F ($36.76) to 155F ($71.22), while doubles cost between 140F ($64.33) and 260F ($119.47), depending on the season and the plumbing. These tariffs include half board. An extra bed in any accommodation costs an additional 25F ($11.49) per person daily.

Sporthotel Montana (tel. 5-34-44) lies in a sunny position near the train station. Its facade is white, with big arched windows and a gabled roof. The inside has massive beams supporting the roof of one of the taverns, and an elegant lobby area with marble columns and a white plaster ceiling embellished with curved ornamentation. The sun terrace attracts a winter as well as a summer crowd. The bedrooms usually have lots of exposed wood, plus big sunny windows spilling light onto the wall-to-wall carpeting. There's a dancing bar on the premises. *Per-person* rates range from 75F ($34.46) to 130F ($59.74) daily, with half board included.

Hôtel des Alpes (tel. 6-12-61) is a modern, four-story building with a flat roof, a slightly recessed ground floor, and big sunny windows which usually open onto small balconies. The bedrooms are clean and cozily up-to-date. You'll find three restaurants inside—Italian, Swiss regional, and a raclette stube—along with two bowling alleys. Each of the 70 comfortable bedrooms has a private bath, radio, TV, and mini-bar. Singles range between 58F ($26.65) and 105F ($48.25), while doubles cost from 48F ($22.06) to 105F ($48.25) per person daily, with breakfast included. Half board is another 25F ($11.49) per person daily, and an extra bed can be added for between 25F ($11.49) and 40F ($18.38), according to the season.

Hotel Dischma (tel. 5-33-23) has an attractively simple facade of white concrete with brown trim around its three floors of windows. The front of the ground-floor restaurant is marked with well-illuminated red-and-white striped awnings. A disco is reached by entering through a side door in the cellar. The interior is heavily rustic, filled with reproduction chalet beams and chairs along with hanging lamps. The bedrooms are sunny and somewhat cramped, partly because they're filled with comfortably modern chairs and settees. Singles range from 52F ($23.89) to 100F ($45.95), while doubles cost from 98F ($45.03) to 210F ($96.50), with half board included. Prices depend on the season and the plumbing.

Sporthotel Bristol (tel. 3-59-42). Mrs. Bieri is the attentive owner of this attractively old-fashioned building near the ski lifts and the Parsenn. She serves well-prepared food to clients who choose to stay here on the board plan. Rooms are sunny and very clean. Singles range from 60F ($27.57) to 88F ($40.44), and doubles cost between 115F ($52.84) and 161F ($73.89), with half board included.

Sporthotel Bellavista (tel. 5-42-52) is a flat-roofed, five-story, balconied building with wood detailing and an arched entranceway. There's a comfortable collection of public rooms. A fire usually burns in the sitting room and bar area, which is outfitted with Windsor chairs, Oriental rugs, and a simple but cozy collection of furnishings. With half board included, singles rent for between 47F ($21.60) and 115F ($52.84), while doubles cost from 84F ($38.60) to 220F ($101.09), depending on the season and the plumbing. Special discounts are sometimes made in summer for senior citizens who take half board.

Hotel Meisser (tel 5-23-33) is a sunny hotel with a brown-and-white facade accented by stone detailing around the front door and regional designs painted onto the panels between the windows. Some of the accommodations have private balcony. The dining room is appropriately paneled, with a scattering of regional antiques. The hotel is only a few steps from the funicular. Ralf and Kathrin Meisser are the busy owners, charging from 58F ($26.65) to 78F ($35.84) in a single and from 94F ($43.19) to 164F ($75.36) in a double, with half board included.

Hotel Anna Maria (tel. 5-35-55) is a family-run pension off the main road of town. You'll go up a gently winding road until you see this modern balconied building with a southern exposure turned toward the mountains. At the top of a long flight of stairs you'll reach the stone-and-stucco facade. The building is very tall, affording excellent views from the top floors with their redwood balconies. The Buchman family owns this hotel, which is well known to virtually every resident of town. Singles range from 42F ($19.30) to 78F ($35.84), and doubles cost from 72F ($33.08) to 140F ($64.33), with half board included.

Gasthaus Brauerei (tel. 5-14-88). Many local youth groups use this hotel's 60-bed dormitory during their sports outings, yet the chances are that you can rent one of the 20 comfortable beds placed in private accommodations with private baths. A single is 55F ($25.28), a double costs 115F ($52.85). The hotel is a simple white structure with a flowery balcony and a parasol-covered sun terrace. Breakfast in included, and there's a pleasant restaurant on the premises.

Staying in Davis-Schatzalp

Berghotel Schatzalp (tel. 3-58-31) is the ideal choice for those who want to get away from it all. The only public access is by funicular, whose departure point is at the edge of the resort. A concierge on the downhill side will tell you about the availability of rooms (hopefully, you'll have made a reservation in high season). The last car usually leaves at 9 p.m. Aside from the usual access to it, you'll know you're in a special hotel as soon as you see the front entrance. It's an arched wrought-iron door with a Grisons-style gray-and-white foliage painted on the plaster around it.

This is an extravaganza of a hotel, made all the more opulent by its inaccessibility. It has long colonnades where guests can sunbathe even in winter. The terrace and its restaurant are called "Snow Beach." The sunny and well-decorated public rooms almost never seem to end. Many of the bedrooms have exquisitely carved Swiss-style beds, as well as balconies with views of Davos and the Alps. Inside you'll find a heated swimming pool, massage and therapy facilities, a vast wine cellar, and a very good restaurant with painted alpine scenes between the white paneling on this elegant dining room.

Singles range from 75F ($34.46) to 192F ($88.22), while doubles cost between 119F ($54.68) and 350F ($160.85), depending on the season and the accommodation. It's not uncommon for more adventurous guests to return to Davos at the end of their stay on a toboggan. There's a run just outside the hotel. The management will arrange for the transport of your luggage.

WHERE TO DINE: Hublis Landhaus, Kantonsstrasse, in Laret (tel. 5-21-21), is the kind of place where you'll have to drive far out into the country, to an out-of-the-way area between Davos and Wolfgangpass. There you'll find a family-run establishment decorated in a cozy regional style. Felix Hubli and his wife Elfie create a light and savory nouvelle cuisine that seems to have called forth many of their creative powers. Specialties include rack of lamb with wild thyme, beefsteak with home-grown cabbage, turbot in a light mushroom sauce, filet mignon of veal with lime sauce, sliced breast of duckling with Brouilly, and duck liver with leeks. Don't miss out on the fanciful desserts either. These include a changing array of such items as passionfruit soufflé or pastries made with a combination of kiwi and figs. Fixed-price meals range from 65F ($29.87) to 110F ($50.55), while à la carte dinners cost from 47F ($21.60) to 124F ($56.89). Always call ahead for a reservation.

Trattoria des Alpes, 136 Promenade, in Davos-Dorf (tel. 6-12-61). Fish and pasta dishes dominate the menu of this sympathetic restaurant with an Italian flavor. Clients sit on comfortable chairs or on upholstered banquettes, under a ceiling of heavy beams and unusually curved café lights emblazoned with the name of the restaurant. The grilled meats are very tasty, usually cooked to your specifications over a wood fire. Pasta includes tortellini, cannelloni, lasagne, and ravioli. The restaurant is open all day except Monday, and reservations are suggested. À la carte meals range from 25F ($11.49) to 50F ($22.98).

Restaurant Post, Frauenkirche (tel. 3-61-04), is one of the Davos bastions of nouvelle cuisine. Owner and chef Christian Conrad prepares a light array of specialties which include pasta stuffed with fresh mushrooms, goose-liver pâté, turbot in Chablis sauce, mignon of beef with marrow sauce, and a dessert menu filled with such delicate treats as vanilla parfait with fresh black currants. The restaurant is closed on Tuesday and from mid-May until June, and also for most of November. Fixed-price meals cost from 13F ($5.97) to 42F ($19.30), while à la carte dinners stretch from 30F ($13.79) to 60F ($27.57).

Bündnerstübli, in Davos-Dorf (tel. 5-33-93). Very little of the wall and ceiling area of this cozy place is not covered with local scotch pine, polished and mellowed by the presence of hundreds of local diners. The menu reads like a history book of local recipes. The staff might help you translate some of the items, including "Maluns," served with applesauce and local cheese. Other dishes include a fondue with grated potatoes, a richly flavored barley soup, and a daily farmer's menu with copious amounts of simple, well-prepared food served at a reasonable price. You'll also find grilled specialties and a variety of cold platters. The restaurant shuts down on Wednesday. Otherwise, fixed-price meals begin at 13F ($5.97), while à la carte dinners range from 15F ($6.89) to 45F ($20.68).

Europestübli (tel. 3-57-67) is a spacious sunny room on the main street of Davos-Platz. It has light olive-colored tablecloths, a beamed ceiling with maroon panels between the timbers, brass chandeliers, and a friendly English-speaking staff. If you want to, you can dine on a large terrace in front which in summer has red parasols and a view of the street. A backroom opens for business in winter only. The menu has excellent appetizers and soups, and good grilled meats. Most main courses are served with pommes frites, spaghetti maison, or riz Casimir. A good choice might also be piccata with risotto. Set meals range from 20F ($9.19) to 25F ($11.49), while à la carte dinners cost from 30F ($13.79) and up. The restaurant serves from 11 a.m. to 11 p.m.

Restaurant Gentiana (tel. 3-56-49) is housed in a gold-colored building on the main street of Davos-Platz, diagonally across from the Hotel Schweitzerhof. The menu features seven types of fondue, as well as a wide variety of air-dried meats from the Grisons, along with rumpsteak Madagascar, a satisfying selection of hearty soups. A specialty of the house is the apple salad. Inexpensive daily specials are also posted. Fondue begins at 13F ($5.97), while à la carte meals range from 30F ($13.79) and up.

DAVOS AFTER DARK: This resort rivals St. Moritz for the brightest lights in the Alps, with lots of après-ski fun. Drinks cost from 7F ($3.22) to 18F ($8.27), but could go even higher if some special live entertainment has been booked, particularly around New Year's and the Christmas holidays.

Cabanna Club, Hotel Europe (tel. 3-59-21), has a disco with video, live bands, and a series of pink spotlights that make everybody look terrific. Dancing begins at 9 p.m. Sometimes there are cabaret-type shows on a revolving schedule, which you can check at the hotel or tourist office.

Cava Grischa-Kellerbar-Dancing, also in the Hotel Europe, offers the only folkloric nightclub in Davos. Chances are within the hour you'll be swaying to the rhythmic melodies of the flüghelhorn and alpine guitar. Order beer for the evening show, which begins at 9 p.m., followed by dancing.

La Ferme, Steigenberger Hotel Belvedere (tel. 2-12-81), is an elegantly rustic dancing restaurant and bar in the most opulent hotel at the resort. The management prefers gentlemen to wear a coat and tie. The music usually begins at 7 p.m. every evening, lasting until 2 a.m.

Palüda Grill, in the Hotel Derby (tel. 6-11-66), has a dinner-dance every evening in high season beginning at 7:30. The clientele tends to be a distinguished older crowd. There's a rustic ambience in the Grisons style. The bar area offers raclette, apéritifs, snails, and regional specialties from 4 to 6:30 p.m., with beer on tap. There's also a large open grill.

Sporthotel Central (tel. 3-65-22) offers nightly dancing in a vaulted room with wood paneling and dozens of gaily striped chairs and banquettes. Musical groups include such local artists as the Dominoes, which might evoke some nostalgia. Music begins at 9 nightly. Most of the informally dressed dancers are under 30.

Hotel Dischma (tel. 5-33-23) has a disco with live bands who perform all kinds of rollicking music. The place attracts mostly younger people in an ambience of darkly timbered rustic walls and an occasional garland of party decorations. The restaurant serves meals until 11 p.m.

Montana-Stübli, Hotel Montana (tel. 5-34-44), offers a rustically cozy, distinguished ambience to an older crowd who listen to the music from the piano bar.

Davoserhof (tel. 3-68-17) is a disco attached to this hotel, and it's indicated with an illuminated sign leading to a side entrance. The Jakobshorn Club is the name of the place. It attracts a younger crowd of drinkers and dancers, who enjoy the colored spotlights and the logs burning in the massive fireplace. Disco action lasts from 9 p.m. to 2 a.m. Happy hour is every day from 5 to 8 p.m. Dinner is served until closing.

Pöstli Club (tel. 2-11-61) is a Grisons-style nightclub with an international orchestra. It opens at 8:30 p.m.

La Bohème (tel. 5-36-56) is a Grisons-style room attracting a fairly elegant, older crowd. It's considered one of the leading stopovers on the après-ski circuit.

PRACTICAL FACTS: The **tourist office** is at 67 Promenade, Davos-Platz (tel. 3-51-35).

Children's public *playgrounds* are found in the Kurpark at Davos-Platz and opposite the lower terminal station of the Parsenn Funicular at Davos-Dorf.

Buses run from Davos-Dorf to Davos-Platz every 20 minutes from 7 a.m. to 10:40 p.m. all year; every 10 minutes from 8 a.m. to 6:40 p.m. from mid-December till late April. A single ride costs 1F (46¢); a book of tickets for 12 rides, 10F ($4.60). Children ride for half fare.

For information on **curling,** call the Davos Curling Club, 46 Promenade, Davos-Platz (tel. 3-67-30), or the Davos-Village Curling Club, Derby Hotel, Davos-Dorf (tel. 6-11-66). The charge is 10F ($4.60) per day or 100F ($45.95) for a season ticket.

Want to go **swimming?** Call 3-64-63 for information on either indoors in winter or summer or outdoors when it's warm enough. Adults are charged 4F ($1.84) and children pay 2F (92¢), including changing room facilities. With use of the sauna included, adults pay 10F ($4.60).

The **postal bus** leaves from Davos-Platz railway station. Check the timetable for when to show up. Organized excursions are available via postal bus also. For information, go to the nearest post office.

To make a reservation or get information on the **Rhaetian Railway,** phone 3-50-50. Numerous excursions are offered.

Golf course information is available by calling the clubhouse, 5-56-34.

For information on **ice skating** on the Davos-Platz rink, the largest natural ice rink in Europe, phone 3-73-79. Admission costs 3.50F ($1.61) for adults, 2F (92¢) for children. For the Davos-Dorf ice rink, opposite the Parsenn funicular station, phone 5-29-79. Admission is the same as for the Davos-Platz rink.

To reach the **Parsenn Rescue Service,** 7 Lehenweg, Klosters, phone 4-48-48; first aid station Weissfluhjoch, phone 5-38-01. There are SOS telephone stations on all principal ski routes: Pischa (tel. 5-17-28), Strela (tel. 3-67-57), and Gotschna (tel. 4-13-91). For the **Bränabüel/Jakobshorn Rescue Service** first aid station and information, phone 3-59-59; for Rinerhorn, 4-92-58.

5. Scuol/Tarasp/Vulpera

One of the eastermost extremities in this guide is represented by a string of resorts which, viewed as a whole, form a fine holiday center of the Lower Engadines.

Bad Scuol (Schul on some maps) is the leading and most historic center. This old Engadine town, the most active part of the trio of resorts being explored, was for many decades a famous spa, surrounded by beautiful woodland. Lying on the left bank of the River Inn, it's on the major road from St. Moritz to Landeck bypass. Scuol gets lots of sunshine, even in winter, and while many people come here for the treatment of gastrointestinal problems, others come just to relax and have a vacation.

Tarasp, a hamlet in a sheltered locale in the Valley of the Inn, is actually the spa center. The springs here have often been compared to those at Karlsbad.

The most important man-made site in the area is the gleaming white hilltop **Castle of Tarasp,** which commands a view of the valley. The castle is considered one of the most impressive of all alpine strongholds. Dating from the 11th century, it became part of the Grisons in 1803. A Dresden industrialist purchased the castle and restored it in the years before World War I. At present it's owned by the Grand Duke Ernest Ludwig of Hesse-Darmstadt, who uses it as a private residence.

The duke allows guided tours to be given in summer daily from May 15 to the end of May at 2:45 p.m.; weekdays in June at the same time; daily from July 1 to August 20 at 10:30 a.m. and at 2:15, 3:15, and 4:15 p.m.; and weekdays from August 21 to mid-October at 2:45 p.m. Admission costs 6F ($2.76) per person. The castle can be reached by postal bus from Scuol/Tarasp.

You should also visit the **Kreuzberg belvedere** (4846 feet) from which you have an excellent view of the castle as well as of the Lower Engadine.

Vulpera, a mini-resort, is little more than a cluster of first-class hotels, German and Swiss holiday-type chalets, on a terraced hillside alive with flowers in summer. This is essentially a summer resort, but it's starting to make a bid for winter business.

FOOD AND LODGING: **Hotel Belvedere** (tel. 9-10-41) is a salmon-colored extravanza that sprawls across several hundred feet of forested hillside. Because of its six-sided tower, its colors, and its symmetry, it could almost be somewhere in Italy. All of the rooms, both public and private, are unusually spacious. The public salons are covered with paneled ceilings and contain surprisingly informal furnishings. The bedrooms are sometimes painted in cheerful shades of sunny colors and are filled with contemporary pieces. You might want to spend some time on the covered terrace with its art nouveau iron columns. The view of the mountains from here is beautifully tinged with greens and purples. *Per-person* rates with half board range from 70F ($32.17) to 120F ($55.14).

Hotel Guardaval (tel. 9-13-21) is filled with charming touches that make it a really pleasant place at which to stay. A well-placed scattering of antiques (among them an old spinning machine with a small wheel) decorate the public rooms. Most of the lower floors are tastefully accented with light-grained wood paneling which, when coupled with the painted chests, make a very attractive format. The hotel is about ten minutes away from the Motta Naluns railway station, next door to the Trü sports center. It offers a panoramic terrace and a regular clientele that seems to return year after year. *Per-person* rates range from 70F ($32.17) to 115F ($52.84) daily, with half board included. Prices depend on the season and the plumbing.

Hotel Bellaval (tel. 9-14-81). The stonework of the exterior of this building could make any mason proud of his craft. It rises five red-shuttered stories, and is constructed entirely of beautifully textured rocks. It's capped with a red tile roof and has summertime café tables set up on the surrounding lawn. The hotel seemingly could withstand any storm, and that knowledge, coupled with the coziness of the renovated public rooms inside, should make you feel safe and snug. The Willy family charges from 58F ($26.65) to 85F ($39.06) in a single and from 105F ($48.25) to 165F ($75.82) in a double, with half board included. Prices depend on the season.

Pension Silvana (tel. 9-13-54) is an older house in the middle of Vulpera with an undistinguished addition off the back and a glass-walled restaurant stretching like a greenhouse toward the front. A café terrace is sheltered from the road by carefully maintained greenery. This is very much a conservative family-run pension with a popular restaurant on the ground floor. Prices range from 45F ($20.68) to 75F ($34.46) in a single and from 80F ($36.76) to 140F ($64.33) in a double, with half board included.

6. S-chanf and Zuoz

These two Engadine resorts can provide an attractive alternative for living in the region without having to pay the high prices of St. Moritz, which is directly to their southwest. Heading south from our last stopover in the tri-resort of Scuol/Tarasp/Vulpera, I recommend a visit to—

S-CHANF: This village with a most unusual name is a summer and winter resort at the entrance to the Swiss National Park, about 5100 feet above sea level. It's a choice starting point for excursions and tours in the Upper and Lower Engadine and in the park. Valley Trupchun is the park hunting ground abounding in the indigenous game of the Grisons.

S-chanf is a peaceful, relaxing village with easy access to several busy sports centers, including St. Moritz. It lies on the Engadine cross-country ski marathon trail.

After a brief visit here, head directly south to the far more interesting town of—

ZUOZ: This old-world village, once the chief place in the Engadine, lies near the River Inn amid alpine meadows and lush forests, its view of the Inn Valley and mountain range backdrop making it look almost like a stage setting brought to life.

This is the best preserved village in the Upper Engadine, where you can see the most striking collection of Engadine houses to be found anywhere in the valley. The houses appear to be decorated for some festival, but they're like that all the time. The best known is the famed **Planta House** (two houses, actually), on the main square of the village, with an outdoor staircase and a rococo balustrade. The Planta family, historically important in the Grisons, built most of the spectacular structures in town. The slender-towered church merits a visit. Inside, look for the severed bear's paw theme, a heraldic symbol of the Plantas. Augusto Giacometti designed some of the church's modern stained-glass windows. The Planta family bear symbol also appears on a fountain in the main square.

For most of the 1200 inhabitants of Zuoz, Romansh is their ancestral language.

A fledgling summer resort, Zuoz offers tennis, climbing and mountaineering, horse-drawn carriage rides, fishing, swimming, horseback riding, and summer skiing.

At 5740 feet above sea level, this minor winter sports center has a ski school for beginners, including children, as well as for advanced pupils. Experienced skiers will gravitate to the heights of the Piz Kesch region or else journey ten miles by train to St. Moritz. Numerous cross-country tracks lead through Zuoz in all directions, and the village is the finishing point of the Engadine ski marathon. Curling, ice skating, and sledging are other winter sports pursued here.

Because of its location at the entrance of the Swiss National Park, many people use Zuoz as a base for visits to the fascinating habitat of alpine birds, animals, and plants.

FOOD AND LODGING: Both of these tiny resorts offer accommodations and dining rooms, should you decide to stay over.

In S-chanf

Parkhotel Aurora (tel. 7-12-64) has a modern addition stretching toward the front yard, which someone has painstakingly planted with seasonal flowers. The hotel was recently renovated into a format of paneled and gently vaulted ceilings, rustic niches, and Oriental rugs. Even the double-laned bowling alley has a paneled ceiling and an alpine format. Mrs. Dora Langen, your hostess, does everything she can to be hospitable. Singles range from 45F ($20.68) to 88F ($40.44), while doubles cost between 80F ($36.76) and 166F ($76.30), with half board included.

Hotel Scaletta (tel. 7-12-71) is one of the best selections in the moderately priced range. You're welcomed by the Schemmekes-Rocca family, who go out of their way to make you feel comfortable in either summer or winter. Their rooms are snug, cozy, and comfortable, and their food is good and hearty, with plenty of it. This quiet, central hotel is very sports oriented. Half board ranges from 44F ($20.22) to 48F ($22.06) per person daily, a good bargain for what you get.

In Zuoz

Hotel Engiadina (tel. 7-10-21) has seven floors (if you count the double row of gables) and a beautifully preserved baroque facade which is painted a pretty pink. The hotel is more than 100 years old, and is today managed by the Arquint family. The public rooms remain faithful to the style of their original construction, but have been charmingly updated with original murals covering the space between paneled ceilings and half-paneled walls. They show 19th-century gentry amusing themselves on a winter landscape. The management has been careful to preserve some of the original plaster detailing of the ceilings. On the premises you'll find a heated swimming pool, tennis courts, a sauna, curling rinks, a dance bar, plus two restaurants which serve both Swiss and Italian specialties. Singles range from 69F ($31.71) to 123F ($56.52), while doubles cost between 122F ($56.06) and 123F ($85.47), with half board included.

Hotel Crusch'Alva (tel. 7-13-19) is housed in an Engadine-style building, with an uncomplicated roofline, generous proportions, and stone detailing. It's not far from the village church and couldn't be more central. The interior is carefully crafted of fine woods and ornate plaster, with the solid construction you've come to expect in Switzerland. Each of the accommodations has a private bath. This is very much of a family-run hotel, and the Max Klarer family are your hosts. Singles range from 58F ($26.65) to 86F ($39.52), with doubles costing between 106F ($48.71) and 162F ($74.44), half board included.

7. Samedan and Celerina

These twin resorts lie virtually at the doorstep of St. Moritz. Many Swiss and German tourists know of their charms and amenities and seek them out instead of being guests of their high-priced neighbor to the north. Both have been referred to as suburbs of St. Moritz, but that's an unsuitable and somewhat demeaning label, as Samedan and Celerina have much Engadine style, and each has its own special character. First—

SAMEDAN: Originally a Roman settlement, Samedan survived to become a principle village of the Upper Engadine. Over the years many well-known Swiss families have made their homes here. Seek out the **Planta House** (the same family who made its mark on Zuoz), and note its large roof and impressive library of Romansh works.

The village (5160 feet) has its own ski lift and ice-skating rink, plus a ski school. In summer it's ideal for mountain walks and climbing. Visitors can fish or play tennis and golf. When there's snow it's possible to take a horse-drawn sleigh to St. Moritz in less than an hour, and all mountain transportation can be reached in a short time.

Food and Lodging

Hotel Quadratscha (tel. 6-42-57). From the outside this rambling balconied hotel looks like other resort hotels you might see in Europe, but from the inside the painted murals covering some of the walls are authentically Engadine. The lobby is dramatically engineered for a double-tiered effect of natural woods, rough-stone detailing, and big windows. On the premises you'll find a large covered swimming pool, a solarium, a fitness room, and massage facilities, plus easy access to the other sports locales of the village. You'll be able to choose from two in-house restaurants, one typically Engadine, the other more international in its cookery. Each of the bedrooms has a balcony, private bath, phone, and a comfortable decor of simple furniture and huge windows. Singles range from 80F ($36.76) to 130F ($59.74), while doubles cost from 140F ($64.33) to 240F ($110.28), with half board included.

Hotel Bernina (tel. 6-54-21) was built in 1865 and today maintains much of the grand manner associated with it then, although in a vastly modernized format. Its symmetrical facade curves in a gentle arc, embracing a series of low-lying extensions in front. The entire edifice is painted white, with gray accents and Italianate detailing over the windows. The comfortable bedrooms are outfitted in a warmly rustic Engadine style, with patterned carpeting and big windows. On the premises you'll find a tennis court, a dance bar, a summertime terrace, a private park, and an immaculately maintained vegetable garden which supplies the well-staffed restaurant. *Per-person* prices with half board in a double room range from 68F ($31.25) to 118F ($54.22), with a supplement of 7F ($3.22) added to the above tariffs for single occupancy. Prices vary according to the season, the accommodation, and the plumbing.

Hotel Donatz (tel. 6-46-66) has a simple green-shuttered facade capped with a flat roof. You'll see a sun terrace on top of the extension attached to the front, and regional designs faintly painted onto the second and third floors. Inside are a series of wood-paneled public rooms, with intricate carving on some of the horizontal posts and lots of sunlight. A restaurant, La Padella, serves regional specialties in an alpine setting. The paneling of the downstairs extends into many of the bedrooms, which are brightly carpeted and comfortable. Each of the accommodations has a private bath, costing from 66F ($30.33) to 85F ($39.06) in a single and from 120F ($55.14) to 150F ($68.93) in a double, with half board included.

Sporthotel (tel. 6-53-33) is an undistinguished-looking balconied building with a yellow facade and a parking lot a few steps away. The interior is comfortable, with brightly patterned carpeting throughout. The bedrooms have loudly tiled bathrooms, conservatively modern furniture, partially paneled walls, and bright colors. The Luzi family charges between 60F ($27.57) and 90F ($41.36) in a single and between 125F ($57.44) and 175F ($80.41) in a double, with half board included.

Hotel Hirschen (tel. 6-52-74) is a small and personalized hotel which has been run by the same family for almost 40 years. The public rooms are spacious and vaulted, sometimes covered with paneling, and tastefully decorated with stone floors, a scattering of antiques, and Oriental rugs. The bedrooms are pleasing, comfortable, and warmly inviting. Each has its own bathroom. A ground-floor pizzeria offers rustic comfort and musical entertainment. An Engadine manor house, with its 16th-century vaults, is connected to the hotel. Singles range from 60F ($27.57) to 85F ($39.06), while doubles cost between 110F ($50.55) and 160F ($73.52), with half board included.

For dining, try **Le Pavillon** in the already-recommended Hotel Bernina (tel. 6-54-21), a pleasant restaurant with a garden terrace, a dancing bar, and a nightclub attached. Directed by Val Candrian, it serves such delectable items as homemade fresh goose liver and, when available, fresh mushrooms made into several delicious dishes. Fixed-price meals range from 21F ($9.65) to 30F ($13.79), with à la carte dinners averaging about the same. The restaurant is closed from mid-April to mid-June and from the first of October until the first of December. The service is as good as the food. Reservations are advised.

CELERINA: This small hamlet on the River Inn (about 5675 feet) has long been overshadowed by its more celebrated neighbors, St. Moritz, less than two miles away, and Pontresina, about three miles distant. But for those in search of local color, Celerina is a worthy choice as a resort center for a holiday, either in winter or summer. Known for its charming Engadine houses, this little village on a sunny plain is sheltered from bitter winds. Besides the houses, Celerina also has an old Romanesque church, **St. John's** (San Gian), with a painted ceiling dating from 1478. The Romansh name of the town is Schlarigna.

The Cresta run, a mecca for bobsledders, starts from St. Moritz and terminates near Celerina. The village also has ice rinks for curling and skating, a toboggan run, and a ski school.

Several interesting conducted **tours** are offered in summer through the Tourist Information Office (tel. 3-39-66). An experienced guide will take you on an exploration tour through the **Swiss National Park** for 5F ($2.30) per person, or you can join a botanical excursion to see alpine flowers in bloom, 10F ($4.60). Strenuous geological and mineralogical tours cost 17F ($7.81), and you can make an exciting journey from the Diavolezza over the glacier to Morteratsch for 12F ($5.51), with an experienced guide.

Celerina is known for its belvederes which give stunning panoramic vistas. One is **Piz Nair** at 10,000 feet. Departures are from nearby St. Moritz every 20 minutes from 8:30 a.m. to 4 p.m. for a combined fare of 22F ($10.11). You take the funicular to Corviglia, then hike the rest of the way (about 20 minutes on). The circular panorama takes in the Bernina summits.

You can also visit **Muottas Muragl** (8040 feet). From the lower station at Punt Muragl, funicular departures are about every 30 minutes. The round-trip fare is 14F ($6.43). You will have stunning views of the Upper Engadine gap, and in the distance you can see the peaks of the Bernina massif, each with "Piz" in its name. Ibex and marmots inhabit the lofty plateau. You'll probably see them as you take mountain walks.

Food and Lodging

Cresta Palace Hotel (tel. 3-35-64) is a very large building that was probably constructed at the turn of the century. It has three frontal gables that you'll notice immediately, and several smaller ones which contribute to an overall effect of grandeur. The inside contains all the public rooms you'd expect, including a bar and an elegant restaurant, as well as a swimming pool, a sun terrace where (if the weather's right) you might have breakfast, and a skating rink. The bedrooms are brightly colored, with rustic pine furnishings. Singles range from 75F ($34.46) to 179F ($82.25), while doubles cost from 70F ($32.17) to 165F ($75.82) per person. Prices vary according to the season, but always include half board.

Hotel Cresta Kulm (tel. 3-33-73) is an unusually designed hotel, with a series of irregularly shaped indented windows inserted into a white concrete facade. The building is set on a grassy lawn, where summertime guests take chairs out for sunbathing. The interior is filled with modern curves and well-crafted stone floors, white stucco walls, and comfortable furniture. Singles rent for between 65F ($29.87) and 100F ($45.95), and doubles cost from 70F ($32.17) to 115F ($52.84), half board included. Prices, of course, depend on the season. The finish of the famous Cresta run and the St. Moritz Bobsleigh run are in front of the hotel.

Hotel Misani (tel. 3-33-14). From the front, the shape and detailing of this lovely hotel look vaguely like that of an oversize American Federal-style house, except that this one has been painted a dark pink. The building is in the shape of a cube, with heavy molding around the roofline and a symmetrical placement of the white-shuttered windows. The interior has some regional antiques, lots of full-grained paneling, and comfortable and sunny bedrooms. You'll be only a three-minute walk from the ski lifts and cable car. Depending on the plumbing and the season, doubles rent for between 54F ($24.81) and 106F ($48.71) per person daily, with half board included. Residents of singles pay an additional charge of 10F ($4.60) per person daily. Parking is nearby.

8. St. Moritz

St. Moritz is the *ne plus ultra* of winter glamour, a haven for the aristocracy (what's left of it) from Germany and Italy and the gathering place of chic jet-setters who arrive in early February and stay until March. Elegance is the password that admits you to this prestigious resort, and money is the key to participation in the lifestyle that exists here. St. Moritz may well be the most fashionable resort in the world.

On the southern side of the Alps in the Upper Engadine, at an altitude of 6000 feet, St. Moritz (San Murezzan in Romansh, the native language of the area) was originally known for its mineral springs, which were discovered, probably by the Celts, some 3000 years ago. From Roman times through the Middle Ages visitors came here in summer to experience the curative powers of the spring waters. The then-tiny hamlet first appears in written history in an official document referring to the sale of the Upper Engadine by a count to the bishop of Chur in 1138. It was first referred to as a spring by the Swiss-born alchemist and physician known as Paracelsus.

Use of the spring waters was a summer pursuit, and it was not until 1834 that the first winter guest stayed in the area. The first skiers appeared on the Upper Engadine scene in 1859 (the natives thought they were nutty), and in 1864 a pension owner brought a group of English people to St. Moritz to spend the winter, starting what has grown into a flood of tourism.

Although snow skiing in all its forms is the premier sport engaged in in this resort area today, other winter sports activities, including curling, ice skating, tobogganing, bobsledding, and an early form of ice hockey were enjoyed by most winter visitors in the last part of the 19th century. With the introduction of competitive skiing and ski jumping, this sport forged ahead in popularity and is likely to remain in the no. 1 spot.

Winter is now the top season in St. Moritz, with its "champagne climate" and attractions for top-flight winter sports figures drawing a cosmopolitan and very well-heeled clientele annually. Long a favorite of movie stars, St. Moritz also attracts persons prominent in the higher economic, cultural, and political echelons of the Western world. Then, too, as the author Peter Viertel once wrote, it attracts "the hangers-on of the rich . . . the jewel thieves, the professional backgammon players and general layabouts, as well as the high-class ladies of doubtful virtue (if such a thing still exists)."

The world's oldest ski school is at Moritz-Dorf, founded in 1927. A total of five ski complexes encircles St. Moritz, the nearest being Corviglia–Piz Nair, which has some challenging, mile-long runs back to the base. There's an abundance of snow in winter on 250 miles of downhill ski runs, 100 miles of cross-country ski trails, and the Olympic ski-jumping hill. For skiing here, you have a choice of five mountains, all of which can be skied on one lift pass. Corvatsch, with 5800 feet of height, is known for the open-bowl skiing which is possible on top. Corviglia has broad runs attracting fledgling and intermediate skiers and is the staging area for skiing Piz Nair, the highest skiable mountain, 10,837 feet, with a vertical drop of 4748 feet. Nearby, in Pontresina, a neighbor resort to be visited in the next section, are the steep Piz Lagalb and Diavolezza with skiing for all levels of experience, including a run over the Morteratsch glacier.

In all, St. Moritz has a total of 34 gondolas and 60 ski lifts as well as mountain railways. A ski pass costs $94 (U.S.) for adults, $70 for children.

The groomed and tracked cross-country runs in the Upper Engadine valley include a tame one-mile loop near the cross-country center, and trails are laid out between the valley resorts. A one-mile segment is lit for night skiing. The Engadine cross-country ski marathon is a major annual event. And of course, in this chic and elegant ambience, the après-ski social activities are always special.

Horse racing on the frozen lake of St. Moritz is also popular, or you can take taxi rides on the bobsled natural-ice run. There are 30 curling rinks, winter golf played on the frozen lake, and tobogganing on the Cresta run. Indoor tennis and squash can be played.

Instruction in cross-country skiing, available in groups on Monday, Tuesday, and Wednesday from 10 a.m. to noon, costs 18F ($8.27) for a half day, 34F ($15.62) for two half days, and 48F ($22.06) for three half days. Private lessons of 55 minutes each given from 1 to 2 p.m. cost 40F ($18.38). A day's excursion costs 25F ($11.49).

If you're interested in curling but don't know how, you can have a first training session free (40 minutes). Individual lessons thereafter cost 20F ($9.19). Playing for half a day will cost 10F ($4.60), but the stones and broom per set comes to 20F ($9.19).

A bobsled ride costs 95F ($43.65), but you get your picture taken (for you to keep), a drink, and a certificate in addition to the ride.

The spa section of this resort is called **St Moritz-Bad,** where you can take mud and carbon dioxide mineral-water baths, physical therapy, and physiotherapy while you enjoy the stimulating alpine climate in a modern Health Spa Center. From Roman times to now, "taking the waters" has been a popular pursuit for persons seeking natural curative treatment for relief from pain and stress. The charge for a mineral-water bath is 17F ($7.81); for a peat-mud bath, 28F ($12.87); and for a massage, 36F ($16.54). For additional treatments you can get a special price list.

In summer, in this area with 25 sparkling mountain lakes, there are many pursuits for visitors, including walking on scenic panorama trails. A rich cultural program and all types of sports activities are offered.

Windsurfing at St. Moritz and on the lakes of nearby resorts has boomed in popularity, with the Engadine surf marathon in July drawing competitors from all over the world. The lake is also a **sailboat** lure. Rentals for a one- to three-person sailboat are 20F ($9.19) to 35F ($16.08) for an hour, 40F (18.38) to 70F ($32.17) for half a day, 70F ($32.17) to 130F ($59.74) for a whole day, or 200F ($91.90) to 350F ($160.80) weekly (Monday to Friday). A motorboat taxi ride costs 40F ($18.38).

Greens fees on the 18-hole **golf course** are 35F ($16.08) on weekdays, 40F ($18.38) on Saturday and Sunday. Rates at the 25 tennis courts vary. Excursions to **Diavolezza-Morteratsch** cost 12F ($5.51) for adults, 6F ($2.76) for children. There's also summer skiing on Corvatsch, costing 30F ($13.79) for all day, and on Diavolezza, 21F ($9.65) for a half day.

You can get a glimpse of the history of St. Moritz and the Engadines by visiting the **Engadine Museum,** open from mid-June until the end of September on weekdays from 9:30 a.m. to noon and 2 to 5 p.m., on Sunday from 10 a.m. to noon. For the remainder of the year it's open only Tuesday to Friday from 2:30 to 5:30 p.m. Admission is 2F (92¢) in summer, 3F ($1.38) in winter. Here you will learn about *sgraffito* (designs in plasterwork) on Engadine buildings, local styles of architecture, and see a collection of Engadine antiques and regional furniture. The elegantly decorated state room shows how noblemen in the area lived. Artifacts from the Bronze Age when Druids lived in the land are also on display, including the 3000-year-old encasement of the spring of Mauritius. St. Moritz stands on a former "mystic place" of the Druids.

Segantini Museum displays works by the artist Giovanni Segantini of Savognin, another little resort hamlet to be visited later in this chapter. He died at the end of the 19th century. Segantini's works are beloved by the Swiss. His most important work is a triptych called *To Be, To Pass, and To Become.* The museum is open weekdays from 9 a.m. (10 a.m. in winter) to 12:30 p.m. and 2:30 (3 in winter) to 5 p.m. On Sunday it's open from 10:30 a.m. to 12:30 p.m. and 2:30 to 4:30 p.m. (3 to 5 p.m. in winter). It's closed on Monday. Admission is 3F ($1.38).

PRACTICAL FACTS: The **Kur- und Verkehrsverein** (tourist office) in St. Moritz may be visited or phoned (tel. 3-31-47) for a wealth of information.

Day **nursery care** for children costs 8F (3.68) for a half day, 10F ($4.60) for a whole day without lunch, 13F ($5.97) with lunch. Ask at the tourist office for nursery locations.

Fishing may be done only by persons over 16, with special permission.

You can arrange for excursions by postal bus at the post office.

SHOPPING: St. Moritz has a concentration of boutiques and shops rivaling those of Paris and London, with prices in line with those charged in the big cities. You can stroll along the inner village streets and find all the shops easily. Some of the most important ones are on the **Via Maistra** (main shopping street) and in the **Palace-Arcades.**

You'll find dozens of fashionable bars and cafés, and St. Moritz is a place where women wear "fun furs." If you don't have any with you, you can certainly purchase them here.

Relax with a cup of coffee and a piece of pastry in one of the world-renowned *Konditoreien* (coffeehouses).

WHERE TO STAY: St. Moritz is well equipped with accommodations, with dozens of hotels, pensions, and chalet-style apartments. But because it's expensive, you may prefer to anchor in at one of several neighboring resorts, such as Pontresina, Silvaplana, Sils Maria, Samedan, or Celerina, all of which are recommended in this chapter. For those who want to be right in the heart of the action, here goes:

The Deluxe Choices

The **Palace Hotel** (tel. 2-11-01) might be a pastiche of seven or eight building styles ranging from medieval Teutonic to art nouveau, but regardless of any confusion about architecture, the Palace is known in powerful circles around the world as one of *the* most desirable resorts. It was built by Caspar Badrutt, who was supposedly the first hotelier in Europe to install private baths in the more expensive suites, an unheard-of luxury at the time.

Today the Great Hall could be called the electrical connection of the haute monde's most delicious exchange of gossip, and the scene of an occasional quietly intense game of bridge. On the grounds is a big outdoor pool, tennis courts (which become skating and curling rinks in winter), a well-equipped gym, a sauna, and a masseur. On the premises you'll find no fewer than five restaurants, ranging from the very formal where a dark suit is required for men (but many go in black tie) to a less formal salon with a view of the pool. The paneling from one of the more rustic dining rooms was imported almost intact from a house built in 1480.

Elizabeth Taylor might be among the more famous people visiting here, but everyone still speaks about the visits of Onassis during the Maria Callas period.

Today the hotel will help to arrange rail transport on a private line for passengers who embark at Chur. Meals are served in a vintage 1930s dining car covered with mahogany. The excellent service in the car is a precursor of what awaits you at the hotel. Of course, the management will dispatch a private limousine if you want.

If you're traveling with children, you can leave them with an in-house kindergarten teacher, or with a resident swimming, skating, or tennis coach, or a member of an well-organized babysitter service.

One of the mottos of the management is "your room is your palace." At the prices charged, you'd certainly expect that! Singles cost from 160F ($73.52) to 440F ($202.18) while doubles range from 285F ($130.96) to 680F ($312.46) daily, with half board included. These rates are only for the small and medium-size rooms. Tariffs for the large doubles and a plethora of suites are available only on request, and in peak season they spiral into the horrifyingly expensive upper strata.

Kulm Hotel (tel. 2-11-51) is an elegant collection of three buildings, the oldest of which was built around 1760. The hotelier who took it over in 1856 was named Joseph Badrutt, and he's credited with the imaginative effort of getting British visitors to come to the Alps in wintertime, thereby launching a major industry. Residents claim that it was during this period at the hotel that skiing, curling, bobsledding, and Cresta (skeleton) was introduced to middle Europe. Today a large part of the bob run, Cresta run, and curling rinks of St. Moritz are on the grounds of this historic hotel, which was also the first building in Switzerland to be lit by electric lights (1878).

Since then the Kulm has witnessed the arrival and departure of royalty from all over the world, including the kings and queens of industry and entertainment. It was the center of the Olympic Games in 1928 and 1945. Today the Sunny-Bar is one of the most popular rendezvous points in town (usually with live music). The public rooms are beautifully paneled, and left in their natural grain with occasionally vaulted ceilings. In the case of the elegantly high-ceilinged dining room, the ceiling was painted a light-reflecting ivory. One of the salons has pumpkin-colored walls and dazzlingly white detailing which emphasize the Doric columns and the molded ceilings.

On the premises are an indoor swimming pool with views of the mountains, a sauna, massage facilities, tennis courts, and an ice rink. There's also a children's playground with a playroom. *Per-person* rates in a double with half board range from 120F ($55.14) to 305F ($140.15). Single occupants pay a supplement of 10F ($4.60) to 15F ($6.89), depending on the season.

Carlton Hotel (tel. 2-11-41) sits in a position regally isolated from the rest of the village. With a view of the lake and the mountains, it's one of the loveliest hotels in St. Moritz. It has a château-like facade covered with ocher paint, bay windows, and balconies. A gloriously elegant set of public rooms gives off a formalized kind of warmth and well-being. Aside from the plaster and wood-paneled detailing, the best part about the sitting room is the tall and narrow fireplace, covered with classical designs and bas-relief that stretch up to the ceiling. Sporting facilities on the premises include a large glass-walled swimming pool with a wood ceiling and tile floor, a skating and curling rink, a sauna, and massage. You'll find three in-house restaurants, plus a disco with live music. Free bus service is available to ski lifts and the center of town. *Per-person* rates, double occupancy, range from 97F ($44.57) to 275F ($126.35), breakfast included, depending on the season. All accommodations contain private baths. Singles require a supplement of 20F ($9.19).

The Upper Bracket

Chantarella House (tel. 2-11-85) is a palatial 19th-century building set 500 feet above the resort. It's designed like a château, with a round tower rising vertically from one end and an enormous expanse of arched and balconied windows looking over a wide expanse of grass. A concert orchestra and dance band provide music for guests who enjoy the ample sunlight on the open-air terrace. The public rooms are outfitted with comfortable and practical furniture. You have to reach this hotel by funicular from the village below. A three-minute ride leaves from 7 a.m. to 1 a.m. On the premises are a skating and curling rink, and there's nearby access to miles of mountain trails. The hotel is open only in winter, when it charges from 90F ($41.36) to 185F ($85.01) in a single and from 160F ($73.52) to 345F ($158.53) in a double, with half board included.

Hotel Monopol (tel. 3-44-33) has a white stucco facade built within the last 20 years, with an occasional bay window extending above the busy street below. Inside you'll find a nightclub and restaurant (the Grischuna), and an elegant series of public rooms furnished with French-style pieces, a few oil paintings, and well-polished wood detailing. The spacious bedrooms are colorfully designed around Louis XV, Louis XVI, or rustic furniture. There's a large covered pool on the top floor, along with a sunny roof terrace. Each of the accommodations has a private bath, costing between 83F ($38.14) and 193F ($88.68) in a single, between 150F ($68.93) and 415F ($195.29) in a double, with half board included. Prices, of course, depend on the season and the room assignment.

Hotel Crystal (tel. 2-11-65) is a large white building with curved corners that looks oddly futuristic when you see it next to the 19th-century buildings around it. The interior combines comfortable alpine rusticity with knotty-pine cabinets and ceiling beams, along with such up-to-date touches as wall-to-wall carpeting and cozy informal furniture. The bedrooms are outfitted with a combination of walnut and lighter grained woods, along with an occasional carved headboard. The in-house Grotto restaurant serves Italian specialties. A nearby piano bar provides midafternoon entertainment. Residents have free access to the swimming pool in the neighboring Kulm Hotel. With half board included, singles range from 105F ($48.25) to 175F ($80.41) and doubles cost from 175F ($80.41) to 315F ($144.74). All accommodations contain private baths.

Hôtel Belvédère (tel. 3-39-05) is on the main road of town, between St. Moritz and St. Moritz-Bad. In the lobby you'll see some antiques, Oriental rugs, stucco arches, and tile steps. The lake side of the hotel retains the Victorian bay windows that were part of the original design. However, the road side (which is the first part you'll probably see) has been unattractively remodeled with a buff-colored stucco facade which, while practical, gives no hint that the hotel is as old as it is. Erwin Degiacomi and his family charge between 70F ($32.17) and 115F ($52.84) in a single and between 130F ($59.74) and 220F ($101.09) in a double, with breakfast included.

Hotel Schweizerhof (tel. 2-21-71) has been owned since it was built in 1896 by the von Gugelberg family. It's considered one of the ten best hotels in town. Its lobby is built in a transitional style that might be art deco or art nouveau, but is nonetheless extravagant in its use of plaster detailing and glowing woods. The establishment contains three bars, one restaurant, a sauna, a fitness room, and lots of niches and cubbyholes where, drink in hand, you might have a few intimate conversations. The rooms, spread out over five floors, cost between 85F ($39.06) and 195F ($89.60) per person daily, with half board included. These rates are for either single or double occupancy, and depend on the season and the room assignment. All the units contain private bath, radio, phone, and mini-bar.

Hotel Steffani (tel. 2-21-01) was built in 1869 by a man named Steffani. It eventually ended up in the hands of the Märky family, who today welcome an elegant clientele into the rustic lobby where beams resembling railroad ties form the balconies of the two-tiered lobby. If you like soft-grained woods carved into regional designs, you'll find plenty of it here, especially in one of the restaurant areas. The management added a fitness room and an indoor swimming pool in the winter of 1982. Doubles range between 55F ($25.27) and 130F ($59.74) per person daily, depending on the season (breakfast is included). Singles require a supplement 5F ($2.30) to 15F ($6.89), depending on the season. Half board is offered for an additional 15F ($6.89) to 25F ($11.49) per person daily.

Hotel Albana (tel. 3-31-21). A hostelry was established at this site in 1644, although the building you see today has been under the same management since 1971. This is a very popular hotel, painted a salmon color with white trim, and decorated inside with regional designs and an occasional hunting trophy. The ceilings are rustically beamed and painted, the bar area has stenciled primative illustrations, and the lobby is filled with leather sofas, and lots of wrought iron and room dividers. On your way to your bedroom you'll probably pass a suit of armor and stenciled pieces of history and pithy wisdom written on the stucco walls. The bedrooms are rustically elegant, usually with ceiling beams or elaborate paneling and an occasional regional armoire. On the premises are a sauna, fitness room, whirlpool, two restaurants, and a bar. Heinrich Weinmann and his family, your hosts, charge between 85F ($39.06) and 180F ($82.71) in a single and between 65F ($29.87) and 175F ($80.41) per person in a double, with half board included. Prices vary according to the season and the exposure of the room assigned.

Neues Posthotel (tel. 2-21-21) is one of the few establishments with a lobby which could in itself be a visitor's social center during his or her stay in St. Moritz. Invitingly furnished, with lots of wood, the hotel has a blazing wintertime fireplace. There are lots of comfortable armchairs, and in all, the place is designed for conviviality. The restaurant has savory food and a good view of the lake through the pointed arches of the huge windows. A smiling cherub greets you inside the front door of this gracious hotel, where doubles with half board included rent for between 60F ($27.57) and 170F ($78.12) per person, with a single supplement ranging from 10F ($4.60) to 15F ($6.89) extra.

The Middle Range

Hotel Soldanella (tel. 3-36-51). The comfortable and fairly spacious bedrooms are weatherproofed in a way that any North American homeowner would be wise to imitate. The doors and windows are both double-hung, which of course adds to the soundproofing as well. The stairwells are decorated with Oriental rugs, and curve around the wrought-iron bars of the old elevator shaft. The reception area opens onto a bar beautifully paneled in polished pine with carefully crafted trim. A curved row of bay windows at the far end allows lots of sunlight to flood into the room. If you choose a half-board plan, you'll have your meals served in the sunny downstairs are nouveau dining room, which has a view of the lake and some turn-of-the-century steel chandeliers. There's limited parking in front of the hotel. The *per-person* rates, with half board, range from 65F ($29.87) to 125F ($57.44) daily, depending on the season.

Hotel Languard (tel. 3-31-37) is a sunny family-run hotel a few buildings away from the main street of town. It has a thermometer with three different gauges set into the granite of the entryway, so you can check the day's temperature before leaving your room every morning. Its pine-paneled interior is clean and very charming, with a breakfast room that overlooks the valley and the lake. The staff is old-fashioned, very Swiss, and conservative, but willing to make your stay as comfortable as possible. Some of the accommodations have private balconies, and many contain private baths as well. The Trivella family charges between 54F ($24.81) and 76F ($34.92) in a single and between 44F ($20.22) and 88F ($40.44) per person in a double, depending on the season. Breakfast in included in the price. The hotel is usually closed during all of May and November.

Hotel Bellevue (tel. 2-21-61) is a white and buff-colored building with an occasional balcony to relieve the unadorned boxiness of its facade. Some of the public rooms extend along one of its sides, with panoramic views which justify the hotel's name. The inside is functionally attractive, with patterned carpeting, the obligatory paneling over some of its surface, and comfortable bedrooms with wood-grained furniture, sometimes upholstered in leather. Doubles rent for between 53F ($24.35) and 105F ($48.25) per person daily, with breakfast included. Singles cost an additional supplement of 15F ($6.89) to 23F ($10.57) per day, depending on the season and the room assignment.

Sporthotel Bären (tel. 3-36-56). My favorite part about this hotel is the 54-foot swimming pool with the fireplace set where another hotel might have placed a diving board. The other public rooms are tastefully decorated with Oriental rugs and ceiling beams, with a lot of rough-hewn stones set into decorative areas to remind you that the mountains are indeed very near. Bedrooms are simple and comfortable, usually with views out over the hillside where the hotel is planted. *Per-person* rates with half board range from 80F

($36.76) to 125F ($57.44) daily, with an additional supplement of 10F ($4.60) required for residents of single rooms. Each of the accommodations has a private bath.

Hotel Eden (tel. 3-61-61) is a very pleasant hotel off a quiet street in the center of town. It was built more than 100 years ago, and has been in the Degiacomi family for the past 28 years. It has 50 modern and comfortable rooms, all with private bath. A covered skylight in the wood-and-stucco lobby illuminates the intricate wrought-iron balustrades of the upper two stories. *Per-person* rates, with breakfast, range from 55F ($25.27) to 90F ($41.36) in a double, with an additional charge of between 5F ($2.30) and 9F ($4.14) for a single.

Hotel Nolda (tel. 3-64-33) is a stucco building with a front section partially covered with weathered paneling. It has grandly arched ground-floor windows and a riverside location next to a cable car and one of the popular ski runs (Corviglia). The interior is heavily beamed and filled with Engadine-style designs around some of the fireplaces and around the cozy bar area. The spacious lobby has curved banquettes of leather-covered couches. The sunny bedrooms rent for between 60F ($27.57) and 170F ($78.12) in a single and for between 45F ($20.68) and 110F ($50.55) per person in a double. Triples cost from 45F ($20.68) to 90F ($41.36) per person. All accommodations contain private baths, and are priced according to the season and their size. Half board goes for an additional 25F ($11.49) per person daily.

Budget Living

Hotel Bernina (tel. 3-60-22) is very close to the lake in St. Moritz-Bad. It has a pleasant, earth-colored lobby with warm textiles and lots of wood. Its format is low-key and unpretentious, with a reception area you'll reach after crossing through a cozy restaurant. This has been under the management of the Herrman family for several generations. They charge between 55F ($25.27) and 175F ($80.41) per person in a double, between 45F ($20.68) and 80F ($36.76) in a single, with half board included. Prices, of course, depend on the season.

Hotel National (tel. 3-32-74) is an old-fashioned, symmetrically proportioned hotel with neoclassical detailing around its windows and wrought-iron balconies. The interior has a scattering of Oriental rugs and informal furniture. *Per-person* rates with half board included range from 65F ($29.87) to 80F ($36.76) daily.

SJH Stille (tel. 3-39-69) is one of the biggest youth hostels in Switzerland. It has 40 bedrooms with four beds apiece and 15 accommodations with two beds apiece. You'll find it in St. Moritz-Bad, at the end of the Via Surpunt. Each of the units has a sink, with toilets and showers on each floor. Accommodations cost 12.50F ($5.74) a night.

WHERE TO DINE: Chances are, you'll be staying on some sort of boarding arrangement at your hotel, but you may want to escape occasionally for a change-of-pace meal, if only to sample the wares at another hotel. There are also some good independent eateries in St. Moritz.

Chesa Veglia (tel. 3-35-96). Chesa means "house" in Romansh, and that's exactly what this Engadine-style building once was. Built of stone, stucco, and carved hand-hewn wood in 1658, it still retains much of its original paneling and carving, as well as entire rooms removed piece by piece from the houses of constantly feuding local leaders who would be horrified if they knew that many of their possessions are today under the same roof. You'll enter a massively arched door made of carved oak, and there you'll find two bars and three restaurants, each on a different floor, all of them rustically decorated. The Chadafö Grill cooks your meat over a wood fire visible from the dining room. The Patrizier-Stube and the Hayloft offer regional specialties and Viennese cookery. Local musicians will probably be playing folkloric music while you eat, which many clients consider reason enough for coming here. This is, by the way, the only authentically Engadine house remaining in St. Moritz. À la carte meals range from 40F ($18.38) to 80F ($36.76), and might include foie gras Chesa Veglia, veal steak Chesa Veglia, or caviar Chesa Veglia. The restaurant is closed from the beginning of April till the end of June and from mid-September until the beginning of December. It's owned and operated by the Palace Hotel.

Restaurant Chesa Pirani, La Punt-Chamues (tel. 7-25-15), is a charming Engadine-style house about 12 miles from the center of St. Moritz. The Hitzbergers are the attractive couple who have set up this first-class restaurant with excellent cuisine and service. You'll be shown into one of a series of dining rooms, none of them holding more than four or five tables. Mr. Hitzberger prepares his original recipes in the kitchen, and these might include an avocado salad with shrimp and a sour vinegar sauce, a delicate cabbage soup, foie gras made by himself, and a wide range of seafood along with lamb cutlets in a goulash sauce. The quiet dining rooms are supervised by Mrs. Hitzberger, who spares no effort to be of service. Dessert might be a champagne sorbet. À la carte meals range from 70F ($32.17) to 110F ($50.55), while fixed-price dinners cost between 70F ($32.17) and 87F ($39.98). The restaurant is closed on Monday and on Tuesday for lunch. Otherwise it's open from 11 a.m. to 3 p.m. and 6 p.m. to midnight. It's also closed the last week in April until mid-June.

Corviglia (Marmite), Bergstation (tel. 3-63-55). You'll need to take the funicular to reach this woodsy restaurant, and once you're there you'll probably be tempted to ski home after your meal. The locale is appropriately rustic, with excellent service and a sophisticated menu choice offered by the Mathys family. There's also a less expensive cafeteria on the premises which in midwinter is usually crowded with skiers. A meal in the more elegant room will range from 30F ($13.79) to 45F ($20.68) à la carte. It might include grilled salmon, calf foot in a truffle sauce, or a bone-warming bouillon, perfect for a cold day, flavored with marrow, vegetables, sherry, and meat. If you're in the mood, you might ask for the six-course caviar menu (the caviar even goes into the potatoes), or else a seafood omelet. Desserts might be figs soaked in a liqueur called grappa, although a buffet is available if you prefer a less potent dessert. The restaurant is open daily from November 20 until April 20 and from early June until mid-October.

Rôtisserie des Chevaliers, Hotel Kulm (tel. 2-11-51), is the dining room of one of the most historic hotels in St. Moritz. In addition to the square yards of exquisite paneling, there are mementos of the Cresta bobsled run decorating some of the walls outside the main room. The smaller of the two menus lists changing daily specialties which include seasonal food such as asparagus, along with terrine of goose liver, lobster bisque flambeed with champagne, grilled seabass flambé, and a unique stuffed veal Hotel Kulm. Dessert might be an apple sherbet or a flambeed fruit. The restaurant is closed from mid-September until the end of November and from mid-April until the end of June. Fixed-price meals range from 38F ($17.46) to 48F ($22.06), while à la carte dinners stretch from 32F ($14.70) to 80F ($36.76).

Veltliner-Keller (tel. 3-40-09). Evening meals are served on the elegant first floor, where many of St. Moritz's wintertime ski bums always seem to have a good time. Specialties include mushroom salad, trout with mushrooms, spaghetti, a wide selection of meats and fish, along with a tasty risotto. Desserts include just about every in-season fruit in Europe. Fixed-price meals range from 12F ($5.51) to 22F ($10.11), while à la carte dinners cost from 20F ($9.19) to 38F ($17.46).

Grotto, Hotel Crystal (tel. 2-11-65), is the best place in St. Moritz for Ticino-style food in a house that, if you didn't know you were in the Engadine, you'd swear was in the Italian-speaking part of the country. Many of the hors d'oeuvres are laid out on a buffet. Main courses might include rabbit with thyme, an array of pasta dishes, spinach gnocchi, and roast veal. You get friendly service in a mildly disorganized format. À la carte meals range from 25F ($11.49) to 50F ($22.98). Closed in November.

Restaurant Engiadina, in the center of town. The decor here is simple and unpretentious enough to be the kind of place for a stimulating conversation. It's filled with white napery, and simple tables and chairs. The location is on a traffic intersection in the heart of the resort. It has a white stucco facade with lots of windows you can look through before choosing the place as your dinner spot. Meals range from 25F ($11.49) and could go as high as 40F ($18.38) or more. Specialties include various steak dishes, fondue, and escargots, as well as a limited but well-prepared list of daily specials. This is very much a local restaurant, with daily platters priced from 13F ($5.97).

ST. MORITZ AFTER DARK: The nightlife here in winter is the most glamorous in Switzerland, centering around the Palace, but there are dozens of other bars, restaurants, and taverns. In some chic discos you might see a man and woman at one table in formal attire, while a couple at the next table will be clad in jeans. Nightlife is chic and very expensive, and case after case of French champagne is hauled into some of these dives, especially in February. But no one looks askance if you should order a beer.

Immediately after a skier returns from the slopes, he or she heads for **Hanselmanns Erben,** 8 Via Maistra, which is open from 7:30 a.m. to 7 p.m., serving afternoon tea and the best cakes, pastries, and chocolates in town.

After a rest and dinner, it's time for fancier action:

King's Club, Palace Hotel (tel. 2-11-01), has every advantage of a big-city disco with few of the drawbacks. It's the most sophisticated club in the Engadine, run by women imported from London's most glamorous clubs. They seem to make a fetish out of collecting bestselling records (by the last count, they had more than 4000 of them). The dress code here, as in almost every other part of the Palace, requires a dark suit and tie for men after 7 p.m. The decor is filled with modern paintings. Entrance is not permitted to everyone, and some memorable hearts have been broken by the hotel's exclusive admission policies. Be sure you have a backup club in mind if you're turned away at the hotel. A more low-key crowd usually congregates around the live jazz of the Grand Bar. If you're allowed inside the King's Club, the only cover charge is collected on weekends and during the Christmas holidays when expensive entertainment will be imported. Finally, the hotel has a quiet bar called the Renaissance which is good for conversation. It was named in the naïve hope that after a night inside, some of the guests would be ready and eager to be off skiing early the following morning.

Au Reduit (tel. 3-66-57) is a futuristic nightclub with lots of ambience. It has a decor of starburst lights and comfortable banquettes for talking and drinking, as well as a small dance floor where you might not be able to be too exuberant, but can nevertheless express yourself. The establishment often has a live pop/rock band playing to an appreciative audience. There's no cover charge, but the first drink costs between 8F ($3.68) and 12F ($5.51), with a food menu available as well. It includes a large pasta selection, eight types of pizza, and specialties of veal and beef. Meals begin at 25F ($11.49) and range upward. A smaller menu, mostly snacks such as burgers, omelets, and soups, is also offered, with prices beginning at 6F ($2.76). This is the place where many members of the St. Moritz hotel staffs go to relax after work, which usually makes for a younger, attractive crowd.

Suvretta House (tel. 2-11-21). A series of steps surround the large dance floor of this popular disco in a five-star hotel. People are usually seated on these steps for a better view of the dance floor, which gets some of the hottest action in town. The decor is in toreador red and black. The establishment is slightly outside of town. Live orchestras most often perform here in winter.

Vivai, Hotel Steffani (tel. 2-21-01), is a very modern disco with bars at either end of this metallic room. A disco is reached by going down a carpeted stone staircase. It's pretty loud even by disco standards, attracting a younger crowd.

Sunny Bar, Hotel Kulm (tel. 2-11-51), is one of the most popular rendezvous points in town, and certainly one in a hotel with a long history. Guests dance beneath the yellow representation of the signs of the zodiac. No entrance fee is charged, but drinks can cost from 15F ($6.89).

Grischuna Restaurant, Hotel Monopol (tel. 3-44-33), has a rustic ambience and an orchestra for dancing.

Cascade Bar, Via Somplax, is an art nouveau establishment with stained and etched glass. It can get quite rowdy at times, but it's a lot of fun. The posters are unabashedly explicit, at least for Paris of 1903. Music lovers will appreciate the unsolicited groups of men singing spontaneous choruses of everything from barbershop quartet to operatic trios. Cordon Rouge chills invitingly in Plexiglas buckets near the naturalistic sculpture on the zinc bartop, although beers costs from 2.50F ($1.15). A restaurant is attached. The place is closed on Sunday.

9. Pontresina

It doesn't have the fame of St. Moritz, but Pontresina (5916 feet) is nonetheless one of the leading headquarters for hiking and mountaineering in the area. It lies in the Upper Engadines on the road to the Bernina Pass, at the mouth of the Bernina Valley, surrounded by woodland made up of larches and stone pines. The towering peaks of the Alps surround and shelter it. From Pontresina you have views of the glacier amphitheater of the Roseg.

This was first a summer resort, the early tourists being attracted to the fresh mountain air, but now it's a leading ski resort, known for its huge jump. The village today is filled with hotels and shops. Unlike St. Moritz, Pontresina has much old Engadine architecture.

The long hours of sunshine in winter and the easy accessibility of all the noted ski sites in the greater St. Moritz area have shown visitors that it's not necessary to stay in crowded St. Moritz, unless they have a real yen to do so. Sites that are lures for skiers in winter are attractive for sightseeing tours in summer. Many trips are possible. The **Diavolezza** tour, which starts at 5765 feet and passes over four glaciers on the way down, is one of the major attractions of the Engadines. You go by road toward Bernina as far as the lower station of the Diavolezza cable car, which takes you up to where you can go on to 10,000 feet by drag lift if your purpose is skiing. From the 9765-foot height there's a celebrated ski run down to the valley or down the glacier to

Morteratsch. If you go with a guide for this glacier walk, allow about three hours. In season the Diavolezza cable car is likely to be crowded, the journey up taking about half an hour. Round-trip fare is 16F ($7.35). In summer beautiful alpine tours are made from here.

Closer at hand is the **Languard,** rising to some 8500 feet, directly above Pontresina with slopes for young and old. You reach it by ski lift. **Muottas Muragl,** about a 12-minute bus ride from Pontresina, has panoramic views, nursery slopes, and easy runs, and **Piz Lagalp** is steep and challenging. Hiking trails in the mountains lead to the little way stations, huts of the Swiss Alpine Club. Horse-drawn sleigh and coach rides in the Val Roseg and to Morteratsch are popular.

WHERE TO STAY: **Hotel Kronenhof Bellavista** (tel. 6-63-33) is set on a gently sloping hillside where a double row of tennis courts separate you from an alpine stream a few hundred yards away. The hotel has both an indoor and an outdoor swimming pool, and a very grand 19th-century facade that retains many of the original super-elegant details of its construction. The main salon (and every other room on the ground floor, for that matter) has a high ceiling ornamented with elaborate classical detailing that has been painted a refreshingly simple white. The Oriental rugs and English furniture complement it beautifully. The hotel is not without its share of full-grained paneling, in a series of public dining rooms that seem to go on forever, serving food and drink in a congenial atmosphere that may tempt you to return another year. An outdoor biseasonal terrace serves lunch beside a skating rink. One of the bars has an orchestra for nighttime dancing. Singles range from 120F ($55.14) to 190F ($87.31), while doubles cost between 210F ($96.50) and 350F ($160.85), with half board included. Prices, of course, depend on the season and the plumbing.

Hotel Walther (tel. 6-64-71). The ground-floor rooms have ceilings high enough to give a baronial impression of 19th-century spaciousness. If you tear yourself away from the piano bar for a walk onto the lawns surrounding the hotel, you'll see a facade that looks like a cross between a stronghold of the Knights Templar and a Wagnerian fantasy of Disneyland. Despite the medieval aspects of the facade, the bar area inside couldn't be more 20th century, with long rows of bottles lined up behind the serving area, plus a candlelit restaurant with good service and tasty food. Tennis courts are within view of the central tower. There's also a nightclub on the premises, along with a sauna and a children's playroom. *Per-person* rates in a double range from 100F ($45.95) to 170F ($78.12), with half board included. The supplement for single occupancy is an additional 10F ($4.60) daily. Each of the accommodations has a private bath, and is priced according to the season and the size.

Hotel Schweizerhof (tel. 6-64-12). The lobby of this hotel is walled with hewn stone and capped with a ceiling of weathered wood slats set about a foot apart from one another. Coupled with the bright carpeting, it gives an airy, comfortable impression of relaxed grandeur that is repeated throughout the rest of the hotel. The dining room has illustrations, Engadine style, painted under the arches, and a paneled and beamed ceiling that give an attractive update to the conception of "rustic." The outside has long rows of white walls accented with yellow balconies, and a stone foundation with big windows and a limited amount of decorative embellishment. All accommodations contain private bath, ranging in price from 95F ($43.65) to 145F ($66.63) in a single and from 180F ($82.71) to 270F ($124.07) in a double, with half board included.

Sporthotel (tel. 6-63-31) is a tall, symmetrical Victorian building in the center of the resort. The manager speaks English, and offers the best breakfast buffet in town. Many residents eat so much they can afford to skip lunch. The comfortable bedrooms offer good views, and are colorful, tasteful, and most often equipped with a private bath. The beamed dining room has alpine chairs and Engadine-style illustrations of animals and plants. Much of the rest of the place is cozily paneled and filled with softly upholstered armchairs. Singles cost from 67F ($30.79) to 114F ($52.38) and doubles range from 62F ($28.49) to 102F ($46.87) per person daily, with half board included. Prices depend on the season and the plumbing.

Rosatsch Hotel (tel. 6-63-51) is an elegantly rustic, old-fashioned building with six floors of brown-shuttered windows, a small cupola, and a carefully crafted vertical row of bay windows rising at one corner. The Albrecht family recently added a modern annex connected to the main building by a passageway leading to a swimming pool with its bar. There's a sauna as well as a squash hall and a massage cabin. The hotel is in the middle of the village, with proximity to everything. The sitting rooms are paneled and comfortable. Both an elevator and a parking garage are on the premises. Singles range from 70F ($32.17) to 120F ($55.14), while doubles cost between 118F ($54.22) and 210F ($96.50), with half board included.

Hotel Bernina (tel. 6-62-21) is a boxy rectangular building with a slightly recessed top floor and attractively patterned wood shutters. A low-lying extension stretches off to one side. Much of the interior has been disciplined into a rustic framework of half-paneling and wrought-iron lighting fixtures. The modern bedrooms are spacious and sunny, renting for between 70F ($32.17) and 110F ($50.55) in a single and between 130F ($59.74) and 200F ($91.90) in a double, with half board included.

Hotel La Collina and **Soldenella** (tel. 6-64-21) is an elegant, white-walled hotel with gables and a corner turret that makes the entire construction look somewhat like a château. The inside has lots of knotty-pine paneling, a few regional antiques, and beamed ceilings stretching over a scattering of Oriental rugs. Bedrooms are conservatively modern, spacious, and decorated in attractive colors. Singles range from 70F ($32.17) to 105F ($48.25), while doubles cost from 110F ($50.55) to 190F ($87.31), with half board included. Prices depend on the season and the plumbing.

Hotel Bahnhof (tel. 6-62-42) is a family-run guest house which sometimes gives the impression you're in a home instead of a hotel. The public rooms are decked out in regional furniture and bright colors, while the bedrooms are comfortable, unpretentious, and attractively simple. Betty and Jean-Pierre Scherz, your genial hosts, charge from 55F ($25.27) to 59F ($27.11) per person in bathless accommodations, with half board included.

WHERE TO DINE: **Sarazena** (tel. 6-63-53) is an old-fashioned Engadine-style house with an Austrian manager, Josef Haas. It serves a classical French repertoire of dishes among its other offerings. You're likely to be presented with a choice of tomato soup flambé, filet of sole "tout Paris," foie gras maison, turbot of the house, and rack of lamb "patron." À la carte dinners range from 27F ($12.41) to 65F ($29.87). A pizzeria on the premises is less expensive, with meals costing from 26F ($11.95) to 37F ($17). This 17th-century building has a number of restaurants, including a bierstube. Many of the antiques are from the 18th century. You're likely to run into just about everybody here, including Fiat's Agnelli. This was once a private home, but has been handsomely converted to receive the public. There's a minstrel's gallery where diners can perch and "oversee" the orchestra and the dancers on the floor below. The management often presents live rock or country-western music. It also shows vintage silent flicks. The restaurant is closed from mid-April to mid-June and from mid-October to mid-December.

Hotel Schweizerhof (tel. 6-64-12). The dining room reeks of regional charm, with primitively drawn characters painted on many of its walls. An open fireplace grills meats as you watch. Other house specialties include fresh lobsters and oysters, filet of beef, ravioli maison, lobster bisque in champagne, noodles with a salmon cream sauce, and smoked river trout, along with such game dishes as roebuck (in season). Dessert might be a satisfying portion of flambeed raspberries with cream. In summer there's dining on a garden terrace. The restaurant is closed in November and in May. Fixed-price meals range from 28F ($12.87) to 110F ($50.55), with à la carte dinners beginning at 50F ($22.98). Reservations are suggested.

Kronenstübli (tel. 6-63-33) is one of the most popular restaurants on the central square in the heart of the resort. The decor is filled with well-polished brass and pewter, and everything (such as paneling) that goes well with it. You might enjoy the paupiettes of sole in a cognac-flavored shrimp sauce with truffles, or pike or salmon (if available), perhaps lobster in cream sauce. Many of the chef's innovations are inspired by nouvelle cuisine cookery. Dessert might be a sorbet of fresh figs. À la carte dinners range from 28F ($12.87) to 52F ($23.89).

APRÈS SKI: It is no longer necessary to head over to St. Moritz for after-dark action. Pontresina has plenty of nighttime diversions, although life here is decidedly more informal than it is in St. Moritz.

The most popular place in town, the **Sarazena,** a combined nightclub and restaurant, has already been recommended.

One of the most frequented bar and restaurant selections at the resort is the Stuev'Alva at the already-recommended **Rosatsch Hotel.** This place is warm, charming, and cozily decorated, with wood paneling and candlelight.

The Restaurant Locanda, at the also-recommended **Hotel Bernina,** is another preferred spot. You can order both raclette and fondue here.

The Nordeska Bar at the well-recommended **Sporthotel** has a tranquil and pleasant atmosphere, with a small dance floor if you're so inclined.

In season, some hotels also have candlelight buffet dinners accompanied by piano music.

10. Silvaplana

Lying on Lake Silvaplana, in sight of Lake Champfèr, the little village of Silvaplana (5900 feet) is at the foot of Piz (mount) Corvatsch (11,338 feet) at the beginning of the Julier Pass. This village is about four miles from St. Moritz, and visitors from that more celebrated resort go windsurfing on Lake Silvaplana. The tiny hamlet of Silvaplana is one of the most unspoiled resorts in the Engadine, with a parish church in the late Gothic style having been built one year before Columbus made his sea voyage west and found America.

Whether you're a skier, a mountaineer, a nature lover, or just a traveling sightseer, you visit **Corvatsch.** From Silvaplana, go across the narrow neck of water where Lake Champfèr and Lake Silvaplana join, and take an aerial cable car at Surlej. In just 15 minutes you'll reach the mountain station from which you have a view of the lakes, meadows, forests, and villages of the Upper Engadine. From the lookout terrace you take in a panorama of what appears to be an infinity of mountain peaks, with the giant glacier of the Bernina group looking close enough to touch.

From November to May skiers find nearly 50 miles of snowy runs, while in summer they can take advantage of the glacier ski lifts and a summer ski school. Swimming, sailing, riding, and fishing are lots of fun for Silvaplana's summer visitors.

FOOD AND LODGING: **Hotel Albana** (tel. 4-92-92) is a recently constructed building with well-insulated windows, chalet-style balconies with patterned wood slats, and regional-style monochromatic stencils running vertically up the corners of the facade. The design is charmingly repeated around many of the ground-floor archways. Inside you'll find a warm collection of beamed ceilings, stone fireplaces, half-timbered walls, and wrought-iron accents. The bedrooms are streamlined of any rusticity, but are appealing and colorful, and always have a private bath. Singles range from 70F ($32.17) to 115F ($52.84), while doubles cost between 112F ($51.46) and 200F ($91.90), depending on the season, the room size, and exposure.

Hotel Sonne (tel. 4-81-52) is an elegantly detailed, four-story rectangular building. The facade has been relieved with louvered shutters, flowerboxes, regional monochromatic designs above a reddish-colored extension, and neoclassical detailing over a few of the many windows. The interior is rustically modern, and very elegant with white settees in the salon and old-fashioned wallpaper and paneling in the dining rooms. You'll also find a pleasantly maintained garden and a dancing bar. *Per-person* rates with breakfast cost 55F ($25.27) to 80F ($36.76), depending on the season and the plumbing. Half board usually goes for another 20F ($9.19) per person daily.

Hotel Julier (tel. 4-81-86) is a red-shuttered, four-story building with gently curved steps and a warmly traditional interior. It sits in front of a fountain with a statue of an ibex on its pedestal. The bedrooms contain knotty-pine furniture, bright colors, pleasant proportions, and private baths. In the public rooms you'll see lots of half-timbering, a handful of antiques, and a friendly staff. *Per-person* rates range from 35F ($16.08) to 70F ($32.17), based on double occupancy with breakfast included. Tariffs depend on the season and the plumbing. Half board is another 18F ($8.27) per person daily, and single occupancy carries a supplement of 9F ($4.14) a day. The same family, the Schaerens, maintain a more modern hotel nearby, the **Ches'Arsa,** where singles range from 56F ($25.73) to 105F ($48.25) and doubles cost from 48F ($22.06) to 65F ($29.87) per person daily, depending on the season, with breakfast included.

Hotel Chesa Grusaida (tel. 4-82-92) is a simple Engadine-style house with white walls, a gently sloping roof, and a location in the middle of a grassy lawn. It's popular with skiers. The interior is rustically simple, with white walls, a scattering of ceiling beams, and a restaurant that serves well-prepared meals. *Per-person* rates range from 35F ($16.08) to 57F ($26.19) daily, based on double occupancy, with breakfast included. Prices depend on the season and the plumbing. Half board is another 20F ($9.19) per person, and the supplement for a bathless single is 3F ($1.38) daily.

Restaurant Albana, in the Hotel Albana (tel. 4-92-92), has a warmly appealing decor of wrought iron, heavy timbers, and richly striped fabrics stretched over chairs and comfortable banquettes. The Mettler family, along with their chef, Herr Koerper, prepare such specialties as terrine of foie gras, fish from the nearby lake covered with a savory chive sauce, rack of lamb with herbs, brochette Albana, and fish fondue Albana, along with veal kidney in Chablis. À la carte meals range from 40F ($18.38) and up, while fixed-price menus cost from 25F ($11.49) all the way to 100F ($45.95). The restaurant is open from 7 a.m. to midnight, but closed from early May until mid-June and from mid-October to mid-November.

11. Sils-Maria (Baselgia)

Lying at an altitude of nearly 6000 feet beside the lakes of the Upper Engadine are two townships at the beginning of the Inn Valley—**Sils-Baselgia,** a tiny hamlet with some hotels, and **Sils-Maria,** which is slightly larger. A church in Sils-Baselgia dates from 1446. Many "dollarwise" European travelers stay here and then take the bus to all the ski facilities in the greater St. Moritz area, but this resort has its own attractions as well, with many winter and summer sports filling its crowded agenda.

There are some excellent hotels in this resort area, with reasonable prices. Nietzsche lived in Sils-Maria in the summer from 1881 to 1889. Beside the Edelweiss Hotel, there's a small house where he lived while he wrote *Thus Spake Zarathustra.* This has been turned into a little museum with some mementos of the German philosopher on display.

A modern cableway takes you to **Furtschellas** (about 7500 feet), where skiers can use ski lifts and 25 miles of runs without having to line up and wait their turn. The Sils resort provides opportunities for hiking via footpaths in all directions, curling, sailing, windsurfing, horseback riding, and tennis. If you're here in summer, why not try a horse-drawn bus excursion trip up the Fex Valley? I found it an enjoyable experience.

HOTELS IN SILS-MARIA: **Hotel Waldhaus** (tel. 4-53-31) is a very comfortable, extravagantly designed hotel built in 1908. You'll reach it by riding or climbing to the top of a forested hill whose conifers come almost to the front door. It's designed like a residential palace, with square towers rising at either end of a long white center section. The interior has a collection of dramatically high-ceilinged rooms such as the reception area, whose wrought-iron staircase railing curves alongside a red-and-black patterned Oriental rug, and a dining room whose massive chandeliers look like art nouveau gilded steel. The oversize bedrooms are filled in part with elegant furniture, including some antiques, and usually have good views of the surrounding mountains. On the premises is a large covered swimming pool, plus facilities to amuse children while their parents are playing. An orchestra usually plays dance music in the bar area, while a wintertime bus service provided by the hotel transports guests to and from the alpine ski slopes. With half board included, singles range from 85F ($39.06) to 170F ($78.12), and doubles cost between 140F ($64.33) and 320F ($147.04), depending on the season, the plumbing, and the room assignment.

Hotel Pensiun Privata (tel. 4-52-47) is a five-story, ocher-colored building with wood-grained shutters and a flagstone roof. Its central position is not far from the village church. The Giovanni family, your hosts, charge between 140F ($64.33) and 165F ($75.82) for a double and between 70F ($32.17) and 87F ($39.98) in a single, with half board included. Prices depend on the season and the plumbing.

HOTELS IN SILS-BASELGIA: **Hotel Margna** (tel. 4-53-06) is a former private house which was built in 1817 in the baroque style. Since then it's had many extensions and additions. It's covered in pink stucco, and still retains its wrought-iron detailing and patrician staircase in front. Inside, vaulted ceilings and well-polished paneling embellish the temporary home for the hundreds of visitors who enjoy the good food in the two restaurants and the rustically attractive cellar bar. An outdoor terrace, sauna, fitness room, and lots of trees in the summertime garden are included among the facilities. Sepp and Dorly Müssgens are the owners of this pleasant establishment, charging between 100F ($45.95) and 155F ($71.22) per person, with half board included, depending on the season and the room assignment.

Chesa Randolina (tel. 4-51-51) is a rambling Engadine-style house with stucco that appears either orange, salmon, or pink colored according to the light and the time of day. The front doorway has a massively arched area covered with gray-and-white regional designs, and a herringbone-shaped pattern built into the rustic front door. The interior is filled with knotty-pine built-in furniture, as well as a healthy share of wall paneling and brightly colored carpeting. The building used to be a farmhouse, but now it's owned by Wally and Hans Clavadetscher, who charge between 75F ($34.46) and 95F ($43.65) per person in a bathless room and between 85F ($39.06) and 125F ($57.44) per person with bath. These tariffs include half board, and the hotel is closed from October, reopening in December.

Pensiun Chastè (tel. 4-53-12) is an old Engadine house on Lake Sils. It has three floors of buff-colored stucco accented with red shutters. Miss Godly is the owner and manager, charging between 55F ($25.27) and 63F ($28.95) in a single and from 105F ($48.25) to 121F ($55.60) in a double, with half board included. Rooms are simple and comfortable.

WHERE TO DINE: **Waldhaus Restaurant,** in the Hotel Waldhaus (tel. 4-53-31), is set in a forested area a slight distance from the center of Sils-Maria. The dining room has a very high ceiling, big-windowed views of the larchwood forest outside, and elegantly simple chairs covered in white. Its menu is proclaimed by many as the finest in the village. You might enjoy turbot with hollandaise sauce or tournedos, perhaps a salmon ragoût or filet of sole poached in white port. A Lake Sils specialty is a sauteed pork steak prepared from an old Engadine recipe. Every other Saturday night the management serves specialties from any one of four Swiss regions, including the Ticino. Fixed-price meals range from 30F ($13.79) to 50F ($22.98), with à la carte dinners costing from 30F ($13.79) to 60F ($27.57). The restaurant is closed from mid-April until early June and from mid-October until mid-December. Otherwise, meals are served between noon and 2:15 p.m. and 7 to 9:30 p.m.

Chesa Marchetta (tel. 4-52-32) is maintained by two sisters, Christine and Maria Godly, who cook and act as hostess. Their restaurant is in the center of the village on the town square in an old building with steep eaves and a prominent stone foundation. The menu is small and select, offering only a few well-prepared dishes which include a tasty gastronomic menu with five courses. Specialties include such items as liver with spinach, polenta, fondue, and other regional dishes. À la carte meals range in price from 25F ($11.49) to 56F ($25.73). Reservations are suggested.

MALOJA PASS: South of Sils you reach the famous Maloja Pass or crossing. This historic pass connects the Engadine with the Lake Como region in Italy. At the pass belvedere stands the old Maloja Kulm Hotel. Even if you're just passing through, every motorist stops here for a look at the Bergell Valley. This "pass" is reached by hairpin roads.

For food and lodging, try the **Hotel Maloja Kulm** (tel. 4-31-05), a historic hotel at the top of the pass. It has a spectacular view of the winding road you just came up on, and a few contented cows grazing near the observation platform. The building has a Victorian hipped roof on one section and on the other the kind of flagstone roof you might have noticed on other buildings in the Grisons. Inside you'll see animal skins decorating the paneled and stucco walls, stone floors, and a simple restaurant and bar serving nourishing alpine meals. The management has recently constructed a new wing. Singles cost from 50F ($22.98) to 85F ($39.06), while doubles range from 90F ($41.36) to 170F ($78.12), with half board included.

12. Flims (Laax)

The following resort area, close to Chur, is actually a triumvirate of resorts consisting of not only Flims but also Falera and Laax. Of the three, Flims and Laax are the most developed.

FLIMS: Very much a European family resort not much known to North Americans, Flims (3450 feet) is the most important holiday resort of the Grisons Oberland. Tourists have been coming to this small Swiss town, about an hour and a half from Zurich's Kloton airport and 20 minutes from Chur, since the late 19th century, but Flims is considered a modern resort, experiencing a tourism boom during the last 20 or so years. This "sun terrace" of the Grisons lies on a scenic route leading over the Oberalp Pass and has good bus and train connections. Leave the main highway at Reichenau, six miles west of Chur, and you'll find Flims after a seven-mile drive onward.

This resort, with an exposure due south, is in two sections—Flims-Dorf, the original mountain village lying at the foot of the Flimserstein cliffs, mostly residential; and Flims-Waldhaus, a little more than half a mile south in a woodland of conifers, with many hotels. Flims lies on a sunny, protected plateau overlooking the Rhine Valley, the result of the biggest landslide brought to Switzerland. This gargantuan slide blocked the river valley, forcing the Rhine to find another course. The result of this convulsion of nature is some rather bizarre topography, the resulting "debris" of the landslide being scattered over a 16-square-mile area.

The southern exposure of Flims brings mild winter temperatures, and visitors find a wealth of sports activities possible. You can go alpine skiing from 30 different locations with their 134 miles of slopes plus 35 miles of cross-country skiing trails and a special ski run for children. You can take the chair lift to **Foppa** (4660 feet), with a second stage going to **Alp Naraus** (6035 feet), and a final swing into heaven taking you by tiny cableway to **Cassons Grat** (8560 feet). In case you get hungry during the ascent or on your way down, there's a restaurant at each of the three stages.

A second major area is **Startgels** and **Grauberg.** A gondola you board in the southwestern section of Dorf takes you to Startgels (5200 feet), where there's a restaurant at which you can stoke up before you continue by cableway to Grauberg (7300 feet).

Other winter frolic includes curling, ice skating, tobogganing, horseback riding, horse-drawn sleigh riding, indoor swimming, and 30 miles of hiking trails.

Unlike most parts of Switzerland, you can swim outdoors here from May to September from the bathing beach at Lake Cauma, which is warmed by underground hot springs. You can also go boating on the lake, play tennis, or try the fitness tracks.

Don't expect to find a typical Swiss village if you go to Flims, as most of the buildings are modern.

Food and Lodging

Park Hotel Waldhaus (tel. 39-01-81) is the finest hotel in Flims, with an elegance and a service worthy of the name "Grand Hotel." It's actually a big complex of at least five buildings, which are joined by covered walkways. The snow gets so deep here that piles on either side create a series of tunnels. In summer the complex is surrounded by green lawns and conifers which come almost to the edge of the nine outdoor tennis courts, the outdoor swimming pool, and a separate curling hall. An indoor swimming pool is framed with a curved row of glass windows set into metal struts, giving a futuristic look to the 19th-century buildings near it. Two indoor tennis courts are set under a roof of laminated wood.

Throughout the complex you'll find comfortable and elegant lounges, often with old-fashioned fireplaces, fieldstone detailing, and heavy beams and paneling. The restaurant, Pavilion, is one of the finest in town, decorated in a modern format of clustered lights held together in geometric brass chandeliers and lots of plants. A less formal charcoal grill, an Italian-style trattoria, and a Spanish restaurant complete the dining facilities, while a live orchestra often performs in the Tschaler bar. Bedrooms are a little on the small side in many cases, but are nonetheless immaculate and comfortable. I prefer the high-ceilinged older rooms. Singles range from 110F ($50.55) to 200F ($91.90), while doubles cost between 210F ($96.50) and 400F ($183.80), with half board included. Prices depend on the season and the accommodation.

Apart-Hotel des Alpes (tel. 39-01-01) has a concrete-and-glass facade with lots of windows in a format that looks like an updated chalet. The gardens around it provide guests with a place to sunbathe in summer, especially since the management has placed flowerboxes on top of the ornamental walls. The interior is what might be called "newly created rustic," with patterned carpeting, wooden post-and-lintel construction in the dining room, and low-key colors of brown and russet. A covered swimming pool, outdoor tennis courts, and fitness facilities are all on the premises. Each of the accommodations has a private bath, costing between 90F ($41.36) and 142F ($65.25) in a single and between 150F ($68.93) and 244F ($112.12) in a double, with half board included.

Hotel Adula (tel. 39-01-61) is a modern hotel with lots of sunny balconies fashioned, chalet style, from weathered planking. The interior is filled with mellow paneling, brass candlesticks, intimate lighting, and stucco vaulting. The popular bar area usually provides a live piano player, and the hotel organizes weekly romantic dinners with regional-style buffet meals. A glass-walled indoor swimming pool is part of the hotel, as well as three outdoor clay-surfaced tennis courts. The 121 rooms are reached via two elevators, while a nearby annex holds the hotel's overflow. The Hotz family even organizes the three-times-weekly guided nature walks lasting half or full days. Singles range from 90F ($41.36) to 140F ($64.33), while doubles cost between 85F ($39.06) and 130F ($59.74) per person, with half board included. Prices depend on the season and room assignment. These tariffs assume a minimum stay of three days, and week-long special packages can often be arranged in advance.

Schlosshotel (tel. 39-12-45). The Romanesque revival facade with the steep gabled roof and the well-proportioned tower could inspire just about everyone from a reader of gothic romances to a ghost-story writer. It really is a marvel of the mason's craft, completely fashioned from rough-textured rocks into a château-like building where you should be very comfortable. The Burkhart family maintains this place, where the simply furnished bedrooms look like something from a much more modern house and where the public rooms are attractively paneled and rustic. The overflow from the main building is housed in one of the two adjoining annexes, the villas Gentiana and Auricula. The hotel's rates usually fall at the lower end of the price scale. *Per-person* tariffs range from 70F ($32.17) to 100F ($45.95), with half board included, depending on the season and the plumbing.

Hotel National (tel. 39-12-24) is a family-run hotel in the center of the village. It has a plain white facade with a few rows of balconies to relieve the monotony. An orange awning covers the sidewalk café in summer. The interior is functionally furnished with a few rustic touches in the less formal of the two restaurants. In winter the Eigenmann family hosts a lunchtime ski barbecue in a rented alpine hut near the slopes. Recent renovations have given each of the comfortable bedrooms a private bath. Singles rent for between 59F ($27.11) and 89F ($40.90), while doubles range from 94F ($43.19) to 168F ($77.20), with half board included.

Restaurant Barga in the Hotel Adula (tel. 39-01-61), is the warmly rustic dining room inside the attractive chalet-style hotel described earlier. Its specialties include a delectable selection of appetizers, along with such dishes as salmon in a fragrant seafood mousse, filet of sole "Las Palmas," Chinese fondue, medallion of veal "3 Musketeers style," and veal in a sour lemon sauce, along with a tempting variety of desserts that might include a chocolate parfait. Fixed-price meals range from 27F ($12.41) to 47F ($21.60), while à la carte dinners cost between 25F ($11.49) and 50F ($22.98). The restaurant is closed from mid-October to mid-December.

LAAX: About three miles from Flims, Laax, whose ski area reaches out to take in the hamlets of **Falera** and **Murschetg**, is at the foot of the "White Arena," a vast ski lift and trail network shared by Flims. Murschetg lies nearest to the lifts, and Falera is less than two miles from Laax, the biggest of the three villages. A good ski bus connects the trio of resort hamlets.

Major ski areas include the **Murschetg–Crap Sogn Gion.** From Crap Sogn Gion (7280 feet), which you reach by cableway from Murschetg, you can go to **Crap Mesegne** (8120 feet), which is a connecting point with the Vorab glacier.

If you have little experience in skiing, you can take the two-stage gondola from Crap Mesegne to the Vorab glacier restaurant. From the restaurant site, a two-way ski lift goes to the loftiest citadel in the whole section, a height of 9900 feet.

The Vorab area is a popular ski center in winter and summer. During the 1982 Christmas season, Prince Charles and Princess Diana were taken by helicopter to the glacier when Scotland was short of snow.

Food and Lodging

Sporthotel Happy Rancho (tel. 39-22-56) is a sports and relaxation complex housed in a very attractive, very large building, with a shape that looks vaguely like a bird poised for flight. The hotel offers access to practically every sport you could pursue in this region, including those that come to mind quickly: hiking, canoeing, horseback riding, swimming, cricket, bowling, cycling, and skiing. But also a few others that you might not have thought of: Frisbee, archery, crossbow shooting, cross-country running, gymnastics, and ice-stick throwing.

The hotel is divided into eight separate units housed under the same roof. Nine elevators connect the divisions. The establishment has 60 doubles and 40 apartment units, some of which contain their own fireplaces. One of the trained sports instructors will videotape your performance on the slopes to help you improve it. Facilities exist for babysitting and for organizing children's activities. Under 6 years old, they get a 50% reduction; from the ages of 7 to 16, a 30% reduction. If you include the sun terrace, the hotel has seven different restaurants, many with their own bar. The public rooms are decorated with monochromatic stencils, Grisons style, and are attractively outfitted with tile floors and a scattering of Oriental rugs. A wide selection of bedrooms is available. With half board included, the cost for a small room in low season begins at 65F ($29.87) per person, ranging upward to 179F ($82.25) per person for a suite in high season.

Sporthotel Signina (tel. 39-01-51) is a large, chalet-style hotel with detailed craftsmanship throughout. Some of the balconies are fashioned of patterned wooden slats, while the interior has beamed and patterned ceilings of well-polished local woods. Two bar areas sometimes offer live entertainment. Sports facilities include seven tennis courts, a bowling alley, a covered swimming pool, and a tavern. The 120 bedrooms are comfortable and well furnished. Singles on half board range from a low of 84F ($38.60) to a high of 110F ($50.55). Doubles, also on half board, cost from a low of 148F ($68.01) to a high of 200F ($91.90). Prices depend on the season and the room assignment.

Berghotel Crap Sogn Gion (tel. 39-21-93) is a ten-minute cable-car ride from the valley below. The 40 rooms at the top are comfortably modern, often with paneled ceilings. Surprisingly, there are plenty of diversions inside this remote place, including a covered swimming pool, a sauna, two restaurants, a cafeteria, two bowling alleys, a news kiosk, and a sun terrace with lounge chairs. From the downhill side the construction looks like one huge solar panel, with a curved metallic-and-glass area directed toward the valley below. Singles range from 75F ($34.46) to 110F ($50.55), while doubles cost from 120F ($55.14) to 190F ($87.31), with half board included. Prices depend on the season and the plumbing.

Hotel Larisch (tel. 2-21-26) looks like a double chalet connected by a center section with balconies. It lies just outside the center of Laax, and offers a lovely view from its dining room. It has 20 double bedrooms plus five apartments suitable for families. Guests can use the swimming pool at the hotel next door, although there's a sauna on the premises. Bedrooms are simple, colorful, and very clean. They range in price from 55F ($25.27) to 80F ($36.76) per person, single or double occupancy, depending on the season. Half board is included in the price. The Kern family are your helpful hosts.

APRÈS SKI IN THE AREA: The **Sardona Club** is a nightclub and bar, catering mainly to the young (unlike the older clientele at many of the hotels). It's owned and run by a man introduced to me only as "Heinz." The club is a good spot for dancing and plenty of socializing should you find yourself all alone at Flims.

The Tschaler dance bar at the previously recommended **Park Hotel Waldhaus** is a major nighttime rendezvous. Hopefully, that band of five middle-aged Polish women I saw on my most recent visit will be brought back for an encore. They were terrific! It didn't matter if their music missed the beat—their flamboyant costumes and music made up for it.

The **Hotel Adula** is known for its Barga dining room, one of the most popular at the resort. A pianist entertains while guests dine in front of an open fire.

The **Hotel Bellevue** (tel. 39-31-31), run by Rolf Joos, also has a nightclub, the Caverna, which on certain snowy nights is the most action-packed place in town.

13. Splügen

This is a mountain village on the route to the Splügen Pass where many noted personages have visited, not so much for its own attractions but because it's on the way to somewhere else. The village lies in the Hinterrhein and controls alpine passes. From here, the highway to the San Bernardino Pass leads to Switzerland's Italian-speaking section, the Ticino. it also leads to the Zapport glacier, the source of the Rhine.

Splügen lies in a wide valley at the foot of the Kalkberg and is both a winter and a summer holiday center. You can take ski lifts to Danatzhöhe (7080 feet).

The little village has many attractive stone-built homes and a parish church dating from 1690.

For food and lodging, try the **Posthotel Bodenhaus** (tel. 62-11-21), a large symmetrical building near the village church. It has four floors of black-shuttered windows below a gently sloping Mediterranean-style roof. It was built in 1722, and still retains many of the charming architectural features that were there originally, including flagstone floors, stone-trimmed vaultings, smallish windows, and geometrically paneled ceilings. Famous guests from the past have included Queen Victoria, Napoleon, the kings of Württemberg, and Lady Hamilton. The public rooms have small collections of Empire-style chairs, while the modernized bedrooms contain light-grained pine accents and provincial chalet furniture. There's an elevator, along with a sun terrace, restaurant, and pub. Singles range from 40F ($18.38) to 75F ($34.46), while doubles cost between 65F ($29.87) and 120F ($55.14) with breakfast included. Half board is offered for another 20F ($9.19) per person daily.

14. Valbella/Lenzerheide

Lying beside Lake Heid (the Heidsee) in a settling of alpine scenery at an altitude of 4757 feet, these two resorts make a good center for seeing the mountains or taking part in sports. The two attractive villages, about a mile and a quarter apart separated by the lake, are on the major road to the Julier Pass.

Dozens of bus and mountain railway excursions are offered, and you can stop off for a fine meal in one of the several mountain restaurants where you can dine on piquant cheese and air-dried Grisons beef. On a two-stage cableway journey up to Rothorn (9400 feet), I found a good restaurant at the first station at 6230 feet, and there's another dining room at the top. You can also go to the top of Schwarzhorn by chair lift, where you'll have beautiful views of the Hörnli Valley. A good lift system allows exploration of the western part of the resort area. The Tgantieni drag lift goes to 5675 feet (there are dining facilities here), and you can then proceed, still by drag lift, to Piz Schalottas (7635 feet).

In winter skiers can enjoy some 90 miles of ski runs of all grades, made accessible by 34 cable cars and elevators. There's a children's ski school with its own elevator and ski garden, which attracts families to these resorts. About 25 miles of cross-country ski trails, more than ten curling rinks, and a huge natural ice-skating rink draw winter sports crowds.

In summer, water sports are popular on the Heidsee, with rowing, swimming, sailing, windsurfing, and fishing taking center stage. This is good country for horseback riding, and there's an 18-hole golf course. Lenzerheide has more than 85 miles of signposted footpaths.

FOOD AND LODGING AT LENZERHEIDE: **Grand Hotel Kurhaus Alpina** (tel. 34-11-34) is built in a pastiche of styles that had its core in an alpine dairy farm a century ago. The main building was constructed at the beginning of this century, but many alterations and additions later, the hotel is a mixture of old masonry and elegantly crafted modern extensions. The building lies in a quiet sunny position behind a cluster of fir trees. A restaurant, a sympathetic bar, and a disco (the Tic-Tac) often have live entertainment. There's a heated swimming pool, as well as a sauna, on the premises. Singles range from 85F ($39.06) to 180F ($82.71), while doubles cost from 150F ($68.93) to 330F ($151.64), with half board included.

Schweizerhof (tel. 34-11-81). Very little of what you've seen before will prepare you for the dimensions and shape of some of the rooms of this hotel. It is, both at the same time, rustic and super-modern. Light-grained paneling covers many of the walls, and many of the accessories, such as hanging lamps, are made of polished brass. The full-length windows often open onto ground-level terraces or upper-level wood-trimmed balconies. The dining room is outfitted with hanging Tiffany-style lamps and knotty-pine paneling, and the other rendezvous points are universally conducive to good music and conversation. On the premises you'll find a swimming pool, a sauna, indoor tennis courts, squash courts, a bowling alley, a table-tennis room, massage facilities, and a fitness room. With half board included, singles range from 65F ($29.87) to 150F ($68.93), while doubles cost from 120F ($55.14) to 270F ($124.07), depending on the season and the room assignment.

Sunstar Hotel (tel. 34-24-91) is a modern hotel with a flat roof, well-defined balconies, and well-furnished rooms of ample size. It's opposite the ski school and has its own garage. The rustically comfortable lobby is filled with leather chairs. Many of the bedrooms overlook the ice-skating rink. An indoor swimming pool will give you the chance to lose some of the weight you might have gained in the attractively rustic dining room, whose stucco and paneled walls are intimately lit with hanging lamps that look almost like origami sculpture fashioned from metal and glass. Each of the 95 bedrooms has its own private bath, phone, and radio. Singles range from 56F ($25.73) to 130F ($59.74), while doubles cost between 102F ($46.87) and 255F ($117.17), with half board included. Prices, of course, depend on the season and the plumbing.

Familienhotel Lenzerhorn (tel. 34-11-05) is a symmetrical 19th-century building with ruddy-colored shutters and a modern extension stretching off to one side. The interior has a pumpkin-colored bar with a heavily timbered ceiling and short Doric columns made of granite supporting its thick stucco arches. A sun terrace with a striped awning sits within view of the buff-colored facade. A wide range of summer and winter sports are available nearby. The dancing bar closes in winter every night at 2 a.m. Paul Bossi and his family charge between 42F ($19.30) and 89F ($40.90) in a single and between 74F ($34) and 158F ($72.60) in a double, with half board included. Prices depend on the plumbing and the season.

Hotel Guarda Val (tel. 34-22-14) is in the remote hamlet of Sporz in a collection of buildings that used to be way stations for alpine farmers on their way with their herds up into the summertime Alps. The hamlet is a three-minute bus ride from the center of Lenzerheide, on transportation which the hotel runs frequently. The hotel is spread out over eight rustic buildings, and contains 70 beds in renovated rooms that have an undeniable charm. Each accommodation has a private bath, plus a variety of floor plans that include rustic beams and irregular shapes. A Japanese bath (Ofuro Taneo) and sand tennis courts are on the grounds. If you're a hiker, you'll find dozens of nearby foot trails. In winter you'll appreciate the several fireplaces and the masses of snow that almost engulf the village. This is not a typical hotel, and might prove to be just what you're looking for if you desire rustic peace, quiet, and calm. Singles range from 95F ($43.65) to 165F ($75.82), while doubles cost from 95F ($43.65) to 160F ($73.52) per person, with half board included. Prices depend on the season and the accommodation.

Hotel Mira Val (tel. 39-12-50), run by the Häusel family, offers 22 handsomely furnished accommodations, each with balcony and private shower and toilet, along with a radio and direct-dial phone. The hotel is among the latest to be erected at Flims, lying on a little hill in a settling of forests and meadows, overlooking the village and the valley beyond. It's constructed directly by the ski slope. Nearby are outdoor tennis courts in summer, or in winter, ice fields where you can skate and curl. The Mira Val also has a comfortable lounge, a dining room, and a small restaurant. The atmosphere is friendly, and the cookery is old-fashioned "home style." Depending on the season, doubles range from 110F ($50.55) to 150F ($68.93) and singles from 55F ($25.27) to 75F ($34.46), each tariff including half board.

Restaurant Guarda Val, in the hotel just recommended (same phone), is the best place for dining in the area, and is often visited by guests from the other hotels. The walls of this restaurant are a white stucco, with a heavily rustic balcony and stairway leading to it. The chef prepares such specialties as grilled meats over the open wood fire, grilled salmon, filet of sole, crayfish, grilled hare, and seabass in a fennel cream sauce. Another deluxe dish is Bresse hen in puff pastry, served with a truffle sauce. lamb is also prepared in several different ways. Meals range in price from 65F ($29.87) to 85F ($39.06). The restaurant is closed from April until some time in mid-June, and it also shuts down from mid-October to mid-December.

FOOD AND LODGING AT VALBELLA: Posthotel Valbella (tel. 34-12-12) is a well-managed, comfortable hotel with dark balconies that contrast attractively with the light yellow of the concrete superstructure. The interior is finished with well-buffed hardwoods, skillfully set masonry, and bright colors. If you count the sun terrace, the establishment contains three different restaurants and three separate bars, all of them rustically paneled in glowing woods. In wintertime guests usually dance to live musical groups. In summer the bar turns into a disco. A large indoor swimming pool, a sauna, a massage room, and two outdoor tennis courts are part of the sports facilities. *Per-person* rates with half board included are between 80F ($36.76) and 170F ($78.12) in a single and between 70F ($32.17) and 180F ($82.71) in a double, depending on the season, the plumbing, and exposure. Walter and Miriam Trösch, your hosts, are conscientious and friendly.

Valbella Inn (tel. 34-36-36) is about a hundred yards off the main street of Valbella, in a modern chalet with beautiful views, plus a restaurant guaranteed to make you feel at home. It has colorful yellow walls below a beamed ceiling, and chalet chairs pulled under tables with red napery. The indoor swimming pool has plants growing near its panoramic windows, while the main sitting room is very large and has a fireplace usually crackling out heat in wintertime. Facilities include a dancing bar, a sauna, two tennis courts, and a sun terrace, plus a cafeteria providing snacks. There's also a children's playroom staffed with a professional kindergarten teacher. All the comfortable rooms contain private bath, ranging from 75F ($34.46) to 150F ($68.93) in a single and between 130F ($59.74) and 286F ($131.42) in a double, with half board included. Prices depend on the season and the exposure of the room.

APRÈS SKI: Check out the previously recommended **Hotel Kurhaus Alpina,** in Lenzerheide, which has a stube bar and dancing to a live band in season. You might begin your evening with an apéritif in the Steivetta Bar, later gyrating to the action in the Tic-Tac disco.

The other "hot spot" at the resort is the just-recommended **Valbella Inn,** whose Heini Hemmi Bar (you remember the Olympic gold medalist) provides music and dancing. It's an ideal place to meet people and relax.

15. Savognin

If you go to this small, unpretentious winter resort, your friends are likely to ask, "How's that, again?" Savognin is something of a discovery, and it's not spoiled. Yet!

A major town in the Oberhalbstein, it lies at the mouth of the Val Nandro. Three of its churches are from the 17th century. Savognin was the home of the painter Giovanni Segantini.

The small resort has a good system of chair lifts and ski lifts, some going as high as 8900 feet. It advertises itself as the biggest snowmaker in Europe, producing fake snow for ski trails with a "snow cannon" when necessary. There are 50 miles of ski slopes, a ski school, and 12 miles of cross-country ski trails, plus tobogganing, a natural ice-skating rink with two curling rinks, sleigh and horseback riding, and lots of signposted walking paths. This is a good family resort, conducting ski races for children. Those too small to ski can be left at the Pinocchio Club (nursery).

Savognin has surprisingly good hotels with reasonable prices for rooms.

FOOD AND LODGING: **Hotel Cresta** (tel. 74-17-55) is a modern four-star hotel in the center of town. The Taverna bar is an active disco usually filled with young dancers who boogie in a red-draped ambience to live bands. A sun terrace and a swimming pool offer panoramic views, while a rustically beamed restaurant has yellow walls and hanging lamps. The bedrooms are simple and attractive, and often have spread-out views of the countryside around the hotel. Singles range from 65F ($29.87) to 135F ($62.03), while doubles cost between 100F ($45.95) and 228F ($104.77), breakfast included. Half board is another 15F ($6.89) per person. Prices depend on the season and the room assignment, although each unit has a private bath.

Hotel Danilo (tel. 74-14-66) is a country-style hotel in the center of the village. On the premises you'll find a dining room for hotel guests only, two restaurants, and two bars (one of them with dancing). The hotel was built in 1970, and furnished in a newly constructed rustic format of heavy stained beams, overstuffed modern leather armchairs, and bright-orange carpeting. With half board included, the *per-person* rate in a double ranges from 40F ($18.38) to 71F ($32.62), with supplements ranging from 7F ($3.22) to 15F ($6.89) charged for single rooms and those with balconies.

Hotel Romana (tel. 74-15-44) is a rustic family-run hotel with heavy beams, lots of polished wood, and a gently sloping staircase leading to the accommodations from the conservatively decorated reception area. A dancing nightclub gives wintertime diversion to guests, while three restaurants serve regional à la carte specialties. The hotel is in the center of town, on the main street, with all the sports facilities close at hand. Singles range from 38F ($17.46) to 55F ($25.27), while doubles cost between 66F ($30.33) and 100F ($45.95), with breakfast included.

Chapter XII

LUGANO, LOCARNO, AND THE TICINO

1. Airolo
2. Faido
3. Bellinzona
4. Locarno
5. Vira-Gambarogno
6. Ascona
7. Brissago
8. Lugano
9. Morcote

IF YOU DON'T NORMALLY think of palm trees in Switzerland, you haven't seen Ticino, the Italian-speaking part of Switzerland. Also called "The Tessin," it's the so-called Swiss Riviera. Although Italian is the major language, many of its people also speak German, French, and English. It's very international, owing to its diverse number of visitors.

Officially, Ticino begins at Airolo, which is the exit of the St. Gotthard Tunnel, and the St. Gotthard railway traverses the canton for about 75 miles from Airolo, at the southern mouth of the tunnel. But most vacationers head instead for the major resorts of Locarno, Lugano, and fast-rising Ascona. As Switzerland goes, they find the prices much cheaper in this canton, especially outside those three just-named resorts and in the little villages and hamlets of the canton, where the people are among the friendliest in the country.

Both Lugano and Locarno share the magnificent lakes of Lugano and Maggiore with Italy, their neighbor to the south. Relations between the two countries weren't as peaceful as they are today, and Ticino was the setting of many a battle between the Swiss and the Lombards. Essentially, the canton was carved out of Swiss conquests of the Duchy of Milan.

Ticino is the most southerly of the cantons, and its name is taken from the Ticino River, a left-bank tributary of the Po. Its weather is almost guaranteed between March and November. The balmy climate produces much subtropical vegetation. The rest of the year can be damp and cold.

The architecture is remarkably different in Ticino from that of the rest of Switzerland. It shows the influence of northern Italy, particularly in its buildings of natural stone. The food and wine are also different. You eat Lombard-style here, but with a definite Swiss accent. Sometimes in the same trattoria along a lakeshore, you'll have a German husband and his wife of Italian origin, and the cuisine they turn out is an amazing concession to both culinary traditions.

You could spend two weeks at least just touring through the valleys of the canton. In almost every case they offer tranquil seclusion and rustic charm. Every visitor soon adopts his or her favorite village.

If you're like most visitors you'll come to the Ticino after leaving central Switzerland, perhaps having visited Andermatt. If so, you'll cross through St. Gotthard, arriving in Ticino. The first town you'll hit is—

1. Airolo

This little hamlet in the heart of the Alps gets all the traffic from the St. Gotthard highway or through the tunnel, lying within easy reach of the pass and the Nufenen road. It has amenities making it pleasant in both summer and winter, including a cableway and ski lift. Airolo is a convenient spot for an overnight stopover.

FOOD AND LODGING: **Hôtel des Alpes** (tel. 88-17-22) is an attractive cube of a building, with a gently sloping, gabled roof and louvered shutters in natural-grain wood. It has a modern extension going off to one side, plus a summertime sun terrace surrounded by flowerboxes. The bedrooms are filled with sunny colors, newly constructed furniture, and an occasional antique. There's also an elevator. Singles range from 45F ($20.68) to 55F ($25.27), while doubles cost between 70F ($32.17) and 80F ($36.76), with breakfast included. For sojourns of more than three days, half board is an additional 18F ($8.27) per person daily.

Hotel Motta & Poste (tel. 88-23-88) is a nondescript white-walled building whose exterior has suffered from a modernizing facelift. It lies on a busy street in the center of town. Inside you'll find masonry walls with copper-flanged chimneys, a paneled dining room, and a sitting room filled with seats made of lime-green upholstered cubes. Bedrooms are filled with molded plastic furniture and colorful bedspreads. A double without bath is only 50F ($22.98), going up to 80F ($36.76) and 90F ($41.36) with shower and bath. Half board is another 22F ($10.11) per person daily.

2. Faido

Faido lies to the south of Airolo and might be another stopover for travelers using the St. Gotthard highway or car and rail tunnel. It's the major town in the beautiful Valle Leventina. You'll see here an architectural mix of stone houses and half-timbered buildings.

If you're driving from the north to go south through the tunnel, you'll notice in Faido the mulberry trees and other vegetation which suggest the dramatic contrast of the Ticino with the rest of Switzerland. A convenient rest stop between St. Gotthard and Bellinzona, Faido is also a good center for exploring the charming village of Giornico.

FOOD AND LODGING: **Hotel Milano** (tel. 38-13-07) has a grandly proportioned loggia with a triple arch soaring above the rest of the building. It looks undeniably Italian, especially with the exotic vegetation growing around it. The interior is filled with streamlined furniture in bright colors. This is one of the best bargains around, with a friendly management, the Lentini family. The location is quiet, lying a few hundred yards off the main road. The clean and simple accommodations rent for 37F ($17) to 47F ($21.60) in a single, while doubles cost from 31F ($14.25) to 40F ($18.38) per person, with breakfast included.

Pedrinis, Piazza Fontana (tel. 38-12-41), has the best food in the area, and should be considered if you're only a motorist passing through. The owner, Mr. Biasca, has hired a fine chef, Mr. Giuseppe, who cooks such delectable specialties as noodles Pedrini, spaghetti Scalinada, risotto with seafood, entrecôte with green peppercorns, a brochette of three kinds of well-flavored meat, and such regional dishes as braised beef with polenta. The restaurant is closed on Sunday in winter and from mid-December to mid-January. Fixed-price meals begin at 20F ($9.19). It's open in summer from 11:30 a.m. to 2:30 p.m. and 6:30 to 10 p.m. In winter they usually close about an hour earlier.

3. Bellinzona

The political capital of the canton of Ticino, Bellinzona lies 14 miles from Locarno. The town may have been of Roman origin, although mention is first made of it in 590. As the key to the St. Gotthard, San Bernardino, and Lukmanier Passes, it loomed large in the history of Lombardy. In the 8th century it was owned outright by the bishop of Como, and jockeying for ownership went back and forth between Como and Milan in the 13th and 14th centuries. But by 1798 it had become the capital of its own canton, Bellinzona. Five years later it was united with the newly formed canton of Ticino, and has remained so ever since, in spite of its turbulent past.

Between the 13th and 15th centuries Bellinzona was fortified by three castles, which form a trio of its three major sightseeing attractions today: the Schwyz, the Unterwald, and the Uri.

The most ancient of the castles, the **Castle of Uri** (Castello Grande, in Italian) now houses administrative offices, but its towers are open to the public. This castle is also known by yet another name, San Michele. At any rate, it dates from the 13th century. Visits, which should be done mainly for the view, are possible from Easter to mid-September from 9 a.m. to noon and 2 to 5 p.m.

Schwyz Castle (Castello di Montebello, in Italian) has been turned into a museum devoted to history and archeology. If you have time to visit only one of the trio of medieval fortifications, make it this one, as it's clearly the most outstanding. It has a 13th-century château with a courtyard, but other additions were made in the latter half of the 15th century. At the turn of this century it was totally restored after having fallen into great disrepair. You can drive to it from the Viale Stazione, following the steep ramp up to this huge citadel. The museum, frankly, is of very minor interest. It's open Easter to mid-September daily from 9 a.m. to noon and 2 to 5 p.m.

The third member of the fortification, the **Castle of Unterwald** (Castello di Sasso Corbaro, in Italian), built in 1479, can be reached on the same road that goes up to the Schwyz. The view from the terrace here is the finest in Bellinzona. You'll see not only the lower valley of the Ticino, but on a clear day (or night), a view of Lake Maggiore as well. The museum (again of minor interest) contains costumes of the canton and some arts and crafts of the region. Its hours are Easter to October daily from 9 a.m. to noon and 2 to 5 p.m. (closed on Tuesday).

Also of note, the collegiate **Church of SS. Peter and Stephen** dates from the 16th century. It's a fine Renaissance structure, with a richly embellished baroque interior.

FOOD AND LODGING: **Hotel Unione** (tel. 25-55-77) was a fairly nondescript white rectangular building until someone added a balconied extension in pink marble. It's surrounded by gardens, some of them with fountains, and has a series of simple modern accommodations with flowery carpeting or beige-colored tiles. Singles range from 42F ($19.30) to 72F ($33.08), while doubles cost between 72F ($33.08) and 103F ($47.33), with breakfast included.

Corona, 5 via Camminata (tel. 25-28-44), serves specialties such as veal steak Daniela, filet of sole parisienne, filet of veal Goccia d'oro, mushrooms with polenta, fresh tortellini with butter and sage sauce, and a gratin of seafood upon special request. The Ticino specialties are very good here, and the management is friendly and welcoming. The prices make the place a bargain, with fixed-price meals ranging from 15F ($6.89) to 21F ($9.65). À la carte meals cost roughly the same. The restaurant is open daily except Sunday from 7 a.m. to midnight.

A GIORNICO POSTSCRIPT: For those traveling the St. Gotthard road, a worthwhile excusion might be at the village of Giornico, lying on both banks of the Ticino River. This, in my judgment, is the most charming stopover on the road.

The hamlet lies in a setting of vineyards. In the middle of the river is a small island with stone roofs, aged by time. It's reached by a pair of old arched bridges. On the right bank are two Romanesque churches.

The finest of these is the **Church of San Nicolao,** from the 12th century. The columns of the gateway are supported by sculptured mythical beasts, showing a marked Lombard influence. Try, if possible, to explore the crypt, with its sculptures. The other church is higher up in a vineyard setting, **Santa Maria di Castello.**

Incidentally, Giornico was the battleground on which 600 Swiss defeated more than 10,000 Milanese soldiers in 1478. A monument in the village commemorates that long-ago victory.

4. Locarno

This ancient Ticinese town sprawls at the north end of Lake Maggiore (which also washes up on the shores of Italy). A holiday resort, it's known for its mild climate, which produces a rich, Mediterranean vegetation even though still in Switzerland. Camellias and magnolias bloom in the spring, as do mimosa and wisteria, azaleas and oleander. Palm fronds flap in the lake wind, and you'll spot eucalyptus like the kind grown in Italy. Olives, figs, and pomegranates flourish in this climate, and myrtle blooms in August. Spring and fall are the ideal times to visit.

Locarno is 14 miles southwest of Bellinzona by rail. Since 1923 the town has been connected by electric railway with Domodossola and the Simplon via the Centovalli (the latter name derived from the hundred valleys that slope down toward the river, on whose banks lie small villages). This international railway, called the Locarno–Domodossola, serves as a link between the Gotthard and the Simplon lines. To cover this difficult terrain required audacious bridge constructions.

Beyond the Italian frontier at Carnedo, the railway climbs up to the plateau of Santa Maria Maggiore, a wide, barren, and solitary district that stretches out for about six miles at 2800 feet above sea level. A steep descent leads down to the railway junction of Domodossola.

From there, one can continue to Brig in the Rhône Valley by railway through the Simplon tunnel. From Brig, one travels on, either to Berne through the Loetschberg tunnel, or to the Lake of Geneva. By direct trains the journey from Lausanne or Berne to Locarno is about four hours.

Locarno itself entered world history books in 1925 because of a series of agreements known as the Pact of Locarno. It was in Locarno that the former enemies of World War I committed themselves to a peaceful policy, even though it wasn't to last. Locarno was chosen over Lucerne, reportedly, because the mistress of the French minister preferred it and persuaded him to demand that the meeting be held on Lake Maggiore. Mussolini arrived and so did Chamberlain, along with the other statesman, including Stresemann from Germany.

Hitler made a mockery of this pact when in March of 1936 he sent troops into the Rhineland, which France considered a "flagrant violation." Britain declined to act, however. But the real flagrant violations were to follow, so this pact is best confined to grandfathers who tell their offspring in Locarno of that long-ago day on October 16, 1925, when they actually saw Il Duce.

Today a host of international celebrities continue to arrive in Locarno, but for a very different reason. They're here to attend the **International Film Festival** which takes place every summer against the backdrop of the **Piazza Grande,** the main square of the town. From here you can walk under the arcades, sheltering you from the hot August sun, to explore the shops on the piazza's north side. Here you're likely to find high fashion (often from Milan), antiques, art galleries, and both Swiss and Italian handicrafts.

From the Piazza Grande, follow the curvy **Via Francesco Rusca** (note all the Italian street names), to the old town. Along the way, you can visit the **Castello Visconti,** a late medieval castle, the sole survival of a former extensive stronghold where the Dukes of Milan lived before it was largely destroyed in 1518. It's now a Museum Civico, which displays many Roman artifacts excavated in the area and some modern paintings, including Dadaists. It's open from the first of April until the end of October from 9 a.m. to noon and 2 to 4 p.m. (closed on Monday). The modern art collection was initially formed by Hans Arp, who died in 1966.

On a tree-studded crag above Locarno, the **Church of the Madonna del Sasso** is the resort's most important site. If you're a devout pilgrim, you can climb up to it (the church stands at an elevation of 1165 feet). However, I'd recommend the funicular, which leaves about every 15 minutes between 7 a.m. and 11 p.m., a round-trip fare costing 3.50F ($1.61). Founded in 1480, the church was reconstructed in 1616. The basilica has been filled with much artwork, the most enticing being Bramantino's *Flight into Egypt* of 1536. The views from the terrace certainly compete with the ecclesiastical treasures inside. The glory of Lake Maggiore lies before you. The church was built after a friar, Bartolomeo da Ivrea, reportedly saw a vision of the Virgin in 1480.

EXCURSIONS: After visiting this pilgrimage site, you can continue by cable car to the **Alpe Cardada,** at 4430 feet. The one-mile trip takes ten minutes, but the view, once you get there, is worth it. From Cardada, a chairlift goes to the summit of **Cimetta** at 5480 feet, from which a magnificent sweep of Lake Maggiore and the Alps unfolds. There's good skiing here, with several ski lifts. The total round-trip fare from Orselina—reached by cable railway—to Cardada to Cimetta is about 18F ($8.27). Service is from 7:30 a.m. to 5 p.m. in season.

The other popular excursion is the **Ronco Tour,** which can also be done easily from the competitive resort of Ascona, as can a trip to the island of **Brissago** (see later in this chapter for a description).

The tourist office in Locarno will outline a number of full- or half-day trips possible from the resort, especially through valleys and up steep, hairpin mountain roads which only very skilled drivers should explore on their own.

One of these, and some say the most fascinating, is to the **Val Verzasca,** a distance of about 20 miles. This Ticinese valley, with its tile-roofed houses and old churches with campaniles, could easily be in some valley in northern Italy. The valley itself (get a good map before striking out) is relatively uninhabited, except for some very wise people who retreat here in summer to enjoy their vacation homes in a most tranquil atmosphere.

To reach it, leave Locarno on the road to Bellinzona. At Gordola, a village at the entrance to the valley, continue on to Sonogno. Along the way you'll see the Verzasca Dam, which was built in the 1960s to prevent flooding in the area. The dam made a lake, called the Lago di Vogorno.

Skirting the lake, you'll pass through seven tunnels. Eventually you'll arrive at Brione, at the head of the Valle d'Osola. The hamlet has a four-towered castle but is known mainly for its church, with its frescoes dating from the 14th century. The post road—so called because postal coaches make this run—terminates at Sonogno, a mountain hamlet at an elevation of 3020 feet.

WHERE TO STAY: Locarno has a number of good accommodations which can be most desirable if you're coming to or from Italy. Many are pleasant if you want to spend a lakeside holiday in the Italian-speaking part of Switzerland. During the International Film Festival in August, you'll neeed a reservation way in advance.

The Upper Bracket

Hotel la Palma au Lac, 29 viale Verbano (tel. 33-01-71), at Muralto, sits beside the lake in a sparkingly white building with vivid green awnings covering the long modern balconies. The lawns leading down to the water are dotted with sun chairs and chaise lounges, while indoors guests can use the sauna, the swimming pool, or a rooftop terrace. The public rooms are furnished in an updated fashion that retains an air of 19th-century grace, thanks in part to the oil paintings and tapestries. There's also a dancing bar, along with eating places, both indoors and outdoors (The Coq d'Or is the premier restaurant in town). The elegantly furnished bedrooms reveal an unmistakable Italian flair. *Per-person* rates range from 88F ($40.44) to 200F ($91.90), depending on the season, the accommodation, and the plumbing. Half board is another 30F ($13.79) per person daily.

Hotel Esplanade (tel. 84-61-46) is a very large ocher-colored building in an Italian Renaissance format of double towers connected by long rows of covered loggias. The interior is as high-ceilinged and elegant as its outside would imply. A grand piano in one of the salons plays evening music. There's also a sun terrace, along with a large outdoor swimming pool, as well as three outdoor tennis courts with an instructor. The establishment is set in the middle of a large park filled with flowers. *Per-person* rates in a double room range from 45F ($20.68) to 100F ($45.95), while singles cost between 50F ($22.98) and the 105F ($48.25), with breakfast included. Prices depend on the season, the exposure of the room, and the plumbing.

Hotel Muralto, Lungolago (tel. 33-88-81), is a white-walled rectangular block pierced with long horizontal rows of silvery windows. From the promenade along the lake you'll see dozens of summertime parasols tilted at angles above the sun chairs on the modern balconies. The bedrooms are clean and gracefully furnished with desirable reproductions of older pieces. They're invariably sunny, and outfitted with clear and pleasant colors. Each of the accommodations has a private bath, TV, phone, and radio. One of my favorite parts of this hotel is the tiled sun terrace, raised above ground level on a cement platform and surrounded by semitropical plants. Singles range from 72F ($33.08) to 140F ($64.33), while doubles cost between 72F ($33.08) and 98F ($45.03) per person, with breakfast included. Half board is available for an additional 28F ($12.87) per person.

Hotel Arcadia al Lago, Lungolago G. Motta (tel. 31-02-82), is one of the newest hotels in Locarno. It's separated from the water only by an expanse of greenery and a whimsically fashioned wrought-iron fence, dividing the grounds from the lakeside promenade. The dozens of balconies give residents a chance to improve their suntans. The bedrooms are filled with full-grained angular modern furniture, wall-to-wall carpeting, and lots of sunlight. *Per-person* rates, with a copious breakfast included, cost between 50F ($22.98) and 90F ($41.36), double occupancy according to the season, with a 15F ($6.89) supplement for single occupancy.

Hotel Reber au Lac (tel. 33-02-02) has been owned by a family with the same name since 1886. It has a Spanish bar and grill room outfitted in shades of scarlet, with a French restaurant with Corinthian columns, high ceilings, and pink leather chairs. You'll enjoy the lakeside sun terrace, the outdoor heated pool, the private pier, and the large semitropical garden, along with a private tennis court. The American bar has sophisticated colors and a psychedelic dance floor. The rest of the hotel is attractive and comfortable. The entire complex is set in a garden with flowers that bloom in every season. Singles range from 55F ($25.27) to 155F ($71.22), while doubles cost between 90F ($41.36) and 275F ($126.35), according to the season, the exposure, and the plumbing. These tariffs include breakfast. Half board is available for another 40F ($18.38) per person daily.

Hotel Quisisana (tel. 33-01-41) is a rambling white-walled hotel with blue trim, a top floor of big-windowed sliding doors surrounded by balconies, and gracefully curved balustrades outside the windows of the lower floors. The entire building is surrounded with exotic vegetation that always seems to be flowering and looks like something you'd find much farther south. Oriental rugs cover many of the floors of the interior. The public rooms have a comfortable but unimpressive collection of conservatively upholstered armchairs and lots of light. The comfortable bedrooms are simple, modern, and attractive. Other facilities include an indoor swimming pool, a solarium, and a fitness room. You'll be only a few minutes away from the railway station. Singles range from 63F ($28.95) to 108F ($49.63), while doubles cost from 120F ($55.14) to 200F ($91.90), with breakfast included.

The Middle Bracket

Hôtel Beau-Rivage, Lungolago (tel. 33-13-55). A Doric colonnade supports the sun terrace just above the main entrance, with masses of shrubbery growing between the pillars. Above that, the white facade is usually festooned with masses of flowers which thrive in the lakeside sunshine. Each of the balconies is crafted of white wrought iron. The interior is furnished in an elegant simplicity that includes vaulted ceilings, floors set with salmon-colored marble, and a few touches of neoclassical gilt-edged mirrors. A terrace restaurant is popular in summer. Singles range from 55F ($25.27) to 85F ($39.06), while doubles cost between 95F ($43.65) and 155F ($71.22), breakfast included. Half board is another 20F ($9.19) per person daily. Prices depend on the plumbing and the season.

Hotel du Lac (tel. 31-29-21) is a rambling white-painted building with a gently sloping Mediterranean-style roof and a functionally updated interior. The dining room is divided almost in two by a grandly arched stucco wall. It has immaculate white napery and a big row of windows. The bedrooms are comfortably modern, with bright colors and big windows which usually face south. The hotel not only has an elevator, but a good cuisine. Singles range from 55F ($25.27) to 70F ($32.17), and doubles cost between 105F ($48.25) and 132F ($60.65), with breakfast included.

Remorino Hotel, 29 via Verbano, (tel. 33-10-33), is a recently constructed, balconied building two minutes from the lake. It's in an area called Minusio, which is full of residential homes surrounded by flowers. The sun terrace behind the hotel is shaded with colorful parasols, while the tasteful bedrooms are simply and attractively furnished in a design that might be called Italian provincial. An outdoor swimming pool is set into the well-maintained gardens, with all the folding chairs you'd need to entertain one friend or ten. Singles rent for between 70F ($32.17) and 90F ($41.36), while doubles cost between 65F ($29.87) and 85F ($39.06) per person, with breakfast included. Each of the accommodations contains a private bath.

Hotel Atlantico, 6 via Cattori (tel. 31-18-64), is a clean and attractive balconied hotel built 25 years ago. It's one of the safest bets in town for a fairly priced, clean, and attractive lodging. It has a green neon sign over the top floor which you can see from the center of the old town a few blocks away. The bedrooms are sunny and very spacious, often with pleasingly irregular shapes, and usually with a balcony offering a view of the lake. The owner is a charming Italian, Tullio Merizzi, who personally greets his guests each morning at breakfast. You'll usually find parking on one of the side streets nearby, or near the extravagantly beautiful fountain a block away. The lake is only three minutes away, and the surrounding neighborhood is filled with old houses. Singles range from 45F ($20.68) to 78F ($35.84), while doubles cost between 81F ($37.22) and 105F ($48.25), with breakfast served by a charming member of the family. The building has an elevator, and very satisfactory shared baths for those in rooms without.

The Budget Range

Conca d'Oro, 7 Riva Paradiso (tel. 54-31-31), in Paradiso, sits at the edge of the lake in a tall white building with a gently sloping roof. Its low-lying outbuildings contain bathing facilities and a sun terrace with waiter service. You can swim in the lake if you wish, but a public swimming pool and a sauna are right next door. Bedrooms are simple and unpretentiously furnished in bright colors and spartan furniture. Singles rent for between 65F ($29.87) and 90F ($41.36), while doubles cost between 110F ($50.55) and 150F ($68), with breakfast included. All units contain private bath.

Rosa Seegarten (tel. 33-87-31) is a cream-colored, old-fashioned hotel which sits right on the lake. It represents a bargain for expensive Locarno. Half board is encouraged by the friendly management. Meals are taken on a lakeside terrace under a grape arbor. Many of the older clients prefer to eat inside, which is attractively outfitted with white walls and wood tones. The hotel lies only three minutes from the train station. An elevator will take you to your comfortable bedroom. *Per-person* rates, in a single or double, range from 44F ($20.22) to 68F ($31.25), with breakfast included. Prices depend on the season and the plumbing.

Hotel dell'Angelo (tel. 31-81-75) is a clean, attractive hotel with a central location and bedrooms which represent a good bargain. It has lots of atmosphere and simply furnished accommodations, renting for between 40F ($18.38) and 65F ($29.87) in a single and between 68F ($31.25) and 108F ($49.63) in a double, with breakfast included. Your friendly host has the wonderfully resonant name of Dado Pierantonio.

WHERE TO DINE: For many visitors, Locarno will represent their introduction to an unfamiliar type of cookery: Swiss-Italian. It's best represented at the establishments recommended below.

La Centenario, 15 Lungolago (tel. 33-82-22), in Muralto. This restaurant bases its menu on the availability in the market of the various fish, meats, and vegetables which go into its recipes. The creations that emerge from the kitchen of Gérard Perriard are as colorful as they are delectable. The austere white walls of the simple dining room reflect the rainbow-colored food to an even better advantage. You'll be seated in a straight-backed chair by the Catalán-born co-owner, Jordi Giner, who will hand you a menu, listing such specialties as seabass with fennel (like that served on the French Riviera), foie gras of duck with salad, roast lamb with aromatic herbs, filet of roebuck (in season) with mushrooms, roast guinea fowl with sauerkraut and truffles, lobster bisque, and shrimp St. Jacques. All these dishes are exquisitely prepared and served. But for a really unusual first course, ask for a cold comsommé of quail eggs swirled into colorful patterns of various natural colors caused by the vegetables contained within. All of this is garnished with caviar. Fixed-price meals range from 40F ($18.38) to 85F ($39.06), while à la carte dinners cost from 42F ($19.30) to 65F ($29.87). The restaurant is closed on Monday and for a month every year sometime in midwinter.

Le Coq d'Or, Hotel la Palma au Lac, 29 viale Verbano (tel. 33-01-71), at Muralto. You might choose to have a drink in the huge bar area before going in to dinner. The bar is marble-floored, with a pianist tinkling melodies in the corner. Almost everything here is in Valentine red, including the textured ceiling, the leather armchairs, and the accessories. The restaurant opens spaciously off the bar, and it too is covered in red walls with accents of well-polished paneling. Even the candles are red. This place is not done in the best of classical tastes, but it's attractive and comfortable, and best of all, it has an exposed kitchen area with an elegant layout where you can see the uniformed chefs preparing your dinner. The head chef is Artino de Marchis, who delighted gourmets at the Ritz and Prunier in London before bringing his talents to the Ticino. The prices are paralyzing, but for many gourmets it's worth it. An à la carte meal could cost 140F ($64.33), while the fixed-price menu gastronomique ranges between 80F ($36.76) and 100F ($45.95). Specialties include a salad with "mushrooms of the woods," a pâté of pheasant with quince jelly, avocado soup with mint, mussel soup with watercress, a mousseline of crayfish with artichoke hearts, lobster sauteed in provençal butter, veal kidney with morels, and poached oysters with truffles.

Restaurant Cittàdella, 18 via Cittàdella (tel. 31-58-85), lies in the center of the old town on a cobblestone street behind an arcade concealed from traffic by vines and granite columns. You'll find a pizzeria downstairs, with timbered ceilings and stucco walls, which gives a rustic quality to the informal atmosphere. Pizzas begin at 7F ($3.22). Upstairs, however, you'll find a chic enclave of nouvelle cuisine. Specialties include a goose-liver terrine, a combination plate of sole, salmon, and turbot, and a salad of large shrimp with nuts and mango. One specialty is a mixed grill with both salt- and freshwater fish. Another favorite is risotto with "fruits of the sea." A special gourmet menu with a choice of four main courses is presented for 62F ($28.49) per person, or you might order à la carte at an average price of 50F ($22.98). The restaurant is open from 8:30 a.m. to 2 p.m. and 5 p.m. to midnight. It's closed for three weeks in June.

Ristorante Zurigo (tel. 33-16-17) serves savory food to a loyal clientele every day from 7 a.m. to midnight. It's right on the lakefront, in an attractive Mediterranean-style building with flowered balconies and shuttered windows. The establishment was built at the beginning of the 20th century, and has a gregarious and friendly staff who work in an art nouveau framework filled with charm. The flagstone terrace is dotted with chestnut trees and festive lights which make it one of the finest dining choices in Locarno on a summer night. There's also a green-and-white interior, with lots of its own kind of turn-of-the-century appeal. Meals are served from 30F ($13.79). One specialty is three types of pasta served on one platter. Many Italian specialties such as risotto verde and saltimbocca appear on the menu, although you may prefer the grilled beefsteak, a regular feature. The veal dishes are also excellent, and moderately priced. For dessert, the chef prepares a superb zabaglione. A children's menu is offered for 6F ($2.76). The Zurigo is also a hotel, offering comfortably furnished and reasonably priced rooms for 68F ($31.25) in a single and from 145F ($66.63) in a double.

Restaurant Carbonara, Piazza Stazione (tel. 33-67-14). You're greeted by the sight of a plentifully stocked bar area, with one side opening onto the outdoors. Behind a glass wall is a heavily beamed ceiling, with hanging ornate lamps, white stucco walls, and lots of visual distraction from the many art objects, such as copper pots, hanging from the walls. Specialties include veal kidney with grappa and mushrooms, veal served piccata style, saltimbocca, and a large pasta menu, featuring macaroni with four different types of cheese. You'll also be served braciola alla pizzaiola, as well as grilled shrimp. Meals cost from 35F ($16.08). About 15 different types of pizza are also offered, costing from 7F ($3.22) to 10F ($4.60). Downstairs, with an entrance from the street, you'll find a cellar bar in stark moderno.

Mövenpick Oldrati, Lungolago (tel. 33-85-44), is one of the best and most elegant members of this popular chain. Its two floors open right onto the lake. A stairwell inside is carpeted with an Oriental runner and covered in fabric woven like an American needlepoint sampler. It leads to a room slightly more formal than the restaurant downstairs. There's also sidewalk dining. Many daily specials cost from 30F ($13.79). The chef specializes in curry dishes, and the Italian kitchen predominates, as reflected by the good pasta courses and the saltimbocca (literally, "jump in your mouth"). The kitchen also does very good terrines if you haven't already settled for an appetizer of the air-dried beef of the Grisons. The sole meunière is among the more favored dishes.

Restaurant Cervo, 11 via Toretta (tel. 31-41-31). You'll recognize it by the pink stucco facade with a wrought-iron bracket holding a replica of a deer's head. The sign advertises, medieval style, the brown-shuttered hotel with the summertime flower boxes. This is a well-kept, smallish hotel with a separate restaurant. Everything is rustically decorated. The kitchen, in the main, turns south to Italy for its inspiration. Specialties include gnocchi in the style of the chef, minestrone Ticinese, grilled shrimp, saltimbocca, risotto with mushrooms, and a special dessert "del padrone." Expect to spend around 30F ($13.79) or more for an excellent, typical meal here.

Restaurant Al Fagiano, 7 via Toretta (tel. 31-75-39). You climb a small street to the pink and granite-trimmed facade of this rustically decorated restaurant. In the vestibule you'll see antique bins filled with fresh vegetables, country style, which makes the whole place seem like a veritable cornucopia of good things to eat. From the street you'll be able to see the uniformed staff through a ground-floor window as they slice vegetables and stuff pasta. The establishment is owned by the Salizia family, who prepare such specialties as cream of shrimp soup with brandy, minestrone Ticinese, pizza in the style of Naples, grilled Florentine beef, and veal piccata Piemontese with risotto. Meals cost from 25F ($11.49) to 50F ($22.98).

Restaurant Locarnese, 1 via Bossi (no phone), isn't the chicest spot in Locarno, but the food is plentiful and good. Going here will give you a chance to eat with the locals. The interior is massively rustic, with a big stone fireplace lined with wine bottles, a smokey ceiling that long ago had designs painted between its timbers, and grayish walls hung with copper pots and knickknacks. You can eat here for only 20F ($9.19), savoring such Italian dishes as green lasagne, cannelloni, and ravioli, as well as four types of spaghetti, unless you prefer tagliatelle. Look for the specialties posted daily on the blackboard. You can also order steak or veal. The restaurant is closed Monday and for all of June.

AFTER DARK: You'd better turn in with a good book and get an early start on sightseeing the following day. Nightlife in Locarno doesn't impress me. Drag out dinner, have a nightcap in a bar at your hotel, and save your money. After checking out several clubs, and getting ripped off for a beer in each of them ("the Ticino is very expensive, sir"), I decided to tear up my notes and head back to my room. However, for that nightcap, I'd recommend either of the following two establishments where you can spend a relaxing hour or two:

Arcadia Bar and Café, Hotel Arcadia, Lungolago G. Motta (tel. 31-02-82), is one of the most attractive rendezvous points in Locarno. Built in the spring of 1983, it's decorated with black and pink marble flooring, palm trees, and rattan chairs that evoke the Caribbean. Every evening from 8 to midnight, they offer live music and dancing on the floor. The big windows open onto panoramic views of the verdant gardens, and you can sit around the curved bar area if you prefer. When I was last there the hotel played Marilyn Monroe records interspersed with Italian favorites. Beer costs from 2.50F ($1.15), while mixed drinks range between 8F ($3.68) and 13F ($5.97).

Café de Barcadero (tel. 31-52-52) is a bar/café/restaurant right on the lakeside at Lungolago G. Motta. It stands next to the embarkation point where you can purchase tickets for those cruises on Lake Maggiore. You'll see café tables under an orange-and-yellow awning. Inside the unpretentious room you'll find comfortable wood chairs. The big sunny windows let in lots of light and open onto a side view of the lake. A gin and tonic goes for only 7F ($3.22), and beer begins at 1.40F (86¢).

5. Vira-Gambarogno

For seekers of tranquility, this secluded spot on Lake Maggiore is ideal. Gambarogno and Vira are twin resorts on the opposite side of the lake from Locarno. The whole area is filled with small lakefront villages built of stone, with red roofs. You can go sightseeing in the small hamlets or hike through the protected Bolle di Magadino area to see its rare plants and waterbirds.

FOOD AND LODGING: **Touring Mot-Hotel Bellavista** (tel. 61-11-16) is a pumpkin-colored collection of villas set in a subtropical garden above the shores of Lake Maggiore. With its vistas of the mountains, its masonry detailing, and its rustic decor of paneled ceilings and modern rattan furniture, you could as easily imagine yourself in the Caribbean as in Europe. The Berger family, your friendly owners, supervise the grounds and the well-planned cuisine served in the sunny dining room. Doubles range from 51F ($23.44) to 99F ($45.49) per person daily, with singles costing from 65F ($29.87) to 99F ($45.49). These tariffs include a buffet breakfast and dinner. Prices depend on the accommodation and the season, although all units contain a private bath.

Hotel Viralago (tel. 61-15-91) is a balconied, salmon-colored building many of whose rooms look over the lake shore. The interior is uncluttered and streamlined, with light neutral colors picked up by the accents of the Oriental rugs and the leather furniture. An indoor pool and a sauna are on the premises, along with rustically stuccoed walls in the snack restaurant. A more formal restaurant serves grilled specialties. Musical entertainment is frequently provided. Singles range from 83F ($38.14) to 103F ($47.33), while doubles cost between 73F ($33.54) and 103F ($47.33) per person, with half board included. If you just want bed and breakfast, the management deducts 18F ($8.27) from the per-person room tariff.

6. Ascona

Only 2½ miles from Locarno, and a rival resort, Ascona lies snugly on Lake Maggiore. Once it was a tiny and sleepy fishing port, but it has grown into one of the most popular destinations in the Ticino. The town has long been a popular rendezvous point for painters, writers, and other celebrities. Lenin found the place ideal, as did Isadora Duncan and Carl Jung. Rudolf Steiner, likewise, was attracted to Ascona, and so were Hermann Hesse and Paul Klee. Erich Maria Remarque, the German novelist who wrote *All Quiet on the Western Front,* also lived here.

Much of the old town that these famous people knew has now been swallowed up by new developments which have seemed to devour the place like a Minotaur. But the heart of Ascona is still worth exploring, with its colorful little shops, art galleries (some good but some tawdry art), and antique stores.

Because of its mild climate, Ascona has subtropical vegetation. All year round, even in the middle of winter, some flowers are in bloom. The resort is well equipped with sports facilities, including a "lido" and its Kursaal. There's also a golf course in the interior. September is a month that music lovers circle on their calendars, for that's the time of the annual Ascona Music Weeks.

The **Collegio Pontificio Papio,** dating from 1584, has one of the most beautiful Renaissance courtyards in the country, with two-story loggias in the Italianate style. The **Church of Santa Maria della Misericordia,** on which construction began in the closing year of the 14th century, belongs to a Dominican monastery. Its chief treasure is one of the most mammoth late Gothic frescoes in Switzerland.

The 1620 **Casa Serodine** (also called Casa Borrani) has one of the most richly embellished facades of any secular structure in the country.

If you're in Ascona in the right season, the **Isole di Brissago,** reached by a boat trip, contains a botanical garden of Mediterranean and subtropical flora. Palm fronds rustle in the lake breezes, and there's also a small Roman bath. Admission is only 2F (92¢). Ask at the tourist office in Ascona if the gardens are open, and also about what boats are likely to go there on any given day.

You can also journey to the colorful little village of **Ronco,** reached by following the road to Verbania. Built on the flank of a slope, this very Italian-style village has one of the most charming settings in all of the Ticino. From the belvedere of the church, you'll have a good view.

WHERE TO STAY: If you like colorful, regional-style inns, you may prefer Ascona to most of the accommodations in Locarno or Lugano. It's the third most popular base for exploring the lake, from one of the hotels recommended below.

The Upper Bracket

Castello del Sole (tel. 35-02-02), about 1½ miles from the center, is the grandest place to stay. In the last few years it has been completely rebuilt. Surrounded by its large park and green meadows, it stands quite near the spot where the Maggia River falls into Lake Maggiore. As such, it offers perfect tranquillity and peace. Lodging here evokes life on a private estate, with a good beachfront and an 18-hole golf course a mile away. The hotel, with its many courtyards, was constructed around an antique palazzo. Spacious vaulted public rooms are set off by granite columns, marble-covered terraces, and charming accents ranging from 19th-century wrought iron to modern and tasteful decorative accessories. The hotel operates from March 30 until the end of October. A farm belonging to the hotel provides much of the produce served in the dining room (the hotel even produces its own wine). The Barbarossa restaurant serves many savory specialties. In summer, buffets are often served (the chefs specialize in grilled meats). There are also five outdoor tennis courts, plus two courts in a modern tennis hall. The hotel also has an indoor and outdoor swimming pool, as well as a sauna and massage facilities. All accommodations contain private balconies, and are beautifully furnished and well equipped. For half board, the cost ranges from 140F ($64.33) to 190F ($87.31) per person daily.

Hotel Losone (tel. 35-10-31), at Losone, on the outskirts, is an intelligently designed, one-story building that sprawls across a landscaped garden dotted with trees and flowerbeds. The various wings of the establishment curve at right angles around a free-form swimming pool which, with its nearby terrace, serves as the social center of the hotel. Inside, the decor is dramatically filled with massively paneled ceilings that look far older than they are, thanks to the regional designs painted between the beams. You'll also find masonry detailing, flagstone floors, Oriental rugs, and open bedrooms, each with a private bath and an access directly onto the lawns outside. The hotel lies midway between Locarno and Ascona, and is maintained by the Glaus family. With half board included, singles rent for between 140F ($64.33) and 180F ($82.71), while doubles range between 125F ($57.44) and 155F ($71.22) per person daily.

Hotel Eden Roc, via Albarelle (tel. 35-01-71), was designed around its location at the entrance to an indentation in the shoreline of the lake. The grounds around the hotel have been disciplined into terraces and flowerbeds, all of them leading gently down to the water. A swimming pool is surrounded by palm trees and a short expanse of well-maintained lawn. The interior is lightheartedly modern, decorated with a sense of style that is more Italian than Teutonic. Bedrooms are sunny and fairly spacious, some of them frilly and romantic, others more angularly modern. Each of the accommodations contains a private bath, balcony, TV, radio, phone, and mini-bar. Doubles range between 240F ($110.28) and 350F ($160.85), depending on the season, the exposure, and the size of the unit.

Albergo Casa Berno (tel. 35-32-32) is a very large hotel with several outcroppings of different balconied wings rising up from the steep hillside into which it's been built. The setting is dramatically forested, with the lake dominating the view from most of the bedrooms. An outdoor swimming pool is cantilevered behind a stone embankment which, because of the steepness of the hill, places it close to the flower-covered roof terrace of the main building. The comfortable bedrooms are filled with elegant furniture, including some painted Louis XVI–style chairs, and flowery curtains. Facilities include a sauna and massage room, two restaurants, and a bar. Each of the accommodations contains a private bath, balcony, southern exposure, and a mini-bar. Singles range from 110F ($50.55) to 155F ($71.22), while doubles cost between 105F ($48.25) and 165F ($75.82) per person daily, with half board included.

Hotel Al Sasso Boretto (tel. 35-71-15). The entire balconied superstructure of this establishment seems to be set on top of cement columns. Glass windows frame the ground floor, which is surrounded by red brick terraces and Mediterranean trees. Inside you'll find a swimming pool decorated with abstract wall murals and a sauna, along with restaurants and garden cafés, as well as a modern bar. The bedrooms, for the most part, are in brown and beige. The larger accommodations are decorated with Italian flair, while the more nondescript smaller ones are cozy and comfortable. You can park in the underground garage. B. Nötzli, the director, organizes once-a-week sightseeing tours in the environs. Singles range from 85F ($39.06) to 110F ($50.55), while doubles cost between 70F ($32.17) and 90F ($41.36) per person, with breakfast included. From November 1 until March 20 the hotel is closed, but its restaurant and apartments remain open.

Hotel Europe au Lac (tel. 35-28-81) looks like a charmingly designed modern rendition of an Italian villa. You'll pass some stone-banked flowerbeds before reaching the massive Romanesque arch of the front entrance, which leads past glass doors to the arched atrium at the interior of the house. This is planted with subtropical flowers and surrounded by an arcade covered with half-rounded teracotta tiles. The dining room repeats the Mediterranean theme, with light colors, lots of flowers, immaculate napery, and touches of wrought iron. Bedrooms are spacious and comfortable, tastefully appointed, and most often charming. Both the indoor and outdoor swimming pool are reached by the elevator from the bedrooms. The hotel has its own beach and a grassy lawn for sunbathing, and lies near a golf course and tennis courts. Its bar area has a live pianist to entertain guests. The hotel is a good choice for a stay in Ascona, especially since the service provided by Richard Diggelmann and his family is conscientious and friendly. With half board included, singles range from 175F ($80.41) to 195F ($89.60), while doubles cost between 255F ($117.17) and 325F ($149.34), depending on the season.

Hotel Acapulco au Lac (tel. 35-45-21). From almost everywhere in this elegant hotel you'll have a sense of being on the water. It's set between the road and the lake, on a hill that's so steep you'll park your car on the roof before heading down to the reception desk. A terrace has been built out over the lake, as well as a marina for wasterskiing. The lake might tempt you for a swim, but the heated indoor pool might suit you better. The rustic restaurant overlooks the water, and is gaily filled with curtains in pink, violet, red, and white stripes. Each of the pleasant bedrooms has its own balcony (or else a terrace facing south), as well as a private bath, TV, phone, mini-bar, and radio. The lounge and bar area is elegantly and lightheartedly filled with rattan furniture and summer colors. Singles range from 89F ($40.90) to 155F ($71.22), while doubles cost between 70F ($32.17) and 135F ($62.03) per person daily, including breakfast.

Budget to Medium-Priced Accommodations

Seeschloss-Castello (tel. 35-18-03). The tower you see today was constructed in 1250 by a countess of Milan from the Ghiriglioni family. It was the fortified dwelling of the clan who eventually controlled most of the navigation on the lake. For the past 50 years this building has been a hotel. Today palms and palmettos surround the flagstone terrace, and the stone entrance curves gracefully up to an antique-filled lobby. You'll pull a wrought-iron bell handle to call the receptionist, who will assign you one of the smallish rooms, which open onto the backyard pool or the lake in front. They're as clean and comfortable as the rooms in any modern hotel anywhere. Singles range from 66F ($30.33) to 103F ($47.33), while doubles cost from 122F ($56.06) to 196F ($90.06), with half board included. Tariffs depend on the season and the plumbing. Across from the hotel is a private park bordering the lake.

Hotel La Perla, 14 via Collina (tel. 35-35-77), is a white-walled balconied hotel with stone retaining walls built around it to hold the terraced gardens in place. It isn't located on the water, but still has a good view of the mountains and there's a swimming pool on the grounds. The homes around it usually date from the 19th century, with lots of deciduous trees set nearby. Each of the attractive units has a balcony, phone, radio, and private bath. There's also an elevator, plus a parking garage on the premises. Singles range from 75F ($34.46) to 95F ($43.65), while doubles cost from 75F ($34.46) to 85F ($39.06) per person daily, with half board included. Accommodations in the nearby annex are slightly cheaper.

Hotel Panorama (tel. 35-11-47). The view from this hotel perched above the lake might be among the best in the city, even though the decor inside is fairly unimaginative. Owned by the Barra family, it's relatively inexpensive for Ascona. A darkly patterned carpet covers the narrow stairway leading to the upper floors. You'll be on the edge of town here, beside a road winding beside the lake. Singles cost 40F ($18.38), while doubles rent for 40F ($18.38) to 47F ($21.60) per person daily, with breakfast included.

Hotel Tamaro (tel. 35-39-39). A welcoming greeting is painted in Latin above the massive arch leading into the flagstone hall of the lounge and reception area where warm jazz often is played softly. If you go a few steps farther you'll be in a skylit central courtyard with vines growing over the massive vaults of its surrounding arcade. Tables have been set up inside this area, which makes the already charming layout even better. This is a former hospice and abbey. Today the furnishings are far more secular, but still include some antiques and some romantically seasoned artifacts. Everywhere you'll find complicated ceiling structures that in themselves identify the building as a very old one. From the street the establishment with its café looks like many of the other Mediterranean-style, pastel-colored buildings along the quays. Some of the bedrooms in the rear open from under a covered arcade onto a pleasant garden. Annette and Paolo Witzig, the owners, charge between 60F ($27.57) and 105F ($48.25) per person, with half board included. Prices depend on the plumbing and the season.

Albergo Elvezia (tel. 35-15-14) has a terrace on the cobblestones facing the lake, with an indoor restaurant just behind it. The upper-story terrace is surrounded by a verdant collection of vines, which even grow above the flowerboxes set onto the balustrade. The ground-floor restaurant looks typically rustic, with Oriental rugs, wooden tables, and hanging chandeliers with pink lampshades. Meals begin at 25F ($11.49), and include many Italian specialties, such as very good pasta (especially one made with four different kinds of cheese), fritto misto (fried mixed fish), scampi prepared in several different ways, osso buco, and veal piccata. Bathless rooms upstairs rent for between 70F ($32.17) and 86F ($39.52) for a double, and between 40F ($18.38) and 48F ($22.06) in a single, depending on what floor you're on.

WHERE TO DINE: Ascona has many fine restaurants—in fact the harborfront is lined with them. Most guests dine al fresco on a summer's night, looking at the lake. However, you shouldn't overlook the many excellent establishments found on the cobblestone streets of the old town either. My favorites follow:

Ristorante Da Ivo, 141 via Collegio (tel. 35-10-31). A trip through the winding streets of the old town might be an adventure in itself, even if it didn't eventually lead to the sophisticated cuisine of Ivo Balestra. If you're looking for nouvelle cuisine, you've come to the right place. It's graced with a large fireplace in a rustically pretty house, with light-grained paneling and dozens of folkloric artifacts covering the cream-colored walls. The menu varies, according to the availability of the ingredients at the market on any particular day. But specialties include such delicacies as suckling lamb with local cabbage, turbot à l'orange with pink peppercorns, baby veal with white truffles in puff pastry, local lakefish, warm foie de canard with broccoli, and salmon flan with leaf lettuce. The tagliatelle alla panna is an excellent pasta selection. A menu gastronomique is offered for 70F ($32.17). The restaurant is closed Monday and Tuesday, and during all of January and February. Otherwise its hours are from noon to 2 p.m. and 6:30 to 10 p.m.

Al Pontile, 31 Piazza G. Motta (tel. 35-46-04). Many restaurants along the quays look alike, and have almost the same menu choices, but the decor at this one seems a little warmer and more intimate than that of its neighbors. The darkly rustic interior has hanging orange lamps and candlelight. But most guests in fair weather prefer to dine outside on the terrace, opening onto the lake. Meals here cost from 25F ($11.49) and could include quail with risotto, osso buco, saltimbocca, Venetian-style calf liver, veal scallopine with tagliatelle, and good pasta dishes such as lasagne, ravioli, or spaghetti. Fish dishes include scampi, sole, and salmon.

Ristorante Borromeo, 16 Collegio (tel. 35-12-98), is one of the most crowded restaurants in the old town, and with good reason. The tables are filled with local people who seem to know each other. It has three rooms of rustic, high-ceilinged charm, and many more if you count the garden terraces. The rooms are joined by a central entryway where the maître d', usually a member of the Bacchi family, stands guard over the flock, much the way the Catholic priests stood guard at the door when this was a monastery and one of the biggest church schools in the region. Meals, costing from 20F ($9.19), might include risotto milanese with saffron, zabaglione, a mixed grill, piccata Marsala, trout, minestrone, calf liver, scampi, or osso buco. Always look for the daily specials that are posted.

Osteria Nostrana (tel. 35-51-58) is one of the most active harborfront restaurants. It has an invitingly rustic interior, and its sidewalk tables overlook the lake and the fashionable promenade. The well-prepared food items that come out of the kitchen might include 11 different types of spaghetti (try the carbonara), although you can also order lasagne verdi, cannelloni, tortelloni alla ricotta, and tagliatelle. The chef also does veal and beefsteak well. When the tomatoes are vine ripened in the summer, the best salad is the insalata di pomodori with mozzarella. The restaurant closes from November 1 until just before Christmas, but is open at other times from 9 a.m. to midnight. Meals begin at 25F ($11.49).

Al Torchio, Contrada Maggiore (tel. 35-71-26). Many guests choose to eat in the first room they see, which has a warm rustic decor, red candles, and imaginative designs painted onto the plaster walls. However, if it's a warm night, you might continue past the American-style salad bar in the back of the restaurant and turn left into the vine-covered courtyard. There, stone pillars support a grape arbor in a Mediterranean ambience. An average meal here will cost about 34F ($15.62). It could include calf liver Venetian style, veal piccata, scampi, osso buco, a wintertime fondue, spaghetti with clams, and a host of other typical Italian specialties. Dessert might be a gelato misto (a mixed selection of ice cream) or a sorbet with vodka.

AFTER DARK: **Nightclub Cincilla,** via Brissago (tel. 35-51-71), is a popular disco with a DJ who is something of a local celebrity. The club is painted in dark colors, with cutout patterns of white trees decorating the walls. Everything is carpeted, and the owners seem to have gone out of their way to create an iconoclastic urban ambience. There's no cover charge, and drinks cost about 15F ($6.89) apiece. The club opens at 9 p.m., closing at 3:30 a.m. A sign warns that "Proper dress is required."

Happyville Night Club, Lungolago (tel. 35-11-58), is a disco and cabaret with a polite management, an orchestra, and seven artists performing a mixture of striptease with song and dance. A tiny dance floor accommodates disco lovers between shows, which are put on every night at 11:30 p.m. and again at 1:30 a.m. The ambience is one of comfortable banquettes with red carpeting covering the walls and most of the floor. The cover charge is 3F ($1.38), and most drinks cost from 13F ($5.97) to 15F ($6.89). Closing time is 4 a.m.

7. Brissago

This little town opening onto Lake Maggiore near the Italian border might be considered if you prefer not to lodge in either Ascona or Locarno. It's on the mainland (and not to be confused with the Island of Brissago), and is reached by heading southwest from Ascona, bypassing Ronco on the way.

Lying at the foot of Monte Limidario (7180 feet), Brissago is the lowest spot in Switzerland, 679 feet above sea level. Only a mile from the border, it's popular with summer vacationers from Italy. Much of the village's activity centers on the lake, where waterskiing, swimming, and sailing prevail. A long, thin Virginia-type cigar, known as the "Brissago," is manufactured here.

FOOD AND LODGING: **Hotel Mirto au Lac** (tel. 65-13-28) is a small, family-run hotel built in the early '50s between the lakeshore and the village church. Each of the accommodations has a private bath, radio, and phone. The simple public rooms are sunny and clean, and decorated in conservatively modern furniture. The Uffer family rents motorboats and bicycles on request. *Per-person* rates with half board included cost between 70F ($32.17) and 84F ($38.60) daily, depending on the room's exposure and its plumbing. The hotel is closed in winter.

Giardino, Strada Cantonale (tel. 65-13-41), is considered one of the finest dining rooms in Switzerland, certainly in the Ticino. Many gourmets drive all the way from Milan to enjoy the excellent cuisine served here. Some of the furniture in this small and unusual town house came from a nearby cloister.

You'll be warmly greeted by Myriam Conti-Rossini, who will hand you a menu listing specialties preferred by her husband, the master chef Angelo, the resident culinary genius of the Ticino. A surprise menu at 80F ($36.76) might include a crayfish salad, suckling lamb à l'orange, or a gratin of fish. À la carte meals cost from 60F ($27.57) to 95F ($43.65), and reservations are essential. The restaurant is closed in August and from around Christmas until mid-February.

8. Lugano

Because of its geographical configuration, Lugano is called the "Rio de Janeiro of Europe." But that could be a very misleading comparison. What it is, is a Swiss town with a decided Italian flavor, as reflected by its alfresco cafés, sun-filled piazzas, arcaded cobblestone streets, and terracotta roofs.

The cultural center of Ticino—also the major town—Lugano has long been a haven for artists. However, as a resort it's patronized almost solely by Germans, and seems relatively undiscovered by the Americans who visit Switzerland.

On Lake Lugano, which the Italians call Lake Ceresio, Lugano is spread out between the peaks of San Salvatore and Monte Brè. Its low mountains protect it from cold alpine winds, and it enjoys an ideal climate from March to November.

The **Parco Civico** (city park) lies by the water. Within this park sit the Palazzo dei Congressi (the convention center) and the Casino of Lugano. In good weather, open-air concerts are staged here.

The **Cattedrale di San Lorenzo** (cathedral of St. Lawrence), in the old town, was built as a Romanesque church but was mainly reconstructed in the 13th and 14th centuries, then massively renovated again in the 17th and 18th centuries. It has an outstanding trio of Renaissance doorways, and inside the decoration is baroque. Look for the 16th-century tabernacle at the end of the south aisle, designed by the Rodari brothers of Maroggia.

The other important church of Lugano is the **Chiesa di Santa Maria deglo Angioli** (Church of St. Mary of the Angels), on the south side of the resort. This convent church was built in the closing year of the 15th century and is celebrated throughout the Ticino for its frescoes by Bernardino Luini, the Lombard painter. His huge fresco, *The Crucifixion,* is from 1529. Many critics have compared the beauty of his work to that of Leonardo da Vinci. Latter-day admirers, including John Ruskin, found an "unstudied sweetness" in Luini's work. Until 1848 the church was occupied by Franciscans.

In Castagnola, to the east of Lugano, the 17th-century **Villa Favorita** contains one of the great private art collections of Europe. The Schloss Rohoncz Collection belongs to Baron Heinrich von Thyssen-Bornemisza, who shares it with the public in his luxuriously furnished villa on Friday and Saturday, mid-April to mid-October, from 10 a.m. to noon and 2 to 5 p.m., charging an admission of 7F ($3.22) for adults and 3F ($1.38) for students.

The collection covers the period from the Middle Ages to the 19th century, including many Flemish and German works. You'll be able to view paintings by Cranach the Elder, Dürer, Holbein the Younger, Memling, and Van Eyck (see his masterpiece, *The Annunciation*). The Italian school is well represented by Titian, Raphael, Fra Angelico, Caravaggio, and Correggio.

The home of noted architect Wilhelm Schmid is maintained as the **Schmid Museum** at the Lugano suburb of Brè, where many of his works and documents are displayed. The city of Lugano received the house as a legacy on the death of Schmid's widow. The architect was deeply involved in the "new objectivity" of the '20s and '30s, and a significant selection of his paintings from that period are on display, together with ceramics, work tools, furniture decorated by Schmid, and books and other papers which reveal his artistic interests and his awareness of the political events that saw him driven out of Nazi Germany in 1936, back to his native Switzerland. The museum is open Easter to mid-October, Tuesday to Sunday from 10 a.m. to noon and 3 to 5 p.m. Brè is about 5½ miles from Lugano and can easily be reached by car, bus, or the funicular. Admission is 6F ($2.76). For more information, phone 23-83-50.

On a very different note, especially if you have a child in tow, you may want to visit the **Swiss Miniature Village** at Melide-Lugano (tel. 68-79-51). Artisans have created small copies of the major buildings in all the Swiss cantons, including the twin castles at Sion. All of them are set into a labyrinth of asphalt paths, and you'll have to buy the official guidebook if you want detailed explanations. Entrance fee is 6F ($2.76) for adults, 2.50F ($1.15) for children under 14. The village is open from 8 a.m. to 10 p.m. seven days a week in July and August, and to 6 p.m. from March until the end of October. It's closed in winter.

WHERE TO STAY: Lugano is better equipped with hotels than any other resort in the Ticino, and they come in all price ranges. Many are located in the outskirts in the districts of Paradiso, Cassarate, and Castagnola, but wherever you're located, know that you're only a few minutes from the heart of town.

The Upper Bracket

Grand Hotel Eden, 7 Riva Paradiso (tel. 54-26-12), at Lugano-Paradiso, is a large contemporary hotel, with an unbroken facade of lakeside balconies angling toward the sunlight. A deluxe establishment, it's considered the finest hotel in the area of Lugano. A low-lying, flat-roofed extension rests on the sun terrace built out over the lake. Inside, a large swimming pool has panoramic views of the café tables and chaise lounges inside. The entire complex is fully air-conditioned, while each of the handsomely furnished accommodations has color TV, radio, TV-video, mini-bar, phone, and safe. Singles range from 120F ($55.14) to 190F ($87.31), while doubles cost between 210F ($96.50) and 320F ($147.04), with breakfast included.

Hotel Splendide Royal, 7 Riva A. Caccia (tel. 54-20-01). Parts of this hotel are indeed splendid, as its name implies. The balconied lake side with a mansard roof is elegantly 19th century, but my favorite part of the outside is the side entrance with the wrought-iron and glass canopy hanging over the door. A covered swimming pool is shaped like an oyster, with grandly arched modern walls opening onto the rock garden. The public rooms are appropriately filled with columns, crystal and gilt chandeliers, Venetian furniture, and Oriental rugs. The most magnificent bedrooms even have ceiling frescoes in some cases. There's a restaurant and bar on the premises. With breakfast included, singles range from 120F ($55.14) to 180F ($82.71), while doubles cost from 200F ($91.90) to 290F ($133.26). Half board is offered for another 40F ($18.38) per person daily.

Grand Hotel Villa Castagnola au Lac, 31 viale Castagnola (tel. 51-22-13), is styled like a Mediterranean villa, with flagstone terraces, exotic trees and plants, and carefully groomed lawns. The facade is ocher-colored, with lime-green shutters that make the whole setting look vaguely Neopolitan. An indoor swimming pool is in a separate ground-floor extension, with sliding panoramic windows overlooking banana plants, palms, evergreens, cactus, and severely pruned topiaries. Four tennis courts are shielded from view by a row of hedges.

The public rooms have polished marble floors in gray, pink, and beige. Other rooms have parquet floors, big fireplaces, a baronial decor, with lots of elegant nooks and crannies for having tea or before-dinner drinks. The clientele is mainly an older crowd. All of this physical plant sits across the street from the lake, where the hotel maintains a private beach. With half board included, singles range from 80F ($36.76) to 145F ($66.63), while doubles cost from 75F ($34.46) to 145F ($66.63) per person per day, the rates depending on the season.

Hotel Bellevue au Lac, 10 Riva Caccia (tel. 54-33-33), is a large white-walled hotel turned sideways to the lake so that only a limited number of bedrooms have frontal views of the water. As it turns out, the other accommodations contain balconies with lots of sunshine and a pleasant view of the garden with a big swimming pool and sun terrace. Each of the accommodations has a balcony, private bath, phone, radio, and refrigerator. With the half board plan, the Foery family includes a sangría party followed by a candlelight dinner, plus weekly barbecue parties. With a generous breakfast included, overnight rates range from 100F ($45.95) to 125F ($57.44), while doubles cost between 165F ($75.82) and 205F ($94.20). Half board is an additional 25F ($11.49) per person daily.

Hotel Europa, 1 via Cattori (tel. 54-36-21), is a well-organized hotel presenting a handsomely proportioned facade of almost pure white to its flowered garden. An indoor swimming pool opens its glass doors during warm weather to a terraced view of the lake. The interior is simple, modern, and informal, with touches of streamlined elegance amid the contemporary furnishings. A cabaret and nightclub offers an international ambience in a darkly wood-covered setting. Well-furnished singles range from 130F ($59.74) to 170F ($78.12), while doubles rent for between 190F ($87.31) and 230F ($105.69), with breakfast included. All the accommodations have private bath, phone, air conditioning, radio, and mini-bar.

Hotel Meister, 11 via San Salvatore (tel. 54-14-12), at Lugano-Paradiso, is a very grand building with five floors of white walls and blue shutters, with a white wrought-iron balcony in front of almost every window. Many of the bedrooms look down over the grassy lawns and swimming pool, and all of them contain private bath, phone, and radio. The public rooms have ornate plaster ceilings, marble or parquet floors, and simple conservative furniture. The dining room is grandly 19th century, with gilt-framed antique mirrors and crystal chandeliers. The hotel is in the suburb of Paradiso, a two-minute walk from the lakeshore. If you're driving, get off at the exit marked "Lugano-Sud." There's parking behind the hotel, as well as covered parking at the nearby Hotel Admiral where guests at the Meister are allowed free use of their indoor swimming pool. Singles rent for between 100F ($45.95) and 125F ($57.44), while doubles range from 90F ($41.36) to 115F ($52.84) per person, with half board included.

Hotel Commodore, 6 Riva Caccia (tel. 54-39-21), is a well-designed modern hotel with two very large wings extending toward the lake. Their balconies are usually covered with flowers, while a series of sun terraces has been built into the central area between the different sections. The hotel sits on the lakeshore promenade in the center of town. The Neptune restaurant inside offers an airy and sunny atmosphere, with burgeoning terrace shrubs just outside its windows and a decor of blue and green with glossy white Chinese Chippendale-style chairs. The lounges are filled with plush armchairs and light colors. The comfortable bedrooms are well furnished in summertime colors and accents of wood and brass. Singles range from 100F ($45.95) to 150F ($68.93), while doubles cost between 150F ($68.93) and 210F ($96.50). Half board is an additional 35F ($16.08) per person daily.

Hotel Belmonte, 5 Strada di Gandria (tel. 51-40-33), at Lugano-Castagnola, is in a suburb of Lugano about a two-minute ride from the center by trolleybus. The facade is a typically balconied structure, a very grand format of big-windowed comfort, with palm trees growing from the front lawn and a view of the nearby lake. The outdoor swimming pool is designed in a narrow angled format that stretches a long distance along the accommodating chaise lounges of the flagstone borders around it. Singles range from 85F ($39.06) to 130F ($59.74), while doubles cost between 145F ($66.63) and 205F ($94.20), with breakfast included. Prices depend on the season.

Hotel Admiral, 15 via Geretta, (tel. 52-23-24), at Lugano-Paradiso, was built in 1975, and it's one of the finest hotels in this little satellite resort of Lugano. It rises seven concrete-and-glass floors above an area near the Lugano-Sud exit from the main highway. Many of the public rooms are outfitted with red leather accents and wood trim, while a showplace salon has French-style armchairs, Oriental rugs, and big windows with a view of the garden. An indoor and a rooftop outdoor swimming pool are the most dramatic of the hotel's facilities, which also include a sauna, a private garage, a bar, two restaurants, and a cafeteria. The comfortable accommodations have private bath, radio, refrigerator, and phone. The nightly rate ranges from 100F ($45.95) to 150F ($68.93) in a single and between 130F ($59.74) and 220F ($101.09) in a double, with breakfast included. Half board is included for another 30F ($13.79) per person daily.

The Middle Bracket

Hotel Ticino, 1 Piazza Cioccaro (tel. 22-77-72), presents a narrow facade to one of the most charming squares in the old town of Lugano. It was a former convent whose present owners have carefully maintained the arcaded central courtyard which today burgeons with verdant plants. They've covered the small area that used to be open to the sky, and now a glass ceiling allows year-round comfort. Antique cupboards and chests have been installed in the stairwell area. Each of the small bedrooms is uniquely furnished, usually with 19th-century provincial pieces. There's a private bath with each chamber, along with a phone, radio, and mini-bar. With breakfast included, singles range from 110F ($50.55) to 170F ($78.12), while doubles cost between 160F ($73.52) and 190F ($87.31). Triples are available for between 180F ($82.71) and 220F ($101.09).

Strandhotel Seegarten, 24 viale Castagnola (tel. 54-23-21), at Lugano-Cassarate, is a symmetrical white hotel which sprawls over an elongated section of lakefront property near the Lido. The management has built a swimming pool out over the water, planting it with the subtropical vegetation that grows so well in Lugano. There's a private parking lot and garage, for which you'll be grateful. The location is about a five-minute walk from the center of town. The Huber family charges between 50F ($22.98) and 80F ($36.76) in a single, between 85F ($39.06) and 155F ($71.22) in a double, with breakfast included. Half board is another 20F ($9.19) per person daily.

Hotel Nizza, 14 via Guidino (tel. 54-17-71), at Lugano-Paradiso, is an elegantly furnished hotel a few blocks from the lake on a forested hillside which gives the sun terraces and the attractive dining room a panoramic view. You'll see lots of Oriental rugs covering the floors, and the bedrooms upstairs are painted in shades of pleasing colors. There's lots of parking nearby thanks to the isolation of the hotel. The swimming pool is heated with solar panels. The bar area is reached by elevator, and has a nighttime view of the lights of Lugano. The Quadri family run frequent bus service to the lakeside promenade, even though it's only a ten-minute walk from your bedroom. The hotel closes from October until April, but in summer rates range from 70F ($32.17) to 98F ($45.03) per person for full board. If you want only half board, you're granted an 8F ($3.68) reduction daily.

Hotel Delfino, 6 via Cassarinetta (tel. 54-53-33), is a dramatically designed hotel built in 1972. It looks especially attractive at night, when it's illuminated from the outside. It has a swimming pool below the angled corners of its facade, and modern balconies decorated with clusters of cascading plants. The interior has certain elegant touches, including an elaborate carving and antique pewter that decorate the hardwoods of the reception desk. An ornate baroque chest and Oriental rugs make the place even more appealing. The hotel lies on a side street a few blocks from the lake, and has a bar as well as a dining room with chandeliers and pink napery. For stays of more than three days, half board is offered for between 100F ($45.95) and 110F ($50.55) in a single and between 90F ($41.36) and 105F ($48.25) per person in a double. Bed and breakfast costs between 75F ($34.46) and 85F ($39.06) per person daily.

Hotel Torre, 1 via delle Scuole (tel. 51-56-21), at Lugano-Cassarate, is housed on a petit skyscraper, at least in Lugano terms. It will give you superb views from the top-floor terrace. Actually the hotel occupies only the top four floors of the building, with business offices on the floors below. Some attempts have been made inside for a rustic feeling, but the format is usually streamlined and modern, with the emphasis on that view of the lake down below. Facilities include a restaurant, tearoom, and snackbar. Singles range from 48F ($22.06) to 65F ($29.87), while doubles cost between 44F ($20.22) and 58F ($26.65) per person, with a breakfast buffet included.

Hotel Colorado, 19 via Maraini (tel. 56-16-31). The name of the hotel might inspire nostalgia for Americans traveling abroad, and the balconied eight-story building might remind you of those you've seen back home. The masses of flowerboxes, however, and the views of the lake from the rooms and from the sun terrace are sights you'll find only in Lugano. The hotel was recently remodeled, placing a TV, radio, mini-bar, phone, and private bath in each of its comfortable bedrooms. The Tavernette Grill inside is attractive, with red brick accents, a rustic ceiling, and a tasty selection of meat, fish, and pasta dishes. An à la carte meal costs from 40F ($18.38). Singles range from 75F ($34.46) to 95F ($43.65), while doubles cost between 120F ($55.14) and 170F ($78.12), with breakfast included.

La Residenza, 16 Piazza della Riscossa (tel. 52-18-31), at Lugano-Cassarate. If you're fond of radically modern architecture and shades of beige and brown, you'll love this hotel. Its facade looks like a monochromatic op-art by Warhol. The dun color of the textured concrete is repeated in dozens of places throughout the interior. Furniture is comfortable, providing color accents of flame orange and deep red. The dining room has wicker chairs, white tablecloths, and hanging lamps shaped like inverted tulips. The bar area has two-dimensional cutouts hanging erratically from the ceiling, painted in what are probably supposed to be appealing dramatic colors. Each of the bedrooms, also dun colored, have private baths, phones, radios, and TVs. Singles range from 75F ($34.46) to 85F ($39.06), while doubles cost between 65F ($29.87) and 75F ($34.46) per person nightly, with breakfast included.

Hotel Arizona, 20 via Massagno (tel. 22-93-43), is an attractive modern hotel at the north end of the city, its facade composed of alternate areas of reddish brick and white concrete. A sun terrace with an above-ground swimming pool is built into the roof stretching above the ground-floor lobby, which is tastefully furnished in graceful modern chairs, textured ceilings, and Oriental rugs. An attractive bar area with flattering lighting and Scottish plaid carpeting offers guests a quiet place to get away from it all. A restaurant and bridge room are also on the premises. Many of the bedrooms, thanks to the angled facade, have irregular shapes, big windows facing south, and unusually large sizes. The Brunner family, your hosts, charge between 70F ($32.17) and 95F ($43.65) in a single and between 95F ($43.65) and 155F ($71.22) in a double, with a very generous breakfast buffet included. To get there, get off the autobahn at the Lugano-Nord exit and turn left at the first traffic light in the direction of Massagno. Then follow the signs to Lugano, which will turn you left at the via San Gottardo, which should eventually lead you to signs indicating the hotel.

Hotel Everest, 7 via Ginevra (tel. 22-95-55), is a modern balconied hotel with white walls, lots of glass, and a fresh interior decorated with springtime colors and comfortable modern furnishings. The chairs in the lobby area are upholstered in leather with chrome swivel bases, while the bedrooms are often covered with flowery wallpaper. A very pleasant street-level café is separated from the sidewalk with masses of pink and red flowers, an iron railing, and an arched awning stretching over the tables. Singles range between 60F ($27.57) and 95F ($43.65), while doubles cost between 90F ($41.36) and 145F ($66.63), with breakfast included.

Holiday Hotel Select, 4 via G. Zoppi (tel. 23-61-72). The concrete balconies of this white-walled hotel rise from a quiet position near the business center of Lugano, only a few minutes from the lake. The lobby is filled with lighthearted furniture, sometimes of upholstered plastic, and some of the functional bedrooms have views of the lake. Singles range from 55F ($25.27) to 85F ($39.06), while doubles cost between 90F ($41.36) and 135F ($62.03), with breakfast included.

Carlton Hotel Villa Moritz, 9 via Cortiva (tel. 51-38-12), at Lugano-Castagnola, is housed in at least two 19th-century buildings set in a verdant park with its well-maintained masonry retaining walls. A free-form swimming pool is set into gray flagstones, receiving a maximum amount of sunlight because of its location on the sunny side of Mount Brè. The hotel is some distance from a main road, so peace and quiet are assured. The public rooms are attractively up-to-date, with well-designed stone accents in the fireplaces and around the bar area. Public buses can carry guests to the center of Lugano in ten minutes. The Wernli family, your hosts, charge between 48F ($22.06) and 66F ($30.33) per person daily, with breakfast included.

The Budget Range

Hotel Panorama, 7 via Maraini (tel. 22-94-33), is an attractively symmetrical building that sits on a bluff a few blocks from the lake. Its balconies are sheltered with red awnings, and the interior is warmly covered with large areas of light-grained paneling. The bedrooms have wall-to-wall carpeting and an informal ambience of upholstered headboards, wood trim, and either flowered or striped fabrics. On the premises is a bistro, along with a restaurant, and a private nightclub, the Epicurean, The views from the sun terrace encompass a panoramic sweep of the lake, hence the name of the hotel. Singles range from 54F ($24.81) to 86F ($39.52), while doubles cost from 80F ($36.76) to 135F ($62.03), with breakfast included.

Hotel Minerva, 12 via Clemente Maraini (tel. 54-27-31), is a contemporary building with curved corners and enveloping balconies. The interior has a wood-grained and maroon-colored bar, a sunny dining room with red accents, and a panoramic sun terrace. Singles range from 38F ($17.46) to 50F ($22.98), while doubles cost between 70F ($32.17) and 115F ($52.84), with breakfast included.

Albergo Domus, 24a Riva Paradiso (tel. 54-34-21), at Lugano-Paradiso, lies on the main road to Paradiso from Lugano. It's a balconied building with red brick walls and an imposing modern format that's hard to miss. The attractive and airy interior is decorated with a light touch of neutral-colored furniture, potted palms, and Oriental rugs. The uncluttered bedrooms are outfitted with a lighthearted southern touch of clear colors and big windows. Singles range from 40F ($18.38) to 44F ($20.22), while doubles cost between 75F ($34.46) and 115F ($52.84), with breakfast included.

Hotel Marina, via della Scuole (tel. 51-45-14), in Lugano-Cassarate, is a flat-topped, solid-looking building with symmetrical rows of concrete balconies. The entrance hall is attractively austere, with a marble floor and marble facing over part of it. The rest of the public rooms are outfitted in pastel colors and contrasting patterns of Oriental rugs, tile floors, and flowered curtains. The bedrooms are spacious and sunny, with wood-grained furniture, homey knick-knacks, and clean sheets. Singles range from 50F ($22.98) to 70F ($32.17), while doubles cost from 83F ($38.14) to 145F ($66.63), depending on the season, the plumbing, and the exposure. Breakfast is included. The Külling family are your honest and congenial hosts, who prove to be friendly and helpful.

Hotel Monte Ceneri, 44 via Nassa (tel. 23-33-40), is the hotel attached to one of the best of the inexpensive restaurants in Lugano (see the dining recommendations). You'll walk up a big skylit staircase to the reception area, as there is no elevator (expect some stains on the carpet). The location is only a block from the lake and your room, which is likely to be slightly shabby and a little run-down, but fairly clean, sunny, and safe. The place is a real bargain in an expensive city, charging only 33F ($15.16) in a single and 60F ($27.57) in a double.

Hotel Astoria, Piazza Molino Nuovo (tel. 22-97-22), is a modern urban hotel with big windows looking out over a commercial street. The bedrooms inside are filled with geometrically patterned wallpaper and slightly dated wood-grained furniture. Doubles range from 60F ($27.57) to 85F ($39.06), while singles cost between 35F ($16.08) and 50F ($22.98), with breakfast included. The management is friendly and conscientious.

WHERE TO DINE: Lugano is well equipped with independent restaurants, ranging from nouvelle cuisine to Italian dishes. Many of its restaurants are expensive, but others are real bargains.

Ristorante Al Portone, 3 viale Cassarate (tel. 23-59-95). If you have a passion for nouvelle cuisine Italian style, or especially if you don't know what that means, you can head toward this elegantly sophisticated restaurant, the domain of Roberto and Doris Galizzi. He cooks and she supervises the service, a winning combination of talents. A fixed-price menu—"according to the wishes of Roberto"—is served for 65F ($29.87), and you might be better off ordering it, although you can also venture into the uncharted waters of the à la carte listings. Like all nouvelle cuisine restaurants, many of the combinations might sound bizarre—fresh salmon with rhubarb, for example—but the taste is usually sensational. Salmon also comes in a ragoût with asparagus. The sole in the style of Roberto is a palate-pleaser, as is the veal liver with champagne. The desserts are also exceptional. The restaurant is open from noon to 2 p.m. and 7 to 9:30 p.m. It's closed on Sunday, until dinner on Monday, and also for the month of August.

Bianchi, 3 via Pessina (tel. 22-84-79), has an unpretentious forest-green turn-of-the-century facade set symmetrically between red carved-stone pillars.

It's on a narrow street in the old town, and has a decor which includes rounded belle-époque ironwork and a single carriage lamp hanging over the door. The service is very formal and old world. Your meal might include Italian dishes such as scampi with curry, filet of sole in white wine, veal cutlet milanese, and calf liver Venetian style, as well as risotto with fresh mushrooms and a selection of grilled barbecue meats. A specialty is the Florentine steak, which is priced by the gram. Fixed-price meals begin at 30F ($13.79), and à la carte dinners cost about 50F ($22.98). The restaurant shuts down on Sunday and for the month of August.

Ristorante Orologio, 2 via Nizzola (tel. 23-23-38), is a high-quality restaurant on the ground floor of a buff-colored building with a restrained exterior. A view of the inside reveals leaded-glass windows, French-provincial 19th-century chairs, immaculate napery, and darkly patterned tartan carpeting. You'll also see lots of copperware on the window ledges above the banquettes, plus an exposed ice chest for the display of salads and condiments. Amusing illustrations advertise the menu items, including such things as a bare-breasted mermaid "discreetly" suggesting the fish courses. Mario Campanile and his family are the owners, and they charge from 28F ($12.87) for a well-prepared meal which might include five kinds of spaghetti, four kinds of scampi, osso buco, chicken curry, good liver and trout dishes, smoked fish, the inevitable minestrone alla Ticinese, and a springtime celebration of certain seasonal vegetables such as asparagus and melon. Some noonday fixed-price meals begin at 22F ($10.11). The restaurant is closed on Saturday.

Al Piccolo Grill, 34 via C. Maraini (tel. 54-26-98), in Loreto, serves a limited but well-prepared Italian menu which includes grilled shrimp, good steaks, pasta, carpaccio, scaloppine with melon, and gnocchi. A café is on the ground floor of this pleasant place, with the restaurant installed upstairs. It's closed on Wednesday. The service is exceptionally good (usually), and the chef is very skilled. He turns out a special gourmet menu at only 110F ($50.55) for two persons which should be ordered only if you're very hungry. Fixed-price meals begin at 18F ($8.27).

Gambrinus, Piazza Riforma (tel. 123 (tel. 23-19-55), is housed in an 18th-century building in a recessed corner of the Piazza Riforma. It's usually laden with masses of flowers, and has two carved cherubs holding up a fluted column above the main doorway, which is set at an angle to the facade. If you're not careful you might crash into a waiter scurrying out the door laden with food for customers waiting at the outdoor café. Most of the interior curves around the windowed section of this place, with a central bar forming a big rectangle inside. The restaurant is open from 10 a.m. till midnight in summer and from 11:30 a.m. to 11 p.m. during the rest of the year. It's closed for three weeks in February. Specialties include macaroni with gorgonzola, typical meat selections such as cutlets, steak, and liver, grilled shrimp, osso buco with risotto, and different types of spaghetti, along with flank steak Vivaldi. Meals start at around 27F ($12.41).

Mövenpick Ristorante Parco Ciani, Piazza Indipendenza, at the Palazzo dei Congressi (tel. 23-86-56), is decorated to look like a village restaurant filled with an abundant Italian harvest. You'll find two distinct dining areas here, one with modern bentwood armchairs and another with reproduction Empire-style rush-bottom antiques. Vines cover the rafters of one room, and bunches of ripened corn in another. The entire complex is housed in a modern concrete building with irregular balconies and big windows at the edge of a city park. You can have drinks or coffee on the terrace while overlooking the manicured shrubs and flowers. The friendly staff serves wild game in season, very good veal-and-rice dishes, tortellini, three kinds of risotto, good curry dishes, and a mixed medley of boiled meats. Meals cost from 25F ($11.49) and up. Service is daily from 9 a.m. to midnight.

Ristorante Galleria, 4 via Negezzi (tel. 23-62-88). The entrance to this elegant place is under an old-fashioned covered passageway that you could easily imagine as being in Naples. The facade of the restaurant is painted a memorable fire-engine red with gilt trim and big windows. You'll see an informal bar area on your left as you enter, and on your right a well-furnished room with white stucco arches, a beautifully textured wood ceiling with heavy beams, and original prints and lithographs by well-known artists, usually Italian. Luigi Rampinelli is the polite owner, and he welcomes many local bankers and business people at lunch, a clientele that gives way to a more fun-loving crowd at night. You can have coffee or a drink at any time outside at a café table set on a mosaic floor under the arcade. Meals, however, are served from noon to 2 p.m. and 7 to 10:30 p.m. The restaurant is closed on Sunday and during all of August. Specialties include brochette Galleria, kebabs, fondue bourguignonne (or else chinoise), duck à la orange, and five kinds of scampi. Fixed-price meals begin at 20F ($9.19), and à la carte dinners are likely to cost from 40F ($18.38).

Huguenin au Lac, 1 Riva Albertolli (tel. 23-37-66), has a multicolored marble floor in gray, white, and pink geometric patterns, as well as elaborately high ceilings. One of the walls is covered with mirrors and dozens of small Swiss flags. You can easily imagine yourself back in the 19th century when you visit this place, especially since the streetside arcade is as massively grand as it was when it was constructed more than a century ago. The uniformed staff serves such specialties as macaroni with four different kinds of cheese, three kinds of risotto, three kinds of trout, and five kinds of scampi, along with osso buco with risotto, filet of sole Basque style, and all the standard grilled meats. Fixed-price meals begin at 23F ($10.57), while à la carte dinners cost from 34F ($15.62). This is also very much of a tearoom and café, so no one will mind if you just drop in for a drink.

Ristorante Monte Ceneri, 44 via Nassa (tel. 23-33-40), has an ornate plastic ceiling, red-checked tablecloths, big windows, and a friendly and gregarious setting that quickly lets you know that this is very much a local eatery. It's a family-run and a family-style establishment where people bring their friends, their lovers (often their wives or husbands), and most definitely their pet dogs. The Campanile family offers one of the best bargains in town: 13F ($5.97) for a fixed-price meal which might include an array of typically Italian local specialties, such as fresh mushrooms, polenta, or risotto. Try one of their four different kinds of fondue or a penciled-in special of the day that's usually very good. My favorite, when featured, is a delectable platter of fresh mushrooms with polenta, costing 22F ($10.11).

Ristorante Piazette Hotel Dante, 5 Piazza Cioccaro (tel. 23-79-43), is at the corner of one of Lugano's prettiest squares in the old town, on the ground floor of an inexpensively priced hotel. It has a garishly modern sign and a decor of trendy Italian-inspired furniture, with heavily angular chairs and rustic overtones. Next to the funicular stop, Bartolo and Antonio welcome you, offering a complete menu for only 15F ($6.89), one of the best bargains in Lugano. It might include spaghetti with tomato sauce (flavored with fresh basil), followed by roast veal with cauliflower and new potatoes, climaxing with a mixed selection of ice cream. If you want to order à la carte, you'll find all the classic specialties, plus some unusual ones (such as frog legs). But be prepared to spend from 25F ($11.49) or more for this indulgence.

A PHARMACY AND A SHOP: **Farmacia San Luca,** 9 vis Pioda (tel. 23-84-55), is a friendly pharmacy right in the center of Lugano. It can take care of most minor ailments, and allows you to stock up on much-needed supplies. English is spoken.

Frankly, you don't come to Lugano to shop. However, there is one store that's exceptional if you're seeking not only souvenirs, but good handicrafts. It's **Bottega dell'Artigiano,** 18 via Canova (tel. 22-81-40), selling such Ticino-made goods as textiles, woodcarvings, pottery, and metalware. You get friendly service in a small area filled with displays.

NIGHTLIFE: Everybody heads to Italy! Not really—but the major gambling casino for Lugano is on Italian soil, a curious hunk of Italian geography completely surrounded by Switzerland. The men of Campione were famous for their stonework, and many buildings in Milan are a testament to their skill. However, very few people go there to admire their handiwork—they go to gamble. The Italians, wanting to pick up some badly needed Swiss francs (West German marks, American dollars, whatever), have installed a gambling casino in Campione.

It's the **Casino Municipale** (tel. 68-79-21), and it offers such games as blackjack and chemin de fer, along with the inevitable slot machines. The casino lies across the lake from Lugano, and is reached by frequent ferry service, only 20 minutes away from your chance with Lady Luck. The casino is a glittering, glamorous establishment where Swiss citizens and seemingly all foreign visitors go to take their chance with baccarat and roulette, among other games. Here, unlike in Switzerland, the stakes are unlimited! However, the currency is Swiss. Long ago the imperial fiefdom of Campione was presented to a Milanese monastery. It has remained Italian ever since, in spite of incredible political turmoil in the area.

Back in Lugano, you can also try your luck at the **Casino Kursaal** (tel. 23-32-81), but here the betting ceiling is limited to 5F ($2.30). Mainly, however, you may look upon this establishment as a place of entertainment, as it often offers cabaret, everything from girlie acts to magic. Drinks cost from 15F ($6.89).

However, your nighttime stroll might begin at the famous **Piazza Riforma** of Lugano. This is a flagstone square, a huge one at that, where practically everyone in town shows up at one time or another. You'll be surrounded by arcaded buildings with masses of flowers that might remind you of the Piazza San Marco in Venice.

Many cafés surround this square, but the favorite one is the **Café Olimpia,** Piazza Riforma (tel. 22-74-88), housed in an elegant stone building with hundreds of chairs set out front. It sometimes has live music (on occasion Mexican). Two Campari and sodas are likely to cost from 6F ($2.75), a small amount to pay for the entertainment.

Recommending nightclubs and discos in Lugano is risky business. Their life span is often short. However, here goes—

Dancing Cecil, in Paradiso (tel. 54-21-21), attracts an under-30 crowd for dancing or whatever. Drinks begin at around 11F ($5.06).

Europa 1001 Notte, also in Paradiso (tel. 54-21-21), attracts an older, more sophisticated and well-dressed crowd for its cabaret shows, where drinks cost around 12F ($5.51).

Dancing Capo San Martino, again in Paradiso (tel. 54-15-31), also draws an older crowd similar to that of Europa 1001 Notte. There's a restaurant on the premises.

Dancing Zappia, Paradiso (tel. 54-14-04), is a mildly punk-rock place for a late teenage crowd of mildly rebellious dancers. A beer costs around 8F ($3.68).

Dancing La Romantica, at Melide (tel. 68-75-21), is an elegant establishment, with both a restaurant and an orchestra, catering to an over-35 crowd of well-dressed night owls.

Caprino-Felsenkeller (tel. 23-98-73) is a summertime disco for lovers. Drinks cost around 10F ($4.60).

Pegasus/Morandi, 56 via Trevano (tel. 51-22-91), is a very modern place that plays lots of recently released discs. It's one of the most popular discos in Lugano, with attractively dressed youngish dancers and drinkers. Drinks cost around 10F ($4.60).

La Piccionaia, via Pioda (tel. 23-45-46), is an elegant and modern establishment for young nymphets and trendily fashionable 25-year-olds. Drinks go for around 10F ($4.60).

La Rustica, at Cassarate (tel. 51-30-66), is one of the better and more popular discos in Lugano. Its decor is rustic and woodsy, and the disco music is up-to-date. Drinks cost from 10F ($4.60), and when a live group appears you can expect a cover charge.

La Canva, at Paradiso (tel. 54-12-18), attracts a very young crowd to its music and summertime precincts. It's inexpensive fun if you're under 20.

EXCURSIONS: Lugano is not only ideal for excursions on its own lake, but on Lake Como and Lake Maggiore as well. The **Società Navigazione del Lago di Lugano** (tel. 51-52-23) operates morning, midday, afternoon, and even evening cruises. Gandria and Morcote are among the favored destinations. **Gandria** is a Ticinese terraced village, built on a steep slope and rising from the lake. Artists have long been drawn to its arcades and narrow lanes against a backdrop of vineyards.

A one-day ticket on the boat line costs 20F ($9.19), but if you plan to vacation in Ticino, you may want to purchase a 35F ($16.08) ticket, allowing you unlimited free boat trips for three days.

If you like belvederes with viewing platforms, you'll find Lugano rich in mountain scenery. The most exciting is generally conceded to be the funicular to **Monte San Salvatore,** a round-trip ticket costing about 10F ($4.60). From the top of the mountain you'll have a great view of all three lakes, as well as both the Swiss and French Alps (Matterhorn, Monte Rosa). The funicular operates from mid-March to mid-November, and leaves from Paradiso.

The funicular to Monte Brè is almost as impressive, leaving from Cassarate, a round-trip ticket costing about 11F ($5.06). Monte Brè is called the sunniest mountain in Switzerland. From its peak you'll have a view of the Valaisan and Bernese Alps, including Monte Rosa and the Matterhorn. From Lugano you can take a trolleybus to Cassarate where you board the funicular for the ascent.

You can also take a cog-wheel train to **Monte Generoso.** From Lugano you go by boat or train to Capolago, and from there by cog-wheel train to Monte Generoso. At 5590 feet, the summit offers a peerless panoramic view of the lakes of Ticino and into northern Italy. A round-trip ticket is about 20F ($9.19).

PRACTICAL FACTS: The **Lugano Tourist Office** is at 5 Riva Albertolli (tel. 21-46-64).

Some important phone numbers are: **police,** 117; **fire department,** 118; **ambulance,** 22-91-91; **doctor or dentist,** 111; **first aid,** 58-61-11; **road service,** 140; **taxi,** 51-21-21 or 54-44-66.

To use the Lugano city **transport facilities,** get an information leaflet at the Public Transport Board, Azienda Communale del Traffico, via Carducci (tel. 21-22-22), or at the tourist office. It costs .50F (23¢) and tells you all about fares and the use of ticket machines. As in other Swiss cities, you must get a valid ticket *before* boarding a transport vehicle, or you'll have to pay a 20F ($9.19) penalty.

Guided **walking tours** are organized by the tourist office in the spring and the fall. From late March to mid-April and in October, the walks are arranged in groups of three, although you can take a single tour if you can't make them all. For the three spring walks the charge is 25F ($11.49), 50F ($22.98) in the fall. A single spring walk costs 10F ($4.60), with the cost in the fall rising to 18F ($8.27).

SPORTS: Sports activities in Lugano are largely water oriented, although there are facilities for golf, tennis, cycling, and many fitness pursuits.

You can **swim** at Lido Beach (tel. 51-40-41), a bathing resort surrounded by green lawns, with a restaurant on an outside terrace. The charge, with use of a changing cabin, is 3F ($1.38) for adults, 1F (46¢), for children from 2 to 14. The beach is open from 9:30 a.m. to 6 p.m. Many hotels have heated pools, some with salt water. Swimming in the lake is also possible at the public bath, riva Caccia (tel. 54-20-35), and at Lido San Domenico, Castagnola (tel. 51-66-66), both charging 2F (92¢) for adults, 1F (46¢) for children. At Lido Piscina Comunale, Paradiso (tel. 54-75-62), the charge is 3F ($1.38) for adults, 1F (46¢) for children.

Waterski at Club Nautico-Lugano (fra Lugano e Melide) (tel. 68-61-39) for an hour at a cost of 120F ($55.14); Scuola Club Migros (tel. 22-76-21) for 100F ($45.95) for 50 minutes; Club Sci Nautico Ceresio (tel. 54-19-21) which also gives instruction in the sport, an hour's skiing costing 132F ($60.65); and Saladin, Piazza B. Luini (tel. 23-57-97) at 55F ($25.27) for a half hour, 95F ($43.65) per hour.

Sailing is also possible at Saladin. A boat for up to four persons costs 25F ($11.49) for an hour or 100F ($45.95) for a full day.

Windsurfing on the lake can be arranged at Club Nautico-Lugano (fra Lugano e Melide) (tel. 68-61-39); Albergo Lago di Lugano, Paradiso (tel. 54-19-21); or Circolo Velico, Lago di Lugano, Foce Cassarate (tel. 51-09-75). The charge is 15F ($6.89) for an hour's fun.

Rowboats and motorboats are available for rental at many spots along the lakefront.

Underwater swimming is a possibility at Lugano-Sub, G. Bucher, 3 Corso Elvezia (tel. 22-96-29).

9. Morcote

Morcote, reached either by boat or car, is considered one of the most idyllic and charming villages of Switzerland. Its arcaded houses and old streets are built on the southern slopes of Monte Arbostora at 2755 feet. Cypresses stud the vine-clad slopes. The pilgrimage **Church of the Madonna del Sasso** dates from the 13th century, although it was reconstructed much later and given a baroque overlay. It has some beautiful 16th-century frescoes. At the church you can take more than 400 steps down to the village on the shores of the lake. Many famous persons were buried in the Morcote cemetery.

Of special interest is **Scherrer Park,** with its typical Ticino trees and vegetation, along with artistic and architectural objects of interest, including sculpture from the Far East. It's open from 9 a.m. to 5 p.m. except on Tuesday and Thursday. The entrance fee is 2.50F ($1.15). On Tuesday and Thursday there are conducted tours with a guide who explains everything. This, of course, is the best time to visit. He conducts tours at 10 a.m., 1:30 p.m., and again at 3:30 p.m., charging an entrance fee then of 5F ($2.30).

FOOD AND LODGING: **Olivella au Lac** (tel. 69-17-31). From the lakeside road passing beside this establishment it won't look very impressive. Once you park, however, and look over the edge of the road, you'll see a lovely oasis of green lawns, flowers, and terraced elegance. Going down several flights, you'll reach the spacious and intimate ambience of what is acknowledged as one of the top restaurants of Switzerland. Service here is impeccable, and chef Mario Sancassani has elevated Ticino cookery to a fine art. You might begin your meal with foie gras or a lobster cocktail, perhaps turtle soup, either selection a proper introduction to this outstanding restaurant, **La Voile d'Or.** The chef might recommend a cassoulet of barbue with small lobster, or a filet of sole Caruso. Game dishes such as roebuck are featured in season. Specialties of the house include duck à la orange and beef Wellington. Blue trout meunière is also outstanding, and scampi and lobster are prepared pretty much as you desire them. A menu gastronomique is offered for 85F ($39.06).

If you want to spend the night, or else make this place a headquarters for your Ticino holiday, it would be an excellent choice. The hotel has two swimming pools, along with waterskiing and windsurfing facilities. There's plenty of atmosphere, and at the piano bar in the evening you're likely to meet your fellow guests. A resident nurse will care for your children as part of your accommodation fee. Singles range from 95F ($43.65) to 175F ($80.41), while doubles cost between 195F ($89.60) and 265F ($121.77), with breakfast included. All rooms have private bath, and most of them have a balcony as well, along with radio, phone, and mini-bar. The hotel is closed in January and February.

Albergo Carina (tel. 69-11-31). The hotel lobby has many happily contrasting colors and patterns woven into the Oriental rugs and upholstery. Even the facade repeats the lighthearted theme, with its Italianate design and pink- and cream-colored trim and its lime-green shutters. The many terraces are filled with potted plants and small tables, where local residents often stop in for coffee. The former owner of this charming place was the Morcote-born architect Gaspare Fossati, who died in 1883. He helped direct the renovations on the mosaics and superstructure of Sancta Sophia in Istanbul. Some of the awards he received from the Ottoman sultan are displayed in the lobby. Heidi and Horst Echsle have directed this place for several years. Their elegant bedrooms are filled with provincial furniture, some of it antique, which rent for between 75F ($34.46) and 140F ($64.33) in a single and between 110F ($50.55) and 200F ($91.90) in a double, with breakfast included. Half board costs an additional 30F ($13.79) per person daily. There's a swimming pool as well as a waterside restaurant on the premises.

Hotel Rivabella (tel. 69-13-14) is housed in an old Italian-style country house some distance down the lakefront from the most congested part of Morcote. It has a terrace built out over the water, beneath which sailboats and motorboats are moored. The Tamborini family have planted flower boxes filled with begonias and geraniums that thrive in the sunshine of the rustically covered porches. Rooms are comfortably and pleasantly furnished. Singles range from 35F ($16.08) to 50F ($22.98), while doubles cost from 62F ($28.49) to 98F ($45.03). Half board is an additional 10F ($4.60) per person daily.

Ristorante della Posta (tel. 69-11-27). This unusual restaurant is housed on a terrace built out over the lake. Waiters scurry with food-laden trays from the kitchens across the street. The setting is charming, but because of the traffic, a little hectic. Specialties include risotto with mushrooms, osso buco with polenta, trout, minestrone Ticino style, and lake fish. Meals cost from 30F ($13.79). The restaurant is closed on Wednesday and during December and January.

Chapter XIII

LIECHTENSTEIN

IF YOU WANT to come back from Europe and let your friends think you've toured a remote and obscure place in that much-traveled continent, pay a visit to Liechtenstein. This tiny principality, nestled snugly between a small portion of Austria with a short stretch of the Rhine River dividing it from Switzerland, is one of the smallest independent sovereign states of Europe, ranking along with San Marino in Italy and Andorra in the Pyrenees between Spain and France. The whole country encompasses only about 60 square miles. It's separated on its western border from the Swiss canton of St. Gallen by the Rhine River, its eastern frontier borders the Austrian province of Vorarlberg, and its southern boundary is a strip less than ten miles long dividing it from the Grisons of Switzerland. The country is cradled in the Three Sisters (Dreï Schwestern) mountains.

Actually, Liechtenstein is not as isolated as it's often made out to be. In fact, if you're touring through eastern Switzerland, it's easily reached by good roads. It lives up to its cliché image of fairytale castles (one inhabited by a real prince), Rhine meadows, and geranium-bedecked chalets in small villages high up in the Alps. It was once on the Grand Tour, at least in Queen Victoria's day, but in spite of its accessibility it still tends to be thought of as remote, so that a visit there almost constitutes an offbeat adventure. Since border guards rarely stamp passports to travelers coming nowadays from Austria, and since there's no Customs to clear if you're motoring in from Switzerland, if you want to prove you've been there, you'll have to get someone at the tourist office to stamp the Liechtenstein seal on your passport. They'll do it for .50F ($23¢).

If you're based in Switzerland you can make Liechtenstein in an easy morning's drive, and unless you choose to stay in one or the other of the towns or villages, it doesn't take long to motor through this 16-mile-long, four-mile-wide country. There are no formalities at the Swiss border for passing into Liechtenstein.

1. Getting Acquainted

Low taxes and low unemployment linked with carefully planned industrial development and a high standard of living make the Principality of Liechtenstein almost a phenomenon in today's world, but this is a development dating from the end of World War II, as a look at the past will show.

HISTORY: The region which today is Liechtenstein was in a part of Europe that for centuries was inextricably connected with Switzerland and Austria, and its history follows the same paths for long eras. Tribal settlements, particularly those of the Celts, left traces showing habitation of the section from about 4000 B.C., with the Romans occupying the Rhine Valley in 15 B.C. and holding control until the middle of the fifth century A.D. What is today Liechtenstein was part of the Roman province of Rhaetia, and establishment of a military and trade route by the Emperor Augustus preceded the coming of the Alemanni, Germanic tribes, who settled here over the centuries from A.D. 300 to 700.

When Charlemagne made all the alpine region a part of the Holy Roman Empire, the area now comprising Liechtenstein became portions of royal estates, as shown in a document drawn up in about A.D. 850, called the *Rhaetican Register.* Descendants of family connections of Charlemagne owned rich estates in the region of Lake Constance and the Lower Alps, which were continually broken up through hereditary claims, resulting in the formation of the County of Vaduz on the east side of the Rhine. Vaduz, the name of the present capital of Liechtenstein, was under the immediate rule of the Roman Empire and not of any territorial lord.

Since 1437 both parts of the country, the old County of Vaduz (called Oberland, or the Upper Country) and the Lordship of Schellenberg (Unterland, or Lower Country) have been united, with the same boundaries of the principality that exist today. The many wars in which the little state became involved during the Middle Ages saw dependency changing from Switzerland to Austria and the country beset with religious strife and the plague. Many of the rulers were tyrants who wrested devastating taxes or by other means brought misery to the land. This sometimes-peaceful, sometimes-wartorn country passed from count to count and lord to lord through inheritance and outright sale of the Schellenberg and Vaduz estates. Finally, Prince John Adam Andrew of Liechtenstein was able to purchase first the estates of Schellenberg and then the County of Vaduz, and in 1719 the two territories were given the title "Imperial Principality of Liechtenstein," becoming thus a member of the Holy Roman Empire and not just a possession of some other ruler. As a result, if you're crossing from Switzerland into Liechtenstein, it's commonly pointed out to tourists that they are leaving one of the world's oldest democracies and entering the last remaining outpost of the Holy Roman Empire.

Under the old German Empire, Liechtenstein was under obligation to provide five men for the Imperial Army, a figure finally raised to 80 under the German Confederation. After a tour of duty in 1866 lasting six weeks on the Tyrol-Italian frontier, during which time they never set eyes on the enemy, the Liechtenstein contingent was never again called up, and in 1869 the principality's army was disbanded permanently by Prince John II.

Until the end of World War I the country had a close alliance with Austria, but in 1921 it signed a postal treaty with Switzerland, followed in 1924 by adoption of Swiss currency and inclusion in the Swiss Customs Union. Since 1959 Switzerland has been Liechtenstein's diplomatic representative abroad. This political marriage with Switzerland was a smart move by the principality. It did not have to suffer Austria's fate when World War II came, and because of its close ties with Switzerland and the same neutrality stance, Liechtenstein escaped occupation by Nazi troops.

Prince John II had the longest reign of any Liechtenstein ruler, 71 years, ending with his death in 1929. He lavished part of his vast fortune on improving life in the principality.

The present ruler is the first to make his permanent home in the country, after becoming ruling prince in 1938. He and his wife, Princess Gina, are the parents of five children, four of them sons. The present ruler's full name is Prince Franz Joseph II Maria Alois Alfred Karl Johann Heinrich Michael Georg Ignatius Benedictus Gerhardus Majella, and he is Prince of Liechtenstein, Duke of Troppau and Jaegerndorf, Knight of the Golden Fleece, and Count of Reitberg.

Although his family has lost vast tracts of its lands in eastern Europe, Prince Franz Joseph II is still one of the wealthiest men in Europe. Yet, we are told, he wears casual clothes and drives around his little principality in a relatively modest vehicle. Obviously he doesn't believe in flaunting his wealth.

The Principality of Liechtenstein celebrated its 250th anniversary in 1969.

THE PEOPLE: Most of the population of this tiny country is of German origin and therefore, of course, German speaking. However, English is understood all over Liechtenstein. It's a predominantly Roman Catholic principality. You'll search hard to find anyone who is unemployed in the country. In fact a citizen of Liechtenstein today enjoys one of the highest standards of living in the world, although many oldtimers remember World War I, when the little principality was virtually cut off from food supplies because of blockades and suffered much hunger and hardship.

Since the end of World War II Liechtenstein has had a social and economic growth period exceeding that of any other Western-world country. Citizens pay relatively little in taxes, and they have an export revenue of some $14,000 annually per citizen.

The people of Liechtenstein enjoy a flourishing cultural ambience, benefiting from royal patronage and cooperation of neighboring countries. Sports, trades and crafts, and agriculture also are actively promoted among the citizenry.

Considered today to be one of the most industrialized countries in the world, Liechtenstein, with some 26,000 citizens scattered throughout 11 communities, has been careful to keep the country attractive. The industrial development is hardly noticeable if you're touring the principality, as factories and workshops are hidden among orchards, meadows, and woodlands in order to have them blend with the environment. There are no factory smokestacks or fumes to pollute the atmosphere. Agriculture and industry are the two top economic resources of the country (one of its commercial specialties is the manufacture of false teeth).

When you hear about all this good life, you may want to become a citizen of Lichtenstein immediately. Forget it! Citizenship is almost impossible to obtain, and unless you're a woman who marries a man of the country, it would require an act of the state's parliament.

GOVERNMENT: The Principality of Liechtenstein is a constitutional hereditary monarchy on a democratic and parliamentary basis. The state power is vested in the prince and the people. The prince's state prerogatives derive from hereditary succession to the throne and are independent of the will of the people. The people, on the other hand, are invested with a right to participate in the guidance of state affairs independently of the prince. Therefore both parties must work together in accordance with the constitution.

The parliament, called the Diet, is elected by the people in national general elections, with the right to vote being constitutionally universal, equal, secret, and direct. Referendum is a vital part of the Liechtenstein people's right. Any law passed by the Diet which is not declared as urgent may be put to referendum.Besides the universal and equal right to vote, the constitution assures Liechtenstein citizens of freedom of expression of opinion, freedom of the press, and freedom of assembly, among other privileges.

Liechtenstein has a prime minister and four government councillors. They act as a connecting link between the prince and the Diet.

STAMPS: Liechtenstein is known all over the world for her postage stamps, finely engraved issues that are an important source of revenue (about 25%) for the country. The design and quality of these stamps are appreciated by philatelists and by other collectors with artistic interests. The stamps depict the special features of the principality, taking subjects from the religion, monarchy, art, history, landscape, nature, work, and leisure of the country. The Postal Museum at Vaduz, the capital, displays both the issues of Liechtenstein from the first ones in 1912 and those received from other members of the Universal Postal Union, formed in 1921, plus many other items of interest to stamp collectors. The post office frequently issues new stamp series.

PRACTICAL FACTS: The **Liechtenstein National Tourist Office** address is 37 Städtle, Vaduz (tel. 2-14-43).

The country's **mail and phone rates** are the same as those of Switzerland. You can **telephone** any number you want in Liechtenstein from Switzerland by dialing 075, followed by the number you want.

The Swiss franc is legal tender. The same rates of exchange prevail (see Chapter II, "The ABC's of Switzerland."

All **travel documents** recognized by Swiss authorities are valid in Liechtenstein. However, you'll encounter the formalities of any western European border crossing if you enter through Austria.

Express **trains** don't actually stop in Liechtenstein, although many such trains cross its borders. If you go by rail, take the train from Buchs in the canton of St. Gallen in Switzerland. Postal buses also run from Switzerland into Vaduz. The bus ride from Buchs takes exactly 18 minutes. From Austria, you can take a train near the border at Feldkirch.

A cost of a holiday in Liechtenstein is about the same as one in Switzerland. Perhaps prices are a little lower in the principality, but in general they're not as low as the tariffs charged in Austria.

2. Vaduz

Vaduz (pronounced Va-dootz), capital of the Principality of Liechtenstein, is a friendly little town at the foot of the castle where the royal family makes its home. Surrounded by sunlit vineyards, Vaduz was once a rural community known mainly for its good wines. Today it's a hospitable, sociable town with attractions for tourists. The baths of Vaduz are popular with spa users, and there are many entertainment and sport facilities, including a riding school, miniature golf course, tennis courts, discos, and a swimming pool.

The main street of the town is **Städtle,** which has one-way traffic flow. The Rathaus (town hall) stands in the center of the capital.

Schloss Vaduz, the prince's castle, has origins dating back to the 12th century, the keep and buildings on the east side being the oldest surviving parts. The castle was burned down by Swiss troops in 1499 and rebuilt at the beginning of the 16th century with round bastions at the northeast and southwest Once a bleak and gloomy fortress, the castle is now much improved, and visitors report on its lavish furnishings and antiques, as well as near-priceless artworks.

Although you can't visit the castle of the prince, you can climb up to it (allow about 20 minutes). A wooded footpath or trail begins at the tourist office (see below). If you don't want to climb, you can take a bus from the Städtle. Some locals visit the terraces and meadows around the castle with a picnic lunch. Once up there, you'll have a sweeping vista that will make the trip worthwhile.

Before you begin exploring, you might visit the **National Tourist Office,** 37 Städtle (tel. 2-14-43), where you'll be given free brochures and information about the country.

In the same building as the tourist office are the National Art Gallery and the Post Office and Postal Museum.

Princes of the House of Liechtenstein have been art collectors since the 17th century, and their treasures were in a palace in Vienna until 1940. The present prince decided to display his collection to the world, and it has become the highlight of many a visitor's trip to Liechtenstein. The prince's collection occupies the top floor of the **National Gallery** above the tourist office. It's well lit and handsomely exhibited, showing to advantage the Rubens collection, considered the greatest on earth, including a cycle of nine large paintings illustrating the history of a Roman consul. See also his *Toilet of Venus.* The gallery also displays works of Van Dyck, Botticelli, Brueghel, and Rembrandt. In my opinion, this is the country's most outstanding attraction. Many of the pictures shown here are reproduced on the famous stamps of Liechtenstein.

The art gallery is open from the first of April to the end of October from 10 a.m. to noon and 1:30 to 5:30 p.m. In winter the hours are from 10 a.m. to noon and 2 to 5:30 p.m. It's closed on Monday, which is unfortunate for the "If it's Tuesday, this must be Belgium" bus crowd who treat Liechtenstein like a luncheon stopover on the way to Innsbruck. Admission for adults is 3F ($1.38), and 1.50F (69¢) for children over 6 years and students.

The **Postal Museum** is the country's biggest attraction, drawing philatelists from all over the world. Founded in 1930 to display the popular Liechtenstein stamps which have grown to be of great value and stamps of member states of the Universal Postal Union, the museum has a wealth of other philatelic objects. Lack of space at present prevents exhibition of all the printing plates, postal and philatelic documents, and other collected items, but special exhibitions are staged from time to time in addition to the 300 permanent showcases. Museum hours are 10 a.m. to noon and 2 to 6 p.m. It's on the ground floor at 37 Städtle.

The **Liechtenstein National Museum,** called Landesmuseum, was founded in 1954 and today has as its contents items from the collections of the prince, the state, and the Liechtenstein Historical Society. Since 1972 the museum has been housed in a completely renovated building which is also of historic interest. Originally it was the Stag Inn on the stagecoach route, later becoming the princely tavern and Customs house. In the early 19th century it was named the Eagle Inn, and then until 1905 it was the seat of government, its basement housing the state prison.

The museum displays artifacts from the prehistoric times of the region, as well as from the Roman period, Alemannic burial articles, records of the early Christian era, medieval coinage and weapons, and some antique Rhineland jewelry.

Hours are the same as those of the National Art Gallery. Admission is 2F (92¢) for adults, 1F (46¢) for children. The museum is closed December 24, December 25, December 31, and January 1.

In the upper village, on the road to the castle, is the **Red House,** the seat of the Vaistlis, vassals of the Counts of Werdenberg, during the Middle Ages. The house, probably in its present form with the exception of the tower, was acquired along with the vineyard by the Monastery of St. Johann in the Toggenburg.

WHERE TO STAY: Most of the hotels, quite naturally, are in the capital.

Park Hotel Sonnenhof (tel. 2-14-43) is the finest hotel in the principality and among the finest in Europe. It has only 33 rooms, beautiful gardens, and the best clientele in Vaduz. Diplomatic receptions are held here frequently, and the Princess of Liechtenstein comes over about once a week to use the swimming pool. The establishment is built in the late 19th century, but has been modernized into a streamlined chalet-style format with balconies and awnings. It has entertained everyone from J. Paul Getty to the crowned heads of virtually everything.

Only hotel guests, regrettably, are allowed in the dining room. Emil Real is the chef and he's celebrated. (He's the brother of another distinguished chef, Felix Real, who owns the Hotel Real.) Emil Real is at home entertaining royalty or Mr. and Mrs. Smith from Kansas. A native of Italy, he was once a chef at Maxim's in Paris. He and his brother were flown by the Shah of Iran in 1972 to cook at that great bash he tossed at Persepolis. His English-speaking wife, Jutta, is the charming hostess.

Rooms are handsomely decorated and furnished. Singles range from 95F ($43.65) to 125F ($57.44), while doubles cost from 160F ($73.52) to 195F ($89.60). Half board is another 40F ($18.38) per person.

Hotel Real, 21 Städtle (tel. 2-22-22), is an extremely well-maintained hotel on the main street of Vaduz. It sits at the bottom of a forested bluff, on top of which is the fortress-like palace of the prince. The hotel is modern, its boxy facade decorated with summertime flower boxes. The rooms are clean and comfortable. Singles range from 95F ($43.65) to 130F ($59.74), while doubles cost between 105F ($48.25) and 155F ($71.22). The restaurant inside is covered in the dining recommendations.

Hotel Schlössle (tel. 2-56-21) is an ocher-colored hotel with medieval-style Teutonic turrets designed into the roofline. It sits on the main route from Vaduz to the prince's castle. The facade has a clock tower with gingerbread trim, and a small carillon of bells hanging above the statue of a Liechtenstein couple in regional garb. The bedrooms are charmingly outfitted with painted furniture. Singles range from 95F ($43.65) to 108F ($49.63), while doubles cost between 128F ($58.82) and 175F ($80.41), with breakfast included. Triples go for anywhere from 195F ($89.60) to 215F ($98.79).

Hotel Engel (tel. 2-10-57) is a small hotel with a convincing decor of rustic artifacts, such as an antique winescrew in the grill room. The well-maintained public rooms include a covered terrace and an intimate French restaurant. The hotel rises four modern stories, with summertime flowers filling many of its balconies. The 17 bedrooms are priced between 55F ($25.27) and 70F ($32.17) in a single and from 75F ($34.46) to 98F ($45.03) in a double.

Löwen Hotel, 35 Herrengasse (tel. 2-14-08), was built in the 17th century as a farmer's private house. He and his family cultivated the vineyards which still grow behind the house. This mellow old hotel sits only two feet from the busy traffic of the street outside, although at night most of the cars stop running in sleepy Vaduz. You'll turn a heavy brass handle to enter the darkly tiled central hallway with low lintels above the wide doors, each of which has a different alpine design painted onto its panels. The house contains an odd mixture of very old furniture, which sits in hallways and in nooks and crannies throughout the hotel. Each of the 14 rooms is furnished with antiques, some of them startingly grand. If it's available, and if you can afford it, ask for Room 4, which has its own ceramic stove, a private bath, and ornately impressive furniture.

The restaurant has a glass walled extension with a view of the prince's castle and the Swiss mountains in the distance. It's open from 7 a.m to midnight, and serves such specialties as smoked trout, air-dried Grisons beef, five kinds of soup, jumbo shrimp, and calf liver, along with farmer's-style lamb chops with beans and potatoes. Meals range from 15F ($6.89) to 25F ($11.49) for dinner. Hilda Vogt is the disciplined owner of this place, and she extends her establishment's hospitality to the prince himself, who shows up just like everyone else in Vaduz about once a month. The wine list contains vintages made from grapes grown on the property. These include Riesling Sylvaner and Beerliwein. Singles are inexpensively priced from 30F ($13.79), while doubles range from 62F ($28.49) to 90F ($41.36).

Hotel Vaduzerhof Wienerwald, 3 Städtle (tel. 2-84-84), is a large white-painted hotel with shutters and a flat roof. It sits in the center of town, with a yellow canopy above the front door crowned by masses of flowers. The rooms are filled with wood-grained, pleasantly designed furniture. Singles range from 48F ($22.06) to 62F ($28.49), while doubles cost between 40F ($18.38) and 62F ($28.49) per person. The metal tables of a sidewalk café ring the trunk of an old tree planted in its center. A Wienerwald restaurant inside is attractively rustic and well maintained, with an older crowd of dignified diners at the red cloth-covered tables. A quick lunch costs 9F ($4.14), while fixed-price meals range from 15F ($6.89).

Hotel Landhaus Vaduzerhof, 16 Zollstrasse (tel. 2-46-64), is a newly built modern hotel about 800 yards from the center of town. It's outfitted like a large country house, with heavy timbers in the lobby area. It also has an elevator and a rustic dining room with Windsor chairs and a big fireplace, plus an on-site swimming pool. The bedrooms are simple and clean, with private baths and balconies. Owned by the Wienerwald chain, the hotel charges from 60F ($27.57) to 66F ($30.33) in a single and from 50F ($22.98) to 56F ($25.73) per person in a double.

WHERE TO DINE: **Restaurant Real,** 21 Städtle (tel. 2-22-22). As you approach this restaurant on the main street of Vaduz, you'll see the prince's castle looming on top of a cliff almost directly above it. The outside has café tables and chairs in plastic rattan, while inside, the wood-paneled rooms are usually filled with contented diners. The lighting fixtures are shaped like grape garlands, while the entire place gives the impression of well-polished and understated prosperity.

The room upstairs offers the same menu as below, in a slightly more formal setting. This establishment is operated by the second famous Real brother, Felix. (His older brother, Emil, owns the already-recommended Sonnenhof.) Felix is a celebrated chef, a native of Italy. Even the prince drops in for dinner here from time to time. The food is very capably cooked, and might include coquilles St. Jacques with Noilly Prat and leeks, or duck liver salad followed by any one of six lobster dishes, wild game specialties, filet of wild trout with Riesling, salmon with champagne, or a good range of meat and chicken dishes. The management offers a fixed-price "menu of the month" with five courses for 88F ($40.44). However, an à la carte dinner will likely cost you around 65F ($29.87) and up.

Restaurant Torkel, 9 Hintergasse (tel. 2-44-10), is a country inn owned by the prince. It's on the site of an old wine press, with a location right outside of town in the midst of a vineyard. You park your car in a lot designated, then follow the signs a short distance to a low-lying building which is today one of the most charming restaurants in Vaduz. The chefs prepare good veal dishes, filet goulash Stroganoff, and a specialty called Torkelsteak, along with noodle and rösti dishes. À la carte meals cost from 35F ($16.08), although a light snack goes for around 20F ($9.19). Closed Wednesday

Old Castle Inn, 22 Aeulestrasse (tel. 2-10-65), in downtown Vaduz, is a popular place for locals, who usually sit around the long, half-timbered bar on stools to drink and gossip. Italian and German folk/rock music plays on the sound system. The place is brightly lit to the point where you can see across the bar, yet it's dim to the point you can feel intimate with whomever you happen to be with. Black-skirted waitresses and black-vested waiters will take your order, which you'll eat on green leatherette banquettes at wood tables. Outside, you'll discover a geranium-bordered terrace with a striped canopy. Hot food is served from 11 a.m. to 2 p.m. and 6 to 11 p.m. The special Italian menu might include some antipasti, risotto with mushrooms, or other good-tasting dishes, a meal costing from 25F ($11.49). There's also a good selection of würst and steak dishes, or you might drop in for just a sandwich. One good bargain is the paprika schnitzel with pommes frites and a salad, costing only 11F ($5.06). Set meals range from 13F ($5.97), which could include minestrone, spaghetti, lasagne, polenta with gorgonzola, and veal liver Venice style.

Café Wolff, 29 Städtle (tel. 2-23-21), is about as schizophrenic an establishment as you're likely to find in Vaduz. It has two floors with a different clientele on each. Upstairs is a tearoom, with an inviting display of open-faced sandwiches and pastries in a glass window. It seems to cater to a gentle older crowd as well as to visitors. Downstairs is a youth-oriented bar with rock music playing to a nighttime crowd of Liechtenstein punk-rockers in leather and sneakers. It has red fabric walls, cramped groupings of closely arranged tables, video games, and a long bar with chrome and leatherette stools. If you thought Vaduz might be a backwater capital of cows and regional garb, look again. Pizzas cost from 7.50F ($3.45), sandwiches from 2.40F ($1.12), and soups from 2.40F ($1.12). There's friendly service.

A SHOPPING NOTE: Most visitors stop off here just to purchase stamps. But if the bus isn't pulling out, you may have time to drop into at least one shop. The best is **L'Atelier,** 36 Städtle (tel. 3-21-64). Even the script of the orange neon sign announcing this shop is chic and in good taste. The place specializes in handicrafts such as lamps, dolls, stoneware, pewter, sculpture, and virtually anything else that's labored over by hand. It has a beautifully polished stone floor and a cork ceiling dotted with pin lights. The store is run by Hélène de Marchi, who opens it from 9:30 a.m. to noon and 2 to 6:30 p.m. on weekdays, from 9 a.m. to noon and 1 to 4 p.m. on Saturday.

3. The Unterland

Formed by the Rhine Valley, Liechtenstein's Unterland (lowland) contains eight villages on or around the slopes of the Eschnerberg at the foot of the Three Sisters (Drei Schwestern) mountains. The little hamlets comprise five parishes: Ruggell, Schellenberg, Eschen-Nendeln, Gamprin-Bendern, and Mauren-Schaanwald. The rugged country of the Unterland is unspoiled, still having tracts of virgin landscape with flora and fauna that are not common elsewhere. Even the pockets of agricultural and industrial development have not been allowed to damage the environment. You'll find wooded hills sheltering wildlife, broad expanses of fields and meadows with wildflowers, clean brooks, and attractive villages.

An extensive footpath network, the **Eschnerberg Historical Trail,** a joint project of the Unterland localities, and a nature trail offer pleasant and informative exercise. The Eschnerberg hills were a secure refuge for prehistoric settlers, offering an island-like setting in the then-marshy Rhine Valley some 5000 years ago. Hiking the mountain track, you'll learn the history of the people who have lived in this region through the centuries.

RUGGELL: This village was first recorded in A.D. 933 in documents conveying a farm, or a *run* (cleared land) in the Rhaeto-Romanic terminology. The locality has been known for efficient farms, although the number has dropped with the springing up of various small industries. The landscape of the parish is mostly water meadows. Some 225 acres of this meadowland is designated as a protected area to prevent the extinction of the plant and animal life peculiar to the area. Ruggell is the northernmost village of Liechtenstein and the lowest geographical spot.

SCHELLENBERG: This second-smallest parish in the principality, (population 577), with the smallest surface area, is the only place in Liechtenstein to bear a wholly German name. It was already settled when the New Stone Age arrived. Some of the Iron Age artifacts displayed in the National Museum in Vaduz were unearthed here. The Herren von Schellenberg built two castles here in the Middle Ages, the ruins of one of which, the **Obere Burg Schellenberg,** have been restored and are a popular excursion spot with views attracting visitors. Schellenberg is a starting point for the Eschnerberg Historical Trail.

MAUREN-SCHAANWALD: In the midst of more rolling meadows, these two villages lie about a mile apart, in a parish covering only three square miles. Mauren, known as the "village of the seven hillocks" because of its location and topography, is in one of the loveliest settings in Liechtenstein. It was first mentioned in recorded history in 1178 under the name of Muron, but the remains of Roman baths and a second-century farmhouse or outbuilding have been excavated here. The village is also known for its fine parish church, dating from 1787. Between Mauren and Schaanwald, which lies on the Schaan-Feldkirch road leading into Austria, the meadows and woodlands have been designated a bird sanctuary. This contains a pond biotope under conservation and a nature trail.

GAMPRIN-BENDERN: This small parish, almost a cliché of picture-postcard charm with the Rhine flowing by, embraces two hamlets on the west spur of the Eschnerberg. Being rich in archeological discoveries, it's one of the best documented localities in Liechtenstein. Excavations have shown that the area was inhabited continuously from about 2500 B.C. to the Roman era. Discoveries around Gamprin have yielded a wealth of information on the culture of the New Stone Age, and remains of a farm and a small church dating from A.D. 55 have been found on the hill on which the Bendern church stands today. This church belonged to the convent of Schänis (St. Gallen) from 809 to 1177 and to the monastery of St. Luzi (Chur) from 1200 to 1816. After the Reformation, the St. Luzi monks built a larger structure, which included the abbot's quarters. Recently restored, this building now serves as a vicarage for the Bendern church.

Bendern's **Kirchhügel** is a favorite local scenic place. It was on this site in 1699 that the men of the lowlands swore loyalty to the Prince of Liechtenstein. You'll find an intersport keep-fit track and a camping site here, as well as a path following a trail of local history. The **Mariengrotte** (Mary's Grotto) at Bendern is the only shrine of its kind in the country.

ESCHEN-NENDELN: The existence of Eschen, main locality in the Liechtenstein Unterland, was first noted in the Carolingian land registry about A.D 850 under the name Essane, which is believed to be derived from the Celtic word *esca,* meaning "by the water" and referring to the nearby brook, the Esche. The parish incorporates Nendeln, a village of equal economic importance. Flint artifacts from the Middle Stone Age, about 5000 B.C., have been found, and excavations at the sites of the prehistoric settlements at Malanser and Schneller have provided evidence of New Stone Age culture. At Nendeln the foundation of a Roman villa and a prehistoric settlement have been discovered. In medieval times the area was owned by monasteries and counts.

Buildings of interest are the Pfrundhaus (prebend structure), Holy Cross Chapel on the Rofenberg (formerly a place of public assembly), the restored church at Eschen with the original walls of the old church laid bare, and the St. Sebastian and Rochus Chapels at Nendeln. Liechtenstein's first industrial enterprise was a tile factory founded at Nendeln in 1836, which for a century was the only industrial plant in the Unterland.

The upper part of Eschen, Schönbühl, is one of the country's most attractive residential sections. You can enjoy swimming in a pool open to the public at Eschen and a nature health-cure trail at Nendeln, as well as the peaceful mountain footpaths on the Eschnerberg trail.

Food and Lodging

Hotel Landhaus (tel. 3-20-11), at Nendeln, is on the road from Vaduz to the Austrian border. It has a large antique wine press in the yard and a dark modern facade. Inside, the large ground floor contains two rooms, paneled with both unpolished and uncut saplings, with a few deer antlers to remind you you're in game country. If you happen to get there on a Sunday morning, you'll see friendly groups of older men reminiscing together. The international menu has foods such as beef goulash with spaetzli, spaghetti carbonara, sole meunière, wienerschnitzel, and steak au poivre, with fixed-price meals beginning at 35F ($16.08). Less expensive meals are also available for around 20F ($9.19), including, for example, a cold würst and cheese salad at 10F ($4.60). If you drop in here at night, a downstairs bar is exotically painted in burnt orange with unusual weavings and South Seas artifacts. Bedrooms inside the hotel cost between 39F ($17.92) and 45F ($20.68) in a single and from 70F ($32.17) in a double, with breakfast included.

4. The Oberland

Besides the capital, Vaduz, the Oberland or Upper Country of Liechtenstein, formerly the region owned by the Count of Vaduz, is made up of five parishes or communes: Planken, Schaan, Triesen, Triesenberg, and Balzers. Looking at the map, you may have difficulty placing this southern part of the country as "upper" and the Unterland (Lower Country) as being really that.

But the explanation is to be found in the topography. The major portion of the Unterland is mainly meadows and hills gently rising from the Rhine Valley, whereas the Oberland, from Planken south, consists of higher country, reaching up to the Liechtenstein Alps.

Towered over by the Three Sisters, the Oberland is rich in woodlands and mountain trails, and most of its parishes provide numerous sports activities for visitors as well as for the locals. Domestic traditions and indigenous customs are followed, especially in the settlements founded by Swiss immigrants some 700 years ago.

Throughout this part of the principality you can find colorful alpine flowers and protected animal species. A wealth of nature trails vary from easy walking to more rugged hiking. The winter sports attractions of Liechtenstein are centered in the alpine portion of the Oberland.

PLANKEN: Three miles from Nendeln lies Planken, the smallest parish in Liechtenstein (population 285), on a natural terrace in a woodland setting. The name of this little hamlet is from the Rhaeto-Romanic word *planca* or *plaunca*, meaning a pasture or meadow upland. Planken was settled by immigrants from the Valais in Switzerland in the latter part of the 13th century, and the inhabitants still speak a dialect quite different from that of the valley people. The village is the starting point for excursions to the Three Sisters (Drei Schwestern) area. From here you have an outstanding panorama of the Rhine Valley and the Swiss mountains, having a view from the Pizol section to Lake Constance. A chapel dedicated to St. Joseph contains copies of old masters and a bronze cross by Georg Malin in the chancel.

SCHAAN: The Carolingian land registry (circa A.D. 831) contains mention of Liechtenstein's second-largest parish under the name Scana. Archeological finds, however, reveal that this was the site of a Roman fort, and digs have yielded two Roman legionnaires' helmets from the first century of the Christian era as well as an Alemannic decorative shield from the sixth or seventh century A.D. See also the 12th-century Romanesque church.

Schaan, just two miles from Vaduz, is the country's main communications center, with its railroad station on the Arlberg line. It lies at the foot of the Three Sisters massif and is the site of much of Liechtenstein's industry. Besides hikes into the mountains, Schaan also has a sports center by a forest, where you'll find tennis courts, a health center, an indoor swimming pool, public baths, and a children's playground. Schaan's **Theater am Kirchplatz** is one of the important cultural centers of the region, with performances by international artists. The town is also the center of the Liechtenstein carnival.

Food and Lodging

Schaanerhof (tel. 2-18-77) is a modern hotel with balconies facing different exposures and a valentine-colored facade of pink and white. A swimming pool is inside, along with a sleek bar near the reception area. The inside is uncommittedly modern, comfortable, and warm. Singles range from 58F ($26.65) to 85F ($39.06), while doubles cost from 70F ($32.17) to 130F ($59.74), depending on the plumbing and the season.

Hotel Dux (tel. 2-17-27) is a white stucco building with a large sun terrace, a flat roof, and an uninterrupted length of wrought-iron balconies which give it a vaguely Spanish look. Its lawns are dotted with old oak trees. The wood-ceilinged bedrooms are modern, with gaily striped curtains and clean sheets.

In the restaurant the chef specializes in regional cookery and French dishes (fondue is a particular favorite). Singles range from 38F ($17.46) to 60F ($27.57), while doubles cost between 75F ($34.46) and 90F ($41.36), with breakfast included.

Hotel Linde (tel. 2-17-04) has a semi-baroque facade with a single ornate gable. A pumpkin-colored extension stretches off to one side, with well-pruned hedges guarding the sun terrace from the street traffic on the other side. Bedrooms inside are outfitted with big-patterned wallpaper in colors you might find overwhelming, but which are nonetheless comfortable and clean. Singles range from 48F ($22.06) while doubles cost from 68F ($31.25) and 73F ($33.54), with breakfast included.

TRIESEN: Already a settlement in Roman times, Triesen was first recorded in 1155 and can be called the oldest compact community in the principality. It lies at the foot of the Falknis cliffs in beautiful country between the Rhine and the Liechtenstein alpine areas, a pleasant setting which caused noble families from the Roman days on to make their homes here until fairly recent times. It's within easy walking distance of Vaduz, to the north.

Of special interest are the old quarter of the Upper Village, the St. Mamerten and Maria Chapel, and the large Kosthaus, built more than a century ago. Health enthusiasts will enjoy tennis courts, a swimming pool, bicycle paths, and attractive footpaths. There's also a children's playground, a nature reserve with a small lake, and two large camping sites. Hikes and mountain tours are offered along a wild gorge to the high alp of Lawena.

Food and Lodging

Hotel/Restaurant Meierhof (tel. 2-18-36) lies on the main road about a mile south of Vaduz. It's laid out in a forgettable format of a conservatively modern main building with an annex. A swimming pool is behind the hotel, while the dining room inside has a geometrically patterned wooden ceiling and high-backed straight chairs. Doubles range from 80F ($36.76) to 85F ($39.06), while singles cost 62F ($28.49).

Hotel/Restaurant Sonne (tel. 2-15-05) has only four bedrooms, which almost ensures a close relationship with your hosts, the Stalder family. A granite arch leads from the outside into the main hallway, which is full of deer heads and rustically decorated paneling. Singles average 34F ($15.62) and doubles cost 56F ($25.73), with breakfast included.The rustic in-house restaurant serves such savory dishes as filet Stroganoff and entrecôte, and such Italian dishes as spaghetti al pesto and piccata milanese. Meals cost from 35F ($16.08), although less expensive snacks are also available. These might include pizza at 8F ($3.68). Dessert might be an apple strudel.

Restaurant Adler (tel. 2-13-57) was taken over three years ago by a former lab technician who abandoned science to set up one of the most popular restaurants in Liechtenstein. It attracts a contemporary and youngish crowd of loyal fans, some of whom show up in a Rolls-Royce or Mercedes. Norma Bargetze is the sympathetic hostess. With her unshakeable sense of humor, she has an appearance somewhat like a thin Cass Elliott. You might drop in only for a beer, costing from 2F (92¢), and a light meal or snack from 10F ($4.60). Or you may want to order some of the hearty fare, including peppersteak, fondue bourguignonne, serveral types of the inevitable schnitzel, and goulash soup. Meals cost from 35F ($16.08).

TRIESENBERG: This largest and highest parish of Liechtenstein has big sections of woodland and scrub, arable land and pasture, a small portion of unproductive land, and a village of just over 2000 inhabitants high above the Rhine Valley at an altitude of 2600 feet, making it the starting point for the principality's alpine world. Triesenberg was settled in the late 13th century by the same immigration wave from the Swiss Valais as was Planken, and the dialect of the two parishes is similar. Many Triesenberg residents wear colorful regional garb, and the style of some of the houses, although of modern construction, dates from the early 14th century and shows the Valaisian influence.

Within recent decades Triesenberg has changed from a predominantly farming community to a rapidly growing light industry center. A restored and elegant town hall and a community center with a local museum and exhibition of wood engravings may interest you, but perhaps its increasing popularity as a tourist resort within easy reach of the Liechtenstein Alps will be more of a drawing card.

Fine highways and well-tended hiking trails lead from Triesenberg to the alpine resorts: Masescha (4100 feet), Silum (5000 feet), Gaflei (5000 feet), Malbun (5350 feet), and Steg (4600 feet). Steg is on the way to Malbun and features the Valüna-Lopp cross-country skiing center and a ski lift. The half-mile-long Gnalp-Steg tunnel connects the valley with the alpine area.

Food and Lodging

Hotel Martha Bühler (tel. 2-57-77) is one of my favorite hotels in the upper reaches of Liechtenstein. It was founded in 1976 by the beautiful and charming Martha Bühler, who was the first Liechtenstein woman to participate in the winter Olympic Games in Grenoble (1968) and Sappora (1972). In winter she offers free weekly ski lessons to the guests of her hotel. Her cozy establishment is set close to a baroque tower, and has a sweeping view of the valley below from many of the tastefully paneled rooms. The public rooms are cozy and filled with elaborate wood detailing and warmly inviting colors and textures. Today with her children and her world-traveled husband, Gerald Tschikof, she welcomes guests, especially foreigners, with all of the sophistication that Olympic competition has taught her.

Her eight double rooms cost from 70F ($32.17) to 82F ($37.68), depending on the season. Each of the units has a private bath, and breakfast is included. A double can occasionally be rented as a single for around 45F ($20.68) a night, with breakfast included. The restaurant serves a limited menu of simple and well-prepared meals, with snacks costing from 10F ($4.60) and a full dinner starting at 30F ($13.79).

Hotel Kulm (tel. 2-87-77) is in the center of the village with a wide view of the valley. It was built in 1980, with a pink and light-grained wood facade with blossoms cascading down the front balconies in spring. A sidewalk café has been set up in front, while the interior alternates between rustically modern and rough-hewn regional. Singles range from 60F ($27.57) to 70F ($32.17), while doubles cost from 85F ($39.06) to 95F ($43.65), with breakfast included. Half board is another 18F ($8.27) per person daily.

Hotel Steg (tel. 2-21-46), at Steg/Triesenberg, is very much a well-kept and family-run hotel, the director of which is a pretty blonde named Uschi Honold, who with her husband, Hans-Rudolf, and their three children, do everything they can to provide a good cuisine and comfortable lodgings for their loyal guests. The hotel lies on the road to Steg, in a chalet-style building with lots of paneling and unpretentious comfort. Singles range from 18F ($8.27) to 27F ($12.41), while doubles cost from 37F ($17) to 55F ($25.27).

None of the accommodations has a private bath. The restaurant serves traditional foods of savory specialties such as veal, steak, and pork, along with two kinds of spaghetti and lots of different cheese and meat salads. Full dinners range from 15F ($6.89).

Kurhaus Silum (tel. 2-19-51) has wooden porches where you can have a meal or just a drink and look at most of the bluish valley below you. The double-grained chalet offers 16 beds in comfortable rooms with southern exposure for around 28F ($12.87) per person, with breakfast included.

MASESCHA: This small resort hamlet lies about two miles to the north of Triesenberg and is a favorite goal for hikers and mountaineers who want to enjoy the beauties of the alpine world high above the Rhine Valley. Sheer cliffs, spreading woods, lush meadows, and clear mountain brooks provide the hiking nature lover with a memorable experience. Of special interest in the village is the restored medieval Theodul's Chapel.

MALBUN: Fast rising as a winter ski area, Malbun is the center of winter sports in Liechtenstein, with ski lifts, chair lifts, a ski school, and hotels with indoor swimming pools. You can take the chair lift up to the Bettlerjoch Peak, at 6900 feet. The Prince of Wales and Princess Anne learned to ski here many years ago. In summer this is an ideal starting point for mountain walks.

Food and Lodging

Hotel Malbunerhof (tel. 2-29-44) is a four-story, modernized chalet near the ski lifts. It has a swimming pool, a sauna, a bowling alley, a disco, and a comfortable bar with padded armrests. The dining room has orange, yellow, and black tartan carpeting, along with original artworks. A wintertime fire is usually blazing in the timbered lounge area where rustic farm implements decorate the stucco walls. The comfortable bedrooms all have private baths, renting for between 55F ($25.27) and 65F ($29.87) per person in double rooms, with a generous breakfast included.

Hotel Montana (tel. 2-73-33) is a well-maintained building with wood balconies and a white stucco facade. A sun terrace and restaurant extend to one side of the low building. The interior is paneled and filled with orange- and magenta-colored upholstered chairs along with functionally practical wooden furniture. The bedrooms rent for between 60F ($27.57) and 80F ($36.76) in a single, between 50F ($22.98) and 70F ($32.17) per person in double, with breakfast included. Half board is offered for another 20F ($9.19) per person daily.

Alpen Hotel (tel. 2-11-81) is one of the oldest hotels in Malbun. It's been in the same family for more than 75 years, and is filled with such charming details as chandeliers made from deer antlers. The wooden ceilings are painted with alpine floral designs, and the heavy timbers are carved with regional reliefs. The owners are among the loveliest people I've met in Liechtenstein: Jacob and Elsa Vögeli-Schroth. Eager to contribute to the well-being of their guests, they maintain 30 bathless rooms in the main hotel and 15 accommodations with bath in a nearby modern annex. On the premises is a covered swimming pool. *Per-person* rates in the main hotel are 30F ($13.79), going up to 40F ($18.38) in the annex. A very attractive restaurant on the premises serves savory food in a panoramic setting. The hotel is closed from the end of October until mid-December and from Easter until mid-May.

BALZERS: If you've looked all over the high country in Switzerland and Liechtenstein for Heidi tending her flock and picking edelweiss, maybe in your mind's eye you'll see her here, as Balzers was her home in the storybook. The parish comprises the communities of Balzers and Mäls, both first listed in the Carolingian land registry sometime after A.D. 850. Artifacts from various eras indicate that people have lived here since about 3000 B.C. Archeologists have identified a Rössener jug, figurines from the Celto-Etruscan era, and early Roman coins, graves, and buildings.

This southernmost parish in the principality was once a staging post on the old Lindau–Milan post road, and a tablet on the tower of the old cemetery honors a Milanese emissary who died making the trek. Balzers was the first official philatelic center in Liechtenstein, established in 1817.

The Gutenberg Castle, privately owned, dominates the town. Built above a prehistoric mound during the Middle Ages, it belonged to the Habsburgs until 1824. Other places of interest are the Mariahilf and St. Peter Chapels with belfries, the restored Old Vicarage, and the old schoolhouse where you'll find a local museum and library.

There are good sports facilities and a public indoor swimming pool. Nature reserves contain unusual plant species.

Food and Lodging

Hotel Römerhof (tel. 4-19-60) is a modern balconied hotel on the main road to Vaduz from Switzerland. It has masonry columns supporting part of the building. Set in a rather bleak parking lot, it was built by the owner, Arthur Vogt, who spent a part of his career as chief cook at the International Hotel in Las Vegas during his explorations of the world. The restaurant inside is paneled with light-grained woods, and farmers' artifacts hang from the ceiling. A nightclub is in the basement, attracting a strictly local crowd of escapees from home. Simple meals cost from 25F ($11.49). Singles rent for 35F ($16.08), doubles from 55F ($25.27), with breakfast included. All units have private bath or shower.

Hotel Post (tel. 4-12-08) represents a good bargain, even though Balzers is somewhat out of the way from what you might want to see in Vaduz. For a one-night stopover, it's clean, simple, and attractive. The friendly management speaks English, and charges from 66F ($30.33) in a double and from 40F ($18.38) in a single. Half board is another 11F ($5.06) per person daily.

5. Nightlife in Liechtenstein

You won't go broke in the nightclubs of Liechtenstein. All are inexpensively priced. Hours in general are from 8:30 p.m. to 1 a.m. (until 2 a.m. on Friday and Saturday). There's rarely a cover charge, and when there is it's small. Drinks cost from 7F ($3.22).

Here's a brief run-down of after-dark diversions:

Hotel Engel (tel. 2-10-57) in Vaduz has a live orchestra playing nighttime dance tunes for an under-30 crowd of lively Liechtensteiners.

Maschlina Bar (tel. 2-26-90) in Triesen offers disco music in the rustic ambience of the provinces.

Restaurant Palazoles (tel. 4-10-10) in Balzers is a youth-oriented disco. But you'll have to travel from Vaduz south to Balzers toward the Swiss border to see this one.

While in the area, you might also check out the already-recommended **Hotel Römerhof** (tel. 4-19-60), also in Balzers. It's on the ground floor of the hotel. Music is strictly disco, the crowd strictly local.

Hotel Gorfion (tel. 2-43-07) in Malbun caters to an older crowd, often featuring regional music in a rustic country ambience.

Gasthof Landhaus (tel. 3-20-11) in Nendeln also caters to an older crowd, who go here to dance.

Roxy Bar (tel. 4-12-82), back in Balzers, is outfitted in strident shades of red, with lots of mirrors, leather chairs, and a big bar counter. The music is disco, and the crowd tends to be under 30.

Hotel Turna (tel. 2-34-21) in Malbun has a very small dance floor, very small tables near banquettes, and lots of candlelight. The music is disco.

Tiffany Bar (tel. 3-13-43) in Eschen has a wood-paneled rustic ambience of lots of couches and dim lights.

Derby Bar (tel. 3-22-11) at Schaanwald attracts a younger, under-30 crowd.

Étienne Bar (tel. 2-20-22) at Schaan also attracts a younger crowd. But don't expect Studio 54.

FROMMER/PASMANTIER PUBLISHERS **Date________________**
1230 AVE. OF THE AMERICAS, NEW YORK, NY 10020

Friends, please send me the books checked below:

$-A-DAY GUIDES

(In-depth guides to low-cost tourist accommodations and facilities.)

- ☐ Europe on $25 a Day $10.95
- ☐ Australia on $25 a Day $9.95
- ☐ England and Scotland on $25 a Day $9.95
- ☐ Greece on $25 a Day $9.95
- ☐ Hawaii on $35 a Day $9.95
- ☐ Ireland on $25 a Day $7.95
- ☐ Israel on $30 & $35 a Day $9.95
- ☐ Mexico on $20 a Day $8.95
- ☐ New Zealand on $20 & $25 a Day $9.95
- ☐ New York on $35 a Day $8.95
- ☐ Scandinavia on $25 a Day $7.95
- ☐ South America on $25 a Day $8.95
- ☐ Spain and Morocco (plus the Canary Is.) on $25 a Day $8.95
- ☐ Washington, D.C. on $35 a Day $8.95

DOLLARWISE GUIDES

(Guides to tourist accommodations and facilities from budget to deluxe, with emphasis on the medium-priced.)

- ☐ Egypt $9.95
- ☐ England & Scotland $7.95
- ☐ France $8.95
- ☐ Germany $9.95
- ☐ Italy $7.95
- ☐ Portugal (incl. Madeira & the Azores) $9.95
- ☐ Switzerland $9.95
- ☐ Canada $10.95
- ☐ Caribbean (incl. Bermuda & the Bahamas) $10.95
- ☐ California & Las Vegas $7.95
- ☐ Florida $9.95
- ☐ New England $9.95
- ☐ Southeast & New Orleans $9.95

THE ARTHUR FROMMER GUIDES

(Pocket-size guides to tourist accommodations and facilities in all price ranges.)

- ☐ Amsterdam/Holland $3.95
- ☐ Athens $3.95
- ☐ Boston $3.95
- ☐ Hawaii $3.95
- ☐ Dublin/Ireland $3.95
- ☐ Las Vegas $3.95
- ☐ Lisbon/Madrid/Costa del Sol $3.95
- ☐ London $3.95
- ☐ Los Angeles $3.95
- ☐ Mexico City/Acapulco $3.95
- ☐ Montreal/Quebec City $3.95
- ☐ New Orleans $3.95
- ☐ New York $3.95
- ☐ Orlando/Disney World/EPCOT $3.95
- ☐ Paris $3.95
- ☐ Philadelphia/Atlantic City $3.95
- ☐ Rome $3.95
- ☐ San Francisco $3.95
- ☐ Washington, D.C. $3.95

SPECIAL EDITIONS

- ☐ How to Beat the High Cost of Travel $4.95
- ☐ New York Urban Athlete (NYC sports guide for jocks & novices) $9.95
- ☐ Where to Stay USA (Accommodations from $3 to $25 a night) $8.95
- ☐ Fast 'n' Easy Phrase Book (Fr/Sp/Ger/Ital. in *one* vol.) $6.95
- ☐ Marilyn Wood's Wonderful Weekends (NY, Conn, Mass, RI, Vt, NJ, Pa) $9.95
- ☐ Museums in New York (Incl. historic houses, gardens, & zoos) $8.95
- ☐ Travel Guide for the Disabled $10.95

In U.S. include $1 post. & hdlg. for 1st book; 25¢ any add'l. book. Outside U.S. $2 and 50¢ respectively.

Enclosed is my check or money order for $________________

NAME________________

ADDRESS________________

CITY________________ STATE________ ZIP________